HUMAN BEHAVIOR THEORY
and
SOCIAL WORK PRACTICE

Second Edition

MODERN APPLICATIONS OF SOCIAL WORK

An Aldine de Gruyter Series of Texts and Monographs

SERIES EDITOR
James K. Whittaker

Paul Adams and Kristine E. Nelson (eds.), **Reinventing Human Services: Community- and Family-Centered Practice**

Ralph E. Anderson and Irl Carter, with Gary Lowe, **Human Behavior in the Social Environment: A Social Systems Approach** (Fifth Edition)

Richard P. Barth, Mark Courtney, Jill Duerr Berrick, and Vicky Albert, **From Child Abuse to Permanency Planning: Child Welfare Services Pathways and Placements**

Dana Christensen, Jeffrey Todahl, and William C. Barrett, **Solution-Based Casework: An Introduction to Clinical and Case Management Skills in Casework Practice**

Marie Connolly with Margaret McKenzie, **Effective Participatory Practice: Family Group Conferencing in Child Protection**

Kathleen Ell and Helen Northen, **Families and Health Care: Psychosocial Practice**

Marian Fatout, **Models for Change in Social Group Work**

Mark W. Fraser, Peter J. Pecora, and David A. Haapala, **Families in Crisis: The Impact of Intensive Family Preservation Services**

James Garbarino, **Children and Families in the Social Environment** (Second Edition)

James Garbarino, and Associates, **Special Children—Special Risks: The Maltreatment of Children with Disabilities**

James Garbarino, and Associates, **Troubled Youth, Troubled Families: Understanding Families At-Risk for Adolescent Maltreatment**

Roberta R. Greene, **Social Work with the Aged and Their Families**

Roberta R. Greene, **Human Behavior Theory: A Diversity Framework**

Roberta R. Greene, **Human Behavior Theory and Social and Social Work Practice** (Second Edition)

André Ivanoff, Betty J. Blythe, and Tony Tripodi, **Involuntary Clients in Social Work Practice: A Research-Based Approach**

Jill Kinney, David A. Haapala, and Charlotte Booth, **Keeping Families Together: The Homebuilders Model**

Gary R. Lowe and P. Nelson Reid, **The Professionalization of Poverty: Social Work and the Poor in the Twentieth Century**

Robert M. Moroney and Judy Krysik, **Social Policy and Social Work: Critical Essays on the Welfare State** (Second Edition)

Peter J. Pecora, Mark W. Fraser, Kristine Nelson, Jacqueline McCroskey, and William Meezan, **Evaluating Family-Based Services**

Peter J. Pecora, James K. Whittaker, Anthony N. Maluccio, Richard P. Barth, and Robert D. Plotnick, **The Child Welfare Challenge: Policy, Practice, and Research**

John R. Schuerman, Tina L. Rzepnicki, and Julia H. Littell, **Putting Families First: An Experiment in Family Preservation**

Madeleine R. Stoner, **The Civil Rights of Homeless People: Law, Social Policy, and Social Work Practice**

Albert E. Trieschman, James K. Whittaker, and Larry K. Brendtro, **The Other 23 Hours: Child-Care Work with Emotionally Disturbed Children in a Therapeutic Milieu**

Harry H. Vorrath and Larry K. Brendtro, **Positive Peer Culture** (Second Edition)

Betsy S. Vourlekis and Roberta R. Greene (eds.), **Social Work Case Management**

James K. Whittaker, and Associates, **Reaching High-Risk Families: Intensive Family Preservation in Human Services**

HUMAN BEHAVIOR THEORY
and
SOCIAL WORK PRACTICE

Second Edition

Roberta R. Greene

ALDINE DE GRUYTER
New York

About the Author

Roberta R. Greene is retired Dean and full Professor at Indiana School of Social Work. She is the author of *Human Behavior Theory: A Diversity Framework; Social Work with the Aged and Their Families;* coauthor with Marie Watkins of *Serving Diverse Constituencies: Applying the Ecological Perspectives;* and coeditor with Betsy S. Vourlekis of *Social Work Case Management.* In addition, Dr. Greene is widely published on the application of conceptual frameworks to social work practice.

Copyright © 1991, 1999 by Walter de Gruyter, Inc., New York
All rights reserved. No part of this publication may be reproduced or transmitted in any form or by any means, electronic or mechanical, including photocopying, recording, or any information storage or retrieval system, without prior permission in writing from the publisher.

ALDINE DE GRUYTER
A division of Walter de Gruyter, Inc.
200 Saw Mill River Road
Hawthorne, New York 10532

This publication is printed on acid free paper ⊚

Library of Congress Cataloging-in-Publication Data

Human behavior theory and social work practice / [edited
   by] Roberta R. Greene. — 2nd ed.
      p.   cm.
   Includes bibliographical references and index.
   ISBN 0-202-36119-5 (cl. : alk paper). — ISBN
0-202-36120-9 (pa. : alk. paper)
      1. Social service.   2. Human behavior.   I. Greene,
Roberta R. (Roberta Rubin), 1940–   .
HV40.H783   1999
361.3'2—dc21   99-39969
                                                    CIP

Manufactured in the United States of America
10 9 8 7 6 5 4 3 2

*This book is dedicated to David Greene
whose unconditional love and support
helped this project come to fruition.*

R.R.G.

CONTENTS

Preface   *xi*

1   Human Behavior Theory, Person-in-Environment,
    and Social Work Method
        Roberta R. Greene   1

2   Human Behavior Theory and
    Professional Social Work Practice
        Roberta R. Greene   31

    CRITIQUE

    Professional Tools for Religiously and
    Spiritually Sensitive Social Work Practice
        Ann P. Conrad   63

3   Classical Psychoanalytic Thought,
    Contemporary Developments, and Clinical
    Social Work
        Roberta R. Greene   73

    CRITIQUE

    Freudian Theory:
    New Developments
        Allen Rader and Ruth Rader   102

4   Eriksonian Theory:
     A Developmental Approach to
     Ego Mastery
          Roberta R. Greene   107

     CRITIQUE

     Moral Development over the Life Cycle:
     Another View of Stage Theory
          Allen Rader and Ruth Rader   137

5   Carl Rogers and the Person-Centered Approach
          Roberta R. Greene   145

     CRITIQUE

     Carl Rogers and the Person-Centered Approach:
     Social Work Applications Now and for the Future
          Judith S. Lewis   166

6   Cognitive Theory for Social Work Practice
          Betsy S. Vourlekis   173

     CRITIQUE

     Cognitive Theory for Social Work Practice:
     Context, Applications, and Questions
          Nancy Poe Wingfield   206

7   General Systems Theory
          Roberta R. Greene   215

     CRITIQUE

     Usefulness of General Systems Theory in
     Social Work Practice
          J. Paul Gallant and Bruce A. Thyer   250

8 Ecological Perspective:
   An Eclectic Theoretical Framework for
   Social Work Practice
      Roberta R. Greene   259

   CRITIQUE

   The Search for Social Work Coherence:
   The Ecological Perspective
      Gerald T. Powers   301

9 Social Construction
      Robert Blundo and Roberta R. Greene   309

   CRITIQUE

   How Useful is the Social Constructionist Approach?
      Irene Queiro-Tajalli   341

10 Feminist Theories and Social Work Practice
      Rebecca Morrison Van Voorhis   351

   CRITIQUE

   Feminist Theory and Social Work:
   Lost in Space?
      Carol T. Tully   382

11 Genetics, Environment, and Development
      Joyce G. Riley   389

   CRITIQUE

   Nature and Nurture
      Joan Esterline Lafure   414

Index   421

PREFACE

This text is intended as a source book in human behavior for students preparing for professional social work careers. The opportunity to critique a select number of human behavior theories is provided. Each chapter provides an introduction to the theory's basic terms and assumptions and discusses the theory's utility for understanding the person-in-environment, explaining development across the life cycle, understanding cultural differences, and understanding how humans function as members of families, groups, communities, and organizations. The theory's usefulness to social work practice in various helping situations is examined through case studies.

This learning opportunity is dependent on a student's willingness to establish a critical posture in which a theory's contributions to the profession are examined and the theory's potential for enhancing the student's social work practice skills is explored. It also requires that the student read selections from the many journal articles and books cited in each chapter to further clarify how a particular theory may shed light on different aspects of human functioning.

A theory has inherent usefulness to the degree that it gives direction to a social work plan of action. However, learning human behavior for social work practice means that the student first must become well grounded in the theory and be able to distill its basic assumptions. To evaluate a theory's utility for his or her social work practice, a student also must examine his or her values and skills and determine if the theory is congruent with personal beliefs and helping style.

In the final analysis, most social workers practice is eclectic or a creative selection of theories and techniques. An eclectic approach to social work practice brings with it the responsibility to integrate effectively a number of theories and to determine the theoretical orientation's suitability for what Fisher (1978) terms intervening in "the client–problem–situation configuration" (p. 237).

I hope that this text will contribute in some small way to the education and service delivery skills of future professional social work colleagues.

Roberta R. Greene

1

Human Behavior Theory, Person-in-Environment, and Social Work Method

ROBERTA R. GREENE

Practice is always shaped by the needs of the times, the problems they present, the fears they generate, the solutions that appeal, and the knowledge and skill available.
—B. C. Reynolds, *Learning and Teaching in the Practice of Social Work*

Social work is a young, evolving profession characterized by a dynamic helping process and a diversity of roles, functions, and career opportunities. The aims of social work—to improve societal conditions and to enhance social functioning among individuals, families, and groups—are put into action across all fields of practice and realized through a variety of methods in a range of settings.

For today's social worker to pursue a career in any one of the profession's diverse service arenas, he or she will need to acquire conceptual frameworks that provide the context for understanding the complexities of contemporary practice. Throughout the profession's history, social workers have turned to a number of theoretical approaches for the organizing concepts needed to define their practice base. This book is concerned with the application of knowledge about human behavior in the social environment that serves as the theoretical underpinning for direct practice in social work. This book focuses on selected conceptual frameworks that have made a major contribution to the profession's understanding of human functioning and examines the ways in which these frameworks have shaped social workers' approach to enhance client functioning. The main theme of this book is that the person-in-environment perspective has been a central influence in the formation of the profession's knowledge base as well as its approach to practice. The chapters explore ways in which specific theories have contributed to understanding the person-in-environment construct and examine the idea that all clinical social work intervention is anchored to a common paradigm: to reshape the context of the person-in-environment configuration (Bartlett, 1970; Saleeby, 1993; Van Den Bergh, 1995).

This book also explores the manner in which a particular theory offers explanations about the biopsychosocial development of individuals across the life cycle and on their functioning as members of families, groups, organizations, and communities. The book addresses a theory's universality, its utility in addressing cultural and ethnic diversity, and its assumptions about what constitutes adaptive behavior. Each chapter outlines the central frames of reference and concepts of a particular theory. Its salient constructs are then applied to practice approaches in selected settings with various client populations. Suggestions are provided about the ways in which practitioners may use the various frameworks to structure professional activities, to guide the practitioner through the social work processes of conducting assessments and selecting interventive strategies, and to create new meanings through discourse. Studies illustrate different ideas for helping individuals, families, and groups.

ORGANIZATION OF THE CHAPTERS

This chapter introduces the organizing principles of the book. Chapter 2 discusses the relationship between human behavior theory and professional social work practice. Chapters 3 through 10 present a series of theories (or a selection from a particular school of thought). The historical context, its philosophical roots, and major assumptions of each theory are discussed. The chapters examine how social workers can use a theory to shape direct social work practice by increasing the practitioner's understanding and potential to enhance human situations. The chapters also explore the challenges and limitations of each theory and address the following questions:

- What does the theory offer for understanding development across the life cycle? Life course?
- What does the theory suggest about the interaction among biological, psychological, and sociocultural factors of human development and functioning?
- What does the theory suggest about healthy/functional and unhealthy/dysfunctional behaviors or wellness?
- What does the theory say is adaptive/maladaptive? How does the theory present stress factors and coping potentials?
- Is the theory universal in its application? How does the theory lend

itself to cross-cultural social work practice or various life contexts? Does the theory address social and economic justice?
- What does the theory propose about individuals as members of families, groups, communities, and organizations?
- How does the theory serve as a framework for social work practice?
- How does the theory lend itself to an understanding of individual, family, group, community, or organizational behavior?
- How does the theory suggest the client and social worker go about defining presenting situations, problems, or concerns? Does the theory suggest a strengths perspective?
- What are the implications of the theory for social work interventions or practice strategies? Do the principles of the theory emphasize a client's capabilities and resources?
- What does the theory suggest the social worker do? What does it suggest the client (system) do?
- What role does it propose for the social worker as change agent? What is the aim of treatment / intervention or meaning creation? What does it suggest enhances functioning or promotes change in the client? In society? In societal institutions?

The chapter also provides examples in which a theory is used to "direct" or guide the social worker-client interchange. Each situation suggests how the theory can be used to shape the social worker's role . Examples use individual, family, and group methodologies and are chosen from among the fields of practice. Clients in a variety of contexts—setting, age, and culture—are addressed.

CHANGES IN EPISTEMOLOGICAL APPROACHES

It is rather as if the professional community had been suddenly transported to another planet.
                    —T. Kuhn, *The Structure of Scientific Revolutions*

The use of human behavior theory needs to be understood within the context of the history of scientific thought. That history suggests that the social work profession has moved from a position of little practice theory to more than twenty major theoretical approaches (Turner, 1995). Each theory stems from a particular *paradigm*, the configuration of beliefs, values, and techniques that are shared by members of a professional community. Each paradigm is a reconstruction of prior thinking (Schriver, 1995) and may have dramatically different philosophical assumptions.

Guba (1990) has described the shifts in paradigm—from positivism, to postpositivism, to constructivism—that have most affected social work practice. Social work's interest in science and the scientific method brought the profession into a world of inquiry and technology. Entry into the university setting in the early 1900s—an era of positivist science—meant that social workers adopted theories that rest on the belief that universal laws guide human behavior. It also meant that the social worker's role was to discover objective facts and to use preestablished theoretical assumptions to understand client concerns. Positivists also argued that objective laws and universal truths discovered through scientific-like activity, logic, and reason would lead to objective social work practice (see Burrell & Morgan, 1979; Martin & O'Connor, 1989). Postpositivists suggest that although natural laws exist, people cannot possibly perceive them. Social worker objectivity would be an ideal. On the other hand, constructionists have proposed that many realities are created at the local level through human interaction (Foucault, 1980). Therefore, no social work endeavor is value free, but must be understood through individual mental frameworks. These philosophical assumptions, as they relate to the role of the social worker, are explored further in the following chapters.

HUMAN BEHAVIOR THEORY, POSITIVIST TRADITION, AND RELIANCE ON SCIENTIFIC THOUGHT

At the very least we ought to know what concepts we are utilizing, and where the concepts come from, and the state of their verification.
                    —S. Firestone, "The Scientific Component in the
                                       Casework Field Curriculum"

Social workers who use theories of human behavior that stem from positivist tradition, such as Freudian theory and systems theory, rely on information, facts, and data to guide their clinical practice. They view *theory*—a logical system of concepts that provides a framework for organizing and understanding observations—as the primary tool in planning assessment and intervention processes (Table 1.1). Theories—intended to offer comprehensive, simple, and dependable principles for the explanation and prediction of observable phenomena—assist practitioners in identifying orderly relationships (Hempel, 1960; Newman & Newman, [1979] 1987).

Theories provide the framework for organizing social work practice.

Just as social scientists used theories to deal with vast quantities of data by formulating significant questions, selecting and organizing data, and un-

Table 1.1. Definitions of Theory

Author	Definition
Chess and Norlin (1988)	A theory offers an explanation for an idea and a set of related assumptions and concepts that explain a phenomenon being observed. Theory should give meaning and clarity to what otherwise would appear to be specific and isolated cases.
Compton and Galaway (1994)	A theory is a coherent group of concepts or propositions that explain or account for phenomena and their interrelationships. A theory may contain both confirmed and assumptive knowledge and provide a rational way of ordering and linking observed phenomena.
Kelly (1955)	A theory offers a way of binding together a multitude of facts so that one may comprehend them all at once.
Newman and Newman ([1979] 1987)	A theory is a logical system of general concepts that provides a framework for organizing and understanding observations. Theories help identify the orderly relationships that exist among many diverse events. They guide us to those factors that will have explanatory power and suggest those that will not.
Saleebey (1993)	Theories are perspectives, not truths. Theories are texts, narratives, and interpretive devices.
Shaw and Costanzo (1982)	Theories allow us to organize our observations and to deal meaningfully with information that would otherwise be chaotic and useless. Theory allows us to see relationships among facts and to uncover implications that otherwise would not be evident in isolated pieces of data. Theories also stimulate inquiry about behavior.
Specht and Craig (1982)	Theories provide us with a means of formulating significant questions, to select and organize data, and to understand the data within a larger framework.

5

derstanding the data within a larger framework, social workers also sought theories to help guide and organize their thinking about a client's presenting problem. Theories also helped social workers explain why people behave as they do, to better understand how the environment affects behavior, to guide interventive behavior, and to predict what is likely to be the result of a particular social work intervention (Fischer, 1981). For example, those social workers who base their practice on Freudian theory may choose to help a client examine the uses of defense mechanisms in the belief that modification of overly rigid or particularly deficient defenses will lead to a healthier personality configuration (see Chapter 3). In contrast, the practitioner who bases practice on a social systems approach may evaluate the relative closed or open quality of a family system with the perspective that helping a family communicate more openly will improve its functional capacity (see Chapter 7). Each theory has a set of assumptions about the cause of the presenting problem and its resolution. Questions that guide the interview suggest that the social worker has an understanding about what constitutes a healthy individual or well-functioning family.

Positivist theorists suggest the social worker take a neutral stance during the helping process and that theory can help the social worker guard against the temptation to act on personal bias. Briar and Miller (1971) underscored the idea that a social worker needs to be able to separate fact from inference and to make explicit his or her assumptions about human behavior to make sound professional judgments:

> The choice for the practitioner is not whether to have a theory but what theoretical assumptions to hold. All persons acquire assumptions or views on the basis of which they construe and interpret events and behavior, including their own. These assumptions are frequently not explicit but are more what has been called "implicit theories of personality." Thus, the appeal for practitioners to be atheoretical amounts simply to an argument that theory ought to be implicit and hidden, not explicit and self-conscious. It is difficult, however, to defend an argument favoring implicit theory that, by definition, is not susceptible to scrutiny and objective validation and therefore cannot be distinguished from idiosyncratic bias. (pp. 53–54)

The usefulness of theory to social work practice can be viewed in a number of ways (Table 1.2). Social workers often turn to those theories of human behavior in the social environment they believe will provide a knowledge base for understanding and action (Bloom, 1984). Those theories that help in understanding the

| The use of theory is the hallmark of professional helping. |

causal dynamics of behavior that has already occurred and in predicting future behavioral events meet this definition for action-oriented knowledge. In short, theoretical frameworks are useful to those in the helping profes-

Table 1.2. Value of a Theoretical Framework

Author	Value
Bloom (1984)	The study of human behavior (theory) is an attempt to provide a knowledge base for understanding and action.
Compton and Galaway (1994)	The social work knowledge base should encompass concepts that explain how human systems develop, change, and dysfunction, and how the interrelationships work among systems.
Newman and Newman (1987)	Theories should provide explanations about the mechanisms that account for growth from conception to old age, and the extent that these mechanisms vary across the life span. They should account for stability and change, the interactions among cognitive, emotional, and social functioning, and predict the impact of the social context on individual development.
Specht and Craig (1982)	Theories should be universal and apply to different ethnic, racial, and social class. This allows for the understanding of general cultural differences in child rearing, cognitive training, and family structure. Theories also account for the particular, thus enabling an understanding of similarities and differences.
Turner (1986)	A theory by virtue of its ability to explain should better enable practitioners to offer responsible, effective intervention.
Zanden (1985)	Theory is a tool. The value of the knowledge yielded by the application of theory lies in the control it provides us over our experience. It serves as a guide to action.
Zastrow and Kirst-Ashman (1987)	Theories of human behavior in the social environment provide a foundation knowledge for assessment and intervention.

sions to the extent that they provide a conceptual foundation that shapes the direction of professional activities and gives context to specific actions.

Whatever the choice of theory, a social worker's actions are not random but tend to reflect the theories, implicit or explicit, that he or she accepts and uses. Theory tends to shape the practitioner's viewpoint, what he or she makes of it, and what he or she decides to do about it. How the practitioner defines a need, situation, or problem largely determines the action he or she will take. If the practitioner views the problem as being within the person, he or she will take a different course of action than if the problem resided within the environment. The social worker who does not believe in a problem-laden social work approach will take another course of action.

During the past three decades, there have been several concerns about the use of theory. There are, of course, limitations to the rigor of scientific theories and their capacity to explain or account for events. No single theoretical construction can encompass all aspects of a phenomenon (Turner, 1995). By their very nature, theories are selective about the factors they emphasize and those they ignore. In addition, a growing number of social work theorists have challenged positivist tradition. This challenge has involved an interest in and a shift to theories that are more *contextualized*, that is, theories that emphasize multiple, individualized perspectives.

The complexity of human concerns with which social workers deal argues against a "hit or miss" approach to their solution. Rather, this complexity makes imperative the need for a consciously held and purposeful conduct of practice. The conscious, explicit application of human behavior theory enables the social worker to carry out his or her responsibility to assist individuals, families, and groups by improving or preventing loss of functioning through a planned, professional process. This approach contrasts with a friendly, helping relationship that may be caring, but is not guided by an awareness of how intervention skills are "used selectively and differentially as determined by a body of theory and a process of deciding" (Compton & Galaway, 1994, p. 34).

DIFFERENT VIEWS ON THEORY

Because a large number of combinations of value orientations exist . . . the search for a proper and helpful fit between client, social worker, and theory of intervention is complex. . . . It presents a highly exciting potential for enhancing effectiveness in a multicultural society.
—F. J. Turner, "Social Work Practice: Theoretical Base"

Over the past two decades, social work theorists have challenged the philosophical assumptions of the traditional use of theory (Dean & Fenby,

1989; Wakefield, 1996). While Marxism and critical theory have received some attention, a major shift in theoretical emphasis has been to equate and further delineate the person-environment with the ecological perspective. The ecological perspective provides a holistic framework; is inclusive of various theory bases and strategies; includes attention to larger geographic, political, and economic environments;

> Social workers have historically sought theory that provides a contextual understanding of human behavior.

and is suitable for practice across cultural and diversity groups. Because the ecological perspective addresses culture, historical eras, gender, ethnicity, and other diversity dimensions relative to political power and worldview, it is thought to expand the contextual variables included in social work practice (Germain, 1979; Germain & Gitterman, 1987; Greene & McGuire, 1998).

Among the other benefits thought to derive from the ecological perspective are the transactional approach, referring to the person and environment as one inseparable unit; a positive view of growth, reinforcing the innate healthy nature of human development; the conception of adaptiveness across the life course, relating to the attainment of well-being as a lifelong process of active person-environment exchanges; and its emphasis on a multilevel assessment and intervention, guiding the activity of the social worker to multiple systems analysis for understanding client functioning (Greene & McGuire, 1998; see Chapter 7).

Social work theorists also have challenged the hegemony of Eurocentric models of social work practice (Schiele, 1996; Swigonski, 1996). For example, Schiele (1996) has contended that Eurocentric theories of human behavior emphasize concepts developed in Europe and in the Anglo-American culture and "are implicitly oppressive" (p. 286). On the other hand, *Africentricity* (as spelled by Schiele) offers an emerging paradigm that infuses the values of people of color. From an Africentric perspective, one theory cannot explain all human phenomena and provide explanations of peoples' similarities and differences. The emphasis of Africentricity is on the collective nature of human identity, involving interconnectedness and group ethos; the spiritual component of people's lives, encompassing the link between humanity and the universe; and the validity of affect in understanding life events, including an acceptance of emotions as well as rationality. Africentric theory also can be used to understand how certain groups in society are privileged or have unearned advantage, whereas others are marginalized or have less access to social, economic, and political resources (Swigonski, 1996). Swigonski (1996) has suggested that privilege is invisible unless social workers make a particular effort to ask "what are some of the advantages of being white, male, middle-class, and so forth" (p. 154; see Table 1.3) At the same time,

Table 1.3. Types of Privilege Reflected in Statements from McIntosh, *White Privilege and Male Privilege* (1988)

Type of Privilege	Sample Statement
The freedom to associate exclusively or primarily with members of your own group	I can, if I wish, arrange to be in the company of people of my race most of the time. (p. 5)
The level of social acceptance one can presume across varying contexts	If I should need to move, I can be pretty sure of renting or purchasing housing in an area in which I want to live. (p. 5)
	Whether I use checks, credit cards, or cash, I can count on my skin color not to work against the appearance of financial reliability. (p. 6)
	I do not have to educate my children to be aware of systemic racism for their own daily protection. (p. 6)
The ability to see members of your groups in a positive light, in the records of history, in texts, in media, and as role models	When I am told about our national heritage or about civilization, I am shown that people of my color made it what it is. (p. 6)
The freedom from stereotyping	I can be pretty sure that if I ask to speak to the person in charge, I will be facing a person of my own race. (p. 7)
	I can swear, or dress in second-hand clothes, or not answer letters, without having people attribute these choices to the bad morale, poverty, or illiteracy of my race. (p. 7)
	I can do well in a challenging situation without being called a credit to my race. (p. 7)
	I can be late to a meeting without having the lateness reflect on my race. (p. 8)
The ability to be oblivious of other groups	I can remain oblivious of the language and customs of people of color who constitute the world's majority without feeling in my culture any penalty for such oblivion. (p. 7)
	My culture gives me little fear about ignoring the perspective and powers of people of other races. (p. 8)
The ability to feel at home in the world	I will feel welcome and normal in the usual walks of public life, institutional and social. (p. 17)

Source: McIntosh, P. (1988). *White Privilege and Male Privilege: A Personal Account of Coming to See Correspondences through Work in Women's Studies* (Working Paper 189, pp. 5–8). Wellesley, MA: Wellesley College Center for Research on Women. Copyright 1988. Adopted with permission.

Africentric theory is based on the values of Africans and African-Americans, and uses their history, culture, and worldview as a frame of reference.

Postmodern theorists, such as some branches of feminism, also have a strong interest in how personal and societal power is distributed. Events that the client describes are to be understood within the client's particular sociopolitical context. This strategy is based on the idea that the "personal is political"—or that there is an inevitable connection between individual concerns and societal power structures and institutions (Van Den Bergh & Cooper, 1986, p. 9). The feminist practitioner seeks to combat oppression, particularly of women, redress societal inequities, and empower persons who may be marginalized (Van den Bergh, 1995; see Chapter 10).

Feminists and other postmodern thinkers reject the idea that there are universal truths or laws (Gordon, 1984). Most of the knowledge used in social work practice, including systems and ecological theories, ego psychology, object relations, self-psychology, and cognitive theory, is based on a positivist view of fixed theoretical assumptions (Fleck-Henderson, 1993; Van Den Bergh, 1995). Social workers who use postmodern theory argue that content—information or facts—is only the starting point in the helping process. Practitioners may view different theories as providing more or less useful ways of helping clients. The idea is to avoid clinging to one theory; rather, the emphasis is on alternative explanations and multiple meanings of events and on preserving those aspects of theories that "focus on the viability of multiple perspectives" (Dean, 1993, p. 59).

Postmodern theorists question the linear (deterministic) or cause-and-effect thinking of the positivists. Postmodern thinkers do not subscribe to the view that behavior *a* causes *b*; rather, behavior is an outcome of complex personal, social, cultural, and historical contexts and meaning is personal—created through language and social interactions. "Social workers should not expect to know in advance what the outcome of clinical interactions will be" (Pozatek, 1994, p. 397). Social workers should take a "not-knowing" stance.

Another shift in emphasis from the constructionists viewpoint is the importance of intuitive knowing (Van Den Bergh & Cooper, 1986; Weick, 1993). Social work theorists are increasingly engaged in a debate about whether social work is an applied science based on empirical knowledge or a process or an art understood by analyzing and codifying the performance of master practitioners (Weick, 1993). Postmodern thinkers have proposed that knowledge is created through social discourse within a historical and sociopolitical context. That is, practitioners may create knowledge at the local level or at the front line of practice. Knowledge thus becomes a process of creation in the client-social worker interaction, or what Schon (1983) has so aptly called "knowing-in-practice" (p. 62). From this perspective, social work may be considered an art: students learn knowledge and skills from master artists (Weick, 1993).

> Human behavior theory must be used in conjunction with critical thinking and reflection.

Schon (1983), who examined paradigms for professional practice, has acknowledged the need for specialized knowledge in professional education. However, he has contended that the types of real-world problems that are at the core of the profession require "reflection-about-action":

> Increasingly we have become aware of the importance to actual practice of phenomena—complexity, uncertainty, instability, uniqueness, and value conflict—which do not fit the model of Technical Rationality [positivism]. (p. 39)

Postmodern theory does not accept the premise that the social worker is an expert; rather, it proposes that social workers view clients as experts on their own behavior. Postmodern practitioners maintain that the central purpose of the therapeutic relationship is creating a therapeutic partnership and new client meaning through dialogue or conversation. This approach is in contrast to a client-social worker relationship in which the client may gain insight into his or her behavior through many practitioner interpretations. In such a positivist stance, the social worker promotes insight based on questions derived from his or her theoretical orientation. In contrast, the postmodern practitioner's goal is to obtain client-generated meaning to enable a positive reframing of events (Duncan, Solovey, & Rusk, 1992). Clients' ability to re-create their life story or rename their problem also enables them to gain a sense of empowerment (White & Epston, 1990).

The practitioner's goal is to set in motion a change process to help the client revise the negative internalized meaning of problems, develop a sense of agency, and find solutions—a client-directed therapy (Lax, 1992). The social worker assumes that each client has unique personal resources as well as the ability to create new stories or life views. Therefore, the practitioner adopts a learning stance and acts as a "participant manager of the conversation" (Anderson & Goolishian, 1990, p. 384). That is, the practitioner is in the position of being informed.

Postmodern theorists have argued that theories as social constructions created during a particular time and place have inherent biases and cannot be value free. Rather, human behavior content may often reflect prevailing social and political contexts (Allen, 1993). For example, feminist practitioners are particularly concerned with how negative ideas about women intrude into the client-social worker relationship. If such biases are understood, social workers can try to avoid mirroring these stereotypes and societal power structures in their practice (Greene, 1994). In short, practitioners must examine all theory for its political biases and ethical implications (Allen, 1993; Weick, 1993). Postmodern practitioners are among an increasingly large number of social workers who, no matter what their theoretical base, aspire to culturally competent social work practice by equalizing power in the client-social worker relationship, creating personalized meaning in the helping relationship, and taking responsibility for their biases. In these ways, practitioners focus on both the person and the environment.

CRITIQUE OF HUMAN BEHAVIOR THEORY

[Use of theory involves] a constant critical stance toward one's own ideas as well as those embedded in the formal theories. . . . [A]ll of our theories, our "texts", our "codes," our languages, contain built-in biases
—J. Laird, *Revisioning Social Work Education:*
A Social Constructionist Approach

Critiquing theories and the paradigm from which they are derived is a key requirement of human behavior and the social environment curriculum (CSWE, 1992; see Table 1.4). Evaluation of theory may take several forms including a critique of its underlying paradigm, its usefulness in serving diverse constituencies, and its underlying value base.

A critique of theory involves a process of "thinking paradigm" or a process of "continually asking questions about what the information . . . we send and receive reflects about our own and others' views of the world" (Schriver, 1995, p. 7). For example, theorists should not view the descriptions of positivist and postmodern theoretical approaches as absolute. Many theorists have looked for ways to consider variables important to social work, such as social class, ethnicity, and gender as well as the ethical implications of social work practice. Therefore, when coming to grips with whether knowledge is "real or socially constructed, the best a practitioner can

> By critically evaluating theories, practitioners can make the choice of what theory(ies) best work for them.

do is to thoughtfully and critically analyze each theory" (Robbins, Chatterjee, & Canda, 1998). A review of the theory may allow for consideration of both positivist and postmodern viewpoints (Dean & Fleck-Henderson, 1992). The ability to join alternative helping strategies holds the promise of

Table 1.4. Theory Critique

- Describe the author's background, credentials, and demographic characteristics.
- When was the model developed? What prompted the author to develop it? What important social, cultural, or historical events surrounded the model's development?
- Are the ideological biases of the theory or model articulated? If so, what are they (e.g., differential emphasis on person and the environment, use of a particular knowledge base)? What psychological or social sciences theory or theories does the model draw?
- What is the purpose of the model?
- What is the real value system of the model? What consideration does the model give to the role of race/ethnicity, gender, sexual orientation, age, physical or mental challenge, or socioeconomic class?
- What are the client characteristics (e.g., demographics, skills, knowledge, personality type) thought to be necessary for appropriate use of the model?
- What unit(s) of attention is/are addressed by the model?
- How are problems defined?
- What causes psychological or interpersonal problems according to the model?
- How is assessment defined and conducted within the model?
- What interventions are described within the model? What skills are required by the practitioner of the model?
- What is the role of the practitioner and what is the role of the client? How is the professional relationship defined and described?
- What is/are the desirable outcome(s)/goals of the model?
- How is time structured within the model?
- Are there any personnel exclusions stated or implied by the model?
- Is the model consistent with collaboration and referral to other agencies or practitioners?
- To what extent can the model be evaluated for effectiveness? What research has been done to evaluate it?
- How is the model similar to or different from social work's person-in-situation paradigm?
- How is the model consistent or inconsistent with the social work code of ethics?

Source: Meyer (1983).

developing the reflective practitioner, one who is both artistic and disciplined (Dean, 1993, p. 57).

Saleeby (1993) has suggested ideas to consider in that regard:

- Theories are associated with power and the dominant culture. The origins of theories of human behavior are sociocultural, political, and relational.
- Theories offer multiple, not singular, views. Practitioners must considered theories in light of the uniqueness of individuals and cultures.
- Theories best address individuals as social phenomena. Theories need to address people as interdependent beings or as persons-in-environments.

• Theories reflect language and intersubjectivity. Language is the basis for the exchange and creation of meanings. Theories imply or reflect values. (pp. 205–212)

Another aspect of evaluating theories is recognizing that they may be culture-bound. For example, Trader (1977) has suggested practitioners use the following four criteria for effective social work practice with oppressed minorities, particularly African-Americans:

(1) Pathology-Health Balance: Does the theory have a balance among well-being, strengths and illness, and deficits?

(2) Practitioner-Client Control Balance: Does the theory allow for shared control?

(3) Personal-Societal Impact Balance: Does the theory take into account the historical, political, and economic influences on behavior?

(4) Internal-External Change Balance: Does the theory emphasize internal change in preference to societal change?

Robbins et al. (1998) have pointed out the importance of understanding the philosophical underpinnings of a theory. Are people assumed to be basically good or evil? Is behavior primarily shaped by nature or nurture? In evaluating a theory's usefulness for social work practice, it is also important to examine the theory's values and ethical base. The Council on Social Work Education (1992) has delineated the values inherent to social work practice as follows:

• Social workers' professional relationships are built on regard for individual worth and dignity and are furthered by mutual participation, acceptance, confidentiality, honesty, and responsible handling of conflict.

• Social workers respect people's right to make independent decisions and to participate actively in the helping process.

• Social workers are committed to assisting client systems to obtain needed resources.

• Social workers strive to make social institutions more humane and responsive to human needs.

• Social workers demonstrate respect for and acceptance of the unique characteristics of diverse populations.

• Social workers are responsible for their own ethical conduct, the quality of their practice, and seeking continuous growth in the knowledge and skills of their profession. (p. 7)

A working knowledge of human behavior theory will allow practitioners to ethically carry out their profession's mission to help individuals, families, and groups. The conscious use of a theory requires that the practitioner become well-grounded in it and distill its basic assumptions. A practitioner then must critically evaluate what he or she thinks about that theory's utility and its connection to social work's value base. This critical posture involves becoming sufficiently knowledgeable to decide whether the theory is one that the practitioner can adopt for practice. If indeed the theory is, or a number of theories are, congruent with the social worker's personal practice approach, he or she can begin to think about how to apply different theoretical constructs in a particular context.

The following sections examine the relationship among the knowledge of human behavior theory, the use of social work method, and ability to intervene effectively in the person-in-environment configuration (Figure 1.1).

PERSON-IN-ENVIRONMENT: THE
DUAL FOCUS OF SOCIAL WORK

The enhancement of interaction between people and environments can be strongly reaffirmed as the primary mission of social work.
                            —P. Ewalt, NASW Conference Proceedings: Toward
                                       a Definition of Clinical Social Work

A continuing and unifying theme in the historical development of social work has been its interest and concern for the person-in-environment.

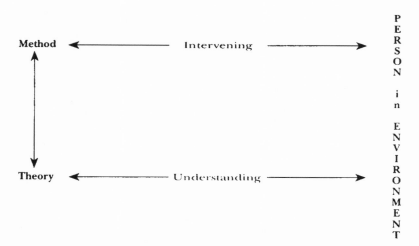

Figure 1.1.   Person-in-environment, theory, and method.

The person-in-environment perspective has been a central influence on the profession's theoretical base and its approach to practice. This perspective is based on the belief that the profession's basic mission requires a dual focus on the person and the environment and to a common structured approach to the helping process (Gordon, 1962). By serving as a blueprint or an organizing guide for social work assessment and intervention at a multiple systems level, the person-environment focus has allowed for social workers to intervene effectively "no matter what their different theoretical orientations and specializations and regardless of where or with what client group they practice" (Meyer, 1987, p. 409). The person-environment is a multisystems, eclectic mind-set that allows social work educators to build curricula within the broad context of all pertinent social systems. In short, the person-environment perspective has established social work's conceptual reference point and has delineated the practitioner's role (Greene & Watkins, 1998).

The dual concern and need for effective intervention in the person and situation has been expressed by a number of critical thinkers. For example, Bartlett (1970) emphasized the relationship between the coping activity of people and the demand from the environment. Germain (1979) focused on the duality of the adaptive potential of people and the nutritive qualities of their environment, whereas Germain

> Through the use of the person-environment perspective, social workers are able to attain their dual mission of personal and societal change.

and Gitterman (1980) stressed the interplay of human potential and the properties of the environment that support or fail to support the expression of that potential.

Furthermore, postmodern social work theorists have remained steadfast to social work's person-in-environment approach (Collins, 1986; Freeman, 1990; Gould, 1988; Wetzel, 1986). For example, Van Den Bergh (1995) has argued that the person-environment "many layered" approach is "syntonic" with postmodern thought (p. 8), and Land (1995) has contended that "the cardinal principles of clinical social work as we know them today: the biopsychosocial approach, the person-in-situation paradigm, and empowerment practice can be attributed to feminist pioneers" (p. 4).

No single theory to date has been able to provide the organizing principles to meet the challenge of understanding fully the person as well as the systems with which he or she interacts. The dual goals of improving societal institutions and assisting clients within their social and cultural milieu has led to the mining of concepts from different disciplines. Each concept or theory attempts to explain the complex interplay of physical, psychological, cognitive, social, and cultural variables that shape human behavior. As a result, the profession's theoretical base has come to incorporate a number of theories, each with its own constellation of values, purposes, assumptions, and prescriptions for interventive behavior (Northen, 1982).

Contemporary social work practice covers a wide range of purposes, organizational structures, client systems, and specific fields. As is expected, each field has its own history. Some, such as the health care field, antedate modern professional social work by millennia. Others are still in the process of emergence. Still others, such as the prevention and amelioration of child abuse, were part of social work's history but disappeared from prominence for a period, only to be rediscovered. What makes a social problem visible is itself a complex question (Blumer, 1969); the answers certainly involve the macrosocial processes of history, human ecology, and economics.

This book explores the way in which particular theories have contributed to the person-environment view of social work practice. The remaining chapters explore the way in which specific theories have contributed to the profession's understanding of the person-in-environment construct "to effect the best possible adaptation among individuals, families and groups and their environments" (Meyer, 1987, p. 409).

DIRECT PRACTICE IN SOCIAL WORK: INTERVENING IN THE PERSON-SITUATION TO ENHANCE PSYCHOSOCIAL FUNCTIONING

At that level of abstraction, . . . the different modes of practice share a common methodological framework, . . . that is, study, diagnosis, and treatments.
—N. Gilbert and H. Specht, "Social Planning and Community Organization"

Historically, social workers in the direct practice of social work have tended to be identified by a particular method, field of practice, or agency function. More recently, many social workers have come to believe that it is inappropriate to base a definition of social work on method—case work, group work, community organization—on the number of people with whom the social worker interacts. Rather, they have proposed that method be defined as so aptly stated by Schwartz (1961)—as "a systematic process of ordering one's activity in the performance of a function" (p. 148).

Direct practice in social work today is characterized by a wide diversity of immediate professional activities designed to help individuals, families, groups, or communities improve their social functioning. Because the profession has become so broad in scope, commonalities and centrality of purpose may be obscured. Nonetheless, common features bind the profession and are constant no matter what the setting or service. These features include the social worker's purpose and his or her comprehensive professional role (Anderson, 1981; Meyer, 1987). Guideposts also include a foundation of shared knowledge, values, and skills (Bartlett, 1970; CSWE, 1971, 1974, 1984) (Figure 1.2). In addition, it generally is accepted that the purpose of social work is to promote a mutually beneficial interaction between individuals and society (Karls, Lowery, Mattaini, & Wandrei, 1997).

In a discussion of the status of direct practice in social work, Meyer (1987) underscored the central purpose of the profession:

> The central purpose of social work practice is to effect the best possible adaptation among individuals, families, and groups and their environments. This psychosocial, or person-in-environment, focus of social work has evolved over the last 70 years to direct the explorations, assessments, and interventions of practitioners—no matter what their different theoretical orientations and specializations and regardless of where or with what client group they practice. (p. 409)

In essence, all social work method is grounded in a common paradigm: to intervene effectively in the person-in-environment configuration. Ex-

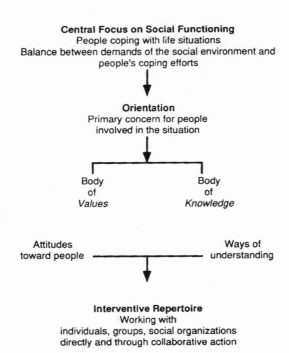

Figure 1.2. The common base of social work practice. From Bartlett (1970).

panding on this point, Germain and Gitterman (1980) insisted that the social worker should be competent enough to intervene in any part of the person-group-environment gestalt.

A person-environment perspective is also well accepted among postmodern theorists, as expressed by feminist Barbara Collins (1986):

> Social work's integrated thinking with its ecological view (person-environment) of process between individual and the environment is consonant with feminist thought. Both ideologies envision the desirable as transactions between people and their environments that support individual well-being, dignity, and self determination. (p. 216)

Although both positivist and postmodern theorists have accepted the centrality of the person-environment perspective, they may disagree about the therapeutic method. Positivist theorists have suggested that a unified perspective of social work practice also implies that there are core professional tasks. The idea of core professional tasks calls for a closer examination of the historically described phases of the helping process. Beginning with the work of Mary Richmond in 1917, if not earlier, the general approach to practice has been to collect the "nature of social evidence" and to interpret the data leading to the "social diagnosis" (pp. 38–40, 342–363). Perlman (1957) later echoed this theme in the following description of social casework: Casework begins with a study phase to clarify the facts of the problem, followed by a diagnosis during which the practitioner analyzes the facts; casework finishes with treatment, during which the practitioner and client attempt to resolve the problem (pp. 88–95).

Ewalt (1980) made a similar proposal that the concern of clinical social work is the ability to conduct a biopsychosocial assessment of the person-in-situation and to carry out interventions based on this assessment. Likewise, Meyer (1987) argued that the "core professional task" in the direct practice of social work is

> to assess the relationships among the case variables. The practitioner must determine what is salient or prominent and in need of intervention, what is relevant and therefore appropriate to do, and what balance or imbalance must be maintained or introduced. Thereafter, the introduction of interventions can be drawn from the repertoire of approaches. (p. 415)

The assertion that social work methods involve common elements that cut across all professional divisions and boundaries is based on the idea that there is a common structured approach to the helping process. Although phases of the change process have been conceptualized somewhat differently over the years, most conceptualizations found in methods texts have retained the study-diagnosis-treatment format originally described by Richmond (Germain & Gitterman, 1980; Hepworth & Larsen, 1982; O'Neil, 1984; Sheafor, Horejsi, & Horejsi, 1988; Siporin, 1975; see Figure 1.3). However, with the emergence of postmodern forms of practice, a new view of direct practice has been suggested. Postmodern practitioners have questioned the traditional social work assessment and intervention process. Dean (1993) captured the postmodern view:

> The expressions "diagnosis," "assessment," "therapy," and "treatment" derived from the medical and research models . . . suggest that the client is sick and needs to recover. In addition, these terms turn the client or problem into a finite entity to be studied and diagnosed. Similarly problematic, the term "interventions" defines a process in which the clinician does something to the client (or situation). (p. 60)

The following section broadly differentiates the relationship of positivist and postmodern human behavior theory to the helping process.

SOCIAL WORK METHOD AND HUMAN BEHAVIOR THEORY

To intervene effectively in the person-in-environment configuration, the social worker must be guided by theoretical understanding.
—H. S. Strean, *Social Casework Theories in Action*

Practitioners and students alike often are puzzled by what questions to ask during interviews: Should I encourage the client to talk? Should I interrupt with a question? Is some information more relevant than other information? What do I need to know about the client to properly understand the problem or situation? The social worker may answer such questions more easily if he or she comes to the interview with sufficient guidelines for helping strategies. No matter what the practice paradigm,

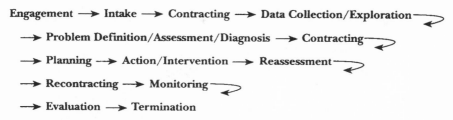

Figure 1.3. Phases of the social work helping process.

theories of human behavior influence the social worker's thinking about the helping process in important ways.

Having an orientation to the helping process is one of the most critical aspects in the professional use of self (Greene, 1986). A theoretical model of human behavior is a point of departure in social work practice. Having a working knowledge of a theory's assumptions provides guidelines about how to carry out the social work role. Whom to include in an interview, how to conduct it, and what activities and resources the social worker may use successfully are among the issues that may be answered by the practitioner's chosen theoretical orientation.

Assessment and the Positivist Tradition

Meyer (1982) best summed up the need for a set of human behavior assumptions, a system for data collection, and a basis for making decisions in the situation. She suggested that "what one is trained to see one addresses in assessment and intervention" (pp. 19–20). For social workers who have chosen a positivist theoretical practice approach, *assessment* is a procedure used to examine and evaluate the client's problem or situation. Through assessment, the social worker identifies and explains the nature of a problem or dysfunction, appraises it within a framework of specific elements, and uses that appraisal as a guide to action (Perlman, 1957). The purpose of an assessment, whether the problem originates with an individual, family, or group, is to bring together the various facets of a client's situation, and the interaction among them, in an orderly, economical manner and to then select salient and effective interventions (Greene, 1986).

Assessment is "differential, individualized, and accurate identification and evaluation of problems, people, and situations and of their interrelations, to serve as a sound basis for differential helping intervention" (Siporin, 1975, p. 224). Accurate assessment requires sufficient information about a problem or situation. It also requires theoretical frameworks to guide how the practitioner will gather, analyze, and interpret the information.

An appraisal of a problem depends on achieving a process through which the practitioner obtains clarity about what "the client and the caseworker both hold in the center of focus" (Perlman, 1957, p. 119). Maintaining that focus is made possible not only through proper interviewing techniques but through an explicit assessment format that is based on a theoretical orientation. Throughout assessment, the practitioner collects data or "facts" about the client's situation. The theoretical assumptions adopted by the practitioner should guide how the practitioner selects pertinent data, and how he or she evaluates and relates the data to problem solving (Greene, 1986). From the initial client contact, the perception of information and professional decisions in response to this information are shaped by the social worker's theoretical orientation. That orientation allows the practitioner to select from the data he or she has gathered about the client those that are important and suggest what additional information needs to be gathered to complete the assessment.

Practitioners need to know, at least in general terms, what it is they hope to accomplish, what information (data) they need to obtain, and what plan for successive interviews they need to implement. For example, the social worker who uses a social systems approach knows that he or she wants to obtain information about the family's interactive and communication styles and that the goal is to educate the fam-

> Human behavior is used in conjunction with social work methods to assess and intervene on behalf of clients.

ily about what is dysfunctional about these patterns so that the family may change or modify those patterns. "Assessment is a process and a product of understanding on which action is based" (Siporin, 1975, p. 1).

In essence, assessment in the positivist tradition is an information-gathering process in which the ordering of data gives direction to the action to be taken by the social worker and client. An important value orientation in social work is the participation of clients in the development of an intervention or treatment plan. Although there is no clear-cut demarcation of phases, there usually is a time when client and social worker agree on treatment goals.

Assessment and the Postmodern Tradition

Postmodern practitioners have challenged social work's traditional approach to assessment and problem solving. For the postmodern therapist, the major goal is to help the client externalize the problem rather than view the problem as an inherent or fixed part of self:

> Questions are introduced that encourage clients to map the influence of the problem in their lives and relationships. . . . This identifies the problem-saturated description of . . . life. This practice facilitates a mutually acceptable definition of the problem, and the exploration of new possibilities. (White, 1994, p. 89)

In the postmodern approach, the social worker generally does not ask predetermined interview questions, but encourages a search for understanding (for an invaluable description of postmodern ideas, see Laird, 1993). That is, the practitioner explores the client's ideas about the nature of "individual dysfunction" (McNamee & Gergen, 1992). Social workers who have adopted a postmodern approach to "assessment" focus on the client's definition of the situation, emphasize the client's unique meaning of events, and ask questions that lead to a collaborative view of solutions.

The manner in which the practitioner works with the client to define the situation may be portrayed as circular (Figure 1.4). Tomm (1994), who has provided an example framework of circular questioning, has distinguished four major groups of questions that practitioners may ask:

Lineal orienting questions: those that presuppose normative data can be collected about each client provided, such as "What problems brought you to see me today?"

Circular questions: primarily exploratory, "How is it we find ourselves together today?"

Strategic questions: based on an assumption the practitioner holds about the client, such as "When are you going to take charge of your life and start looking for a job?"

Reflexive questions: intended to place the client in a reflexive position or to trigger the consideration of new options, such as "If your depression suddenly disappeared, how would your life be different?"

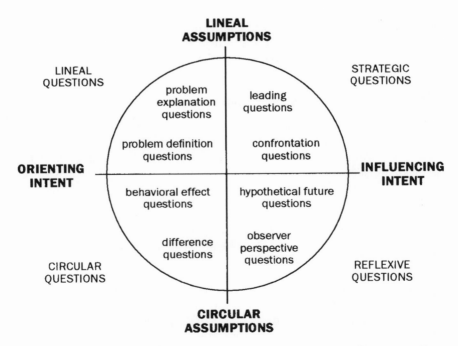

Figure 1.4.   A framework for distinguishing four major groups of questions. From Tomm (1994).

Treatment/Intervention in the Positivist Tradition

As with assessment, social workers use different approaches to intervention according to the theoretical framework that guides their helping process. Intervention strategies also differ according to their specific purpose, a client's problems or life situation, and the organizational or agency context. A spectrum of activities, ranging from interventions aimed at making social institutions more responsive to the needs of people to therapies focused on developing individual insight, compose social work treatment.

Generally, treatment that begins at the initial client-social worker contact should seek to enable clients to improve their psychosocial functioning. Helping people increase their problem-solving and coping capacities, obtaining resources and services, facilitating interaction among individuals and their environments, improving interpersonal relationships, and influencing social institutions and organizations all come under the rubric of social work treatment (Lowy, 1979).

In the complex practice world, the seasoned practitioner may use an eclectic orientation that involves "the technical flexibility of selecting interventions on the basis of specific client/problem/situation configuration" (Fischer, 1978, p. 237). An eclectic orientation also carries with it the need for the effective integration of a number of theories. Nonetheless, those helping strategies must be guided by the disciplined and continuous effort to make explicit how human behavior theory rather than personal bias influences the decision-making process.

Renaming a Postmodern Tradition

In the postmodern tradition, the therapeutic conversation is the primary vehicle for helping the client be more efficacious. The client-social worker dialogue sets in motion a helping process that reframes a problem-laden client narrative with little or no sense of agency to a new story with a client sense of empowerment (McNamee & Gergen, 1992). Postmodern theorists Duncan, Solovey, and Rusk (1992) have suggested that the common thread uniting client-centered therapies is the practitioner's suggestions that help the client formulate "competing experiences—[those] that compete in some way with the client's actual experiences of the presenting problem" (p. 92, see Figure 1.4)

To create competing experiences, the practitioner adopts a nonpathological posture and focuses on client resources, learns client goals or what the client wants, collaborates with the client in the description of the problem and selection of solutions, interrupts negative solutions or counterproductive behavior, helps seek new meaning of events, and validates client experiences.

The major therapeutic tool in client-centered postmodern approaches is the conversational question. Anderson and Goolishian (1988) described this approach:

> The therapist develops the art of asking questions that are not focused on discovering information and collecting data. Questions are not considered interventions, searches for preselected answers or checking out hypotheses. Questions are the tools of the therapist in a therapeutic conversation, and they are to be guided and informed by the views of the clients so that the conversation is geared toward maximum production of new information, understanding, meaning, and interpretation. (p. 383)

Meaning and understanding comes about through therapeutic conversations between client and social worker. "Not-knowing questions" are central to helping a client "bring into the open something unknown and unforeseen into the realm of possibility" (Anderson & Goolishian, 1992, p. 34). Thus, the reconstruction of the client's story or narrative and the client's ability to carry these new meanings forward into action is the major goal. In the ultimate sense, this is the use of the *strengths perspective*— an empowering process by which clients transform themselves personally and collectively (Albrecht & Brewer, 1990; Saleeby, 1992; Sullivan, 1992; Weick, Rapp, Sullivan, & Kisthardt, 1989).

REFERENCES

Albrecht, L., & Brewer, R. M. (1990). *Bridges of Power: Women's Multicultural Alliances.* Philadelphia: New Society.

Allen, J. (1993). The constructivist paradigm: Values and ethics. In J. Laird (Ed.), *Revisioning Social Work Education: A Social Constructionist Approach* (pp. 31–54). New York: Haworth.

Anderson, H., & Goolishian, H. (1988). Human systems as linguistic systems. *Family Process, 27*, 371–395.

Anderson, H., & Goolishian, H. (1992). The client is the expert: A not-knowing approach to therapy. In S. McNamee & K. J. Gergen (Eds.), *Therapy As Social Construction* (pp. 25–39). Newbury Park, CA: Sage.

Anderson, J. (1981). *Social Work Methods and Processes.* Belmont, CA: Wadsworth.

Bartlett, H. M. (1970). *The Common Base of Social Work Practice.* New York: Putnam.

Bloom, M. (1984). *Configurations of Human Behavior.* New York: Macmillan.

Blumer, H. (1969). *Symbolic Interactionism: Perspective and Method.* Englewood Cliffs, NJ: Prentice-Hall.

Briar, S., & Miller, H. (1971). *Problems and Issues in Social Casework.* New York: Columbia University Press.

Burrell, G., & Morgan, G. (1979). *Sociological Paradigms and Organizational Analysis.* London: Heineman.

Chess, W. A., & Norlin, J. M. (1988). *Human Behavior and the social Environment.* Boston: Allyn and Bacon.

Collins, B. G. (1986). Defining feminist social work. *Social Work, 31*(3), 214–219.

Compton, B., & Galaway, B. (1994). *Social Work Processes.* Pacific Grove, CA: Brooks/Cole.

Council on Social Work Education (1971). *Undergraduate Programs in Social Work: Guidelines to Curriculum Content, Field Instruction, and Organization.* New York: Author.

Council on Social Work Education (1992). *Handbook of Accreditation Standards and Procedures* (rev. ed.). Alexandria, VA: Author.

Council on Social Work Education (1974). *Standards for the Accreditation of Baccalaureate and Degree Programs in Social Work.* New York: Author.

Council on Social Work Education (1984). *Handbook of Accreditation Standards and Procedures* (rev. ed.). New York: Author.

Dean, R. (1993). Teaching a constructivist approach to clinical practice. In J. Laird (Ed.), *Revisioning Social Work Education: A Social Constructionist Approach* (pp. 55–75). New York: Haworth.

Dean, R. G., & Fenby, B. L. (1989). Exploring epistemologies: Social work action as a reflection of philosophical assumptions. *Journal of Social Work Education, 25*(1), 46–53.

Dean, R. G., & Fleck-Henderson, A. (1992). Teaching clinical theory and practice through a constructivist lens. *Journal of Teaching in Social Work, 6*(1). 3–20.

Duncan, B. L., Solovey, A. D., & Rusk, G. S. (1992). *Changing the Rules: A Client Directed Approach to Therapy.* New York: Guilford.

Ewalt, P. (Ed). (1980). *NASW Conference Proceedings: Toward a Definition of Clinical Social Work.* Washington, DC: National Association of Social Workers.

Firestone, S. (1962). The scientific component in the casework field curriculum. In C. Kasius (Ed.), *Social Casework in the Fifties* (pp. 311–325). New York: Family Service Association of America.

Fischer, J. (1978). *Effective Casework Practice: An Eclectic Approach.* New York: McGraw-Hill.

Fischer, J. (1981). The social work revolution. *Social Work, 26*(3), 199–207.

Fleck-Henderson, A. (1993). A constructivist approach to "Human Behavior and the Social Environment I." In J. Laird (Ed.), *Revisioning Social Work Education: A Social Constructionist Approach* (pp. 219–238). New York: Haworth.

Foucault, M. (1980). *Power/Knowledge: Selected Interviews and Other Writings.* New York: Pantheon.

Freeman, J. (1990). Beyond women's issues: Feminism and social work. *Affilia, 5*(2), 72–89.

Germain, C. B. (Ed.) (1979). *Social Work Practice: People and Environments.* New York: Columbia University Press.

Germain, C. B., & Gitterman, A. (1980). *The Life Model of Social Work Practice.* New York: Columbia University Press.

Germain, C. B., & Gitterman, A. (1987). Ecological perspectives. In A. Minahan (Editor-in-Chief), *Encyclopedia of Social Work* (Vol. 1, 18th ed., pp. 488–499). Silver Spring, MD: National Association of Social Workers.

Gilbert, N., & Specht, H. (1987). Social planning and community organization. In

A. Minahan (Editor-in-Chief), *Encyclopedia of Social Work* (Vol. 2, 18th ed., pp. 602–619). Silver Spring, MD: National Association of Social Workers.

Gordon, W. (1962). A critique of the working definition. *Social Work, 7*(4), 3–13.

Gordon, W. E. (1984). The obsolete scientific imperative in social work research. *Social Work, 29*(1), 74–75.

Gould, K. H. (1988). Old wine in new bottles: A feminist perspective on Gilligan's theory. *Social Work, 33*(5), 411–415.

Greene, R. R. (1986). *Social Work with the Aged and Their Families.* Hawthorne, NY: Aldine de Gruyter.

Greene, R. R. (1994). *Human Behavior Theory: A Diversity Framework.* Hawthorne, NY: Aldine de Gruyter.

Greene, R. R., & McGuire, L. (1998). Ecological perspective: Meeting the challenge of practice with diverse populations. In R. R. Greene & M. Watkins (Eds.), *Serving Diverse Constituencies. Applying the Ecological Perspective* (pp. 1–29). Hawthorne, NY: Aldine de Gruyter.

Greene, R. R., & Watkins, M. (Eds.) (1998). *Serving Diverse Constituencies. Applying the Ecological Perspective.* Hawthorne, NY: Aldine de Gruyter.

Guba, E. G. (Ed.) (1990). *The Paradigm Dialog.* Newbury Park, CA: Sage.

Hempel, C. G. (1960). Operationalism, observation and theoretical terms. In A. Danto & S. Morgenbesser, (Eds.), *Philosophy of Science* (pp. 101–120). Cleveland: World.

Hepworth, D. H., & Larsen, J. (1982). *Direct Social Work Practice.* Homewood, IL: Dorsey.

Karls, J., Lowery, C., Mattaini, M., & Wandrei, K. (1997). The use of the PIE (person-in-environment) system in social work education. *Journal of Social Work Education, 33*(1), 49–59.

Kelly, G. S. (1955). *The Psychology of Personal Constructs.* New York: W. W. Norton.

Kuhn, T. (1970). *The Structure of Scientific Revolutions.* Chicago: University of Chicago Press.

Laird, J. (1993). Introduction. In J. Laird (Ed.), *Revisioning Social Work Education: A Social Constructionist Approach* (pp. 1–10). New York: Haworth.

Land, H. (1995). Feminist clinical social work in the 21st century. In N. Van Den Bergh (Ed.), *Feminist Practice in the 21st Century* (pp. 3–19). Washington, DC: NASW Press.

Lax, W. D. (1992). Postmodern thinking in a clinical practice. In S. McNamee & K. J. Gergen (Eds.), *Therapy as Social Construction* (pp. 69–85). Newbury Park, CA: Sage.

Lowy, L. (1979). *Social Work with the Aging: The Challenge and Promise of the Later Years.* New York: Harper & Row.

Martin, P. Y., & O'Connor, G. G. (1989). *The Social Environment: Open Systems Applications.* New York: Longman.

McIntosh, P. (1988). White privilege and male privilege: A personal account of coming to see correspondence through work in women's studies. Working paper 189, Wellesley College for Research on Women, Wellesley, MA.

McNamee, S., & Gergen, K. J. (Eds.) (1992). *Therapy As Social Construction* (pp. 25–39). Newbury Park, CA: Sage.

Meyer, C. (1982). Issues in clinical social work: In search of a consensus. In P. Caroff

(Ed.), *Treatment Formulations and Clinical Social Work* (pp. 19–26). Silver Spring, MD: National Association of Social Workers.

Meyer, C. (1983). Selecting appropriate practice models. In A. Rosenblatt & D. Waldfogel (Eds.), *Handbook of Clinical Social Work* (pp. 731–749). San Francisco, CA: Jossey-Bass.

Meyer, C. (1987). Direct practice in social work: Overview. In A. Minahan (Editor-in-Chief), *Encyclopedia of Social Work* (Vol. 1, pp. 409–422). Silver Spring, MD: National Association of Social Workers.

Newman, B., & Newman, P. R. ([1979] 1987). *Development through Life: A Psycho Social Approach.* Homewood, IL: Dorsey.

Northen, H. (1982). *Clinical Social Work.* New York: Columbia University Press.

O'Neil, M. J. (1984). *The General Method of Social Work Practice.* Englewood Cliffs NJ: Prentice Hall.

Perlman, H. H. (1957). *Social Casework: A Problem-Solving Process.* Chicago: University of Chicago Press.

Pozatek, E. (1994). The problem of certainty: Clinical social work in the postmodern era. *Social Work, 39*(4) 396–403.

Reynolds, B. C. ([1969] 1985). *Learning and Teaching in the Practice of Social Work.* Silver Spring, MD: National Association of Social Workers.

Richmond, M. (1917). *Social Diagnosis.* New York: Russell Sage Foundation.

Robbins, S. P., Chatterjee, P., & Canda, E. R. (1998). *Contemporary Behavior Theory: A Critical Perspective for Social Work.* Boston: Allyn & Bacon.

Saleeby, D. (1992). *The Strengths Perspective in Social Work Practice.* New York: Longman.

Saleeby, D. (1993). Notes on interpreting the human condition: A constructed HBSE curriculum. In J. Laird (Ed.), *Revisioning Social Work Education: A Social Constructionist Approach* (pp. 197–217). New York: Haworth.

Schiele, J. H. (1996). Afrocentricity: An emerging paradigm in social work practice. *Social Work, 41*(3), 284–294.

Schon, D. (1983). *The Reflective Practitioner.* New York: Basic Books.

Schriver, J. M. (1995). *Human Behavior and the Social Environment: Shifting Paradigms in Essential Knowledge for Social Work Practice.* Needham Heights, MA: Allyn & Bacon.

Schwartz, W. (1961). Social worker in the group. Paper presented at the National Conference on Social Welfare, Social Welfare Forum, New York.

Shaw, M. E., & Costanzo, P. R. (1982). *Theories of Social Psychology* (2nd ed.). New York: McGraw-Hill.

Sheafor, B. W., Horejsi, C. R., & Horejsi, G. A. (1988). *Techniques and Guidelines for Social Work Practice.* Boston: Allyn & Bacon.

Sheafor, B. W., & Landon, P. S. (1987). Generalist perspective. In A. Minahan (Editor-in-Chief), *Encyclopedia of Social Work* (Vol. 1, 18th ed.). Silver Spring, MD: National Association of Social Workers.

Siporin, M. (1975). *Introduction to Social Work Practice.* New York: Macmillan.

Specht, R., & Craig, G. J. (1982). *Human Development: A Social Work Perspective.* Englewood Cliffs, NJ: Prentice Hall.

Strean, H. S. (Ed.) (1971). *Social Casework Theories in Action.* Metuchen, NJ: Scarecrow.

Sullivan, P. W. (1992). Reclaiming the community: The strengths perspective and deinstitutionalization. *Social Work, 27*(3), 204–209.

Swigonski, M. E. (1996). Challenging privilege through Africentric social work practice. *Social Work, 41*(2), 153–161.

Tice, K. (1990). Gender and social work education: Directions for the 1990s. *Journal of Social Work Education, 26*, 134–144.

Tomm, K. (1994). Interventive interviewing: Part III. Intending to ask lineal, circular, strategic, or reflexive questions? In K. Brownlee, P. Gallant, and D. Carpenter (Eds.), *Constructivism and Family Therapy* (pp. 117–156.). Thunder Bay, Canada: Lakehead University Printing Services.

Trader, H. P. (1977). Survival strategies for oppressed minorities. *Social Work, 22*(1), 10–13.

Tully, C. T. (1994). Epilogue. Power and the social work profession. In R. R. Greene (Ed.), *Human Behavior Theory: A Diversity Framework* (pp. 235–243). Hawthorne, NY: Aldine de Gruyter.

Turner, F. J. (Ed.) (1986). *Social Work Treatment: Interlocking Theoretical Approaches.* New York: Free Press.

Turner, F. J. (1995). Social work practice: Theoretical base. In R. L. Edwards (Editor-in-chief), *Encyclopedia of Social Work* (Vol. 3, 19th ed., pp. 2258–2265). Washington, DC: NASW Press.

Van Den Bergh, N. (1995). Feminist social work practice: Where have we been. . . . Where are we going? In N. Van Den Bergh (Ed.), *Feminist Practice in the 21st Century* (p. xi). Washington, DC: NASW Press.

Van Den Bergh, N., & Cooper (Eds.) (1986). *Feminist Visions for Social Work.* Silver Spring, MD: National Association of Social Workers.

Wakefield, J. C. (1996). Does social work need the eco-systems perspective [Part 1]? *Social Service Review, 70*, 1–32.

Weick, A. (1993). Reconstructing social work education. In J. Laird (Ed.), *Revisioning Social Work Education: A Social Constructionist Approach* (pp. 11–30). New York: Haworth.

Weick, A., Rapp, C., Sullivan, P. W., & Kisthardt, W. (1989). A strengths perspective in social work practice. *Social Work, 34*(4), 350–356.

Wetzel, J. (1986). A feminist world view conceptual framework. *Social Casework, 67*, 166–173.

White, M. (1994). The externalizing of the problem and the re-authoring of lives and relationships. In K. Brownlee, P. Gallant, & D. Carpenter (Eds.), *Constructivism and Family Therapy.* Lakehead University, Canada: Lakehead University Press.

White, M., & Epston, D. (1990). *Narrative Means to Therapeutic Ends.* New York: W. W. Norton.

Zanden, J. W. V. (1985). *Human Development.* New York: Knopf.

Zastrow, C., & Kirst-Ashman, K. (1987). *Understanding Human Behavior and the Social Environment.* Chicago: Nelson Hall.

2

Human Behavior Theory and Professional Social Work Practice

ROBERTA R. GREENE

The purpose of human behavior and the social environment content within the social work curriculum is to provide us with knowledge for practice.
—J. Schriver, *Human Behavior and the Social Environment: Shifting Paradigms in Essential Knowledge for Social Work Practice*

[T]he human behavior sequence . . . requires all educational programs to develop a coherent approach to selecting research and theories in the social, behavioral, and biological sciences, and to present them in a way that will illuminate divergencies and interrelationships.
—C. Germain, *Human Behavior in the Social Environment: An Ecological View*

The expansive person-in-environment perspective, which is central to the social work human behavior and the social environment theoretical base and the profession's approach to practice, has led to an equally broad knowledge base. Meyer (1982) noted that what the social worker is supposed to do should dictate the boundaries of the profession's knowledge base. However, the definition of social work activities is so broad that "there are hardly any boundaries to knowledge that social workers need to get through the working day" (p. 27). Goldstein also (1980) defined the lack of precise knowledge boundaries as a concern: "It becomes necessary for each practitioner to be expert in understanding individuals, their environment, the society, and the transactions among people and environments. One might ask, what else is there?" (p. 43).

Postmodern theorists have further complicated the question of what theories—knowledge—are needed for social work practice. Because they have given less credence to normative theories based on a specific body of scientific knowledge and, rather, have emphasized individual knowledge and belief, postmodern theorists also have taken exception with the view that universities are the only seats of learning. Instead, postmodernist thinkers have argued that knowledge is a process or art involving intuitive thinking and interpretation developed within a cultural, historical, and sociopolitical context (Weick, 1993).

Despite the lack of consensus about how social workers acquire the knowledge of human behavior needed for social work practice, answers are suggested in the widely accepted person-in-environment perspective reflected in the Council on Social Work Education (CSWE, 1992) curriculum policy statement:

> The professional foundation must provide content about theories and knowledge of human bio-psycho-social development, including theories and knowledge about the range of social systems in which individuals live (families, groups, organizations, institutions, and communities). The human behavior and social environment curriculum must provide an understanding of the interactions between and among human biological, social, psychological, and cultural systems as they affect and are affected by human behavior. The impact of social and economic forces on individual and social systems must be presented. Content must be provided about the ways in which systems promote or deter people in the maintenance or attainment of optimal health and well-being. Content about values and ethical issues related to bio-psycho-social theories must be included. Students must be taught to evaluate theory and apply theory to client situations. (p. 8)

This chapter outlines and critiques the broad content areas noted in the policy statement and discusses their relationship to social work practice.

EXPLAINING DEVELOPMENT ACROSS THE LIFE CYCLE

[The concern of clinical social work is] the assessment of interaction between the individual's biological, psychological and social experience which provides a guide for clinical intervention.
—J. Cohen, "Nature of Clinical Social Work"

The idea is . . . that these [family] stages, with some acknowledgment of biological realities, are social constructions that have political, economic, social, and ethnic meaning.
—D. Saleebey, "Notes on Interpreting the Human Condition: A Constructed HBSE Curriculum"

Developmental Theory: A Positivist/ Traditional View

Positivist theorists have proposed that developmental theory offers a means of understanding the client's behavior within the broader context of the life span and within the complex of biopsychosocial events. The aim of developmental theory is to account for both stability and change of human behavior across the life cycle (Table 2.1). Before 1940, most social scientists believed that development did not occur after people became physically mature. Today, it generally is accepted that development, particularly in the cognitive and affective spheres, occurs across the life cycle (Kastenbaum, 1979; Newman & Newman, [1979] 1987).

Life span development draws from a collection of theories and, because of the complexity of the subject matter, involves many scientific disciplines. Life span developmental theory addresses all aspects of human development within an environmental context; this approach to human development considers the individual's genetic endowment, physiology, psychology, family, home, community, culture, education, religion, ethnicity / race, gender, sexual orientation, and economic status (Rogers, 1982). Developmental theory falls within the scope of the person-in-the-situation construct and often serves as a useful body of information for social workers. It contributes to social work practice by providing the broad parameters for understanding a client's growth, development, and behavioral changes, from conception to death. It offers a biopsychosocial approach to assessment, which allows a social worker to view the client's functioning both longitudinally over time and cross sectionally in the light of stage-specific factors.

> Many theorist consider development to be continuous and cumulative, moving in a direction that is increasingly complex.

Developmental theory can

- provide a framework for ordering the life cycle
- describe a process that is both continuous and changing from conception to death
- address stability and change in the unfolding of life transitions
- account for the factors that may shape development at each specific stage
- discuss the multiple biopsychosocial factors shaping development
- explore the tasks to be accomplished at each life stage
- consider each life stage as emerging from earlier stages
- explain successes and failures at each stage as shaped by the outcome of earlier stages
- recognize personal differences in development

Life Span Development: Different Lenses

Positivist theorists have called for universal principles of psychological and social functioning. Because universal principles may not always give

Table 2.1.   Summary of Definitions of Human Development

Author	Definition
Birren and Woodruff (1973)	Development is a process whereby the individual goes from a less differentiated to a more differentiated state, from a less complex to more complex organism, from a lower or early stage to a higher or later stage of an ability, skill, or trait.
Greene (1986)	Developmental theory encompasses biopsychosocial variables and accounts for stability and change across the life cycle.
Kastenbaum (1979)	Development is the unfolding of potential.
Schell and Hall (1979)	Development is an orderly, ever-increasing, more complex change (in behavior) in a consistent direction.
Specht and Craig (1982)	Human development is a process blending biological and cultural factors and refers to changes over time in the structure, thought, and behavior of a person. These changes, which begin at conception and continue through old age, are usually progressive and cumulative, and result in enlarged body size, increasingly complex activity, and greater integration of functions.
Zanden (1985)	Development is the orderly and sequential changes that occur with the passage of time as an organism moves from conception to death. Development includes both hereditary and environmental forces and the interaction between them.

credence to gender, ethnic/racial, cultural, and sociopolitical differences, and generalized human behavior theory may overemphasize commonality and universality without giving sufficient attention to individual variations, postmodern thinkers may shy away from universal explanations of the complex interaction of biopsychosocial factors. Postmodern thinkers have questioned a fixed approach to describing the life cycle (Weick, 1983). Particularly at a time when social workers serve an increasingly heterogeneous population, postmodern theorists have contended that practitioners should explore diversity and differences. Each life cycle is best understood within a client's cultural milieu and the broader social context. Furthermore, social workers may best approach differences in factors such as gender by exploring socialization behaviors and relationship building (Land, 1995).

Stage theories examine the development of specific underlying biopsychosocial structures and propose that development moves in one direction, with each stage building on the preceding one. There are defined "normal"' behaviors at various stages. Although social workers continue to use developmental theory, they increasingly are recognizing that the timing of events, both in a personal and sociocultural sense, has a strong influence on the progression and mastery of developmental tasks (Kropf & Greene, 1994). For example, persons living with human immunodeficiency virus (HIV) may find it difficult to experience tasks occurring at other than the "usual stage" (Greene, 1994, p. 6). Hale (1992) described an experience with a young mother who attempted to grasp the meaning of her HIV diagnosis on her young child:

> The first thing she said to me . . . "So I have to die?" . . . I thought, of course, everybody has to die. But that wasn't the question she was asking. She was twenty-one years old. She was really asking "[D]o I have to die soon?" She really wanted to see her child grow up. (p. 8)

Another example of the limitations of the life span model is seen in the phenomenon of aged African-American women parenting grandchildren (Burnette, 1997; Queiro-Tajalli & Smith, 1998). Multiple factors, such as the rate of adolescent pregnancy and increases in addiction and substance abuse as well as HIV disease among young mothers, have contributed to this seemingly inappropriate life task. "The question then becomes whether any fixed, determined sequence of life tasks adequately addresses an understanding of human development during changing cultural, social, and political eras" (Kropf & Greene, 1994, p. 81).

Postmodern and ecological theorists have argued that practitioners should understand each life cycle and also that development is context specific (Boxer & Cohler, 1989; Germain, 1994). An alternative approach to studying how people live out their lives is called the *life course* (Bronfenbrenner, 1989) "The concept of life course is concerned with the timing of life events in relation to the social structures and historical changes affecting them" (Haraeven, 1982, p. 16; see Chapter 8).

> Ecological and postmodern theorists suggest that development is best understood by exploring the context of an individual's life course.

Postmodern theorists have also questioned the idea of developmental stages. Gergen (1982) argued that there is no universal standard for human behavior:

> It is becoming increasingly apparent to investigators in this domain that developmental trajectories over the life span are highly variable; neither with respect to psychological functioning nor overt conduct does there appear to

be transhistorical generality in life span trajectory. . . . A virtual infinity of developmental forms seems possible. (p. 161)

In essence, an alternative view of development and another lens for understanding the lifespan suggest that human growth is an innate, common life force that "revolve[s] around the capacity for intimacy, the capacity to nurture, engagement in productive activity, establishment of balance between dependence and independence, and the capacity to transcend personal concerns" (Weick, 1983, p. 134).

ACCOUNTING FOR BIOPSYCHOSOCIAL FUNCTIONING

Because difficulty in any one area may lead to a request for social work services, understanding the interplay of biological, psychological, social, and cultural elements of development in the life space of individuals has traditionally been a central feature of clinical social work practice (Caroff, 1982). Historically, an understanding of biological factors includes an exploration of genetic endowment, as well as the physiologically induced changes and functional capacities of vital organ systems that contribute to health, well-being, and life expectancy. Consideration of social factors involves the capacity for carrying out social roles with respect to other members of society, whereas psychological components deal with the coping strategies and adaptive capacities of the individual vis-à-vis environmental demands (Birren, 1969; Greene, 1986).

Biological Development

Biological development is the process that traditionally is most closely associated with the individual's capacity for survival or position along his or her life span. An understanding of physiological development includes all time-dependent changes in structure and function of the organism, allows for a general prediction of a person's growth rate, and, allows for whether a person is "older" or "younger" than other individuals of the same chronological age (Birren & Renner, 1977). This prediction, in turn, permits an understanding of whether the individual has the characteristic physiological changes, health, and life expectancy of people of the same age, for example:

"She weighs half the normal birth weight."
"He is shorter than everyone in his class."
"He has the heart of a forty-year-old."
"She has the stamina of a woman half her age."

In the strictest sense, biological age is a measure of the vital life-limiting organ systems closely associated with the client's current state of health, health history, and health habits (Zarit, 1980). In a broader context, biological processes involve the client's characteristic rates of energy output, of fatiguing, of recovery from fatigue, and characteristic rhythms of activity and rest; how the individual uses his or her body, including sports skills; and attractiveness of face, physique, and grooming in terms of their impact on others. Biological processes may also encompass physical strengths, limitations, and challenges, including how the individual manages them and how the individual thinks and feels about them. This resolution also involves psychological and social processes and illustrates the interplay among these factors (Butler, Lewis, & Sunderland, 1997; Havighurst, 1972).

Sociocultural Development

Social workers are much more attuned to and have had a long history of concern about the sociocultural aspects of clients' lives. Traditional theories about how social processes influence development have focused on how the individual becomes integrated into society. An understanding of this development requires that the practitioner become familiar with the client in relationship to other members of the client's social groups. Knowledge of rituals, cultural myths, social expectations, communication rules, family forms, political and religious ideologies, and patterns of economic well-being is critical (Newman & Newman, [1979] 1987). Every society, and different subcultures within that society, has a system of social expectations regarding appropriate behavior for each life stage (Neugarten & Datan, 1973). Those expectations are experienced differentially as a person grows up and grows older, and he or she generally knows what is expected: when and how to go to school, to work, to marry, to raise children, to retire, and even to "grow old" and to die:

"My mother doesn't think I should date yet. She says I'm not old enough."

"My friends say my biological clock is running out. I just don't know if I want to start a family."

"I just don't feel old enough to retire, but I guess it's time."

From a positivist viewpoint, social work assessment involves the individualized attention to the client's role performance within his or her social reality. From this perspective, development can be viewed as the passage from one socially defined position (status) to another throughout the culturally recognized divisions of life—from infancy to old age—and the obligations, rights, and expectations (roles) that accompany these var-

ious positions (Bengston & Haber, 1983; Riley, Foner, Hess, & Toby, 1969).
An evaluation of the sociocultural aspects of development also requires
that the social worker become knowledgeable about the changes in social
structure that accompany an individual's life transitions. It is often the demands that accompany these life expectations that lead individuals to seek
social work services.

Sociocultural development focuses on the processes by which a person
negotiates a succession of roles and changing role constellations, learning
the behaviors appropriate to his or her
gender, social class, ethnic group, and
age. At each stage of life, as people perform new roles, adjust to changing
roles, and relinquish old ones, they are,
in effect, attempting to master new social situations. An understanding of
these complex processes is essential to sound social work practice.

> Biological, psychological, and social
> development is a unitary process.

Psychological Development

Another characteristic feature of social work practice is understanding
the way in which it integrates information on biological and social functioning with psychological functioning. The direct practice of social work
is distinguished by its interest in an individual's intrapersonal and interpersonal functioning in relation to his or her relative capacity to function
productively in a given society. This orientation places psychological developmental theory within the context of the person and situation configuration, with "person" referring to the individual's "inner states" (Cohen,
1980, p. 27). The study of psychological development encompasses a wide
range of behavioral, affective, and cognitive aspects of human experience.
Although language and terminology vary considerably, psychological developmental theory generally has come to refer to mental functioning and
those processes central to thinking and reasoning (Newman & Newman,
1987). Psychological development includes such diverse factors as an individual's perception, learning, memory, judgment, reasoning, problem-
solving ability, language skills, symbolic abilities, self-awareness, and
reality testing (ibid.).

An individual's abilities to acquire new information or concepts, to alter behavior as a result of experience, and to develop new skills are cognitive and sensory processes related to psychological development. This
development involves all five senses: (1) hearing, (2) taste, (3) smell, (4)
sight, and (5) the somatosensory (touch, vibration, temperature, kines-
thetics, and pain). Elements of cognitive functioning also include intelligence: the capacity and ability to learn and perform cognitive and
behavioral tasks; memory: the ability to retain information about specific

events that have occurred at a given time and place; and learning: the ability to acquire knowledge about the world (see Chapter 6).

Biopsychosocial Development: New Lens

Human behavior and the social environment curriculum continues to emphasize content on the interactions between and among biological, social, psychological, and cultural systems. However, approaches other than a positivist theoretical approach are available. Traditionally, psychological aspects of human behavior have been viewed as either intrinsic to the person or socially created (Pardeck, Murphy, & Min Choi, 1994). An alternative view of the self that has moved away from structure and life span trajectory suggests that personality development occurs through interaction with others, that the self arises through social interaction (Ephross & Greene, 1991; Gergen, 1985; Weick, 1993). For example, postmodern theorists have a fluid view of the self or, as Hoffman (1992) said, the self is "a stretch of moving history, like a river or stream" (p. 10).

Historically, social workers have focused on structural metaphors such as role behaviors and the fulfilling of role expectations for understanding the social dimensions of human behavior. That is, what is understood to be appropriate behavior stems from the structure of society, a person's educational attainment, family of origin, or social class, and people's obligations to one another (Thompson & Greene, 1994. Theorists such as symbolic interactionists and social constructivists have proposed an alternative view that "the social world cannot be treated as an objective system" (Pardeck et al., 1994, p. 343). Rather, behaviors and their meaning are subjective, developed through discourse. Meaning, then, is a social product created by people as they interact (Blumer, 1969; see Chapter 9).

Although the incorporation of biopsychosocial content remains a well-recognized feature of clinical social work practice, there have been a number of challenges in terms of the adequacy of the concept (Johnson et al., 1990). For example, Saleebey (1992) has called for a much greater appreciation and articulation of the biological component of human behavior. The extension of the biopsychosocial con-

> Postmodern theorists suggest that the development of the self is best understood as an ongoing interactive process.

cept to include the spiritual dimension is also under debate (Amato-Von Hemert & Clark, 1994; Cascio, 1998; DiBlasio, 1993; Joseph, 1987). On the one hand, social work has been seen as a secular profession; on the other hand, there is growing concern that clinical social workers should integrate a spiritual perspective into their social work practice (Canda, 1988, 1989; Cornett, 1992; Joseph, 1987; Yamashiro & Matsuoka, 1997). For example,

Cornett (1992) has proposed that when the social worker does not explore the spiritual aspects of a client's life situation, he or she may diminish the potential for client growth. Cornett went on to state that a social worker who infuses such a broad definition of spirituality into the social worker–client relationship gains a better understanding of the client's response to life events.

Adaptation

The literature has suggested that there is little consensus about what constitutes mental health and mental illness, and each theory may begin with a different conception (Goldstein, 1987). Definitions of mental illness tend to be vague, ill-defined, and reflective of diverse theoretical positions. These definitions include the viewpoint that there is no such thing as mental illness (Szaaz, 1960; Termerlin, 1979), the perspective that "there are no universally accepted definitions of health and illness" (Lieberman, 1987, p. 112), and the view that specific criteria for defining mental illness can be established (Jahoda, 1958). Nonetheless, as members of one of the mental health professions, social workers have had a long-standing concern with issues of personality development as they relate to mental health and have had a need to keep abreast of contemporary perspectives about the causative factors related to mental illness (Williams, 1995).

The concept of adaptiveness most often is understood to be the goodness-of-fit between the individual and his or her environment and vice versa. From a social work standpoint, adaptiveness is transactional in nature and involves the reciprocal influence of the environment and the individual, with both the individual and his or her environment making mutual demands on and influencing the other (Germain & Gitterman, 1995). Reynolds (1933) drove this point home as early as the 1930s, when she stated, "The essential point seems to be that the function of social casework is not to treat the individual alone nor his environment alone, but the process of adaptation which is the dynamic interaction between the two" (p. 337). The enhancement of the person-environment reciprocal relationship continues to be at the heart of direct practice in social work.

Meeting life's biopsychosocial transitions successfully is another key feature long associated with adaptability. This process, too, is reciprocal with each transition involving personal development and a changing environment. Among the behaviors considered adaptive are those that contribute to effective modes of dealing with reality, lead to a mastery of the environment, resolve conflict, reduce stress, and establish personal satisfaction (Bloom, 1984; Maddi, 1972). Mastery of the environment, or adaptability, also has been linked to the concepts of stress, crisis, and coping

(Compton & Galaway, 1994; Newman & Newman, 1987). Because so much of social work practice involves engaging with a client (system) who is in a state of crisis, an awareness of how individuals develop the capacity to shape their environment is critical. Caroff (1982) has suggested that finding a means of reducing stress, strengthening coping resources, and releasing adaptive capacities provides the basis for formulating social work intervention strategies.

Social workers have also turned to standards set among the mental health professions for formulations for determining what constitutes mental health and mental illness. Practitioners need a basic knowledge of psychopathology in many social work practice settings. For example, social workers use the American Psychiatric Association's (1994) *Diagnostic and Statistical Manual of Mental Disorders Fourth Edition, Revised* (DSM-IV) to arrive at multiaxial psychiatric diagnoses, often for the purpose of filing insurance claims (Williams, 1995). The DSM-IV is an atheoretical manual produced by a task force of mental health practitioners to arrive at standard terminology and precision in diagnostic classifications (Frances, Pincus, First, & Widiger, 1990). The reliance on diagnostic categories has had both supporters and critics (Kirk & Kutchins, 1992; Kutchins & Kirk, 1995; Tomm, 1990; Williams and Spitzer, 1995). For example, Johnson (1987) cautioned that, without the knowledge of diagnostic categories, the social worker would likely focus almost exclusively on interpersonal transactions, which might be effects rather than causes: "Only when an in-depth evaluation indicates that nothing can be done about the causes themselves should attention be directed exclusively to effects. In the absence of such an evaluation, attention to interpersonal effects may simply impede the identi-

> The concept of what is "normal" is defined by historical place, time, and culture. There also appears to be an underlying biological basis for major mental illnesses.

fication of causes" (p. 848). In contrast, Allen (1993) has stated that, when using diagnostic categories, "it is all too easy inadvertently to impose the 'normal' view of the dominant society even though the practitioner is well-intentioned" (p. 40).

Although for some practitioners the use of medical and psychiatric diagnoses may be controversial, it is important for social workers to be alert to and recognize the symptoms of physical and mental disease. It is increasingly necessary for social workers to engage in informed consideration of the possible causes of the various physical and personality disorders, psychosocial stressors, and issues of adaptive functioning associated with mental health and mental illness (Williams, 1987).

The viewpoint that biological causative factors are associated with serious mental illnesses is one that is increasingly accepted (Johnson, 1986;

Northen, 1987; Sullivan, 1998). According to Sullivan, for example, there is little variance in universality and prevalence rates for severe mental illness:

> The preponderance of evidence points to very real neurobiological involve-
> ment in human conditions that are labeled in a variety of ways worldwide.
> Thus, these conditions require attention and care, and this care extends be-
> yond the identified individual to include family and community. (p. 222)

In addition, he contended that assessment of severe mental illness requires culture sensitivity and a focus on strengths.

Adaptiveness: New Lens

Postmodern theorists have challenged the positivist view of what constitutes mental health or adaptation. Fleck-Henderson (1993) suggested
that "any references to 'normal,' 'healthy,' 'well-adjusted,' or their oppo-
sites be explored for the normative system from which they arise" (p. 224).
As an alternative to a normative approach, postmodern theorists have
used a strengths perspective to examine each person's particular attributes and needs, respect a client's cultural patterns, and avoid negative labels
(Saleebey, 1992). The idea is to listen to client stories or recounting of events
and to shy away from labels and diagnoses. In addition, the practitioner
focuses on how social structures contribute to a client's situation. The
essence of strengths-based social work practice is to mobilize the client's
strengths and resources (Sullivan, 1992; Weick, Rapp, Sullivan, & Kisthardt,
1989).

When practicing from the strengths perspective, practitioners emphasize resilience, healing and wellness, and empowerment. "A sense of hu-
mor, loyalty, insight, and other virtues might very well become the source
of energy for successful work with clients" (Saleebey, 1996, p. 299). Cowger
(1994) has proposed twelve practice guidelines for assessing client
strengths:

1. Give preeminence to the client's understanding of the facts.
2. Believe the client.
3. Discover what the client wants.
4. Move the assessment toward personal and environmental
    strengths.
5. Make the assessment of strengths multidimensional.
6. Use the assessment to discover uniqueness.
7. Use language the client can understand.
8. Make assessment a joint activity between social worker and client.
9. Reach a mutual agreement on the assessment.
10. Avoid blame and blaming.

11. Avoid cause-and-effect thinking.
12. Assess; do not diagnose.

The concept of adaptiveness continues to evolve. For example, Germain and Gitterman (1987) have suggested that transactions are adaptive when they support people's growth, development, and emotional well-being and are supported by significant others as well as by social institutions (p. 489). Their observation extends the meaning of adaptiveness by incorporating a macrodimension that involves organizations, political and economic structures, and policies. Simultaneously, some postmodern theorists believe the expansion of the definition of adaptiveness to include macrodimensions insufficient to erase the stigma of mental illness or change oppressive societal structures. For example, Witkin (1993) has contended that "descriptions of mental health and mental illness are not pure linguistic representations of empirical reality, but reflect ideological beliefs, values, institutional relationships, and cultural mores" (p. 242).

Finally, there is a small, but growing body of literature on wellness theory (Jones & Kilpatrick, 1996). Wellness theory focuses on biological, psychological, social, and spiritual dimensions of the person-environment from a strengths perspective and suggests that the social worker examine client resilience and assets. Research in this area has suggested that wellness is related to a person's capacity to keep long-term close relationships, emotional expressiveness, and responsiveness to others (Gilgun, 1996a,b).

USING HUMAN BEHAVIOR, UNDERSTANDING DIVERSITY: CULTURALLY COMPETENT SOCIAL WORK PRACTICE

Practice is an intersection where the meanings of the worker (theories), the client (stories and narratives), and culture (myths, rituals, and themes) meet.
    —D. Saleebey, "Culture, Theory, and Narrative:
        The Intersection of Meanings in Practice"

Because social workers are serving increasingly diverse constituencies, the expectation that practitioners be culturally competent in the delivery of social services has never been so great (Devore & Schlesinger, 1996; Hooyman, 1996; Nakanishi & Rittner, 1992; Saleebey, 1994). There is no one definition of cultural competence. For example, Cooper (1973) proposed that social workers who are culturally aware value differences and have "the capacity to value differences as a positive phenomenon, and to guard against the need to measure everyone by a single standard of behavior" (p. 78). Crompton (1974) defined cultural competence as social workers' ability to work effectively with people and communities other than their own. Whereas Hooyman (1996) contended that for practitioners "to fully incorporate diversity is to promote the full humanity of all voices which have been marginalized in our society" (p. 20).

Because human diversity is not unidimensional, but multidimensional, many sources of knowledge are needed to engage in culturally competent social work practice (Greene, Watkins, McNutt, & Lopez, 1998). The profession has an array of perspectives and practice approaches dealing with diversity (Goldenberg, 1978; Norton, 1976, 1978; Pinderhughes, 1976, 1989; Solomon, 1976). "Each of these works approaches related issues from a different conceptual or practice perspective" (Schlesinger & Devore, 1995, p. 907). These sources of knowledge include practice models, social work professional documents, and human behavior theories.

Social workers may turn to two widely used practice models to become more culturally competent. Green's (1995) model for ethnic competence in social work practice places the responsibility on the practitioner to conduct himself or herself in a way that is congruent with the behavior and expectations that members of the group being served see as appropriate among themselves. Green's model of ethnic competence requires that the social

> Social work has increasingly expanded the definition of diversity to encompass people who are of different cultures, are in varying power positions, or may be marginalized in society.

worker use a knowledge base for cross-cultural human services work that begins with what is salient in the client's culture and definition of the problem; be honest in addressing the personal meaning of racial and cultural differences; understand different worldviews, individualize the client accord to those differences, and explore ways of developing analytical insight and appropriate empathy; and find culturally appropriate interventions (ibid., pp. 46–48). Social work's professional organizations reflect the commitment to diversity content as well. For example, CSWE (1992) through its curriculum policy statement has mandated that content on groups who had advocated and sought redress for societal inequities be infused into the social work curriculum. Each program is required to include content about population groups such as those distinguished by race, ethnicity, culture, class, gender, sexual orientation, religion, physical or mental ability, age, and national origin. The curriculum policy statement also requires schools of social work to present content on social and economic justice and content on populations at risk (Table 2.2).

The National Association of Social Workers (NASW, 1997) code of ethics (see Table 2.3) also encompasses the profession's commitment to diverse constituencies, including practice competence with respect to "race, ethnicity, national origin, color, sex, sexual orientation, age, marital status, political belief, religion, and physical disability" (pp. 22–23). The code of ethics definition of the mission of the social work profession addresses the needs of people "who are vulnerable, oppressed, and living in poverty" (p. 1) and mandates that social workers focus change efforts on "issues of poverty, unemployment, discrimination, and other forms of social justice" (p. 5).

Clearly, not all theories of human behavior in the social environment have equal utility in addressing diversity and cross-cultural and ethnic concerns. To effectively deliver cross-cultural social work services, practitioners must be armed with theories that are as flexible as possible in their application. The extent to which theories of human behavior can be applied throughout the diversities that characterize U.S. society and allow for human differences within cultures is an important issue explored in this book.

Table 2.2. CSWE Curriculum Policy Statement for Master's Degree Programs in Social Work Education Diversity

---

M6.6. Professional social work education is committed to preparing students to understand and appreciate human diversity. Programs must provide curriculum content about differences and similarities in the experiences, needs, and beliefs of people. The curriculum must include content about differential assessment and intervention skills that will enable practitioners to serve diverse populations.

Each program is required to include content about population groups that are particularly relevant to the program's mission. These include, but are not limited to, groups distinguished by race, ethnicity, culture, class, gender, sexual orientation, religion, physical or mental ability, age, and national origin.

Promotion of Social and Economic Justice

M6.7. Programs of social work education must provide an understanding of the dynamics and consequences of social and economic injustice, including all forms of human oppression and discrimination. They must provide students with the skills to promote social change and to implement a wide range of interventions that further the achievement of individual and collective social and economic justice. Theoretical and practice content must be provided about strategies of intervention for achieving social and economic justice and for combating the causes and effects of institutionalized forms of oppression.

Populations-at-Risk

M6.8. Programs of social work education must present theoretical and practice content about patterns, dynamics, and consequences of discrimination, economic deprivation, and oppression. The curriculum must provide content about people of color, women, and gay and lesbian persons. Such content must emphasize the impact of discrimination, economic deprivation, and oppression upon these groups.

Each program must include content about populations-at-risk that are particularly relevant to its mission. In addition to those mandated above, such groups include, but are not limited to, those distinguished by age, ethnicity, culture, class, religion and physical or mental ability.

Source: From Commission on Accreditation (1992). *Handbook of Accreditation Standards and Procedures* (p. 140). Alexandria, VA: Council on Social Work Education. Reprinted with permission.

Table 2.3.   Ecological and Diversity Principles: Tenets for Practice as Evident in the
       NASW Code of Ethics

Preamble

The primary mission of the social work profession is to enhance human well-
       being and help meet the basic human needs of all people, with particular
       attention to the needs and empowerment of people who are vulnerable,
       oppressed, and living in poverty. A historic and defining feature of social
       work is the profession's focus on individual well-being in a social context
       and the well-being of society. Fundamental to social work is attention to
       the environmental forces that create, contribute to, and address problems
       in living.
Social workers promote social justice and social change with and on behalf of
       clients. "Clients" is used inclusively to refer to individuals, families, groups,
       organizations, and communities. Social workers are sensitive to cultural and
       ethnic diversity and strive to end discrimination, oppression, poverty, and
       other forms of social injustice. These activities may be in the form of direct
       practice, community organizing, supervision, consultation, administration,
       advocacy, social and political action, policy development and implementa-
       tion, education, and research and evaluation. Social workers seek to enhance
       the capacity of people to address their own needs. Social workers also seek
       to promote the responsiveness of organizations, communities, and other
       social institutions to individuals' needs and social problems.
The mission of the social work profession is rooted in a set of core values. These
       core values, embraced by social workers throughout the profession's history,
       are the foundation of social work's unique purpose and perspective:

   • service
   • social justice
   • dignity and worth of the person
   • importance of human relationships
   • integrity
   • competence

Ethical Principles

The following broad ethical principles are based on social work's core values of
       service, social justice, dignity and worth of the person, importance of human
       relationships, integrity, and competence. These principles set forth ideals to
       which all social workers should aspire.

Value: Social Justice

Ethical Principle: Social Workers Challenge Social Injustice

Social workers pursue social change, particularly with and on behalf of vulner
       able and oppressed individuals and groups of people. Social workers' social
       change efforts are focused primarily on issues of poverty, unemployment,
       discrimination, and other forms of social injustice. These activities seek to
       promote sensitivity to and knowledge about oppression and cultural and
       ethnic diversity. Social workers strive to ensure access to needed informa-
       tion, services, and resources; equality of opportunity; and meaningful partic-
       ipation in decision making for all people.

continued

Table 2.3. (Continued)

Ethical Standards

The following ethical standards are relevant to the professional activities of all social workers. These standards concern. . . . social workers' ethical responsibilities in practice settings, . . . social workers; ethical responsibilities as professionals, . . . social workers' ethical responsibilities to the social work profession, and . . . social workers' ethical responsibilities to the broader society.

Some of the standards that follow are enforceable guidelines for professional conduct, and some are aspirational. The extent to which each standard is enforceable is a matter of professional judgement to be exercised by those responsible for reviewing alleged violations of ethical standards.

1.05   Cultural Competence and Social Diversity

   (a) Social workers should understand culture and its function in human behavior and society, recognizing the strengths that exist in all cultures.
   (b) Social workers should have a knowledge base of their clients' cultures and be able to demonstrate competence in the provision of services that are sensitive to clients' cultures and to differences among people and cultural groups.
   (c) Social workers should obtain education about and seek to understand the nature of social diversity and oppression with respect to race, ethnicity, national origin, color, sex, sexual orientation, age, marital status, political belief, religion, and mental or physical disability.

4.   Social Workers' Ethical Responsibilities as Professionals

4.02   Discrimination

Social workers should not practice, condone, facilitate, or collaborate with any form of discrimination on the basis of race, ethnicity, national origin, color, sex, sexual orientation, age, marital status, political belief, religion, or mental or physical disability.

Source: National Association of Social Workers (1997). *Code of Ethics* (pp. 1–25). Washington, DC: Author. Copyright 1977 by National Association of Social Workers. Reprinted with permission.

UNDERSTANDING HOW HUMANS FUNCTION AS MEMBERS OF FAMILIES, GROUPS, ORGANIZATIONS, AND COMMUNITIES

A person may be viewed as a biopsychosocial system who, from, birth is a member of a family and an extended family and who subsequently becomes a member of friendship, educational, recreational, religious, and cultural groups, and civic associations.
            —H. Northen, *Social Work with Groups*

Direct social work practice, which continues to be identified as social treatment, views clients as members of interacting social systems (Pinderhughes, 1995). Concern with individuals as members of social systems has resulted in an ongoing effort to refine the person-in-situation perspective to attain a more comprehensive practice approach (Germain & Gitterman, 1980; Meyer, 1983; Northen, 1982, 1987). Falck's (1988) call for a new paradigm to address the "individual-collectivity relationship" (p. 22) is an example of such thinking. His view that social work should approach the study of human behavior from the perspective that "every person is a member" (p. 30) is an effort to come to a holistic view of social work and to overcome the potential theoretical split in the person-in-environment metaphor.

Today, the teaching of social work practice is characterized increasingly by a unified approach to methods, which emphasizes the commonalities among the types of direct practice, whether with individuals, families, or groups (Meyer, 1987; Middleman & Goldberg, 1987). Among the practice models are Germain and Gitterman's (1980) ecological practice model, which examines reciprocal causality in the transactions between persons and their environment and Northen's (1988) intersystem approach, which considers the "multiple and complex transactions that occur among persons, families, other membership and reference groups, and organizations" (p. 5).

THE FAMILY AND SOCIAL WORK PRACTICE

Family-centered practice is a model of social work practice which locates the family in the center of the unit of attention or field of action.
    —A. Hartman and J. Laird, *Family-Centered Social Work Practice*

Since its beginnings, the social work profession has had a concern for the well-being of families. Assistance to families can be traced to the Relief and Aid and Charity Organization Societies of the 1880s, when volunteers and early social workers regularly met with families in their homes to help resolve social and emotional problems (Richmond, 1917). Since that time, family-focused social work has come to encompass a broad spectrum of services and methods of intervention, including therapy, problem-solving guidance, environmental intervention and advocacy, family life education, as well as homemaker service, financial relief, or other tangible assistance.

Today, this mode of service is distinguished by its stated concern with the family and all of its members. The aim of service is to enhance the psychosocial functioning of all and the focus is on those "transactions among person, family, and environment that affect individuals, families, and even larger social forces and systems in which families are enmeshed" (Sherman, 1977, p. 446). The intent to locate the family at the center of attention reflects social work's person-in-environment stance and places family practice "squarely within its traditional domain" (Hartman, 1995; Hartman & Laird, 1987).

New Lenses

Postmodern theorists have had a profound effect on how social workers practice with families. During the 1960s and 1970s, postmodern practitioners began to question the ideas of a fixed family structure and typical life cycle. Cultural differences and the effects of larger societal systems came to the forefront of practice. Definitions of what constitutes a family were revised (Carter & McGoldrick, 1999). The family literature also discussed the ethics and values of family treatment (Doherty & Boss, 1992; Klein, 1982; Margolin, 1982). These discussions are an example of the need to evaluate and critically apply theory to the client situation.

Human behavior theory for social work practice with families in large measure is based on a positivist structural approach, and is increasingly sensitive to understanding various family forms, gender, age, ethnic differences, and the intrusion of political and economic bias (Greene & Frankel, 1994). For example, understanding of the family life cycle has increasingly addressed the influence of gender and variations in family life cycle patterns (Carter & McGoldrick, 1999). A knowledge of human behavior theory that elucidates the nature of the family group within its cultural context is a necessary prerequisite.

> Families of all forms provide people with their first sense of the meaning of connectedness.

Changes in family size and forms also have brought about change in family treatment approaches (Pennekamp & Freeman, 1988). Since the nineteenth century, family size in the United States has declined steadily (Johnson & Wahl, 1995). In the past three decades "the structure and the functioning of U.S. families have continued to undergo rapid and far reaching changes" (Billingsley, 1987, p. 520). Among those changes discussed by Billingsley are the increase in single-parent households, remarriage, and the two-career family, the commuter family, and stepfamilies. These changes, along with other social factors, have led to a variety of family forms and a seeming lack of consensus about how to define the family (Table 2.4). Definitions have ranged from the traditional family, a nuclear unit comprising blood relatives, to the self-defined family unit comprising individuals bound together by emotional relationships. Each of the chapters that follows explores how a particular human behavior theory addresses the changing family scene.

Table 2.4. Definitions of Family

Author	Definition
Billingsley (1968)	The nuclear family includes three types: (1) the incipient, consisting only of married pair; (2) the simple, consisting of marital pair and minor children; and (3) the attenuated, consisting of one parent and minor children. The extended family may include other relatives added to the nuclear household. The augmented family includes types of family situations wherein unrelated family members are incorporated into the household.
Boulding (1972)	The expanded family comprises either biologically related extended family or those who voluntarily associate as such.
Butler and Lewis (1973)	The nuclear family comprises a married pair with dependent children and an independent household bound to outside kin by voluntary ties of affection and duty. The extended family is all persons related to one another by blood and marriage. A family comprises those who consider themselves economically and emotionally related to each other by blood (consanguinity) or by marriage (conjugality).
Stack (1974)	In traditional terms, the family is considered a basic economic unit comprising husband, wife, and offspring who provide sexual, economic, reproductive, and educational functions. The family in kin-communities may be considered the smallest, organized, durable network of kin and nonkin who interact daily, providing domestic needs of children and assuring their survival. The family network may be diffused over several kin-based households.
Terkelsen (1980)	A family is a small social system comprising individuals related to each other by reason of strong reciprocal affection and loyalties and comprising a permanent household (or cluster of households) that persist over the years and decades.
White House Conference on Aging (1981)	A family is a system of related and unrelated individuals integrated by patterns of social relationships and mutual help.

Source: R. Greene (1988). *Continuing Education for Gerontological Careers.* Washington, DC: Council on Social Work Education. Copyright 1988 by Council on Social Work Education. Adapted with permission.

Groups and Social Work Practice

Group work began in such diverse settings as settlement houses, boys clubs, YMCAs, and Jewish community centers (Middleman & Goldberg, 1987). Group work theory emerged during the 1930s and 1940s as part of a movement that had its origins in efforts to Americanize immigrants (Papell, 1983). Values centered around a commitment to social change and justice for oppressed groups (Meyer, 1987; Middleman & Goldberg, 1987). Later, during the 1950s and 1960s, the social group work method incorporated a remedial approach grounded in psychoanalytic concepts, ego psychology, and social role theory. During this time social group work was seen as a distinct method.

By the late 1960s and 1970s, there was a trend to unify casework and group work in a generic approach to social work practice (Middleman & Goldberg, 1987). Although the reaction to an integrated methods approach has been mixed, the emphases on a common direct practice base continues. Northen (1988), who proposed that all social work service focus on forces that have disrupted the balance among "the client-group-situation gestalt" (p. 63), represents this perspective. She has suggested that an integrated approach to social work practice, which would include social work practice with groups, would tap individual, family, group, and community modalities.

A group work perspective proceeds from a somewhat different starting point. Falck (1988) argued that the concept of membership is a central one for social work. In social work, the concept of person-in-environment can be seen as recognizing that individuals learn, develop, construct their realities, learn to perceive, and participate in social institutions as members of groups, with their families as the first (and, for a long time, the most influential) of these groups. Societal perspectives, adaptive and otherwise, are transmitted to individuals in and through their participation in groups. Without small group participation, membership in a society remains an abstraction.

Today, almost all social workers are involved in group work, whether it be participation with a board of directors or a treatment group (Schopler & Galinsky, 1995). A group perspective, then, leads social work to focus on processes that are sociopsychological in their nature, both to understand people and to design preventive and remedial experiences (Garvin, 1987a). For example, sex roles certainly proceeded from a biological starting point. As many researchers have pointed out (e.g., Bern, 1980), however, the relatively small core of biologically determined limits is surrounded by a much broader aura of attitudes, expectations, and constructions of reality; norms; and behaviors that are learned, largely in and through a series of small group experiences. A series of attributions—for example, what is masculine and what is feminine—as well as a self-concept—how well do

I do being masculine or feminine—result from membership in various groups and the learnings that result from experiences in these groups.

From the viewpoint of social work practice, such learning affects interpersonal relationships, attitudes, and behaviors toward violence, norms of sexual behavior, senses of personal inadequacy, expectations around marriage, behavior within families, parenting, care of the elderly, and political attitudes toward social welfare. Other questions exist about what constitutes social work practice with groups. Garvin (1987b) rejected the idea that any and all work with groups is social work. He suggested that when groups are consistent with self-determination, they enhance social functioning, are useful to diverse client groups, and fall into the category of the "professional heritage of social group work" (pp. 59–60).

Middleman and Goldberg (1987) suggested that social work with groups must "include attention to helping the group members gain a sense of each other and their groupness" (p. 721). The focus is on group process, collective support, and interaction as a means of enabling individual members to grow and develop or to achieve a task. The group provides the vehicle by which individuals may improve their interpersonal relationships and their environmental or societal conditions. It is this emphasis on group development that characterizes social work with groups.

Lang (1981) characterized the social work group as a unique social form that operates as a mutual aid system that promotes autonomy and benefits the individual members through the effective action of the whole group. She also suggested that the social work group is defined by professional and group norms that reinforce acceptance, respect, open communication, tolerance of differences, and democratic group functioning.

Anderson and Carter (1984) suggested that, as an arena of social interaction, social work groups have the potential for meeting a number of human needs that cannot be met through individual help. These needs include the need to belong and be accepted, the need to be validated through group feedback, the need to share common experiences with others, and the need to work with others on common tasks. Other intrinsic properties of group interaction include the opportunity to share, to explore the universality of human problems, and to work toward making decisions.

> Membership—or the ability and opportunity to form associations—is a critical aspect of personal and societal well-being.

Social work practice in groups, like other modalities, should be grounded in human behavior theory. To date, there has been no unified theoretical approach to small group practice; rather, a number of theoretical orientations, such as social exchange theory, field theory, and social systems theory, have contributed to practice perspectives (Garvin, 1987a).

SOCIAL WORK PRACTICE IN ORGANIZATIONS

Human organizations exist in a changing community environment.
—T. P. Holland & M. Petchers, "Organizations:
Context for Social Service Delivery"

Organizations are of interest to social workers for a number of reasons. For example, human services organizations are designed to fulfill basic human functions (Holland & Petchers, 1987). As such, changes in American institutions and the organizational structures that support them have an impact on social work practice. In recent decades, forces in the larger society have radically altered the shape, delivery, and financing of human services. To understand the way in which such changes influence the direct practice of social work, it is necessary to first examine the factors defining the delivery of social work services.

The human services field has been increasingly affected by the resurgence of the belief in capitalist principles of competition and private-sector free enterprise. Among the factors that may be contributing to the transformation of the social work profession is an increased reliance on entrepreneurship and a trend toward privatization, a greater focus on quality assurance and outcome measures, deregulation and job reclassification, and demands for cost-containment and cost-effectiveness. The effect of these trends is evident in many fields of social work practice. Perhaps the most dramatic example of the way in which human services delivery systems have been redefined by broad societal influences is in the health and mental health arena. Social workers, employed by health maintenance organizations, capitated health plans, and employers who use fixed contracting for services are commonplace. Simultaneously, programs owned and managed by social workers are competing successfully for private foundation money and publicly funded contracts to offer innovative community-based services to homeless, chronically mentally ill, and frail elderly people.

The family services field, which deals with families, children, and elderly people, also has witnessed dramatic changes in social work service patterns. Changing demographics and the demand for appropriate interventions to meet a diverse range of families have given impetus to new modes of service delivery. The rapid increase in the segment of the population that is more than seventy-five years old will increase the demands for a host of family, social, and emotional supports and services.

Organizations are of interest to social workers because a large proportion of these practitioners will spend much of their careers delivering services within a human services or health organization (Anderson & Carter,

1984; Blau and Meyer, 1987; Chess and Norlin, [1988] 1997). Social workers today work in hospitals, counsel traffic controllers, conduct support groups for new parents, provide fertility and genetic counseling, offer psychotherapy for the adult children of alcoholics, teach vocational skills to blind people, participate on emergency rescue teams, and serve as consultants in human resources development programs, all within complex organizational settings. Practitioners also continue to be employed in traditional social work roles such as adoption, foster care, and protective services.

In addition, organizations are of interest to social workers because organizations are vital parts of each person's person-in-environment gestalt. Individuals spend a significant part of their lives in organizations; what happens on the job is strongly related to an individual's (and his or her family's) well-being. Thus, social workers increasingly are concerned with client needs in the workplace (Akabas & Kurzman, 1982; Davis-Sacks & Hasenfeld, 1987; Ephross & Vassil, 1990; Van Den Bergh, 1995). Among the specific concerns are substance abuse and child and elder care.

Furthermore, organizations are of interest to social workers because the structure of delivery systems is related to service accessibility. A social worker is a member of the organizational structure and, as such, is mandated to carry out organizational goals. Simultaneously, social work values suggest, the social worker acts as an advocate or ombudsman, working to confront institutional barriers to services delivery.

Social Planning, Community Organization, and Administration

Social planning and community organization are established social work methods (Harrison, 1995; Kahn, 1995; Weil & Gamble, 1995). These methods reflect the profession's interest in social change and betterment of "community action systems" (Gilbert & Specht, 1987, p. 602–619) and historically have focused on the initiation of targeted program efforts, the allocation of funds and their efficient use, the management of social welfare organizations, and the enlistment of community action to combat poverty and a range of other social problems .

Social workers in the direct practice of social work should not become isolated from their colleagues in the arms of the profession. An awareness of the reciprocal relationship among macrosystems and microsystems is necessary. Clients are deeply affected by the ways in which service delivery organizations are developed and managed, and by the policies they adopt. The theoretical concepts that underpin the sociopolitical processes and technical tasks needed for social planning, community organization, and administration are beyond the scope of this text. However, many human behavior concepts that address the nature and functions of community and how individuals interact as community and organization members are discussed.

REFERENCES

Akabas, S. H., & Kurzman, P. A. (Eds.) (1982). *Work, Workers and Work Organizations: A View from Social Work*. Englewood Cliffs, NJ: Prentice-Hall.

Allen, J. (1993). The constructivist paradigm: Values and ethics. In J. Laird (Ed.), *Revisioning Social Work Education: A Social Constructionist Approach* (pp. 31–54). New York: Haworth.

Amato-Von Hemert, K., & Clark, J. (1994). Should education address religious issues? Yes or No. *Journal of Social Work Education, 30*(1), 7–17.

American Psychiatric Association (1994). *Diagnostic and Statistical Manual of Mental Disorders* (4th ed.). Washington, DC: Author.

Anderson, R. E., & Carter, L. (1984). *Human Behavior in the Social Environment*. Hawthorne, NY: Aldine de Gruyter.

Bengston, V., & Haber, D. (1983). Sociological perspectives on aging. In D. Woodruff & J. E. Birren (Eds.), *Aging: Scientific Perspectives and Social Issues* (pp. 72–90). Monterey, CA: Brooks/Cole.

Bern, S. L. (1980). Beyond androgyny: Some presumptuous prescriptions for a liberated sexual identity. In M. Bloom (Ed.), *Life Span Development* (pp. 310–318). New York: Macmillan.

Billingsley, A. (1987). Family: Contemporary patterns. In A. Minahan (Editor-in-chief), *Encyclopedia of Social Work* (Vol. 1, 18th ed., pp. 520–529). Silver Spring, MD: National Association of Social Workers.

Billingsley, A. (1968). *Black Families in White America*. Englewood Cliffs, NJ: Prentice-Hall.

Birren, J. E. (1969). The concept of functional age, theoretical background. *Human Development, 12*, 214–215.

Birren, J. E., & Renner, V. J. (1977). Research on the psychology of aging: Principles and experimentation. In J. E. Birren & K. W. Schaie (Eds.), *Handbook of the Psychology of Aging*. New York: Van Nostrand Reinhold.

Birren, J. E., & Woodruff, D. (1973). Human development over the life-span through education. In P. Baltes & K. W. Schaire (Eds.), *Life-Span Developmental Psychology: Personality and Socialization* (pp. 306–334). New York: Academic Press.

Blau, P. & Meyer, M. W. (1987). *Bureaucracy in Modern Society*. New York: Random House.

Bloom, M. (1984). *Configurations of Human Behavior*. New York: Macmillan.

Blumer, H. (1969). *Symbolic Interactionism: Perspective and Method*. Englewood Cliffs, NJ: Prentice-Hall.

Boulding, E. (1972). The family as an agent or social change. *Futurist, 6*(5), 186–191.

Boxer, A. M., & Cohler, B. J. (1989). The life course of gay and lesbian youth: An immodest proposal for the study of lives. *Journal of Homosexuality, 17*(3/4), 315–355.

Bronfenbrenner, U. (1989). Ecological systems theory. *Annals of Child Development, 6*, 187–249.

Burnette, D. (1997). Grandparents raising grandchildren in the inner city. *Families in Society, 78*(5), 489–501.

Butler, R. N., & Lewis, M. (1973). *Aging and Mental Health Positive Psychological Approaches.* St. Louis, MO: C. V. Mosby.

Butler, R. N., Lewis, M., & Sunderland, T. (1997). *Aging and Mental Health: Positive Psychosocial and Biomedical Approaches.* Boston: Allyn & Bacon.

Canda, E. R. (1988). Spirituality, religious diversity, and social work practice. *Social Casework, 5*, 238–246.

Canda, E. R. (1989). Religious content in social work education: A comparative approach. *Journal of Social Work Education, 25*(1), 36–45.

Caroff, P. (Ed.) (1982). *Treatment Formulations and Clinical Social Work.* Silver Spring, MD: National Association of Social Workers.

Carter, E. A., & McGoldrick, M. (Eds.) (1999). *The Expanded Family Life Cycle: Individual, Family, and Social Perspectives* (3rd ed.). Boston: Allyn & Bacon.

Cascio, T. (1998). Incorporating spirituality into social work practice. *Families in Society 79*, 523–531.

Chess, W. A., & Norlin, J. M. (1988, 1997). *Human Behavior and the Social Environment.* Boston: Allyn & Bacon.

Cohen, J. (1980). Nature of clinical social work. In P. Ewalt (Ed.), *NASW Conference Proceedings: Toward a Definition of Clinical Social Work* (pp. 23–32). Washington, DC: NASW Press.

Compton, B., & Galaway, B. (1994). *Social Work Processes.* Pacific Grove, CA: Brooks/Cole.

Cooper, S. (1973). A look at the effect of racism on clinical work. *Social Casework, 54*(2), 76–84.

Cornett, C. (1992). Toward a more comprehensive personology: Integrating a spiritual perspective into social work practice. *Social Work, 37*(2), 101–102.

Council on Social Work Education (1992). *Curriculum Policy Statement for Master's Degree Programs in Social Work Education.* Alexandria, VA: Author.

Cowger, C. D. (1994). Assessing client strengths: Clinical assessment for client empowerment, *Social Work, 39*(3), 262–268.

Crompton, D. W. (1974). Minority content in social work education—Promise or pitfall? *Journal of Education for Social Work, 10*(1), 9–18.

Davis-Sacks, M. L., & Hasenfeld, Y. (1987). Organizations: Impact on employees and community. In A. Minahan (Editor-in-chief), *Encyclopedia of Social Work* (Vol. 2, 18th ed., pp. 217–225). Silver Spring, MD: National Association of Social Workers.

Devore, W., & Schlesinger, E. G. (1996). *Ethnic-Sensitive Social Work Practice.* Boston: Allyn & Bacon.

DiBlasio, F. A. (1993). The role of social workers' religious beliefs in helping family members forgive. *Families in Society, 74*(3), 163–170.

Doherty, W. J., & Boss, P. G. (1992). Values and ethics in family therapy. In A. D. Gurman & D. P. Kniskern (Eds.), *Handbook of Family Therapy* (pp. 606–637). New York:Brunner/Mazel.

Ephross, P. H., & Greene, R. R. (1991). Symbolic interactionism. In R. R. Greene &

P. H. Ephross (Eds.), *Human Behavior Theory and Social Work Practice* (1st ed., pp. 203–226). Hawthorne, NY: Aldine de Gruyter.

Ephross, P. H., & Vassil, T. V. (1990). The rediscovery of "real-world" groups. In S. Wenoceer (Ed.), *Proceedings of the Tenth Annual Symposium on Social Work with Groups* (pp. 15–25). New York: Haworth.

Falck, H. S. (1988). *Social Work: The Membership Perspective.* New York: Springer.

Fleck-Henderson, A. (1993). A constructivist approach to "Human Behavior and the Social Environment I." In J. Laird (Ed.), *Revisioning Social Work Education: A Social Constructionist Approach* (pp. 219–238). New York: Haworth.

Frances, A., Pincus, H. A., Widiger, T. A., Davis, W. W., & First, M. B. (1990). DSM-IV: Work in progress. *American Journal of Psychiatry, 147,* 1439–1448.

Garvin, C. D. (1987a). *Contemporary Group Work* (2nd ed.). Englewood Cliffs, NJ: Prentice-Hall.

Garvin, C. D. (1987b). Group therapy and research. In A. Minahan (Editor-in-chief), *Encyclopedia of Social Work* (Vol. 1, 18th ed., pp. 682–696). Silver Spring, MD: National Association of Social Workers.

Gergen, K. J. (1982). *Toward Transformation in Social Knowledge.* New York: Springer.

Gergen, K. J. (1985). The social constructionist movement in modern psychology. *American Psychologist, 40,* 266–275.

Germain, C. (1991). *Human Behavior in the Social Environment: An Ecological View.* New York: Columbia University Press.

Germain, C. (1994). Human behavior and the social environment. In F. G. Reamer (Ed.), *The Foundation of Social Work Knowledge* (pp. 88–121). New York: Columbia University Press.

Germain, C., & Gitterman, A. (1980). *The Life Model of Social Work Practice.* New York: Columbia University Press.

Germain, C., & Gitterman, A. (1987). Ecological perspectives. In A. Minahan (Editor-in-chief), *Encyclopedia of Social Work* (Vol. 1, 18th ed., pp. 488–499). Silver Spring, MD: National Association of Social Workers.

Germain, C., & Gitterman, A. (1995). Ecological perspective. In R. L. Edwards (Editor-in-chief), *Encyclopedia of Social Work* (Vol 1, 19th ed., pp. 816–824). Washington, DC: NASW Press.

Gilbert, N., & Specht, H. (1987). Social planning and community organization. In A. Minahan (Editor-in-chief), *Encyclopedia of Social Work* (Vol. 2, 18th ed., pp. 602–619). Silver Spring, MD: National Association of Social Workers.

Gilgun, J. F. (1996a). Human development and adversity in ecological perspective, Part 1: A conceptual framework. *Families in Society, 77*(7), 395–402.

Gilgun, J. F. (1996b). Human development and adversity in ecological perspective, Part 2: Three patterns. *Families in Society, 77*(8), 459–476.

Goldenberg, I. I. (1978). *Oppression and Social Intervention.* Chicago: Nelson-Hall.

Goldstein, E. (1980). Knowledge base of clinical social work. In P. Ewalt (Ed.), *NASW Conference Proceedings: Toward a Definition of Clinical Social Work* (pp. 42–53). Washington, DC: National Association of Social Workers. Washington, DC: NASW Press.

Goldstein, E. (1987). Mental illness. In A. Minahan (Editor-in-chief), *Encyclopedia of Social Work* (Vol. 2, 18th ed., pp. 102–109). Silver Spring, MD: National Association of Social Workers.

Green, J. W. (1995). *Cultural Awareness in the Human Services: A Multi-Ethnic Approach.* Boston: Allyn & Bacon.

Greene, R. (1986). *Social Work with the Aged and Their Families.* Hawthorne, NY: Aldine de Gruyter.

Greene, R. (1988). *Continuing Education for Gerontological Careers.* Washington, DC: Council on Social Work Education.

Greene, R. (Ed.) (1994). *Human Behavior Theory: A Diversity Framework.* Hawthorne, NY: Aldine de Gruyter.

Greene, R. R., & Frankel, K. (1994). A systems approach: Addressing diverse family forms. In R. R. Greene (Ed.), *Human Behavior Theory: A Diversity Framework* (pp. 147–172). Hawthorne, NY: Aldine de Gruyter.

Greene, R. R., Watkins, M., McNutt, J. & Lopez, L. (1998). Diversity defined. In R. R. Greene & M. Watkins (Eds.), *Serving Diverse Constituencies: Applying the Ecological Perspective* (pp. 29–62). Hawthorne, NY: Aldine de Gruyter.

Hale, W. (1992). Impact of roles, relationships, and boundaries. Paper presented at the HIV Positive Persons, Friends, and Caregivers Conference, Athens, GA, May.

Haraeven, T. K. (1982). The life course and aging in historical perspective. In T. K. Haraven & K. J. Adams (Eds.), *Aging and Life Course Transitions: An Interdisciplinary Perspective* (pp. 1–27). New York: Guilford.

Harrison, W. D. (1995). Community development. In R. L. Edwards (Editor-in-chief), *Encyclopedia of Social Work* (Vol. 1, 19th ed., pp. 555–562). Washington, DC: NASW Press.

Hartman, A. (1995). Family therapy. In R. L. Edwards (Editor-in-chief), *Encyclopedia of Social Work* (Vol. 2, 19th ed., pp. 983–991). Washington, DC: NASW Press.

Hartman, A., & Laird, J. (1983). *Family-Centered Social Work Practice.* New York: Free Press.

Hartman, A., & Laird, J. (1987). Family practice. In A. Minahan (Editor-in-chief), *Encyclopedia of Social Work* (Vol. 1, 18th ed., pp. 575–589). Silver Spring, MD: National Association of Social Workers.

Havighurst, R. J. (1972). *Developmental Tasks and Education.* New York: David McKay.

Hoffman, L. (1992). *A Reflexive Stance for Family Therapy.* New York: Basic Books.

Holland, T. P., & Petchers, M. (1987). Organizations: Context for social service delivery. In A. Minahan (Editor-in-chief), *Encyclopedia of Social Work* (Vol. 2, 18th ed., pp. 204–207). Silver Spring, MD: National Association of Social Workers.

Hooyman, N. R. (1996). Curriculum and teaching: Today and tomorrow. In *White Paper on Social Work Education—Today and Tomorrow* (pp. 11–24). Cleveland, OH: Case Western Reserve University Press.

Jahoda, M. (1958). *Current Concepts of Positive Mental Health.* New York: Basic Books.

Johnson, G. B., & Wahl, M. (1995). Families: Demographic shifts. In R. L. Edwards (Editor-in-chief), *Encyclopedia of Social Work* (Vol. 1, 19th ed., pp. 936–941). Washington, DC: NASW Press.

Johnson, H. (1987). Human development: Biological perspective. In A. Minahan (Editor-in-chief), *Encyclopedia of Social Work* (Vol. 1, 18th ed., pp. 835–850). Silver Spring, MD: National Association of Social Workers.

Johnson, H., Atkins, S. P., Battle, S. F., Hernandez-Arata, L., Hesselbrock, M., Libassi, M. F., & Parish, M. (1990). Strengthening the "bio" in the biopsychosocial paradigm. *Journal of Social Work Education, 26*(2), 109–123.

Johnson, L. C. (1986). *Social Work Practice.* Boston: Allyn and Bacon.

Jones, G., & Kilpatrick, A. C. (1996). Wellness theory: A discussion and application to clients with disabilities. *Families in Society, 77*(5), 259–268.

Joseph, M. V. (1987). The religious and spiritual aspects of social work practice: A neglected dimension of social work. *Social Thought 13*(1), 12–23.

Kahn, S. (1995). Community organization. In R. L. Edwards (Editor-in-chief), *Encyclopedia of Social Work* (Vol. 1, 19th ed., pp. 569–576). Washington, DC: NASW Press.

Kastenbaum, R. (1979). *Human Development: A Lifespan Perspective.* Boston: Allyn & Bacon.

Kirk, S., & Kutchins, H. (1992). *The Selling of DSM.* Hawthorne, NY: Aldine de Gruyter.

Klein, M. H. (1982). Feminist concepts of therapy outcome. In H. Rubenstein & M. H. Block (Eds.), *Things That Matter: Influences on Helping Relationships* (pp. 304–318). New York: Macmillan.

Kropf, N. P., & Greene, R. R. (1994). Erikson's eight stages of development: Different lenses. In R. R. Greene (Ed.), *Human Behavior Theory: A Diversity Framework* (pp. 75–92). Hawthorne, NY: Aldine de Gruyter.

Kutchins, H. & Kirk, S. (1995). Should DSM be the basis for teaching social work practice? No. *Journal of Social Work Education, 31*(2), 148–168.

Land, H. (1995). Feminist clinical social work in the 21st century. In N. Van Den Bergh (Ed.), *Feminist Practice in the 21st Century* (pp. 3–19). Washington, DC: NASW Press.

Lang, N. (1981). Some defining characteristics of the social work group: Unique social form. In S. L. Abels & P. Abels (Eds.), *Social work with groups. Proceedings, 1997 Symposium.* Louisville, KY: Committee for the Advancement of Social Work with Groups.

Lieberman, F. (1987). Mental health and illness in children. In A. Minahan (Editor-in-chief), *Encyclopedia of Social Work* (Vol. 2, 18th ed., pp. 111–125). Silver Spring, MD: National Association of Social Workers.

Maddi, S. (1972). *Personality Theories.* Homewood, IL: Dorsey.

Margolin, G. (1982). Ethical and legal considerations in marriage and family therapy. *American Psychologist, 7,* 789–801.

Meyer, C. (1982). Issues in clinical social work: In search of a consensus. In P. Caroff (Ed.), *Treatment Formulations and Clinical Social Work* (pp. 19–26). Silver Spring, Maryland: National Association of Social Workers.

Meyer, C. (Ed.) (1983). *Clinical Social Work in the Ecosystems Perspective.* New York: Columbia University Press.

Meyer, C. (1987). Direct practice in social work: Overview. In A. Minahan (Editor-in-chief), *Encyclopedia of Social Work* (Vol. 1, 18th ed., pp. 409–422). Silver Spring, MD: National Association of Social Workers.

Middleman, R. R., & Goldberg, G. (1987). Social work practice with groups. In A. Minahan (Editor-in-chief), *Encyclopedia of Social Work* (Vol. 2, 18th ed., pp. 714–729). Silver Spring, MD: National Association of Social Workers.

Nakanishi, M., & Rittner, B. (1992). The inclusionary cultural model. *Journal of Social Work Education, 28*(1), 27–35.

National Association of Social Workers (1997). *Code of Ethics of the National Association of Social Workers*. Washington, DC: Author.

Neugarten, B., & Datan, N. (1973). Sociological perspectives on the life cycle. In P. B. Baltes & K. W. Schaie (Eds.), *Life-Span Developmental Psychology* (pp. 53–68). New York: Academic Press.

Newman, B., & Newman, P. R. ([1979] 1987). *Development through Life: A Psycho Social Approach*. Homewood, IL: Dorsey.

Northen, H. (1982). *Clinical Social Work*. New York: Columbia University Press.

Northen, H. (1987). Assessment in direct practice. In A. Minahan (Editor-in-chief), *Encyclopedia of Social Work* (Vol. 1, 18th ed., pp. 171–183). Silver Spring, MD: National Association of Social Workers.

Northen, H. (1988). *Social Work with Groups* (2nd ed.). New York: Columbia University Press.

Norton, D. G. (1976). Working with minority populations: The dual perspective. In B. Ross & S. K. Khinduta (Eds.), *Social Work in Practice* (pp. 134–141). New York: National Association of Social Workers.

Norton, D. G. (1978). *The Dual Perspective: Inclusions of Ethnic Minority Content in the Social Work Curriculum*. New York: Council on Social Work Education.

Papell, C. (1983). Group work in the profession of social work: Identity in context. In N. Lang & C. Marshall (Eds.), *Patterns in the Mosaic: Proceedings of the 4th Annual Symposium for the Advancement of Social Work with Groups* (pp. 1193–1209). Toronto: Committee for the Advancement of Social Work with Groups.

Pardeck, J. T., Murphy, J. W., & Min Choi, J. (1994). Some implications of postmodernism for social work practice. *Social Work, 39*(4), 343–346.

Pennekamp, M., & Freeman, E. M. (1988). Toward a partnership perspective: Schools, families, and school social workers. *Social Work in Education, 10,* 246–259.

Pinderhughes, E. (1976). Power, powerlessness and empowerment in community mental health. Paper presented at the annual Convocation of Commonwealth Fellows, Chestnut Hill, MA, Oct.

Pinderhughes, E. (1989). *Understanding Race, Ethnicity, and Power*. New York: Free Press.

Pinderhughes, E. (1995). Direct practice overview. In R. L. Edwards (Editor-in-chief) *Encyclopedia of Social Work* (Vol. 1, 19th ed., pp. 740–751). Washington, DC: NASW Press.

Queiro-Tajalli, I., & Smith, L. (1998). Provision of services to older adults within an ecological perspective. In R. R. Greene & M. Watkins (Eds.), *Serving Diverse Constituencies: Applying the Ecological Perspective* (pp. 199–220). Hawthorne, NY: Aldine de Gruyter.

Reynolds, B. C. (1933). Can social work be interpreted to a community as a basic approach to human problems? *Family, 13,* 336–342.

Richmond, M. (1917). *Social Diagnosis*. New York: Russell Sage Foundation.

Riley, M. H., Foner, A., Hess, B., & Toby, M. (1969). Socialization for the middle and later years. In D. A. Goslin (Ed.), *Handbook of Socialization Theory and Research* (pp. 951–982). Chicago: Rand McNally.

Rogers, C. R. (1982). *Life-Span Human Development.* Monterey, CA: Brooks/Cole.

Saleebey, D. (Ed.) (1992). *The Strengths Perspective in Social Work Practice.* New York: Longman.

Saleebey, D. (1993). Notes on interpreting the human condition: A constructed HBSE curriculum. In J. Laird (Ed.), *Revisioning Social Work Education: A Social Constructionist Approach* (pp. 197–217). New York: Haworth.

Saleebey, D. (1994). Culture, theory, and narrative: The intersection of meanings in practice. *Social Work, 39*(4), 351–359.

Saleebey, D. (1996). The strengths perspective in social work practice: Extensions and cautions. *Social Work, 41*(3), 296–305.

Schell, R., & Hall, E. (1979). *Developmental Psychology Today.* New York: Random House.

Schlesinger, E. G., & Devore, W. (1995). Ethnic-sensitive practice. In R. L. Edwards (Editor-in-chief), *Encyclopedia of Social Work* (Vol. 1, 19th ed., pp. 902–908). Washington, DC: NASW Press.

Schopler, J. H. & Galinsky, M. J. (1995). Group practice overview. In R. L. Edwards (Editor-in-chief), *Encyclopedia of Social Work* (Vol. 2, 19th ed., pp. 1129–1142). Washington, DC: NASW Press.

Schriver, J. M. (1995). *Human Behavior and the Social Environment: Shifting Paradigms in Essential Knowledge for Social Work Practice.* Needham Heights, MA: Allyn & Bacon.

Sherman, S. N. (1977). Family services: Family treatment. In A. Minahan (Editor-in-chief), *Encyclopedia of Social Work* (Vol. 1, 18th ed., pp. 435–440). Silver Spring, MD: National Association of Social Workers.

Solomon, B. B. (1976). *Black Empowerment: Social Work in Oppressed Communities.* New York: Columbia University Press.

Specht, R., & Craig, G. J. (1982). *Human Development: A Social Work Perspective.* Englewood Cliffs, NJ: Prentice-Hall.

Stack, C. B. (1974). *All Our Kin.* New York: Harper & Row.

Sullivan, P. W. (1992). Reclaiming the community: The strengths perspective and deinstitutionalization. *Social Work, 27*(3), 204–209.

Sullivan, P. W. (1998). Culturally sound mental health services: Ecological interventions. In R. R. Greene & M. Watkins (Eds.), *Serving Diverse Constituencies: Applying the Ecological Perspective* (pp. 221–241). Hawthorne, NY: Aldine de Gruyter.

Szaaz, 1. (1960). The myth of mental illness. *American Psychologist, 15*(1), 13–18.

Terkelsen, G. (1980). Toward a theory of the family cycle. In E. A. Carter & M. McGoldrick (Eds.), *The Family Life Cycle: A Framework for Family Therapy* (pp. 21–52). New York: Gardner.

Termerlin, M. (1979). The inability to distinguish normality from abnormality. In W. S. Sahakian (Ed.), *Psychopathology Today* (pp. 23–28). Itasca, IL: F. E. Peacock.

Thompson, K. H., & Greene, R. R. (1994). Role theory and social work practice. In R. R. Greene (Ed.), *Human Behavior Theory: A Diversity Framework* (pp. 93–114). Hawthorne, NY: Aldine de Gruyter.

Tomm, K. (1990). A critique of the DSM. *Dulwich Centre Newsletter: Reflections on Our Practices* (Part 1, No. 3), 5–8.

Van den Bergh, N. (Ed.) (1995). *Feminist Practice in the 21st Century.* Washington, DC: NASW Press.

Weick, A. (1983). A growth-task model of human development. *Social Casework, 64*(3), 131–137.

Weick, A. (1993). Reconstructing social work education. In J. Laird (Ed.), *Revisioning Social Work Education: A Social Constructionist Approach* (pp. 11–30). New York: Haworth.

Weick, A., Rapp, C., Sullivan, P. W., & Kisthardt, W. (1989). A strengths perspective in social work practice. *Social Work, 3*(4), 350–356.

Weil, M., & Gamble, D. (1995). Community practice models. In R. L. Edwards (Editor-in-chief), *Encyclopedia of Social Work* (Vol. 1, 19th ed., pp. 577–593). Washington, DC: NASW Press.

White House Conference on Aging (1981). *Report of the Technical Committee on Family Social Services and Other Support Systems.* Washington, DC: Department of Health and Human Services.

Williams, J. (1987). Diagnostic and statistical manual. In A. Minahan (Editor-in-chief), *Encyclopedia of Social Work* (Vol. 1, 18th ed., pp. 389–393). Silver Spring, MD: National Association of Social Workers.

Williams, J. (1995). Diagnostic and statistical manual of mental disorders. In R. L. Edwards (Editor-in-chief), *Encyclopedia of Social Work* (Vol. 1, 19th ed., pp. 729–739). Washington, DC: NASW Press.

Williams, J., & Spitzer, R. (1995). Should DSM be the basis for teaching social work practice? Yes. *Journal of Social Work Education, 31*(2), 148–168.

Witkin, S. L. (1993). A human rights approach to social work research and evaluation. In J. Laird (Ed.), *Revisioning Social Work Education: A Social Constructionist Approach* (pp. 239–253). New York: Haworth.

Yamashiro, G., & Matsuoka, J. K. (1997). Help-seeking among Asian and Pacific Americans: A multiperspective analysis. *Social Work, 42*(2), 176–185.

Zanden, J. W. V. (1985). *Human Development.* New York: Alfred A. Knopf.

Zarit, S. (1980). Group and family intervention. In S. Zarit (Ed.), *Aging and Mental Disorders* (pp. 322–349). New York: Free Press.

CRITIQUE

Professional Tools for Religiously and Spiritually Sensitive Social Work Practice

ANN P. CONRAD

As part of the global consciousness that has come to characterize the end of the twentieth century, religion and spirituality have taken on a new and expanded meaning. Spirituality is now widely accepted as an integral dimension of human development (Assagioli, 1991; Fowler, 1995). Similarly, within social work and related professions, knowledge and skill in the area of religion and spirituality are recognized as essential competencies for practice. Within this context, spirituality has been defined in various ways (Carroll, 1998; Hugen, 1998). Broadly, it is the underlying dimension of consciousness that strives for meaning, union with the universe, and with all things (Joseph, 1988). This means that spirituality is multidimensional. That is, it includes environmental, interpersonal, personal, transpersonal, and transcendental dimensions. The purpose of this critique is to provide an overview of the meaning and place of religion and spirituality in its historical and contemporary context in social work. It examines the renewed interest in the spiritual within society and the profession and considers the implications for religiously and spiritually sensitive social work practice.

The long held practices of diverse indigenous groups such as Native Americans (Coggins, 1998), Asians (Koenig & Spano, 1998), African-Americans (Wiredu, 1992; Gyekye, 1987), and the ancient Celts (Chadwick, 1991; O'Donohue, 1997) that have emphasized that interrelatedness and harmony with the environment—both animate (i.e., animals, plants) and inanimate (air, fire, water)—are a central part of life and well-being. In a very broad sense, this relatedness at the core of human consciousness is deeply spiritual in nature. Typically, religious belief systems hold that loving and compassionate human exchanges (such as between friends or colleagues

or between professionals and clients) can mirror this transcendent relationship, and that something of the divine is actually present in each human encounter (Rahner, 1973, 1974). Whatever the faith or religious
tradition of the person, whether he or she claims a belief system or not, Rizzuto (1979) holds that each person has an internalized representation of
God that should be acknowledged and respected as an important dimension of personhood.

DIFFERENTIATING BETWEEN FAITH, RELIGION, SPIRITUALITY, AND THE GOD REPRESENTATION

To understand the nature of spirituality and its implications for social
work practice, Joseph (1987) advised that it is helpful to differentiate
between faith, religion, spirituality, and the God representation. *Faith* can
be understood as an inner system of beliefs that relate one to the transcendent or ultimate reality. In contrast, *religion* is the external expression
of a person's faith. It comprises beliefs, ethical codes, and worship, all of
which unite people to a moral community. *Spirituality* differs from faith
and religion in that *spirit* is at the core of people's being, an integral part
of each person that seeks to transcend the self in order to discover meaning, belonging, and relatedness to the infinite. For some persons, the distinctions between faith, religion, and spirituality may be quite seamless.
However, others find the distinctions important and meaningful in their
lives.

The research of Rizzuto (1979) on the *God representation,* a psychody-
namic concept that draws from object relations theory, is important to the
understanding of God. She explained the God representation as a precipitate of internal weavings, unconscious feelings, and ideas around significant internal objects, such as parents, siblings, and friends. Whether or
not a person is a religious believer and regardless of whether she / he has
become aware of a spiritual consciousness, religious symbols and images
are all around us. We pass churches in our neighborhood / communities;
society recognizes religious celebrations; we may have friends whose
faith tradition is very meaningful for them. From an object relations perspective, these very real images in the lives of most persons converge in a
notion of God. In other words, whether a person has a faith tradition or a
spiritual consciousness, it is most likely that she / he has some form of a
God representation. Competent professional practice requires that social
workers recognize and are sensitive to these very complex multidimensional phenomena in ourselves and in our clients (Kilpatrick & Holland,
1990).

POSTMODERN INFLUENCES ON THE RISE
OF INTEREST IN SPIRITUALITY

The rise of the contemporary interest in all forms of spirituality—ranging from a reemergence of ancient and medieval traditions, such as Celtic spirituality and Gregorian chant to contemporary new age adaptations of Eastern and Native American rituals and practices—can be traced to a dissatisfaction with key characteristics of the modern age. As a result, there is an escalating preference for the beliefs and attitudes of the postmodern era. Briefly, modernism embraces a set of attitudes and beliefs associated with an industrial/scientific society. It has been characterized by a belief in unending progress, confidence in universal reasoning, reliance on the power of the self-contained individual, human control over nature, and the use of empirically based knowledge as the sole source of truth. In view of a rather pervasive dissatisfaction with these tenets, postmodern thinkers have offered an alternative perspective, which draws attention to the limitations of human progress and human reason, places emphasis on universal connectedness, and affirms cultural and environmental sensitivity and concern for the vulnerable.

Postmodern perspectives emphasize the importance of community; sharing a sense of solidarity with the poor and oppressed; honoring plurality and sensitivity to cultural difference; recognizing suppressed voices and their stories; working for a more just and peaceful universe; and committing oneself to the realization of a greater spiritual consciousness while rejecting exaggerated materialism (Johnson, 1994). These themes are clearly echoed in contemporary social work knowledge development and practice (Pozatek, 1994; Saleebey, 1994; Pardick, Murphy, & Choi, 1994; Kelley, 1995; Saleebey, 1997; Rapp, 1998).

THE PLACE OF RELIGION/SPIRITUALITY IN
THE SOCIAL WORK PROFESSION

Religion and spirituality have had a place in the social work literature and practice since its earliest beginnings, although the consistency and depth of this content has varied considerably. Carroll (1997) reviewed the early social work literature and found important contributions of some of our social work pioneers. As early as 1922, Mary Richmond expressed interest in Jung's work on spirituality as containing appropriate concepts for use in social work practice. In 1925, Lucille Corbett referred to the human spirit as embodying a principle of life and vital energy, whereas Bertha Reynolds, in 1926, referred to religion as a material, social, and spiritual resource for clients. In the 1960s and following, Keith-Lucas suggested that the religious basis of social work served to strengthen both commitment and service. By the 1970s, professional journals on religion / spirituality in social work had emerged. These included the *Journal of Jewish Communal Service, Social Work and Christianity,* and *Social Thought.* By the latter part of the 1980s, an expanding volume of conceptual and empirical literature on such areas as the nature of spirituality (Keith-Lucas, 1989), the differentiation of faith, religion, or spirituality (Joseph, 1988), the religious-spiritual dimension in practice (Joseph, 1987; Lowenberg, 1988), the contributions of comparative religions (Canda, 1988), and the compatibility of religion and social work (Sanzenbach, Canda, & Joseph, 1989) appeared. Also, it is important to note that the North American Association of Christian Social Workers developed in the 1970s with a focus on "integration of the Christian faith and social work practice." During the mid-1990s, the Society for Spirituality and Social Work emerged from a network of social workers concerned to promote "spiritually sensitive social work practice and non-religious forms of spirituality." These groups have substantial membership across the United States and Canada and hold annual conferences.

Within the profession itself, renewed attention has been given to religiously and spiritually sensitive practice. The revised Code of Social Work Ethics of the National Association of Social Workers (1996) includes understanding of and respect for religious beliefs as part of our responsibility to clients, to colleagues, to professionals, and to the broader society . The Council on Social Work Education (CSWE) had included content on religion in its 1953 and 1962 Curriculum Policy Statements but this was eliminated from the 1970 and 1984 statements. However, the 1992 Curriculum Policy Statement requires that all social work programs include content on religion as part of the student's preparation for working with diversity and with populations at risk (CSWE, 1992). And so, religiously and spiritually sensitive social work practice is no longer a choice or special interest of some professionals. It has become an imperative for twenty-first century practice.

TOOLS FOR RELIGIOUSLY/SPIRITUALLY SENSITIVE PRACTICE

A burgeoning menu of tools for religiously sensitive social work practice has begun to be conceptualized and implemented in practice, presented in the literature, and discussed and debated at social work conferences and workshops. Some have been empirically tested and their findings reported in the literature. The bulk of these contributions have been developed for direct practice with clients for use in assessment, intervention, termination, and service evaluation processes (Cornett, 1998; Richards & Bergin, 1998; Sherwood, 1998; Stroup, 1972).

Before addressing religious/spiritual issues in practice, it is important to establish some general guidelines (Cascio, 1998). These include maintaining a nonjudgmental, accepting attitude about diverse spiritual beliefs and practices; acknowledging that one cannot be familiar with all beliefs and practices; encouraging clients to explain unfamiliar beliefs and practices; and giving careful attention to professional self-awareness (p. 525). Moreover, practitioners should become knowledgeable of the religious/spiritual resources in the community.

In direct practice, attention has been given to the *religious/spiritual assessment* of clients, groups and families. Here, the distinctions discussed earlier between faith, religion, spirituality, and the God representation can be especially useful. Understanding these dimension of human development can be particularly helpful in establishing meaningful relationships with clients and in crafting appropriate intervention strategies. Traditionally, social service agencies have recorded the religious affiliation of clients (if available) as part of the identifying information germane to the case history. This information was used to make appropriate referrals for pastoral care and for the material and social supports that might be available through the client's local congregation. Values histories or a knowledge of the evolution of a client's belief system have been particularly helpful in health care settings where strategic medical decisions about life supports and life sustainment are sometimes made.

Boyd (1998) developed a comprehensive religious/spiritual assessment tool that involves exploring the client's religious upbringing, religious/spiritual life-shaping experiences, conversion/peak/mystical experiences, spiritual crises and emergencies, and current religious/spiritual relationships. Bullis (1996) suggested constructing a genogram with clients that charts the most significant persons and events in one's spiritual development and ways in which they have affected spiritual growth and development. He also considered how a person's spiritual stance has changed in the last five years; any particular experience(s) that had a lasting impact; and the current spiritual ideas, books, authors, persons, or events that have been most influential for a particular client (p. 35). Lewandowski and Canda (1995) presented a typological model for assessing religious groups that is designed to assist social workers and their clients in reflecting on the possible helpful or harmful implications of participation in religious groups. Griffin (1986) highlighted the importance of assessing the God-family relationship in working with religiously committed families.

Models for religious/spiritual intervention have also been developed. Smith (1995) conceptualized and empirically tested a transpersonal model of social work intervention to address the psychospiritual distress of death. Others have considered the strengths and cautions of such interventions as prayer with clients, guided reflection, journaling, engaging in rituals, and religious/spiritual bibliotherapy (Garland, 1998; Cascio, 1998).

Understanding the significance of faith, religion, and spirituality in the lives of clients has been helpful for many social workers in evaluating the effectiveness of practice interventions and anticipating the kinds of prognoses that may be expected. For example, Freeman (1997) found that recidivism in domestic violence was significantly reduced when male abusers reported having an active faith/spirituality. These and other social work initiatives hold much promise for integration of the religious/ spiritual dimension in direct practice in all forms of intervention from case management to psychotherapy and for practice research.

In light of the current enthusiasm for the integration of the religious/ spiritual dimension, a word of professional caution needs to be raised about the importance of carefully addressing the ethical issues that can emerge in this area. For example, it is essential that clients have all the opportunities for informed consent in dealing with religious and spiritual issues as they would in any other developmental or problem area addressed. Further, the practitioner must be aware of the boundary issues that can arise between working with spiritual issues and providing spiritual direction (Ausubel Danzig, 1998; Ressler, 1998).

In the *social policy* arena, social workers need to be aware of the policy statements issued by churches of many denominations on the various social issues of the times. Many of these are congruent with the social justice interests of social workers (Netting, Thibault, & Ellor, 1990). For example, the national policy statements of the American Catholic Bishops on the U.S. economy (National Conference of Catholic Bishops, 1986) and on the responsibility of parents and society to respect all persons regardless of sexual orientation (United States Catholic Conference, 1998) have potential for collaborative social action in areas that are consistent with the advocacy positions taken by the social work profession on behalf of the poor and those who experience violence and discrimination (Ressler, 1998). Reciprocally, social workers need to be aware of their responsibility to advocate for consideration of the needs of the whole person, including the religious/ spiritual dimension, as well as to include this dimension in planning social policy initiatives at the local, state, and national levels (Anderson, 1998).

In summary major initiatives to include the religious/spiritual dimension as an integral aspect of professional social work practice are emerging. Current efforts are under way to transform current theological, spiritual, and human development knowledge for use in strengthening the competencies of social workers to integrate the spiritual dimension into their professional practice. Social workers need to be proactively engaged in these processes "not only because they are ubiquitous aspects of our clients' and our own lives, but also because to do otherwise would be to neglect the very basis of what it is to be human" (Canda, 1994, p. 177).

REFERENCES

Anderson, G. (1998). The field of child welfare: Suffer the little children. In B. Hugen (Ed.), *Christianity and Social Work*. Botsford, CT: North American Association of Christians in Social Work.

Assagioli, R. (1991). *Transpersonal Development*. San Francisco, CA: Aquarian.

Ausubel Danzig, R. (1998). Linking spirituality and diversity: Towards a fluid fountain of unity, respect, and pluralism. *Society for Spirituality and Social Work Newsletter, 5*(2), 1,6–9.

Boyd, T. A. (1998). Spiritually sensitive assessment tools for social work practice. In B. Hugen (Ed.), *Christianity and Social Work*. Botsford, CT: North American Association of Christians in Social Work.

Bullis, R. (1996). *Spirituality in Social Work Practice*. Washington, DC: Taylor and Francis.

Canda, E. R. (1988). Conceptualizing spirituality for social work: Insights from diverse perspectives. *Social Thought, 14*(1) 30–46.

Canda, E. R. (1994). Does religion and spirituality have a significant place in the Core HBSE Curriculum. In M. Bloom & W. Klein (Eds.), *Controversial Issues in Human Behavior in the Social Environment*. Boston: Allyn & Bacon.

Carroll, M. (1997). Spirituality and clinical social work: Implications of past and current perspectives. *Arete, 22*(1), 25–34.

Carroll, M. (1998). Social work's conceptualization of spirituality. *Social Thought, 18*(2), 1–14.

Cascio, T. (1998). Incorporating spirituality into social work practice: A review of what to do. *Families in Society: The Journal of Contemporary Human Services, 79*(6), 523–531.

Chadwick, N. (1991). *The Celts*. London: Penguin.

Coggins, K. (1998). *The Recovery Medicine Wheel: An Alternative Pathway to Healing and Wellness*. Boston, VA: Ventajas.

Cornett, C. (1998). *The Soul of Psychotherapy*. New York: Free Press.

Council on Social Work Education (1994). *Handbook of Accreditation Standards and Procedures*. Alexandria, VA: Author.

Fowler, J. (1995). *Stages of Faith: The Psychology of Human Development and the Quest for Meaning*. New York: Harper Collins.

Freeman, D. (1997). *The Relationship between Spiritual Wholeness and Physical Violence*. Washington, DC: Catholic University of America Press.

Garland, D. (1998). Church social work. In B. Hugen (Ed.), *Christianity and Social Work*. Botsford, CT: North American Association of Christians in Social Work.

Griffin, J. (1986). Employing the God-family relationship in therapy with religious families. *Family Process, 25*, 609–618.

Gyekye, K. (1987). *An Essay on African Philosophical Thought*. New York: Cambridge University Press.

Hugen, B. (1998). Calling: A spirituality model for social work practice. In B. Hugen (Ed.), *Christianity and Social Work* (pp. 91–106). Botsford, CT: North American Association of Christians in Social Work.

Johnson, E. A. (1994). Between the times: Religious life and the postmodern experience of God. *Review for Religious*, 6–28.

Joseph, M. V. (1987). The religious and spiritual aspects of clinical practice: A neglected dimension of social work. *Social Though, 13*(1), 12–23.

Joseph, M. V. (1988). Religion and social work practice. *Social Casework, 69*(7), 443–452.

Keith-Lucas, A. (1989). *The Poor You Have with You Always*. St. Davids, PA: North American Association of Social Workers.

Kelley, P. (1995). Integrating narrative approaches into clinical curricula: Addressing diversity through understanding. *Journal of Social Work Education, 31*(3), 347–357.

Kilpatrick, A., & Holland, T. (1990). Spiritual dimensions of practice. *Clinical Supervisor, 8*, 125–140.

Koenig, T. L., & Spano, R. N. (1998). Taoism and the strengths perspective. *Social Thought, 18*(2), 47–66.

Lewandowski, C. A., & Canda, E. R. (1995). A typological model for the assessment of religious groups. *Social Thought, 18*(1), 17–38.

Lowenberg, F. M. (1988). *Religion and Social Work Practice in Contemporary American Society*. New York: Columbia University Press.

National Conference of Catholic Bishops (1986). *Economic Justice for All*. Washington, DC: Author.

National Association of Social Workers (1996). *Social Work Code of Ethics*. Washington, DC: NASW Press.

Netting, E. E., Thibault, J., & Ellor, J. (1990). Integrating content on organized religion into macropractice courses. *Journal of Social Work Education, 26*(15–24).

O'Donohue, J. (1997). *Anam Cara*. New York: HarperCollins.

Pardick, J. T., Murphy, W. W., & Choi, M. M. (1994). Some implications for postmodernism for social work practice. *Social Work, 39*(4), 343–346.

Pozatek, E. (1994). The problem of certainty: Clinical social work in the postmodern era. *Social Work, 39*(6), 396–403.

Rahner, K. (1973). Practical theology and social work in the church. *Theological Investigations* (Vol. 10, pp. 349–370). Translated by D. Bourke. London: Darton, Longman & Todd.

Rahner, K. (1974). Church of real spirituality. In *The Shape of the Church to Come* (pp. 82–89). New York: Seabury.

Rapp, C. A. (1998). *The Strengths Model*. New York: Oxford University Press.

Ressler, L. (1998). When Social Work and Christianity Conflict. In B. Hugen (Ed.), *Christianity and Social Work*. Botsford, CT: North American Association of Christians in Social Work.

Richards, P. S., & Bergin, A. E. (1998) *A Spiritual Strategy for Counseling and Psychotherapy.* Washington, DC: American Psychological Association.

Rizzuto, A. (1979). *The Birth of the Living God.* Chicago: University of Chicago Press.

Saleebey, D. (1994). Culture, theory and narrative: The interpretation of meanings in practice. *Social Work, 39*(4), 351–359.

Saleebey, D. (1997). *The Strengths Perspective in Social Work Practice* (2nd ed.). New York: Longman.

Sanzenbach, P., Canda, E. R., & Joseph, M. V. (1989). Religion and social work: It's not that simple! *Social Casework, 70*(9), 571–757.

Sherwood, D. A. (1998). The relationship between beliefs and values in social work practice: Worldviews make a difference. In B. Hugen (Ed.), *Christianity and Social Work.* Botsford, CT: North American Association of Christians in Social Work.

Smith, E. (1995). Addressing the psychospiritual distress of death as reality: A transpersonal approach. *Social Work, 40*(3), 402–413.

Stroup, H. (1972). The common predicament of religion and social work. *Social Work, 7*(2), 89–93.

United States Catholic Conference. (1998). *Always Our Children.* Washington, DC: Author.

Wiredu, K. (1992). The African American concept of personhood. In H. E. Flock & E. D. Pelegrino (Eds.), *African American Perspectives on Biomedical Ethics.* Washington, DC: Georgetown University Press

3

Classical Psychoanalytic Thought, Contemporary Developments, and Clinical Social Work

ROBERTA R. GREENE

Freud's conceptualization of the development, structure, and functioning of the personality ushered in a new era in understanding behavior
and in treating the human mind (Baker, 1985). Many view Freud, whose
theory offers an explanation of human development and a method of treatment, as a pioneer whose far-reaching concepts provided ideas "central to
nearly every approach to treating psychological problems via psychotherapy" (ibid., p. 20).

The influence of Freud's psychoanalytic theory has been so dramatic
that it has left a legacy of ideas that has shaped the direction of much of
twentieth-century psychology and social science. Freud's psychoanalytic
theory has influenced almost every arena of modern life—literature, art,
and law, as well as political, social, and economic systems—to such an extent that his "concept and terminology have infiltrated the thinking even
of those who most repudiate his views" (Wood, 1971, p. 46).

Psychoanalytic theory, which is about a century old, and its contemporary offshoots have been important influences on social work practice.
Some believe that these influences have been so strong that they have "per-
meated not only the casework method, but also the social reality within
which social casework is embedded" (ibid.). This chapter presents selected classical psychoanalytic tenets, outlines the major shifts in emphases
that have led to the development of ego psychology and the object relations schools of thought, and discusses some of the major contributions of
these bodies of thought to clinical social work practice. The case study involves a young adult with problems of ego identity. Chapter 4 continues in
the psychoanalytic tradition and discusses Eric Erikson's ego psychology.

In large measure, social workers' interest in Freudian theory came about because of the profession's struggle to find a scientific base for practice (Hamilton, [1940] 1951; Hollis, 1964). Germain (1970) suggested that the premise laid out in *Social Diagnosis* by Mary Richmond (1917)—"that uncovering the cause will reveal the cure"—led to a strong interest in the medical model or "disease metaphor" (as conceived by Freud) and with it a "study- diagnosis-treatment framework" (pp. 10–13). Because of this historical commitment to the *medical model,* a perspective with an emphasis on diagnosis, treatment, and cure, it is sometimes said that Freudian theory "transformed casework from a trial-and-error art" to a more precise or scientific framework for helping people (Wood, 1971, pp. 45–46).

Members of the diagnostic and psychosocial schools of social casework particularly have been affected by Freudian theory (Hamilton, 1958; Hollis, 1970; Perlman, 1957a). The assumption that "there must be pain-staking social study, followed by a diagnostic formulation leading to a plan of treatment" (Hollis, [1964] 1967, p. 191), is a major principle of these schools that is based on Freud's medical model.

> Freud's theory of human behavior permeates western thought and was adopted by social workers to guide the diagnostic process.

Among the most important assumptions that many clinical social workers adopted from psychoanalytic theory is the view that all behavior is determined in a purposeful and orderly way. That is, everything a person says or does, even words or actions that are seemingly irrational, is meaningful and capable of explanation. Freud was among the first students of human behavior who took all forms of behavior as meaningful expressions that could ultimately be understood. In other words, Freud proposed that all mental phenomena made sense. By sense, he meant "'meaning,' 'intention,' 'purpose' and position in a continuous psychical [psychological] context" (Freud, [1920] 1966, p. 61). According to Hollis ([1964] 1967), Freud's conceptualizations, which help caseworkers "to understand causation in the developmental sense of how the person came to be the way he [or she] is . . . made a major contribution to the social work profession" (p. 168).

Although not without dispute, another major approach to practice that many clinical social workers have borrowed from psychoanalytic theory is the idea that there are unconscious mental processes and that these processes are of great significance. For example, Hamilton ([1940] 1951) contended that "caseworkers must sometimes bring to the attention of the client ideas and feelings, whether acceptable or not, of which he [or she] was previously unaware" (p. 73). Lieberman (1982), in a discussion of the place of unconscious determinants of behavior in social work practice, stated that "for a clinician there should be only one answer. The client needs to be understood in depth, beyond the immediate presentation" (p. 28).

The wide-scale adoption of the idea that a client may not be aware of important unconscious or irrational feelings and thoughts affected how many social workers saw their role. Using a psychoanalytic model meant that the social worker's techniques would be geared to interpreting the client's behaviors and motivations as well as helping the client to understand the meanings of symptoms. The use of self in the helping relationship also was affected by psychoanalytic theory. "Almost over-night, advanced practitioners who had now been brought under 'the influence' learned to listen . . . [and] to observe the client's verbal and nonverbal activity in a more productive way" (Hamilton, 1958, p. 25).

> Social workers of the 1960s and 1970 were greatly influenced by the idea that human behavior is unconsciously motivated.

Freud's assumption that adult pathology has its roots in early childhood experiences also had a pervasive influence on social casework (Lowenstein, 1985). As a result of the influence of psychoanalytic thought, uncovering hidden childhood motivations for behavior became an important aspect of many social casework assessments. An acceptance of the subjective meanings clients attribute to events has been a consistent theme in both psychoanalytic treatment and social casework. The role of many social workers increasingly came to be one of interpreting a client's motivations and present difficulties in light of past experiences.

The idea that the clinical social worker has the responsibility to understand his or her own psychological self also can be traced to Freud's ideas about what transpires in the helping relationship. Because Freud believed there was the potential for both client and therapist to relive significant irrational aspects of their developmental histories within the helping relationship, he suggested that self-awareness was of great importance to the helping person. The classical psychoanalytic principle that a helping person must first be self-aware before he or she is able to assist a client has been an important influence on social work practice. Although most social workers today do not follow orthodox psychoanalytic methods and may employ a number of different human behavior theories, contemporary styles of direct practice still reflect influences of Freudian tradition. "From our contemporary point of view, the question is not so much 'What did Freud say?' but 'What has Freud's work led to?'" (Baker, 1985, p. 19).

THE PERSON-IN-ENVIRONMENT HISTORICAL CONTEXT: FREUD'S PSYCHOANALYTIC THEORY

A neurologist by training, Freud was educated to view all symptoms as stemming from some organic disorder or brain malfunction. Although Freud began his scientific work with a recognition of the biological aspects of psychiatry, he later came to believe that the science of his day was insufficiently advanced to study organic diseases of the nervous system. He therefore turned to an investigation of psychological functioning or what he termed "the workings of the mind." Through his study, Freud came to believe that people become psychologically or physically ill because of conflicts in human relationships. That is, mental illness could be a functional disturbance—in this case, a product of a disturbed relationship. He hoped that psychoanalysis would give psychiatry "its missing psychological foundation" and that the "convergence of physical and mental disorder" would become intelligible (Freud, [1920] 1966, p. 21).

Freud was concerned that others in the scientific community thought that there was "no objective verification of psychoanalysis" and doubted the credibility of the psychoanalytic method (ibid., p. 19). He refuted this position by stating that "one learns psycho-analysis on oneself, by studying one's own personality" (ibid.).

> Early in Freud's career, he hoped to demonstrate that human behavior was, in large measure, biologically based.

Freud's theoretical views challenged so much of the scientific thinking and norms of his day that he himself saw his ideas as controversial.

Freud began his work when psychology emerged as an independent discipline in the mid–nineteenth century. In the scientific tradition of his day, the explanation of complex experiences was reduced to a number of elementary phenomena, an approach known as *reductionism* (Hall & Lindzey, 1957). The major scientific focus in psychology at that time was the identification and study of the structural elements of the conscious mind. Psychologists of Freud's day clearly placed the unconscious beyond the realm of serious scientific analysis (Nye, 1975). Freud, who made the concept of the unconscious the cornerstone of his theory and believed that a person's unconscious could be an object of scientific study, brought an entirely different and controversial dimension.

Another reason for Freud's controversial reception was his treatment of sexuality, which, for his day, was "novel to the point of scandal" (Wood, 1971, p. 51). Most shocking was his attribution of sexuality to the young child. Today it is clear that some of the controversy was based on misunderstandings of Freud's statements. Freud did not equate infant and adult sexuality. Rather, he suggested that personality was developed in psychosexual stages during which there was movement of psychic energy from one erogenous, or gratifying, zone of the body to the next, with each stage presenting psychological conflict and gratification.

Freud was ahead of his day in foreseeing that the laws of chemistry and physics could be applied to humans. Although some of his concepts have become outdated, many of his central ideas, when modified, have made important contributions to social work practice. For example, early systems theory influenced Freud to posit the view that there is a fixed sum of psychic energy available to the personality that must be exchanged among the id, ego, and superego. As Hamilton (1958) noted, psychological energy "was likened to steam in a boiler, and could only be diverted or discharged" (p. 1552). Today, the idea that the mind is a closed system governed by a finite amount of energy is no longer accepted. However, ego psychologists have extended Freud's ideas about ego functioning, suggesting that the ego has its own psychic energy, is relatively autonomous, and plays a critical role in assuming coping strategies. This point of view was seen by many as more congruent and useful in social work practice, where a central issue is a client's strategies for meeting the demands of his or her environment (Compton & Galaway, 1994; Fromm, 1959; Goldstein, 1986; Lowenstein, 1985).

Darwinian theory also influenced Freud. It led to the adoption of the notion that instincts have an important place in human evolution and play a strong role in personality development. Freud believed that two major drives, sex and aggression, were inborn, and that an inclination for war and destructiveness also was innate (Freud, [1933] 1964). These views about human nature were challenged by those who believed that it was more congruent with social work philosophy to see personality features as molded by the cultural environment (Wood, 1971).

Freud's critics have suggested that for several decades (1920–1960) social workers became too immersed in psychoanalytic theory. They argued that the profession's strong emphasis on intrapsychic phenomena created a schism within the profession—dividing it between those who were more interested in the "person" and those who placed a stronger emphasis on the "environment" (Woodroofe, 1971). On the other hand, it has been argued that the profession's understanding of intrapsychic phenomena has been strengthened through an eclectic use of psychoanalytic principles, and that, despite this strong interest in the "person," the profession has remained equally environmentally concerned (Caroff, 1982; Cohen, 1980). During World War II and postwar years, when an interest in political and social factors came to the fore, social work practitioners focused their interest on how a client learns to master his or her environment.

Contemporary Applications

Contemporary psychoanalytic thinking, for the most part, tends to be based on *ego psychology* (Corey, 1986; Hogan, 1976). Although ego psychology does not deny the existence of intrapsychic conflict, it places a greater emphasis on the striving of the ego for mastery and control over the environment than does orthodox Freudian thought. The view of ego psychologists, who examine the functioning of the ego throughout the life cycle, thus represents a critical change in emphasis. Their emphasis on the impact of the environment and the more rational and problem-solving capacities of the ego in fostering adaptive behavior has been an important perspective in social work practice (Goldstein, 1984, p. xvii).

For many, the ego psychology school of thought marked the return to a better balance between personality and situational factors in social work practice. For example, Wood (1971) suggested that ego psychology renewed the profession's focus on the person-environment constellation. Hamilton (1958) proposed that ego psychology had developed "a fresh orientation to [casework] treatment" by refocusing casework practice on the ego as an autonomous, separate, and distinct personality structure. She went on to state that by emphasizing ego strengths, "the casework method was fundamentally reorganized" to be concerned with the "stresses of reality" (p. 22). The view of human functioning proposed by ego psychologists is still a prevalent one in the direct practice of social work. Erik Erikson, whose theory made a major contribution to this perspective, is discussed in Chapter 4.

Another contemporary offshoot of Freudian theory, developed over the past twenty years, is *object relations*. Among the latest revisions of Freud's theory beginning in the late 1960s to the 1970s is object relations theory (Bowlby, 1980; Hamilton, 1988, 1989; Hartmann, 1939; Karen, 1990; Mahler, 1968). The path to object relations theory led through the work of several of Freud's students and disciples, notably his daughter, Anna Freud. Anna Freud made major contributions to the development of psychoanalytic theory by shifting her focus to an elaboration of the defenses and how they operate. Rather than being concerned primarily with drives, she devoted a great deal of attention to defining the ego and how it operates to protect its own integrity (Freud, 1936).

Object relations theorists acknowledge their debt to psychoanalysis. They view themselves as developers, elaborators, and carriers of the psychoanalytic tradition (for example, Bion, 1962; Fairbairn, 1954; Kernberg, 1976; Kohut, 1971). Object relations is an outgrowth of these theorists' view that personality structure is a result of the nature of interpersonal experiences. Their contributions have enabled modern psychoanalytic thought to relate itself especially to the outpouring of studies about the early development of young children (Bowlby, 1969, 1973; Brazelton, 1969; Mahler, Pine, & Bergman, 1975; Spitz, 1965;). By observing the similarities between the normal, developmental behaviors of young children and the ways in which disturbed adult patients behave toward both external and internal objects or people, object relations therapists have been able to draw important practice insights for understanding the meanings of patients' behaviors. Object relations theorists emphasize separation and individuation through the process of internalizing representation of self and others.

BASIC ASSUMPTIONS AND TERMINOLOGY

Freud's Psychoanalytic Theory

As constructed originally by Sigmund Freud from about 1895 to 1932, psychoanalytic theory is *deterministic*. That is, earlier events control (determine) later events. This assumption underlies all of his conceptualizations. For example, Freud ([1905] 1953) saw infants as having drives that are directed toward certain goals, most notably attaining oral gratification (see the section on Explaining Development across the Life Cycle). Freud's most general purpose, and another underlying assumption, was to demonstrate or prove that all experiences, feelings, thoughts, fantasies, and dreams make sense.

Freud was a prolific writer who elaborated his theory of personality for more than forty years. During that time, he produced a number of models to explain psychic structures and the meaning of behavior. Although for purposes of clarity, each of Freud's models is described separately, his theory is best understood through the integration of the information from each model (Table 3.1). Freud's theory has led to the elaboration of contemporary uses of his concepts.

Economic Model

The economic model—which is the foundation for future models—proposed two major ideas: (1) There is a fixed amount of psychic energy shared among id, ego, and superego, and (2) behavior is affected by the quantity and quality of instinctual demands. In the economic model, Freud suggested that all behavior is governed by drives and the purpose of all behavior is to dispose of psychological, instinctual energy.

Topographic Model

Perhaps Freud's greatest contribution to understanding personality is his suggestion that there are three levels of consciousness (Corey, 1986). Mental processes that are conscious are within awareness; *preconscious* mental processes are capable of becoming conscious "without much ado" or are fairly accessible; and *unconscious* mental processes are outside awareness and cannot be studied directly (Freud, 1960a, p. 5). Freud stated that consciousness is transitory and that it is the exception rather than

Table 3.1. Psychoanalytic Theory: Basic Assumptions

All mental life is meaningful.
Nothing happens randomly or by chance.
Each psychic event is determined by preceding events.
As a three-part energy system, the personality is fueled by psychic energy that
    can be invested in varying degrees in objects.
Behavior is biologically based, propelled by tensions created by innate sexual or
    aggressive drives.
Society is a necessary controlling influence on primitive biological needs,
Each psychosexual stage is an outgrowth of and recapitulates earlier ones.
Personality is an outgrowth of all five stages. The major events in personality for-
    mation occur in the first 5 to 6 years of life.
Consciousness, or being aware of one's own thoughts and feelings, is the excep-
    tion rather than the rule; therefore, the individual is unaware of most of his
    or her mental processes.
Unconscious or unknown motivations in large measure are responsible for con-
    scious actions, feelings, and thought.
The helping process involves uncovering underlying causes of abnormal or de-
    structive behavior. Motivations that are symbolic of unconscious needs and
    desires can be interpreted through an understanding of overt behaviors.
The helping process is a corrective emotional experience.

the rule. The three states of consciousness or layers of awareness should
not be thought of as distinct or absolute categories, but as matters of degree. The assumption that most of a person's thoughts and feelings are outside awareness became the bulwark of Freud's psychoanalytic theory.

Freud gave as evidence of unconscious processes at work the human
tendencies to forget (names, impressions, and experiences), to lose and
mislay belongings, to make errors, slips of the tongue, and slips of the pen,
to misread, and to bungle actions. His belief in the predominance of unconscious processes led to his interest in free association, resistance, patterns of likes and dislikes, life patterns, jokes and errors, works of art, and
neurotic symptoms. Freud's interest in unconscious mental life also led to
a study of *dreams* (residues of waking mental activity). He viewed dreams
as the "distorted substitute for something else, something unconscious,"
and that the task of interpreting a dream is to discover this unconscious
material (Freud, [1920] 1966, p. 114).

The perspective that behavior and motivation have roots in different
levels of awareness, that is, that the individual may not be aware of his or
her motivations or causes of behavior, has had an important influence on
social casework. The theme that the social worker needs to take an active
role in interpreting the underlying meanings of behavior cuts across the social work literature (Perlman, 1957b). For example, Cohen (1980) stated
that in clinical social work practice behavior needs to be understood in

terms of "ideas, wishes, feelings, and fantasies, and conflicts that are both in and out of awareness" (p. 28). Kadushin (1972), although modifying this thought slightly, proposed that social workers follow the dictum that "no communication is without meaning" (p. 35). Shulman (1984) proposed that "putting the client's feelings into words" so that he or she "knows the worker understands" is a critical aspect of the social worker–client relationship (pp. 27–28).

> Freud's various models describe the origins of mental activity and how practitioners may understand and interpret behaviors.

Structural Model

Freud's topographical model was followed by the structural model, which integrates many of his earlier ideas. In the structural model, Freud suggested that the personality is made of three major parts or systems: the id, the ego, and the superego. Although each part of the personality has its unique functions and properties, they interact to form a whole and each subsystem makes a relative contribution to an individual's behavior. Needless to say, each part of the personality as described is a conceptualization, and should not be thought of as having an actual existence (Figure 3.1).

The *id* is the original, inherent system of the personality and consists of everything present at birth, including instincts and the reservoir of psychic energy. The id houses drives that produce a state of *tension* that propels the person to activity to reduce the tension. It has only one consideration: to reduce tensions either by activity or by image, such as the formation of dreams and fantasies.

The id is the foundation of the personality, and remains infantile in its

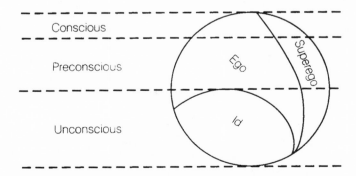

Figure 3.1.   An illustration of Freud's structural model. From Nye (1975). Copyright Brooks/Cole.

functions and thinking throughout life. It cannot change with time or experience because it is not in touch with the external world and does not know about laws, logic, reason, or values. If the id retains control over a large amount of energy in the adult, his or her behavior will be relatively impulsive, primitive, and irrational in nature. Freud made a major contribution in his perspective that irrationality is a regular part of anyone's thought processes. Problems ensue when these irrational thoughts predominate.

Freud believed that there are two modes of thinking: primary and secondary process (Lowenstein, 1985). *Primary process thinking,* according to Freud, originates in the id or unconscious and is characterized by lack of logic, time, and order. This form of mental process or thinking knows no objective reality and is selfish, wishful, and omnipotent in nature. In the infant, this form of thinking means that there is no recognition of anything external to the self and the child believes all needs will be met as if by magic. In the adult, primary process thinking can be recognized in individuals who engage in wishful thinking with little regard for reality. Freud suggested that primary process thinking predominates in early childhood and will occur throughout life. However, Freud considered the predominance of primary process thinking in adults to be pathological. The idea that the image of the object is thought of by the id as if it were the actual object is a central concept in contemporary psychoanalytic thought. Clients who frequently use magical or wishful thinking need help in distinguishing between fantasy and reality. Another important characteristic Freud attributed to the id is that it operates according to the *pleasure principle.* This means the processes of the id are concerned solely with tension reduction and gratification. (When tension is reduced, the person receives gratification.)

The *ego* then "is that part of the id which has been modified by the direct influence of the external world" (Freud, 1960a, p. 15). To take into account the external reality, psychic energy is shifted from the id to form the ego, the executive arm of the personality, which controls and governs the id. The ego becomes differentiated from the id as the individual needs to transact with the objective world. The ego is governed by the *reality principle,* or the ability of the ego to postpone the discharge of energy or seek gratification until it is appropriate. Being able to tolerate tension until a method of discharge is found that is socially appropriate or acceptable and eventually leads to pleasure is a primary function of the ego.

> Freud's concept of ego mastery set the foundation for how social workers approach person-in-environment.

The ego operates by thinking through a plan of action to see if it will work or not. If the mental test does not work out, then it is thought through again until a solution is found. This is known as *"reality testing."* Reality testing allows for greater mastery of impulses and a strengthened ability to distinguish between fantasy and reality. An important aspect of many clinical social workers' approach to practice is to enhance ego functioning and the client's ability to test reality by assisting the client to think through his or her options.

Freud suggested that even the person who has successfully passed through the psychosexual stages of development and is a mature functioning adult will experience conflict between these demands. Such conflict leads to *anxiety,* or an omnipresent state of tension that motivates people to act. In an attempt to deal with anxiety, *ego defenses* are developed. That is, Freud saw anxiety as a normal part of the human condition. When the ego fails in its attempt to use the reality principle and anxiety is experienced, unconscious defense mechanisms that distort reality come into play. Otherwise anxiety can make one feel overwhelmed by "a sense of danger." The more adaptive the *ego defense structure,* or the pattern of use of defense mechanisms, the healthier the individual is said to be. An assessment of a client's defense structure is an important aspect of a psychoanalytically oriented helping process. This allows the social worker to evaluate whether to attempt to work toward interpreting and / or modifying these structures.

Among the defense mechanisms of particular interest to Freud were *regression* (returning to earlier stages of behavior), *repression* (excluding painful or threatening thoughts and feelings from awareness), *reaction formation* (warding off negative impulses by expressing the opposite impulse), *projection* (attributing to others one's own unacceptable desires), *rationalization* (explaining away failures or losses), *introjection* (taking in the values and standards of others), *identification* (seeing oneself as someone else, usually someone successful), *sublimation* (diverting sexual energies to a higher channel or activity), *undoing* (reconstructing previous actions so that they are less threatening), and *denial* (failing to acknowledge reality).

The *superego* is the third and last system of the personality to develop and consists of the values and ideals of society the child derives from his or her parents. The formation of the superego is an important part of the *socialization* process, which consists of placing one's sexual and aggressive impulses under control. This moral or judicial branch of the personality, along with the ego, enables an individual to control behavior.

The Dynamic Model

The dynamic model, based on the view that an individual is propelled by *drives,* or primitive urges, and is conflicted by contradictory societal expectations, dominated classical Freudian thought. Freud [1915, (1933] 1964) suggested that a conflict exists between a person's internal pleasure-seeking forces, which wish to release sexual and aggressive energy, and the social environment, which demands inhibition. Inherited instincts form the core of the personality and, according to Freud, bring about an innate propensity for sexual and destructive behaviors if not checked by ego defenses and societal forces. Freud proposed that psychological activity is determined by a constant need to reduce instinctual tensions and restore psychological balance. This perspective on behavior is called the "dynamic model." The dynamic model influenced object relations theorists, who adopted Freud's idea that psychic energy may become *fixated*, or heavily invested in an object or person.

EXPLAINING DEVELOPMENT ACROSS THE LIFE CYCLE

Freudian developmental theory centers around a dual process involving biological maturation and the development of related psychological structures. Personality patterns are seen as a function of constitutional predispositions and a result of an individual's early life experiences. How an individual has experienced early life stages is said to determine how later life events will be handled. This point of view can be said to minimize conscious choice (Baker, 1985).

Freud proposed that there is a sequence of universal stages from birth to adulthood, which is defined in terms of the region of the body providing primary erotic gratification at that time. In other words, psychoanalytic theory suggests that psychological maturation consists of the unfolding of predetermined phases with specific tasks at each phase involving the transformation of sexual energies. These have been termed *psychosexual* stages. The resolution of each stage centers around a psychological issue (Table 3.2).

Psychoanalytic theory suggests that the orientation of the personality is an outcome of the resolution of psychosexual stages. This perspective is called the "genetic" or developmental model.

The genetic model assumes that there is no clear-cut demarcation of stages and that there may be overlap between stages. At each stage of development the individual concentrates energies on the part of the body that defines that stage. To pass through a developmental stage successfully requires the optimal amount of gratification (there must not be too much or too little gratification). An over-

> Freud revolutionized how we think about child development. That process of reevaluation continues today.

Table 3.2.   Summary of Tasks of Each of Freud's Psychosexual Stages

Stage	Task
Oral	Separate/individuate
	Form object relationships
Anal	Accept responsibility and control
	Negotiate with others in authority
Phallic	Adopt one's gender orientation with a view of ones' place in the family constellation
	Demonstrate a capacity for dealing with the value orientation and ethics of one's society
Latency	Move to more advanced uses of ego defenses
Genital	Work and love successfully

abundance of gratification at a particular stage—or a strong *cathexis*—brings about what Freud called a "fixation."

Fixation occurs when psychic energy is heavily invested in a particular stage. Fixations, particularly minor ones, are a general feature of psychosexual development—"everyone has a fixation of some kind" (Hogan, 1976, p. 38). Because energy that is fixated is not as readily available to the individual to move on to the next stage, the result is that development is frustrated or incomplete. This may impede the individual's capacity to reach full maturity. *Regression* is a predisposition to return to behaviors of earlier stages, particularly under stress. The complementary processes of fixation and regression "give a distinct flavor to a person's interpersonal style" (ibid.).

In this context, a person's developmental history is a critical determinant of later behavior, and much of what an adult does is believed to be determined by early childhood experiences (Baker, 1985; Nye, 1975). Early behaviors that develop during the first six to seven years of life become the prototypes for the characteristics traits and behaviors of adulthood. It is these patterns of behavior that give the social worker clues about the client's developmental history.

The first of Freud's stages is the *oral stage,* which occurs during the first year of life and involves the erotic pleasure or satisfaction derived from nursing. Pleasurable stimulation of the mouth, lips, and tongue is associated with the mother figure. The prototypes or basic patterns of these behaviors, as with the patterns of each stage, can be seen in adulthood. For example, a person who has had his or her oral needs met relatively well during this stage is more apt to reach out to others and not be overly aggressive and acquisitive. Deprivation of oral gratification is assumed to lead to problems in adults such as withdrawal, extreme dependency, and an inability to form intense relationships. The task of this stage of development is to achieve separation and individuation.

During the *anal stage,* which takes place from one to three years of age, the anal zone becomes critical in personality formation. The locus of erotic stimulation shifts to the anus and personality issues center around eliminatory behavior, the retention and expulsion of feces. Again, the manner of resolution of the stage becomes the prototype or pattern for adult behaviors. Freud's idea that strict toilet training leads to compulsive traits such as stinginess and tidiness, called "anal retentiveness," is well-known.

The *Oedipal* or *phallic stage,* which takes place between three and six years of age, is Freud's most complicated, widely discussed, and perhaps most controversial stage. At this time, sexual interest and excitation becomes more intense and centers around the genitalia. According to orthodox psychoanalytic view, the basic controversy during this stage is the child's unconscious desires for the parent of the opposite sex. This conflict is known as the *Oedipus conflict* in boys and the *Electra complex* in girls. Freud believed *identification* (the internalization of another's characteristics) with the parent of the same sex was one of the major outcomes of the phallic stage. This successful resolution of the Oedipus conflict determined an individual's sex role identification and gender identity. In the adult, when these sexual impulses arise, they would be channeled toward sexual union and expressed through a number of emotions, including loyalty, piety, filial devotion, and romantic love. Freud also proposed that the superego was the heir of the Oedipus complex. Identification with the same-sex parent was identified as the mechanism for this socialization process.

The *latency stage,* which occurs between the ages of six and twelve, was viewed by Freud as a time when infantile sexual energies lay dormant. By this time, the major structures of the personality are formed, as are the relationships among its subsystems (id, ego, superego). The *genital stage,* ages twelve through eighteen, marks the return of repressed sexuality. Earlier sources of sexual pleasure are coordinated and have matured. According to Freud, the ability to work productively and to love deeply, or achieve sexual orgasm, are the central characteristics of this stage.

Psychological Health or Adaptiveness

In Freud's model, psychological health is ideal. Freud believed that most individuals do not reach full emotional maturity, but even if they do, they will experience psychological conflicts. Psychopathology in Freud's view was linked to the quality and quantity of instinctual drives, the ef-

> Western psychiatric practices have their origins in Freud's concepts of psychopathology.

fectiveness of the ego defenses in modulating the expression of such drives, the level of maturity of an individual's defensive functioning, and the extent of superego sanctions or guilt. Pathology arises when the drives are excessively frustrated or excessively gratified, and there is early trauma during the oral, anal, and phallic stages. Unresolved unconscious conflicts precipitated during these early stages were thought to be the major cause of psychological problems in adults.

Freud suggested that to achieve mental health in adulthood it was necessary to pass through the psychosexual stages successfully (with minimal tension/conflict). This required an optimal amount of gratification at each stage—not too much or too little. According to Freud, previously well-functioning adults regress under severe stress and, in the process, return to earlier adaptive patterns. This perspective may be said to underlie social work crisis intervention.

In the relatively healthy individual, the parts of the personality are in synchronization and allow the individual to transact well with the world, as demonstrated by the ability to maintain "commerce with the external world," use defenses effectively, delay gratification, and place one's sexual and aggressive impulses under control. It is the social work practitioner's role to help the client achieve a more realistic balance.

The hallmark of the healthy personality, according to Freud, is an ego that is well developed and can deal effectively with anxiety. Ego defenses, which allow instincts to be satisfied without excessive punishment or guilt, are a means of relieving the ego of excessive anxiety. The ultimate indicator of a healthy personality is identified by the capacity to love and work. Freud stressed that being able to love and work is tied to the ability to find socially acceptable outlets for potentially destructive instincts. He suggested a straightforward answer to the question of mental health, stating it is often resolved by deciding the practical issue of the client's "capacity for enjoyment and of efficiency" (Freud, [1920] 1966, p. 457).

UNDERSTANDING CULTURAL DIFFERENCES: CROSS-CULTURAL SOCIAL WORK PRACTICE

Although many of Freud's ideas were tied to the scientific and cultural attitudes of the day, to his credit, Freud also was interested in the basic and exciting discoveries of anthropologists about the nature of human cultures and the differences among them. Many of the basic anthropological studies were published during his lifetime (Benedict, 1934; Malinowski, 1922). However, Freud, educated as a physician during the nineteenth century, tended, in the opinion of many of those who came after him, to underestimate the extent to which cultures influence the development of human personality by the teaching (socialization) that they do. Some of what Freud viewed as basic human nature is seen to be specific to a particular culture when one compares across cultures. Much of what Freud viewed as "inevitable" seems to be specific to his culture and time.

The ways in which Freudian theory dealt with issues about the development of women is an example of a major point of controversy (Firestone, 1971; Miller, 1973; Rice and Rice, 1973). On the one hand, Freud [(1925] 1956, [1931] 1956, 1933) clearly was interested in alleviating women's illnesses, and in training and teaching women professionals the theories and practice of psychoanalysis (Gay, 1988, p. 509). On the other hand, there are many theorists who see Freudian theory as "male oriented" and as emphasizing "the male as a model for normalcy" (Wesley, 1975, p. 121).

Horney (1939) and Jones (1955), both students of Freud and distinguished psychoanalysts in their own right, saw Freud's views of women as both biased and inaccurate (Gay, 1988, pp. 519–521). In the opinions of both Homey and Jones, Freud thought of women as derivative of men, and disregarded the fact that femininity is not just the result of the frustration of women's attempts to be "masculine."

> Many of Freud's critics believe his theory was not universal, but based on a male model in the context of 1920s Vienna.

Rather, both argued that femininity and feminine qualities are the primary birthright of women and have equal validity with those qualities that are identified as masculine. Perhaps the most damning argument about Freud's poor conceptualization of development in women is made by Gilligan (1982), who contends that Freud, although surrounded by women, "was unable to trace in women the development of relationships, morality, or a clear sense of self" (p. 24).

Gould (1984), in a historical analysis of the social work literature, questioned the wide-scale adoption of "antifeminist" psychoanalytic views of women into social casework practice (p. 96). Her review documented that Freud's [(1925] 1956, [1931] 1956, 1933) views on the differential psychosexual development of men and women were widely disseminated into social work without a critical evaluation of Freud's original writings.

Among the challenges about the universality of Freud's theory is his conceptualization of the Oedipus complex. Freud suggested that the Oedipal situation was the central organizing principle in gender identification. Increasingly this view has come to be challenged by modern analysts and Freudian scholars (Goleman, 1990; Wetzel, 1976). This too has come to be seen merely as a reflection of the scientific climate in which Freud worked.

Theorists also have challenged Freud's ideas about homosexuality. Freud suggested that everyone is constitutionally bisexual, by which he meant that an individual's basic makeup includes same-sex and opposite-sex components. Freud believed that the family experience combined with inherited tendencies toward sexual orientation worked together to produce a final sexual identification (Nye, 1975). Freud did believe that homosexuality was not within the "normal" range of behavior and this belief, unfortunately, has continued to shape the thinking and practice of many psychoanalytically oriented therapists. According to Isay (1989), the belief that homosexuality is abnormal has "interfered with our being able to conceptualize a developmental pathway for gay men and thus has seriously impeded our capacity to provide a psychotherapy that is neutral and unbiased by cultural expectations" (p. 5).

UNDERSTANDING HOW HUMANS FUNCTION AS MEMBERS OF FAMILIES, GROUPS, ORGANIZATIONS, AND COMMUNITIES

Freud stressed that there is a major conflict between the pleasure-seeking nature of individuals and the existence of civilized society (Freud, 1936). His view of human nature was such that he argued that it is the innate tendency of humans to exploit each other for sexual and destructive satisfaction. "Society believes that no greater threat to its civilization could arise than if the sexual instincts were to be liberated and returned to their original aims" (Freud, 1936, p. 23). He proposed that the development of civilization rested on the inhibition of primitive urges and their diversion into socially acceptable channels. Freud's (1910) fascination with great men such as Moses and Leonardo da Vinci appears to stem from an interest in how psychological functions were turned to higher social and cultural achievements. He called the process of channeling psychic energy into acceptable alternatives "sublimation."

Family

The applicability of Freud's theory to different family forms or structures is questionable. Cross-cultural research suggests that family styles probably are more a function of culturally shaped variables than the biologically driven forces proposed by Freud (Brislin, 1981). Such field studies seem to indicate that practitioners should cautiously apply principles developed within a specific culture at a particular historical time. By their very nature, classical psychoanalytic methods were concerned with the internal dynamics of the personality and with an analysis of the therapist-client relationship. It is said that Freud "left a legacy of conviction that it was counter-productive and dangerous for a counselor to become involved with more than one member of the same family" (Broderick, 1981, p. 16). Ironically, contemporary family systems work has incorporated many of the ideas originally advanced in orthodox psychoanalytic theory—shifting from a focus on the individual to the family emotional relationship system (Bowen, 1978; Scharff, 1982; Kerr, 1981). Ackerman ([1972] 1984, 1981), a pioneer in this form of treatment, extended the psychoanalytic approach to include the psychodynamics of family functioning and the therapist-client transference.

Groups

Freud (1960b) believed that his conceptualizations about the human personality extended to how people behave in groups. He wrote in *Group Psychology and the Analysis of the Ego* that "individual psychology . . . is at the same time social psychology" (p. 3). For the most part, Freud viewed the psychology of the group, which he believed produced an environment that weakens the power of the superego and in which primary process thinking prevails, as a negative influence. He suggested that, in groups, people tended to behave in a more childlike fashion. He felt that the strong emotional ties that bind the individual to the group members and to the fatherlike leader accounted for the powerful influence of the group.

This view of the power of the group is reflected in most psychoanalytically oriented group treatment approaches (Bion, 1959; Wolf, Schwartz, McCarty, & Goldberg, 1972). Psychoanalytic group treatments build on orthodox thinking about the etiology of mental illness, the nature of psychosexual stages, and the predominance of unconscious processes. Exploring intrapsychic processes, analyzing the interaction between client and helping person, interpreting and overcoming resistance, and developing insight are the key (Table 3.3).

Table 3.3. Some Differences between the Psychoanalytic: Two-Person Situation and the Group Therapeutic Situation

Psychoanalysis	Group therapy
1. Two persons.	Three or more persons.
2. Couch technique.	Face-to-face contact.
3. Temporary subordination of reality	Reality continuously asserted by group though reality takes fluid form.
Analyst reasserts reality according to patient's need.	Patient's impact with reality is immediate.
Analyst is observer; suppresses his own personality.	Group therapist is more real person, participant as well as observer.
Relationship is not social, except in later stages.	Group provides genuine social experience.
Social standards not imposed.	

Continued

Table 3.3. (Continued)

Psychoanalysis	Group therapy
4. Exclusive dependence on therapist.	Group standards emerge, but remain flexible.
Emergence of irrational attitudes and expectations.	Dependent need is divided, not exclusively pointed to therapist.
Magic omnipotent fantasy prominent. Irrational motivation may rise to dominant position.	Irrational attitudes and expectations appear, but checked by group pressures.
5. Direct gratification of emotional need not given.	Magic omnipotent fantasy is controlled.
6. Communication largely verbal; communication less real.	Irrational motivation not permitted dominant position.
Patient communicates deeply with self; also with therapist.	Group offers some direct gratification of emotional need.
Patient feels alone.	Communication less verbal; greater expression in social action and reaction.
7. "Acting out" suppressed; little motor discharge of tension.	
8. Access to unconscious conflict more systematic; greater continuity in "working through."	Higher degree of social communication.
	Patient belongs to group, shares emotional experience, feels less alone.
Emphasis on inner conflict with self; conflict with self mirrors conflict with environment.	Higher degree of "acting out," and motor discharge of tension.
	Access to unconscious conflict less systematic; lesser degree of continuity in "working through."
	Conflict is projected, externalized. Conflict with environment mirrors inner conflict.

With permission from Ackerman, N. (1963). "Psychoanalysis and Group Psychotherapy." In M. Rosenbaum and M. M. Berger (Eds.), *Group Therapy and Group Functions* (p. 299). New York: Basic Books.

DIRECT PRACTICE IN SOCIAL WORK: INTERVENING IN THE PERSON-SITUATION TO ENHANCE PSYCHOSOCIAL FUNCTIONING

Psychoanalysis, designed to deal with the causes and treatment of abnormal behavior, is a therapeutic procedure aimed at investigating the source and the relief of emotional symptoms. In general, psychoanalytic treatments attempt to restructure the client's feelings about the past to de-

velop insight about and correct current difficulties. The goal of psychoanalytic styles of treatment also is to restructure the individual's internal psychological organization so that it is more flexible and mature. To reach this
goal, psychoanalytically oriented treatments aim to bring more mental
processes under conscious control.

Psychoanalytically oriented treatment, however, cannot be easily divided into assessment and intervention phases. Throughout the helping
process the therapist must make several assumptions (Table 3.4). Freud
said of psychoanalysis that it "does not take symptoms of an illness as its
point of attack, but sets about removing its *cause*" (Freud, [1920] 1966,
p. 436). The ultimate goal of intervention then is to provide accurate interpretation that will result in insight (Freud, [1920] 1966).

Dream analysis (or the explanation of forbidden wishes) and *free association* (a technique requiring that the
client take responsibility to produce
the content of treatment by saying
whatever comes to mind) were used to
uncover unconscious material. Once
this material was uncovered, it could be dealt with at the conscious level
in the present.

> Freud established the foundation for
> many forms of therapy in which
> practitioners are experts who
> interpret client problems.

The *interpretation* (relating the themes that explain the patterns and origins of behavior) of symbolic meanings is an important aspect of psycho-
analytic-influenced treatments. In this context the *manifest content* —or the
explicit aspects of symptoms or dreams—is conscious and can be related
by the client in treatment. The *latent content*—or hidden, unconscious wishes that cannot be expressed—is interpreted by the therapist.

As a client attempts to recover or relive the past, conflicts emerge. Because this is a painful process, *resistance* (a refusal to allow insight to lead
to the surfacing of unconscious motivations) is to be expected. *Working*

Table 3.4.   Assumptions about Psychoanalytically Oriented Practice

Examining and explaining the symbolic nature of symptoms is the path to recon-
 struction of past events, particularly childhood traumas.
Uncovering pertinent repressed materials and bringing it to consciousness is a
 necessary ingredient in the helping process.
Expressing emotional conflicts helps to free the individual from traumatic memories.
Reconstructing and understanding difficult early life events will be curative.
Using the relationship of the helping person and client as a microcosm of crucial
 experiences is an important part of the helping relationship.
Developing self-awareness and self control are the goals of social work intervention.

through, or the gradual acceptance by the client of unconscious fantasies and expectations, is a lengthy and difficult undertaking. In the process, however, Freud believed a catharsis—a sense of relief—occurred.

Freud extended his interest in self-awareness to the client-therapist relationship. He conceived of the two major concepts to help analyze the therapeutic processes: transference and countertransference. *Transference* is the client's special interest or feelings about the therapist that allow the client to reexperience earlier relationships within the clinical experience. Freud described this process as the client transferring intense feelings of affection (or hostility) toward the therapist, "which are justified neither by the doctor's behavior nor by the situation that has developed during treatment" (ibid., pp. 440–441). Freud believed that as these feelings are reexperienced with the helping person, they can be brought to a more positive resolution.

Time-Limited Psychotherapy

Contemporary psychoanalytic styles of treatments, which contain many of the elements described, have often involved shortening the amount of time needed for each client. As early as 1964, the concern over long waiting lists for treatment led the director of psychiatry at Boston University School of Medicine to develop a short-term treatment protocol (Mann, 1973). Mann (1973) contended that because short forms of psychotherapy awaken the client's "horror of time," time should be central to the helping process (p. 9). The *horror of time* concept suggests that clients experience the force of time in therapy as they did the force of leaving childhood and moving to adulthood. Childhood time is filled with fantasy and pleasure, and is experienced as infinite. Childhood time also is connected to a person's closeness with his or her mother. On the other hand, adult time is linked to reality and the understanding of mortality.

In commonsense terms, Mann believed that practitioners should not foster dependence in the helping process. His structured protocol outlined a twelve-session approach that is clearly presented to and agreed to by the client. There is an intake or consultative interview in which the client and practitioner discuss the central conflict that motivates the client to seek help. Historical data is also collected to formulate the treatment plan. While some interest is taken in the childhood source of the problem, the focus of treatment is the central adaptive issue relevant to the client's immediate use. The urgency of time place the practitioner and client in a therapeutic alliance necessary to solve the issue in the given time. The practitioner's skill in selecting the central issue and in interviewing the client will determine the success of treatment.

REFERENCES

Ackerman, N. ([1972] 1984). Family psychotherapy theory and practice. In G. D. Erikson & T. P. Hogan (Eds.), *Family Therapy: An introduction to Theory and Technique* (pp. 165–172). Monterey, CA: Brooks/Cole.

Ackerman, N. (1981). Family psychotherapy—Theory and practice. In G. D. Erikson & T. P. Hogan (Eds.), *Family Therapy: An Introduction to Theory and Technique* (pp. 290–300). Monterey, CA: Brooks/Cole.

Baker, E. (1985). Psychoanalysis and a psychoanalytic psychotherapy. In S. J. Lyn & J. P. Garske (Eds.), *Contemporary Psychotherapies* (pp. 19–68). Columbus: Charles E. Merrill.

Benedict, R. (1934). *Patterns of Culture*. New York: Mentor.

Bion, W. R. (1959). *Experiences in Groups*. New York: Basic Books.

Bion, W. R. (1962). *Learning from Experience*. London: Heinemann.

Bowen, M. (1978). *Family Therapy in Clinical Practice*. New York: Jason Aronso.

Bowlby, J. (1969). *Attachment and Loss* (Vol. 1). New York: Basic Books.

Bowlby, J. (1973). *Attachment and Loss* (Vol. 2). New York: Basic Books.

Bowlby, J. (1980). *Attachment and Loss* (Vols. 1–3). New York: Basic Books.

Brazelton, T. B. (1969). *Infants and Mothers: Differences in Development*. New York: Delacorte.

Brislin, R. (1981). *Cross Cultural Encounters*. New York: Pergamon.

Broderick, C. B. (1981). The history of professional marriage and family therapy. In A. S. Gurman & D. P. Kniskern (Eds.), *Handbook of Family Therapy* (pp. 5–35). New York: Brunner/Mazel.

Caroff, P. (Ed.) (1982). *Treatment Formulations and Clinical Social Work*. Silver Spring, MD: National Association of Social Workers.

Cohen, J. (1980). Nature of clinical social work. In P. Ewalt (Ed.), *NASW Conference Proceedings: Toward a Definition of Clinical Social Work* (pp. 23–32). Washington, DC: NASW Press.

Compton, B., & Galaway, B. (1994). *Social Work Processes*. Pacific Grove, CA: Brooks/Cole.

Corey, G. (1986). *Theory and Practice of Counseling and Psychotherapy*. Monterey, CA: Brooks/Cole.

Fairbairn, W. R. D. (1954). *An Object Relations Theory of the Personality*. New York: Basic Books.

Firestone, S. (1971). *The Dialectic of Sex: The Case for Feminist Revolution*. New York: Bantam.

Freud, S. ([1905] 1953). Three essays on the theory of sexuality. In J. Strachey (Ed.), *Complete Psychological Works* (standard ed., Vol. 7). London: Hogarth.

Freud, S. ([1910] 1957). The future prospects of psychoanalytic therapy. In J. Strachey (Ed.), *Complete Psychological Works* (standard ed., Vol. 11). London: Hogarth.

Freud, S. (1915). *General Introduction to Psychoanalysis*. New York: Liveright.

Freud, S. ([1920] 1966). *Introductory Lectures on Psychoanalysis*. New York: Norton.

Freud, S. (1910). *Leonardo Da Vinci: A Study in Psychosexuality*. New York: Random House.

Freud, S. ([1925] 1956). Some psychological consequences on the anatomical distinction between the sexes. In. J. Strachey (Ed.), *Collected Papers* (Vol. 5, pp. 186–197). London: Hogarth.

Freud, S. ([1931] 1956). Female sexuality. In J. Strachey (Ed.), *Collected Papers* (Vol. 5, pp. 252–272). London: Hogarth.

Freud, S. (1933). The Psychology of Women. Lecture III. In *New Introductory Lectures on Psychoanalysis* (pp. 1534–1595). New York: Norton.

Freud, S. ([1933] 1964). Why War? In J. Strachey (Ed.), *Complete Psychological Works* (standard ed., Vol. 22). London: Hogarth.

Freud, A. (1936). *The Ego and Its Mechanisms of Defense.* New York: International Universities Press.

Freud, S. (1960a). *The Ego and the Id.* New York: Norton.

Freud, S. (1960b). *Group Psychology and the Analysis of the Ego.* New York: Bantam.

Fromm, E. (1959). *Sigmund Freud's Mission.* New York: Harper and Brothers.

Germain, C. B. (1970). Casework and science: A historical encounter. In R. W. Roberts & R. H. Nell (Eds.), *Theories of Social Casework* (pp. 3–32). Chicago: University of Chicago Press.

Gay, P. (1988). *Freud: A Life for Our Time.* New York: Norton.

Gilligan, C. (1982). *In a Different Voice.* Cambridge, MA: Harvard University Press.

Goldstein, E. G. (1984). *Ego Psychology and Social Work Practice.* New York: Free Press.

Goldstein, E. G. (1986). Ego psychology. In F. J. Turner (Ed.), *Social Work Treatment* (pp. 375–406). New York: Free Press.

Goleman, D. (1990). As a therapist, Freud fell short, scholars' find. New York Times, March 6,1,12.

Gould, K. H. (1984). Original works of Freud on women: Social work references. *Social Casework, 65,* 94–101.

Hall, C. S., & Lindzey, G. (1957). *Theories of Personality.* New York: Wiley.

Hamilton, G. (1940). *Theory and Practice of Social Casework.* New York: Columbia University Press.

Hamilton, G. (1958). A theory of personality: Freud's contribution to social work. In H. J. Parad (Ed.), *Ego Psychology and Casework Theory* (pp. 11–37). New York: Family Service of America.

Hamilton, N. G. (1988). *Self and Others: Object Relations Theory in Practice.* New York: Jason Aronson.

Hamilton, N. G. (1989). A critical review of object relations theory. *American Journal of Psychiatry, 146,* 12.

Hartmann, H. (1939). *Ego Psychology and the Problem of Adaptation.* New York: International Universities Press.

Hogan, R. (1976). *Personality Theory: The Personological Tradition.* Englewood Cliffs, NJ: Prentice-Hall.

Hollis, F. (1964). Social casework: The psychosocial approach. In J. B. Turner (Ed.), *Encyclopedia of Social Work* (Vol. 2, 17th ed., pp. 1300–1308). Washington, DC: NASW Press.

Hollis, F. (1970). The psychosocial approach to the practice of casework. In R. W. Roberts & R. H. Nee (Eds.), *Theories of Social Casework* (pp. 33–76). Chicago: University of Chicago Press.

Horney, K. (1939). *New Ways in Psychoanalysis.* New York: Norton.

Isay, R. (1989). *Being Homosexual: Gay Men and Their Development.* New York: Farrar Straus Giroux.

Jones, E. (1955). *The Life and Work of Sigmund Freud.* New York: Basic Books.

Kadushin, A. (1972). *A Social Work Interview.* New York: Columbia University Press.

Karen, R. (1990). Becoming attached. *Atlantic Monthly, February,* 35–70.

Kernberg, O. F. (1976). *Object Relations Theory and Clinical Psycho-Analysis.* New York: Jason Aronson.

Kerr, M. (1981). Family systems theory and therapy. In A. S. Gurman & D. P. Kniskern (Eds.), *Handbook of Family Therapy* (pp. 226–264). New York: Brunner/Mazel.

Kohut, H. (1971). *The Analysis of the Self.* New York: International Universities Press.

Lieberman, F. (1982). Differences and similarities in clinical practice. In P. Caroff (Ed.), *Treatment Formulations and Clinical Social Work* (pp. 27–36). Silver Spring, MD: National Association of Social Workers.

Lowenstein, S. F. (1985). Freud's metapsychology revisited. *Social Casework, 6*(3), 139–151.

Mahler, M. S. (1968). *On Human Symbiosis or the Vicissitudes of Individuation.* New York: International Universities Press.

Mahler, M. S., Pine, F., & Bergman, A. (1975). *The Psychological Birth of the Human Infant.* New York: Basic Books.

Malinowski, B. (1922). *Argonauts of the Western Pacific.* London: Routledge and Keegan Paul.

Mann, T. (1973). *Time limited psychotherapy.* Cambridge, MA: Harvard University Press.

Miller, J. B. (1973). *Psychoanalysis and Women.* New York: Brunner/Mazel.

Nye, R. D. (1975). *Three Views of Man: Perspectives from Freud, Skinner and Rogers.* Monterey, CA: Brooks/Cole.

Perlman, H. H. (1957a). Freud's contribution to social work. *Social Service Review, 31,* 192–202.

Perlman, H. H. (1957b). *Social Casework: A Problem-Solving Process.* Chicago: University of Chicago Press.

Rice, A. K. (1965). *Learning for Leadership.* London: Tavistock.

Rice, J. K., & Rice, D. G. (1973). Implications of the women's liberation movement for psychotherapy. *American Journal of Psychiatry, 130*(2), 191–195.

Richmond, M. (1917). *Social Diagnosis.* New York: Russell Sage Foundation.

Scharff, D. E. (1982). *The Sexual Relationship: An Object Relations View of Sex and the Family.* New York: Routledge.

Shulman, L. (1984). *The Skills of Helping: Individuals and Groups.* Itasca, IL: Peacock.

Spitz, R. A. (1965). *The First Year of Life.* New York: International Universities Press.

Wesley, C. (1975). The Women's movement and psychotherapy. *Social Work, 20*(2), 120–124.

Wetzel, J. W. (1976). Interaction of feminism and social work in America. *Social Casework, 57,* 235.

Wolf, A., Schwartz, E. K., McCarty, G. J., & Goldberg, I. A. (1972). Psychoanalysis in groups: Contrasts with other group therapies. In C. J. Sager (Ed.), *Progress in Group and Family Therapy* (pp. 47–53). New York: Brunner/Mazel.

Wood, K. M. (1971). The contribution to psychoanalysis and ego psychology. In H.

S. Strean (Ed.), *Social Casework Theory in Action* (pp. 45–117). Metuchen: NJ: Scarecrow.

Woodroofe, K. (1971). *From Charity to Social Work in England and the United States.* Toronto: University Toronto Press.

GLOSSARY

Anal retentive.   A personality style characterized by extreme orderliness and / or compulsive behavior.

Anal stage.   Freud's psychosexual stage during which the focus of tension and gratification shifts to the anal area and toilet training activities are central.

Anxiety.   A state of tension that is always present at some level that motivates one to act.

Catharsis.   Emotional expression and release brought about by talking through problems.

Cathexis.   A great degree of psychic energy, which is limited in total quantity, that is attached or bound to an object.

Conscience.   A subsystem of the superego that deals with what is considered morally bad, thereby producing guilt.

Conscious.   Mental processes of which one is aware.

Countertransference.   The irrational emotional reactions or fantasies that practitioners experience in response to a client.

Death instincts.   Unchecked aggressive impulses.

Determinism.   The belief that behavior is a function of certain preceding variables that bring about action in an orderly or purposeful way.

Dream analysis.   An interpretation of the underlying meaning of dreams.

Dreams.   An expression of the most primitive workings or content of the mind.

Dynamic model.   Freud's ideas about the competition between innate drives and societal demands.

Ego defense mechanisms.   Unconscious mental processes that distort reality to ward off anxiety and safeguard the ego from id impulses and pressures of the superego.

Ego defense structure.   The pattern of use of ego defenses.

Ego functioning.   The ability of the ego to cope adaptively and to master reality effectively.

Ego ideal.   A subsystem of the superego that deals with what is morally good.

Ego.   The executive arm of the personality, whose chief function is to interact with the environment.

Electra complex.   The female counterpart of the Oedipal conflict, in which the little girl expresses interest in the parent of the opposite gender and rivalry with the parent of the same gender. The resolution of this conflictual situation is gender identification.

Erogenous zones.   The body area that is the focus of the discharge of tension and sensual pleasure.

Fixated.   To be arrested at an early stage of development; to overly concentrate on ideas interfering with maturation.

Free association.   A technique in counseling requiring the client to say whatever comes into consciousness no matter how inappropriate it may seem.

Genetic point of view.   An approach that retrospectively reconstructs an individual's psychological history to define the infantile roots of adult behavior and pathology.

Genital stage.   Freud's final psychosexual stage during which psychological identity is integrated.

Id.   The innate subsystem of the personality made up of unconscious representations of sexual and aggressive drives.

Identification.   Taking over the personality features of another person; matching mental representation with physical reality.

Insight.   Conscious recognition of previously repressed memories or fantasies.

Interpretation.   The process of the helping person listening, observing, and clarifying a client's meaning of events.

Introjection.   An ego defense mechanism in which one unconsciously takes another's feelings and or ideas into oneself.

Latent content.   Unconscious or hidden content in feelings and dreams.

Libido.   Sexual energy and drive.

Life instincts.   Drives equated with sexual energy and positive life forces.

Manifest content.   Conscious or explicit content of feelings and dreams.

Medical model.   A perspective with an emphasis on diagnosis, treatment, and cure.

Neurosis.   Mental illnesses defined by Freud as caused by extreme anxiety brought about by overwhelmingly threatening id impulses. To be arrested at certain levels of development short of maturity.

Object choice.   The investment of psychic energy in an action, person, or image that will gratify an instinct.

Object relations theory.   A body of concepts of individual personality development emphasizing attachment and separation in the final individuation of the self.

Object.   An internal representation of a person, place, or symbol.

Oedipal conflict.   The conflict that occurs during Freud's phallic stage when a little boy expresses interest in the parent of the opposite gender and rivalry with the parent of the same gender; the resolution of this conflictual situation is gender identification.

Omnipotence.   A sense of being all powerful derived from the id's inability to test reality.

Oral aggressive.   A personality style characterized by lashing out in an immature fashion.

Oral dependent.   A personality style characterized a strong longing for maternal support.

Oral stage.   Freud's psychosexual stage covering the period from birth to eighteen months, when activity and gratification are centered around the mouth, lips, and tongue.

Phallic stage.   Freud's psychosexual stage occurring at about age three years, when tensions and gratification shift to the genitals; gender identification and superego formation occur as a result of the resolution of the Oedipal conflict.

Pleasure principle.   A means of operation of the id in which tension reduction and gratification are paramount.

Preconscious.   Mental processes that an individual is capable of making conscious.

Primary process.   Unconscious, primitive mental functioning that attempts to fulfill a wish or discharge tension by producing an image of the desired goal.

Projection.   A defense mechanism in which the source of anxiety is attributed to something or somebody in the external world rather than to one's own impulses; attempts to get rid of one's own unacceptable characteristics by assigning them to someone else.

Projective identification.   A defense mechanism in which one places aspects of the self on another.

Psychic determinism.   A philosophy that describes behavior as occurring in an orderly, purposive manner and as an outcome of specified variables.

Psychoanalysis.   A method of psychotherapeutic treatment for emotional disturbance; a method of studying and developing a theoretical explanation for behavior.

Psychosexual stage.   A period of predetermined time in which there is a shift in the focus of sexual and aggressive energy during the course of maturation; as each stage unfolds, emotional patterns are formed that determine the adult personality.

Rationalization.   A defense mechanism in which there is an offering of reasonable sounding explanations for unreasonable, unacceptable feelings or behavior.

Reaction formation.   A defense mechanism in which there is a replacement in consciousness of an anxiety-producing impulse or feeling by its opposite.

Reality principle.   A means of operation of the ego in which there is an attempt to control anxiety by mastering the environment. Postponement of gratification is delayed until it is appropriate through this process.

Reality testing.   A mental test to weigh whether a plan of action is best for warding off anxiety.

Reductionism.   A thought process that reduces an explanation of complex events to elementary phenomenon or events.

Regression.   A defense mechanism in which there is a return to behavior patterns characteristic of earlier levels of functioning, often precipitated by stress.

Repression.   A basic defense mechanism in which ideas are pushed out of awareness.

Resistance.   A defense mechanism used to avoid facing reality. Often used in therapy to avoid the helping person's interpretations.

Secondary process.   An ego-based mental process that involves forming plans of action to determine how best to delay gratification appropriately.

Structural model.   Freud's concepts about the three major subsystems of the personality: the id, ego, and superego.

Sublimation.   An ego defense mechanism in which there is a diverting of sexual drives to lofty purposes.

Superego.   The subsystem of the personality dealing with values and moral issues.

Tension.   That which propels the individual to activity to gratify needs.

Topographic model.   Freud's ideas about the three levels of consciousness: the unconscious, preconscious, and conscious.

Transference.   The irrational feelings the client has for the helping person brought about by the irrational intrusion of early childhood relationships.

Unconscious.   Mental processes outside awareness and not subject to direct observation.

Undoing.   A defense mechanism in which there is a reconstruction of events or previous actions so that they are distorted but less threatening.

Whole object relations.   The capacity to hold positive and negative feelings about the same person, thereby sustaining the relationship.

Wish fulfillment.   Unconscious thought processes of the id in which a mental representation of a wanted object (person or idea) is substituted for the real object.

Withholding.   A personality pattern in which objects are kept for oneself.

Working through.   The process of gaining insight and coming to terms with emotional conflicts.

CRITIQUE

Freudian Theory
New Developments

ALLEN RADER and RUTH RADER

Although Freud's basic theory focused on the individual mind and psychic apparatus, he also tied the development of a significant part of the tripartite model of character organization to outside social influences (Freud, 1960, 1966). Psychoanalytical theory led the way to current relational theories in which the self is viewed as being constructed and reconstructed out of a relational processes. That is, theories such as interpersonal theory, object relations, and self psychology have come to view relationships as the primary source of psychological change. Subsequent theorists have elaborated on the influence of social interaction and have moved theory toward the stance that interactional processes—a person's relational field—are a primary factor in character development. Implicit in this argument is an appreciation for the effect of relationships on the development, maintenance, and expression of the self.

An example of the relational field and its influence on self processes is Mahler's phase of separation and individuation that occurs during infancy. This stage spans the ten-twelve- to the sixteen-eighteen-month period of growth. In the later part of this period, the child experiences free upright locomotion. To reach this point, children experience the differentiation of their bodies from their mother or primary caregiver, establish a specific bond with him or her, and develop an autonomous ego that functions in close proximity to their mother or caregiver (Mahler, Pine, & Bergman, 1975). These developments are strongly influenced by the child's mother, who must be supportive to this individuation process.

Understanding the formation of relational patterns can help social workers who may work with clients whose early experiences were chaotic or oppressive. These clients have had an array of experiences in their relational developmental process that have resulted in unproductive behaviors. For example, some practitioners are puzzled by the seemingly irrational response of a battered woman who returns to a situation in which physical harm is predicted and nearly assured. They are puzzled that children frequently prefer to return to abusive parents rather than to the safer foster care environments. Relational theorists contribute a valuable perspective. They suggest that "the central motivation in human experience is the seeking out and maintaining an intense relationship with another person" (Fairbairn, 1954, p. 27). Although it is puzzling to see that painful feelings, and self-destructive relationships are re-created, these patterns arise because people perpetuate early ties to significant others. This hypothesis may help social workers understand why there is a bond between abused children and their abusers. Even if these experiences are negative, the person is inclined to seek out and repeat similar experiences in service of their need for intense relationships (Mitchell, 1988).

Relational models posited that the mind (self) is developed out of the relational matrix. It is through disturbances in these interpersonal relationships that psychopathology is developed. Because early experiences have an effect on the structure and the relational patterns of the person, it is appropriate to assume that such patterns can be changed within a supportive relational field set up between the social work practitioner and the client.

Relational theories provide social workers with a foundation for clinical work based on the curative elements of relationships in the here and now. Development does not halt at some given time during the life span. On the contrary, over the life span humans remain deeply involved in the complex development of the self, and some relational theorists regard "the establishment and preservation of a sense of self as the primary human motivation" (Mitchell, 1988, p. 30). Therefore, clinical social workers can bolsters the client's sense of self and raises self-esteem through the therapeutic relationship. It is within this therapeutic relational matrix that the client can become a new self, one in which he or she no longer relies totally on past experiences for behavioral direction, but can create them anew in current relationships.

SCIENTIFIC PERSPECTIVES ON PSYCHOANALYSIS

Psychoanalytic theory has led to a greater interest in the socioemotional development of the child, specifically the relationship among early social environments, the actions of primary caregiver, and the evolution of structures of the brain (Schore, 1994). The convergence of knowledge in a number of fields such as developmental psychology, neurology, genetics, and a multitude of related disciplines can suggest some answers. For example, the child psychology movement out of which Jean Piaget, John Bowlby, Margaret Mahler, and David Stern evolved provides alternative methods for understanding children. These theorist started with observations of the child and theorized how the observed experiences influenced the child's personality development. This is in contrast to the traditional psychoanalytic approach of reconstructing the history of an adult's personality development after he or she has developed problems in functioning (Bowlby, 1982).

As scientific inquiry in cognitive science and genetics continues to expand, a new wave of knowledge is influencing psychoanalytic thinking (Borden, 1998). Studies have shown that the organs of the human body, including the infant brain, develop in stages over critical periods. These stages are sequential and governed by genetic and biological influences; yet they are also influenced by the environment. During the critical periods of maturation and growth, the organs involved are extremely susceptible to an arrest in their growth due to environmental influences (Schore, 1994). Current research suggests that the mother does not only use nonverbal cues and affective expression to modulate and regulate the child's internal states. The mother also influences the child's brain chemistry and affects the brain's maturation, setting the future of socioemotional functioning. Based on these study findings, social workers interested in prevention now have additional support for the importance of effective early parenting programs. Parenting education and support teach the parents skills not only so they will be able to help their children develop emotionally and behaviorally, but also to enable them to directly influence the growth and development of the child's brain.

Considering such research about early brain development can assist policymakers in considering (1) what is the potential damage done by removing the child from the home; (2) is there another primary caregiver to give the adequate developmentally appropriate responses during these critical periods; and (3) what are the possible long-term ramifications of doing either. Some children may need to be removed more quickly during periods of early neglect as the result of the developmental damage that can ensue by waiting for the parent to develop the skills necessary to care for the child.

Modern genetics is another scientific discipline that has influenced traditional psychoanalysis. "It is often not appreciated that an individual's genetic inheritance which encodes the unvarying sequence of development is only partially expressed at birth" (Schore, 1994, p. 3). The development—from an infant dependent on his or her mother to modulate the child's emotional functioning to one in which the child is capable of his or her own self-regulation—is a genetically influenced process. The capacity to develop may be constrained by an immature central nervous system.

The child's higher brain centers can only process a small amount of information in any given amount of time compared with an adult's faster processing speed. By regulating the excessive positive and negative emotions, the mother assists in the gradual unfolding of her child's neurological and psychological development. This process shapes internal states and influences the person's capacity to self-organize.

Finally, psychoanalysis has clearly evolved since Freud originally proposed the drive theory. Many psychoanalysts now look to the relational matrix as the key to understanding the way biological or genetic aspects of humanity uniquely manifest themselves. Through relationships, our sense of self evolves. This evolution can more accurately be described as a co-evolution between the quality of our relationships and our biological or genetic makeup in which both interact and influence each other. Psychoanalysis is no longer the bastion of individual development based on instincts, drives, defenses, and intrapsychic conflicts. Many psychoanalyst now see the individual in the person's relational environment.

REFERENCES

Borden, W. (1998). The place and play of theory in practice: A Winnicottian perspective. *Journal of Analytic Social Work, 5*(1), 25–40.

Bowlby, J. (1982). *Attachment* (2nd ed.). New York: Basic Books.

Freud, S. (1960). *The Ego and the Id* (Joan Riviere, transl.). New York: Norton.

Freud, S. (1966). *The Complete Introductory Lectures on Psychoanalysis* (James Strachey, transl.). New York: Norton.

Mahler, M. S., Pine, F., & Bergman, A. (1975). *The Psychological Birth of the Human Infant: Symbiosis and Individuation*. New York: Basic Books.

Mitchell, S. A. (1988). *Relational Concepts in Psychoanalysis: An Integration*. Cambridge, MA: Harvard University Press.

Schore, A. N. (1994). *Affect Regulation and the Origin of the Self: The Neurobiology of Emotional Development*. Hillsdale, NJ: Erlbaum.

4

Eriksonian Theory: A Developmental
Approach to Ego Mastery

ROBERTA R. GREENE

Eric Erikson, although originally part of the mainstream of psychoanalytic thought, made critical departures from orthodox Freudian theory.
These deviations from classical psychoanalytic thinking, which included
understanding the healthy personality across the life cycle and the development of the ego as a social phenomenon, allowed for new, important emphases in many forms of psychotherapeutic practice (Table 4.1). Erikson's
major contribution—the conceptualization of a developmental approach
to ego mastery—is the focus of this chapter. The case study illustrates a
client experiencing difficulty with the psychosocial crisis generativity versus stagnation.

Erikson possessed an optimistic, biopsychosocial view of development.
A positive outlook about people's ability to change, the belief that clients
possess a sense of inner unity, good judgment, and a capacity to do well
predominated in Erikson's philosophy. For example, Erikson believed that
the healthy ego of the child propelled the child toward the next stage of development, with each stage offering new opportunities. He emphasized
that "there is little in inner developments which cannot be harnessed to
constructive and peaceful initiatives if only we learn to understand the
conflicts and anxieties of childhood" (Erikson, 1959, p. 83). The interest of
the social work profession in Erikson's principles has contributed to a more
hopeful, less fatalistic view of personality development.

Erikson was one of the very few great personality theorists (Jung was another) to view development as occurring throughout the life cycle (Hogan,
1976). Erikson proposed that development takes place in eight life stages,
starting with the infant at birth and ending with old age and death. He
viewed each stage of development as a new plateau for the developing self

Table 4.1. Framework for Personality Development: According to Freud and Erikson

Theorist	Personality development is
Freud	Based on a relatively closed energy system
	Impelled by strong sexual and aggressive drives
	Dominated by the id
	Threatened by anxiety and unconscious needs
	Dominated by behaviors that attempt to reduce anxiety and to master the environment
	Conflicted by contradictory urges and societal expectations
	Intended to place impulses under control
	Formed in early childhood stages, culminating in early adulthood
Erikson	Based on a relatively open energy system
	Shaped by weak sexual and social drives
	Governed by the ego
	Based on social interaction
	Bolstered by historical and ethnic group affiliation
	Formed through ego mastery and societal support
	Based on the historical and ethnic intertwining of generations
	Intended to prepare a healthy member of society who can make positive contributions to that society
	Shaped over the life cycle
	Intended to convey principles of social order to the next generation

or ego to gain and restore a sense of mastery. A life cycle perspective on development drew new attention to middle and old age, and refocused research and treatment issues. For example, many researchers have seen their findings as refining Erikson's propositions about midlife generativity (Goleman, 1990; Levinson, 1978), and Butler (1963), a geriatric psychiatrist, turned to Erikson's unified theory of the life cycle as the basis for his conception of life review, a clinical technique used in therapy with older adults.

In contrast to Freud, who believed that individuals are impelled by unconscious and antisocial sexual and aggressive urges that are basically biological in their origin, Erikson (1975) proposed that individuals are influenced positively by social forces about which they are highly aware. Although Erikson agreed that the individual must face unconscious conflicts, he emphasized that the study of personality development should focus on the interaction of the individual in his or her environment.

Unlike Freud and other classical psychoanalysts who emphasized id (the innate source of tension in the personality) impulses in their study of personality, Erikson primarily was concerned with a theoretical framework that addressed the capacity of the *ego* (the executive arm of the personality) to act on the environment. A focus on the interaction between the striving ego and mastery of the environment was the key to Erikson's formulation of personality development.

To account for social forces, Erikson moved to a more open energy system, and hypothesized that there existed a "mutual complementation of ethos and ego, of group identity and ego identity" (Erikson, 1959, p. 23). Erikson's restatement of the nature of identity, linking the individual's inner world with his or her unique values and history, placed him among the vanguard of *ego psychologists* (Hogan, 1976).

Erikson turned to social anthropology, ecology, and comparative education for social concepts that would complement his concept of ego identity. In keeping with his emphasis on the social world, Erikson reformulated the concept of *ego identity* to encompass the mutual relationship between the individual and his or her society. An understanding of the natural, historical, and technological environment was among the factors Erikson thought to be part of ego identity and necessary for a true appraisal of the individual. Central to Erikson's (1964a) philosophy was the idea that a "nourishing exchange of community life" is key to mental health (p. 89). "All this makes man's so-called biological adaptation a matter of life cycles developing within their communities' changing history" (Erikson, 1959, p. 163).

Erikson proposed that membership identities, comprising social class, culture, and national affiliation, provided people with the collective power to create their own environment. Society, through its ideological frameworks, roles, tasks, rituals, and initiations, "bestow[ed] strength" and a sense of identification on the developing individual (Erikson, 1964b, p. 91). Social influences, including economic, historical, and ethnic factors, were stressed, as was the view that people are socialized positively to become part of the historical and ethnic "intertwining of generations" (Erikson, 1964a, p. 93).

Erikson's approach to personality development is highly compatible with social work's philosophy and values, and lends itself to the profession's interest in how social institutions foster development. During the 1940s, as social work moved away from a linear "medical" model, Erikson's emphasis on the individual's social order offered a supporting

> Erikson, a psychoanalytic thinker, brought an optimistic and social view to his theory.

knowledge base for a psychosocial approach to social work practice (Hamilton, 1940; Newman & Newman, [1979] 1987).

PERSON-IN-ENVIRONMENT HISTORICAL CONTEXT: ERIKSON'S DEVELOPMENTAL THEORY

Erikson often is credited with bringing more attention to social factors in contemporary psychoanalytic thought and thereby a more balance person-in-environment perspective. Erikson credited Freud with taking monumental steps in applying contemporary concepts from physics to describe personality as an energy system. However, Erikson believed that Freud did not go far enough in conceptualizing the importance of environmental influences on the individual (Compton & Galaway, 1994; Corey, 1986; Erikson, 1968a). Erikson argued, for example, that although Freud was able to demonstrate that sexuality begins with birth, he only laid the groundwork for demonstrating that "social life also begins at the very start of life" (Erikson, 1959, p. 20).

Erikson (1968a, p. 44) urged that the relationship between "inner agency and social life" be better understood. His interest in the psychosocial is illustrated in the following statement in which he reaffirms the need for more attention to the functioning of the ego in the social environment:

> The word psychosocial so far has had to serve as an emergency bridge between the so-called "biological" formulations of psychoanalysis and newer ones which take the cultural environment into more systematic consideration. . . . In psychoanalytic writings the terms "outer world" or "environment" are often used to designate an uncharted area which is said to be outside merely because it fails to be inside. (Erikson, 1959, pp. 161–162)

Erikson (1959) continued by saying that such a vague description of environment, which "threatens to isolate psychoanalytic thought from the rich ethological and ecological findings of modern biology," does not provide an understanding of the major way in which "man's ecology" shapes the individual ego (p. 162).

Erikson's changes in orthodox psychoanalytic perspective—from an emphasis on the "inner world" to a focus on the "outer life"—provided social work practitioners with an expanded knowledge base to assess and intervene in the person-situation, and reflected the historical evolution of social work thought (Germain & Hartman, 1980). For the social work profession that has long struggled with how to account for the relationship between the person and his or her environment, Erikson's call for a reconceptualization of personality development lent itself and has contributed to a new balance between person-environment factors.

BASIC ASSUMPTIONS AND TERMINOLOGY
OF ERIKSON'S DEVELOPMENTAL THEORY

Erikson (1975) viewed development as a biopsychosocial process (Table 4.2). He stated that clinical evidence suggested the biopsychosocial nature of identity, and the following three "orders in which man lives at all times":

1. The *somatic order,* by which an organism seeks to maintain its integrity in a continuous reciprocal adaptation of the *milieu interieur* and other organisms.
2. The *personal order,* that is, the integration of "inner" and "outer" world in individual experience and behavior.
3. The *social order,* jointly maintained by personal organisms sharing a geographic-historical setting. (Erikson, 1975, p. 46)

Erikson adopted Freud's postulates that behavior has basic biological origins and is motivated by the search for sexual and/or aggressive release. However, Erikson proposed that personality development also begins with three social drives: (1) a need for social attention, (2) a need for *competence* (the need to master one's environment), and (3) a need for structure and order in one's social affairs. The idea that thought was social in origin, and not removed from social and cultural conditions, has made an important contribution to the study of the nature of mental health (Hogan, 1976).

Erikson modified Freud's idea of the unconscious, expanding on Freud's belief that the unconscious was biological in origin and consisted of mental

Table 4.2. Eriksonian Theory: Basic Assumptions

Development is biopsychosocial and occurs across the life cycle.

Development is propelled by a biological plan; however, personal identity cannot exist independent of social organization.

The ego plays a major role in development as it strives for competence and mastery of the environment. Societal institutions and caretakers provide positive support for the development of personal effectiveness. Individual development enriches society.

Development is marked by eight major stages at which time a psychosocial crisis occurs. Personality is the outcome of the resolution—on a continuum from positive to negative—of each of these crises. Each life stage builds on the success of former, presents new social demands, and creates new opportunities.

Psychosocial crises accompanying life stages are universal or occur in all cultures. Each culture offers unique solutions to life stages.

The needs and capacities of the generations are intertwined.

Psychological health is a function of ego strength and social supports.

Confusions in self-identity arise from negative resolution of developmental crises and alienation from societal institutions.

Therapy involves the interpretation of developmental and historical distortions and the curative process of insight.

elements repressed as a defense against anxiety. Erikson proposed two additional concepts: that expectations from each developmental stage in the life cycle were repressed and remained in the unconscious, and that a *sociological unconscious,* comprising cultural factors outside conscious awareness, existed. Erikson urged both theorist and helping professionals to understand how factors related to a person's culture and social class could influence behavior. He also challenged his mental health colleagues to analyze sociological sources of repressed anxiety and distortions with the same vigor with which they addressed sexual and aggressive content.

Development across the life cycle is the focus of Eriksonian *psychosocial theory,* a theoretical approach that involves social and environmental factors, which produced changes in thought and behavior. The tendency of an individual's life to form a coherent, lifetime experience and to be joined or linked to previous and future generations, known as a *life cycle approach,* was his primary focus. His interest centered on the way in which the individual changed to a more refined or specialized biological, psychological, and / or social state *(differentiation).*

Erikson's perspective on development was derived from the biological principle of *epigenesis,* or the idea that each stage depends on resolutions of the experiences of prior stages. Epigenesis suggests that "anything that grows has a ground plan, and out of that plan *parts* arise, each part having its *time* of special ascendancy—until all parts have arisen to form a *functioning whole*" (Erikson, 1959, p. 53). Erikson (1982) defined epigenesis as

> a progression through time of a differentiation of parts. This indicates that each part exists in some form before "its" decisive and critical time normally arrives and remains systematically related to all others so that the whole ensemble depends on the proper development in the proper sequence of each item. Finally, as each part comes to its full ascendance and finds some lasting solution during its stage, it will also be expected to develop further under the dominance of subsequent ascendancies, and most of all, to take its place in the integration of the whole ensemble. (p. 29)

That is, personality development follows a proper sequence, emerges at critical or decisive times, progresses through time, and is a lifelong integrative process.

Erikson's thinking about epigenesis is reflected in his discussion of the *superego* (the moral arm of the personality) and moral development. Erikson proposed that although the superego is a biological given, further moral development occurs later in life during three critical periods or stages of development: (1) the stage of initiative, when one acquires moral tendencies, (2) the stage of identity, when one perceives universal good, and (3) the stage of intimacy, when a truly ethical sense firmly emerges (Hogan, 1976).

Personality from an Eriksonian epigenetic perspective develops through a predetermined readiness "to interact with a widening social radius, beginning with the dim image of a mother and ending with mankind" (Erikson, 1959, p. 54). The healthy personality, according to Erikson begins in infancy when the healthy child, "given a reasonable amount of guidance, can be trusted to obey inner laws of development, laws which create a succession of potentialities for *significant interaction* with those who tend him" (ibid., p. 54).

Not all contemporary theories and research findings on human development concur with Erikson's epigenetic view that there are predetermined, sequential stages to emotional and social development (Germain, 1987). For example, Riley (1985) has suggested that to establish universal stages of emotional and social development many different cohorts at different times and in different places would have to be studied. Therefore, there may not be critical periods of development during which fixed stages and tasks must be negotiated. And Bronfenbrenner (1979) proposed a nonstage theory in which the individual experiences various levels of the environment and shifts in ecological settings (Chapter 8). Nonetheless, because of Erikson's ability to shed light on normal developmental processes, his theory of human development based on the epigenetic principle is now in wide use in social work education and practice (Brennan & Weick, 1981; Lowenstein, 1978).

The role of caretakers and institutions in shaping the outcome of psychosocial crises, and thereby personality development, was another principle emphasized by Erikson (1982). He used the concept of a "radius of significant relationships" to explain the developing individual's expanding number of relationships through life. These relationships begin with the maternal person, parental figures, basic family, neighbors and schoolmates, peer group, and partners in friendship and love, and expand to one's own household, and finally one's fellow human beings. Through a series of psychosocial crises and an ever-widening circle of significant relations, the individual develops "an expanded radius of potential social interaction" (Erikson, 1959, p. 21). Although social interactive patterns may vary from culture to culture, development, nonetheless, is said to be governed by proper, predetermined rates and sequences. The idea that the infant starts life with a proclivity toward social interaction, and that thought is social, and not instinctual, was an important contribution Erikson made to understanding the development of the ego, and played a central role in his motivational theory.

> Erikson's theory, while biopsychosocial, emphasizes social interactions.

The process by which an individual develops his or her *ego identity*, or the learning of effectiveness as a group-psychological phenomenon, was the major focus of Erikson's work (1959, p. 22). *Identity formation* is a developmental task involving the formation of a personal philosophy of life and an integrated system of values. It centers around a personal struggle to define who one is and where one is going, and reaches its height in adolescence (Corey, 1986).

Erikson, whose discussion of identity formation has made a major contribution to understanding adolescence, believed that the process of identity formation was a lifelong process. The process of psychosocial identity also encompassed what Erikson (1964a) termed a "psycho-historical side" (p. 20), meaning that "life histories are inextricably interwoven with history" or "the ideologies of the historical moment" (ibid.). Erikson's delineation of the way in which the ego continues to strive for self-mastery and self-expression within the framework of the individual's social group can be a useful perspective that complements social work's person-in-environment stance.

Erikson argued that identity not only emerges in stages, but also involves restructuring or resynthesis. The view that personality development involves new configurations at different life stages is called "hierarchical reorganization." *Hierarchical reorganization* is the concept that development over time is not only linear, but has changing structures and organization over time that permit new functions and adaptations (Shapiro & Hertzig, 1988):

> From a *genetic point of view,* [a point of view that examines the source of behavior], the process of identity formation emerges as an *evolving configuration*—a configuration which is gradually established by successive ego syntheses and resyntheses throughout childhood; it is a configuration gradually integrating constitutional givens, idiosyncratic libidinal needs, favored capacities, significant identifications, effective defenses, successful sublimations, and consistent roles. (Erikson, 1959, p. 125)

Through a series of psychosocial crises and an ever-widening circle of significant relations, Erikson (1959) believed the individual developed "a new drive-and-need constellation" and "an expanded radius of potential social interaction" (p. 21).

EXPLAINING DEVELOPMENT ACROSS THE LIFE CYCLE

Erikson's (1959) most important and best known contribution to personality theory is his eight stages of ego development. In this life cycle approach, Erikson proposed that development is determined by shifts in instinctual energy, occurs in stages, and centers around a series of eight psychosocial crises. As each stage emerges, a psychosocial crisis fosters development within the person and in his or her expanding interconnections between self and environment. Crises offer the opportunity for new experiences, and demand a "radical change in perspective," or a new orientation

> Erikson's theory offers a normative approach to development across the life cycle.

toward self and the world (Erikson, 1963, p. 212). The result is an "ever-new configuration that is the growing personality" (p. 57).

Erikson emphasized that one stage of development builds on the successes of previous stages. Difficulties in resolving earlier psychosocial issues may predict difficulties for later stages. Each stage of development is distinguished by particular characteristics that differentiates it from preceding and succeeding stages (Newman & Newman, 1987). The notion that development occurs in unique stages, each building on another and having its own emphasis or underlying structural organization, is called *stage theory* (Figure 4.1).

Erikson argued that personality is a function of the outcome of each life stage. The psychological outcome of a crisis is a blend of ego qualities resting between two contradictory extremes or polarities. For example, although an individual may be characterized as trusting, the outcome of the first psychosocial crisis is truly a mixture of trusting and mistrustful personality features. The idea that the outcome of a psychosocial crisis is a

	1	2	3	4	5	6	7	8
Old Age								Integrity vs Despair. WISDOM
Adulthood							Generativity vs Stagnation. CARE	
Young Adulthood						Intimacy vs Isolation. LOVE		
Adolescence					Identity vs. Identity Confusion. FIDELITY			
School Age				Industry vs. Inferiority. COMPETENCE				
Play Age			Initiative vs Guilt. PURPOSE					
Early Childhood		Autonomy vs Shame, Doubt. WILL						
Infancy	Basic Trust vs Basic Mistrust. HOPE							

Figure 4.1.   Erik Erikson's psychological crises. From Erikson (1982).

blend of ego qualities should be clearly understood. Erikson did not mean that an individual exhibits psychological properties of only one polarity. Rather, the qualities associated with one pole will predominate or be more apparent. Another important distinction made by Erikson was that a crisis may be considered a *normative event*, that is, a crisis in this connotation is an expected, universal time when the individual must reestablish his or her ego functioning or equilibrium (Table 4.3).

The developmental sequences that Erikson described parallel in some ways the classic Freudian stages of psychosexual development. However, Erikson's discussion presented major differences. One such difference was Freud's view that personality development culminates in adulthood. In contrast, Erikson argued that personality continues to develop throughout life. The role that institutions play in personality development was another point of disagreement. Freud suggested that social institutions are designed to play an inhibiting socialization role to contain the aggressiveness and sexuality of human nature. Erikson suggested the contrary, and stated that when societal institutions fail to support and nurture personal effectiveness, the individual's development is adversely affected.

Another of Erikson's breaks with Freudian theory concerned the relationship between psychosexual and psychosocial development. Erikson contended that *psychosocial development* (development that focuses on social interaction) occurs together with *psychosexual development* (development that revolves around sexual and aggressive needs). He proposed that social forces play a critical role in personality development, and suggested that development occurs within an expanding social sphere, or a widening radius of social interaction.

Erikson also believed that there is always opportunity for healthy personality growth. He challenged traditional psychoanalytic thinking when he argued that successes of each stage and the support of social institutions can contribute to the development of a healthy personality throughout life. Erikson offered a process orientation to identity formation, in which he stressed renewed opportunity to integrate personality function at each stage. For example, he argued that although "the tension between trust and mistrust reaches back to the very beginnings of life," the individual continues to grapple with reconciling "opposing tendencies toward trust and assurance, on the one hand, and toward wariness and uncertainty, on the other" (Erikson, Erikson, & Kivnick, 1986, pp. 218–219). That is, although the development of trust is the major focus of the first stage of life, there will be opportunities to revisit and resolve this psychosocial issue. Erikson believed that teachers, clergy, friends, and therapists could play a critical role in providing new experiences in which a sense of trust could be developed further.

Erikson believed that an exploration of expressed feelings and behav-

Table 4.3. Erikson's Psychosocial Crises

Stage	Age	Psychosocial crises	Radius of significant relations	Basic strengths	Core pathologies	Psychosocial modalities	Psychosexual stage
I	Infancy's birth to 2 years	Trust vs. mistrust	Maternal person	Hope	Withdrawal	To get / To give in return	Oral
II	Early childhood: 2–4 years	Autonomy vs. shame	Parental persons	Will	Compulsion	To hold on / To let go	Anal
III	Play age: 4–6 years	Initiative vs. guilt	Basic family	Purpose	Inhibition	To make (going after) / To make life (play)	Infantile genital
IV	School age: 6–12 years	Industry vs. inferiority	Neighborhood, school	Competence	Inertia	To make things / To make things together	Latency
V	Adolescence: 12–22 years	Identity vs. identity confusion	Peer group	Fidelity	Repudiation	To be oneself (or not to be) / To share being oneself	Puberty
VI	Young adult: 22–34 years	Intimacy vs. isolation	Partners in friend-ship, sex, competition, cooperation	Love	Exclusivity	To lose and find oneself in another	Genitality
VII	Adulthood 34–60	Generativity vs. stagnation	Divided labor and shared household	Care	Rejectivity	To make be / To take care of	
VIII	Old age: 60–death	Integrity vs. despair	"Mankind"; "my kind"	Wisdom	Disdain	To be, through having been / To face not being	

Source: Summarized from Erikson (1982, pp. 32–33; 1959, pp. 178–179), Erikson and Kivnick (1986, p. 45).

ioral patterns would glean clues that allowed for the reconstruction of an individual's developmental history. The therapist's reconstruction of the client's developmental successes or failures lent itself to an assessment of the roots of adult behavior and disorders. An assessment of how successfully a client moved from stage to stage was a necessary precondition for selecting treatment interventions.

Erikson's principles regarding the need for a developmental history are highly compatible with many social workers' approaches to clinical practice. For example, the first aspect of history taking when using an Eriksonian framework is to assess the relative success with which a client has resolved each of the psychosocial crises. Trust versus mistrust, the first crisis, occurs from birth to age two years and corresponds with Freud's oral stage. Erikson retained Freud's point of view that psychosexual activity during this stage centers around the mouth and that "to get" and "to give in return" are important psychosocial modalities or behavioral interactions. (Erikson assumed that psychosocial growth occurs together with psychosexual development.)

Freud's oral stage is recast by emphasizing the infant's strong innate readiness for social interaction with the mothering caretaker. Through positive interaction with a caretaking figure, Erikson (1959) believed that "enduring patterns for the balance of basic trust over basic mistrust" were established (pp. 64–65). He viewed the establishment of trust as the "cornerstone of the healthy personality" and the primary task during the stage of trust versus mistrust.

The resolution of each psychosocial crisis, according to Erikson (1959), resulted in a basic strength or *ego quality*. He indicated that the first psychosocial strength that emerges is *hope*, the enduring belief in the attainability of primal or basic wishes. Hope is related to a sense of confidence and, according to Erikson, primarily stems from the quality of maternal care. Although Erikson focused on the development of healthy personalities, he acknowledged that the resolution of each crisis produced both positive and negative ego qualities. He identified a tendency toward *withdrawal* (becoming socially detached) from social relationships as the negative outcome of the first life crisis. Tendencies later in life toward low self-esteem, depression, and social withdrawal are indications that there may have been difficulty during the first stage of trust versus mistrust.

> Each of Erikson's stages is resolved on a positive to negative continuum, that is, a blend of qualities.

Erikson's (1982) second stage, which corresponds to Freud's anal stage, is autonomy versus shame. *Autonomy,* or a sense of self-control without a loss of self-esteem, involves the psychosocial issues of "holding on" and "letting go." On the other hand, *shame,* the feeling of being exposed or estranged from parental figures, involves a child feeling that he or she is a failure and lacking in self-confidence. Erikson accepted Freud's view that this life stage is associated with the child's assertiveness during toilet training, and is resolved through interaction with parental figures. However, he extended the classical psychoanalytic perspective to encompass an interest in the child's general assertiveness in his or her home and culture.

A successful resolution of the psychosocial crisis of autonomy versus shame results in the positive ego quality, will. *Will,* or the unbroken determination to exercise free choice, first exhibits itself in the child's determined cry, "Mine." Will's antipathic counterpart, *compulsion,* or repetitive behavior used to restrict impulses, is the negative outcome of autonomy versus shame. Erikson warned that the child who is overly shamed may turn against him- or herself, and go through life with a burdensome sense of shame. The adult who has positively resolved this stage develops a sense of justice.

A well-developed sense of autonomy is exhibited in the individual's behavior throughout the life cycle and, according to Erikson et al. (1986), may result in a renewed sense of willfulness in old age. In a study of personality and living patterns among older adults, Erikson et al. found that elderly individuals who have a lifelong pattern of willfulness exhibit "an assertive accommodation to disability" (p. 191).

Erikson's third stage of life, which corresponds to Freud's infantile genital stage, is initiative versus guilt. Erikson (1959) retained the traditional psychoanalytic view connected with infantile genitality and the Oedipal conflict (see Chapter 3). Erikson echoed Freud's view when he stated that girls "lack one item: the penis; and with it, important prerogatives in some cultures and classes" (p. 81). As is typical of Erikson, he identifies the source of the inequality he notes not to some form of biological determinism, as did Freud, but rather to the inner workings of some societies.

Erikson departed from traditional psychoanalytic thought, however, when he proposed that, during this stage, children are more concerned with play and with pursuing activities of their own choosing than they are with their sexuality. Erikson (1963) stressed that,

> The resolution of the crisis of each Eriksonian stage is *not* final. New opportunities to revisit the crisis may arise throughout life.

at this time, the child engages in an active investigation of his or her environment, and that the family remains the radius of significant relations.

During the stage of initiative versus guilt, as a result of being "willing to go after things" and "to take on roles through play," the child develops a sense of purpose. However, if he or she is overly thwarted, a feeling of *inhibition,* or restraint that prevents freedom of thought and expression, will predominate. Long after the person has matured, the individual displays, as part of his or her "work ethos as well as in recreation and creativity, behaviors relevant to rebalancing of initiative and guilt" (Erikson et al., 1986, p. 169). "An energetic involvement with diverse aspects of the world may be conveyed in a spectrum of activity in healthy adults throughout life" (ibid., p. 173).

Corresponding to Freud's latency stage, Erikson's fourth psychosocial crisis of *industry versus inferiority* occurs between ages six and twelve years (see Figure 4.2). Classical psychoanalysts believed that this was a time when the sexual drive lay dormant (or was sublimated), and children enjoyed a period of relative rest (Corey, 1986, see Chapter 3). Erikson (1959) broke with psychoanalytic thinking. He suggested that the central task of this time was to achieve a sense of industry. Developing *industry* is a task involving "an eagerness for building skills and performing meaningful work" (p. 90). The crisis of industry versus inferiority can result in a sense of competence or a blend of its opposite counterpart, *inertia* (a paralysis of thought and action that prevents productive work). Success at making things and "making things together" with one's neighbors and schoolmates is a critical task in the child's expanding physical and social world at this time (Erikson, 1982; Newman & Newman, 1987). Of course, the pleasure that is possible from creative work is evidenced throughout the life cycle, and can be evaluated during history taking.

Play

is a

child's work.

Play is how children figure out the world.

Through play children

explore and learn

about things, animals, places, and people.

Play is the way children learn what no one can teach them.

Figure 4.2. Industry versus inferiority. Source: Children's Museum, Indianapolis, Indiana.

Identity versus identity confusion, the fifth psychosocial crisis of adolescence, occurs from ages twelve through twenty-two years. According to Erikson (1968a), *identity* depends on social supports that permit the child to formulate successive and tentative identifications, culminating in an overt identity crisis in adolescence. During adolescence, an individual struggles with the issues of how "to be oneself" and "to share oneself with another" (Erikson, 1959, p. 179). The peer group becomes the critical focus of interaction.

The person who forms a relatively healthy identity views the world of experience with a minimum of distortion, a minimum of defensiveness, and a maximum of mutual activity. *Fidelity,* or the ability to sustain loyalties, is the critical ego quality that emerges from this stage. *Identity confusion* is based on a summation of the most undesirable and dangerous aspects of identification at critical stages of development (Newman & Newman, 1987). Severe conflicts during the stage of identity versus identity confusion can result in *repudiation,* or a rejection of alien roles and values.

Erikson (1964a) viewed identity as "a new combination of old and new identification fragments" (p. 90). He stated that identity is more than the sum of childhood identifications. The individual's inner drives, his or her endowments, and opportunities, as well as the ego values accrued in childhood come together to form a sense of confidence and continuity about "inner sameness" and in "one's meaning for others" (Erikson, 1959, p. 94). Absorption of personality features into a "new configuration" is the essence of development during this stage (Erikson, 1959, p. 57). Erikson proposed that identity formation is a lifelong developmental process. Therefore, the ability to retain belief in oneself as well as one's life-style and career, often a focus of therapy, can be enhanced throughout life.

Intimacy versus isolation, Erikson's sixth stage involving a mature person's ability to form intimate relationships, occurs between the ages of twenty-two and thirty-four years. Corresponding to Freud's genital stage, the stage of intimacy versus isolation focuses on the psychosocial modality of "being able to lose and find oneself in another" (Erikson, 1959, p. 179). The radius of significant relations expands to include partnerships in friendship and love, and encompasses both cooperative and competitive aspects. Love, or a mutual devotion that can overcome "the antagonisms inherent in a divided function," is the emerging ego strength (Erikson, 1968a, p. 289). Shutting out others, or exclusivity, is a sign that an individual has not been as successful in reaching intimacy (Newman & Newman, 1987).

Erikson (1968a) subscribed to Freud's view that the criterion of a mature person is the ability to "love and work" (p. 289). Erikson also agreed with Freud that intimacy includes mutuality of orgasm with a loved partner of the opposite sex, with whom one shares mutual trust, and the continuing cycle of work, recreation, and procreation. But he also perceived of inti-macy as more than sexual intimacy, including an interest in another's well-being and intellectually stimulating interactions. On the other hand, Erik-son (1959, p. 102) suggested that the psychoanalytic perspective on mature genitality "carries a strong cultural bias," and that societies might define differently the capacity for mutual devotion.

> Erikson conceived of the personality as a dynamic, evolving blend of each stage resolution or outcome.

Erikson's seventh psychosocial crisis, *generativity versus stagnation*, a stage that occurs in adulthood between ages thirty-four and sixty years, is concerned with "establishing and guiding the next generation" (Erikson, 1968a, p. 290). The psychosocial crisis centers around "the ability to take care of others" (Erikson, 1959, p. 179). The radius of significant relations extends to dividing labor and sharing households. Broadly framed, gen-erativity encompasses creativity through producing a family, mentoring a student, colleague, or friend, and engaging in a career and leisure activity.

Generativity versus stagnation involves the ability to take care of oth-ers. The inability to care for others sufficiently or to include them signifi-cantly in one's concerns results in the negative ego quality rejectivity. As can be seen in the following case vignette, what is commonly called a "midlife crisis" may be an inability to satisfactorily resolve Erikson's stage of generativity versus stagnation:

Mr. K., a 53-year-old male employee of a large organization consulted a ca-reer counselor. Mr. K., a vigorous, well-dressed, extremely articulate person, complained that it had been difficult for him to find interesting things to do in his job. He was disappointed and frustrated with the progress of his ca-reer.

Following graduation from college with a degree in journalism, Mr. K. be-gan working as a journalist. He recalled these times as "exciting" and "chal-lenging." He stated that he has become disenchanted with his current job because of its "nonsubstantive nature" and "remoteness from the central ac-tivities of the organization." Mr. K's supervisor had given him the under-standing that he would be given every consideration for promotion. Despite the assurances and recommendations of superiors, he has not been promot-ed. Mr. K. admires his colleague and friend who, based on his growing dis-illusionment with the organization, decided to seek a second career as a school counselor.

Mr. K. does not understand "what went wrong with his career and why he is unable to get the promotion that he feels he deserves." Mr. K's frustra-tion may be exacerbated by the continued progress of his wife (who now out-ranks him) in the organization. When asked to define his career goals, Mr. K.

denied that promotion was the issue, and said he was only concerned about having an "interesting job." He felt his lack of progress was related to "being too honest and independent to politic for a better position" and "not quite fitting into the organizational mold for managers." He expressed a vague interest in environmental issues, possibly leaving the organization to return to journalism or going into the catering business (cooking being his hobby). The social worker's role was to help Mr. K. resolve these issues in light of his midlife and other life stages.

There are conflicting images of midlife. The popular press and other media often depict this phase of life as a time of crisis, one that generally is assumed to center around an abrupt, if not drastic, career change. Included in the descriptions of midlife are gloomy accounts of the growing emotional awareness of mortality and now limited opportunities for reaching one's life goals. Nevertheless, research seems to indicate that most people do not experience a midlife crisis. Rather, a persuasive body of literature suggests that midlife may actually be a time of calm transition, perhaps because many individuals have developed the necessary coping skills (Hunter & Sundel, 1989).

Integrity versus despair, the eighth psychosocial crisis concerns old age, which Erikson designates as beginning at age sixty years and lasting until death. The issue of this psychosocial crisis is "how to grow old with integrity in the face of death" (Erikson, 1959, p. 104). *Integrity* is achieved by individuals who have few regrets, have lived productive lives, and cope as well with their failures as with their successes. The person who has successfully achieved a sense of integrity appreciates the continuity of past, present, and future experiences. He or she also comes to have an acceptance of the life cycle, to cooperate with the inevitabilities of life, and to experience a sense of being complete. Wisdom, or the active concern with life in the face of death, characterizes those who are relatively successful in resolving this stage.

Despair, on the other hand, predominates in those who fear death and wish life would give them another chance. The older person who has a strong sense of despair feels that life has been too short and finds little meaning in human existence, having lost faith in himself or herself and others. The person in whom a sense of despair predominates has little sense of world order or spiritual wholeness. *Disdain,* a scorn for weakness and frailty, characterizes those who are relatively unsuccessful in resolving integrity versus despair.

Erikson's notion that one stage of life is intimately related to all others comes full circle at the end of life. His view that the needs and capacities of the generations intertwine is reflected in his statement that the development of trust in children depends on the integrity of previous generations: "Healthy children will not fear life if their elders have integrity enough not to fear death" (Erikson, 1950, p. 269).

UNDERSTANDING CULTURAL DIFFERENCES:
CROSS-CULTURAL SOCIAL WORK PRACTICE

Erikson's psychosocial theory contains a number of principles that provide the practitioner with useful perspectives for cross-cultural social work practice. Erikson viewed the psychosocial crises accompanying the eight stages of development as universal, that is, as existing in all cultures throughout history. He allowed that each culture may offer different solutions and institutional supports to life stages, but believed that all people would pass through the various critical periods at the prescribed time. For example, because Erikson described several roads to generativity—pursuing hobbies, careers, and teaching as well as procreation—his theory is seen as holding special promise for understanding and assisting gay men in midlife development (Cornett & Hudson, 1987).

Erikson's (1964a,b) view about the universality of his "eight stages of man" was revealed when he related how he felt when he discussed psychiatry with an old shaman (a priest or priestess in some Native American tribes):

> We felt like colleagues. This feeling was based on some joint sense of the historical relativity of all psychotherapy: the relativity of the patient's outlook on his symptoms, of the role he assumes by dint of being a patient, of the kind of help which he seeks, and of the kinds of help which are eagerly offered or are available (p. 55).

Erikson (1959) was interested in the psychodynamics of prejudice. He suggested that psychoanalytic thought take into account "the sad truth that in any system based on suppression, exclusion, and exploitation, the suppressed, excluded, and exploited unconsciously believe in the evil image which they are made to represent by those who are dominant" (p. 30). He suggested that an understanding of "the unconscious associations of ethnic alternatives with moral and sexual ones are a necessary part of [understanding] any group formation" (ibid.). This understanding of ethnic factors, Erikson believed, could contribute to the knowledge of "the unconscious concomitants of prejudice" (ibid.). Historical movements and the political and economic power associated with them also were of interest to Erikson. He shared Freud's fascination with the biographies of great men and their impact on *the historical moment,* a person's place in the historical, political, and economic ideologies of his or her day (Erikson, 1975,

p. 172). However, Erikson's (1975) concern, which is illustrated in his attraction to the life of Gandhi, went beyond the "sexual" and the "repressed" as can be seen in the following quote from a lecture he gave in 1968:

> I hope before this lecture is over to have given you some proof that South Africa may have every reason to be as proud of this export, the Gandhian method, as it is proud of its gold, its diamonds, and its stamina; for whatever the long-range political fate of militant nonviolence may be, the spirit of its origin has, I believe, added lasting insights into our search for truth. (p. 172)

Erikson proposed that psychoanalytic thought needed to incorporate an understanding of the cultural factors that shaped personality. He argued that only psychoanalysis and social science together could eventually chart the life cycle as it relates to the history of the community (Erikson, 1959). Without an understanding of cultural phenomena that shape the sociological unconscious—or the cultural factors outside conscious awareness that can influence behavior—Erikson believed that a therapist could not be aware of why "men who share an ethnic area, a historical era, or an economic pursuit are guided by common images of good and evil" (Erikson, 1959, p. 1).

> Theorists—who seek a more context-specific approach to human behavior—continue to question the universality of Erikson's stage theory.

Although Erikson has done much to infuse psychoanalytically oriented theory with sociocultural concepts, there are those who believe he has not gone far enough. Whether Erikson sufficiently explored sex differences in developmental processes is a key example. Erikson has been challenged for his observations that differences in attitude and worldview are rooted in biological predispositions (Huyck & Hoyer, 1982). Particularly under question are Erikson's suggestions that patterns of identity formation are based on biological-reproductive potential (for a different perspective, see McGoldrick, 1989). The following quote captures Erikson's (1964b) sense that differences in human potential often are part of the "ground plan of the human body" (p. 301):

> Clinical observations suggest that in female experience "inner space" is at the center of despair even as it is at the very center of potential fulfillment. Emptiness is the female form of perdition—known at times to men of the inner life, but standard experience for all women. (ibid., p. 305)

Erikson's perceptions about women's identity centering around the wish to bear children and men's identity formation focusing on the capacity to work productively will continue to come under question. For example, Bern (1980) suggested that her own research on the concept of psychological androgyny, in which individuals experience both "masculine" and "feminine" emotions, has been very fruitful and needs to be further explored, whereas Gilligan (1982) has contended that "despite Erikson's observation of sex differences in life cycle phases, . . . the male experience continues to define his life-cycle conception" (p. 12). She goes on to state that

> the discovery now being celebrated by men in mid-life of the importance of intimacy, relationships, and care is something that women have known from the beginning. However, because that knowledge in women has been considered "intuitive" or "instinctive," a function of anatomy coupled with destiny, psychologists have neglected to describe its development. (ibid., p. 17)

Theorists also have pointed out the need to give more attention to differential development of heterosexuals and homosexuals (Crawford, 1987). For example, Roth and Murphy (1986) have proposed that because a positive lesbian identity involves some processes unique to that subculture, such as a more complex relationship with the family of origin, a different developmental model is needed. They go on to state that the model needs to address "repeated decisions about risking loss, initially the loss of a previously held self-image, and repeatedly the loss of others" (p. 80). The importance of pair bonding between lesbian women and recognizing this different family form also is underscored.

Erikson also has been challenged for his incomplete description of identity processes in ethnic and minority children. For example, Spencer and Markstrom-Adams (1990) suggested that although Erikson was correct in his view that the establishment of identity is a major developmental task of all adolescence, his theory fell short. They go on to argue that further research is needed on early childhood development to better understand the developmental precursors of racial and minority identity.

UNDERSTANDING HOW HUMANS FUNCTION AS MEMBERS OF FAMILIES, GROUPS, ORGANIZATIONS, AND COMMUNITIES

Erikson suggested that there is a strong mutual interaction between an individual and his or her social organization that should not be "shunted off by patronizing tributes to the existence of social forces" (Erikson, 1959, p. 18). Rather, he suggested that sufficient attention should be paid to the mutual positive interaction between an individual and society. How each society develops institutions appropriate to the developmental needs of the individual, the way the developing individual enriches society, and the manner in which caretakers and societal institutions provide positive support for the development of personal effectiveness should be the focus of concern.

Erikson (1959) believed that the methodology of psychoanalytic thought made an artificial differentiation between the "individual-within-his family" and the "individual-in-the-mass" (p. 18). In contrast, Erikson saw the family and other social groups as a central force in human development. He suggested that personality development occurred through a "child's satisfactory interaction with a trustworthy and meaningful hierarchy of roles as provided by generations living together in some form of family" (Erikson, 1959, p. 172).

> Erikson hoped his theory would address people as participating members of various societal institutions, and as part of their historical time.

Erikson contended that an individual is a contributing member of his or her society as well as part of a historical chain between generations. He emphasized the "interplay of successive and overlapping generations, living together in organized settings" (Erikson, 1964a, p. 114). Erikson (1964a) argued that the "cogwheeling" stages of childhood and adulthood involved a "system of generation and regeneration . . . to which the institutions and traditions of society attempt to give unity and permanence" (p. 152). That is, Erikson viewed human strength as being related to a combined function related to the ego as regulator, the sequence of generations, and the structure of society. In many ways, Erikson's view of human development is compatible with those of the social actionist.

DIRECT PRACTICE IN SOCIAL WORK: INTERVENING IN THE PERSON-SITUATION TO ENHANCE PSYCHOSOCIAL FUNCTIONING

Erikson acknowledged his debt to Freud's conceptualization of the psychoanalytic method, and adopted many Freudian principles in his treatment approach. Central to Erikson's perspective on therapy are the importance of the therapeutic relationship as a "patient's first steps of renewed social experimentation" (Erikson, 1959, p. 149), the *genetic perspective*, or retrospective description of childhood roots of adult behavior and pathology, and the development of insight into repressed mental elements that are a defense against anxiety—all concepts derived from a Freudian approach to therapy.

Erikson's major contribution to the psychoanalytic method was a statement of the need for interpretation of the client's developmental and historical distortions. *Insight,* or an understanding of the stage of development and the "normative crisis" of the client's age group, was Erikson's primary therapeutic goal. This goal reflects his belief that clients seek therapy when they cannot cope with the tensions and conflicts generated by the polarities of life stages. Because of these conflicts, Erikson argued, many patients struggle with their sense of identity: "The cured patient has the courage to face the discontinuities of life . . . and the polarities of [his or her] struggle for an economic and cultural identity" (Erikson, 1959, p. 36).

> Erikson suggested that practitioners enhance client insight through interpretation of life events.

Erikson's clinical work also involved the therapist giving "free-floating attention," refraining from undue interference, allowing the patient to "search for curative clarification," and providing interpretation (Erikson, 1964a, p. 58). The interpretation of dreams and transference also are features of the clinical encounter.

Erikson assumed, as did Freud, that the patient is unconscious of the meanings communicated in the therapeutic encounter. Therefore, interpretation is curative or healing "through the expansion of developmental and historical insight" (Erikson, 1982, p. 98). It is the role of the therapist to assist the client in feeling and speaking more clearly. *Interpretation,* a "private language developed by two people in the course of an intimate association," involves the therapist looking for a "unitary theme" that cuts across the patient's symptomatology, relationship with the therapist, an important conflict in his or her childhood, and to facets of his or her work and love life. Interpretations, which are not "suggestions" or "clinical slaps on the back," move the therapy forward and "join the patient's and the therapist's modes of problem-solving" (Erikson, 1964a, p. 72).

According to Erikson (1964a), developing a treatment history, through which the therapist's interpretation supports a systematic self-analysis, is "the core of the clinical encounter" in psychoanalytic therapy (p. 52). The analysis of ego function includes the individual's ego identity "in relation to the historical changes that dominate his childhood milieu" (Erikson, 1959, p. 50). By taking a combined psychosexual and psychosocial perspective, Corey (1986) suggested that helping professionals can find a useful conceptual framework for understanding developmental issues as they appear in the helping process. Corey (1986) raises the following questions:

- What are some major developmental tasks at each stage in life, and how are these tasks related to counseling?

- What are some themes that give continuity to this individual's life?
- What are some universal concerns of people at various points of life?
- How can people be challenged to make life-giving choices at these points?
- What is the relationship between an individual's current problems and significant events from earlier years?
- What influential factors have shaped [a client's] life? What choices were made at these critical periods, and how did the person deal with these various crises? (p. 26)

The ultimate goal of therapeutic interpretations is the development of insight in service to the ego. Self-awareness is described by Erikson (1964a) as "a fundamental new ethical orientation of adult man's relationship to childhood: to his own childhood, now behind and within him; and to every man's children around him" (p. 44). Through the use of self-awareness, the client (ego) is able to interact actively and positively with the environment (Table 4.4). As a result of this process, Erikson believed the client restores the functioning of his or her ego, and comes to terms with phenomenal reality—to be freed from distortions and delusions, defensiveness, or offensive acting out.

Life Review: A Group Intervention with Older Adults

The notion of developing a history through the client's self-analysis has been an important influence on contemporary therapies and services for older adults (Ott, 1993; Vachon, 1995). Butler (1963) coined the term "life review" to refer to the natural process of reminiscing in old age. He posited a therapy involving a "restructuring" of past events. Butler suggested that the progressive return to consciousness of past experiences was an attempt to resolve and integrate them and was related to the resolution of the crisis integrity versus despair, Erikson's final life task. Since it was first advanced, life review therapy has become a widely accepted social work technique, and is thought to serve an important intrapersonal and adaptive function in helping older adults cope with the aging process (Greene, 1982, 1986; Kivnick, 1996; Merriam, 1993; Pincus, 1970).

Recent research demonstrates the continued examination of reminiscence as a therapeutic tool (Bass & Greger, 1996; Stevens-Ratchford, 1993). For example, the 1988 Georgia Centenarian Study sponsored by the National Institute of Mental Health explored the use of reminiscence among 288 study participants. While reminiscence was found to have storytelling and enjoyment value, its dominant function was found to be therapeutic (Merriam, 1993). Among the areas in which reminiscing is thought have therapeutic results are enhancing family coping (Comana, Brown, &

Table 4.4.   Guidelines for the Eriksonian-Style Practitioner

---

Understand that your client is engaged in a lifelong process of personality
    development in which you as the practitioner can be instrumental in
    promoting growth.
Engage the client in a self-analysis that results in a developmental history.
Distinguish with the client his or her relative successes and difficulties in
    resolving psychosocial crises.
Determine areas of development that have led to a distortion of reality and a
    diminution in ego functioning.
Interpret the client's developmental and historical distortions. Ask for client
    confirmation of your interpretations.
Develop the client's insight and understanding about unresolved normative
    crises and their historical as well as present implications.
Identify ways in which the client can use his or her ego strengths to cope more
    effectively with his or her environment. Explore how these coping strategies
    can be put into action.
Clarify how and in what ways various social institutions support or fail to
    support the client's psychosocial well-being.
Seek means of enhancing the client's societal supports.
Promote the client's developing a new orientation to his or her place in the social
    environment.

Thomas, 1998; Rosenblatt, 1990), working with depression (Youssef, 1990),
clarifying adult roles (Greene, 1982), and forming self-help groups (Andrada & Korte, 1993; Creanza & McWhirter, 1994).

Reminiscing groups in nursing homes also are popular (Burnside, 1990).
Burnside (1984) has suggested a group framework of six to ten group participants who would meet twice a week for ten weeks. Each session would
meet for forty-five to sixty minutes and is intended to promote reminiscence about a specific time in an older adult's life and the positive experiences that occurred. Events are presented in chronological order. The
following format was used:

1.   Group leaders presented a prepared unit designed to stimulate reminiscing about a particular person, event, or era.
2.   Group members were encouraged to discuss materials presented and
to relate events in their own lives to the materials presented. Leaders asked
questions such as "How did your family celebrate Thanksgiving?"
3.   Group leaders helped the resident identify positive elements in the recalled experiences (p. 301)

Andrada and Korte (1993) have described a reminiscing group for Hispanic elderly that is designed to capture the rich oral tradition of storytelling, riddles, poetry, folklore, and songs. The social worker introduces
the group as a *platica* group—one in which everyday conversation is used

to maintain social and cultural affiliation. The social worker presents the group members with auditory stimulation through song and imagery, tactile stimulation through the examination of antique items such as irons and radios, taste stimulation through special cultural foods, and visual stimulation through pictures from the past. A particularly poignant group session recalled a past *Dia de Gracia*—Thanksgiving:

> Group members were asked to visualize the meal, relate who was there, and talk about the smells and sounds they remembered. . . . For the elderly in the group this was a time to be in the center and recount experiences significant to them. In reaching out to the elders and encouraging their *platica,* they could take satisfaction in their history, their knowledge and their feelings were still important. It was their time for *resolana* albeit in the confines of a nursing home. (Andrada & Korte, 1993, pp. 32–41)

REFERENCES

Andrada, P. A., & Korte, A. O. (1993). En aquellos tiempos: A reminiscing group with Hispanic elderly. *Journal of Gerontological Social Work, 20*(3/4), 25–42.

Bass, B., & Greger, L. (1996). Stimulus complexity in reminiscence therapy and scores on the Beck Depression Inventory of a small group of nursing home residents. *Perceptual and Motor Skills, 82,* 973–974.

Bern, S. L. (1980). Beyond androgyny: Some presumptuous prescriptions for a liberated sexual identity. In M. Bloom (Ed.), *Life Span Development* (pp. 310–318). New York: Macmillan.

Brennan, E. M., & Weick, A. (1981). Theories of adult development: Creating a context for practice. *Social Casework, 62,* 13–19.

Bronfenbrenner, U. (1979). *The Ecology of Human Development.* Cambridge, MA: Harvard University Press.

Burnside, I. (1984). *Working with the Elderly: Group Process and Technique.* Monterey, CA: Wadsworth.

Burnside, I. (1990). Reminiscence: an independent nursing home intervention for the elderly. *Issues in Mental Health Nursing, 11*(1), 33–48.

Butler, R. N. (1963). The life review: An interpretation of reminiscence in the aged. *Psychiatry, 26,* 65–76.

Compton, B., & Galaway, B. (1994). *Social Work Processes.* Pacific Grove, CA: Brooks/Cole.

Corey, G. (1986). *Theory and Practice of Counseling and Psychotherapy.* Monterey, CA: Brooks/Cole.

Cornett, C., & Hudson, R. A. (1987). Middle adulthood and the theories of Erikson, Gould, and Vaillant: Where does the gay man fit? *Journal of Gerontological Social Work, 10*(3/4), 61–73.

Crawford, S. (1987). Lesbian families: Psychosocial stress and the family-building process. In *Baston Lesbian Psychologies Collective Edition* (pp. 195–214). Champagne, Urbana: University of Illinois Press.

Comana, M., Brown, V., & Thomas, J. (1998). The effect of reminiscence therapy on family coping. *Journal of Family Nursing, 4*(2), 182–198.

Creanza, A. L., & McWhirter, J. (1994). Reminiscence: A strategy for getting to know you. *Journal for Specialists in Group Work, 19*(4), 232–238.

Erikson, E. H. (1950). *Childhood and Society.* New York: Norton.

Erikson, E. H. (1959). *Identity and the Life Cycle.* New York: Norton.

Erikson, E. H. (1963). *Childhood and Society,* 2nd ed. New York: Norton.

Erikson, E. H. (1964a). *Insight and responsibility.* Toronto: George J. McLeod.

Erikson, E. H. (1964b). Inner and outer space: Reflections on womanhood. *Daedalus, 93.*

Erikson, E. H. (1968a). *Identity youth and crisis.* New York: W. W. Norton.

Erikson, E. H. (1968b). Life cycle. In D. L. Sills (Ed.), *The International Encyclopedia of the Social Sciences* (Vol. 9, pp. 286–292). New York: Crowell, Collier Macmillan.

Erikson, E. H. (1975). *Life History and the Historical Moment.* New York: Norton.

Erikson, E. H. (1982). *The Life Cycle Completed.* New York: Norton.

Erikson, E. H., Erikson, J. M., & Kivnick, H. Q. (1986). *Vital Involvement in Old Age.* New York: Norton.

Germain, C. B. (1987). Human development in contemporary environments. *Social Service Review, 61*(4), 565–580.

Germain, C. B., & Hartman, A. (1980). People and ideas in the history of social work. *Social Casework, 61*(6), 323–331.

Gilligan, C. (1982). *In a Different Voice.* Cambridge, MA: Harvard University Press.

Goleman, D. (1990). As a therapist, Freud fell short, scholars' find. *New York Times,* 6 March, 1.

Greene, R. (1982). Life review: A technique for clarifying family roles in adulthood. *Clinical Gerontologist, 2,* 59–67.

Greene, R. (1986). *Social Work with the Aged and Their Families.* Hawthorne, NY: Aldine de Gruyter.

Hamilton, G. (1940). *Theory and Practice of Social Casework.* New York: Columbia University Press.

Hogan, R. (1976). *Personality Theory: The Personological Tradition.* Englewood Cliffs, NJ: Prentice-Hall.

Huyck, M. H., & Hoyer, W. J. (1982). *Adult Development and Aging.* Belmont, CA: Wadsworth.

Hunter, S., & Sundel, M. (1989). *Midlife Myths.* Newbury Park, CA: Sage.

Kivnick, H. Q. (1996). Remembering and being remembered: The reciprocity of psychosocial legacy. *Generations, 20*(3), 49–54.

Levinson, D. J. (1978). *The Seasons of a Man's Life.* New York: Ballantine.

Lowenstein, S. F. (1978). Preparing social work students for life transition counseling within the human behavior sequence. *Journal of Education for Social Work, 14,* 66–73.

McGoldrick, M. (1989). Women through the family life cycle. In M. McGoldrick, C. M. Anderson, & F. Walsh (Eds.), *Women in Families: A Framework for Family Therapy* (pp. 200–226). New York: Norton.

Merriam, S. B. (1993). The uses of reminiscence in older adults. *Educational Gerontology, 19,* 441–450.

Newman, B., & Newman, P. R. ([1979] 1987). *Development through Life: A Psychosocial Approach.* Homewood, IL: Dorsey.

Ott, R. L. (1993). Enhancing validation through milestoning with sensory reminiscence. *Journal of Gerontological Social Work, 20*(1/2), 147–159.

Pincus, A. (1970). Reminiscence in aging and its implications for social work practice. *Social Work, 15,* 47–53.

Riley, M. W. (1985). Women, men and lengthening life course. In A. S. Rossi (Ed.), *Gender and the Life Course* (pp. 333–347). Hawthorne, NY: Aldine de Gruyter.

Rosenblatt, P. C. (1990). Shared reminiscence about a deceased parent: Implications for grief education and grief counseling. *Family Relations, 39*(2),206–211.

Roth, S., & Murphy, B. C. (1986). Therapeutic work with lesbian clients: A systemic therapy view. In J. C. Hanse & M. Ault-Ricke (Eds.), *Women and Family Therapy* (pp. 79–89) Rockville, MD: Aspen.

Shapiro, T., & Hertzig, M. E. (Eds.) (1988). Normal growth and development. In *American Psychiatric Press Textbook of Psychiatry* (pp. 91–121). Washington DC: American Psychiatric Press.

Spencer, M. B., & Markstrom-Adams, C. (1990). Identity processes among racial and ethnic minority children in America. *Child Development, 61,* 290–310.

Stevens-Ratchford, R. G. (1993). The effect of life review reminiscence activities on depression and self-esteem in older adults. *American Journal of Occupational Therapy, 47*(5), 413–420.

Vachon, M. (1995). Cognitive therapy and life review therapy: Theoretical and therapeutic implications for mental health counselors. *Journal of Mental Health Counseling, 17*(2)157–123.

Youssef, F. A. (1990). The impact of group reminiscence counseling on a depressed elderly population. *Nurse Practitioner, 15*(4), 32–38.

GLOSSARY

Autonomy.   A sense of self-control without loss of self-esteem.

Care.   A concern with adhering to irreversible obligation that overcomes self-concern.

Competence.   The ability and skill to complete tasks successfully.

Conflict model.   A view that an individual is driven by primitive urges, impelled by unconscious, antisocial sexual and aggressive urges, and must face contradictory societal expectations.

Core pathologies.   The negative qualities that emerge as a result of severe negative resolutions of psychosocial crises.

Crisis.   A critical period that demands that the individual become reoriented, make a radical change in perspective, and face new opportunities.

Despair.   A feeling of lack of integration and meaninglessness.

Development.   A maturational process involving social and environmental factors that produces changes in thought and behavior.

Developmental stage.   A period in life with an underlying organizational emphasis involving the need to adopt a new life orientation.

Differentiation.   Change to a more refined or specialized state in biological, psychological, and or social properties.

Ego identity.   The mutual relationship between the individual and his or her society.

Ego psychology.   A school of psychology that places an emphasis on the striving ego and the individual's efforts to attain mastery of his or her environment across the life cycle.

Ego strength.   The capacity to unify experience and take actions that anticipate and overcome self-concerns.

Ego.   The executive arm of the personality that relates to the outer world.

Epigenetic principle.   A principle that suggests that one stage of development grows out of the events of the previous stage and that development is propelled by a biological plan.

Fidelity.   An ability to sustain loyalties despite contradictions in value systems.

Generativity.   Concern with establishing and guiding the next generation.

Genetic perspective.   To retrospectively describe the childhood roots of adult behavior and pathology.

Guilt.   A feeling of fear that punishment will occur.

Hierarchical reorganization.   The view that development is not only linear, but rather involves a new configuration of structures and functions.

Historical moment.   A person's place in the historical, political, and economic ideologies of his or her day.

Hope.   Belief in the attainability of primal or basic wishes.

Id.   The impulsive part of the personality that houses aggressive and sexual urges or drives.

Identity crisis.   A sense of urgency; a disturbance in the experience of time; a disruption in workmanship.

Identity.   Accrued confidence gathered over the years.

Industry.   Possession of a sense of the technology of one's culture.

Inferiority.   A feeling of being unworthy or unprepared to deal with technology.

Initiative.   The ability to move independently and vigorously.

Integrity.   The ability to transcend the limits of self-awareness and the relativity of all knowledge.

Intimacy.   An ability to commit to affiliations and partnerships even though they may call for significant sacrifice and compromise.

Isolation.   The avoidance of contacts that commit to intimacy.

Life cycle.   A developmental perspective that explores the tendency of an individual's life to form a coherent, lifetime experience and be joined or linked to previous and future generations.

Life review.   A natural process of reminiscing in old age involving a "restructuring" of past events. A helping process based on the progressive return to consciousness of past experiences in an attempt to resolve and integrate them.

Love.   A mutuality of devotion that is greater than the antagonisms and dependency needs inherent in a relationship.

Mutuality.   A complex pattern of interdependence between the generations.

Normative event.   An expectable, universal time when the individual must reestablish his or her ego functioning.

Prime adaptive ego qualities.   Features that emerge as a result of positive resolution of psychosocial crises.

Psychological health.   A condition characterized by a strong ego and congruence with social institutions.

Psychosexual stage.   A stage of development revolving around sexual needs.

Psychosocial crises.   A crucial period or turning point in life when there is increased vulnerability and heightened potential; a time when particular efforts must be made to meet a new set of demands presented by society.

Psychosocial stage.   A stage of development focusing on social interaction.

Psychosocial strengths.   The abilities developed through a lifelong process of positive interaction with one's environment.

Psychosocial theory.   A theoretical approach that explores issues of growth and development across the life cycle as a product of the personality interacting with the social environment.

Psychosocial.   The relationship between "inner agency and social life."

Purpose.   An ability to pursue valued and tangible goals guided by conscience.

Radius of significant relationships.   The developing individual's expanding number of social relationships through life.

Shame.   A feeling of being exposed and of being looked at disapprovingly.

Sociological unconscious.   Aspects of culture and social class that influence behavior, but are outside conscious awareness.

Superego.   The moral arm of the personality.

Trust.   A feeling of certainty about one's social ecology.

Unconscious.   Mental elements repressed as a defense against anxiety, and the expectations left over and repressed from previous stages in the life cycle.

Will power.   The unbroken determination to exercise free choice and self-control.

Wisdom.   Active concern with life in the face of death; mature judgment.

CRITIQUE

Moral Development over the Life Cycle
Another View of Stage Theory

ALLEN RADER and RUTH RADER

Erikson and Kohlberg both studied personality development from a biopsychosocial and life span perspective: Erikson focused his efforts on the mastery of the ego and the development of identity; Kohlberg explored moral development. This critique suggests that Kohlberg has contributed more than any other theorist to the study of moral development and his name is nearly synonymous with the field. To quote Loevinger (1986), "in the broad field that is ego development as I see it, Kohlberg's contribution has been magnificent. He has revolutionized the way many social scientists see moral development" (p. 192). Kohlberg combined systematic research and clinical sensitivity to explore intersubjective experience and meaning discernment with a rigor that previously did not exist. In addition, he combined psychology and philosophy in a manner that not only explained development but also addressed treatment goals and interventions, and enhanced the ability for future theorists to build on and expand their knowledge (Gielen, 1991; Kegan, 1982; Puka, 1994; Rest, 1991).

It is important for social workers to have an understanding of Kohlberg's theory. Although there has been continued research into the realm of moral development since Kohlberg, his work remains the foundation for any cogent discussion of the topic. This critique provides a brief description of Kohlberg's stage theory of moral development and the implications his theories have for social work today. It also discusses some limitations and new directions in Kohlberg's research.

BACKGROUND

Kohlberg's work was influenced by philosophers, psychological theorists, and psychoanalytic, and romantic theorists. Psychoanalytic and romantic traditions characterized the development of morals as a gradual unfolding or maturation of the individual. The individual has all the important innate elements necessary for growth, and the environment provides the necessary nourishment for the unfolding to occur. Romanticists also posited that the environment—rather than being the formative ingredient—adds the nourishment to allow the expression of innate elements (Kohlberg, 1981). These romantic theorists and educators advocated a permissive environment in which good and spontaneity are allowed to unfold and the inner bad is kept under control.

On the other hand, theorists such as social learning and behavioral theorists have characterized the development of morals as a process of cultural transmission. They view the environment as an input by which information or energy is transmitted to the person, who responds with an output (Hayes, 1991). Thus the culture, through its rules and standards, transmits to the individual the lists of virtues that he or she is to practice to improve moral character.

Kohlberg believed that the interface between the environment and the person was much more interactional than any of these theories proposed. Kohlberg saw innate structures unfolding through this biological/environmental interaction without development being solely determined by either biological or environmental influences. In the end, Kohlberg developed a cognitive-developmental model of moral development. He delineated stages of development that encompass cognitive/moral structure and reasoning. Each stage is transformed through interactions with the environment and results in a new stage that has a qualitatively different worldview. Kohlberg (1984) assumed that "the child's active moral constructions, as distinct from passively learned assertions of adult moral cliches, would center on the child's sense of justice" (p. xxvii).

KOHLBERG'S FRAMEWORK FOR MORAL DEVELOPMENT

The philosophical stance of Socrates contributed a fundamental basis for Kohlberg in the areas of virtue and democratic education. Kohlberg used Socratic questioning and discussions of moral dilemmas as effective methods to enhance moral development (Kohlberg, 1981). From Socrates, Kohlberg learned that "the way to stimulate stage growth is to pose real or hypothetical dilemmas to students in such a way as to arouse disagreement and uncertainty as to what is right" (Kohlberg, 1981, p. 27). This type of questioning, which encourages students to explore their values, is the foundation of Kohlberg's theoretical approach to education and moral development. Coupled with the appropriate cognitive development, these questions enhance the growth of moral reasoning.

Kohlberg's stages have the following general characteristics: each stage implies a distinct or qualitatively different mode of thinking or of solving problems; these different modes of thought have an invariant sequence that may be sped up, slowed down, or stopped by cultural factors; however, their sequence will not change; each of the different modes of thought forms a structural whole; and stages are hierarchical integrations. That is, stages form a sequence of increasingly differentiated and integrated structures. Table 4C.1 details each of the stages and the accompanying social perspective.

Progress through Kohlberg's stages rests upon the child's concern for the welfare of others. At each stage, children perceive basic values and empathize by taking the roles of other people or living things. Justice becomes part of the cognitive-structural transformation when this basic value is experienced in ever more sophisticated ways as the person develops through the stages. Role-taking and the increasing sophistication with which roles are experienced becomes the method of developing this increasingly sophisticated relationship to justice and competing moral perspectives. Thus, moral stages form a process whereby increasingly sophisticated lev-

Table 4C.1. Kohlberg's Stages of Moral Development

Level 1: Preconventional
Stage 1: Heteronomous Morality

What Is Right
> Failing to break rules to avoid punishment, being obedience for its own sake, and avoiding physical damage to persons and property.

Reasons for Doing Right
> To avoid punishment, and the superior power of authorities.

Social Perspective of Stage
> Egocentric point of view: Doesn't consider the interests of others or recognize that they differ from the actor's; doesn't relate two points of view; actions are considered physically rather than in terms of psychological interests of others; confusion of authority's perspective with your own

Stage 2:   Individualism, Instrumental Purpose, and Exchange

What Is Right
> Following rules only when it is to someone's immediate interest; acting to meet your own interests and needs and letting others do the same; right is also what's fair, what's an equal exchange, a deal, an agreement

continued

Table 4C.1. (Continued)

Reasons for Doing Right
>   To serve your own needs or interests in a world in which you have to recognize that other people have their interests, too

Social Perspective of Stage
>   Concrete individualistic perspective; aware that everybody has his or her own interests to pursue and these conflict, so that right is relative (in the concrete, individualistic sense)

Level II: Conventional

Stage 3:   Mutual Interpersonal Expectations, Relationships, and Interpersonal Conformity

What Is Right
>   Living up to what is expected by people close to you or what people generally expect of people in your role as son, brother, sister, friend, etc; "Being good" is important and means having good motives, showing concern for others; it also means keeping mutual relationships, such as trust, loyalty, respect, and gratitude

Reasons for Doing Right
>   To fulfill a need to be a good person in your own eyes and those of others; your caring for others; your belief in the Golden Rule; your desire to maintain rules and authority that support stereotypical good behavior

Social Perspective of Stage
>   Perspective of the individual in relationship with other individuals; awareness of shared feelings, agreements, and expectations that take primacy over individual interests; relates points of view through the concrete Golden Rule; putting yourself in the other person's shoes; does not yet consider the generalized system perspective

Stage 4:   Social System and Conscience

What Is Right
>   Fulfilling the actual duties to which you have agreed; upholding laws except in extreme cases in which they conflict with other fixed social duties; right is also contributing to society, the group, or institution

Reasons for Doing Right
>   To keep the institution going as a whole, to avoid the breakdown in the system "if everyone did it" or the imperative of conscience to meet your defined obligations (easily confused with stage 3 belief in rules and authority)

Social Perspective of Stage
>   Differentiates societal point of view from interpersonal agreement or motives; takes the point of view of the system that defines roles and rules; considers individual relations in terms of place in the system

Level III: Postconventional or Principled

Stage 5:   Social Contract or Utility and Individual Rights

What Is Right
>   Being aware that people hold a variety of values and opinions, that most values and rules are relative to your group; these relative

continued

Table 4C.1. (Continued)

rules should usually be upheld, however, in the interest of impartiality and because they are the social contract; some nonrelative values and rights such as life and liberty must be upheld in any society and regardless of majority opinion

Reasons for Doing Right

To fulfill a sense of obligation to law because of your social contract to make and abide by laws for the welfare of all and for the protection of all people's rights; to honor a feeling of contractual commitment, freely entered into, to family friendship, trust, and work obligations; to address a concern that laws and duties be based on rational calculation of overall utility, "the greatest good for the greatest number"

Social Perspective of Stage

Prior-to-society perspective; perspective of a rational individual who is aware of values and rights before social attachments and contracts; integrates perspectives by formal mechanisms of agreement, contract, objective impartiality, and due process; considers moral and legal points of view; recognizes that they sometimes conflict and finds it difficult to integrate them

Stage 6:   Universal Ethical Principles

What Is Right

Following self-chosen ethical principles; particular laws or social agreements are usually valid because they rest on such principles; when laws violate these principles, you act in accordance with the principle; principles are universal principles of justice: the equality of human rights and respect for the dignity of humans as individuals

Reasons for Doing Right

To follow the belief as a rational person in the validity of universal moral principles and a sense of personal commitment to them

Social Perspective of Stage

Perspective of moral point of view from which social arrangements derive; perspective is that of any rational individual who recognizes the nature of morality or the fact that persons are ends in themselves and must be treated as such

Source: Kohlberg (1984, pp. 174–176).

els of equality and reciprocity between people develop as they continue to more effectively differentiate and universalize their reasoning from the preceding stage (Kohlberg, 1981, 1994).

IMPLICATIONS FOR SOCIAL WORK

Kohlberg's work has several implications for social work practice and fits well with social work's traditional mission of a dual focus of the person-in-environment. Social workers need to be cognizant that they can develop interventions that promote moral growth. That is, "counseling can be seen as a process of social influence and by their very nature a moral activity" (Hayes, 1991), p. 173). Using the underlying principles delineated by Kohlberg in his paper "Stage And Sequence: The Cognitive-Developmental Approach to Socialization," Richard Hayes (1991) has suggested seven specific conditions that the practitioner should promote:

1.   Consideration of fairness and morality. The environment for counseling should promote trust for the clients as well as others.
2.   Exposure to cognitive conflict, which promotes the development of the cognitive structures needed for development and exposes clients to others' viewpoints.
3.   The provision of role-taking opportunities, which allows for self-development.
4.   Allowing active participation in decision-making, which stimulates self-development by helping clients realize the consequences of their actions.
5.   Exposure to higher levels of thinking, which enhances clients' capacity to solve their own problems.
6.   Intellectual stimulation, which helps clients make meaning out of their experience.
7.   Group counseling and democratic education, which takes advantage of the power of peers to provide an environment for the other six conditions. (For a complete discussion, see Hayes, 1991.)

Kohlberg's theories also calls for a reexamination of the role of family and peer groups in the development of moral and social development. Kohlberg viewed the family's participation as not "unique or critically necessary for moral development and the dimensions on which it stimulates moral development are primarily general dimensions by which other primary groups stimulate moral development" (Kohlberg, 1984, p. 75). Thus for Kohlberg, the rules, authority, and modeling of the family formed a general foundation for development; however, the actual evolution of moral thought came from the taking of roles in social situations. Through this process of examining the situation, *empathizing* with the different conflicting viewpoints, and discovering what is fair and just, children develop their moral reasoning. This is different from the passing down of rules and regulations or the incorporation of models of behavior (Kohlberg, 1984).

This lessening of the traditional role of the family in development is one of the most controversial aspects of Kohlberg's theory. Yet, like all of the rest of his work, he backed these assertions up with research. His work in the *kibbutz* showed that *kibbutz* children show normal moral development even though they have a marked reduction in their interaction with their parents. Kohlberg attributed this result to the *kibbutz* children's having intense peer interaction with group leaders, which assists in the process of developing a sense of community. Because social workers are involved with the decisions that influence children's development, Kohlberg's finding may point to different solutions concerning the placement of children and the role of the school and the family in the development of values.

Another area in which Kohlberg's research has influenced social work is in the growing area of spirituality and religion. Although much of Kohlberg's focus has been on the educational system in which the separation of church and state made it critical that spiritual issues be separated from moral development, his work has helped to lay a foundation of legitimacy for further incorporation of values into the practice of social work (Kohlberg, 1981).

Kohlberg's influence can also be helpful for those social workers who are working with diverse populations. Kohlberg found that the stages of moral development could be duplicated across cultures, enabling those social workers who deal with the value systems and standards of different cultures to be able to search for a common ground of fairness and justice to help in the reconciliation of conflicting cultural value systems (Kohlberg, 1984). In addition, social workers can listen for signs of the different stages of cognitive, social, and moral development to assist them in helping these clients with their personal moral dilemmas.

However, Kohlberg has been criticized for not researching his model and applying it to the development of girls and women (Langdale, 1993). One concern is that Kohlberg did not consider that girls and boys may play differently. Another issue is that some girls' games have fewer rules than those of boys; Carol Gilligan (1982) has been among the most vocal critics to point to the "male bias" in Kohlberg's work. Gilligan argued that Kohlberg's emphasis on justice as a core component of morality and his use of hypothetical dilemmas is biased and limited. Justice is only one of two perspectives. The other is care (Gilligan, 1982). Therefore, had Kohlberg been inclusive of women, his theory might have evolved differently: "In contrast to the justice orientation, the emphasis in the voice of care is on themes of attachment, connection, interdependence, and the responsiveness of human beings to one another" (Langdale, 1993, p. 32).

Another area of controversy has been Kohlberg's reliance upon invariant stages (Locke, 1986; Loevinger, 1986; Tomlinson, 1986). For example, Thomas (1997) has suggested that there are multiple moralities that interconnect leading to different ultimate virtues. Although his theories have met with early criticism and continue to be attacked and revised, Kohlberg laid the foundation for the study of morals. The value of his work is undeniable.

REFERENCES

Gielen, U. (1991). Kohlberg's moral development theory. In L. Kuhmerker, U. Gielen, & R. L. Hayes (Eds.), *The Kohlberg Legacy for the Helping Professions* (pp. 18–38). Birmingham, AL: R.E.P.

Gilligan, C. (1982). *In a Different Voice: Psychological Theory and Women's Development.* Cambridge, MA: Harvard University Press.

Hayes, R. L. (1991). Counseling and clinical implications of Kohlberg's developmental psychology. In L. Kuhmerker, U. Gielen, & R. L. Hayes (Eds.), *The Kohlberg Legacy for the Helping Professions* (pp. 173–187). Birmingham, AL: R.E.P.

Kegan, R. (1982). *The Evolving Self: Problem and Process in Human Development.* Cambridge: Harvard University Press.

Kohlberg, L. (1981). *The Philosophy of Moral Development: Moral Stages and the Idea of Justice* (Essays on Moral Development). San Francisco: Harper & Row.

Kohlberg, L. (1984). *The Psychology of Moral Development: The Nature and Validity of Moral Stages* (Essays on Moral Development). San Francisco: Harper & Row.

Kohlberg, L. (1994). Stage and sequence: The cognitive-developmental approach to socialization. In B. Puka (Ed.), *Defining Perspectives in Moral Development* (Vol. 1, pp. 1–134). New York: Garland.

Langdale, S. (1993). Moral development, gender identity, and peer relationships in early and middle childhood. In A. Garrod (Ed.), *Approaches to Moral Development: New Research and Emerging Themes* (pp. 30–58). New York: Teachers College Press.

Locke, D. (1986). A psychologist among the philosophers: Philosophical aspects of Kohlberg's theories. In S. Modgil & C. Modgil (Eds.), *Lawrence Kohlberg: Consensus and Controversy* (pp. 21–38). Philadelphia: Falmer.

Loevinger, J. (1986). On Kohlberg's contributions to ego development. In S. Modgil & C. Modgil (Eds.), *Lawrence Kohlberg: Consensus and Controversy* (pp. 183–193). Philadelphia: Falmer.

Puka, B. (Ed.) (1994). *Kohlberg's Original Study of Moral Development* (Vol. 3). New York: Garland.

Rest, J. (1991). Kohlberg in perspective: A backward and a forward look. In L. Kuhmerker, U. Gielen, & R. L. Hayes (Eds.), *The Kohlberg Legacy for the Helping Professions* (pp. 201–204). Birmingham, AL: R.E.P.

Thomas, R. M. (1997). *An Integrated Theory of Moral Development.* Westport, CT: Greenwood Press.

Tomlinson, P. (1986). Kohlberg's moral psychology: Any advance on the present stage? In S. Modgil & C. Modgil (Eds.), *Lawrence Kohlberg* (pp. 107–121). Philadelphia: Falmer.

5

Carl Rogers and the Person-Centered Approach

ROBERTA R. GREENE

Carl Rogers, founder of the person-centered approach, is best known for his principles on the conditions that facilitate a therapeutic relationship. The central idea in the Rogerian approach is that if the practitioner is empathetic, accepts the client with unconditional positive regard, and is genuine in his or her respect for the client, positive change will occur. This view continues to be a widely accepted, if not "obvious" aspect of helping relationships (Mitchell, 1998). A commitment to self-determination and the integral worth of the individual, as well as a recognition of the importance of social responsibility, also are central principles important in the person-centered approach that are equally compatible with social work philosophy and code of ethics (NASW, 1997; Rowe, 1986). In addition, Rogers's approach to helping, which is acknowledged almost universally, is associated with the importance of the social worker–client relationship to personality growth, change, or development.

Rogers (1959) stated:

In a wide variety of professional work involving relationships with people— whether as a psychotherapist, teacher, religious worker, guidance counselor, social worker, clinical psychologist—it is the quality of the interpersonal encounter with the client which is the most significant element in determining effectiveness (p. 85).

The nature of the helping relationship as described by Rogers is of great importance to social work practice. Many social work theorists also have viewed the relationship as the keystone of the casework process and as basic to all treatment (Hollis, 1972; Perlman, 1957a,b). For example, Biestek (1957) viewed the relationship as an integral part of the communication between client and social worker—the "soul of social casework" (p. 18).

145

while Fischer (1978) and Kadushin (1972) emphasized that the relationship is the communication bridge between people and the context for effective learning.

Another major Rogerian assumption important to social work and most schools of counseling and psychotherapy is that individuals possess vast resources for self-understanding and growth, which can be realized through a warm and caring therapeutic relationship (Raskin, 1985). This view of the therapeutic encounter grew out of an existential-humanistic philosophy. A consistent theme in Rogers and other existential writings is a deep faith in the individual worth of all human beings and in clients' potential to use help if a positive climate is provided.

> Building a warm and caring client– social worker relationship is the cornerstone of social work practice.

Exploring the mechanisms by which people construct meaning out of life's experiences and, as a result, make decisions is central to *existential philosophy*. Existentially based theorists believe everything is in the realm of possibility, and that life is a series of unfolding experiences and choices. If an individual accepts responsibility for his or her life and risks the future, meaningful growth can occur (Maddi, 1985). *Humanistic philosophy*, with its deep faith in the tendency of humans to develop in a positive manner and its emphasis on self-determination and self-actualization, which underlies Rogers' person-centered approach, has had a central influence on social work values.

The key to a person-centered approach, and also central to much of social work practice, is this optimistic perspective and belief in the client's ability to achieve self-awareness. Rogers (1980a) suggested that each client brings the same need to achieve self-awareness to the therapeutic relationship: "It seems to me that at bottom each person is asking: Who am I really? How can I get in touch with this real self, underlying all my surface behavior? How can I become myself?" (p. 357).Therefore, the goal of the helping process, according to Rogers, is to raise the level of client self-awareness so that the client can perform new and constructive responses in the everyday world (White & Watt, 1981). Through this self-actualization process—a process whereby the individual strives to develop to his or her fullest capacities—the individual (in Rogers's famous words) "becomes a person" (Rogers, 1961, p. 134).

PERSON-IN-ENVIRONMENT HISTORICAL CONTEXT OF THE ROGERIAN APPROACH

Rogers's client-centered approach strongly emphasized the person or the developing self. Although Rogers recognized the need for the environment to be supportive or conducive for self-actualizing tendencies to flourish, he did not explore this notion in depth. For the most part, Rogers did not believe in extensive history-taking in the form of a psychosocial history, nor did he champion diagnostic classification. Rather, Rogers agreed with other humanists who sought to counter Freud's pessimistic outlook on human nature. The term "the third force" has been used to describe this existential-humanistic view of human nature (Rowe, 1986; Turner & Helms, 1983).

Helping professionals grounded in existential humanism (including Rogers) turned their attention to understanding the person in the present and exploring how a client makes decisions in his or her own world. Rogers (1980b) traced his psychological insights to the philosopher Kierkegaard, who wrote during the nineteenth century that the most common despair is to be in despair about not choosing, or willing to be one's

> The Rogerian approach is based on an optimistic, positive view of human nature.

self. This despair can be addressed, and the individual's tendency toward normal growth and adjustment can be released, according to Rogers (1959), if the practitioner offers the client freedom and choice.

Rogers, once again in reaction to the directive nature of traditional approaches to psychotherapy, began by calling his therapeutic method "nondirective counseling." This label was based on the idea that the client, not the counselor, always should take the lead in the helping process. From the beginning, Rogers (1959, 1942) emphasized that the client's inherent potential for growth could be tapped if the helping person focused on the positive side of human nature.

During the 1950s, Rogers's (1951) attention shifted to the development of a theory of personality and its application in counseling. Because of this change in emphasis, he renamed his approach "client-centered therapy." During this phase in Rogers's (1957) work, he redefined his therapeutic goals. He suggested that entering a client's "internal frame of reference" to help the client examine his or her feelings was the central purpose of the helping process. Rogers thought that the client's understanding of his or her feelings led to positive behavioral change within the client's environment.

From the late 1950s to the early 1960s, Rogers and his associates conducted extensive research to test the major assumptions of the client-centered theory. Some researchers concluded that the client-centered method was most helpful for intelligent young people with "no more than mild anxiety complications" (White & Watt, 1981, p. 257). They also suggested that Rogers was valued most for his work in training counselors and psychotherapists in the conditions that facilitate the therapeutic relationship, and that many of Roger's axioms, such as respect for the client, self-determination, and the need for empathic understanding, had become the "common sense" of therapeutic relationships (White and Watt, 1981, p. 257).

Throughout the 1960s and 1970s, Rogers's (1970, 1972, 1977) interest and influence broadened. What first seemed to be a simple model became increasingly complex (Raskin, 1985). Among Rogers's widening interests were the development of personal-growth groups and work with couples and families. Rogers also applied his ideas to administration, minority groups, interracial and intercultural groups, as well as to international relations. As a result of Rogers's growing interest in how people obtain and share power and control, his method became known as the "person-centered approach."

BASIC ASSUMPTIONS AND TERMINOLOGY OF THE PERSON-CENTERED APPROACH

As a therapist who believed in the individual's inherent worth and potential for growth, Rogers (1959) assumed that individuals have within them "vast resources for self-understanding and for altering self-concepts, basic attitudes, and self-directed behavior" (p. 236). Rogers's major contribution to counseling was the idea that these inherent client resources could be tapped if the helping person provided a facilitating climate.

Empathy, unconditional regard, and congruence were proposed as the "necessary and sufficient conditions for therapeutic personality change" (Rogers, 1957, p. 99). Rogers believed that if *empathy* (recognizing a person's feelings and experiences), *unconditional positive regard* (accepting the client with warmth), and *congruence* (offering a genuine and real relationship) were provided in therapy, positive growth would occur naturally (Table 5.1).

Freedom was another important ingredient in Rogers's conceptualization. *Freedom* was "an inner thing, something which exists within the person and quite aside from any of the outside choices of alternatives which we so often think of constituting freedom" (Rogers, 1959, p. 45). The concept of freedom, the idea and feeling that one has the ability to make choices and to determine events, is central to the Rogerian therapeutic relationship (Table 5.2).

> The Rogerian approach to helping taps a person's freedom from within and releases an internal sense of well-being.

Rogers (1980b) believed that when any client first comes into a helping relationship, he or she hides behind a mask. Through the facilitating con-

Table 5.1. The Person-Centered Approach: Basic Assumptions

People are trustworthy, capable, and have a potential for self-understanding and self-actualization.

Self-actualization is a lifelong process.

People develop and grow in a positive manner if a climate of trust and respect is established.

Individual growth is promoted through therapeutic and other types of relationships.

Positive attributes of the helping person, including genuineness, acceptance, and empathetic understanding, are necessary conditions for effective helping relationships.

Respecting the subjective experiences of the client, fostering freedom and personal responsibility and autonomy, and providing options facilitate the client's growth.

The helping person is not an authority. The helping person is someone, who through his or her respect and positive regard, fosters positive growth.

Clients are capable of self-awareness and possess the ability to discover more appropriate behaviors.

Clients, as do all people, have a propensity to move away from maladjustment toward psychological health.

The practitioner should focus on the here-and-now behavior in the client–social worker relationship.

The content of the helping relationship also should emphasize how the client acts in his or her world.

Getting to know the true self is a major goal of the helping relationship.

The aim of the helping relationship is to move the client toward greater independence and integration.

ditions of the helping relationship, a client gradually becomes more and more him- or herself:

> In this attempt to discover his own self, the client typically uses the therapeutic relationship to explore, to examine the various aspects of his own experience, to recognize and face up to the deep contradictions which he often discovers. He learns how much of his behavior, even how much of the feelings he experiences, is not real, is not something that flows from the genuine

Table 5.2. The Rogerian Helping Relationship

Client	Social Work Therapist
Establishes self-trust	Values the client in a free environment
Is open to experience	Establishes a therapeutic climate
Is open to self-evaluation	Promotes the client's self-exploration
Experiences freedom to grow	Provides genuineness, positive regard, and empathy
Moves to a new self-concept	Experiences a renewed sense of caring

reaction of his organism, but is a facade, a front behind which he has been hiding. He discovers how much of his life is guided by what he thinks he *should* be, not by what he is. (p. 358)

Rogers (1980b) assumed that in the warmth and understanding of a facilitating relationship with a helping person an individual explores what is behind the mask he or she presents to the world. As the client's facade begins to crumble in the light of real experiences, the client "becomes a person" (p. 360). The person who emerges becomes more *open to experience* (seeing reality without distortions), *trusts in one's organism* (faith in one's ability to successfully weigh demands and make decisions), feels he or she is in touch with an *internal locus of evaluation* (an inner core or center that is crucial to the process of self-analysis and standard setting), and is more satisfied to be engaged in a *process of becoming* (a lifelong process of self-actualization).

> Mr. B., 45 years of age, was a hospice patient dying of lung cancer. He had a long history of drug abuse and was HIV positive. Mr. B. was divorced from his first wife and had one son, Jim, 22, by that marriage. Jim was an inmate in a local state prison.
>
> During the last days of Mr. B.'s life, he asked to see his son one last time to say good-bye. Wishing to assist her client with his request, the hospice social worker discussed the request with the prison chaplain. The hospice social worker was informed that, according to prison policy, Jim's family needed to make the request. The social worker located Jim's mother who was willing to ask for Jim to be allowed to visit his father. The visit then was arranged through the warden's office.
>
> One day later, Jim arrived on the hospice unit, manacled and accompanied by armed guards. The social worker arranged for the handcuffs to be removed, and "introduced" Jim to his father by saying "I know this must be a difficult time for both of you." Mr. B. enjoyed a two hour visit with Jim who tenderly fed his father, reminisced with him about past events, and finally said good-bye. (Sandra Fink, LCSW, Family Consultant, Stella Maris Hospice Care Program, Baltimore, Maryland)

The person who emerges from a helping relationship, according to the Rogerian tradition, is "open to what exists at this moment in this situation" (Rogers, 1980b, p. 361). For an individual who is open to experience, defensiveness and rigidity are replaced by an *organismic*, or self-evaluating, process. A greater awareness of reality as it exists outside oneself emerges. The individual who emerges from the helping relationship "increasingly discovers that his own organism is trustworthy" (Rogers, 1980a, p. 362). The feeling that one has an ability to be self-governing, to make conscious choices, and to balance demands is the feeling of being trustworthy. This characteristic goes hand in hand with being open to experiences that provide the data or information on which to base behavior.

The person who emerges from a positive helping relationship increasingly comes to recognize that the locus of evaluation lies within him- or herself rather than within others (Rogers & Stevens, 1967). This client posture allows the individual to be the source or locus of choices and decisions and of evaluating judgments. The person who emerges from counseling asks, "Am I living in a way that is deeply satisfying to me and that truly expresses me?"

Rogers (1980a) stated that the process of becoming a person does not end with counseling. The process of becoming is lifelong. Through the helping process, clients learn that goals are not static and that they may continue to grow and experience:

> The whole train of experiencing, and the meanings that I have so far discovered in it, seemed to have launched me on a process which is both fascinating and at times a little frightening. It seems to mean letting my experience carry me on, in a direction which appears to be forward, toward goals that I can but dimly define, as I try to understand at least the current meaning of that experience. The sensation is that of floating with a complex stream of experience, with the fascinating possibility of trying to comprehend its ever-changing complexity. (p. 364)

EXPLAINING DEVELOPMENT ACROSS THE LIFE CYCLE

Humanistic theorists such as Rogers place great importance on an individual being's uniqueness, his or her potential and inner drive. The study of personality development from a humanistic perspective centers around the emergence of an individual's self-concept and his or her ability to maximize potential. Self-theories of personality that tend to reject both the instinctual and dynamic concepts of the psychoanalytic school sometimes are called "phenomenological" or "self-actualizing" theories. *Phenomenological theories* stress that the individual's perception of him-or herself and of life events provides the framework for understanding personality development. The phenomenological orientation considers the individual to be the source of all acts, believes that behavior is the only observable expression of the internal world, suggests that science begin with the study of peoples' experiences, and that people are free to make choices in each situation. In addition, knowledge of the individual's reaction to the environment based on a personal interpretation of events is the key.

Rogers (1961) described the *self* as that aspect of the person that "is consulted in order to understand himself" (p. 113). As such, the self-concept is related to *self-evaluation* (self-approval and self-disapproval) and to personal adjustment. The *self*, according to Rogers (1961), is an

> organized, consistent conceptual gestalt composed of perceptions of the relationships of the "I" or "me" and the perceptions of the relationships of the "I" or "me" to others and to various aspects of life, together with the values attached to these perceptions (p. 200).

Roger's (1961) theory of personality development focuses on the phenomenal self. The *phenomenal self is* the image of the self that each person perceives in his or her own unique way. The picture an individual has of his or her phenomenal self does not necessarily correspond to some external reality. According to Rogers (1961), well-adjusted people are those who have a more accurate perception of how they truly act, think, and experience. Maladjusted individuals, on the other hand, have a greater discrepancy between their self-image and reality, which may lead to higher levels of anxiety (Goldberg & Deutsch, 1977). It is these contradictions between self-image and reality that are addressed in the helping process.

Rogers (1959) went on to use his research on client-centered therapy to develop a theoretical statement about the nature of personality and behavioral change. The way in which an individual experiences his or her world and the respect shown the developing individual are at the core of Rogers's theoretical approach. Rogers

> Rogers believed that because each person has the potential for growth, the practitioner can contribute to a client's self-development.

(1983) believed that an infant possesses an *internal locus of evaluation*, knowing what he or she likes without parental influence. Because the infant is free to value things as he or she wishes, the infant's *organismic valuing processes*, or trust in one's own feelings or emotions, are flexible and open. As the child develops, he or she receives evaluations from the outside world and thereby gradually undergoes a transformation of organismic valuing processes. The child learns to evaluate him- or herself according to what parents, teachers, and finally employers and others in authority think of him or her (Raskin, 1985).

In some instances, this external evaluation process stifles the person's ability to self-actualize or grow. According to Rogers (1959), negative conditions of worth placed by others on an individual can lead to severe psychopathology, involving psychological defenses of denial and distortion:

> The continuing estrangement between self-concept and experiences leads to increasingly rigid perceptions and behavior. If experiences are extremely in-

congruent with the self-concept, the defense system will be inadequate to prevent the experiences from intruding into and overwhelming the self-concept. When this happens the self-concept will break down, resulting in disorganized behavior. (Holdstock & Rogers, 1977, p. 136)

The aim of a Rogerian helping relationship is to provide the facilitating conditions to stimulate the client's exploration and feeling of regard for his or her own world of experience. In this manner, the client has a renewed and heightened sense of his or her self-valuing processes. The individual who is able to move to a position of positive self-regard is characterized by an internal locus of evaluation, is flexible and highly differentiated, and takes into account varied past and present experiences. The goal of the clinical social work relationship from a Rogerian perspective is to promote this self-actualizing process. Rogers based his therapeutic approach on the humanist belief that people are born with a tendency to self-actualize. The belief in the individual's capacity to self-actualize rests on the assumption that all individuals have a healthy drive to attain full development of their potentials, capacities, and talents.

Maslow (1959), a humanist psychologist who is best known for his pyramidal hierarchy of needs—physiological needs, safety, belonging and love, esteem, and self-actualization—found that the tendency to attain a unique sense of self was more profound among individuals who accepted self and others, were spontaneous, possessed strong problem-solving ability, could function autonomously, and appreciated their environment. Maslow attributed personality differences to the manner in which the individual fulfilled his or her self-actualizing potential.

Rogers proposed that the process of self-actualization involved an *organismic valuing process.* Each experience that was perceived as leading toward self-fulfillment was valued positively. Each experience perceived as threatening was evaluated negatively. Rogers suggested that the individual's tendency to self-actualize enabled him or her to make the most of an accepting therapeutic relationship, using it successfully to overcome obstacles to growth.

UNDERSTANDING CULTURAL DIFFERENCES: CROSS-CULTURAL SOCIAL WORK PRACTICE

Because existential philosophy as expressed in Rogerian practitioners places a high value on the personal meaning of a client's experiences, it has several features that make it well suited for cross-cultural social work practice. Rogerian practitioners emphasize the importance of understanding a client's personal systems of meanings and clarifying the nature of change a client is seeking. Goal formulation is an outgrowth of a mutual agreement between client and practitioner. Seeing the client as someone who has the power of free choice gives the client a sense of empowerment that is critical in cross-cultural practice. In addition, "the existential therapist's attitude affirms the inherent value of the client as a unique person with a very special worldview or life-style that is hers alone to charter" (Krill, 1987, p. 518). Furthermore, researchers have often concluded that person-centered therapy is successful when clients perceive their therapists as conveying empathy, congruence, and unconditional regard (Krill, 1987; Raskin, 1985).

Nonetheless, there may be occasions when the practitioner wants to question when his or her comments will be perceived as empathetic (Gibbs, 1985; Greene, 1994; Miller & Stiver, 1991). Gibbs (1985) reminded social workers that achieving empathy in the interview becomes difficult when the practitioner assumes that all people are the same. She cautioned that specified social worker behaviors do not necessarily transmit universal messages with predictable and specified interpretations. On the other hand, Pinderhughes (1979) contended that power differences related to gender, social class, age, ethnicity, and so forth can be overcome if the practitioner imparts genuine empathy.

Rogers (1980b) himself gradually came to realize the "terrific political threat posed by the person-centered approach" (p. 304). In *A Way of Being*, he discussed the idea of "giving away power" as it related to the use of the person-centered approach in education. To make his point that therapists and educators are facilitators who provide a psychological climate in which the learner is able to take responsible control, he tells of a teacher who was fired for refusing to grade on a curve. Rogers's premise was that the teacher who refused to fail a certain percentage of students, no matter how well they accepted their responsibility to learn, became a "political threat" because the teacher bucked the establishment (p. 304).

UNDERSTANDING HOW HUMANS FUNCTION
AS MEMBERS OF FAMILIES, GROUPS,
AND COMMUNITIES

Families

Client-centered therapy has had an important influence on family-centered practice. As early as 1939, Rogers advocated the inclusion of the entire family in work with children. During the late 1950s, through the influence of Rogers and other colleagues, counselors were teaching parents client-centered therapy principles. Rogers also extended his concepts to include married couples. In his book *Becoming Partners,* Rogers (1972) addressed the idea that there was no longer a single, rigid model of the right kind of marriage. He expressed the view that it was important to establish relationships that optimized personal satisfaction and growth for each individual. He stressed the idea that if a couple were willing to strive to develop intimacy and to communicate feelings, they were more likely to grow as individuals and as a couple.

Groups

Rogers, who saw the group as a vehicle for growth-promoting interpersonal communication, was an important influence in the development of encounter groups. The encounter group movement can be traced to Rogers and Lewin, who viewed group experiences as opportunities for personal growth and attitudinal change (Rowe, 1986). Many of the same principles that Rogers espoused in person-centered therapy, such as the need for a climate of safety and mutual trust and the expression of feelings, were followed in various kinds of group experiences. Rogers (1970) believed in the power of the group to provide a positive, growth-producing experience. He proposed that participation in a T group offered a sensitive ability to hear, a deep satisfaction in being heard, an ability to be more real, which in turn brings forth more realism from others, and consequently, a greater freedom to give and receive love (p. 26).

Communities

Person-centered theory also found its way into community development work. Largely through training experiences for participants and the development of conflict resolution techniques, Rowe (1986) noted that experiments using Rogerian principles have been used in "a wide variety of neighborhoods, cultures, religions, and political situations . . . and are most clearly aligned with the principles of locality development" (p. 424). Though from time to time social change advocates have questioned the use of all therapeutic models because of their potential deflection of energies into a search for inner peace that might otherwise have found expression in political and social action, many Rogerians—and Rogers himself—have objected to such a dichotomy. Rather, they have argued, effective social action requires the kind of energized view of one's self and one's potentials, which they help to bring about in the people with whom they work.

DIRECT PRACTICE IN SOCIAL WORK: INTERVENING
IN THE PERSON-SITUATION TO ENHANCE
PSYCHOSOCIAL FUNCTIONING

The philosophy of the person-centered approach to helping suggests that each client is unique and has the capacity for self-actualization. Providing an atmosphere of safety and freedom in which a client can experience true feelings and discover elements of his or her true self is the essence of the person-centered approach. The person-centered approach focuses on how positive growth that occurs within the warmth and understanding of the clinical social work relationship can be transferred into a more full and authentic daily life.

Corey (1986) suggested that the practitioner's role in the Rogerian approach is "to be without roles" (p. 105). Rogerians center on here-and-now experiences that grow out of the client-practitioner relationship. Specific outcomes are not proposed. Acquiring clinically significant information, therefore, is not necessarily the social worker's goal. Rather, the process by which personality change occurs is of interest. The issue is not on the presenting problem per se, but the growth processes that will help the client to cope better with problems. The aim is to engage the client in the valuing process within the helping relationship to assist the client in achieving a greater degree of independence and integration. In this manner, self-evaluation is stimulated and growth occurs.

A process conception of clinical social work involves helping the client to view a problem differently, to accept one's own feelings, to modify cognitive experiences, to recognize life's contradictions, and to modify the nature of relationships. Clients who go through this process, and come to know themselves better, discover more appropriate behaviors. Personality change is evidenced in a shift from negative to positive client attitudes and feelings, and a shift from valuing evaluation by others to self-evaluation. The development of insight, an openness to new experiences, a greater willingness to take a change, an ability to take responsibility for oneself, and an understanding of the consequences of behavior are among other indications of client change (Raskin, 1985).

> The Rogerian practitioner supports the client's natural growth process and ability to self-actualize.

The Rogerian approach to clinical social work does not focus on specific interventions. Rather, the practitioner enters into an egalitarian relationship with the client to facilitate a freeing and unfolding of potential (Raskin, 1985). Letting a client know that the relationship is safe, showing respect, and offering choices are necessary therapeutic conditions for personality growth to occur. Freedom within the helping relationship permits the client to explore "areas of their life that are now either denied to awareness or distorted" (Corey, 1986, p. 105). Empathy, unconditional regard, and congruence are among the key facilitating conditions, strategies, and techniques.

Necessary, Facilitating Therapeutic Conditions

Rogers (1957) hypothesized that "significant personality change does not occur except in a relationship" (p. 98). He considered that empathy, unconditional regard, and congruence were the "necessary and sufficient conditions of therapeutic personality change." From this perspective, the social worker's "total" function is to provide a therapeutic climate that facilitates growth. *Empathy,* a primary therapeutic condition in the person-centered approach, is the recognition of the client's feelings and an appreciation of what he or she is experiencing. Empathy is the practitioner's capacity to feel with the client and the ability to communicate this understanding. The social worker who understands the client's world view and perceptions focuses on both verbal and nonverbal cues, which enables the practitioner to better understand both manifest and latent content and to respond appropriately to the client's meanings.

Empathy enables the practitioner to enter the client's world through his or her own imagination while retaining an objective perspective. The ability to perceive clients accurately and realistically in the ongoing helping process is critical to the integrity of the therapeutic relationship (Greene, 1986). Empathy, which furthers exploration and expression of feelings, "capture[s] exactly what the client is consciously feeling and wishing to communicate, evoking in the client a reaction of "'Yes, that's exactly it!'" (Raskin, 1985, p. 165). The helping person practicing in the Rogerian tradition does more than encourage a client to talk. Clients are helped to express themselves through the social worker's skillful mirroring of feelings. As Shulman (1984) stated, reaching for feelings requires the social worker to step into "the client's shoes and . . . summon an affective response which comes as close as possible to the experience of the other" (p. 67).

A second therapeutic condition of a Rogerian helping relationship is unconditional positive regard, or "nonpossessive warmth" (Rogers, 1957). Rogers (1967) described a practitioner who exhibited unconditional regard as making "no attempt to force conclusions upon the client" and giving the client the "fullest opportunity to express feelings" (p. 240). The social worker who demonstrates nonpossessive warmth accepts and cares about the client in a nurturing but nonpatronizing and nondominating way. Although unconditional regard calls for a nonblaming, nonjudgmental attitude, it does not mean that a social worker condones antisocial or self-destructive acts. A caring approach allows the client to feel respect and to experience him- or herself as a person of worth (Greene, 1986).

The third facilitating therapeutic condition is congruence. *Congruence* is used to "refer to the correspondence between a person's view of self-as-is and self-as-ideal" (Raskin, 1985, p. 170). The goal of a person-centered helping relationship is to achieve a greater congruence between the client's self-evaluation and his or her evaluation by others. Congruence on the part of the social worker refers to genuineness. Genuineness or authenticity in the helping relationship also refers to the social worker's capacity to be open. The social worker who demonstrates genuineness is able and willing to acknowledge his or her own feelings about the client. For example, the genuine practitioner would be able to ask questions that reveal that he or she may not fully understand what a client has said or may share a significant, personal conviction (Raskin, 1985).

Although being genuine implies that social workers be themselves, it does not mean they should disclose their "total" self to the client, nor does it mean that the practitioner loses his or her objectivity. What is involved in being genuine is the development of sufficient self-awareness on the part of practitioners to use constructively their own genuine responses. "The need for achieving professional objectivity through self-management is essential. If the social worker is too involved with his or her feelings, he/she will not be in a position to perceive the client with clarity" (Greene, 1986, p. 41).

If the practitioner provides the necessary and sufficient conditions for change, then, according to Rogers (1961), the other person in the relationship

- will experience and understand aspects of himself or herself that previously have been repressed
- will become better integrated, more able to function effectively
- will become more similar to the person he or she would like to be
- will be more self-directing and self-confident
- will become more of a person, more unique, and more self-expressive
- will become more understanding and more accepting of others
- will be able to cope with the problems of life more adequately and more comfortably. (p. 38)

The Social Worker's Role

Attitude is the central element in the Rogerian practitioner's role. It is critical that the social worker convey a strong interest in the client and in the significance of the client's feelings and experiences. Consistent and respectful treatment of the client is paramount in promoting growth and self-actualization. Rogers (1961) suggested that the following ten questions will assist the therapist in thinking about his or her effectiveness:

1.   Can I be perceived by the other person as trustworthy, as dependable or consistent in some deep sense?

2.   Can I be expressive enough as a person that what I am will be communicated unambiguously?

3.   Can I let myself experience positive attitudes toward this other person—attitudes of warmth, caring, liking, interest, respect?

4.   Can I be strong enough as a person to be separate from the other?

5.   Am I secure enough within myself to permit him [or her] separateness?

6.   Can I let myself enter fully into the world of [the others] feelings and personal meanings and see these as he [or she] does?

7.   Can I accept each facet of this other person which is presented to me? Can I receive [the other] as he [or she] is?

8.   Can I act with sufficient sensitivity in the relationship that my behavior will not be perceived as a threat?

9.   Can I free [the other] from the threat of external evaluation?

10.   Can I meet this other individual as a person who is in process of *becoming,* or will I be bound by [the others] past and by my past? (pp. 50–55)

The following case study between Rogers and a client illustrates Rogers's expertise and the role of the Rogerian-based practitioner. The case study was transcribed from an American Academy of Psychotherapists Tape Library (from Raskin, 1985):

Client:	Take me, for instance, how would you go about . . . like I don't have a goal, like I told you awhile ago. How do you go about helping me find one?
Social worker:	Well, let's talk about it a bit. You say you have no goal.
Client:	No, sir.
Therapist:	None whatsoever.
Client:	Not even one.
Therapist:	There isn't anything you want to do.
Client:	Oh, yeah, I want to keep on living.
Therapist:	Oh?
Client:	That's a goal.
Therapist:	M-hm.
Client:	But otherwise, for picking a career I have none whatsoever.
Therapist:	But you do want to keep on living.
Client:	Yeah, who doesn't?
Therapist:	You feel everybody wants to keep on living.
Client:	No, I don't feel that way, I know quite a few that don't.
Therapist:	OK, so do I. So I'm interested, you say, but for you that is one thing, life somehow in some way or another seems worth living. Is that what you are saying?
Client:	Yes, sir.

Therapist:	It somehow has enough possibilities that give it a chance anyway, or something like that.
Client:	Yes, sir. Uh, if a person didn't want to go on living and had no goal, then that would be a sign of mental trouble, wouldn't it?
Therapist:	Well, it sure would be a sign he wasn't very happy. I don't really go very much for this business of mental trouble, and so on. What I mean is, to me a person seems to be a person, and sure, some of them are doing very well and some of them are very unhappy, and so on, but . . .
Client:	Well, how would you go about getting a person to want to, say, have a brighter outlook on life?
Therapist:	Are you . . . the way I get that is that you are partly asking that for yourself: "How could I have a somewhat brighter outlook on life?"
Client:	Well, my outlook on life isn't dim, but it's not the shiniest thing in the world either.
Therapist:	It's about 15-watt maybe, or something like that?
Client:	Well, maybe 75.
Therapist:	Oh, 75? But you wish it were a brighter outlook on life. In what sense is it dim? Can you tell me?
Client:	Well, uh . . . family.
Therapist:	Family? I don't know whether you would be willing to tell me about that, but I would be very willing to listen.
Client:	It's just the same old story. Mothers and fathers try to tell the kids what to do, and the kids revolt. So, that's the only thing right now, that's between my parents and me.
Therapist:	So I guess you are saying, this is true in general, but it's also true of you, that your parents try to tell you what to do and you feel, "I won't take that."
Client:	Well, I don't feel it. I say it. Of course, what I say and what I do are two different things though.
Therapist:	Uh, huh. I am not quite clear there. You say, you say it but you don't really feel it?
Client:	Well, let's put it this way: If my mother tells me what to do, and whether I like it or not, I have to do it. But, boy, I let her know that I'm not too happy about having to do it, either.
Therapist:	Uh, huh. Are you saying there, "She may be able to make me behave in certain ways or do certain things, but she can't control the way I feel and I let her know how I feel."
Client:	That's exactly it. And about twice . . . after about two times of it straight in a row, I think she usually gives in to save the mess and bother of breaking them dishes and stuff like that.
Therapist:	So that, what you are saying, that when you sort of stand up on your hind legs strong enough a couple of times in a row, then no matter what she thinks she kind of gives in to save the broken dishes.

Client:	Well, not the broken dishes. Just she sees she's gone a little too far.
Therapist:	Ah.
Client:	You see I have a stepfather.
Therapist:	I see.
Client:	Let's put it this way: My stepfather and I are not on the happiest terms in the world. And so, when he states something and, of course, she goes along, and I stand up and let her know that I don't like what he is telling me, well, she usually gives in to me.
Therapist:	I see.
Client:	Sometimes, and sometimes it's just the opposite.
Therapist:	But part of what really makes for difficulty is the fact that you and your stepfather, as you say, are not . . . the relationship isn't completely rosy.
Client:	Let's just put it this way, I hate him and he hates me. It's that way.
Therapist:	But you really hate him and you feel he really hates you.
Client:	Well, I don't know if he hates me or not, but I know one thing, I don't like him whatsoever.
Therapist:	You can't speak for sure about his feelings because only he knows exactly what those are, but as far as you are concerned . . .
Client:	. . . he knows how I feel about it.
Therapist:	You don't have any use for him.
Client:	None whatsoever. And that's been for about eight years now.
Therapist:	So for about eight years you've lived with a person whom you have no respect for and really hate.
Client:	Oh, I respect him.
Therapist:	Ah . . . Excuse me. I got that wrong.
Client:	I have to respect him. I don't have to but I do. But I don't love him. I hate him. I can't stand him.
Therapist:	There are certain things you respect him for, but that doesn't alter the fact that you definitely hate him and don't love him.
Client:	That's the truth. I respect anybody who has bravery and courage, and he does.
Therapist:	I see.
Client:	And I still, uh, though I respect him, I don't like him.
Therapist:	But you do give him credit for the fact that he is brave, he has guts or something.
Client:	Yeah. He shows that he can do a lot of things that, well, a lot of men can't.
Therapist:	M-hm. M-hm.
Client:	And also he has asthma, and the doctor hasn't given him very long to live. And he, even though he knows he is going to die, he keeps working and he works at a killing pace, so I respect him for that, too.

Table 5.3.   Guidelines for the Social Worker Practicing in the Rogerian Tradition

Examine your own belief system. Review your attitudes about the self-worth of
each individual and his or her potential to use the helping relationship
effectively.
Deliberate about whether you have the capacity and are able to promote an
atmosphere of warmth and trust within the helping relationship.
Involve the client in a therapeutic relationship in which he or she takes the lead
in describing his or her experiences and in expressing feelings.
Show respect for the subjective experiences of the client by echoing his or her
concerns accurately.
Focus on the here-and-now experiences within the interview. Develop a process
in which the client can learn that he or she can trust his or her own
experiences.
Use interviewing techniques that express genuineness, empathy, and congruence.
Accept and interpret the client's life experiences that may stand in the way of his
or her positive self-evaluation.
View the helping relationship as an opportunity to facilitate growth (for both
client and therapist) and promote self-evaluation.

Therapist:	M-hm. So I guess you're saying he really has . . .
Client:	. . . what it takes.
Therapist:	quite a few, yeah, he has what it takes in quite a few ways. He has a number of good qualities. But that doesn't mean that you care for him at all. Quite the reverse.
Client:	That is the truth. The only reason I put up with him being around is because for my mother's sake.
Therapist:	M-hm, m-hm.

Epitomizing a process conception of psychotherapy, the above dialogue
illustrates the effectiveness of Rogers's (1957) belief that "the client experiencing himself as being" (p. 363) is "the most precious gift one can give to
another" (Rogers, 1975, p. 10) (Table 5.3).

REFERENCES

Biestek, F. B. (1957). *The Casework Relationship*. Chicago: Loyola University.
Corey, G. (1986). *Theory and Practice of Counseling and Psychotherapy*. Monterey, CA:
Brooks/Cole.
Fischer, J. (1978). *Effective Casework Practice: An Eclectic Approach*. New York: Mc-
Graw-Hill.
Gibbs, J. T. (1985). Treatment relationships with black clients: Interpersonal instru-
mental strategies. In C. B. Germain (Ed.), *Advances in Clinical Social Work Prac-
tice* (pp. 179–190). Silver Spring, MD: National Association of Social Workers.
Goldberg, S. R., & Deutsch, F. (1977). *Life-Span Individual and Family Development*.
Monterey, CA: Brooks/Cole.

Greene, R. (1986). *Social Work with the Aged and Their Families.* Hawthorne, NY: Aldine de Gruyter.

Greene, R. (1994) *Human Behavior Theory: A Diversity Framework.* Hawthorne, NY: Aldine de Gruyter.

Holdstock, T. L., & Rogers, C. R. (1977). Person-centered theory. In R. J. Corsini (Ed.), *Current Personality Theories.* Itasca, IL: Peacock.

Hollis, F. (1972). *Casework: A Psychosocial Therapy* (rev. ed.). New York: Random House.

Kadushin, A. (1972). *A Social Work Interview.* New York: Columbia University Press.

Krill, D. (1987). Existential approach. In A. Minahan (Editor-in-Chief), *Encyclopedia of Social Work* (Vol. 1, 18th ed., pp. 517–519). Silver Spring, MD: National Association of Social Workers.

Maddis, S. (1985). Existential psychotherapy. In S. J. Lynn & J. P. Garske (Eds.), *Contemporary Psychotherapies Models and Methods* (pp. 191–220). Columbus: Charles E. Merrill.

Maslow, A. H. (1959). Creativity in self-actualizing people. In H. H. Anderson (Ed.), *Creativity and Its Cultivation.* New York: Harper & Row.

Miller, J. B., & Stiver, I. P. (1991). A relational reframing of therapy work in progress. No. 52, The Stone Center, Wellesley College, Wellesley, MA.

Mitchell, C. G. (1998). Perceptions of empathy and client satisfaction with managed behavioral health care. *Social Work, 43*(5), 404–412.

National Association of Social Workers (1997). *National Association of Social Workers Code of Ethics.* Washington, DC: Author.

Perlman, H. H. (1957a). Freud's contribution to social work. *Social Service Review, 31*, 192–202.

Perlman, H. H. (1957b). *Social Casework: A Problem-Solving Process.* Chicago: University of Chicago Press.

Pinderhughes, E. B. (1979). Teaching empathy in cross cultural social work. *Social Work, 24*(4), 312–316.

Raskin, N. (1985). Client-centered therapy. In S. J. Lynn & J. P. Garske (Eds.), *Contemporary Psychotherapies Models and Methods* (pp. 155–190). Columbus: Charles E. Merrill.

Rogers, C. R. (1942). Counseling and psychotherapy. Boston: Houghton Mifflin.

Rogers, C. R. (1951). *Client-Centered Therapy.* Boston: Houghton Mifflin.

Rogers, C. R. (1957). The necessary and sufficient conditions of therapeutic personality change. *Journal of Consulting Psychology, 21*, 95–103.

Rogers, C. R. (1959). A theory of personality and interpersonal relationships as developed in the client-centered framework." In S. Koch (Ed.), *Psychology: A Study of Science. Formulations of the Person and the Social Context* (Vol. 3, pp. 184–256). New York: McGraw-Hill.

Rogers, C. R. (1961). *On Becoming a Person.* Boston: Houghton Mifflin.

Rogers, C. R. (1970). *On Encounter Groups.* New York: Harper & Row.

Rogers, C. R. (1972). *Becoming Partners: Marriage and Its Alternatives.* New York: Delacorte.

Rogers, C. R. (1975). Empathetic: An unappreciated way of being. *Counseling Psychologist, 5*(2), 2–10.

Rogers, C. R. (1977). *Carl Rogers on Personal Power: Inner Strength and Its Revolutionary Impact.* New York: Delacorte.

Rogers, C. R. (1980a). What it means to become a person. In A. Arkoff (Ed.), *Psychology and Personal Growth* (pp. 357–365). Boston: Allyn & Bacon.

Rogers, C. R. (1980b). *A Way of Being.* Boston: Houghton Mifflin.

Rogers, C. R. (1983). *Freedom to Learn in the 80s.* Columbus, OH: Merrill.

Rogers, C. R., & Stevens, B. (1967). *Person to Person: The Problem of Being Human.* New York: Pocket Books.

Rowe, W. (1986). Client-centered theory. In F. J. Turner (Ed.), *Social Work Treatment* (pp. 407–431.) New York: Free Press.

Shulman, L. (1984). *The Skills of Helping: Individuals and Groups.* Itasca, IL: Peacock.

Turner, J. S., & Helms, D. B. (1983). *Life-Span Development.* New York: Holt, Rinehart & Winston.

White, R. W., & Watt, N. F. (1981). *The Abnormal Personality.* New York: Wiley.

GLOSSARY

Acceptance.   Truly felt warmth and genuine caring.

Accurate empathic understanding.   The ability or capacity to deal sensitively and accurately with the client's feelings and or experiences.

Congruence.   The correspondence between the client's self-as-is and the self-as ideal. Congruence also refers to genuineness and authenticity on the part of the social worker.

Existential philosophy.   A philosophy that views life as a series of choices, and examines the way in which people construct meaning out of life's experiences.

Experiencing.   A critical aspect of the therapeutic situation that involves a process of receiving and expressing feelings and trust in one's self.

Genuineness.   The practitioner's capacity to be open with the client.

Humanism.   A philosophical school that places emphasis on peoples' inherent tendency to develop in a positive manner.

Ideal self.   The way an individual would like to view him- or herself.

Internal locus of evaluation.   A process of self-evaluation that allows an individual to live up to his or her own standards.

Organismic valuing process.   The tendency to value positively each experience that is perceived as leading toward self-fulfillment. Each experience that threatens self-actualization is valued negatively.

Phenomenal self.   The image of the self that each person perceives in his or her own unique way.

Phenomenological approach. A philosophy of human nature that suggests that individuals structure their lives according to their perceptions of reality.

Relationship. The interactional and emotional bond between the client and the social worker and an integral part of the communication process.

Self-actualization. An inherent tendency or disposition to develop one's capacities in such a way as to maintain and promote growth.

Self-concept. That part of the person's personality that is involved with self-evaluation and self-approval.

Self-determination. The right of the client to make his or her own choices.

Self-evaluation. A process of learning to trust one's own experiences.

Unconditional positive regard. A deep and genuine caring for the client. Such regard means that the social worker is not judgmental about the client's feelings.

Warmth. The social worker's acceptance of the client as an individual.

CRITIQUE

Carl Rogers and the Person-Centered Approach
Social Work Applications Now and for the Future

JUDITH S. LEWIS

The work of Carl Rogers, founder of the person-centered approach to counseling, has had such a major influence on social work practice that his principles and tenets could be viewed as almost synonymous with our own professional standards (Greene & Ephross, 1991). Although Rogers's work and theory of counseling are typically included in social work human behavior and practice courses only as one of many theoretical frameworks for social work practice and thought, his basic assumptions and guidelines for practitioners continue to permeate social work practice and education. For example, social work belief in the intrinsic value of all humans, empathy, and the paramount importance of the social worker–client relationship in fostering positive growth are so basic to social workers' practice and training that we often take them for granted, not thinking about their origins or development, or associating them explicitly with Carl Rogers. However, with the renewed resurgence of a social justice and social change mission in the profession and a focus on macropractice methods such as community development and cause advocacy, one might wonder about the current applicability of a model that has the therapeutic relationship as its primary focus.

This critique examines the Rogerian approach to practice and how it is reflected in a sample of current social work literature. It discusses what promise there is in Rogers's approach for the future of social work practice as it changes in response to myriad social, political, and professional influences and demands. Using Rogers's basic assumptions and guidelines as a lens, four themes in current social work literature are considered: (1) generalist practice with eclectic choice of practice models, (2) the strengths perspective and empowerment, (3) refinement of the ecological perspective, and (4) feminist practice.

GENERALIST PRACTICE

Social workers today are faced with a mind-boggling array of theoretical perspectives and practice models to inform their work (Dorfman, 1988; Turner, 1986; Zastrow, 1992). Their multiple roles and foci in practice settings require creativity and flexibility in thought and action (Pinderhughes, 1995). Criteria for selection of appropriate and relevant practice models are helpful to practitioners. Guidelines for theory selection in social work generalist practice found in the literature include many criteria suggestive of Rogerian principles. For example, client collaboration at each step of the helping process, reciprocity in the social worker–client relationship, and interventions that reflect the client's understanding of the situation are all part of the basic assumptions of the person-centered approach (Compton & Galaway, 1994; Pinderhughes, 1995).

Rogerian principles also can be found among the resurgent phenomenological approaches such as constructivist theory (Fisher, 1991), narrative theory (Laird, 1993), and feminist theory (Gutierrez, 1990). In those approaches, the concept of reality is based on context and meaning for both client and social worker rather than on some form of objective discovery (Blundo, Greene, & Gallant, 1994).

Strengths Perspective

The strengths perspective and empowerment have been major themes in the recent social work literature that also contain clear elements of the person-centered approach (Gutierrez, 1990; Lee, 1994; Saleebey, 1992; Simon, 1994). Particularly relevant is Rogers's emphasis on the client as an active participant, on respecting client's subjective experiences, and not presenting oneself as the expert.

Respect for the client's view and an openness to learn about the client's perspective are basic requirements of a strengths perspective, especially when practice is with members of oppressed groups. According to Pinderhughes (cited in Greene, 1994), empathy, a core Rogerian principle and technique, is the "key ingredient that neutralizes the client's powerlessness" (p. 43). A Rogerian approach is consistent with Saleebey's (1992) description of process as true engagement with clients and their world that requires social workers to make continuing adjustments and to be responsive and alert. "The idea of empowerment is to help people gain (and regain) control and influence over the course of their daily lives, to tap into the inherent resources, knowledge and interests they have, and to help them enhance those and develop other resources" (Saleebey, 1992, p. 177).

168 Judith S. Lewis

Ecological Perspective

The recent social work literature confirms that much work continues on the refinement and expansion of the ecological and the person-in-environment perspective (Germain & Gitterman, 1995; National Association of Social Workers, 1997). Social systems theory has been a part of social work education for more than twenty years and is part of the context for most, if not all of our practice models (Pinderhughes, 1995). An ongoing task for social work is articulating our understanding of environmental systems and how to negotiate them and intervene in them with clients in a way that they can experience as empowering. Part of this process involves clarifying the relationships between skills used in work with individuals and small groups and those needed in the context of larger systems change (Swenson, 1998).

"Although Rogers recognized the need for the environment to be supportive or conducive for self actualizing tendencies to flourish, he did not explore this notion in depth" (Greene, 1991, p. 106). His major emphasis was on practice in the therapeutic context rather than in the arena of broader systems change (Bozarth, 1997). Nevertheless, many principles of his approach seem applicable to human interaction and helping relationships even at the level of environmental intervention. Respect for all persons and belief in their potential for positive growth again seems to be common sense in practice, whether it is in cause advocacy work or the therapeutic practice context.

Feminist Social Work Practice

Feminist social work practice is another theme in the literature in which perhaps the most obvious comparisons can be drawn with the work of Carl Rogers. As social work practice with women has evolved from concerns about sexism and women's issues to the development of models for feminist practice based on feminist theory and scholarship, the similarities between the two seem even clearer than they might have a decade ago (Bricker-Jenkins & Lockett, 1995). Although feminist practice has a political agenda not present in Rogers's work, one cannot help but be struck by the common language appearing in the assumptions of the two approaches. For example, in feminist practice, the social worker places great emphasis on believing the client's story; focusing on the client's meanings, words, and events; and establishing a collaborative relationship with the client as a partner in the helping process (Bricker-Jenkins & Lockett, 1995).

Another basic common belief shared with the person-centered approach is self-actualization as a goal of human existence and a belief in the ability of people to grow and develop given a supportive environment (Miller, Jordan, Kaplan, & Stiver, 1997). Unlike Rogers, however, feminist practice does speak specifically to environmental influences: "The purpose of social work practice is to support collective self-actualization. Given structural and ideological barriers to self-actualization, practice must address itself explicitly to them. All practice is inherently political in consequence; feminist practice is explicitly political in intent" (Bricker-Jenkins & Lockett, 1995).

Although the person-centered approach and Carl Rogers's work does not appear to any great extent in current social work literature, there are theorists and scholars in related disciplines, particularly psychology, whose work contributes to a further elaboration of the Rogerian approach to therapy (Bohart & Greenberg, 1997; Farber & Brink, 1996; Sundararajan, 1995). Sundararajan (1995) analyzed the therapeutic potential of Rogerian reflective listening and viewed it as a significant therapeutic approach rather than a practice technique. Farber and Brink (1996) provided in-depth commentaries of case studies from Rogers's own practice. Notable among feminist theorists is the work of scholars and therapists at the Stone Center for Research on Women at Wellesley College in Massachusetts (Jordan, 1997; Jordan, Kaplan, Miller, Stiver, & Surrey, 1991; Miller & Stiver, 1997). The Stone Center relational model emphasizes the centrality of connection in women's lives, the usefulness of the concepts of self and autonomy in understanding women's experience, and maintains that relationships are in fact the source of psychological health for women. Jordan (1997) has looked at ways women who are marginalized develop strengths that may differ from strengths of privileged women.

FUTURE APPLICATIONS

Social work has undergone considerable change and has met many challenges within the past decade, and there is every reason to expect more of the same (Swenson, 1998). A renewal of social workers' commitment to social justice, environmental change, and greater attention to the client's perspective has contributed to greater pressure to find new ways to use our skills and experience to better serve clients individually, in groups, and in their communities. Although the social work literature does not contain the specific focus on Rogers's work that exists in some related helping professions, practice principles for social work still contain many of the key elements of the person-centered approach of Carl Rogers.

As the profession continues to address applications of the strengths and ecological perspectives, new work is emerging that considers the blending of clinical practice models with social reform efforts (Haynes, 1998; Swenson, 1998). Although current trends in social work may seem far removed from the therapeutic relationship emphasized in the work of Carl Rogers, the basic principles of respect for the person, partnership in the helping process, and authenticity and caring in the working relationship still seem essential if we are to contribute to the empowerment of people and our society's ability to solve serious social problems. The specific ways in which the principles of the person-centered approach will be evident in the future of social work practice may not be entirely clear at this time, but it is hard to imagine any change so radical that we would disown our basic professional beliefs about the person-to-person relationship.

REFERENCES

Blundo, R., Greene, R. R., & Gallant, P. (1994). A constructionist approach with diverse populations. In R. R. Greene (Ed.), *Human Behavior Theory: A Diversity Framework* (pp. 115–132). Hawthorne, NY: Aldine de Gruyter.

Bohart, A. C., & Greenberg, L. S. (Eds.) (1997). *Empathy Reconsidered: New Directions in Psychotherapy*. Washington, DC: American Psychological Association.

Bozarth, J. D. (1997). Empathy from the framework of client-centered theory and the Rogerian hypothesis. In A. C. Bohart & L. S. Greenberg (Eds.), *Empathy Reconsidered: New Directions in Psychotherapy* (pp. 81–102). Washington, DC: American Psychological Association.

Bricker-Jenkins, M., & Lockett, P. W. (1995). Women: Direct practice. In R. L. Edwards (Editor-in-chief), *Encyclopedia of Social Work* (Vol. 3, 19th ed., pp. 2529–2539). Washington, DC: NASW Press.

Compton, B., & Galaway, B. (1994). *Social Work Processes*. Monterey, CA: Brooks/Cole.

Dorfman, R. A. (Ed.) (1988). *Paradigms of Clinical Social Work*. New York: Brunner/Mazel.

Farber, B. A., & Brink, D. C. (Eds.) (1996). *The Psychotherapy of Carl Rogers: Cases and Commentary*. New York: Guilford.

Fisher, D. (1991). *An Introduction to Constructivism for Social Workers*. New York: Praeger.

Germain, C. B., & Gitterman, A. (1995). Ecological perspective. In R. L. Richards (Editor-in-chief), *Encyclopedia of Social Work* (Vol. 1, 19th ed., 816–824), Washington, DC: NASW Press.

Greene, R. R. (1991). Carl Rogers and the person-centered approach. In R. R. Greene & P. H. Ephross (Eds.), *Human Behavior Theory and Social Work Practice* (pp. 105–122). Hawthorne, NY: Aldine de Gruyter.

Greene, R. R. (1994). The social work interview: Legacy of Carl Rogers and Sigmund Freud. In R. R. Greene (Ed.), *Human Behavior Theory: A Diversity Framework* (pp. 35–54). Hawthorne, NY: Aldine de Gruyter.

Greene, R. R., & Ephross (1991). *Human Behavior Theory and Social Work Practice*. Hawthorne, NY: Aldine de Gruyter.

Gutierrez, L. M. (1990). Working with women of color: An empowerment perspective. *Social Work, 35*(2), 149–153.

Haynes, K. S. (1998). The one hundred-year debate: Social reform versus individual treatment. *Social Work, 43*(6), 501–511.

Jordan, J. V. (1997). *Women's Growth in Diversity: More Writings from the Stone Center*. New York: Guilford.

Jordan, J. V., Kaplan, A. G., Miller, J. B., Stiver, I. P., & Surrey, J. L. (1991). *Women's Growth in Connection: Writings from the Stone Center*. New York: Guilford.

Laird, J. (1993). Family-centered practice: Cultural and constructionist reflections. *Journal of Teaching in Social Work, 8*(1/2), 77–110.

Lee, J. (1994). *The Empowerment Approach to Social Work Practice*. New York: Columbia University Press.

Miller, J. B., Jordan, J. V., Kaplan, A. G., & Stiver, I. P. (1997). Some misconceptions and reconceptions of a relational approach. In J. V. Jordan (Ed.), *Women's Growth in Diversity: More Writings from the Stone Center* (pp. 25–49). New York: Guilford.

Miller, J. B., & Stiver, I. P. (1997). *The Healing Connection: How Women Form Relationships in Therapy and in Life*. Boston, MA: Beacon.

National Association of Social Workers (1997). Revitalization of impoverished communities. *Social Work (Special issue), 42*(5), 409–536.

Pinderhughes, E. (1995). Direct practice overview. In R. L. Richards (Editor-in-chief), *Encyclopedia of Social Work* (Vol. 1, 19th ed., pp. 740–751). Washington, DC: NASW Press.

Saleebey, D. (Ed.) (1992). *The Strengths Perspective in Social Work Practice*. New York: Longman.

Simon, B. (1994). *The Empowerment Tradition in American Social Work*. New York: Columbia University Press.

Sundararajan, L. (1995). Echoes after Carl Rogers: "Reflective listening" revisited. *Humanistic Psychologist, 23*(2), 259–271.

Swenson, C. R. (1998). Clinical social work's contribution to a social justice perspective. *Social Work, 43*(6), 527–538.

Turner, F. (1986). *Social Work Treatment: Interlocking Theoretical Approaches*. New York: Free Press.

Zastrow, C. (1992). *The Practice of Social Work*. Belmont, CA: Wadsworth.

6

Cognitive Theory For Social Work Practice

BETSY S. VOURLEKIS

Cognitive theory provides an essential vista in the social work practitioner's requisite broad perspective on human development and functioning in the environment. The theory focuses on the acquisition and function of human thought and knowledge: how and what one comes to think and know, and the role this plays in what one does and feels. Persons' cognitions include thoughts, memories, and reflections of what they feel and do, and of their experiences with their environment, including all of the people in it. It is through cognition that the external environment is rendered uniquely real and meaningful for each individual. Cognitive theory illuminates areas that are central to understanding human personality and behavior, and designing efforts to create change.

There is not one preeminent or unifying theory of cognitive development or cognitive functioning in the behavioral sciences today. One might more accurately write of the cognitive movement, replete with many theories that overlap in assumptions and concepts in some respects, and diverge sharply from each other in others. What this movement represents is a fundamental change in perspective across many fields of psychological inquiry: a redirection of interest from the regulation of what the individual does by instinctual drives and needs (Freudian tradition) or environmental consequences (behaviorist tradition), to a focus on the mediating role of what the individual thinks as an influence on what one feels and does. The success of the movement has led to the notion of a "cognitive revolution" in the behavioral sciences.

If by "revolution," one means a significant and enduring shift in emphasis and conceptual scaffolding, there can be little doubt that a cognitive revolution is well underway in behavior therapy, psychology, psychiatry, and social work (Mahoney, 1988, p. 359). The fundamental ascendance of cognitive processes in psychological theory, research, and clinical treatment was recognized in the 1970s. In the intervening nearly thirty years, cognitive theoretical developments have proliferated, basic research on cognitive development and change through the life course has yielded important new information, and cognitively derived strategies to deal with an increasing array of troubled circumstances have been shown to be effective. The influence of a cognitive perspective and its insights have been far-ranging, including, it has been argued, not just on the psychological and behavioral sciences, but on models of understanding and exploring phenomena in many other basic scientific disciplines (Sperry, 1993).

Cognitive theory is used in this chapter as an umbrella term representing the collective contributions of several theories. These theories share some common assumptions and emphases. Concepts from different theorists that are useful to the social work practitioner in understanding problems of social functioning and engaging in flexible efforts to help are presented. A general guideline to assessment and intervention incorporates these key assumptions and concepts.

The composite view of cognitive theory presented in this chapter draws on three major sources. Developmental theorists and researchers explain the nature and development of the human cognitive system and provide models of cognitive functioning. Basic age-related distinctions in the quality of thought and extent of cognitive capacity and the ramifications of this for social and emotional development and functioning are of interest. Cognitive-learning and cognitive-behavioral theorists illuminate fundamental processes through which a person's thinking influences behavior, as well as the ways in which one's behavior and the environmental response or consequences of that behavior influence thinking. Concepts from these theories have relevance for understanding and influencing human behavior and social functioning in such diverse circumstances as family child rearing, the classroom, agency staff meetings, and even the political arena. Finally is a group of theories that represents an extension of ideas about cognitive development and functioning into the clinical realm. These theories seek to explain why people are upset, troubled, or functioning poorly, and to present strategies for change.

THE PERSON-IN-ENVIRONMENT CONTEXT
AND COGNITIVE THEORY

Paradigms for social work practice have always stressed the need for a broad and encompassing view of the person in the environment. The ecological perspective and life model of practice represent more recent efforts to conceptualize the richness and diversity of this view in the metaphor of the life space (Germain, 1973; Germain & Gitterman, 1980). In turn, social work's focus on the person-environment interface leads to an understanding of social functioning (whether of individuals, families, groups, or organizations) that recognizes the interacting influence of individual(s) capacities and needs and the specific demands and opportunities of the environment. Understanding the life space, with its multiple sources of influence and potential targets for change, requires concepts that help the practitioner recognize and organize information about each of the interacting systems and, ultimately, the interaction itself. How does the social worker describe and understand the individual in a way that captures the contribution of a complex biological and psychological organism (developing across the course of a life) to transactions with the environment? In working with clients, how does the social worker identify the impact of the environment on that client or client system? Social work's attention to the person-environment interaction, or interface, requires concepts and models of what to look for and what is happening that can in turn provide guidance for how to intervene. Cognitive theory, based on the assumption

> Cognitive theorists conceive of person-environment transactions as information exchange.

that human behavior is the product of reciprocal interaction between personal and environmental realities, suggests that such transactions can be thought of as *information exchange* (Berlin, 1980, 1983).

From a cognitive perspective, person-environment interaction is accessible first of all through the meaning that each individual ascribes to the events, circumstances, and behaviors of others that comprise his or her outer world. It is through cognition—mentally processing and constructing personal meaning from information—that the environment is rendered uniquely real and meaningful for each individual, and it is that reality and meaning that comprise a useful person-environment interface. That reality may be distorted as judged by facts as others know them; it may include generalized self-deprecating notions of ability that overlook specific performance success; it may include a set of rules about how to do things that is not shared by a colleague; it may lead to feelings of hopelessness when demands of a task outstrip knowledge and skills; and it also may be a realistic appraisal of an unfair or not welcoming organization or agency. In each case, an imbalance or "poor fit" exists between person and perceived environment, and social functioning is likely to suffer. From a social work practice point of view, such mismatches may describe a self-appointed or designated client, collaborating family member or significant other, representative of another helping system impinging on the client, or the social work practitioner him- or herself. Thus an understanding of individual cognitive factors and functioning does not constrain or prescribe the target for intervention (Goldstein, 1982). It is the case that specific cognitive therapies use helping strategies that place the locus of the problem and change in the client. However, this is not a necessary or inevitable application of the theoretical concepts and insights of cognitive theory.

There is growing social work literature that is suggestive of the utility of cognitive theory and the intervention strategies suggested by it for the diverse clientele and concerns of practice. For example, cognitively derived strategies have been used with abusing parents (Nurius, Lovell, & Edgar, 1988; Whiteman, Fanshel, & Grundy, 1987), individuals confronting serious illness (Levine and Lightburn, 1989; Fobair, 1998), and to enhance independent functioning and life skills for persons with chronic mental illness (Taylor & Taylor, 1989). The prominence of cognitive approaches in psychotherapy is just one prominent area, and should not divert the social work practitioner's attention from the increasing array of thoughtful applications of cognitive principles in strategies and interventions for a wide range of roles and functions, including professional self-awareness (Berlin, 1990). Wingfield's critique of the theory offers many more examples of applications for social work practice.

> Cognitive theorists believe that the client's environment is increasingly accessible and understood as the client enhances his or her cognitive functions.

HISTORICAL CONTEXT OF COGNITIVE THEORY

Although the "cognitive revolution" is a relatively recent phenomenon, the roots of American cognitivism are as diverse and ancient as our preoccupation with the mind. Nevertheless, throughout most of this century, American psychology was overwhelmingly behavioral in orientation, and American psychiatry and psychotherapy were dominated by Freudian and neo-Freudian views that emphasized instinctual motivations and unconscious processes. Sociologists concerned with social psychology, such as symbolic interactionists Cooley and Mead, formulated ideas of the subjective nature of reality, defined as it was through the meaning ascribed to events by individuals in interaction with each other. However, their influence on mainstream psychology, including developmental psychology, was limited.

The person who most influenced the movement of cognitive processes into the central ring of American psychological inquiry that it occupies today was the Swiss philosopher-psychologist Jean Piaget. Beginning in the 1950s, Piaget's work on the development of moral reasoning in children began to stimulate American developmental psychologists' interest in cognition. Although Piaget's theory no longer dominates the field of developmental psychology as it did through the 1970s, his work has had a major impact on our knowledge of cognitive development and growth and study of the child.

In a parallel development, the computer, information, and communication explosion of the 1960s and 1970s influenced cognitive psychology as well. Information-processing models of cognitive functioning use basic systems theory concepts to explain the cognitive "system" as a complex array of interacting parts, similar in some ways to a computer. Environmental input is "information" that is processed or manipulated by the individual in a number of ways. In this view, cognition is information processing. The human mind, like a computer, operates on the basis of complex programming that provides rules and sequenced operations to manipulate information and knowledge in many ways (Siegler, 1983). From this viewpoint, cognitive phenomena of particular interest are not just what the person thinks (content and description) and why one thinks that way (reasoning), but the organizing structures, rules, and problem-solving strategies of the mind with which each individual transforms information in dealing with all aspects of day-to-day life.

Information-processing models provided behaviorally oriented theorists a viable explanatory framework for a mediating role of cognition—in the form of the individual's internalized processing of information—in determining behavioral choices and outcomes (Dember, 1974; Dobson & Block, 1988).

> Cognitive theorists seek to better understand how people process information and learn.

The mediational influence of cognition on behavior became a central area of inquiry for social learning theory (Bandura, 1977; Mischel, 1973).

As noted earlier, the "cognitive revolution" has invaded most areas of behavioral science inquiry. The cognitive perspective increasingly pervades the clinical domain as well. Ellis's (1962) rational-emotive therapy focused on irrational thoughts and beliefs that he believed contributed to self-defeating behavior and emotional distress. Beck's (1976, 1991; Beck, Rush, Shaw, & Emery, 1979; Beck & Emery, 1985) cognitive therapy explored the connections between characteristic patterns of thinking and clinical depression and anxiety disorders. The work of both Ellis and Beck are examples of a cognitive approach to the understanding and treatment of emotional disorders. More recently, the emergence of cognitive-behavioral therapy represents a creative blending of social learning, behavioral, and cognitive theories (Mahoney, 1974; Meichenbaum, 1985), focused on a broad spectrum of behavioral difficulties. Social work theorists have developed cognitive models suited to essential social work practice principles (Berlin, 1983; Goldstein, 1982; Werner, 1982). By the 1990s, over twenty different approaches to cognitively based psychotherapy could be identi-

fied (Mahoney, 1995). Of growing influence in the domain of psychotherapy have been ideas from constructivist philosophy that are more fully explained in Chapter 9.

BASIC ASSUMPTIONS AND CONCEPTS
OF COGNITIVE THEORY

The Cognitive Domain

What is *cognition?* What mental phenomena are of interest to cognitive
theorists? By tradition, all of the so-called higher mental processes—
knowledge, consciousness, intelligence, thinking, imagining, creating, generating plans and strategies, reasoning, inferring, problem solving, conceptualizing, classifying and relating, symbolizing, and even fantasizing and
dreaming—are included. To these are added perception, memory, attention, and learning, leaving one to wonder what psychological processes are
not cognitive (Flavell, 1985). Perhaps that is the important point: virtually
all human psychological activity has a cognitive aspect.

Frequently a distinction is made between cognition, as in thinking, and
emotions, as in feeling. However, the connections between the two are
complex, and the distinction between them is by no means clear (Izard,
1989). What a person knows and perceives, and thinks of that perception,
has a great deal to do with what one feels. Cognitions such as thoughts and
beliefs may be rational or irrational. Ellis (1962) defined irrational thoughts
as those that get in the way of or defeat one's life goals. Thoughts and
knowledge may be in immediate awareness and the person may realize
their influence, or they may be out of awareness yet influencing other cognitive processes, feelings, and behavior. This *tacit* knowing and thinking
has been described as "knowing more than we can tell" (Polanyi, 1966,
p. 4). Thoughts not in immediate awareness are also called *automatic*
thoughts (Beck, 1976). Automatic thoughts are accessible, if the person
monitors thinking processes attuned to look for them. Finally, cognitions
may be about the outside physical world, the interpersonal world, the internal private world, or the abstract logical world. Taken together, these
multiple dimensions of cognition constitute the individual's cognitive
functioning.

Basic Assumptions

Optimistic and Nondeterministic.   Cognitive theory rests on a relatively
optimistic and nondeterministic view of human functioning, growth, and

potential for change. Cognitive growth and change can and will occur throughout the life span as a result of each individual's physical matura- tion and interaction with the environment, providing that the environment provides reasonable conditions and opportunities (Table 6.1).

Active Construction of Personal Knowledge. Knowledge and beliefs are not simply "acquired," as if each person were an empty vessel passively being filled, nor are they merely "processed" out of informational input. Rather, the individual actively and continuously constructs knowledge and meaning out of the interaction of experience and his or her own exist- ing cognitive capacities and knowledge.

Mediating Role of Cognition. Human thinking plays a mediating role in all aspects of functioning. Thought provides meaning to both internal and external events. Mental processes such as selective attention, inference, and judgment influence one's motivation to act, shape the nature of one's action, and color one's feeling about the action after the fact. Thought pro- cesses are viewed as making a causal contribution to behavioral outcomes, including social competence and coping (Bandura, 1986). Likewise, cogni- tive dysfunctions, distortions, or deficits are presumed to interfere with so- cial performance and adaptation, and contribute to dysfunctional moods and psychiatric symptoms (Beck, 1976). This *mediational role* of cognition in human affairs is central, but not a one-way street. That is, behavioral con- sequences, adequacy of performance, physiological states—aspects of one's environment or of one's biology—also influence thinking.

Reciprocal Determinism. This notion of circular causality, with each sys- tem potentially influencing the other, is referred to as *reciprocal determinism*

Table 6.1. Cognitive Theory: Basic Assumptions

Human cognitive growth and change occurs throughout the life span.
At any age, an individual's cognitive competency in a given domain (for example, intelligence, problem-solving ability, decision-making) will vary with the context within which the individual functions.
Cognition (knowledge, thinking, and problem-solving) is a product not only of the person's exposure to environmental events, but of the person's active construction of the meaning of these events.
Individuals act primarily in response to their cognitive representations of environmental events; for example, their selective attention to and inter- pretation of meaning of these events.
Thoughts, feelings, behaviors, and their consequences are all causally interre- lated.
Cognitive representations, including thoughts about oneself, influence social functioning and emotional well-being, and are amenable to change.
Behavior change can be effected through cognitive change.

(Bandura, 1978). As with any dynamic system, the three subsystems of thinking, feeling, and behaving provide feedback to each other; all may contribute to a given outcome or state, and change in one may lead to change in the others. The following case example illustrates the assumption of reciprocal influence and other basic assumptions of cognitive theory.

> An elderly woman who breaks her hip faces the new reality of a nursing home when she leaves the hospital. She is agitated and deeply unhappy in spite of assurances that her apartment will be kept for her. In her thinking, a nursing home is a place from which you never return, for it is a place for people who are going to die. In cognitive terms, she had an expectancy that if she went to a nursing home then she was not going to get better. She cannot be convinced otherwise, for her view of the nursing home is her "reality." In the home, rehabilitation therapy is begun, with a sensitive, persistent therapist who is not discouraged by the woman's pessimism and apathy. After several weeks she is successful at standing and walking a step or two with a walker. At that point she becomes an eager participant in her rehabilitation and begins to make realistic plans for an eventual return home. In this case, her behavioral competence contributed to a change in mood and a change in thinking in the form of new hypotheses about her future.

This vignette also illustrates the assumption of reciprocal influence and interaction between personal and environmental realities. At a given moment, the meaning of the environment is a product of the individual's thinking about it. Initially, our elderly woman saw the nursing home environment very differently than the hospital social worker or the rehabilitation therapist did. That was her personally constructed reality. However, the environmental reality was a source of opportunity and information: in this case rehabilitation and performance feedback. This modified an aspect of her cognition, namely, her expectations concerning performance in the future, with accompanying changes in feeling state and behavior.

> Cognitive approaches focus on how a client's cognitive processes mediate personal feelings and "realities" of the environment.

Cognition plays a mediating role in interpreting reality. Each person's perceptions of others and understanding of the physical world, what is experienced as rewarding or punishing, what is attended to or missed are cognitive processes that contribute to a subjective, individual construction of meaning out of the diverse information provided by the environment. That is "reality" as one knows it.

"Starting where the client is" involves an effort on the part of the practitioner to understand the problem situation as the client views it, and to work on changing a dimension of that situation that the client wants changed. The social worker needs to understand and intervene in the client's "reality." In the same way, working with the goal of improving person-environment fit is not an objective exercise like a child's peg board where round pegs will go into round holes and square pegs will not. How adequate, desirable, or menacing is an environment frequently is best determined by the client's perception of that environment.

The variety of cognitive phenomena suggests caution in evaluating cognitive competence. Global and overly generalized measures or assessment ignore the multiple components of cognitive functioning. Since the field's early efforts to measure intelligence, cognitive theorists have emphasized the importance of context in the demonstration of any given cognitive competency. College board scores are good predictors of college performance, not success in business or in raising well-adjusted children, to make an obvious example. Problem-solving skills with machinery are not the same skills required to deal with interpersonal conflict. Invoking the assumption of reciprocal determinism, it follows that context, which is another way to talk about the environment, will in and of itself contribute to perceived and actual competence. Everyday examples of this abound. Student test performance may be affected by a noisy versus a quiet examination room, as distractions from the environment overwhelm individual cognitive self-regulatory mechanisms such as concentration. The time allowed or available to complete a task will influence performance. A person's strength of belief about his or her likelihood to succeed in the face of multiple, devastating social circumstances, such as frequently confront many of our clients, may well be diminished from a previous life point when circumstances may have been better.

Cognitive Structures and Processes

The complexity of cognitive functioning is challenging for the social work practitioner. Information gathering and assessment of cognitive functioning, whether of the client or other key individuals in the life space, requires more than meaningless global generalizations such as good/bad, high/low, or competent/incompetent. At the same time, more detailed inquiry and assessment of every aspect of cognitive functioning is impossible. An understanding of basic cognitive processes and structures provides an initial framework for assessment and intervention.

The mental processes with which the person perceives, organizes, remembers, and evaluates available information are *cognitive processes*. These can be thought of as "how" the person thinks (Meichenbaum, 1985). Search, retrieval, and storage processes are central to memory. Executive processes contribute to problem-solving. These processes include articulation of a problem and its solution, awareness of what is needed to solve the problem, activation of cognitive rules and strategies, flexibility, and control of anxiety and distraction (Kagan, 1984). Processes such as inference and categorization ascribe meaning to information and events.

Cognitive structures provide the information (content) out of which the person constructs and interprets reality, and engages in problem-solving or other purposeful behavior. Given the current state of knowledge, there is some consensus concerning the basic units of cognition. These are thought to be *schemata, concepts,* and *propositions* (Kagan, 1984). The schema is an abstract representation of the distinctive features of an event or stimulus. A concept results from the organization of information from multiple experiences into a class or category that combines shared features. A proposition is the relating of two or more concepts to form rules, beliefs, and hypotheses. The patterning and organization of information, for example, the application of a belief or rule (proposition) of ideas about oneself (self-concept), result in an interpretive framework that guides perception of others as well as behavior (Markus, Smith, & Moreland, 1985). These interpretive biases, arising out of past experience, are used by the individual to make sense out of current experience and, in some cases, to distort that experience.

The *self-concept* is an example of a cognitive structure that is thought to be particularly important for understanding social functioning. The self-concept illustrates the dynamic interplay, interrelationship, and patterning of structures that are central to understanding cognitive functioning. Multiple schemata of the self develop through interaction with others, experience in the physical world, knowledge, and reflection and insight. Categorized and classified, these schemata form the concept of self. This concept, as any other, is then both the subject and object of numerous propositions such as

• I (self) am fatter than you. The world does not like fat people and so I am not likable. If I try to make friends with you I will be rejected.

Such "thoughts" illustrate propositions involving self-evaluation, beliefs about the world and the self in relation to it, and projections and expectations concerning future consequences for the self in action. These patterns and clusters of thoughts constituting self-appraisal may be an important influence on the quality and effectiveness of coping efforts (Nurius, 1989).

A person's organized self-appraisal propositions can be thought of as a belief system about self. Bandura (1977, 1986) termed this *self-efficacy.* He defined this as

people's judgments of their capabilities to organize and execute courses of action required to attain designated types of performances . . . concerned

> not with the skills one has but with the judgments of what one can do with whatever skills one possesses. (Bandura, 1986, p. 391)

Self-efficacy beliefs can influence choice of behaviors, the degree of effort expended or persistence, emotional reactions to a task, and the organization of thinking about it. In each case, coping and problem-solving may be enhanced or hindered.

As with any other aspect of cognitive functioning, an individual's ideas about self and self-efficacy will vary to some extent according to the situation. In addition, each person has goals and aspirations and views of self for the future. For social workers engaged in helping efforts, both of these perspec-

> Cognitive therapists emphasize cognitive functions dealing with self-efficacy and self-concept.

tives warn against a static or overgeneralized view of a person's self-concept and self-efficacy. Nurius (1989) described the *working self-concept* as that aspect of the self-concept (out of the total self-concept repertoire) operating at a given moment. The working self-concept represents both the variability in self-concept from situation to situation or one time frame to another, as well as the susceptibility to influence and change of the self-concept of the moment. A specific example of a type of working self-concept is the *possible self*. The possible self is the individual's conceptions of what one would and would not like to come to be. It is "cognitive representations of goals, aspirations, motives, fears and threats" (Nurius, 1989, p. 289). Recognition of the possible self provides a framework for connecting an individual's expectations for change with behavior that supports or prevents such change. For clients with multiple and cumulatively devastating life experiences, compounded by stigmatizing conditions, the possible self may represent a critical therapeutic opportunity, as the following case illustrates:

> John is a 24-year-old man with chronic mental illness. His life story, related to the case manager, is one of progression from one institution to another, including prison, with brief interludes of tenuous community existence. After a hospitalization of six months, he is living in a community residence facility, and returns to clinic for medication and monthly meetings with the case manager. The plan is for him to begin a sheltered work assignment. He talks of earning some money and is asked what he would like to do with it. "I'll buy some new clothes and feel like a man." The case manager reflects that John "wants to be a man," and John agrees. In the step-by-step discussion and work that follows in getting John into the work assignment and beyond, the case manager continues to explore and reinforce the linkages between John's own view of the possibility of "being a man," and the behavioral expectations for elements of manhood.

Two additional types of propositions are relevant to understanding social functioning. An individual's *expectancies* are hypotheses about outcomes; they are the anticipated consequences of different behavioral possibilities in a specific situation (Mischel, 1973). Expectancies can be understood intuitively as the "if . . . then . . . " statements the individual mentally formulates on a continuous basis in response to circumstances. In the example above, John has the expectancy that if he earns money, then he can own proper clothes that will place him in a valued status position, that of "being a man." John's desired outcome is the possible self of manhood; his expectancy provides the beginning working link between the outcome and the means he can visualize for achieving it.

Attributions are beliefs about the causes of behavior, particularly behavior that affects performance. A person's perceptions of cause-and-effect relationships influence the emotional meaning of events in the environment, as well as the nature of the response to the environment (Weiner, 1985). Drawing from attribution theory, Fleming (1981, pp. 68–69) outlined three dimensions of attributional beliefs that have particular relevance for social work practice.

Locus of control.   Does the client see the present problem as within or beyond his/her influence or control?

Misattribution.   Has the client inaccurately perceived a sequence of events, ascribing an effect to the wrong cause?

Self-attribution.   Does the client excessively self-blame; internalize socially generated negative labels such as "different" or "crazy"; or view him- or herself as "hopeless"?

Expectancies mediate one's own behavioral choices, but they frequently involve judgments and attributions about the behavior and circumstances of others. Thus, for example, a worker whose client fails to keep an appointment or call decides that the client does not want help. The worker's cognitive mediation of the "reality" of the client's behavior includes the (1) belief that people who really want to work on their problems show up for appointments or call, (2) attribution that the client does not want help, (3) and expectancy that further effort on the worker's part is a waste of time.

The client, on the other hand, may have a different view of the situation. The client may believe that it is important to use others' help only when you "need" it. The client's expectancy on the day of the appointment may be "If I go, it is a waste of my time and the worker's time, since I feel OK and don't need help." Although this different expectancy, unless changed, precludes the client from taking advantage of many traditional forms of helping, including that worker's, it would be a mistake to conclude that the client does not want the worker's help. The worker's labeling of the client as unmotivated is a misattribution.

Expectancies and attributions concerning a client are a component of the cognitive functioning of helping professionals, other representatives of systems with which clients interact, and significant individuals in the client's life. Frequently based on prior experiences with the client or "type" of client, these expectancies and misattributions may need to be the target of exploration and change as well.

EXPLAINING DEVELOPMENT ACROSS THE LIFE CYCLE

In the cognitive sciences there are two influential models of cognitive development in use today: Piaget's stage theory and an information-processing model. The two are complementary in some respects (Flavell, 1985). General elements of Piaget's theory are presented here. The reader is referred to Flavell (1985) and Kagan's (1984) detailed presentation of cognitive growth and development from an integrative perspective. Piaget's theory was dominant and influential to a remarkable degree until recently. Prolific research, spawned from his careful predictions and creative methods, has since suggested important limitations in the theory that will be discussed below.

Nevertheless, Piaget has made a fundamental contribution to the field of child development. His view of the integrity and strength of the mental processes made "cognitive events" important, and worthy of respect and attention, including the most rigorous research. His probing of the thinking of children has led to a basic appreciation of the child's "reality," that is, the impact of events on the child as filtered through his or her cognitive structures as they develop. His connection of maturing cognitive representations and the development of morality and moral thinking remains a seminal contribution to the field.

General Model

As a young man, Piaget got a job with a colleague of Binet (of the Stanford-Binet I.Q. Test). Working on standardizing test questions, he became interested in the similarity of the wrong answers he was seeing. Why did they answer that way? He sought to understand the structure and organization of thought that lay behind such "errors." In a lifelong effort, Piaget elaborated a general theory of intellectual development, as well as its implications for the moral, social, and emotional development of the child (Cowan, 1978).

Piaget's theory proposed an invariant sequencing of stages of cognitive development from birth to late adolescence. Each *cognitive stage* represents a fundamentally new psychological reorganization resulting from the maturation of new functions and abilities. As the child develops, thinking is altered and transformed through the development and transformation of the fundamental structures and processes through which the child "knows" the world, resulting in movement to the next cognitive stage. Progression from one stage to the next is a function of both biological maturation and the child's experience and action in the environment. Cognitive, affective, and social development are inseparable and parallel, and cognitive achievements from stage to stage affect interpersonal relations as well as intrapersonal "thinking" (Piaget and Inhelder, 1969).

Within this stage framework, the process of knowledge acquisition is the same across all stages, and similar for all forms of knowledge. Knowledge is not just "acquired" through experience, but actively constructed by the individual as experience is filtered and organized through existing cognitive structures. All knowledge is the product of the complementary and simultaneous mental processes of *assimilation* and *accommodation*. In this model of cognitive functioning, assimilation represents taking in information from the environment and integrating it with one's preconceived and existing way of thinking about things. Accommodation represents taking into account the actual properties of external events and objects and adjusting accordingly. Both processes are crucial to cognitive growth. Growth is viewed as lifelong, incremental modification in the cognitive system as a result of "daily, virtually continuous assimilation of milieu to mind and accommodation of mind to milieu" (Flavell, 1985, p. 8). These complementary processes represent the ongoing *adaptation* of the individual to the environment, at the cognitive system level.

Stages of Cognitive Development

Piaget postulated the existence of four qualitatively distinct stages in cognitive development, culminating in the acquisition and display of true abstract and logical thought. The stages, major characteristics of thinking for each, and approximate age of movement from stage to stage in normal development are briefly described below.

Sensorimotor Stage. In this period from birth to approximately two years of age, intelligence and knowing are the product of the infant's at first reflexive and then rapidly developing sensory and motor capabilities. Maturation and the infant's actions on, and interaction with, the environment lead to the development of concepts fundamental to further psychological growth, and to the beginning comprehension of the nature of the physical world. This includes the acquisition of the concepts of *object permanence,* or the awareness that objects continue to exist even when they cannot be seen;

causality, as infants begin to demonstrate awareness of cause and effect relationships; and *intentionality,* accompanied by the appearance of goal-oriented behavior. Thinking at this stage is characterized as *representational intelligence,* indicating the achievement of the ability to mentally represent objects and solve sensorimotor problems.

Preoperational Stage. In this period of roughly two to seven years of age, the emergence of language provides the child with a symbolic representational ability and the beginnings of conceptual thinking. Intelligence tends to be dominated by perception (what the child sees), and with this an egocentric perspective in which the child's view and thinking is "right." Thinking is *prelogical* at this stage, and symbolic representation through fantasy and play are important avenues for problem-solving and mastery.

Concrete Operational Stage (Seven to Eleven Years). Development proceeds from prelogical thought to logical thought, when applied to concrete problems, objects, or events. The fundamental logical operations of *conservation, reversibility, seriation,* and *classification* are attained. Conservation is the conceptualization that the amount or quantity of a matter stays the same regardless of any changes in shape or position. Reversibility is the ability to follow a line of reasoning back to where it started. The ability to mentally arrange elements according to increasing or decreasing size is seriation. Classification is the ability to classify objects, taking into consideration simultaneously two or more classes (Wadsworth, 1971). With the achievement of the concrete operations, the child can think logically, but cannot apply this logic to verbal or hypothetical problems.

Formal Operational Stage (Eleven to Fifteen Years). The child now becomes able to apply logical thought to all classes of problems and situations, including those involving the future. Hypothetical and abstract reasoning leads to *scientific thinking.* During this period the adolescent struggles to integrate the discrepancy between what is logical and the functioning of the real world, which is frequently not ordered in a logical way (Wadsworth, 1971).

The relevance of these, or any other, descriptions of age-related differences in children's thinking, competencies, and view of the world to the problems and situations that confront the social worker requires careful and specific connections. The significance of age and stage of cognitive development for a child's understanding of feelings is a useful example:

A four-year-old child who is facing foster care placement will have a very different understanding of his or her own feelings and the causes of them than will a thirteen-year-old. For example, the younger child has great difficulty understanding that a single event, such as visiting the foster mother, could precipitate mixed (more than one) feelings, and will not talk about experiencing them simultaneously. The older child, in addition to being able to conceive of him- or herself having two feelings at the same time, has some ability to understand that others (such as the foster mother) may also. Both children may say they feel unhappy. The younger child's view of the cause of this feeling will be concrete and linked to specific objects: "I want to sleep in my own bed." The older child is more apt to understand that several aspects of the situation may be contributing to feeling unhappy and would need to be dealt with before he or she will feel better.

These cognitive, age-related mediators of the understanding of emotions have implications for how the social worker talks about feelings with children of different ages, and plans interventions to address meaningfully children's felt concerns (Nannis, 1988).

Limitations of Piaget

Piaget's theory has come under question in several important respects. The utility of any stage model, based on the notion of fixed, invariant sequences of social and emotional growth and development for all individuals, has been questioned. Such models may not adequately reflect important cultural differences and are overly deterministic (Germain, 1987). More fundamental yet, Piaget's theory assumes the universality of Western logic. Within Western culture, predicted stagelike differences in children's conceptual thinking in relation to the physical world can be demonstrated in experimental conditions, but may not be generalizable to the range and extent of social and emotional phenomena that fundamental changes in cognitive structures would suggest they should be (Radke-Yarrow, Zahn-Waxler, & Chapman, 1983).

The constructs of assimilation and accommodation are not adequate to explain either what is occurring or how in the fundamental transformations of thinking from stage to stage (Kagan, 1989). As general propositions they reflect the essential active nature of knowledge, that is, the development of mental structure out of action on/in one's environment. However, they do not provide insight into the dynamics of cognitive change.

With respect to the stages themselves, research suggests considerable validity for the distinctive age-related quality of the sensorimotor stage, and of advanced conceptual ability (formal operations stage). However, the middle two stages are far less clear. In general, research suggests that young children are competent in many cognitive tasks earlier, and have more conceptual ability than Piaget's stage theory predicts. Summarizing, Flavell (1985) writes, "[T]here is growing doubt in the field as to whether post-infancy age changes in people's cognitive systems are as fundamental, momentous, qualitative, and stage-like as Piaget and others believed"

(p. 82). Nevertheless, there does seem to be evidence for developmental trends that produce characteristic differences in thought, and these differences are of interest and import to the social work practitioner.

Growth and Development in Adulthood

Cognitive theory assumes ongoing growth and development throughout and then after the achievement of physical maturation. The mediation and reciprocal influence assumptions of the theory presume that the cognitive system is an open, dynamic one and the potential for growth and change is always present. Basic capabilities (structures and processes) invariably will develop in childhood, given an even remotely "expectable" environment and the absence of biological impairments. In this respect, cognitive theory provides an optimistic, nondeterministic view of the individual's ability at any given point in time to construct a new and different (and better) personal reality (Goldstein, 1982).

At the same time, the old saying, You can't teach an old dog new tricks, represents the common, everyday experience of how unyielding to change are many features of a person's cognitive functioning. Belief systems that are rigidly held in spite of evidence to the contrary, irrational ideas that do not give way to logical analysis, and perceptions of others that ignore new information are examples of this. Because individual reality is constructed and endowed with meaning through cognition, holding on to preferred ways of thinking serves an important self-maintenance function. Furthermore, much of what a person thinks and knows—the cognitions that mediate behavior and feeling—is a product of earlier learning. Kagan suggests that both children and adults are prone to resist "retiring hypotheses that have been effective in the past" (Kagan, 1984, p. 220). Thus beliefs about the world and the self that may have been adaptive to another set of circumstances can obstruct thinking in new ways for new circumstances.

The processes and mechanisms that contribute to stability and change in cognitive functioning are still poorly understood. Circumstances that produce cognitive conflict and instability, referred to as *cognitive dissonance*, are likely candidates as motivators for change (Markus & Zajonc, 1985).

Old Age

Common assumptions are made about the inevitable decline of cognitive functioning in old age. It is important, therefore, to understand general features of "normal" cognitive functioning in old age. At the same time, it is true that chronic disease processes, such as Alzheimer's disease and other forms of senile dementia that can produce profound changes in cognitive functioning, are more prevalent among the elderly. However, such diseases, and their consequences, must be differentiated from normal aging. The social work practitioner needs to become familiar with the basic clinical distinguishing features of dementia and to understand the range of possible contributing agents to such conditions. Careful medical assessment and monitoring can detect and in many cases reverse what is too often viewed as "just old age."

Normal Aging.   Longitudinal, large sample population studies of adult intellectual development using standardized tests show that on average performance continues to show gains until the late 30s and early 40s, little change through the early 60s, and a slow process of modest decline beginning in the mid-70s (Schaie, 1996). Research suggests the following important cautionary points in interpreting this information: (1)individual variation in tested capacities is vast at any age; (2) behavioral slowing, including perceptual speed, occurs with aging and affects performance on standardized intelligence tests; and (3) intellectual decline is not necessarily inevitable or irreversible (Schaie, 1996). Neuropsychological testing reveals decline after sixty-five in cognitive processes such as the amount of time it takes to process information or to learn new information. However, such changes are typically not evident at the level of a clinical evaluation (Horvath and Davis, 1990). Thus, although some components of intellectual performance, as measured in abstract and academic tasks, decrease in later life, the real-life products of these same components may not. The time it takes to remember a name may be far less significant in "real life" than the cumulative process of generating and putting to use a list of treasured friends to whom to send holiday greetings. Recent research focuses on "practical intelligence" in older people and finds that older individuals are more rapid and efficient decision-makers than younger people, using informational strategies that are similar to those of "experts" in many fields (Willis, 1996).

> Assessing cognitive function at any age requires client individualization and an appreciation of the strengths perspective.

Research findings underscore the importance for an understanding of cognitive functioning in old age of avoiding overly generalized assessment of cognitive capacity, and looking for strengths. For example, memory is a multifaceted capacity, and change in one aspect of memory does not imply change in another. Evidence suggests that older people will show deficits in explicit memory tasks (being asked to remember something or if they remember something on demand) but not in implicit memory tasks (actually remembering something without a conscious effort at remembering) (Hultsch & Dixon, 1990). In general, memory deficits with aging appear to be much less pronounced the more ecologically valid the memory task is, that is, embedded in and relevant to the life experience and life circumstances of the individual (Hultsch & Dixon, 1990). This underscores the importance of a more context-dependent approach to measuring cognitive capacity in all areas of functioning. Cognitive development and competence in old age, as at any age, can be characterized as a process of individual adaptation to a set of specific environments (Sternberg & Berg, 1987). Not only is capacity to some extent tied to each environment, but the cognitive abilities most critical for successful adaptation may change with age as the demands and opportunities of one's environment change. Moreover, important qualities of the actual context such as the complexity, challenge, or stressfulness of the situation will affect capacity. Much of the actual observed loss of cognitive competence in the elderly (individuals in their 80s and 90s) occurs under these circumstances (Schaie, 1996).

Dementia. In contrast to minor, "normal" decrements in cognitive functioning associated with healthy aging are the global and severe loss of intellectual abilities characteristic of dementia. Dementia is defined by the DSM-IV as "multiple cognitive deficits . . . [which] must be sufficiently severe to cause impairment in occupational or social functioning and must represent a decline from a previously higher level of functioning" (American Psychiatric Association, 1994, p. 134). In DSM IV, the diagnostic classification dementia includes a number of specific disorders, distinguished by their etiology (to the extent it can be determined). For illustrative purposes, diagnostic criteria for dementia of the Alzheimer's type are presented in Table 6.2. Criteria A and B, as shown in the table, are most relevant to the social work practitioner and are the same for each of the specific dementia disorders. Clients presenting this degree of cognitive impairment should be referred for a thorough medical evaluation and diagnosis if this has not already been done.

There are a number of possible causes of dementia, including degenerative diseases (for example, Alzheimer's and Parkinson's diseases), vascular changes, HIV disease, metabolic imbalances, toxic substances, and head trauma. Some conditions are treatable and reversible and others are not (Horvath & Davis, 1990). It is important that the practitioner bear in mind that not all dementia is Alzheimer's disease, as this distinction is frequently not made by the lay public. Drug toxicity from the interaction of multiple medications is frequently implicated in dementia, and may be reversible with proper medical evaluation and intervention.

UNDERSTANDING CULTURAL DIFFERENCES

A cognitive view of the meaning and function of differences in culture and cultural milieu for the individual is composed of two comple-

Table 6.2. DSM-IV Diagnostic Criteria for Dementia of the Alzheimer's Type

A. The development of multiple cognitive deficits manifested by both
    1. memory impairment (impaired ability to learn new information or to recall previously learned information)
    2. One (or more) of the following cognitive disturbances:
        a. Aphasia (language disturbance)
        b. Apraxia (impaired ability to carry out motor activities despite intact motor function)
        c. Agnosia (failure to recognize or identify objects despite intact sensory function)
        d. Disturbance in executive functioning (i.e., planning, organizing, sequencing, abstracting)
B. The cognitive deficits in Criteria A1 and A2 each cause significant impairment in social or occupational functioning and represent a significant decline from a previous level of functioning.
C. The course is characterized by gradual onset and continuing cognitive decline.
D. The cognitive deficits in Criteria A1 and A2 are not due to any of the following:
    1. Other central nervous system conditions that cause progressive deficits in memory and cognition (e.g., cerebrovascular disease, Parkinson's disease, Huntington's disease, subdural hematoma, normal-pressure hydrocephalus, brain tumor)
    2. Systemic conditions that are known to cause dementia (e.g., hypothyroidism, vitamin B12 or folic acid deficiency, niacin deficiency, hypercalcemia, neurosyphilis, HIV infection)
    3. Substance-induced conditions
E. The deficits do not occur exclusively during the course of a delirium
F. The disturbance is not better accounted for by another Axis I disorder (e.g., Major Depressive Disorder, Schizophrenia).

Source: *Diagnostic and Statistical Manual of Mental Disorders* (4th ed.). Washington, DC: American Psychiatric Association. Copyright 1994. Reprinted with permission.

mentary positions: on the one hand, the basic cognitive structures and processes, as well as a certain general predictability to the sequencing of their development in the maturing organism, are presumed to be identical for all individuals. In this respect, it is a theory of *cross-cultural invariance.*

On the other hand, the content of individual thought, and the ongoing personal construction of the meaning of reality through cognitive mediation of external and internal information, will vary from culture to culture. In cognitive terms, culture is a shared belief system. Through child-rearing practices and family life, group rituals and mores, and literature, music, and speech, these shared ideas are a powerful source of information from the environment. A proportion of what each person knows and believes is derived from these shared views of the world, which provide information essential to the individual's successful functioning as a member of one's society (Quinn & Holland, 1987).

In continual interaction with the environment, the individual cognitively processes this information, simultaneously transforming it (assimilation) and being transformed by it (accommodation), while constructing personal knowledge of self and self in relation to the world. Thus, cognitive theory emphasizes the subjective nature, personal, and cultural uniqueness of thought, and individual thinking is culturally relative.

Generally, cognitive theory suggests that the best way to understand and take into account the contribution of cultural differences in person-environment transactions is through the individual's own view of self and reality, a view that has incorporated personally relevant cultural information. This approach avoids stereotypical judgments and interpretations of cultural differences, or assumptions about individual preferences that are based on that individual's cultural, ethnic, racial, or religious group membership.

UNDERSTANDING HOW HUMAN BEINGS FUNCTION AS MEMBERS OF FAMILIES, GROUPS, ORGANIZATIONS, AND COMMUNITIES

In cognitive terms, each person's social interactions with others, whether in the context of family, school, work, or community, are cognitively mediated. That is to say, how one perceives others, the judgments one makes about these perceptions, and the choices one makes about behavior in response to others are all influenced by what and how one thinks (Sherman, Judd, & Park, 1989). Social exchanges and encounters are another form of "information" that is cognitively processed by each individual in constructing one's own unique reality.

At this most general level, social discord and social dysfunction can be understood as disparities among individuals' views of reality, and social cohesion and collaboration as arenas of shared views. Although the application of this general understanding to family, group, and organizational functioning and dysfunctioning is not well developed, several examples can serve to illustrate.

Werner (1982) enumerates ways in which intrafamily problems can be understood as difficulties in the exchange and coordination of information and meaning among the family members:

Unrealistic or differing expectations: between parents and children or spouses; expectations color both behavior and the interpretation of behavior

Misinterpretations of behaviors and intents: for example, differing attributions, misattributions, self-attributions

Deficits in information regarding the "others" in the environment: one may poorly understand or have no information about the other's needs, fears or values.

Another illustration of a cognitive approach to social functioning is group consciousness raising (Chatterjee, 1984). Here group cohesion is built through the development of a new, shared view of "reality" that alters each individual's previously circumscribed view. Members of oppressed groups, or people who are experiencing extreme deprivation, may have self-attributed and self-blamed for difficulties in their life, to the exclusion of recognizing other influential social circumstances. Consciousness raising becomes a means to empowerment through collective meaning and action. Social movements are built prominently on the power of such shared views.

The application of insights and concepts from cognitive theory and science to organizational functioning is still relatively undeveloped (Weick & Roberts, 1993) and is an area of promising work. Its utility for understanding sources of organizational conflict, such as differences in beliefs about the causes of satisfactory or unsatisfactory performance between managers and workers, is being explored (Ilgen & Klein, 1988). Recent work investigates from a cognitive perspective the elements of "smart" people systems—collective mental processes that contribute to an understanding of complex and interrelated task fields and functions—that are viewed as key to reliable organizational performance (Weick & Roberts, 1993).

DIRECT PRACTICE: INTERVENTION IN THE PERSON-SITUATION TO ENHANCE FUNCTIONING

Cognitive theory illuminates aspects of the individual's mental representation of reality and the ways in which this representation influences (and is in turned influenced by) what the individual does and feels. This representation of reality is a point of interface between the person and the situation that can provide a focus for a variety of change strategies. Although intervention is frequently at the individual level, an appreciation of cognitive functioning can assist in identifying and targeting individuals other than the client for an effort at change. Such an individual could be an important part of the client's situation, such as a teacher, foster-mother, or a gatekeeper to a resource needed by the client. Or it could be the worker him- or herself. As discussed above, cognitive change efforts can be implemented with families and groups as well.

Whoever the designated person or person(s) for intervention, there are many aspects of cognitive functioning that potentially could be targeted for change. These can include such relatively accessible phenomena as perceptions, expectancies, and causal attributions, customary distortions in routine information processing such as overgeneralization, minimization and magnification, and personalization, and what are believed to be less accessible or out-of-awareness beliefs and personal schema (Granvold, 1994).

Cognitive theory has generated a broad array of clinical applications ranging from intensive and relatively long-term psychotherapy to short-term skill development exercises. Each approach has specific frameworks for assessment and specific intervention strategies. The social work practitioner will want to develop an awareness of the diversity of approaches from which to choose. In this section basic principles for assessment and intervention generated by a cognitive theoretical point of view are discussed. One general model for practice, Berlin's personal problem-solving process, is presented.

Assessment

Assessment begins with the client's view of the problem and of what needs to change. The assumption of cognitive mediation of reality suggests that the way in which the client interprets events, circumstances, the actions of others, and his or her own behavioral responses is the focus of interest. As Werner (1982, p. 84) states,

> The older child or adult may not be aware of the origins for the problem, his own part in creating it, or its connection with other aspects of his life, but he can and does tell the therapist that he wants something to change—himself, other people, or his situation. Therapy can begin from there.

The worker helps the client explore and articulate beliefs about self, expectancies, and goals, attributions for difficulties and barriers in the current situation, and past and current problem-solving strategies employed by the client. Historical information may help in surfacing important self-beliefs, but assessment generally is present, or here-and-now oriented. The worker inquires about the client's conscious thoughts, and is not concerned with unconscious ideation. The worker may assist the client in identifying and becoming more aware of the thoughts and thinking that underlie

> Enhancing client awareness sets the context for social work assessment and intervention.

his or her views, feelings, and behaviors that were not previously recognized.

Assessment includes efforts to identify aspects of the client's view that are characteristic of his or her cultural environment. This means, as well, taking special care to avoid mislabeling as "irrational," dysfunctional, sick, or abnormal, thoughts and views that, in the context of the client's cultural milieu, reflect adaptive and shared meanings.

Intervention

In general, cognitive approaches to helping are likely to be somewhat structured and time limited. They call for an active and involved stance on the part of the worker who directs and guides the helping effort. Cognitive helping is explicitly educational in emphasis; the worker may function as a "coach" or teacher, and the client may be given "homework" or instructed to practice between sessions.

The client is helped to examine carefully some aspect of cognitive functioning (which aspect or aspects will vary depending on the specific cognitive theory chosen), and to engage in a series of tasks designed to (1) change, modify, or restructure existing ways of thinking, or (2) add on to or augment cognitive functioning through learning new information or new skills. The worker attends to maximizing conditions that facilitate change. These include (1) clear specification of what is to be done or attempted, (2) choosing tasks or behaviors that provide opportunities for feedback to the client, (3) exploring the client's perceptions of risks and consequences resulting from targeted change, and (4) assessing obstacles or restrictions, including a lack of resources or incomplete information or knowledge (Fleming, 1981).

Berlin (1983) outlined one model of intervention for social workers that integrates concepts and techniques from cognitive theory. Given the social work concern for helping people deal with a variety of life problems, Berlin's personal problem-solving model has the advantage over other therapeutic models of being explicitly tied to coping and coping strategies. The model also suggests multiple points of intervention and diverse techniques, both of which are helpful for flexible social work practice.

The nine-step problem-solving process is viewed as both a model for therapeutic intervention and a way of managing one's life. Thus clients can be helped to deal with their immediate concern while at the same time learning more effective problem-solving skills for the future. The model is outlined in Table 6.3. Key aspects of effective and less effective cognitive functioning in a problem-solving sequence are identified. A more detailed explanation of one sequence and the cognitive techniques that can be employed follows.

Berlin points out that lack of awareness of early warning signs of problems or trouble can lead to problems growing to overwhelming proportions, making coping more difficult. Recognition of early internal warning signs of anger allows the person behavioral choices such as leaving the room. External warnings, such as marked behavior changes in children, may go unnoticed or unrecognized as warning signs. Once again, effective coping efforts are not forthcoming or delayed until trouble deepens. Berlin (1983, p. 1100) describes several techniques for enhancing awareness of early warning cues:

- Provide an explanation for the importance of attending to problem antecedents.
- Help clients reflect about events and feeling leading to their awareness of the current problem, and then help them to identify similar sequences of events that led to other related problems.
- Give clients information they are lacking about relevant social, familial, or organizational dynamics, for example, about how the school, the welfare department, or the gas company works; about how babies grow or how women become pregnant.
- Elicit information about the client's emotions; show clients how emotions can be used as information for coping.

The following case excerpt illustrates work with a client focused on defining the problem, generating solutions, and analyzing options and making a decision:

Tom was a 20-year-old, part-time university student who came to the student counseling center complaining that he was anxious, uncomfortable at school, unsure about continuing, and in a quandary about what to do with his life. He expressed critical and hostile feelings toward other students, from whom he felt isolated. He then was self-critical for having such a negative view. He was spending as little time on campus as possible. In a review of his academic performance, the worker learned that Tom was a strong B student in all of his classes except for math. He had received a D in a required math course the previous semester and was retaking it. He was not doing well, and acknowledged that he was not spending much time on the homework and was not attending the math lab. He would need a second math course as well to complete his major. Tom had friends outside of school, and stated that he felt comfortable when he was with people he knew and to whom he was known. He said he enjoyed his other classes. This more differentiated negative and positive view of Tom's situation became apparent when the worker asked Tom to identify the specific environments and circumstances in which he experienced his constellation of negative thoughts, and environments and circumstances when he did not.

With further exploration, it became clearer that Tom's thinking, feeling, and behavior with respect to math and math class provided a more specific instance of the generalized complaints with which he had come to the cen-

Table 6.3. The Personal Problem-Solving Model

	Awareness
Not aware	Aware of early warning cues (internal and external)
	Expectations
Expect that I can't cope with this	Expect I can solve this problem
Expect that nothing I can do will help	Expect I can influence a better outcome
	Defining problem
Stay stuck in a general feeling of unease	Specify exactly *what is* wrong
	Figure out the conditions (inside of you and outside of you) that influence the problem
	Think of solution alternatives
	(Discriminate areas of personal control)
Keep possibilities narrow	Based on probable causes and creative thinking, generate a variety of possibilities, including doing nothing
	Analyze options and decide
Be led by force of habit	Figure out task requirements
	Look at costs and benefits of each option
	Take action and persevere
Don't ever start; get bogged down by anxiety and self-doubt	Review alternatives, prepare, and take action
Give up after a few setbacks	Give new plan a fair trial, expect setbacks, analyze them, and help yourself through them

Attributions	
Look primarily at shortcomings, blame them on personal inadequacy	Take credit for successful efforts and positive abilities
Attribute any successes to luck or factors outside self	Figure out if and how you can cope with remaining problems
Analyze progress and modify plan	
Stay hazy about the effects of new work	Look at what is working, what is not working, and what needs to be changed; modify plan
Attribute failure to inadequate abilities and success to luck or external factors	Attribute success to ability and effort, and attribute other failure to modifiable effort on external factors
Maintenance of change	
Assume success is final or assume failure at first nonmaintenance	Anticipate and prepare for high-risk situations
	Know that one nonmaintenance does not make a failure

Source: Berlin, S. (1983) "Cognitive-Behavioral Approaches." In A. Rosenblatt and D. Waldfogel (Eds.), *Handbook of Clinical Social Work*. San Francisco: Jossey-Bass, Inc., p. 1099. Reprinted with permission.

ter. He had high expectations of himself and his performance, and expected to be able to achieve good results quickly. He felt anxious and uncomfortable around the students in math class, negatively portraying them as "nerds." He then became self-deprecating for holding such negative attitudes. He was avoiding math lab or any other opportunities to work on his math outside of class because of spending as little time as possible on campus.

Problem-solving focused on improving Tom's performance in math. Problem definition moved from one of a more general feeling of unease to a specification of one thing that clearly was wrong. Through exploration of the math situation, Tom acknowledged that the course exams were largely based on the homework assignments, which he was not completing nor getting available help with. The worker suggested getting the homework done as an initial task.

With the worker's help, Tom began to generate possible alternative solutions to his problem beyond his initial stated solution that he needed to spend more time on his homework. Additional solutions included: meeting with the professor after class; attending a tutorial group that was offered; making time available for math lab, which meant spending more time on campus. Tom and the worker analyzed the proposed options and Tom was able to see that his habitual response was to avoid doing the homework, which he could not complete easily and quickly, while chastising himself that he should be able to do this work. He explored the obstacles, risks, and benefits to each of the proposed solutions. He decided to attend the math lab and the tutorial group and recognized that he was avoiding the campus just as he was avoiding the homework. Both the lab and the tutorial would provide interaction with fellow students and a chance to become known.

In helping Tom, the worker used the strategy of monitoring thoughts. The worker asked Tom to pay attention to the content of the negative thoughts that contributed to avoiding homework. Among these were fear of failure, an expectancy of perfection, and self-blame when work was not accomplished easily. These were discussed, and thoughts that were more facilitative of the task were identified and written down on cards so that Tom could refer to them. The worker also provided information to Tom on the impact of avoidance behavior. He coached Tom in monitoring thoughts, and provided specific assignments. The worker used an understanding of context-specific cognitive functioning to identify Tom's strengths, and to identify concrete problems and tasks. The worker also determined that resources were available in the environment that matched the needs of the client.

An understanding of cognitive theory and cognitive change strategies can be a useful component of professional practice whether or not one chooses to follow a cognitive helping model. Carefully integrated into the social worker's conceptual framework, cognitive theory illuminates the personal and subjective aspects of person-environment transactions. These aspects are understandable and accessible, whether the focus of change is the person or the person's environment.

REFERENCES

American Psychiatric Association (1994). *Diagnostic and Statistical Manual of Mental Disorders IV.* Washington, DC: APA Press.

Bandura, A. (1977). Self-efficacy: Toward a unifying theory of behavior change. *Psychological Review, 84,* 191–215.

Bandura, A. (1978). The self system in reciprocal determinism. *American Psychologist, 33,* 344–358.

Bandura, A. (1986). *Social Foundations of Thought and Action.* Englewood Cliffs, NJ: Prentice-Hall.

Beck, A. T. (1976). *Cognitive Therapy and the Emotional Disorders.* New York: International Universities Press.

Beck, A. T., & Emery, G. (1985). *Anxiety Disorders and Phobias: A Cognitive Perspective.* New York: Basic Books.

Beck, A. T., Rush, A. J., Shaw, B. F., & Emery, G. (1979). *Cognitive Therapy of Depression.* New York: Guilford.

Beck, A. T. (1991). Cognitive therapy: A 30-year retrospective. *American Psychologist, 46,* 368–375.

Berlin, S. (1980). A cognitive-learning perspective for social work. *Social Service Review, 54,* 537–555.

Berlin, S. (1983). Cognitive-behavioral approaches. In A. Rosenblatt & D. Waldfogel (Eds.), *Handbook of Clinical Social Work* (pp. 1095–1119). San Francisco: Jossey-Bass.

Berlin, S. (1990). Dichotomous and complex thinking. *Social Service Review, 64,* 46–59.

Chatterjee, P. (1984). Cognitive theories and social work practice. *Social Service Review, 64,* 46–59.

Cowan, P. A. (1978). *Piaget with Feeling.* New York: Holt, Rinehart & Winston.

Dember, W. N. (1974). Motivation and the cognitive revolution. *American Psychologist, 29,* 161–168.

Dobson, K. S., & Block, L. (1988). Historical and philosophical bases of the cognitive-behavioral therapies. In K. S. Dobson (Ed.), *Handbook of Cognitive Behavioral Therapies* (pp. 3–38). New York: Guilford.

Ellis, A. (1962). *Reason and Emotion in Psychotherapy.* New York: Lyle-Stuart.

Flavell, J. H. (1985). *Cognitive Development* (2nd ed.). Englewood Cliffs: NJ: Prentice-Hall.

Fobair, P. (1998). Cancer support groups and group therapies. In J. Williams & K. Ell (Eds.), *Mental Health Research.* Washington: NASW Press.

Fleming, R. C. (1981). Cognition and social work practice: Some implications of attribution and concept attainment theories. In A. N. Maluccio (Ed.), *Promoting Competence in Clients* (pp. 55–73). New York: Free Press.

Germain, C. B. (1973). An ecological perspective in casework practice. *Social Casework, 54*(6), 323–331.

Germain, C. B. (1987). Human development in contemporary environments. *Social Service Review, 61*(4), 565–580.

Germain, C. B., & Gitterman, A. (1980). *The Life Model of Social Work Practice.* New York: Columbia University Press.

Goldstein, H. (1982). Cognitive approaches to direct practice. *Social Service Review,* *56,* 541–555.

Granvold, D. (1994). Concepts and methods of cognitive treatment. In D. K. Granvold (Ed.), *Cognitive and Behavioral Treatment* (pp. 3–31). Pacific Grove, CA: Brooks/Cole.

Horvath, T. B., & Davis, K. L. (1990). Central nervous system disorders in aging. In E. L. Schneider & J. W. Rowe (Eds.), *Handbook of the Biology of Aging* (3rd ed., pp. 306–329). New York: Academic Press.

Hultsch, D. F., & Dixon, R. A. (1990). Learning and memory in aging. In J. E. Birren & K. W. Schaie (Eds.), *Handbook of the Psychology of Aging* (3rd ed., pp. 258–274). New York: Academic.

Ilgen, D. R., & Klein, H. J. (1988). Organizational behavior. *Annual Review of Psychology, 40,* 327–351.

Izard, C. (1989). Studies of the development of emotion-cognition relations. *Cognition and Emotion, 3,* 257–266.

Kagan, J. (1984). *The Nature of the Child.* New York: Basic Books.

Kagan, J. (1989). *Unstable Ideas: Temperament, Cognition and Self.* Cambridge, MA: Harvard University Press.

Levine, K. G., & Lightburn, A. (1989). Belief systems and social work practice. *Social Casework, 70,* 139–145.

Mahoney, M. J. (1974). *Cognition and Behavior Modification.* Cambridge, MA: Bollinger.

Mahoney, M. J. (1988). Cognitive sciences and psychotherapy. In K. S. Dobson (Ed.), *Handbook of Cognitive-Behavioral Therapies* (pp. 357–386). New York: Guilford.

Mahoney, M. J. (1995). Theoretical developments in the cognitive psychotherapies. In M. J. Mahoney (Ed.), *Cognitive and Constructivist Psychotherapies* (pp. 3–19). New York: Springer.

Markus, H., & Zajonc, R. B. (1985). The cognitive perspective in social psychology. In G. Lindzey & E. Aronson (Eds.), *The Handbook of Social Psychology* (3rd ed., Vol. 1, pp. 137–230). Hillsdale, NJ: Erlbaum Associates.

Markus, H., Smith, J., & Moreland, R. L. (1985). Role of the self-concept in the perception of others. *Journal of Personality and Social Psychology, 49,* 1494–1512.

Meichenbaum, D. (1985). Cognitive-behavioral therapies. In S. J. Lyn & J. P. Garske (Eds.), *Contemporary Psychotherapies* (pp. 261–286). Columbus: Charles E. Merrill.

Mischel, W. (1973). Toward a cognitive social learning reconceptualization of personality. *Psychological Review, 80,* 252–283.

Nannis, E. D. (1988). A cognitive-developmental view of emotional understanding and its implications for child psychotherapy. In S. R. Shirk (Ed.), *Cognitive Development and Child Psychotherapy* (pp. 91–115). New York: Plenum.

Nurius, P. S. (1989). The self-concept: A social cognitive update. *Social Casework, 70,* 285–294.

Nurius, P. S., Lovell, M., & Edgar, M. (1988). Self-appraisals of abusive parents: A contextual approach to study and treatment. *Journal of Interpersonal Violence, 3,* 458–467.

Piaget, J., & Inhelder, B. (1969). *The Psychology of the Child.* New York: Basic Books.

Polanyi, M. (1966). *The Tacit Dimension.* Garden City, NY: Doubleday.

Quinn, N., & Holland, D. C. (1987). Culture and cognition. In Holland, D. C. & Quinn, N. (Eds.), *Cultural Models in Language and Thought* (pp. 3–35). Cambridge: Cambridge University Press.

Radke-Yarrow, M., Zahn-Waxler, C., & Chapman, M. (1983). Children's prosocial dispositions and behaviors. In P. H. Mussen (Ed.), *Handbook of Child Psychology* (Vol, IV, 4th ed., pp. 469–545). New York: Wiley.

Schaie, K. W. (1996). Intellectual development in adulthood. In J. Birren & K. W. Schaie (Eds.), *Handbook of the Psychology of Aging* (pp. 266–286). San Diego: Academic.

Sherman, S. J., Judd, C. M., & Park, B. (1989). Social cognition. *Annual Review of Psychology, 40,* 281–326.

Siegler, R. S. (1983). Information Processing Approaches to Development. In P. H. Mussen (Ed.) *Handbook of Child Psychology* (Vol. I., 4th ed., pp. 129–211). New York: Wiley.

Sperry, R. W. (1993). The impact and promise of the cognitive revolution. *American Psychologist, 48,* 878–885.

Sternberg, R. J., & Berg, C. A. (1987). What are theories of adult intellectual development theories of? In C. Schooler & K. W. Schoie (Eds.), *Cognitive Functioning and Social Structure over the Life Course* (pp. 3–23). Norwood, NJ: Ablex.

Taylor, B., & Taylor, A. (1989). Social casework and environmental cognition: Mobility training for community mental health services. *Social Work, 34,* 463–467.

Wadsworth, B. J. (1971). *Piaget's Theory of Cognitive Development.* New York: David McKay.

Weiner, B. (1985). An attributional theory of achievement, motivation, and emotion. *Psychological Review, 92,* 548–573.

Weick, K. E. & Roberts, K. (1993). Collective mind in organizations. *Administration Science Quarterly, 38,* 357–81.

Werner, H. D. (1982). *Cognitive Therapy.* New York: Free Press.

Whiteman, M., Fanshel, D., & Grundy, J. F. (1987). Cognitive behavioral interventions aimed at anger of parents at risk of child abuse. *Social Work, 32,* 469–474.

Willis, S. L. (1996). Everyday problem solving. In J. Birren & K. W. Schaie (Eds), *Handbook of the Psychology of Aging* (pp. 287–307). San Diego: Academic.

GLOSSARY

Accommodation.   Taking into account new information and creating new cognitive schemes.

Adaptation.   Use of cognitive processes such as assimilation and accommodation to increase or enhance person-environment fit.

Assimilation.   The cognitive process by which the person integrates new perceptual information into existing ways of thinking.

Attributions.   Beliefs about the causes of behavior.

Causality.   An awareness of cause and effect relationships.

Classification. One of the concrete operations; the ability to classify objects, taking into consideration simultaneously two or more classes.

Cognition. Knowledge, thinking, and problem-solving; higher mental processes.

Cognitive dissonance. Cognitive conflict and instability.

Cognitive processes. The mental processes with which the person perceives, organizes, remembers, and evaluates available information.

Cognitive structures. That which provides the information to interpret reality and engage in problem-solving behavior.

Concepts. The organization of information from multiple experiences into a class or category.

Concrete operational stage. The third of Piaget's stages occurring between 7 and 11 years of age when the child reasoning becomes logical in concrete situations.

Conservation. One of the concrete operations; the conceptualization that the amount or quantity of matter stays the same regardless of changes in shape or position.

Cross-cultural invariance. An approach that suggests that the sequence of peoples' development is identical for all individuals.

Culturally relative. An approach to development that suggests that a portion of knowledge consists of the shared beliefs of the society of which one is a part and is therefore culturally distinctive.

Egocentric. Preoccupation with one's personal world view, rather than the exchange of ideas.

Expectancies. Hypotheses about outcomes.

Formal operational stage. The fourth of Piaget's cognitive developmental stages occurring from 11 to 15 years of age when the ability to solve all classes of problems develops, including hypothetical and scientific problems.

Information exchange. Reciprocal exchanges between personal and environmental realities.

Intentionality. The initiation of goal-directed behavior.

Locus of control. Locating a problem or decision making within or beyond one's personal control.

Mediating role. Causal networks comprised of events that contribute to behavior and those that influence thinking.

Misattribution. Inaccurate perceptions of the sequence of events.

Object permanence. The child's awareness that objects continue to exist even when they cannot be seen.

Propositions.   Relating of two or more concepts to form rules, beliefs, and hypotheses.

Possible self.   An individual's conceptions of what one would and would not like to come to be.

Preoperational stage.   The second of Piaget's cognitive stage occurring between 2 and 7 years of age during which a conceptual symbolic approach emerges in the child.

Reciprocal determinism.   One system's influence on another.

Representational intelligence.   The ability to internally represent objects and solve problems mentally.

Reversability.   One of the concrete operations; the ability to follow a line of reasoning back to where it started.

Schemata.   Cognitive structures by which individuals intellectually adapt to and organize the environment. Abstract representation of the distinctive features of an event or stimuli.

Self-attribution.   Internalized socially generated labels.

Self-concept.   Ideas about oneself.

Self-efficacy.   The belief system about oneself with respect to capability for performance.

Sensorimotor stage.   The first of Piaget's stages of cognitive development occurring from birth to 2 years of age when reflexive behaviors are noted.

Seriation.   The ability to mentally arrange elements according to increasing or decreasing size.

Stage.   A new psychological reorganization that can result from maturational forces, deep insights, and changed demands and opportunities of the environment accompanying life shifts.

CRITIQUE

Cognitive Theory for Social Work Practice
Context, Applications, and Questions

NANCY POE WINGFIELD

To ascertain the value and relevance of cognitive theory and cognitively derived approaches to contemporary social work practice, it is necessary to consider the current context of professional practice and attendant trends in research, policy, and practice protocols. This critique provides an overview of contextual considerations that frame the use of cognitive theory, and delineates how the theory and its related applications are used in social work intervention.

CONTEXTUAL CONSIDERATIONS

Cognitive theory marked a dramatic divergence from Freudian traditions that emphasized the importance of instinctual drives and needs and from behaviorist traditions that emphasized the importance of environmental consequences in shaping human behavior. Indeed, the incorporation of cognitive theorizing into psychological and social sciences, with its focus on the active role taken by individuals in mediating their own experiences, represents "one of the most powerful developments of the twentieth century" (Mahoney, 1991, p. 67). Accordingly, cognitively derived approaches have been used in ever-widening fields of practice since the 1970s (Beck, 1995; Stadjkovic & Luthans, 1998), with mounting empirical support for their efficacy in helping to effectuate positive change in persons' lives and relationships (Hollon & Beck, 1994).

Even so, scientists remain unsure about the precise nature of "the mind" and its processes (Wilson, 1998), and even more so about how to translate and apply these to "strategic efforts toward human change" (Granvold, 1994, p. 26). Two phenomena are in motion at the close of the twentieth century that will undoubtedly yield significant changes in our understanding of cognition and its role in interventions to allay human suffering: (1) developments in brain research and genetic science and (2) wide-ranging policy initiatives that increasingly determine available and appropriate practice protocols.

Developments in Brain Research and Genetic Science

Knowledge of the human mind, once the realm of philosophers and theologians, is now a matter for investigation in the hard sciences due to overwhelming advances in medical technology. The "cutting edge of this endeavor is cognitive neuroscience . . . an alliance formed by neurobiologists, cognitive psychologists, and a new school of empirically minded philosophers sometimes referred to as neurophilosophers" (Wilson, 1998, p. 99). Concurrent with the formation of new disciplines emerging from the juncture between biology and psychology has been an accumulation of massive amounts of data on mental processes and disorders from the 1990s "Decade of the Brain" federal research initiative (Library of Congress, 1998; National Center for Genome Resources, 1998). Theoretically, the scientific explosion may reveal that the explanations for myriad human difficulties lie in DNA, with solutions found not in effective social work intervention, but rather in chromosomal engineering.

Policy-Practice Curriculum

There has been a movement toward pragmatism and interdisciplinary cooperation within therapeutic fields, ushered in by changes in health care policy, most notably insurance reimbursement schedules and managed care for professional services. As a result, "workers are being encouraged to do 'what works' in the most expeditious manner possible" (Wright & Schrodt, 1989, p. 267). The result has been a growing demand for operationalization and accountability in service delivery systems across disciplines (Shae & Howell, 1998; Stein, 1997). Helping professionals are increasingly engaged in efforts to specify, if not quantify, foci of "treatment," prove results, and to minimize duration and parameters of intervention. These contemporary demands are congruent with cognitive approaches that, as a matter of course, identify and specify targets for intervention and tend to be time-limited.

A corollary to the policy-practice nexus alluded to earlier is the press to acknowledge and address psychosocial difficulties as entailing biophysical underpinnings. Cognitivists have responded in a variety of ways, one of which has been widespread adoption of multimodal treatment strategies that combine pharmacology with traditional cognitive interventions.

Multimodal treatment in mainstream cognitive work, especially for persons with "serious disorders," has been widely recognized (Alford & Beck, 1997; Wright, 1987). Given the current climate of knowledge expansion and service contraction, how are cognitive theory and its derivatives being applied in contemporary social work practice?

Overview of Social Work Applications

The cognitive literature offers many examples of the utility of the theory in designing interventions pertaining to social work with diverse clientele in various fields and concerns of practice. Indeed, cognitive approaches have an established track record in work with individuals who exhibit depression (Hollon & Carter, 1994), anxiety disorders (Street & Barlow, 1994), eating disorders (Craighead & Kirkley, 1994), personality disorders (Freeman & Leaf, 1989), suicidal behavior (Freeman & White, 1989), and seemingly all manner of personal pathologies, mental health problems, or emotional disturbances. Aside from these psychiatric applications, the utility of cognitive approaches in fields more closely aligned with traditional social work practice is gaining ground.

Social workers are using cognitive approaches with clients in home-based, school-based, as well as office settings to deal with problems of child abuse and neglect (Heying, 1985; Hodges & Blythe, 1992; Kowal et al., 1989; Lutzker, 1990; Mueller & Leviton, 1986). New directions in family preservation, foster care intervention, school social work, and comprehensive family services are suggested by applications of cognitive theory to parent-training (Barth, Blythe, Schinke, & Schilling, 1983; Craighead & Kirkley, 1994; Holden, Lavigne, & Cameron, 1990).

Divorce mediation work (Cohen, 1985; Coogler, 1978; Pawson & Russell, 1995; Everett & Volgy, 1989) has direct relevance for cognitively based social work performed in conjunction with juvenile and domestic court systems, including child support enforcement efforts. It is not unreasonable to consider the potential of cognitive approaches for helping to restructure the adversarial practices of marital dissolution, replacing the metaphor of "broken families" and "visitation" with descriptions of "reconstituted families" and "co-parenting."

Emery (1981) has found cognitive theory to be an especially applicable and attractive approach in work with older adults. In Emery's opinion, "Many of the problems that face older adults are strongly determined by maladaptive conceptualizations, beliefs, expectations, interpretations, attributions, role definitions, and values" (p. 477). In addition, social work applications of cognitive approaches can be found in the fields of substance abuse services (King & Lorenson, 1989; Larimer & Marlatt, 1994; Shorkey, 1994). Foci of treatment include family issues of "co-dependency" and "enabling" as well as how to conduct "interventions" to break through client "denial," which cognitivists would refer to as a faulty construct (Thomas, 1994; Thomas & Yoshioka, 1989).

Cognitive theory and its therapeutic derivatives are not beyond reproach, however. A common and significant criticism is that they downplay environmental realities and construe personal difficulty as entirely the product of distorted judgments (Coyne, 1994). Similarly, the locale of trouble, and therefore the target for change efforts in cognitively derived methods, is the mind and mental processes of an individual who is experiencing trouble. This criticism is particularly salient for social work, which distinguishes itself from other helping professions in its ecological perspective and focus on person-environment interfaces for understanding human problems and how to go about ameliorating them. Advocacy, political activism, and striving for social and economic justice—all mainstays of the social work tradition—would seem incongruent with cognitive methods, if not outright irrelevant to cognitive views of human distress. For example, Glantz (1989) refuted the appropriateness of cognitively derived approaches for work with geriatric populations by admonishing, "The elderly are likely to face many real physiological, environmental, and social problems that require direct action for amelioration" (p. 477).

Likewise, intervention with client systems beyond the level of the individual would seem contrary to cognitive methods and a significant drawback of the approach. However, social work literature offers many examples of utility of interventions grounded in cognitive theory for the diverse clientele and concerns of practice including group, family, and macrolevel client systems (Stein, 1997). Cognitive group work is actually a method for doing individual work in a collectivity. It begins with a practitioner's assessment of persons in individual preparatory interviews to develop a conceptualization of each client's situation and a hypothesis for starting intervention (Hollon & Evans, 1983). The social worker then assigns clients to a group format on the basis of either shared characteristics relative to the type of problem being encountered (e.g., posttraumatic stress disorder, substance abuse, sexual abuse, or divorce) or shared cognitive strategies being used by group members. With "insider knowledge" of one another, members can provide the social worker with input that may assist him or her to refine conceptualizations of problems for work and therefore improve the therapeutic process.

In addition, the homework assignments that are central to cognitive interventions (Beck, 1995; Niemeyer & Feixas, 1990) can be practiced on, performed with, and witnessed by fellow group members. In-group experiential exercises can be used to augment homework (Wessler & Hankin-Wessler, 1989). Members, in turn, can provide feedback that supports the work of other clients and the social worker. Extending the "coach" and "director" metaphors used to describe the role of social workers using cognitive approaches, group work allows members to become "assistant coaches" and "deputy directors," all the while having their own process propelled by the work of every other member.

Cognitive-based family work reflects the integration of individual-based cognitive approaches with systems concepts and interpersonal communication theory. Although there are innumerable points of entry in cognitive family work, three primary emphases emerge from the literature. First, cognitive family work involves the social worker in attempts to modify unrealistic expectations that members hold of one another and for the family as an entity. Correcting faulty attributions is the second area of intervention. This involves the social worker in helping members become aware of how they frame others' behavior in negative terms. Third, the social worker makes an effort to teach family members skills in "self-instruction" with the goal of decreasing impulsive reactivity. In other words, the worker helps the family members to bring emotions into check, in order for communication to occur in a more reasoned manner (Epstein, 1983).

A cognitive approach to family work is interesting because it reflects a hybrid intervention that combines two seemingly contradictory perspectives. One the one hand, there is cognitive theory that recognizes that problems are "located" in the psyche of an individual (Bedrosian, 1983). On the other hand, there are systems theory and communication theory, which recognize that problems arise not from a person, but from ineffective patterns generated, shared, and maintained by the family as a whole.

Applications of cognitive concepts and approaches to macrolevel intervention are limited, because it is difficult to conceptualize an organization or community as possessing a cognitive center. Even so, applications of cognitive concepts have a long history in social work efforts to effectuate social change, although they have not typically been delineated as such. Program development interventions at organizational or community levels require social workers to create a change, not in the thoughts of an individual client, but in the views of a *target population.*

One may accurately conclude that cognitive theorizing and related methods occupy a central place in the character and conduct of the social work profession. Cognitive approaches are congruent with social work values and principles in a number of important ways, including ideas about starting where the client is, self-determination, the dignity, worth, and uniqueness of clients, and the ability of people to change and grow.

Yet there are limitations to cognitive theorizing and intervention such as working with persons of diminished cognitive capacity, like very young children and those with mental challenges, e.g., those with brain injury, autism, or various forms of dementia. Nonetheless, the utility of cognitive theory in social work practice is far-reaching. If one is honest, she or he may be hard pressed to raise an issue, problem, or client situation that does not entail and require some measure of cognitive formulation. The scope of cognitive theory is broad indeed; virtually all human experience contains cognitive components to one degree or another, imbuing cognitively based intervention with a fundamental, essential quality.

REFERENCES

Alford, B. A., & Beck, A. T. (1997). *The Integrative Power of Cognitive Therapy*. New York: Guilford.

Barth, R. P., Blythe, B. J., Schinke, S. P., & Schilling, R. F. (1983). Self-control training with maltreating parents. *Child Welfare, 62,* 313–324.

Beck, J. S. (1995). *Cognitive Therapy: Basics and Beyond*. New York: Guilford.

Bedrosian, R. C. (1983). Cognitive therapy in the family system. In A. Freeman (Ed.), *Cognitive Therapy with Couples and Groups* (pp. 95–106). New York: Plenum.

Cohen, S. N. (1985). Divorce mediation: An introduction. In D. H. Sprenkle (Ed.), *Divorce Therapy*. New York: Hayworth.

Coogler, O. J. (1978). *Structured Mediation in Divorce Settlement*. Lexington, MA: D. C. Heath.

Coyne, J. C. (1994). Possible contributions of "cognitive science" to the integration of psychotherapy. *Journal of Psychotherapy Integration, 4*(4), 401-416.

Craighead, L. W., & Kirkley, B. G. (1994). Obesity and eating disorders. In L. W. Craighead, W. E. Craighead, A. E. Kazdin, & M. J. Mahoney (Eds.), *Cognitive and Behavioral Interventions: An Empirical Approach to Mental Health Problems* (pp. 141–156). Boston: Allyn & Bacon.

Emery, G. (1981). Cognitive therapy with the elderly. In G. Emergy, S. Holon, & R. Bedrosian (Eds.), *New Directions in Cognitive Therapy* (pp. 84–98). New York: Guilford.

Epstein, N. (1983). Cognitive therapy with couples. In A. Freeman (Ed.), *Cognitive Therapy with Couples and Groups* (pp. 107–123). New York: Plenum.

Everett, C. A., & Volgy, S. S. (1989). Mediating child custody disputes. In M. R. Textor (Ed.), *The Divorce and Divorce Therapy Handbook*. Northvale, NJ: Aronson.

Freeman, A. (Ed.) (1983). *Cognitive Therapy with Couples and Groups*. New York: Plenum.

Freeman, A., & Leaf, R. C. (1989). Cognitive therapy applied to personality disorders. In A. Freeman, K. M. Simon, L. E. Beutler, & H. Arkowitz (Eds.), *Comprehensive Handbook of Cognitive Therapy* (pp. 403–434). New York: Plenum.

Freeman, A., & White, D. M. (1989). The treatment of suicidal behavior. In A. Freeman, K. M. Simon, L. E. Beutler, & H. Arkowitz (Eds.), *Comprehensive Handbook of Cognitive Therapy* (pp. 321–346). New York: Plenum.

Glantz, M. D. (1989). Cognitive therapy with the elderly. In A. Freeman, K. M. Simon, L. E. Beutler, & H. Arkowitz (Eds.), *Comprehensive Handbook of Cognitive Therapy* (pp. 467–489). New York: Plenum.

Granvold, D. K. (1994). Concepts and methods of cognitive treatment. In D. K.

Granvold (Ed.), *Cognitive and Behavioral Treatment: Methods and Applications* (pp. 3–31). Pacific Grove, CA: Brooks / Cole.

Heying, K. (1985). Family based, in-home services for the severely emotionally disturbed child. *Child Welfare, 5,* 519–527.

Hodges, V. G., & Blythe, B. J. (1992). Improving service delivery to high-risk families: The case for home-based practice. *Families in Society, 73,* 259–265.

Holden, G. W., Lavigne, V. V., & Cameron, A. M. (1990). Probing the continuum of effectiveness in parent training: Characteristics of parents and preschoolers. *Journal of Clinical Child Psychology, 19*(1), 2–8.

Hollon, S. D., & Beck, A. T. (1994). Cognitive and cognitive-behavioral therapies. In A. E. Bergin & S. L. Garfield (Eds.), *Handbook of Psychotherapy and Behavior Change* (4th ed., pp. 428–466). New York: Wiley.

Hollon, S. D., & Carter, M. M. (1994). Depression in adults. In L. W. Craighead, W. E. Craighead, A. E. Kazdin, & M. J. Mahoney (Eds.), *Cognitive and Behavioral Interventions: An Empirical Approach to Mental Health Problems* (pp. 89–104). Boston: Allyn & Bacon.

Hollon, S. D., & Evans, M. D. (1983). Cognitive therapy for depression in a group format. In A. Freeman (Ed.), *Cognitive Therapy with Couples and Groups* (pp. 11–41). New York: Plenum.

Homan, M. S. (1994). *Promoting Community Change: Making It Happen in the Real World.* Pacific Grove, CA: Brooks / Cole.

King, G., & Lorenson, J. (1989). Alcoholism training for social workers. *Social Casework, 70,* 375–382.

Kowal, L., Kottmeier, C. P., Ayoub, C. C., Komives, J. A., Robinson, D. S., & Allen, J. P. (1989). Characteristics of families at risk of problems in parenting: Findings of a home-based secondary prevention program. *Child Welfare, 68*(5), 529–538.

Larimer, M. E., & Marlatt, G. A. (1994). Addictive behaviors. In L. W. Craighead, W. E. Craighead, A. E. Kazdin, & M. J. Mahoney (Eds.), *Cognitive and Behavioral interventions: An Empirical Approach to Mental Health Problems* (pp. 157–168). Boston: Allyn & Bacon.

Library of Congress (1998). *Project on the Decade of the Brain* [On-line]. Available: http: / / lcweb.loc.gov / loc / brain / proclaim.html.

Lutzker, J. (1990). Behavioral treatment of child neglect. *Behavior Modification, 14*(3), 301–315.

Mahoney, M. J. (1991). *Human Change Processes.* New York: Basic Books.

Mueller, M., & Leviton, A. (1986). In-home versus clinic-based services for the developmentally disabled child: Who is the primary client—parent or child? *Social Work in Health Care, 11*(3), 75–88.

National Center for Genome Resources (1998). *What Is the Human Genome Project?* [On-line]. Available: http: / / www.ncgr.org / ncgr / HGP.html.

Niemeyer, R. A., & Feixas, G. (1990). The role of homework and skill acquisition in the outcome of group cognitive therapy for depression. *Behavior Therapy, 21*(3), 281–292.

Pawson, G., & Russell, T. (1995). Social planning: A child welfare exemplar. In J. E. Tropman, J. L. Erlich, & J. Rothman (Eds.), *Tactics and Techniques of Community Intervention* (3rd ed., pp. 187–197). Itasca, IL: F. E. Peacock.

Shae, C. M., & Howell, J. M. (1998). Organizational antecedents to the successful implementation of total quality management: A social cognitive perspective. *Journal of Quality Management, 3*(1), 3–25.

Shorkey, C. T. (1994). Use of behavioral methods in individuals recovering from substance dependence. In D. K. Granvold (Ed.), *Cognitive and Behavioral Treatment: Methods and Applications* (pp. 135–158). Pacific Grove, CA: Brooks/Cole.

Stadjkovic, A., & Luthans, F. (1998). Social cognitive theory and self-efficacy: Going beyond traditional motivational and behavioral approaches. *Organizational Dynamics, 26*(4), 62–78.

Stein, J. (1997). How institutions learn: A socio-cognitive perspective. *Journal of Economic Issues, 31*(3), 729–741.

Street, L. L., & Barlow, D. H. (1994). Anxiety disorders. In L. W. Craighead, W. E. Craighead, A. E. Kazdin, & M. J. Mahoney (Eds.), *Cognitive and Behavioral Interventions: An Empirical Approach to Mental Health Problems* (pp. 71–88). Boston: Allyn & Bacon.

Thomas, E. J. (1994). The spouse as a positive rehabilitative influence in reaching the uncooperative alcohol abuser. In D. K. Granvold (Ed.), *Cognitive and Behavioral Treatment: Methods and Applications* (pp. 159–173). Pacific Grove, CA: Brooks/Cole.

Thomas, E. J., & Yoshioka, M. R. (1989). Spouse interventive confrontations in unilateral family therapy for alcohol abuse. *Social Casework, 70,* 340–347.

Wessler, R. L., & Hankin-Wessler, S. (1989). Cognitive group therapy. In A. E. Bergin & S. L. Garfield (Eds.), *Handbook of Psychotherapy and Behavior Change* (4th ed., pp. 559–581). New York: Wiley.

Wilson, E. O. (1998). *Consilience: The Unity of Knowledge.* New York: Alfred Knopf.

Wright, J. H. (1987). Cognitive therapy and medication as combined treatment. In A. Freeman & V. Greenwood (Eds.), *Cognitive Therapy* (pp. 36–50). New York: Human Sciences.

Wright, J. H., & Schrodt, R. (1989). Combined cognitive therapy and pharmacotherapy. In A. Freeman, K. M. Simon, L. E. Beutler, & H. Arkowitz (Eds.), *Comprehensive Handbook of Cognitive Therapy* (pp. 267–282). New York: Plenum.

7

General Systems Theory

ROBERTA R. GREENE

General systems theory first came to the full attention of the scientific community in the 1960s through the efforts of Bertalanffy, a biologist. General systems theory is not like the other theories presented in previous chapters. It is not in itself a body of knowledge (Janchill, 1969); rather, it is content free and its highly abstract set of assumptions or rules can be applied to many fields of study to understand systemic change (Buckley, 1967, 1968; Stein, 1971; see Table 7.1). This chapter outlines select general systems theory principles and discusses the major contributions of the theory to social work practice. Family therapy involving older adults is emphasized and case illustrations of such interventions are presented.

From its originators' point of view, general systems theory is actually not a theory at all, but "a working hypothesis, the main function of which is to provide a theoretical model for explaining, predicting, and controlling phenomena" (Bertalanffy, 1962, p. 17). Models have been defined in various ways. For example, Kuhn (1970) suggested that modern scientists shared approaches to thinking about problems and assumptions about solutions. Chin (1961) stated that analytical models are "a constructed simplification of reality that retains essential features" (p. 91). Anderson and Carter ([1984] 1999) suggested that models may be described as a way of looking at and thinking about selected aspects of reality that are at a higher level of abstraction than a theory:

> A model is not a description of the real world. . . . It is a map or transparency that can be superimposed on social phenomena to construct a perspective showing the relatedness of those elements that constitute the phenomenon. (Anderson, Carter, & Lowe, [1984] 1999, p. 10)

Models, then, are high-level abstractions that are universal in their application. They may be thought of as simple representations of complex re-

Table 7.1. Systems Theory: Basic Assumptions

A social system comprises interrelated members who constitute a unit, or a
    whole.
The organizational "limits" of a social system are defined by its established or
    arbitrarily defined boundaries and identified membership.
Boundaries give the social system its identity and focus as a system, distinguish-
    ing it from other social systems with which it may interact.
A systems environment is one that is defined as outside the system's boundaries.
The life of a social system is more than just the sum of its participants' activities.
Rather, a social system can be studied as a network of unique, interlocking rela-
    tionships with discernible structural and communication patterns.
There is a high degree of interdependence and internal organization among
    members of a social system.
All systems are subsystems of other (larger) systems.
There is an interdependency and mutual interaction between and among social
    systems.
A social system is adaptive or goal-oriented and purposive.
A change in any one member of the social system affects the nature of the social
    system as a whole.
Transactions or movements across a social systems boundary influence the social
    systems functional capacity and internal makeup.
Change within or from outside the social system that moves the system to an
    imbalance in structure will result in an attempt by the system to reestablish
    that balance.

alities. Analytical models guide the theorist or practitioner in recognizing
what factors to consider in their analysis and in identifying the relationship properties among those factors (Chin, 1961). A comprehensive theoretical model for describing and analyzing any living system, general
systems theory can be applied at all levels of organization, from a cell to
society, and to all forms of human association (Anderson, Carter, & Lowe,
[1984] 1999; Durkin, 1981; Kearney, 1986; Polsky, 1969).

Systems are organized wholes comprising component parts that interact in a distinct way and endure over time (Anderson, Carter, & Lowe,
[1984] 1999). Bertalanffy (1968) intend-
ed general systems theory to be used
in understanding "systems in general,
whatever the nature of their component elements and the relations of focus between them" (p. 37). That is,
general systems theory principles are
intended to be used with all complex,
highly diverse living systems to examine their similar relational properties
(or to understand the interaction within any social system). The notion that
all systems have similar relational properties that can be analyzed using

> Systems theory provides social
> workers with a means of
> simultaneously understanding the
> interrelatedness of several complex
> variables, whether they be physical,
> social, or psychological.

general systems principles may seem "deceptively simple" (Durkin, 1972, p. 11). However, scientists and practitioners have viewed this analytical approach as a revolutionary departure from earlier mechanistic, reductionist thinking—it emphasizes the interrelatedness and mutual interdependence of systems elements (Buckley, 1967, 1968; Durkin, 1972; Hearn, 1958).

Although highly abstract and not applied systematically, systems theory has significantly influenced social work practice (Drover & Shragge, 1977; Hearn, 1958; Leighninger, 1977; Stein, 1971). Systems theory was instrumental in moving social work from a simple "medical model" with a linear view of causation, in which x causes y, to a more multicausal context for understanding human behavior (Petr, 1988). General systems theory provides a conceptual scheme for understanding the interactions among a number of variables, rather than reducing explanations of behavior to one simple cause. By helping the practitioner synthesize information from many different disciplines, systems theory principles were found to be useful as a theoretical framework for examining human behavior (Berger & Federico, 1982). For example, a linear explanation of male / female differences in behavior might attribute such differences to hormonal balance, rather than to a number of interacting biological, social, and psychological factors. In other words, general systems theory is a conceptual tool to help study and explain such complex phenomena as role behavior and gender identity, by considering a number of contributing variables.

In addition, systems theory has been an important influence on social work practice because it drew attention to the need for the social worker to examine the multiple systems in which people function. An example of how to use a systems perspective as an integrating tool for understanding many systems at once is in a social work assessment of an older adult's biopsychosocial functional capacity, which requires that knowledge derived from a number of different systems be placed in a family and community context (Greene, 1986; Martin & O'Connor, 1989).

Because it is an approach that considers the many systems in which people interact, general systems theory gave new direction to the social work assessment and intervention processes. Most important, the theory influenced the way in which the profession defined a "case" or a "client." Meyer (1973a) aptly described how the systems perspective shaped that definition:

> The case may be defined as a person, a family, a hospital ward, a housing complex, a particular neighborhood, a school population, a group with particular problems and needs, or a community with common concerns. . . . The drawing of a systemic boundary rather than a linear one provides for the true psychosocial perception of a case, because it includes the significant inputs into the lives of the individuals involved. (p. 50)

This broader definition of a case allows the social worker to better decide what is the target of change—the individual client, the family, or larger system, or both—or whether it is appropriate to intervene at all.

Because systems theory can be applied to systems of varying sizes and complexity, the theory has been found to be useful at all levels of practice and planning. The principles of general systems theory have been used in social work practice to understand and intervene in an individual's life problems and have also been applied to various forms of social organization, including families, social groups, corporations, and communities. The theory's emphasis on interdependence and interaction among systems components and its interest in what makes social systems adaptive or maladaptive are two important reasons for its usefulness in social work practice.

> Systems theory provides a framework for understanding the organizational qualities of a social system of any size and the dynamic interaction of its members.

General systems theorists have supplied a much needed means of accounting for stability and change within and among various social systems—another reason for the theory's usefulness in social work practice. The concept that social systems are not static, but instead are purposive, goal directed, and in constant states of interchange with their environments is important to keep in mind when problem-solving and determining possibilities for intervention and change.

Systems theory has broadened the social work profession's understanding of human behavior in the social environment and has given it a more value-free orientation. The theory's broad, universal principles that begin with the person-in-environment focus not only allow for, but suggest the inclusion of cross-cultural content. Therefore, systems theory is highly suitable for working with diverse client populations. Bush, Norton, Sanders, and Solomon (1983) supported this view, suggesting that systems theory "is a viable way for conceptualizing transactions between social systems and Blacks . . . as well as developing strategies for change" (p. 110).

The focus of systems theory on the interrelatedness of social phenomena is perhaps its major contribution to social work practice. This perspective has refocused attention from individual behavior to the dynamic interaction among systems members. Behavior from a systems perspective has come to be understood as the product of the dynamic interaction and relationship ties among the people who comprise a system. From a social systems point of view, behavior also is understood as the outcome of the total social situation in which an individual subsystem, group subsystem, or other social unit finds itself (Shafer, 1969, p. 31). A systems view of behavior has had a major effect on the profession's approach to practice by broadening the view of assessment and intervention.

THE PERSON-IN-ENVIRONMENT HISTORICAL CONTEXT
OF SYSTEMS THEORY

It is not surprising that general systems theory has found a home in social work. The theory "provides a scientific framework for the long-standing values of social casework, namely respect for the individual and his self-determination" (Stein, 1971, p. 149). Systems theory also is compatible with the goals of clinical social work—to restore or enhance social functioning—and with the social work profession's interest in the fit between the individual and his or her environment.

The place of systems theory in social work history can be understood, however, only by examining the evolution of how social problems have been perceived. Social workers have defined social problems differently in different historical periods and social contexts. At times, the profession has placed a greater emphasis on the importance of social conditions in examining problems, and at other times, the profession has located problems primarily within the individual (Findlay, 1978; Fordor, 1976).

The dual allegiance of the social work profession to both person and environment began with the founders of the profession. Mary Richmond and Bertha Reynolds are two examples. Mary Richmond (1922) was interested in a casework process that addressed "those processes which developed personality through adjustments consciously affected, individual by individual, between men and their social environment" (p. 98). Bertha Reynolds (1935) first viewed casework as a process of counseling the client on "a problem that is essentially his own" and moved to the position that casework was a "form of social work which assists the individual while he struggles to relate himself to his family, his natural groups, and his community" (p. 235).

According to Findlay (1978), the first stage of the history of social work was pragmatic and "characterized more by direct action than by any concern for the elegance or utility of theory" (p. 54). Caseworkers and group workers assisted individuals and families facing the socioeconomic difficulties arising from the Industrial Revolution. Jane Addams and other early settlement house workers exemplified the approach of assisting clients through advocacy and lobbying efforts.

World War I and the Great Depression saw a change in the perception of and the solution to human problems. When some clients did not respond to advice and material help, caseworkers became increasingly interested in addressing these "resistances" through techniques derived from personality and psychoanalytic theory (Strean, 1971). This shift, which continued throughout the 1940s, directed the attention of the social work profession to "internal" processes and to problems as being primarily psychological in nature.

The second stage in social work practice, beginning in the 1930s and lasting well into the 1960s, was marked by an increase in the number of clients from the middle class and a strong interest in Freudian theory and the "medical model" (see Chapter 3; De Hoyos & Jensen, 1985). Freudian theory shifted the emphasis of social work practice by "affecting the whole process of study, diagnosis, and treatment and recasting the very definition of task . . . by shifting the focus from problem to person" (Janchill, 1969, p. 75).

The 1960s saw an ambivalence about the use of the medical model and its limitations in addressing the impact of the social environment on personal problems. It was at that time that systems theory caught the attention of social work. For example, Meyer (1973a) suggested that "the transition from linear thinking [the medical model] to systemic thinking involved a fundamental change in practice"

> Social work theorists of the 1960s were ready for an approach to social work practice that would allow holistic rather than linear thinking.

(p. 49). Meyer also declared that the day of the medical model was over, or at least on its way to being replaced. Stein (1971) also viewed social work's shift to a person-in-environment focus as one of the major benefits of the systems approach.

The need for a theoretical bridge to address person-in-environment issues and the struggle to overcome the false dichotomy between person and environment have characterized the current stage of social work practice (Berger & Federico, 1982; Hearn, 1979; Janchill, 1969). Systems theory, because of its emphasis on the multiplicity of systems with which people interact, often has been seen as a unifying perspective or conceptual bridge. For example, Hearn (1979) proposed that systems theory would enable social workers to maintain a "simultaneous dual focus on the person-situation-complex" (p. 45). Gordon (1969) suggested that the central focus of social work is to individualize the person-system and the environment-system complex to achieve the best match (pp. 6–7). Weick (1981) has called for "a theoretical base that brings the individual and the social system together in a new partnership, a synthesis that unites divided camps . . . a new amalgam of person and environment" (pp. 140–141).

Writing in the late 1970s, Leighninger (1977, 1978) suggested that the tendency of social work to concentrate on one-to-one interventions with an emphasis on psychological theories was on the wane and that countertendencies to focus on larger social forces of the suprasystem was on the upswing. He went on to say that systems theory had the potential of bridging the gap between micro- and macroforces (Leighninger, 1978). The major contribution of systems theory in this regard was to refocus the location of the "problem" to a more situational or environmental context.

In the 1980s, the profession's interest in systems theory was mixed. Siporin (1980) suggested that systems theory had lost its popularity and was on the way to being replaced by ecological theory (see Chapter 8). On the other hand, Kearney (1986) suggested that the key concepts of systems theory continue to play a pivotal role in understanding the mutual influences of individual and systems behaviors. De Hoyos and Jensen (1985), in a review of the literature, also suggested that social workers continue to pay attention to intersystem phenomena, the person-in-situation concept, and a combination of direct and indirect service. However, throughout the 1990s an examination of the literature and of popular usage suggests that general systems theory is used eclectically and that social workers continue to search for theories that lend themselves to better understanding a client's place in the social environment.

BASIC ASSUMPTIONS AND TERMINOLOGY
OF SYSTEMS THEORY

There are a number of difficulties in sorting out and explicating the basic assumptions and terms of systems theory as they relate to social work. It has been suggested that several confusions confront students of systems theory. Since social work was first introduced to general systems by Hearn (1958, 1979), model building has continued to evolve. Systems theory in its current form contains shared elements with related fields such as cybernetics and communication theory, and has been expanded to encompass an ecological approach (see Chapter 8). In addition, systems theory terms are difficult, complex, and highly abstract, have been popularized, and are not applied systematically. For these reasons, Compton and Galaway (1989) believed that systems theory, at first, may seem strange and unappealing to social workers. Nonetheless, mastery of the basic systems theory vocabulary is necessary before its potential for providing a better understanding of the client in his or her environment can be realized. The following section introduces and defines many of these terms.

Bertalanffy (1974), the founding father of general systems theory, offered the following definition of a system:

> A system is defined as a complex of components in mutual interaction. . . . Concepts and principles of systems theory are not limited to material systems, but can be applied to any [whole] consisting of interacting [components]. (p. 1100)

A system is an organization of objects united in some form of regular interaction or interdependence (Bardill & Ryan, 1973). The components of a system interact with and influence one another. By virtue of this interaction, the component parts form a unique whole. That is, a system comprises united and integrated parts that fit together to form a whole. Systems have a structure, a capacity for performance and relative stability, and exist over time and space. Examples of systems extend from the unity of action among all the cells in the brain that brings about the functioning of the human mind to the pattern of interaction among family systems members that is addressed in family therapy.

A *social system* is a defined structure of interacting and interdependent persons that has the capacity for organized activity. As social systems evolve or develop over time, each system takes on a unique character with each member taking on differentiated roles. Systems theory offers a way of thinking in an organized, integrated way about reciprocal interactions among the system's members. Troubled families, corporate boards, street gangs, state departments of social services, case management teams, and psychiatric wards are among the social systems with which social workers may be involved.

> Systems theory assumes that the world is orderly and that systems can best be understood by examining them as holistic entities.

The family is used throughout this chapter to illustrate the properties of social systems. A *family* is a social system consisting of individuals who are related to each other by reasons of strong reciprocal affection and loyalties, comprising a permanent household or cluster of households that persists over time (Terkelsen, 1980, p. 2). Systems theory assumptions suggest that, to understand a family, each member should not be viewed in isolation. Rather, it is necessary to examine the relationships among family members, and any one individual's behavior is considered to be a consequence of the total social situation (Shafer, 1969):

> A family is far more than a collection of individuals occupying a specific physical and psychological space together. Rather, it is a natural social system, with properties of its own, one that has evolved a set of rules, roles, a power structure, form of communication, and ways of negotiation and problem solving that allow various tasks to be performed effectively. (Goldenberg & Goldenberg, 1980, p. 3)

The translation of general systems theory into family therapy approaches has led to a number of suggestions for the social work practitioner. A family system's structure, organizational properties, its patterns of communication, and its relationship to its environment have become focal points of assessment and intervention with families.

Structure and Organizational Properties

Each family has a unique, discernible structure. *Structure* refers to the pattern of stable relationships among family system members and is based on the functions that each person carries out. In family therapy, the practitioner is helping the family group "take a snapshot" of the system at a given point in time (Anderson, Carter, & Lowe, [1984] 1999). Buckley (1967), a leading systems theorist, recognized "varying degrees of systemness" based on the nature of the organization of the system into systematic relationships (p. 42). He pointed out that the key system's assumption—that the whole is more than the sum of its parts—becomes clear when the unique relational characteristics of the whole are understood:

> The "more than" points to the fact of *organization,* which imparts to the aggregate characteristics that are not only different from, but *not found in* the components alone; and the "sum of the parts" must be taken to mean, not their numerical addition, but their unorganized aggregation. (p. 42)

The idea that the aggregate is not found in the parts becomes more clear through examples. The Big Dipper or the Big Bear constellation cannot be seen when the observer looks at one star at a time. The separate stars take on these images through their arrangement or the manner in which they appear to fit together to form a whole. The principle that the whole is more than the sum of its parts also lends itself to an understanding of why each family takes on a different configuration. Because family systems vary in their interaction and communication, their organizational structure, and their degree of openness to their environment, each family constellation is different. Because no two families are exactly alike, family systems develop discernible and unique communication and structural patterns (Table 7.2). Therefore, the family-focused social worker focuses his or her assessment and intervention processes on the family as a whole and on the particular nature of the relationships among members.

Organization refers to the grouping(s) or arrangement(s) of the system members that facilitates the exchange of energy. The way in which a family system is organized is intimately related to its structure and working order. Organization comes about through the pattern of repetitive exchanges within the family and with the family's environment. Through these repetitive exchanges, roles are differentiated and subsystems and hierarchies are created. A subsystem may be thought of as a *holon* or an entity that is simultaneously a part and a whole. The concept of a holon contributes to understanding that systems or systems members operate or behave at more than one systems level. *Subsystems* (components of a system that are systems of their own) are commonly formed in families by

Table 7.2.   Systems Theory Guidelines for Assessment and Intervention in Family
Social Work

Assume the family is a system with a unique structure and communication
 patterns that can be examined. The purpose of assessment is to work with
 the family to determine what is bringing about its dysfunction.
Define the boundaries of the family system by working with the family to
 ascertain membership. Observe functions and behaviors, and be cognizant
 of cultural forms. Assess the properties related to relative openness or closed
 boundaries by observing and asking about the extent of exchange the family
 has with larger societal systems.
Determine how well the family system fits with its environment. Review what
 additional resources need to be obtained or accessed to improve the family
 system-environment fit.
Develop a picture of the family structure through an understanding of its
 organization. Explore socialization processes, how subsystems are created,
 the nature of their hierarchy or hierarchies, and the way in which roles are
 and continue to be differentiated. Learn from the family how its culture
 influences organizational structure.
Examine the family's communication patterns. Follow the transfer of information
 and resources in and between the system and its environment. Assess the
 relative nature of the systems feedback processes. Determine how this relates
 overall to patterns of interaction. Ask if the family can describe its rules.
 Work with the family to identify dysfunctional triangulation in communication. Ask family members about their specific cultural communication clues.
Determine how responsive the family is to stress. Work with family members to
 identify elements in their structure and communication patterns that
 contribute to entropy, synergy, or achieving a steady state. Explore ways the
 system can decrease stress and move to a new level of adaptation, possibly
 by restructuring.

---

generation, by gender, by interest, and by function. The most enduring of
the subsystems, or subgroups of interacting individuals, usually are the
parental and the sibling subsystems. The dynamic interplay of subsystems
is an important element in a family's functional capacity (Minuchin, 1974).

Throughout the life cycle, family members must be able to negotiate the
required changes, shifting and altering their relationships to meet the
needs of all. This movement through the life cycle is called *family development*. Family development traditional-
ly has involved the phases of the life
cycle connected to childbearing. As
new family forms emerge, family transition points are being rethought
(Davies & Rains, 1995; Kelley, 1996).
Nonetheless, systems theory suggests

> The family is a structure comprised
> of individual, but complementary,
> roles. The family also develops
> subsystems of interacting roles.

that family transitions bring about changes for the individual. Transitions
from worker to retiree, from caretaking mother to mother-in-law, from par-

ent to grandparent, and from spouse to widow or widower are examples (Burnette, 1997; Eggbeen, 1992; Morn, Robinson, & Fields, 1994). To accomplish these tasks, a *differentiation* of family roles within a family occurs (Greene, 1986).

Role is "the sum total of the cultural patterns associated with a particular status" (Linton, [1936] 1976, p. 76). All people occupy "a complex of roles" (Anderson, Carter, & Lowe, [1984] 1999, p. 53). All social systems have two interrelated systems of roles: the instrumental, dealing with socioeconomic tasks, and the expressive, dealing with emotions. Family members may play different roles at different times in the life of the family. The caretaking role, for example, may be fulfilled by the parent for a child or by an adult child for a parent.

Among the issues related to family functioning and role structure, the complementarity of roles is of major importance. *Complementarity* refers to the fit of role relationships and the growth and creative adaptability of the family group (McAdoo, 1993; Sherman, 1974; Spiegel, 1968). To achieve complementarity of roles, one member of the family system acts to provide something that is needed by another. When there is failure in role complementarity, stress is placed on the family system, and the individual experiences role strain, for example, when a person finds him- or herself under pressure to change his or her role in some manner. The outcome of how the individual copes with the pressures depends on his or her capabilities and the adaptability of the family system (Greene, 1986).

The establishment of a *hierarchy*, or the ranking, power, and control of the various members of a system is another organizational property of systems. Even egalitarian or the most dysfunctional of systems have hierarchies. The parental dyad or twosome deciding who can stay up to watch television and when it is time to go to bed is a power alliance often observed in families. This process of defining the

> Family systems theory suggests that family structure may be observed, understood, and changed through planned intervention.

"division of labor" and "pecking orders" associated with family membership is a necessary and key component in establishing a pattern of relationship that is unique to a particular family.

Communication

Communication, the flow of information within and from outside the system, is another important family system's property that is a key to assessment and intervention. Communication can be considered a system of transmitting information between two or more individuals, the cumulative exchanges serving as the basis for evolving relationships between people (Bloom, 1984). When communication occurs between two or more people, it becomes a shared social experience in which interaction and social communication occur. "Interaction is a continuous and reciprocal series of contacts between two or more persons who take each other into account" (Gouldner, 1960, p. 161). In this sense, communication is a shared, complementary process.

By definition, there is always communication within a system, whether it be through a verbal tirade, silence, a pout, a shrug, a formal speech, a smile, or a tear. Interaction is realized through communication, which can be verbal or nonverbal. For example,

> an older uncle reports to the therapist that his new life is unpleasant since he joined the family of his niece. The niece said she thought that he was "getting on in years" and should "not live alone." Now he relates that he is constantly told to do this; don't do that; wash up before dinner; hang up your clothes. This report was given in a calm and measured voice. The therapist noticed that as the uncle talked, he began to tap his fingers on his knee and started to jerk his head nervously. Even though the voice of the client seemed unemotional, his body language communicated agitation. (Greene, 1986, p. 146)

The communication of information sometimes can be so subtle that Bateson (1972) defined it as "a difference that makes a difference" (p. 78). An examination of a system's communication patterns involves content and the processing of information, both verbal and nonverbal. From a social work viewpoint, communication refers to listening, understanding another person, and expressing oneself. Systems take in information and other sources of energy—*input*—as well as give out information—*output*— as they interact with their environment.

Practitioners need to assess how information affects the system's orientation and its organization. How systems gather information about how they are performing and the adequacy of the system's *feedback* (a response to information within the system) are key features in the functional ability of the system. Feedback is "a form of regulating signals" (Janchill, 1969, p. 81). The capacity of a system to establish effective feedback and patterns of communication is of interest because it is strongly related to the system's adaptability.

Family therapists have elaborated on the concept of communication to examine the way in which families are governed (Bowen, 1971). Jackson (1965, 1967) proposed that families operate by following *rules,* many of which are unspoken, and that an understanding of these family rules can lead to a better understanding of family organization. The term "rules" is commonly used to depict the way in which a family strives to maintain or restore defined relationships among its members. For example, "We don't do that" or "No one treats him that way."

Satir (1972), who observed many families in her practice of family-centered social work, suggested that roles in a family, which always are positioned or enacted in pairs, shape communication. These roles fall into three major categories: (1) marital, (2) parental-filial, and (3) sibling. For example, the role of the mother is "attached" to child, brother to sister, wife to husband, and so on. When two members of a family communicate, it is not unusual for a third to join in the interaction, and a family communication triangle is formed. *Triangles,* or communication exchanges among three family members, have the potential of resulting in confusion within the family, sometimes resulting in dysfunctions. Because each family has an identifiable communication system, an analysis of the group's particular patterns can be made. These patterns develop over time and generate shared definitions of norms and roles for family members. Satir (1972) believed that helping families understand dysfunctional patterns of family communication was the essence of family therapy.

In general, functional communication involves the use of messages that are clear and direct. The individual who is a functional communicator may restate, clarify, or modify messages when necessary, and is receptive to feedback, checks his or her perceptions, and asks for examples. Dysfunctional communication is unclear. The

> Systems theory places the person—a biopsychosocial system in his or her own right—within a multisystem context.

dysfunctional communicator leaves out connections, ignores questions, generally responds out of context, and often behaves inappropriately (Satir, 1972).

Relationship to the Environment

Systems boundaries may be thought of as imaginary open borders or dotted lines around a system that distinguish the system from its *environment* (everything external to the system's boundary). The bark of a tree, the skin of a person, or the defined number of people in a parish are examples of boundaries. Boundaries are a conceptual and arbitrary way of defining who participates in the system. Boundaries not only define who is inside or outside the system, but distinguishes the system from its environment. From the viewpoint of family systems therapy, it is important for the client system to define its own membership. Once the social worker has identified the client system, he or she can direct attention toward understanding and intervening in the various communication and structural patterns that may lead to dysfunction.

An important systems property that needs to be understood in this regard is the relative openness or permeability of the system's boundaries.

To picture the relative openness of a system's boundaries, visualize a fishing vessel with its fishnet. Nets may be cast closer or farther away from the vessel, and nets may have smaller or larger holes through which water and fish may pass. Like fishnets, all living systems are *open*.

Relatively open systems have a freer exchange of information and resources within the system and also allow the relatively free passage of energy from and to the outside. Relatively *closed* systems are more self-contained and isolated from their environment. This is an important concept for social workers because it can help them understand why families with relatively open boundaries are more likely to ask for services and to use community resources.

Energy, which deals with the system's capacity to act, to maintain itself, and to effect change, is produced internally and also is imported. To better understand the operation of a family system, it is necessary to assess how energy interchange gives a system its capacity to maintain itself. Energy is a form of information or resource that "keeps the family going." Examples of energy used by family systems include a paycheck, a college education, a magazine subscription, or a visit to a museum. Increasing the amount of energy within a system through increased interaction is known as *synergy* and often occurs when systems join forces.

Family boundaries that are relatively open allow members to "reach out" to surrounding systems to obtain or "import" additional energy or resources when internal energies are insufficient. Relatively open boundaries also permit families to export energy in the way of ideas and resources. Access to the outside world provides sufficient energy for a family to allow for growth and elaboration of the system. All systems must be able to grow or change and, simultaneously, all systems must be able to maintain themselves. Families maintain their internal stability and take on their unique character by selectively allowing inputs from the environment. Through this selective process, families also reorganize internally.

Social systems must maintain a balance between change and maintenance. Despite the lack of consensus about their use, there are several useful terms referring to the balance within a system. *Homeostasis,* the most commonly used term to describe a system's ability to achieve balance, is the inclination of a system to restore its balance when threatened. *Equilibrium* is a system's ability to maintain balance without input from the environment. However, equilibrium may bring about temporary instability that eventually leads to growth and development. *Steady state,* the most desirable term used when speaking about a system's balance, occurs when a whole

> Systems theorists are concerned with the movement of resources within and between systems.

system is in balance and is maintaining a viable relationship with its environment (Anderson, Carter, & Lowe, [1984] 1999). *Entropy,* on the other hand, is the tendency of a system to run down or become disordered or disorganized.

Some level of *tension* (stresses and strains on the internal structural organization) as complex adaptive systems develop over time is characteristic of all social systems. Tension is a natural part of a system's evolution as it interacts with the environment (Stein, 1971). Families that are more open to outside energy sources may feel the stresses and strains, but are capable of handling them and grow as a result of tension. Such families are con-

> The family system needs to be understood within the context of its interaction with other societal social systems such as schools and houses of worship.

sidered to be among the more flexible, adaptable, and goal-achieving systems—*functional:* "Functional refers to a judgment about the utility of a structural or behavioral pattern in achieving objectives" (Walsh, 1980, p, 198).

The more closed the boundaries, the more a family operates within its own boundaries. These more self-contained systems are apt to be inflexible, undifferentiated, and less effective—*dysfunctional* (Goldenberg & Goldenberg, 1980). Dysfunctional systems tend to have insufficient organization for meeting the system's goals.

EXPLAINING DEVELOPMENT ACROSS THE LIFE CYCLE

Individual Development

Individual development is a product of complex biological, psychological, and sociocultural factors. These three major dimensions of human behavior interact in a complex manner that is continually being explored and just beginning to be understood. Although content-free (or a set of abstract principles), a systems theory perspective can be helpful in understanding development across the life cycle in several ways. Systems theory suggests a holistic study of human development. A holistic approach is especially critical in client assessment when the multiple influences on biopsychosocial functioning and the many systems in which people interact are examined. Berger and Federico (1982) proposed that systems theory is the practitioner's integrating tool for synthesizing biopsychosocial information and for understanding the reciprocal interaction between and among systems. The ability to make such an assessment and to arrive at a treatment plan within a theoretical framework is the key to sound clinical social work practice.

A systems theory approach also suggests that the social work practitioner take an interactional view of personal development. The systems theory view of personal development is expressed by Buckley (1967), who suggested that "the behaving individual—the psychological being—was essentially an organization that is developed and maintained only in and through a continually ongoing symbolic interchange with other persons" (p. 44). From a systems perspective, personal behavior is considered goal-directed and is modified in response to environmental demands and is understood within this interactional framework.

A systems theory perspective also would suggest that an interactional framework be used to define what constitutes coping behavior. Hearn (1969), in a discussion about coping behavior from a general systems perspective, stated that it is necessary to consider a broad repertoire of observable behavior that may be directed at and effectively deal with the impinging environment.

> Systems theorists contend that consistencies and changes in human development are orderly and follow observable patterns over time.

The study of human development usually centers around the processes of growth, maturation, and directional change that occur over time. Systems theorists believe that interaction among systems members may result in significant changes in individuals and have important consequences for the system as a whole (Buckley, 1967). In this context, understanding a client's behavior involves more than a static explanation of the client's current functioning. It would need to include an evaluation of how the client participates as a member of his or her major systems, how that participation has changed over time, as well as the nature of change in the systems themselves.

Family Development

General systems theory is one of the conceptual models instrumental in bringing about the study of the family group as a developmental unit (Levande, 1976; Rhodes, 1980). The developmental approach to the family suggests that the family is a unit that passes through normal, expectable life stages that tests the group's adaptive capacity. Each change brings a new set of circumstances to which the family must adapt. Minuchin (1974) proposed that failure to meet life transitions may lead families to seek help from mental health or social services agencies. The contribution of systems thinking to the understanding of this process is that it provided a framework for examining how family change is related to its internal workings as well as its external demands (Levande, 1976).

> As individual family members interact over time, patterns, such as the division of labor, authority structure, and rules for behavior, emerge and evolve over time.

Rhodes (1980) captured the idea that throughout the life cycle of the family, group members learn to cope with developmental or maturational tasks and demands requiring adaptation and changes in internal organization:

> Each stage in the life cycle of the family is characterized by an average expectable family crisis brought about by the convergence of biopsychosocial processes which create stage-specific family tasks to be confronted, undertaken, and completed. These family tasks reflect the assumption that the developmental tasks of individual family members have an overriding influence or effect on the nature of family life at a given time and represent family themes that apply to family members as individuals as well as a group. (p. 31)

Systems theory also is useful in understanding the "interactional impact of individuals at different stages in the life cycle and their reciprocal effect on one another over time" (Rhodes, 1980, p. 303). According to Rhodes (1980), it is necessary to understand the family as a social system that has the following four characteristics:

> 1.   Its members occupy various family positions which are in a state of interdependency. A change in the position, status, behavior, or role of one member leads to change in the behavior of other members.
> 2.   The family is a boundary-maintaining unit with varying degrees of rigidity and permeability in defining the family and nonfamily world. Family composition (who composes the family) differs from culture to culture; moreover, shifts in family composition can be identified at different points in the life cycle.
> 3.   The family is an adaptive and equilibrium-seeking unit with patterns of interaction repeating themselves over time.
> 4.   The family is a task performing unit that meets both the requirements of external agencies representing society and also the internal needs and demands of its members. This reciprocity between individual and social needs is known as socialization of family members. (p. 302)

As new family forms emerge, the idea that family development is fixed and sequential is increasingly being questioned (Hare, 1994; Laird, 1996; Van Voorhis & McClain, 1997). Germain (1994) has argued that normative models—which assume that development is a linear movement through sequential stages—were best suited for the nuclear families of the 1950s, rather than the family forms found in contemporary life. She contended that the concept of the life course is better able to embrace diversity and economic, political, and social variables.

Complex Adaptive Systems

Perhaps the major contribution that systems theory makes to an understanding of human behavior in the social environment is an explanation of how systems maintain stability as they grow or change. Systems theorists have proposed that social systems always live beyond their means in the sense that they must continually face the demands of their environment (Norlin, & Chess, 1997; Schriver, 1995). The energy or "intrusions" from the environment bring about change in the system and the potential for it to operate at a higher level of organization—*morphogenesis*. That is, the effect of environmental demands on a social system is to create tensions that can impact on its structural arrangements. Adaptive systems face the demands of their environment by "structuring, destructuring, restructuring" or becoming more differentiated or complex (Buckley, 1968, p. 494; see Table 7.3).

Explaining what properties of a system contribute to its becoming highly integrated and able to interact successfully with the surrounding environment is the key to understanding how systems adapt. The internal organization of an *adaptive* system acquires features that permit it to discriminate, act on, and respond to the environment. Over time, because of this selective process, the system becomes more elaborated and is selectively matched to its environment (Buckley, 1968, p. 491).

Systems theorists have attempted to explain what makes a system relatively more adaptive [to attain a dynamic steady state and demonstrate an (innate) capacity for growth and elaboration]. The systems model assumes that there is organization, interdependence, and integration among parts. Change rests with how well the internal components fit and their fit with the environment. Tension is the source of change and change brings about a reduction in tension (Chin, 1961). Systems that are more self-regulating and self-directed also are seen as having a greater ability to be adaptive or become more complex (Janchill, 1969; Leighninger, 1978).

> Adaptive families have positive, dynamic interactions with their external environments to optimize their internal organization and communication.

Buckley (1967) stated that "openness is an essential factor underlying a system's viability, continuity, and its ability to change" (p. 50). Open sys-

Table 7.3. Key Features of an Adaptive System

Adaptive systems change, become more complex, and maintain a steady state.
The internal organization of an adaptive system acquires features that permit it to discriminate, act on, and respond to the environment.
Information is a key to organizational operation and adaptiveness.
Feedback loops, or error control, are a key to the viability of an adaptive system.
Adaptive systems develop a pool of alternative ideas and behaviors.
Openness is an essential factor underlying an adaptive system's viability, continuity, and its ability to change.
Open systems
- Have a more permeable or partially permeable boundary.
- Demonstrate an active exchange of energy with the environment.
- Experience significant strains on their structure.
- Are capable of increasing differentiation or increasing number and types of roles.
- Provide the potential for individual development or individuation.
- Have a dynamic interplay of subsystems.

Adaptive systems have a more adequate map of the environment.
Adaptive systems produce effective responses to the demands of the environment.
Adaptive systems become increasingly more selectively matched to their environments.
Over time, the selective process of adaptive systems brings about elaboration or growth.
Shifts in structure allow the adaptive system to act competitively on the environment.
Adaptive systems have the ability to reach the same final state from different initial conditions and in different ways.

---

tems have a more permeable or partially permeable boundary, and demonstrate an active exchange of energy with the environment. Because an open system has an active exchange with its environment, it experiences more strain on its structure. At the same time, it is better able to act to maintain a steady state and achieve a system-environment fit.

Buckley (1967, 1968) is best known for his outline of the features that characterize complex adaptive systems. He proposed that complex adaptive systems must manifest some degree of "plasticity," and "irritability" vis-à-vis its environment, to maintain an interchange, have a source of *variety* or a pool of potential responses to meet the changing environment, establish *selective* criteria to sift through the environment to map or code it, and find a way of *preserving* or *propagating* to continue with successful mapping (Buckley, 1968, p. 63).

Because the family is a complex adaptive system found in some form in every society, there is a strong interest in what makes families adaptive. Among the qualities that are thought to make families more adaptive is a

dynamic interplay among their subsystems, an ability to reach the same final state from different initial conditions and in different ways (equifinality), a capability to increase the number and types of roles (differentiation),
and an ability to provide for individual development (individuation).

UNDERSTANDING CULTURAL DIFFERENCES:
CROSS-CULTURAL SOCIAL WORK PRACTICE

General systems theory is particularly useful in understanding the evolution of culture and in appraising transactions between different cultural systems (Norton, 1976). Interacting, relatively open social systems
exchange more energy with their environment and, as a result, develop a
set of shared meanings that serve as a social foundation for their organized
way of life (Chess & Norlin, 1988). *Culture* refers to the way of life followed
by a group. Culture binds a society together and includes its manners,
morals, tools, and technologies (Anderson, Carter, & Lowe, [1984] 1999).
Culture can be thought of as those elements of a people's history, tradition,
values, and social organization that become implicitly or explicitly meaningful to the participants (Green, 1995). "Cultures differ in their world
view, in their perspectives on the rhythms and patterns of life, and in the
concept of the essential nature of the human condition" (Devore & Schlesinger, 1995, p. 9).

Culture refers to the idea that human groups are distinguishable by the
manner in which they guide and struc-
ture behavior, and in the meaning ascribed. Cultures shape the cycle of
growth of the members of a group.
Within the context of those members,
the family maintains itself throughout
its life by adhering to its own particular values, which are a conception, ex-

> Culture is a property that emerges
> from the interactions among the
> members of a group. It is feature of
> daily living that is based on
> relationships and not on individual
> action, as such.

plicit or implicit, distinctive of an individual or characteristic of a group
that is desirable (Kluckhorn, 1951).

Culture comprises those things that are relevant to communication
across a social boundary, and becomes most important when crossing cultural boundaries (Green, 1995). For this reason, the systems theory approach, which offers a means of conceptualizing transactions among
systems, has been seen as having great potential for understanding cultural differences.

An example of the usefulness of systems theory as a framework for understanding cultural differences across social boundaries is Norton's
(1976) "dual perspective." The dual perspective offers another dynamic

way of describing the relationship between the larger societal system and minority systems (Bush et al., 1983). It is a "conscious and systematic process of perceiving, understanding, and comparing simultaneously the larger societal system with those of the client's immediate family and community system" (p. 3). The concept of the dual perspective uses Chestang's (1972) approach, which recognizes that all clients are part of two systems: (1) the dominant or sustaining system—the source of power and economic resources—and (2) the nurturing system—the immediate social environment of the family and community. Social work practice often focuses on the tensions and conflicts that can be experienced because of the dissonance between the sustaining and the nurturing systems.

In his article "Reflections on the Dual Perspective," Miller (1980) recounted a conversation with a minority student that captures the full meaning of the dual perspective:

> For a Chicano like myself it can be very hard. I have found that I am lonely for a people, a culture, a way of life—I have missed my people. Not just my family, but the Chicanos and the Chicano way of life. I miss speaking our language with a group of people. I miss our food and the many varieties of it, miss seeing others like me at restaurants and the movies, miss my people and culture. But aside from that, there is the matter of rethinking what I know and believe. Minority students who have achieved high success in the educational system are often hurt most, because they have to exchange their way of life and their values so as to fit into the mold of that system. I have had to do that for a little while, but I have not given up my way of life and values. I have only placed them aside for a while. Once I return to San Antonio and the barrio, I will again be myself with one difference: I will know how to think like the people that are in control of things; and I will have credentials which they recognize. I will not think like them all the time; only when I want to communicate with them. (p. 59)

The term *biculturalism*—moving from one culture to another—has been extended. Van Den Bergh (1991) has examined biculturalism related to socializing people to diversity issues in the workplace, whereas Lukes and Land (1990) have suggested that, although sexual orientation may not necessarily involve differences in culture per se, it may be helpful to explore how homosexuality is affected by cultural context.

Another major contribution of the systems perspective in cross-cultural social work practice is that the theory helps the practitioner understand the effects of socioeconomic forces on the lives of minority individuals (Matsuoka & Benson, 1996; Oriti, Bibb, & Mahboubi, 1996). By drawing attention to "how certain patterns of deployment of resources as well as certain legislative and administrative decisions place heavier burdens on minorities than on the general population, simply because of the ethnic status and concomitant life experiences," the systems perspective can lead to a better understanding of how power is distributed in American society (Bush et al., 1983, p. 111; McAdoo, 1993; Pinderhughes, 1995). Solomon's (1976) concept of the ethnosystem addressed the issue of empowerment in social work in oppressed communities. She defined an *ethnosystem* as a "collective of interdependent ethnic groups with each group sharing unique historical and or cultural ties and bound together by a single, political system" (p. 45). As part of her conception, American society is viewed "as an open ethnosystem" in which there is "a continuous interchange of energy with successively more encompassing systems" (p. 46). The definition of ethnosystems in this manner emphasizes the interdependent, interrelatedness of ethnic collectivities in the United States, and makes it possible to study the variations in cultural patterns and social organization, language and communication, the degree of power over material resources, and political power.

The concept of the ethnosystem specifically was used to view black families "within the larger context that is formed by the configuration and interacting elements of values, knowledge, and skills" vis-à-vis the "Anglo" culture (Bush et al., 1983, p. 112). Of particular interest was the manner in which the black ethnosystem interacted with larger societal institutions, and the degree of congruence between the values, knowledge, and skills of the respective systems. According to Solomon (1976), when there is a high degree of congruence among the elements within each family, community, and society, and a more equitable distribution of power, black families will be more likely to experience a sense of control and well-being (Figure 7.1).

Lewis (1980) suggested that understanding how clients seek help should take on a system perspective. He gives as an example the practice of Native Americans, who have a long history of using natural helping systems (Figure 7.2). According to Lewis, it is important for practitioners to remember that when a Native American needs help, he or she prefers to go first to the immediate family. If the problem is not resolved, he or she will go to members of his or her social network, next to the spiritual or religious leader, and then to the tribal council. If all else fails, only then will he or she go to a formal agency.

UNDERSTANDING HOW HUMANS FUNCTION
AS MEMBERS OF FAMILIES, GROUPS,
ORGANIZATIONS, AND COMMUNITIES

General systems theory is a means of conceptualizing the mutual interrelatedness of individuals–families–social groups–communities–

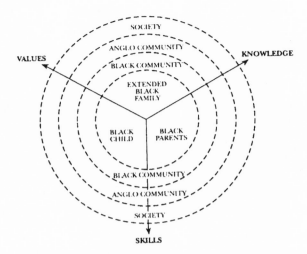

Figure 7.1. A framework for understanding the behaviors of an ethnosystem. From Bush, Norton,
Sanders, & Solomon (1983). Copyright 1983.
Reprinted with permission of Howard University Press.

societies (Fitzpatrick & Gomez, 1997; McKnight, 1997). Because general
systems theory principles apply to all forms of social organization, systems
theory has "major utility for a systems analysis for practitioners of change"
(Chin, 1961, p. 93). Among the processes to be understood is how tension,
stress, and conflict operate within a client system, whether family, group,
or community. In his seminal discussion of the utility of systems theory,
Chin (1961) suggested that a theory of change should answer the following questions:

> How does the theory account for stability and change?
> Where does the model (theory) locate the "source of change"?
> What does the model suggest about how the goals are determined?
> How does the model provide the change-agent with "levers or handles"
> for bringing about the process of change? or What is the role, or place of the
> change-agent? (pp. 100–101)

These broad questions provide a practitioner with a guide for the selection
of interventions with systems of any size.

The value of systems theory for micropractice is that it draws attention
to systems such as schools, employment, medical care, and one's own
agency (Kamerman, Dolgoff, Getzel, & Nelson, 1973, p. 105). For example,

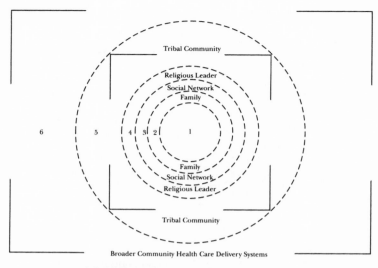

1. Individual
2. Goes to family first
3. Then to extended family (cousins, aunts, uncles, etc.) - social network
4. Religious leader
5. Tribal council
6. Finally formalized health care delivery system

Figure 7.2. Helping methodology must take on a system perspective. Schema: Individual seeking aid, numbered in order of significance for Native Americans and path followed for seeking help. From Lewis (1980). Reprinted with permission of Macmillan Publishing Co., Inc.

Polsky (1969) proposed that "the helping system is the mediator between society and the impaired individual" (p. 19). His observation is a recognition of the idea that the social worker is representative of a community agency, and draws attention to the role of the practitioner as part of the helping system and in the social worker–client relationship system.

Family

Family practice in social work dates back to the inception of the profession. Current practice is a reflection of that earlier commitment and interest and involvement in the family therapy movement with its strong ties to general systems thinking. Although social work has had a long-standing interest in family-centered practice, the profession's approach to working with families was revitalized by family systems thinking (Hartman & Laird, 1987). Currently, many social workers in different fields of practice have adopted family systems concepts and techniques. The goal of social work with families is to alter or facilitate interaction among family members to enhance social functioning (Eyde & Rich, 1983; Silverstone & Bu-rack-Weiss, 1983).

General systems theory concepts may be found with different degrees of emphasis in the major theories of family therapy (Skynner, 1981, p. 49). Herr and Weakland (1979) identified the following six commonalities that stem from systems theory and related disciplines among the various schools of family therapy:

1.   Communication and interaction between people powerfully affects the behavior of every individual involved: their *thoughts, feelings,* and *actions.*

2.   Correspondingly, regardless of past events, characterological and physical traits, or social circumstances, how people interact with each other in the *here-and-now* very significantly influences how they function, for better or worse.

3.   In any durable relationship, patterns of interaction develop, more or less rapidly, and then persist not because any particular behavior is fixed or inherent in itself, but largely because of reciprocal reinforcements . . .

4.   Although such interaction may occur, and be important, in any social organization (a school, a work group, etc.), it is *particularly important in the family,* since this group is ubiquitous and its relationships are long-lasting and of great emotional and practical import for the individual members.

5.   There is a "problem" when some behavior arises and *persists* that is seriously distressing either to the individual himself or to others concerned about the individual's behavior. From a systems view, plainly, *other behavior must be occurring within the system of interaction that provokes and maintains the problem behavior inadvertently and in spite of efforts to resolve it.*

6.   The resolution of a problem requires either some appropriate change of behavior or behaviors within the system of interaction or a change by the participants in their evaluation of the behavior ("Really, that is not such a serious matter after all"). (pp. 51–52)

DIRECT PRACTICE IN SOCIAL WORK: INTERVENING IN THE PERSON-SITUATION TO ENHANCE PSYCHOSOCIAL FUNCTIONING

The use of systems theory as an analytical model provides a broad outline for helping practitioners to decide what to include in their analyses. For example, a systems analysis assumes that the family system has structure and sufficient stability to take "an arbitrary slice" or picture in "frozen time" (Chin, 1961, p. 92). A picture (in the form of an assessment) of the family of later years allows the practitioner to understand how the family is coping with the developmental tasks associated with this life stage. Family systems thinking refocused social workers' attention from the individual and his or her intrapsychic concerns to the functioning of the whole family group. The idea that the family consists of individuals who make up an entity, group, or system is at the heart of this philosophy of treatment.

Family therapy from a systems perspective is an interactional process of planned interventions in an area of family dysfunction. The major contribution of systems theory is that it offers a set of assumptions that examines interrelatedness and mutual interdependence among systems members. The nature and extent of relatedness are matters of assessment. The goal of therapy is to change family structure by altering behavior. This means that family therapy is seen as a means of changing the family relationship structure by modifying members' roles. It also assumes that no one individual is responsible for the behavior of the system, but rather systems behavior is part of a evolving process of interaction. The practitioner's interventions are designed to help family members understand their interactive styles to alleviate dysfunctional family patterns that bring about such "symptoms." In short, family-focused interventions address the structure of the family group and the functions of the individuals within the group (Greene, 1986).

Systems theory calls attention to the various systems in which the client operates, which should be examined. Systems theory offers a conceptual framework for ensuring "a true *transactional* understanding of the person-situation" (Meyer 1973a, p. 51). That is, the social worker will need to consider the broad range of systems that affect the case. The social worker addresses the family or general support system, as well as issues such as housing, income, transportation, health, and health care resources. In this sense, therapy encompasses resource consultation or case management.

Assessment

The use of general systems theory generally requires a broadening of assessment skills (Meyer, 1973b). Assessment involves drawing an arbitrary boundary around the client system, deciding what is the system and what is the environment, and thereby knowing whom to consider. Setting of boundaries to conduct a systems analysis also involves choosing a focal system—or system of attention (Anderson, Carter, & Lowe, [1984] 1999; Greene & Watkins, 1998; Longres, 1990). Assessment requires that the practitioner define how members of a system are related to each other and to be "on the alert for subtle interconnections" (Leighninger, 1978, p. 454). Systems concepts provide a guide for understanding the reciprocal relationship among people, which is necessary information in problem-solving.

Systems theory provides a way of studying the structure of a system. The theory places particular emphasis on communication patterns or the way a system is able to receive, store, process, and recall information. Diagnostic questions that lead to an understanding of the internal and external forces affecting the systems balance are critical to assessment (Chin, 1961). "The most important improvement the change-agent can help a client system to achieve," according to Chin (1961), "is to increase its diagnostic sensitivity to the effects of its own actions upon others" (p. 95). This

> The practitioners use of systems theory guides assessment and intervention toward multiple interactions both within and outside the family system.

improvement involves increasing or unblocking the feedback process that is a long-lasting skill for the client system. With such an understanding, the practitioner can evaluate how internally and externally produced tensions affect the structural dynamics of the system or can lead to structural change. A system is assumed to have this tendency to strive for positive balance. By working with family members to achieve this goal, the practitioner makes his or her most powerful interventions.

Intervention

Stein (1971) suggested that systems theory recasts the role of the social worker as change agent. Systems theory suggests that the social worker as change agent

- brings the client system together to promote self-knowledge about sources of dysfunction and for problem-solving,
- leads the family in an examination of structural and communications patterns,
- points out the here-and-now behaviors that might help the family understand and solve their difficulty(ies),
- asks questions and uses other techniques to coach the family on what behaviors may be more functional,
- works with the family to find and access solutions and resources, and strives to help the family move to a new level of functioning.

Family Therapy with the Family of Later Years

A systems approach to assessment and intervention with the family of later years usually aims to engage the family in problem resolution on behalf of the older adult. Interventions often involve promoting positive interdependence, settling old scores, and arranging and coordinating caretaking plans for the frail older adult (Greene, 1989). The systems properties most examined in the family of later years and that often find their way into therapy are related to issues such as interdependency and intergenerational connectedness. Intervention strategies are aimed at the development of a system of mutual aid and the resolution of "old debts" (Boszormenyi-Nagy & Spark, 1973).

According to Keller and Bromley (1989), a systems approach to therapy with the family of later years suggests that the practitioner have the entire family present for therapy; include an emphasis on joining with the family socially and therapeutically; assume the family is "normal," assess the various sources of physiological and environmental stress; identify the needs, responsibilities, and expectations of all family members; create a context that encourages awareness of underlying "behavioral beliefs"; and develop adaptation options with the family (pp. 34–38; see Table 7.3).

As can be seen in the following case, in family-focused social work, the social worker directs his or her attention toward assisting the family group to sort out what difficulties in normal life events are having an ill-effect on family functioning:

S. was a 75-year-old widow who lived in her own home, located in a community near Baltimore. S. arrived at the nursing home with her son Philip. Her son had called the nursing home and stated this his mother needed placement. Philip, 50, was an only child and now lived and worked in another city in Maryland, a 3-hour drive from Baltimore.

Philip appeared anxious during the social work assessment interview. He expressed concern that his mother could no longer live in the house by herself and required nursing home placement. S. was mortified that her son wanted to put her in a nursing home. Although she admitted she was having a hard time keeping up with the housework, she stated she was able to take care of her personal needs and even took the car out for an occasional shopping trip.

The social worker asked Philip if he agreed with what his mother was saying. He admitted that she did seem to bathe and dress herself, manage her laundry and cook, although he was concerned about what she ate. He also had noticed that the house was messy. Philip remarked that "she just doesn't seem to be able to keep up the house and is so isolated from everyone." The social worker asked about medications. S. piped up and said, "I certainly take that little white pill for my heart every day." The social worker asked if S. was on other medications. S. quickly responded "only an occasional aspirin for my arthritis."

The social worker then asked if both S. and Philip would agree that the only problem S. seemed to be having at this point was in performing household chores. They both agreed. The social worker expressed her concern that although S. was having some difficulty managing at home, she did not need nursing home placement at this time. The social worker explained about homemaker services programs, stating that this service would help S. maintain her home on a regular basis. S.'s face brightened. Relieved, Philip stated that he particularly liked the fact that someone would be checking on his mother. He worried so much about her being by herself. With S. and Philip's permission, the social worker made a referral to a local homemaker service. The program social worker agreed to do a home visit assessment to determine S.'s specific needs. (Colleen Galambos, ACSW, Director of Social Work and Outreach, Cardinal Shehan Center, Baltimore, Maryland)

REFERENCES

Anderson, R. E., Carter, I., & Lowe, G. R. ([1984] 1999). *Human Behavior in the Social Environment*. Hawthorne, NY: Aldine de Gruyter.

Bardill, D. R., & Ryan, F. J. (1973). *Family Group Casework*. Washington, DC: NASW Press.

Bateson, G. (1972). *Steps to an Ecology of Mind*. New York: Ballantine.

Berger, R., & Federico, R. (1982). *Human Behavior: A Social Work Perspective*. New York: Longman.

Bertalanffy, L. (1962). General systems theory: A critical review. *General Systems Yearbook, 7*, 1–20.

Bertalanffy, L. (1968). *General Systems Theory, Human Relations*. New York: Braziller.

Bertalanffy, L. (1974). General systems theory and psychiatry. In S. Axieti (Ed.), *American Handbook of Psychiatry* (Vol. 1, 2nd ed., pp. 1095–1117). New York: Basic Books.

Bloom, M. (1984). *Configurations of Human Behavior*. New York: Macmillan.

Boszormenyi-Nagy, I., & Spark, G. (1973). *Invisible Loyalties*. New York: Macmillan.

Bowen, M. (1971). Aging: A symposium. *Georgetown Medical Bulletin, 30*(3), 4–27.

Buckley, W. (1967). Systems and entities. In W. Buckley (Ed.), *Sociology and Modern Systems Theory* (pp. 42–66). Englewood Cliffs, NJ: Prentice-Hall.

Buckley, W. (1968). Society as a complex adaptive system. In W. Buckley (Ed.), *Modern Systems Research for the Behavioral Scientist* (pp. 490–511). Hawthorne, NY: Aldine de Gruyter.

Burnette, D. (1997). Grandparents raising grandchildren in the inner city. *Families in Society, 78*(5), 489–501.

Bush, J. A., Norton, D. G., Sanders, C. L., & Solomon, B. B. (1983). An integrative approach for the inclusion of content on blacks in social work education. In J. C. Chunn, P. J. Dunston, & F. Ross-Sheriff (Eds.), *Mental Health and People of Color* (pp. 97–125). Washington DC: Howard University Press.

Chess, W. A., & Norlin, J. M. (1988). *Human Behavior and the Social Environment*. Boston: Allyn & Bacon.

Chestang, L. (1972). Character development in a hostile society. Occasional Paper No. 31, School of Social Service Administration, University of Chicago.

Chin, R. (1961). The utility of systems models for practitioners. In W. G. Bennes, K. D. Berne, & R. Chin (Eds.), *The Planning of Change: Readings in the Applied Behavioral Sciences* (pp. 90–113). New York: Holt, Rinehart & Winston.

Compton, B., & Galaway, B. (1989). *Social Work Processes*. Chicago: Dorsey.

Davies, L., & Rains, P. (1995). Single mothers by choice. *Families in Society, 76*(9), 543–550.

De Hoyos, G., & Jensen, C. (1985). The systems approach in American social work. *Social Casework, 66*(8), 490–497.

Devore, W., & Schlesinger, E. G. (1995). *Ethnic-Sensitive Social Work Practice.* St. Louis, MO: C. V. Mosby.

Drover, G., & Shragge, E. (1977). General systems theory and social work education: A critique. *Canadian Journal of Social Work Education, 3*(2), 28–39.

Durkin, H. E. (1972). Analytic group therapy and general systems theory. In C. J. Sager & H. S. Kaplan (Eds.), *Progress in Group and Family Therapy* (pp. 917). New York: Brunner/Mazel.

Durkin, H. E. (1981). *Living Groups.* New York: Brunner/Mazel.

Eggbeen, D. (1992). From generation unto generation: Parent-child support in aging families. *Generations, 16*(3), 45–51.

Eyde, D. R., & Rich, J. (1983). *Psychological Distress in Aging: A Family Management Model.* Rockville, MD: Aspen.

Findlay, P. C. (1978). Critical theory and social work practice. *Catalyst, 1*(3), 53–68.

Fitzpatrick, J. A., & Gomez, T. R. (1997). Still caught in a trap: The continued povertization of women. *Affilia, 12*(3), 318–341.

Fordor, A. (1976). Social work and systems theory. *British Journal of Social Work, 6*(1), 13–42.

Germain, C. B. (1994). Emerging conceptions of family development over the life course. *Families in Society, 75*(5), 259–267.

Goldenberg, I., & Goldenberg, H. (1980). *Family Therapy: An Overview.* Monterey, CA: Brooks/Cole.

Gordon, W. E. (1969). Basic constructs for an integrative and generative conception of social work. In G. Hearn (Ed.), *The General Systems Approach: Contributions toward a Holistic Conception of Social Work* (pp. 5–11). New York: Council on Social Work Education.

Gouldner, A. (1960). The norm of reciprocity. *American Sociological Review, 25,* 161–168.

Green, J. (1995). *Cultural Awareness in the Human Services.* Englewood Cliffs, NJ: Prentice-Hall.

Greene, R. (1986). *Social Work with the Aged and Their Families.* Hawthorne, NY: Aldine de Gruyter.

Greene, R. (1988). *Continuing Education for Gerontological Careers.* Washington, DC: Council on Social Work Education.

Greene, R. (1989). A life systems approach to understanding parent-child relationships in aging families. In G. A. Hughston, V. A. Christopherson, & M. J. Bonjean (Eds.), *Aging and Family Therapy: Practitioner Perspectives on Golden Pond* (pp. 57–70). New York: Haworth.

Greene, R. R., & Blundo, R. (In press). Postmodern Critique Systems Theory in Social Work with the Aged and Their Families. *Journal of Gerontological Social Work, 31*(3/4).

Greene, R. R. & Watkins, M. (Eds.) (1998). *Serving Diverse Constituencies: Applying the Ecological Perspective.* Hawthorne, NY: Aldine de Gruyter.

Hare, J. (1994). Concerns and issues faced by families headed by a lesbian couple. *Families in Society 75*(1), 27–35.

Hartman, A., & Laird, J. (1987). Family practice. In A. Minahan (Editor-in-chief),

Encyclopedia of Social Work (Vol. 1, 18th ed., pp. 575–589). Silver Spring, MD: National Association of Social Workers.

Hearn, G. (1958). *Theory Building in Social Work*. Toronto: University of Toronto Press.

Hearn, G. (1969). Progress toward an holistic conception of social work. In G. Hearn (Ed.), *The General Systems Approach: Contributions toward a Holistic Conception of Social Work* (pp. 63–70). New York: Council on Social Work Education.

Hearn, G. (1979). General systems theory and social work. In F. J. Turner (Ed.), *Social Work Treatment* (pp. 333–359). New York: Free Press.

Herr, J. J., & Weakland, J. H. (1979). *Counseling Elders and Their Families*. New York: Springer.

Jackson, D. D. (1965). Family rules: Marital quid pro quo. *Archives of General Psychiatry, 12,* 589–594.

Jackson, D. D. (1967). The individual and the larger contexts. *Family Process, 6,* 139–147.

Janchill, M. P. (1969). Systems concepts in casework theory and practice. *Social Casework, 15*(2), 74–82.

Kamerman, S. B., Dolgoff, R., Getzel, G., & Nelson, J. (1973). Knowledge for practice: Social science in social work. In A. Kahn (Ed.), *Shaping the New Social Work* (pp. 102–123). New York: Columbia University Press.

Kearney, J. (1986). A time for differentiation: The use of a systems approach with adolescents in community-based agencies. *Journal of Adolescence, 9*(3), 243–256.

Keller, J. F., & Bromley, M. C. (1989). Psychotherapy with the elderly: A systemic model. In G. A. Hughston, V. A. Christopherson, & M. J. Bonjean (Eds.), *Aging and Family Therapy: Practitioner Perspectives on Golden Pond* (pp. 29–46). New York: Haworth.

Kelley, P. (1996). Family-centered practice with stepfamilies. *Families in Society, 77*(9), 535–544.

Kluckhorn, C. (1951). Values and value orientations. In T. Parsons & E. A. Shibs (Eds.), *Toward a Theory of Action*. Cambridge, MA: Harvard University Press.

Kuhn, T. (1970). *The Structure of Scientific Revolutions* (2nd ed). Chicago: University of Chicago Press.

Laird, J. (1996). Family-centered practice with lesbian and gay families. *Families in Society, 77*(9) 559–572.

Leighninger, L. (1977). Systems theory and social work: A reexamination. *Journal of Education for Social Work, 13*(3), 44–49.

Leighninger, R. D. (1978). Systems theory. *Journal of Sociology and Social Welfare, 5*(4), 446–480.

Levande, D. L. (1976). Family theory as a necessary component of family therapy. *Social Casework, 57,* 291–295.

Lewis, R. (1980). Cultural perspective on treatment modalities with native Americans. In M. Bloom (Ed.), *Life Span Development* (pp. 434–441). New York: Macmillan.

Linton, R. ([1936] 1976). *The Study of Man*. New York: Appleton Century Croft.

Longres, J. F. (1990). *Human Behavior in the Social Environment*. Itasca, IL: F. E. Peacock.

Lukes, C. A., & Land, H. (1990). Biculturality and homosexuality. *Social Work, 35*(2), 155–161.

McAdoo, J. L. (1993). The role of african-American fathers: An ecological perspective. *Families in Society, 74*(1), 28–35.

Mailick, M., & Vigilante, F. W. (1997). The family assessment wheel: A social constructionist perspective. *Families in Society, 78*(4), 361–369.

Martin, P. Y., & O'Connor, G. G. (1989). *The Social Environment: Open Systems Applications*. New York: Longman.

Matsuoka, J. K., & Benson, M. (1996). Economic change, family cohesion, and mental health in a rural Hawaii community. *Families in Society, 77*(2), 108–116.

McKnight, J. L. (1997). A 21st Century map for healthy communities and families. *Families and Society, 78*(2), 117–127.

Meyer, C. H. (1973a). Direct services in new and old contexts. In A. J. Kahn (Ed.), *Shaping the New Social Work* (pp. 26–54). New York: Columbia University Press.

Meyer, C. H. (1973b). Purpose and boundaries casework fifty years later. *Social Casework, 54*, 269–275.

Miller, S. (1980). Reflections on the dual perspective. In E. Mizio & J. Delany (Eds.), *Training for Service Delivery to Minority Clients* (pp. 53–61). New York: Family Service of America.

Minuchin, S. (1974). *Families and Family Therapy*. Cambridge, MA: Harvard University Press.

Morn, P., Robinson, J., & Fields, V. (1994). Women's work and caregiving roles: A life course approach. *Journal of Gerontology: Psychological Sciences, 49*, S176–S186.

Norlin, J. M. & Chess, W. A. (1997). *Human Behavior and the Social Environment: Social Systems Theory*. Boston: Allyn & Bacon.

Norton, D. G. (1976). Working with minority populations: The dual perspective. In B. Ross & S. K. Khinduta (Eds.), *Social Work in Practice* (pp. 134–141). New York: National Association of Social Workers.

Oriti, B., Bibb, A., & Mahboubi, J. (1996). Family-centered practice with racially/ethnically mixed families. *Families in Society, 77*(9), 573–582.

Petr, C. G. (1988). The worker-client relationship: A general systems perspective. *Social Casework, 69*(10), 620–626.

Pinderhughes, E. (1995). Direct practice overview. In R. L. Edwards (Editor-in-chief). *Encyclopedia of Social Work* (Vol. 1, 19th ed., pp. 740–751). Washington, DC: NASW Press.

Polsky, H. (1969). System as patient: Client needs and system function. In G. Hearn (Ed.), *The General Systems Approach: Contributions toward a Holistic Conception of Social Work* (pp. 5–11). New York: Council on Social Work Education.

Reynolds, B. C. (1935). Rethinking social casework. *Family, 16*, 235–241.

Rhodes, S. L. (1980). A developmental approach to the life cycle of the family. In M. Bloom (Ed.), *Life Span Development* (pp. 30–40). New York: Macmillan.

Richmond, M. E. (1922). *What Is Social Casework?* New York: Russell Sage Foundation.

Satir, V. (1972). *People Making*. Palo Alto, CA: Science and Behavior Books.

Schriver, J. M. (1995). *Human Behavior and the Social Environment: Shifting Paradigms in Essential Knowledge for Social Work Practice*. Boston: Allyn & Bacon.

Shafer, C. M. (1969). Teaching social work practice in an integrated course: A general systems approach. In G. Hearn (Ed.), *The General Systems Approach: Contributions toward a Holistic Conception of Social Work* (pp. 26–36). New York: Council on Social Work Education.

Sherman, S. N. (1974). Family therapy. In F. J. Turner (Ed.), *Social Work Treatment: Interlocking Theoretical Approaches* (pp. 457–494). New York: Free Press.

Silverstone, B., & Burack-Weiss, A. (1983). *Social Work Practice with the Frail Elderly and Their Families.* Springfield, IL: Charles C. Thomas.

Siporin, M. (1980). Ecological systems theory in social work. *Journal of Sociology and Social Welfare, 7,* 507–532.

Skynner, A. C. R. (1981). An open-systems, group-analytic approach to family therapy. In A. S. Gurman & D. D. Kniskern (Eds)., *Handbook of Family Therapy* (pp. 39–84). New York: Brunner / Mazel.

Solomon, B. B. (1976). *Black Empowerment: Social Work in Oppressed Communities.* New York: Columbia University Press.

Spiegel, J. P. (1968). The resolution of role conflict within the family. In N. W. Bell & E. F. Vogel (Eds.), *Modern Introduction to the Family* (rev. ed., pp. 391–411). New York: Free Press.

Stein, I. (Ed.) (1971). The systems model and social system theory: Their application to casework. In H. S. Strean (Ed.), *Social Casework Theories in Action* (pp. 123–195). Metuchen, NJ: Scarecrow.

Strean, H. S. (Ed.) (1971). *Social Casework Theories in Action.* Metuchen, NJ: Scarecrow.

Terkelsen, G. (1980). Toward a theory of the family cycle. In E. A. Carter & M. McGoldrick (Eds.), *The Family Life Cycle: A Framework for Family Therapy* (pp. 21–52). New York: Gardner.

Van Den Bergh, N. (1991). Managing biculturalism in the workplace: A group approach. *Social Work with groups, 13*(4), 71–84.

Van Voorhis, R. & McClain, L. (1997). Accepting a lesbian mother. *Families in Society, 78,* 642–650.

Walsh, F. (1980). The family in later life. In E. A. Carter & M. McGoldrick (Eds.), *The Family Life Cycle: A Framework for Family Therapy* (pp. 197–222). New York: Gardner.

Weick, A. (1981). Reframing the person-in-environment perspective. *Social Work, 2,* 140–143.

GLOSSARY

Adaptive systems. Systems that discriminate well and act effectively on their environments. Adaptive systems are more complex because they have a greater capacity to grow and to elaborate their structures.

Boundary. Permeable "limits" to the system that define what is considered inside or outside the system; boundaries regulate the flow of energy into (inputs) and out of (outputs) the system.

Closed systems. Systems characterized by a less active exchange with the environment. They are less goal-oriented and have a lesser ability to modify behavior.

Communication.   The flow of information between and among systems' members and between and among systems.

Complementarity of roles.   The fit of role relationships.

Culture.   A way of life that binds a group together.

Differentiation.   The developmental sequencing or elaboration of the system. It is the way in which members take on organizational roles. Differentiation or change in behavior is based on expectations of the members, the needs of the individual, and the system.

Dysfunctional systems.   Systems that have relatively closed boundaries and primarily operate within their own boundaries. These systems are apt to be inflexible, undifferentiated, and less effective.

Energy.   The flow of information and resources in and out of the system that make it able to perform its functions.

Entropy.   Disorganization within the system or the "running down" of performance.

Environment.   Everything external to or outside the systems' boundaries.

Equifinality.   A property of a system that allows it to arrive at its goals from a number of different vantage points or the ability of a system to reach the same final state from different initial conditions and in different ways.

Equilibrium.   The ability of a system to maintain balance without input from the environment. This may bring about temporary instability; this instability, however, may lead to growth and development.

Family developmental tasks.   A major turning point for the family that brings about a new set of circumstances to which the system must adapt.

Family.   A social system of interdependent persons with its own unique structure, pattern of differentiated roles, and communication that may exist in different forms in different cultures.

Feedback loop.   A response to information gathered by the system.

Feedback.   The ability to monitor the system's operation, make a judgment if adaptive action is needed, and, if so, make corrections.

Functional systems.   Systems that are more open to outside energy sources and are more flexible, adaptable, and goal-achieving.

Hierarchy.   The ordering or ranking of people within the system, which is based on power or control.

Holon.   An entity that is simultaneously a part and a whole and refers to the idea that systems or systems members operate at more than one systems level.

Homeostasis. The inclination of systems to maintain a balance and to attempt to restore it when threatened.

Individuation. The ability of a system to provide for individual development.

Interaction. The exchange of information or resources between and among systems and systems members. Interaction is a continuous and reciprocal series of contacts between two or more persons who take each other into account.

Model. An abstraction or a visual representation of reality of how things work under "ideal" conditions. Models present a frame of reference for analyzing a phenomenon.

Morphogenesis. The process of structural elaboration or change of a system. The energy or "intrusions" from the environment bring about change to the system and the potential for it to operate at a higher level of organization.

Open systems. Systems that are characterized by the active exchange of energy (information and materials) with their environment, are more goal-oriented, and have a greater ability to adapt. All living systems are, by definition, relatively open.

Organization. The way in which systems members work together or their established patterns for achieving systems' goals.

Rules. Guidelines for the way in which a family maintains defined behaviors among its members.

Social system. A structure of interacting and interdependent people.

Socialization. A process of bringing about reciprocity between the individual and social needs so he or she may participate effectively in societal systems.

Steady state. A system's dynamic balance. Systems that maintain a steady state are better able to adapt and grow through effective use of inputs and outputs.

Structure. The pattern of stable relationships among family systems members based on the functions that each person carries out.

Subsystem. A component of any system that is a system in its own right.

Suprasystem. A large-size system that contains smaller subsystems. The term is sometimes used to refer to large-scale political and economic macrosystems.

Synergy. Increased positive interaction in a system or among systems.

System. A complex whole made up component parts in mutual interaction.

Tension. Stresses or strains on the structural organization of systems. Tension is more characteristic of complex adaptive systems.

CRITIQUE

Usefulness of General Systems Theory in Social Work Practice

J. PAUL GALLANT and BRUCE A. THYER

The idea that casework needs a superordinate theory or theories is no longer tenable. The knowledge base of future practice will more likely consist of a variety of empirically demonstrated propositions from different perspectives, tied together by at lease one major thread, i.e., their utilization leads to success in helping clients.
—*J. Fischer,* "A Review of Theories of Social Casework"

This critique examines general systems theory in terms of its current literature and usefulness in social work practice. Having concluded that general systems theory appears to have little usefulness, each of the current authors suggests an alternative model. One author argues that a more viable approach to the person-in-environment perspective may be found in social learning theory; whereas the other contends that the integration of clinical and macro dimensions of social work practice are encompassed in social constructionist thought. General systems theory is

> a conceptual orientation that attempts to explain holistically the behavior of people and societies by identifying the interacting components of the system and the controls that keep these components (*subsystems*), stable and in a state of *equilibrium*. It is concerned with the *boundaries, roles, relationships,* and *flow* of information between people. General systems theory is a subset of *systems theories* that focuses on living entities, from microorganisms to societies. (Barker, 1995, p. 148)

The term *theory* itself is fraught with confusion, but for consistency's sake this critique refers to Barker's (1995) definition: a theory is a "group of related hypotheses, concepts, and constructs, based upon facts and observations, that attempts to explain a particular phenomenon" (p. 381).

Among the characteristics of a good theory for social work practice are the following (see Thyer, 1993, for a lengthier treatment):

• It is comprehensive, covering a wide array of social problems, as opposed to just one or a small number.
• It is rational, is consistent with the rules of logic, and does not generate tautological statements or contradictory conclusions.
• It is heuristic, productive in terms of yielding predictive hypotheses, and generates publishable research.
• It is practical, producing effective approaches to social work intervention.
• It is falsifiable, capable of being disproved (this is a more stringent standard, scientifically, than capable of being corroborated).
• It is empirical, consistent with valid observations of psychosocial phenomena.

There can be no doubt, as thoroughly reviewed by Greene in Chapter 7, that general systems theory has had a significant and enduring influence within social work education and to a more limited extent, practice and research, during the past three decades. Contemporary textbooks on social work theory contain prominent chapters dealing with systems theory (e.g., Brandell, 1997; Payne, 1997), but despite its long standing presence among social work conceptual frameworks, general systems theory has not escaped criticism (e.g., Drover & Shragge, 1977; Goldstein, 1975; Leighninger, 1977; Siporin, 1980; Wakefield, 1996a, 1996b, 1996c). Rather than reviewing these earlier criticisms, this critique examines the role of general systems theory in contemporary social sciences and in social work practice.

GENERAL SYSTEM THEORY IN THE SOCIAL SCIENCES

Using the comprehensive computerized databases on journal articles, books, and book chapters to search the social sciences literature, the current authors used the key words *general systems theory* and examined the search results in *PsychINFO*, perhaps the most widely used database in the social work field. A total of 42 hits appeared (as of December 1998), the most recent being a doctoral dissertation published in 1997. The next publication was a chapter in 1996, and the third was an article in a Spanish journal in 1993. From 1990 through 1998, there was a total of only 7 hits. But perhaps this limited response was an artifact or some sort of limitation of PsychINFO as a citation database.

The authors next searched the database *Social Sciences Abstracts* and produced a total of 6 hits, only 3 of which occurred in the 1990s. The database *SocioAbs* (a subset of *Sociofile*) found 48 hits, with 3 produced in the 1990s (the most recent in 1994). The NASW database *Social Work Abstracts* found 28 records associated with general systems theory, of which 1 appeared in 1997, 1 in 1993, 1 in 1991, and 1 in 1990. Only 1 of the 4 articles from the 1990s appeared in a social work journal. The authors then tried alternative models using that *PsychINFO* database: *applied behavior analysis* as a set of key words produced 378 hits; *ego psychology* yielded 630; *attachment theory* resulted in 613; and *cognitive theory resulted in* a total of 917, with many of these hits appearing in the late 1990s. Clearly, then, general systems theory is not a burgeoning field of inquiry in the social and behavioral sciences, particularly in comparison with some alternative theories. Although it perhaps meets the criteria pertaining to comprehensiveness and rationality, general systems theory seemingly fails the test of being heuristic in that little contemporary social sciences research is being derived from it. Also, by omission, it would fail the test of being based on facts and observations, as stipulated by Barker (1995) in the definition of *theory,* because so little systematic empirical work in being conducted on general systems theory

GENERAL SYSTEMS THEORY IN SOCIAL WORK PRACTICE

Kevin Gorey and his colleagues (Gorey, Thyer, & Pawluck, 1998) recently reviewed 13 major social work journals for the years 1990–1994 and extracted all empirically based studies that had evaluated the effectiveness of social work practice. Gorey et al. then categorized the articles in terms of the theoretical model or orientation on which the intervention services were based. Of the 45 studies published, 22 dealt with cognitive-behavioral interventions (the most frequently represented orientation) but only 3 tested interventions derived from general systems theory (one study covered the "ecosystem" model).

An earlier, more comprehensive review by MacDonald, Sheldon, and Gillespie (1992) reviewed 95 empirical outcome studies published between 1979 and 1991, and also categorized them in terms of practice models or theories being evaluated. Thirty-one articles evaluated behavioral / cognitive-behavioral social work practice; 26, some generic form of "casework"; 11, some type of group work; 7 tested family therapy; and the remaining 20 articles were classified as "other" models. The terms *general systems theory* and *systems theory* do not appear in the article by MacDonald et al. (1992). The MacDonald et al. (1995) and Gorey et al. (1998) studies are the most recent reviews providing a look at outcome studies on social work practice. Combining the 45 located by Gorey et al. with the 95 reviewed by MacDonald et al. (undoubtedly there is some overlap among these articles), it appears that of about 140 empirically based outcome studies on social work practice published in the past two decades, only 3 (perhaps 4) apparently concerned systems theory. Thus general systems theory seems to have little impact on contemporary social work practice.

The concept that the usefulness of a theory, model, or conceptual framework is directly tied to its effectiveness in practice is not a new one. Leibniz in 1679 (cited in Easlea, 1980) claimed that "the value and even the mark of a true science consists in my opinion . . . in the useful interventions which can be derived from it" (p. 151). About a century later, R. Thyer (1759) noted that "the end of all knowledge is to understand what is fit to be done; for to know what has been, and what is, and what may be, does but tend to that" (p. 487–488). Even the venerable Karl Marx had the wisdom to have engraved on his tomb "The philosophers have only interpreted the world with various ways. The point however, is to change it."

Payne (1997) noted that one of the features of a good social work practice theory is that "guidance is given to workers on how they should act when doing social work" (p. 2). He further stated that "'theory' is a statement of what social work is and *prescribes* what social workers should do in various situations" (Payne, 1997, p. 24, italics added). How does general systems theory fare by this standard? According to Barker (1995), "the ecosystems perspective offers no prescription for intervention" (p. 114). As Meyer (1988) indicated, "It is not a model, with prescriptions for addressing cases; it does not draw from a particular theory of personality; it does not specify outcomes. It is often misunderstood as being a treatment model" (p. 275). These views are echoed in Greene's chapter (see Chapter 7), which claims that it is a way of thinking rather than a way of working. As the Bible says, "Faith without works is dead" (James, 2:20). The same verdict can be passed on any model of social work practice that does not provide guidance for intervention. A theory without prescriptiveness is dead.

As a concrete example of vagueness in practice, take the following contradiction: Greene noted that in general systems theory, "Assessment involves drawing an arbitrary boundary around the client system, deciding what is the system and what is the environment, and thereby knowing whom to take into consideration." *Arbitrary*? Suppose the problem is a child doing poorly in school. General systems theory offers no advice as to whether the boundary should be around the child-teacher, child-teacher-parent, child-teacher-parent-school, child-teacher-parent-school-grandparent, and so on. How inclusive must one be in encompassing the systems impinging upon a client's life? This question has no right or wrong answer. In what direction should intervention be focused: Academic tutoring for the child? Marital therapy for the troubled parents? Move the child to a new classroom? Have the child's hearing checked? Cultural sensitivity training for the teacher, to take into account the unique circumstances of the immigrant child's past? Does it make any difference? Common sense would suggest so, but any *one* of these options, or all of them, can be justified under general systems theory. No wonder practitioners do not seem to be relying on it much. Wakefield (1996a) summarized this point as follows:

> The perspective's [general systems theory's] influence on assessment, like the Cheshire cat's smile, hangs in the air without any substance. . . . The perspective cannot help in identifying the nature of the problem in any particular case because it makes no substantive assertions about specific causal processes. The perspective's claim to be an assessment instrument is therefore spurious. (p. 14)

Oddly enough, the scientific disciplines underlying general systems theory bear all the stigmata of a mainstream, conventional, quantitative science that is subject to so much abuse in our contemporary social work literature. It has the reductionism characteristic of biology; the mechanistic flavor of cybernetics; and the incomprehensibility (to most social workers at least) of the advanced mathematics so necessary to the study of ecology. Few social workers read systems, cybernetics, or ecological journals for a good reason. Most of us, the current authors included, could not understand them. The attractiveness of general systems theory within social work education is possible attributable to the fact that it provides a veneer of respectability for our field via its tenuous connection to these more credible disciplines.

SOCIAL LEARNING THEORY: AN ALTERNATIVE TO THE PERSON-IN-ENVIRONMENT PERSPECTIVE

Another attractive feature of general systems theory has been its explication of a framework conceptualizing the person-in-environment perspective, which has long characterized social work. It appears to the current author that general systems theory has become an outmoded organizing framework for social work practice. The evolution from psychoanalytic theory, to general systems theory, and in recent years to linguistic systems parallels the growing emphasis from modern to postmodern modes of thought.

Some researchers have suggested that social learning theory—and its applications in behavior analysis and behavior therapy—is a more viable model of person-in-environment than general systems theory. The following representative quotes pertain to the learning theory view of person-in-environment:

> We no longer look at behavior and environment as separate things or events but at the interrelation among them. (Skinner, 1969, p. 10)

The stimulating conditions that constitute the environment produce changes in behavior; these changes alter the environment; . . . the altered environment produces further behavior that again modifies the environment, etc., resulting in the construction of unique cultures (modified environments) on one hand, and unique individual psychological developments on the other. (Bijou & Baer, 1978, p. 12)

Men act upon the world and change it, and are changed in turn by the consequences of their action. Certain processes . . . alter behavior so that it achieves a safer and more useful interchange with a particular environment. When appropriate behavior is established, its consequences work through similar processes to keep it in force. If by chance the environment changes, old forms of behavior disappear, while new consequences build new forms. (Skinner, 1957, p. 1)

Contrast this with the systems / ecological perspective in social work:

The human being and their environment reciprocally shape each other. People mold their environments in many ways and, in turn, they must then adapt to the changes they created. (Germain, 1992, p. 407)

The ecological metaphor of mutual adaptation suggests that the connectedness referred to is reciprocal, that is, a certain adaptiveness takes place between the person and other in the environment they share. (Meyer, 1988, p. 276)

At the very least, it appears that person-in-environment ideas are shared by systems theory and social learning theory. However, the more robust track record of empirical support for social learning theory—and, for that matter, the cognitive/behavioral practices—suggests that practitioners should favor these more empirically-based approaches (see Thyer & Myers, 1998; Thyer & Wodarski, 1998).

INTEGRATION OF MICRO AND MACRO SOCIAL WORK PRACTICE THROUGH SOCIAL CONSTRUCTIONIST THEORY AND NARRATIVE IDEAS FOR CHANGE

It is said that general systems theory strengthened social work's dual purpose to remedy personal dysfunction and enhance social functioning and promote social and economic justice and societal change. However, the current author suggests that the traditionally application of general systems theory has led the profession to a bifurcated approach to practice that is manifested in a seemingly separate clinical orientation and a macro orientation. Most clinical models are taught within frameworks that emphasize social justice and the ending of oppression as contextual values for practice, but do not offer specific methods for the joint application of these values. Typically, the methodological pathways to the social change dimensions are left to macro practice.

The current authors suggest that narrative-deconstructive model of clinical practice, nested in the postmodern paradigm and embodied in the work of social workers Michael White and David Epston (1990), offers a way out of this dilemma and provides a distinct movement away from the mechanistic / objectivist models of general systems and social learning theories. White and Epston have developed a practice model that allows both the client and the social work practitioner to move seamlessly from a focus on individual problems to methods of macro practice, including social action and cause advocacy, that combat oppression (Tomm, 1989). This model integrates techniques for facilitating individual change with methods of macro systemic change. The use of specific clinical methods (such as restorying; see Chapter 9) unmask and personify the large-scale societal narratives that enforce the client's problems. Through this process, the social worker places the controls for change in the hands of clients.

At the heart of White and Epston's therapeutic practice is the innovative process of externalizing the problem (Gallant, 1993; White & Epston, 1990). It involves separating problems from the client's personal identity. The process of objectification and classification is used in the service of establishing a greater sense of personal agency through the location of problems as residing outside the individual, couple, or family and thus opening space in which to take some collective and collaborative action against externalized forces which have negative and often traumatic effects on people's lives.

In conclusion, a review of the current literature indicated that little social sciences research is derived from social work practice grounded in general systems theory. We suggest that social work practice from either the social learning or the narrative / social constructionist / postmodern perspective may provide a more coherent connection with the person-in-environment perspective of social work.

REFERENCES

Barker, R. (Ed.) (1995). *The Social Work Dictionary* (3rd ed.). Washington, DC: NASW Press.

Bijou, S., & Baer, D. M. (1978). *Behavior Analysis of Child Development*. Englewood Cliffs, NJ: Prentice-Hall.

Brandell, J. R. (Ed.) (1997). *Theory and Practice in Clinical Social Work*. New York: Free Press.

Drover, G., & Shragge, E. (1977). General systems theory and social work education: A critique. *Canadian Journal of Social Work Education, 3*(2), 28–39.

Easlea, B. (1980). *Witch Hunting, Magic and the New Philosophy: An Introduction to Debates of the Scientific Revolution 1450–1750*. Sussex, UK: Harvester.

Fischer, J. (1972). A review of *Theories of Social Casework*. *Social Work, 17*, 105–108.

Gallant, J. P. (1993). New ideas for the school social worker in the counseling of children and Families. *Social Work in Education, 15*(2), 119–125.

Germain, C. H. (1992). A conversation with Carel Germain on human development in the ecological context. In M. Bloom (Ed.), *Changing Lives: Studies in Human Development and Professional Helping* (pp. 406–409). Columbia: University of South Carolina Press.

Goldstein, H. (1975). Some critical observations on the relevance of social systems theory for social work practice. *Canadian Journal of Social Work Education, 1*(3), 13–23.

Gorey, K. M., Thyer, B. A., & Pawluck, D. E. (1998). Differential effectiveness of prevalent social work practice models: A meta-analysis. *Social Work, 43*, 269–278.

Leighninger, L. (1977). Systems theory and social work: A re-examination. *Journal of Education for Social Work, 13*, 44–49.

MacDonald, G., Sheldon, B., & Gillespie, J. (1992). Contemporary studies of the effectiveness of social work. *British Journal of Social Work, 22*, 416–443.

Meyer, C. H. (1988). The ecosystems perspective. In R. A. Dorfman (Ed.), *Paradigms of Clinical Social Work* (pp. 275–294). New York: Brunner / Mazel.

Payne, M. (1997). *Modern Social Work Theory* (2nd ed.). Chicago, IL: Lyceum.

Siporin, M. (1980). Ecological systems theory in social work. *Journal of Sociology and Social Welfare, 7*, 507–532.

Skinner, B. F. (1957). *Verbal Behavior*. Englewood Cliffs, NJ: Prentice-Hall.

Skinner, B. F. (1969). *Contingencies of Reinforcement*. Englewood Cliffs, NJ: Prentice-Hall.

Thyer, B. A. (1993). Social work theory and practice research: The approach of logical positivism. *Social Work and Social Sciences Review, 4*, 5–26.

Thyer, B. A., & Myers, L. M. (1998). Social learning theory: An empirically-based approach to understanding human behavior in the social environment. *Journal of Human Behavior in the Social Environment, 1*, 33–52.

Thyer, B. A., & Wodarski, J. S. (Eds.) (1998). *Handbook of Empirical Social Work Practice* (vol. 1). New York: Wiley.

Thyer, R. (Ed.) (1759). *Samuel Butler*. London: J. & R. Tonson.

Tomm, K. (1989). Externalizing the problem and internalizing personal agency. *Journal of Strategic and Systemic Therapies, 8*(1), p. 54.

Wakefield, J. C. (1996a). Does social work need the eco-systems perspective? Part 1. Is the perspective clinically useful? *Social Service Review, 70*, 1–32.

Wakefield, J. C. (1996b). Does social work need the eco-systems perspective? Part 2. Does the perspective save social work from incoherence? *Social Service Review, 70*, 183–213.

Wakefield, J. C. (1996c). Does social work need the ecological perspective? Reply to Alex Gitterman. *Social Service Review, 70*, 476–481.

White, M., & Epston, D. (1990). *Narrative Means to Therapeutic Ends*. New York: Norton.

8

Ecological Perspective

An Eclectic Theoretical Framework for Social Work Practice

ROBERTA R. GREENE

The ecological perspective is a social work practice approach that draws on a multifaceted conceptual base that addresses the complex transactions between people and their environments. A broad framework that synthesizes ideas from a number of human behavior and social work practice theories, the ecological perspective offers a rich, eclectic social work knowledge and practice base. Bronfenbrenner (1979), one of the best known developmental psychologists in the ecological tradition, has defined the ecological approach to human behavior as the "scientific study of the progressive, mutual accommodation, throughout the life course between an active, growing human being and his or her environment" (p. 188). This chapter traces the major roots of the ecological perspective and outlines its primary assumptions. The practice benefits of select concepts encompassed in the perspective for interventions relevant to individual, group, and community enhancement also are discussed.

The growing acceptance of the ecological perspective as a practice approach can be traced to a number of reasons. The ecological approach is a further extension of the social work profession's long-standing interest in service modalities directed toward enhancing both the intrapsychic life of the client and the client's environmental condition or situation (Hamilton, 1940). This interest in the complementarity between person and environment, as embodied in the concepts embraced by the ecological perspective, is, perhaps, *the* distinguishing characteristic of contemporary social work practice. That social work is a form of social treatment committed to an array of direct and indirect intervention is deeply rooted in the profession (Siporin, 1975). For example, as early as 1917 Richmond spoke of the "interdependence of individual and mass betterment" (p. 365). Reynolds

(1933) also clarified that "the function of social casework is not to treat the individual alone nor his [or her] environment alone, but the process of adaptation which is the dynamic interaction between the two" (p. 337). As a perspective that addresses the person-in-environment as one entity, the ecological approach offers the potential of "integrating the treatment and reform traditions of the profession" (Gitterman & Germain, 1976, p. 4).

The concepts emphasized in the ecological perspective focus on the person-environment as a unitary system in which humans and environments reciprocally shape each other:

> Because ecology considers the organism to be inseparable from the environment—together constituting a transacting system—an ecological metaphor can avoid dichotomizing person and situation and direct our attention to the transactions between them. (Germain, 1973, p. 326)

Because social work has such a broad scope of practice, it has been suggested that many theories are relevant to the profession. Confining a practitioner to one theory may limit understanding and, in turn, his or her intervention, which is based on that understanding (Hefferman, Shuttlesworth, & Ambrosino, 1988). However, the ecological approach offers the benefits of an extensive, integrated knowledge base for practice because it focuses on a blend of concepts that describe the degree of person-environment fit, the reciprocal exchange between person and environment, and the forces that support or inhibit that exchange (Germain, 1973).

Another strength of the ecological perspective is that it combines concepts from many disciplines that deal with growth-inducing experiences. The belief that growth may occur through interaction with a helping professional and through positive life experiences, as well as the idea that the helping process is a time of restitution and empowerment, is congruent with social work's humanistic philosophy (Pinderhughes, 1983; 1995). Theorists who have contributed to the ecological perspective are interested in the complex network of forces that positively affect the individual in his or her behavioral setting. They equally are concerned with ameliorating negative life situations that may impair growth, health, and social functioning, such as oppression and poverty, unemployment, and pollution (Germain & Gitterman, 1987, 1995). Furthermore, the social dimensions of the environmental global crisis, such as ozone depletion, deforestation, and species depletion, fall under this rubric (Hoff & Polack, 1993).

| The ecological perspective takes a context-specific view of behavior. |

Social work theorists in the ecological tradition also have been interested in how people successfully interact with others in their environments. These theorists are concerned with social support networks of all sizes and their degree of connectedness (Garbarino, 1983). A focus on the day-to-day social networks in which people live as well as how they achieve success has been translated into practice approaches cutting across all fields, including child welfare, mental health, school social work, and health care (Allen-Meares & Lane, 1983[[?]]; Aponte, 1976, 1979, 1991; Bosch, 1996; Hartman, 1979; Pennekamp & Freeman, 1988; Whittaker & Garbarino, 1983).

Practice in the ecological perspective generally is concerned with "problems in living" that block or interfere with a client's "maximum use of progressive forces. . . . A blend of direct service and environmental actions are aimed at restructuring situations for a better adaptive fit whether the difficulty is primarily with the individual, family, subculture, or larger community" (Germain, 1979, p. 18). Practice models synthesize existing orientations in social work and emphasize a common practice base (Meyer, 1973, 1976, 1983). "A unified method of social work practice is endorsed, with all workers needing to have the skills necessary to intervene at any point that is indicated" (Peterson, 1979, p. 595). Germain (1973) indicated that "the ecological approach to social work service [makes] help available when and where it is needed in the life space of people" (p. 330).

PERSON-IN-ENVIRONMENT HISTORICAL CONTEXT OF THE ECOLOGICAL APPROACH

The ecological social work perspective came to the fore in the 1970s and was part of the trend of increased concern for better environments and quality of life. To best understand this eclectic approach, it is important to trace its theoretical roots. Concepts selected for discussion represent the major converging conceptual trends that formed the practice and knowledge base for the perspective. The ecological perspective in social work practice has adopted so many theoretical concepts that it is difficult to establish precise boundaries for the approach. For example, the perspective has adopted concepts from ecology, ethology, ego psychology, stress theory, the Gestalt school of psychology, role theory, anthropology, humanistic psychology, symbolic interaction theory, general systems theory, and the dynamics of power relationships. Yet the bedrock of ideas for the ecological perspective rests with the founders of the profession who helped clients with material services and tried to remedy economic, social, and health problems (Table 8.1).

Ecology

Concepts adopted from ecology also have had a central influence on the ecological social work approach to practice (Dubos, 1959; Germain, 1968,

Table 8.1. Select Theoretical Foundations of the Ecological Perspective

Time frame	Major theorist(s)	Theory	Major theme	Concepts adopted for practice
1859	Darwin	Evolutionary theory	Evolving match between adapting organism and environment	Goodness of fit
1917	Richmond	Social diagnosis	Improving socioeconomic conditions through personal adjustment	Social treatment
1930	Coyle	Social goals model of group work	Interacting processes of groups	Task roles, reciprocal relations
1932	Murphy & Jensen	Gestalt	Perceiving figure-ground configuration	Analysis of total experience
1934	G. H. Mead	Role theory	Studying social functioning as a transactional process	Pattern of behavior and social positions
1957 1934 [1937] 1969	Perlman G. Mead Blumer	Symbolic interaction	Establishing meaning	Self, generalized other
1940	Gordon Hamilton	Social diagnosis	Improving economic and social conditions as well as intrapsychic functioning	The importance of socioeconomic conditions to personal well-being
1949	M. Mead	Anthropology	Interacting within cultural environments	The importance of ethnographic data and information about personality development
1959	Maslow	Humanistic psychology	Providing growth-inducing life experience	Caring therapeutic relationships

262

Year	Author	Theory	Aim	Key concepts
1961	Rogers	Field theory	Understanding the life space	Person-in-environment
[1931] 1951	Lewin			
1953	Lorenz	Ethology	Studying animals in their natural setting	Critical periods
1956	Selye	Stress theory	Coping with stress	Adaptive mechanisms
1960	Searles			
1963	Bandler	Ego psychology	Promoting the ego's effectiveness, personal competence	Integrity of ego and functions, competence, coping
1958	Hartmann			
1959	White			
1959	DuBos	Environmental biology	Promoting adaptive environments	Transactions
		Human ecology		
1973	Bowlby	Attachment theory	Forming relationships through active transactions	Attachment, relatedness
1968	Bertalanffy	General systems theory	Examining systems change	Synergy, open systems, reciprocal causality
1969	Gordon			
1979	Bronfenbrenner	Ecological development	Developing process-person context	Micro, meso, exo, and macrosystems
1972	Chestang	Empowerment	Affecting one's life space beneficially	Reciprocal power
1976	Solomon			
1978	Pinderhughes			
1980	Germain & Gitterman	Life model	Intervening in the life space	Common practice base life experiences, time, space, ecological maps

1970, 1973; Germain & Gitterman, 1986). The term "ecological" was adopted in social work to convey "a dual, simultaneous concern for the adaptive potential of people and the nutritive qualities of their environments" (Germain, 1979, p. 8). The term "ecosystem," referring to a community of species of plants and animals together with the physical features of their habitat, also has been adopted (Dies, 1955). Ecological concepts about the adaptive capacities of humans in continuous transactions with the environment are particularly suited for social work because they enable the understanding of diverse clients in a variety of life situations and are reflective of social work's definition and professional purpose.

Evolutionary Biology

The ecological social work perspective also has augmented its knowledge base through the adoption of the evolutionary biology concept of adaptation. Adaptation of the species over time as well as adaptation of the individual over the life span is encompassed in the perspective (Hinde, 1989). The concept of goodness-of-fit between organisms and their environments or how a person and his or her environment mutually shape and influence each other is the key to the perspective. How organisms change and change their physical environments as well as how organisms survive and develop satisfactorily are major concepts (Dubos, 1959; Germain, 1979).

Ethology

Another theory base that has influenced the ecological perspective is *ethology,* or the study of animals in their natural settings (Eibl-Eibesfeldt, 1970; Lorenz, 1953). Although the life of human infants is seemingly more complex than that of other species, ecological theorists have borrowed methods from ethologists to describe and analyze behavioral interactions between parents and children in as natural a setting as possible. These theorists view such information as more relevant and less limited than information gained in a laboratory or clinical settings. Among the issues that ecological theorists have investigated using techniques borrowed from ethology is whether human children become bonded to their mothers or other caretakers during a critical period in infancy (Bowlby, 1973a,b).

Anthropology

Anthropologists, such as Margaret Mead (1930), have been looked to by ecological theorists to increase their understanding of personality development across cultures. Ethnographic techniques, such as on-site natural observations of behavior to describe the customs, the kinship systems, and the artifacts found in nonindustrial societies, have been applied to explore urban societies. Of particular interest to social work are studies of child-raising practices.

Ego Psychology

Understanding how people develop competence is another critical component of the ecological social work perspective. Ideas from diverse disciples that address this concept have been adopted. For example, concepts about the autonomous functioning of the ego have been borrowed from ego psychology (Bowlby, 1969, 1980; Erikson, 1959; Hartmann, 1958; White, 1959). Ego psychologists generally define competence as the person's achieved capacity to interact effectively with the environment (White, 1959). Others, such as symbolic interactionists, have conceived of competence in interpersonal terms, defining competence as the ability to perform certain tasks and to control "the outcome of episodes of interaction" (Foote & Cottrell, 1965, p. 53). Working with the progressive forces of the personality and the securing of resources equally are underscored in the ecological approach to competence (Maluccio, 1979). Another related concept, *self-efficacy,* referring to a person's perception of his or her ability to carry out certain behaviors, is increasingly being incorporated into social work practice (Furstenberg & Rounds, 1995; Jung, 1996).

Stress Theory

Concepts related to coping skills and the determinants of stress borrowed from early stress theorists such as Selye (1956) and Searles (1960) also come under the umbrella of the ecological social work perspective. The ecological approach to understanding stress and coping emphasizes a process orientation that centers around exploring a person's continuing relationship with his or her environment and the positive nature of coping (Lazarus, 1980).

Gestalt School of Psychology

Theoretical assumptions from the Gestalt school of psychology also have contributed to the ecological perspective. Gestalt psychologists argue that all elements within a system are part of a harmonious whole and form a larger pattern of reality (Murphy & Jensen, 1932). They also suggest that the way an object is perceived is determined by the total context or configuration in which it is embedded. The best known illustration of this figure-ground principle is the color blindness test that tests the ability of an individual to see a figure among colored dots. The figure-ground principle is among the factors that have interested ecological theorists in the way behavior is perceived within a situational context.

Lewin (1931, 1935, 1951), a psychologist in the Gestalt tradition, was among the first to translate ideas about behavior as a function of its situational context or field into personality theory. By *field,* he meant "the totality of coexisting facts [affecting personality] which are conceived of as mutually interdependent" (Lewin, 1951, p. 240). Lewin's field theory focused on the concept of the interactive effects of the person and environment. He described *personality* as a product of the historical development of the interaction between the physiological organism and the environment, expressed mathematically as $B = f(PE)$, that is, behavior (B) is a function (f) of the person-environment (PE).

The entire psychological field, including the interdependent person and his or her environment, is called the *life space* (Lewin, 1935). The life space is the whole of psychological reality, containing every possible fact that can determine behavior. Lewin (1935) represented this idea in the formula $B = f(L)$, that is, behavior (B) is a function (f) of life space (L). Lewin's work underscored the importance of examining person-environment processes within a total context, rather than explaining phenomena simply by categorizing them. His concepts about the life space have provided important theoretical underpinnings for an ecological approach to development (Bronfenbrenner, 1979; see Explaining Development Across the Life Cycle).

Lewin (1951) also proposed a phenomenological conception of the environment that has been adopted by the ecological perspective. A *phenomenological perspective* on environment suggests that it is impossible to understand the meaning of the environment from an objective point of view. Rather, the meaning must be understood subjectively, that is, as the environment is experienced by a particular individual in a specific setting.

Role Theory

Concepts from role theory, as originally discussed by G. H. Mead (1934) and further elaborated by Perlman (1957a,b), also have been incorporated into the ecological perspective. Issues related to socialization processes, interactional behavioral systems, and mutual role expectations among family or other group members have had a major influence on the ecological approach. The ecological perspective also incorporates ideas of G. H. Mead (1934) and his colleague Blumer (1937) about the way in which the self develops through social interaction. These concepts are known as symbolic interactionism.

Humanistic Psychology

The ecological perspective also has adopted ideas about how positive change can result from life experiences from humanistic psychologists such as Maslow (1970) and Rogers (1961; see Chapter 5). Humanistic psychologists subscribe to the belief that people strive to fulfill their own needs and potential as well as the needs of others (Maslow, 1970). An important social work value in the ecological tradition held in common with humanistic psychology is that theories of motivation and personality should stress healthy development.

General Systems Theory

The ecological perspective has many of its roots in, and often is seen as a form of, general systems theory (Germain, 1979; Germain & Gitterman, 1987; Meyer, 1983; Zastrow & Kurst-Ashman, 1987). Because the ecological approach integrates knowledge and practice information from many different sources, "systems thinking must serve as the integrating tool" (Berger & Federico, 1982, p. 39). The terms "systems framework" and "ecological approach" sometimes are used interchangeably. It has been suggested that the ecological perspective was developed as part of the social work profession's efforts to humanize and integrate general systems concepts (Germain, 1973). Ecological terms were viewed as having the advantage of being less abstract and dehumanizing than general systems theory. In addition, Germain suggested that ecological concepts provided more direction for "when to intervene in a complex field of systems and what planned and unplanned consequences are likely to produce" (1979, p. 6) and offered concepts that are less abstract and closer to human experience than systems theory (Germain & Gitterman, 1995).

Among the major assumptions that general systems theory and the ecological perspective share are an interest in different levels of systems, an emphasis on transactions among people and their environments, the need to examine a system as a whole, and a concern about stress and balance within and among systems (Gordon, 1969; see Chapter 7). The ecological perspective and general systems theory differ in that the ecological perspective focuses on the individual's ability to negotiate with his or her environment, whereas general systems theory emphasizes a system's ability to change (De Hoyos & Jensen, 1985).

Dynamics of Power Relationships

Concepts that examine the dynamics of power relationships also have been incorporated into the ecological perspective. From this conceptual stance, power is related to the goodness-of-fit between person-environment and whether environments are sufficiently nutritive to offer people the necessary resources, security, and support that enhances their development and well-being and that of their community (Greene, 1994; Solomon, 1976). At the heart of this approach is the person's capacity to influence the forces that affect his or her life space (Chestang, 1980; Draper,

1979; Pinderhughes, 1983, 1995; see Understanding Cross-Cultural Differences). These ideas have allowed for a sounder approach to client advocacy within an ecological framework (Gary, 1996).

BASIC ASSUMPTIONS AND TERMINOLOGY
OF THE ECOLOGICAL APPROACH

Ecological theory is concerned with "an adaptive, evolutionary view of human beings in constant interchange with all elements of their environment" (Germain & Gitterman, 1980, p. 5). The idea that the person and environment are inseparable and must be considered jointly is the theory's primary assumption (Bronfenbrenner, 1989; Table 8.2).

Another assumption of the ecological approach to human behavior is that the person and his or her environment form a unitary system or ecosystem in which each shapes the other. In the ecological approach, the focus of inquiry is not the effects of the environment on the person or vice versa, but on the reciprocal nature of the relationship or the transactions between organisms and their environments.

> The ecological view considers the nature of person-environment behaviors as proactive, inseparable, and multisystemic.

This principle can be better understood if one considers that environmental forces affect individual-environment transactions and that the individual brings personal resources and his or her level of development into a situation:

> The individual and the environment negotiate their relationship over time. Neither is constant; each depends on the other in this reciprocal process. One cannot predict the future of one without knowing something about the other. (Garbarino, 1983, p. 10)

Different people may react differently to the same environment and the same environment may interact differently with the same person at different times.

A key assumption of the ecological perspective is that the person and environment mutually influence each other. *Transactions,* or exchanges between a person and his or her environment, bring about change within the person-environment unit. This principle of mutual influence is referred to as *reciprocal causality.* Interest is not on the additive effects of person plus environment, but on their interactive, cumulative effects. From a social work perspective, this concept reflects the idea that people not only adapt to the community in which they live, but also participate in creating the

Table 8.2. The Ecological Perspective: Basic Assumptions

The capacity to interact with the environment and to relate to others is innate.
Genetic and other biological factors are expressed in a variety of ways as a result of transactions with the environment.
Person-environment forms a unitary system in which humans and environment mutually influence each other (form a reciprocal relationship).
Goodness-of-fit is a reciprocal person-environment process achieved through transactions between an adaptive individual and his or her nurturing environment.
People are goal-directed and purposeful. Humans strive for competence. The individual's subjective meaning of the environment is key to development.
People need to be understood in their natural environments and settings.
Personality is a product of the historical development of the transactions between person and environment over time.
Positive change can result from life experiences.
Problems of living need to be understood within the totality of life space.
To assist clients, the social worker should be prepared to intervene anywhere in the client's life space.

conditions to which they must adapt (Hartman, 1958). However, the concept of transaction needs to be distinguished from interaction. In an interaction, two factors, such as person and environment, influence each other but still retain their separate identities. Transaction, on the other hand, implies a mutuality of influence between person and environment as well as "the fusion of person and environment into a unit, a relationship, a system" (Lazarus, 1980, p. 38).

A transactional view also emphasizes *process*, or what happens over time or across encounters. A process orientation to human behavior does not examine a single response, act, or experience. Rather, interest is centered around the flow of events over time. For example, liken the difference between a single still photograph and a real life documentary to the difference between an interaction and a transaction, respectively (Lazarus, 1980).

Another concept central to the ecological perspective is goodness-of-fit. *Goodness-of-fit* refers to the extent to which there is a match between an individual's adaptive needs and the qualities of his or her environment over time. Goodness-of-fit is achieved over evolutionary time in the case of species and over the life span in the case of individuals (Germain & Gitterman, 1987).

Goodness-of-fit comes about through transactions between the person and his or her environment. The match between person and environment is a function of both. Transactions can be either adaptive or maladaptive (see Adaptiveness). To describe this cumulative effect or process, ecological theorists borrowed from general systems theory the term *synergism*, or the process in which joint forces produce an effect greater than the sum of the individual effects.

Transactions between a person and his or her environment often can generate life stress. *Stress* is an imbalance between a person's perceived demands and his or her perceived capability to use resources to meet those demands (Germain & Gitterman, 1986).

> The ecological perspective characterizes the attainment of personal well-being as a lifelong process of numerous person-environment exchanges.

The response to stress need not be negative if the individual has positive self-esteem and feels competent (see Explaining Development Across the Life Cycle). The social worker's practice role from an ecological perspective is to address situations in which goodness-of-fit has not been achieved sufficiently and a lack of fit is causing a client to experience undue stress. In essence, the person-environment perspective is an approach that lends itself to understanding the context of a particular person's behavior (Boxer & Cohler, 1989; Germain, 1994; Greene & McGuire, 1998).

EXPLAINING DEVELOPMENT ACROSS THE LIFE CYCLE

The ecological perspective on development assumes that a human is shaped by his or her species' biology, including the processes of mutation and selection as well as genetic change over evolutionary time. The idea that people are born with genetic potentialities that are either supported or inhibited by transactions with the environment is encompassed in this view.

An ecological approach to human development further asserts that human behavior is a product of the interaction between the growing individual and his or her environment over time. No single characteristic of the person exists in isolation, but the totality of personal characteristics derives its meaning and expression through transactions with the environment (Gitterman & Germain, 1981).

The ecological perspective is one of the few nonstage theory approaches to development. Stage theories tend to focus on life segments or predetermined ages and stages of development. A fixed sequence of stages is assumed in which each stage must be successfully negotiated for the next stage to be addressed successfully (see Chapters 3 and 4). In contrast, the ecological perspective on development offers an examination of the reciprocal role of person and environment across the life course.

Bronfenbrenner (1989) suggested that people are both the products and producers of their development. This stems from the belief of ecological theorists that people are active, goal seeking, purposive beings who make decisions and choices" (Germain, 1979, p. 10). That is, the human infant is not a *tabula rasa*, or blank slate, but is innately predisposed to act on his or her environment. Those "aspects of a person most likely to produce powerful interactive effects" with the environment have been termed "developmentally-instigating characteristics" (Bronfenbrenner, 1989, p. 227). *Developmentally instigating characteristics* are personal qualities that invite or discourage reactions from the environment and thereby foster or discourage growth. In this regard, the individual has the potential not only to create a response from the environment, but also to create the external environment and thereby influence the subsequent course of his or her psychological growth throughout the life course (Bronfenbrenner, 1989).

Life Course

Central to the ecological view of development are the concepts of life course, relatedness, competence, role, environment, habitat, niche, and adaptiveness. The concept of life course is

> concerned with the timing of life events in relation to the social structures and historical changes affecting them. It thus takes into account the synchronization of individual life transitions with collective family configurations under changing social conditions. (Hareven, 1982, p. xiv)

As the time line in Figure 8.1 illustrates, the life course view of development centers around "an interactional, person-environment process [that occurs] . . . over individual, family, and historical time" (Germain, 1987, p. 568). Using such time lines with clients in the assessment process facilitates the collection of information that may encompass such meaningful life events as the invention of the automobile, the death of a president, or the passage of a civil rights bill.

Cohort theory is another example of how a transactional life course conception of development can be used to explain variations in human behavior. Cohort theory suggests that the process of development is not the same for each group of people born in a particular year or era, or cohort. Rather, cohort theory explores differences in the "reciprocal relationship between environment and ideas, and between social change and emotional, social, and behavior development" (Germain, 1987, p. 566). This approach suggests that historical context is important in shaping the person-environment transactions of the time. For example, people born into

> A person's life course is understood within the context of physical, emotional, familial, organizational, political, historical, and economic factors.

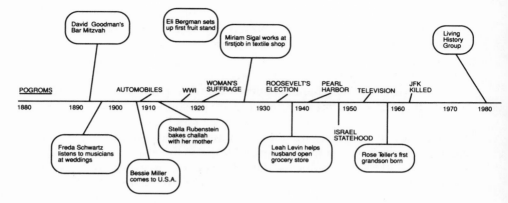

Figure 8.1.   An example of a time line (names used are fictitious). From Guerin and
Pendagast (1976). Reprinted with permission of Gardner Press.

the 1960s generation or the Great Depression were not only influenced by
these events and their own beliefs, but as a result of these events and beliefs now "require society to construct further social changes and changes
in institutions," such as demonstrating to end the Vietnam War (Germain,
1987, p. 566).

Relatedness

The concept of relatedness is another idea central to an ecological view
of development. Relatedness is the ability to form human relationships or
to connect with other people. Occurring both in intimate primary groups,
such as the family, and in less personal exchanges, such as among members of a civic groups, relatedness is a critical aspect of human development. According to ecological theorists, the desire and ability to relate
begin with consistent parenting and result in patterns of reciprocal caretaking behaviors throughout the life course (Ainsworth & Bell, 1974; Germain, 1987).

Competence

Ecological theorists argue that the development of competence is
another ingredient essential to development (White, 1959). From an ecological perspective, *competence,* or the ability to be effective in one's environment, is achieved through a history of successful transactions with the
environment. As the child begins to actively transact with his or her environment by crying, grasping and manipulating objects, crawling, and
walking, he or she experiences a feeling of efficacy, or the power to be ef-

fective (White, 1959). Continued activity combined with consistent mutual caretaking results in a lifelong pattern of effective relationships with others. The ability to make confident decisions, to trust one's judgment, to achieve self-confidence, and to produce one's desired effects on the environment are included in a life course conceptualization of competence. In addition, the availability and purposive use of environmental resources and social supports are integral to this concept (Maluccio, 1979). In instances in which relatedness is a developmental issue, and social isolation and loneliness are of concern, social work treatment may be indicated.

Social workers in the ecological tradition closely link the concepts of self-identity and self-esteem to competence. It is suggested that self-identity and self-esteem arise from the quality of early relationships and attachments and continue to thrive through an ever-widening circle of positive social experiences (Germain & Gitterman, 1987). The ecological perspective subscribes to the view that the capacity to relate and to form a sense of positive self-identity is a lifelong issue that is addressed many times through life events.

Role

The ecological perspective on development also borrows concepts from role theory as a means of understanding how personal and interpersonal processes are guided by cultural and other environmental influences. A role perspective offers an understanding of the social dimensions of development. Role performance encompasses not only expectations about how a person in a given social position is to act toward others, but also how others are to act toward that person (Mead, 1934). Roles are not solely a set pattern of expected behaviors, but a pattern of reciprocal claims and obligations. Feelings, emotions, perceptions, and beliefs are also keys to role performance. In short, roles serve as a bridge between internal processes and social participation (Thompson & Greene, 1994).

Role performance, or social participation, is strongly related to one's sense of self-esteem. For example, the research on the impact of role loss on the coping resources and life satisfaction of the elderly suggests that, although income, health, and the personal characteristics of the individual are important variables, role loss is closely related to both stress and decreased life satisfaction (Figure 8.2).

The ecological perspective on development not only examines personal or individual factors that propel development, but also explores the "complex network of forces that affect the individual through behavioral settings" (Garbarino, 1983, p. 8). The combined situational forces that work to shape the behavior and development of the individual in a particular setting are called the *environment*. Although the environment comprises

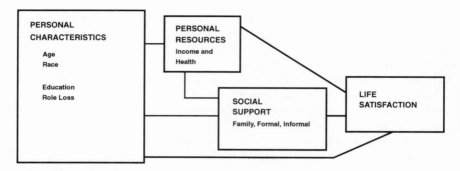

Figure 8.2.   Impact of role loss. From Elwell and Maltbie-Crannell (1981).

many interacting forces that can "press" on the individual, supporting or undermining the processes of personal development, the individual "figures significantly" [in the outcome] as well" (ibid., 1983, pp. 8–9).

Niche and Habitat

The terms "niche" and "habitat" have been borrowed from ecology to describe people's (cultural) environments. *Habitat* refers to the person's physical and social setting within a cultural context (Germain & Gitterman, 1987). *Niche* refers to the individual's immediate environment or statuses occupied by members of the community. Ecological *niches* have been described by Bronfenbrenner (1989) as "regions in the environment that are especially favorable or unfavorable to the development of individuals with particular personal characteristics" (p. 194). The idea that "the outcomes available as possibilities for individual development can vary from one culture or subculture to the next, both within and across time" also is an important element encompassed in the notion of ecological niches (ibid., p. 205).

The concept of niches is not intended to categorize people or to place them into "social addresses" (ibid., p. 194). Rather, the niche is a means of understanding a process that occurs in the person environment unit associated with the niche. According to Bronfenbrenner (1989), this approach to socioeconomic status would suggest that interpreting the data about low birth weights being prevalent among babies born to poor, young, unmarried African-American mothers must be done within a process context. By focusing on the association between low birth weights and certain characteristics of the mother, such as socioeconomic status or race, the *process* by which low birth weights are brought about can be ignored as can issues of access to health care and the fact that low birth weights in infants can be reduced through adequate prenatal care.

Adaptiveness

Adaptiveness is viewed as a process within the person-environment unit involving an active exchange between person and environment. The concept of *adaptiveness* in which the person and environment mutually influence and respond to each other to achieve the best possible match or goodness-of-fit is also central to the ecological view of development. Goodness-of-fit occurs when a preponderance of person-environment transactions are successful, or adaptive, that is, when "significant others, social organizations, and political and economic structures and policies . . . and physical settings . . . [support] peoples' growth, development, and physical and emotional well-being" (Germain & Gitterman, 1987, p. 489). From an ecological point of view, adaptive problems are not defined as pathological states. Traditionally, many social work approaches "largely viewed the presenting problem of the client as pathological. That is, the client was viewed as deviant, behaviorally troubled, or disturbed" (Pardeck, 1988, p. 137). In the ecological approach, there is an evaluation of all the elements of the client's ecological system, including "other people, things, places, organizations, ideas, information, and values" to determine the relative success of person-environment transactions (Germain, 1973, p. 327).

The ecological perspective on adaptiveness reconceptualized individual psychopathologies as a mismatching of individual needs and coping capacities with environmental resources and support (Germain, 1979; Germain & Gitterman, 1980). In her discussion of an ecological approach to the borderline personality, Goldstein (1984) suggested that the ecological approach "relocates the social work point of entry to the transactional area" (p. 354). The salient transactions are among systems such as family and school. She added that this does not obviate the need for understanding intrapsychic developmental issues, but underscores the need to incorporate an examination of the environmental factors contributing to stress and a lack of successful adaptation.

> Self-worth is linked to collective efficacy or a community's willingness to intervene in the lives of its citizens.

As so aptly stated by Coles (1972),

> *to get along* is not to be "sick" and in need of treatment or to be in psychiatric jeopardy and in need of "support" or "evaluation." *To get along* is to live, to manage from day to day—which means one is not a case history, but rather a life-history. (pp. 6–7)

In terms of adaptiveness, an ecological social work approach to practice focuses on the extent to which the environment is supportive or whether it is stress-producing (Germain, 1979). According to this perspective, stress is a biopsychosocial phenomenon resulting from an imbalance in person-environment transactions. At the biological level are the physical stressors encompassing endocrine and somatic changes, on the psychological level are the individual's perception, meaning, and evaluation of the events, and on the social level are the situational demands or strain (Lazarus, 1980; Searles, 1960; Selye, 1956). Stress is not necessarily problematic. However, there are times when the balance between physical and social demands and the individual's potential to deal with those demands is severely upset. Ecological theorists view these upsets in the adaptive balance as problems in living.

According to the life model approach to social work, inspired by the ecological view, people's needs and problems arise from stressful person-environment relationships. Germain and Gitterman (1980), major proponents of this approach, argued that problems in living encompass three interrelated areas of living: (1) life transitions, or new developmentally imposed demands and roles; (2) environmental pressures, which encompass difficulties in organizational and social network resources or physical and social environments; and (3) maladaptive interpersonal processes, which include obstacles in the communication and relationship patterns in one's family or other primary groups.

The ecological social work approach offers adaptive strategies to help people to mitigate problems of living. One major strategy is the enhancement of coping skills. *Coping skills,* evoked naturally by the experiences of stress, are behaviors carried out by an individual to regulate his or her feelings of emotional distress. The ability to cope requires both internal and external resources. *Internal resources* refers to self-esteem and problem-solving skills; *external resources* include family, social network, and organizational supports (McAdoo, 1993). Promoting competence through life experiences is another adaptive strategy of the ecological approach. Working with the progressive forces of the personality and helping to remove environmental obstacles to growth are important means of increasing adaptiveness and life satisfaction (Bandler, 1963; Maluccio, 1979; Oxley, 1971).

Social workers who use the ecological approach to practice also are interested in how problems of living relate to issues in human environments. For example, a study of Vietnamese refugees living in the United States revealed that well-being was moderated by ecological factors such as economics, marital status, education, and premigration stress (Tran, 1993). An interest in how ecological variables affect stress also extends to both the social and physical settings in which people live and the objects and structures that are produced (Tinetti & Powell, 1993). An aspect of environment that critically affects people's well-being is *space.* For example, environments with crowded, deteriorated buildings or streets with noisy, pollution-emitting cars can affect well-being (Germain, 1979).

The concept of space also extends to architectural styles, such as the design of welfare offices, hospitals, public housing, and nursing homes; to territorial relationships, such as peer and gang turfs or age-segregated housing; and to personal perceptions and conceptions, such as distance or emotional space. The ecological perspective on space suggests that these variables are important in the adaptiveness of the person-environment unit, both in urban mass society and in rural settings. The adaptiveness of the person-environment unit in neighborhoods also needs to be understood as a community phenomenon (Butterfield, 1997). For example, Butterfield, a psychiatrist at the Department of Public Health at Harvard University, found that trust within urban environments required that "a sense of social and ownership of public space" (p. 11).

Time, or pacing, duration, and rhythm, is another broad ecological dimension that is important to adaptiveness (Germain, 1976). Time, according to Germain (1976), includes *clock time* (established Greenwich Mean Time); *biological time*, which encompasses internal rhythms such as stomach contractions, menstrual cycles, respiration, pulse, and blood pressure; *psychological time*, or the development of a sense of duration and sequence; *cultural time*, or culturally based beliefs and attitudes about the timing of life events; and *social time*, which deals with lifestyles of a generation or epoch. *Evolutionary time*, which refers to how the species has adapted and evolved over the eons, also is of interest to ecological theorists.

An illustration of the most practical point of view about time from a social work perspective is an agency's approach to the timing of appointments. Whether they are available on weekends or evenings, for example, can be a critical element in service delivery. In creating agency policy and procedures, agency staff need to consider the idiosyncratic issues related to time in the community it serves. "How the rhythm, tempo, and timing of an organization's activities mesh with the temporal patterns of those who use its services" is an important consideration (Germain, 1976, p. 421).

UNDERSTANDING CULTURAL DIFFERENCES: CROSS-CULTURAL SOCIAL WORK PRACTICE

Social workers will increasingly serve diverse constituencies (Ewalt, Freeman, Kirk, & Poole, 1996; Greene & Watkins, 1998; Hooyman, 1996; Suarez, Lewis, & Clark, 1995). This will necessitate an understanding of how clients live in *bicultural environments*—the environment(s) of the client's own ethnic community and the environments of the larger society (de Anda, 1997); the nature of *institutional racism*—how networks of institutions work together to reinforce discrimination (Green, 1995; Pinder-hughes, 1989); and how to advance *social and economic justice*—how to appreciate and intervene to obtain redress regarding societal inequities.

Several basic assumptions of the ecological perspective on human behavior can contribute to these dimensions of cross-cultural social work practice. Among these is the idea that humans must be viewed as a culture-producing and culture-produced species, and therefore must be understood within a broad cultural and historical context (Luria, 1978; Vygotsky, 1929). An ecological approach to understanding the interaction between people and their environments necessitates an examination of the effects of cultural environments.

> Culturally competent social work practice is essential as U.S. society becomes increasingly diverse. The advancement of social justice and economic justice must go hand in hand.

The ecological perspective is particularly concerned with the manner in which certain niches in U.S. society are devalued and the effect of this devalued status on development (Draper, 1979). A critical issue is the quality of environments characterized by "social injustice, societal inconsistency, and personal impotence" (Chestang, 1972, p. 105). Such hostile environments are seen as taking the "psychological toll of second-class citizenship" and impeding "the fulfillment of an individual's potential" (Thomas & Sillen, 1972, p. 47).

The ecological perspective emphasizes a transactional view of coping capacity and power relationships with goodness-of-fit as the underlying paradigm (Draper, 1979; Pinderhughes, 1983). Goodness-of-fit is a reciprocal process that can result in a good fit when there is a good match between organism and environment or a poor fit when the match is poor. It is understood that when environments in which people live are nutritive, people tend to flourish and the match tends to be good. When environments are not nutritive, the match tends to be poor. People then strive to change the environment, themselves, or both, to achieve a better match or goodness-of-fit.

A goodness-of-fit metaphor suggests that nutritive environments offer the necessary resources, security, and support at the appropriate times and in the appropriate ways. Such environments enhance the cognitive, social, and emotional development of community members. Hostile environments, in which there is a lack or a distortion of environmental supports, inhibit development and the ability to cope.

> Further extending social work services to people who are oppressed requires attention to people who are members of marginalized groups.

Minority individuals as well as families learn adaptive strategies to cope and develop competence in their children (DeVos, 1982). Adaptive strategies promote the survival and well-being of the community, families, and individual members of the group. "These [adaptive strategies] are cultural patterns that become part of the ecologies of ethnic minority groups" (Harrison, Wilson, Pine, Chan, & Buriel, 1990, p. 348).

Ecological theorists believe that the ecological challenges facing ethnic minorities are not sudden temporary economic calamities, but derive from a long history of oppression and discrimination. The process of discrimination often leading to poverty can result in a

> cycle of powerlessness in which the failure of the larger social system to provide needed resources operates in a circular manner. . . . [T]he more powerless a community the more the families within it are hindered from meeting the needs of their members and from organizing the community so that it can provide them with more support. (Pinderhughes, 1983, p. 332)

Pinderhughes (1983) suggested that oppression, or the withholding of power by dominant group(s), can be addressed only through empowerment. She defined *power* as the capacity to influence the forces that affect one's desired effects on the environment. This systemic process of empowerment involves influencing the external social system to be less destructive and requires working with extrafamilial systems, such as churches, businesses, or schools. Making surrounding systems more responsive, addressing the power differential, and assisting clients to exert their personal, political, and economic power are the ultimate goals of empowerment.

Draper (1979) suggested that an understanding of the interaction between oppressed people and an oppressing society also must consider the special coping capacities and resources necessary to survive and function in a hostile environment. She applied this understanding of the developmental effects of environment to the development of the language used by African-Americans. She contended that the African-American use of the adjective bad to mean good is an example of culturally based "behavior that is calculated to transform impotence into an active force" (p. 274). Draper furthered her argument by stating that phrases such as "Keep in your place" and "If you're black, stay back" "refer to the boundaries around social space exerted by whites" (p. 272). Ecological thinking suggests that successfully spanning such diverse boundaries is the key to cross-cultural social work practice:

> Ecological and diversity principles are not only complementary but are so interwoven in social work history and philosophy . . . that their tenets can serve as a template for, or nucleus of, 21st century practice (Greene & Watkins, 1998, p. 2).

UNDERSTANDING HOW HUMAN BEINGS FUNCTION
AS MEMBERS OF FAMILIES, GROUPS,
ORGANIZATIONS, AND COMMUNITIES

Ecological approaches emphasize the connections among individuals at various systems levels. Bronfenbrenner (1979) conceptualized the nature of the ecological environment as "a set of nested structures, each inside the next, like a set of Russian dolls" (p. 22). He further described an individual's environment as a hierarchy of systems at four levels that may be thought of as ever-widening concentric circles of environment that surround the individual, moving from the most near to the most remote. The levels Bronfenbrenner (1989) identified are the *microsystem*, which comprises a pattern of activities and roles and interpersonal face-to-face relations in the immediate setting, such as the family; the *mesosystem*, which encompasses the linkages and processes occurring between two or more settings containing the (developing) person, such as the school and the family; the *exosystem*, which encompasses the linkages and processes that occur between two or more settings, at least one that does not ordinarily contain the developing person, such as the workplaces of parents; and the *macrosystem*, which consists of the overarching patterns of a given culture, or broader social context, such as an ethnic group system (Figure 8.3).

The adaptiveness of larger scale systems are of particular importance in the ecological perspective. Even if the social worker is helping an individual client, the assumption is made that the client cannot be understood without taking into account the quality of life within and among the community of systems of which the client is a part. Because social networks are viewed as a "significant variable in the life space of people," behavior from the ecological perspective needs to be understood as a "function of families, groups, organizations, and communities" (Swenson, 1979, p. 215).

By offering the opportunity to relate to others and to exchange resources and social support, social networks have the potential for contributing to growth and adaptation. Social networks also are "a set of relational linkages and communication pathways that influence the behavior of members" (Gitterman & Germain, 1981, p. 46). Friendship groups, family members, work colleagues, college dormitory cliques, and neighborhood councils all may be included among such social groupings.

> The ecological perspective suggests that people connect with and act simultaneously within several systems.

Social networks are of particular interest to social workers because they are a channel of support and nurturance, and may be instrumental in providing mutual aid and sources of intervention (Collins & Pancoast, 1976; Gitterman & Shulman, 1986). Useful means of describing networks of var-

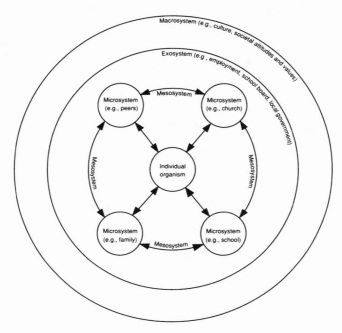

Figure 8.3. The levels of the ecological system. From Hefferman, Shuttlesworth, and Ambroseno (1988).

ious sizes and for visualizing a client's transactions within his or her environment have been developed (Biegel, Shore, & Gordon, 1984; Hartman,
1979). For example, mapping a client's family tree and depicting a client's
support networks are such means.

Swenson (1979) developed a social network map that is useful for visualizing a client in relationship to his or her family, other significant individuals, friends, and neighbors (Figure 8.4). In addition, Biegel et al. (1984)
provided an assessment questionnaire for a social network analysis. *Social
network analysis* is an assessment of the structure and content of a person's
social networks. The structure includes the number of ties, the types of ties
(kin, friends, and neighbors), and the interconnectedness of ties. Content
analysis examines the kind of support or nurturance the individual gives
and receives from these relationships. Table 8.3 provides questions that can
be asked to gather these kinds of data.

Family

The ecological approach mandates that the person be understood in the
context of his or her environment. As Hartman (1979) has aptly stated, "A
salient portion of that environment is the family" (p. 263). Although fami-

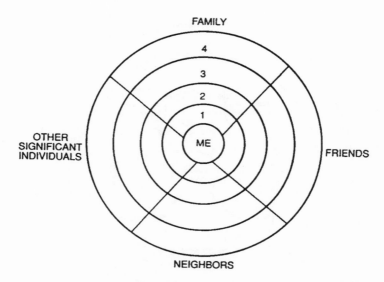

Figure 8.4. Social network map. From Biegel, Shore, and Gordon
(1984). Reprinted by permission of Sage Publications, Inc.

ly-centered social work practice is diverse and can trace its historical roots
to a number of different theoretical orientations, many of its major tenets
are grounded in the ecological perspective. It has been suggested that the
focus of family-centered practice is the "family-environment interface, as
worker and family examine the fit or lack of fit between the family and its
'surround'" (Hartman & Laird, 1987, p. 582; see Chapter 7). Goodness of
family fit is a result of the family's adaptiveness or history of successful
transactions over time.

Hartman (1978, 1979), a pioneer in bringing the ecological perspective
to work with families, suggested that social workers who wish to gain
insight into how a family adapts, and the nature of the family's complex
community interactions, must develop a cognitive map that addresses relationships and events. This strategy of helping the family to study linkages among family members is the "objectification of the family system"
(Hartman, 1979, p. 247). Hartman (1978) also stated that "paper-and-pen-
cil simulations have proven to be particularly useful, not only as assessment tools, but in interviewing, planning, and intervention" (p. 466).
Simulations she has popularized within the social work profession include
the ecological map or "eco-map" and the genogram.

The eco-map simulates the family in the life space, namely the major
systems that are a part of a family's life as well as the nature of those relationships—whether they are nurturant or conflict-laden (Figure 8.5). Con-

nections between the family and the various systems are indicated by drawing different types of lines between the family and those systems: a solid or thick line depicts an important or strong connection; a dotted line, a tenuous connection; and a jagged line, a stressful or conflict-laden connection. Arrows indicate the direction of the flow of energy. Educational, religious, health, recreational, political, economic, neighborhood, and ethnic systems usually are graphically represented (Swenson, 1979). The relative flow of resources to the family is the paramount concern.

The *genogram*, which depicts the contemporary as well as past generations of the family over time, is used as a vehicle to gather information about the dates of births and deaths, marriages and divorces, occupations, and residences of the family (Figure 8.6). Demographics, facts about fami-

Table 8.3. Network Assessment Evaluation Questionnaire

---

1. Is there any one person you feel close to, whom you trust and confide in, without whom it is hard to imagine life? Is there anyone else you feel very close to?
2. Are there other people to whom you feel not quite that close but who are still important to you?
3. For each individual named in (1) and (2) above, obtain the following:
   - Name
   - Gender
   - Age
   - Relationship
   - Geographic proximity
   - Length of time client has known individual
   - How do they keep in touch (in person, telephone, letters, combination)
   - Satisfaction with amount of contact: want more or less? If not satisfied, ask
     What prevents you from keeping in touch more often?
     What does individual do for you?
     Are you satisfied with the kind of support you get?
     Are there other things that you think he or she can do for you?
     What prevents him or her from doing that for you?
     Are you also providing support to that individual? If so, what are you giving?
4. Now, thinking about your network—all the people that you feel close to— would you want more people in it?
5. Are there any members of your network whom you would not want the agency to contact? If so, who? Can you tell us why?
6. Are you a member of any groups or organizations? If so, which ones?
7. Are you receiving assistance from any agencies? If so, what agency and what service(s)?

Source: From D. E. Biegel, B. Shore, & E. Gordon, E. (1984). *Building Support Networks for the Elderly.* Copyright 1984. Reprinted by permission of Sage Publications, Inc., Beverly Hills, CA.

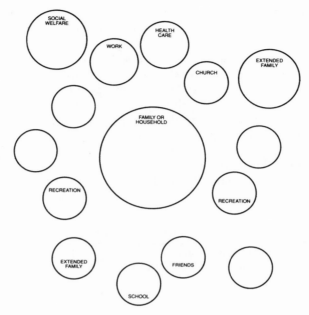

Figure 8.5. A sample ecomap. From Hartman (1978,
p. 473). Reprinted by permission of Social Casework.

ly member's health, ideas about family communication patterns, as well
as role assignments and myths can be obtained. Congres (1994) has extended Hartman's work to provide a means of assessing and empowering
diverse families through the culturagram. The *culturagram* gathers information ranging from a family's reasons for immigration to variables contributing to their ecological well-being since arrival in the United States
(Figure 8.7)

Groups

Most social work practice with groups is based on an intersystem
perspective that is highly compatible with and rooted in an ecological approach (Northen, 1988). This long-standing group work tradition examines the group within the total context of organized groups. This approach
to thinking about groups can be traced to Coyle (1930), who wrote that "the
reciprocal action of individuals, groups, and the total milieu creates each
organization and determines its functions and processes" (p. 27).

Among the more recent practice approaches that have been inspired by
the ecological perspective is a life model, mutual aid approach to group

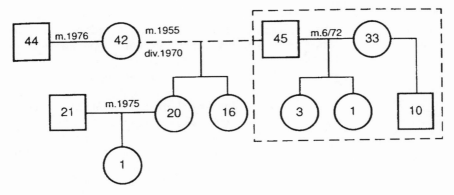

Figure 8.6. Model for a family genogram. From Hartman (1978, p. 473). Reprinted with permission of Social Casework.

work. The mutual aid approach to groups is based on the principle that group members are a source of help and support to each other in coping with life transitions, environmental pressures, or maladaptive interpersonal processes (Gitterman & Shulman, 1986). The group is considered an enterprise of mutual aid or an alliance of individuals who need and help

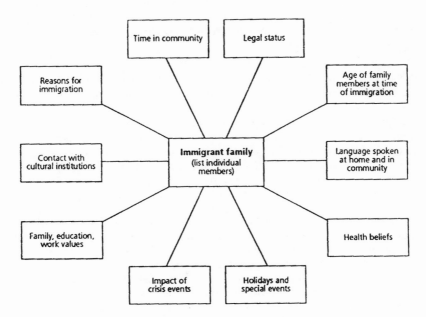

Figure 8.7. Culturagram. From Congress (1994, p. 53). Reprinted with permission of Families in Society.

each other with common problems. The social worker's role is to mediate the individual-group engagement (Schwartz, 1977). A central task is to search out the common ground among the individuals who comprise the group, thus assuring the development of a shared group point of view.

Whether the group is a naturally occurring neighborhood group or one organized by the social worker, it can provide the opportunity for mem-

> Group programs that use an ecological design often engage members of a naturally occurring network.

bers to share data, offering information and facts; engage in a dialectical process, putting forth a tentative idea; discuss taboo topics, such as sexuality or death; feel that they are in the same boat, realizing that they are not alone in their feelings; offer mutual support, realizing that they are not carrying a burden alone; make mutual demands, such as pushing each other to accept responsibility; attempt problem-solving, giving help with an individual problem as a case in point; rehearse solutions, trying out ideas; and experience strength in numbers, experiencing a sense of power (Gitterman & Shulman, 1986; Kramer & Nash, 1995; Strauss & McGann, 1987).

Irizarry and Appel (1986) suggested that social group work using the mutual aid approach can be particularly effective with young adolescents growing up in low-income ethnic minority neighborhoods. Adolescents growing up in an unjust and hostile environment are at a particularly vulnerable life transition and may introject negative prejudices and stereotypes (Chestang, 1980).

The following case study illustrates the power of the ecological social work approach to practice that often calls on the social worker to use multiple service modalities involving numerous systems levels (Figure 8.8).

Magic Me is a nonprofit organization dedicated to developing self-esteem in seemingly unmotivated youngsters by involving them in imaginative community service. Motivating those who are distracted, bored, down on themselves, or too cool to care, Magic Me shows them that they can matter.

Magic Me works primarily with junior and senior high students in public and private schools. Many of the students involved in the program have at one time been identified as either a potential dropout or a behavior problem. Community service is used as a means to develop the students' confidence and to build character. Still other students are involved because they have a desire to serve but cannot find institutions that will train and welcome their support. Magic Me, therefore, meets the needs of a wide range of youths.

Currently, Magic Me has its youths work exclusively with the elderly in nursing homes. By providing unusual interactions—art, poetry writing, drawing, working on murals together, composing rap songs, and so forth—Magic Me helps build relationships in ways that are "fun" and educational.

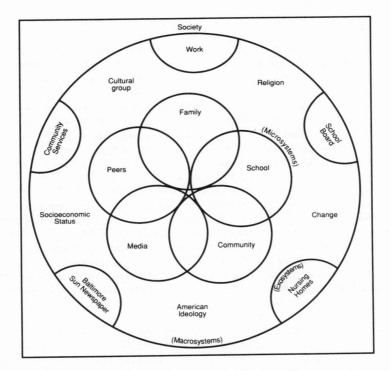

Figure 8.8. An ecological model of human development. Adapted with permission from Bronfenbrenner (1979, p. Q48).

The Magic Me secret is in motivating youths by teaching them through direct experience and unusual classroom seminars to imagine worlds outside their own.

Students are trained before their first visit to a nursing home. This training session usually lasts between 90 minutes and 2 hours. Issues such as what to expect, how to approach nursing home residents, and the special needs of the handicapped are covered. The students are also asked to share their fears about the nursing home and the elderly so that the group can discuss and dispel the myths the students harbor.

Trained students then go on weekly trips during the school day to area nursing homes. There, they are paired with a resident partner. Each pair works together throughout the school year on different projects designed to foster a genuine and meaningful relationship. All nursing home visits are supervised and led by a trained Magic Me staff member or volunteer.

At least once a month, students meet at school with their Magic Me leader [often a university student majoring in social work] to discuss and process their experiences. Students share their successes and failures in befriending their partners and the group plans ways to overcome the failures. During these sessions, the students discuss aging, dying, and overcoming fear and unconventional communication skills. The students are encouraged to use their own creative talents to draw out the residents who are seemingly trapped in sickness and neglect. Very quickly, the students become attuned to the needs of the residents and want to provide what the overburdened nursing home staff cannot—trips to the theater, a walk through the aquarium, a night at the ballpark. Magic Me helps organize and fund these events. Every student is provided a Magic Me journal in which he or she records his or her experiences in the nursing home and processing sessions.

Once students experience the excitement of the activity, they learn how their academic skills can help them serve their partners. They sharpen their grammar skills through weekly entries into their journals and by writing articles and poetry. Students also practice their math skills by participating in various fundraisers and other special activities for which they are responsible for the bookkeeping. Students must use problem-solving skills constantly to analyze the quality of life experienced by their partners and plan strategies in which they might improve it.

The success of Magic Me rests on the students' intrinsic pleasure in dramatically changing someone else's life in a positive direction. Even students who seemed "unreachable" demonstrate a renewed vigor and desire to be heard, to learn, and to reach out.

It is the philosophy of Magic Me that freedom is gained by encouraging independence. Students learn the value of the elderly. They also learn the rewards inherent in helping others not in the impersonal forms of "I-give-you-take" charity, but through personal commitment and mutual exchange.

Magic Me began with more than 500 students. The program hopes to expand to serve nearly 1,000 students and to publish an evaluation of the effects of the program on students' attendance, grades, and attitudes. (Dr. Jim Bembry, UMBC, Baltimore, Maryland, personal communication, 1990)

DIRECT PRACTICE IN SOCIAL WORK: INTERVENING IN THE PERSON-SITUATION TO ENHANCE PSYCHOSOCIAL FUNCTIONING

Although several generations of social work practitioners and theorists have sought to define the professional purpose as enhancing the transactions between a person's coping patterns and the qualities of the impinging environment, direct and conscious applications of the ecological perspective to social work practice are relatively new. Nevertheless, numerous applications of the ecological social work approach exist. In general, the ecological perspective leads the social worker to implement two complementary approaches to practice. On the one hand, it emphasizes individual interventions directed at promoting personal competence. On

the other hand, an ecological approach to helping focuses on environmental concerns aimed at strengthen-
ing or establishing social supports
(Holahan, Wilcox, Spearly, & Campbell, 1979, p. 6). Both approaches must
come together to foster a goodness-of-
fit between the person and the environment.

> Ecological assessment assumes that
> a client's life experiences and
> contexts form a larger pattern of
> reality. Intervention can be directed
> anywhere in that life space.

Whittaker (1983) suggested that the ecological view is an inclusive view
of human service practice that

- recognizes the complementarity of person-in-environment, and seeks
to strengthen each component
- accepts the fact that an exclusive focus on *either* the individual *or* his or
her immediate environment will generally not produce effective helping
- acknowledges that interpersonal help may take many forms, as long
as its goal is to teach skills for effectively coping with the environment
- views social support not simply as a desirable concomitant to professional help but as an inextricable component of an overall helping strategy
- recognizes the distinct and salutary features of both professional and
lay helping efforts in an overall framework for service (pp. 36–37)

Two of the practice models that embody the preceding principles are the
life model and the competence-based approach. The life model directs
practitioners' attention to the way in which a client's particular life tasks
and maturational needs are met as he or she transacts with the environment. The strength of the life model lies in the fact that it "reconceptual-
izes problems and needs of personality or environment into problems of
living" (Peterson, 1979, p. 595).

The ecological perspective as it is applied to the life model suggests that
"strengthening the fit between people and their environments provides social work with a core function" (Germain & Gitterman, 1986, p. 631)

Life itself, its processes and almost infinite successful experiments, can be our
model, and the goals of psychotherapy are to approximate arduously what
is accomplished ideally in living. If we take seriously the proposition that life,
its processes and successful methods of solving problems and resolving conflicts, is our model for psychotherapy, we are confronted by a significant phenomenon. (Bandler, 1963, p. 32)

Thus, the social worker places great value on experiences that are conducive to individual growth. Gaining more confidence and self-esteem
through life experiences, particularly experiences that promote independence in the client, are central (Stredt, 1968). That is, "the way an agency

and therapist set the stage for client action will influence the process of growth" (Oxley, 1971, p. 632).

Life transitions, environmental pressures, and maladaptive interpersonal processes are the focus of attention. In the initial stage of the helping process, the social worker examines salient information about the client's life space that may have an effect on the problem. A mutually developed plan is communicated. In the ongoing phase of treatment, the social worker's goal is to foster the client's coping skills and to further engage the client in positive organizational and social networks. The ending phase of the life model recognizes termination as a time of loss and evaluates with the client the effectiveness of the helping process (Germain & Gitterman, 1979).

The ecological approach to social work also has led to competence-based practice. Maluccio (1981) identified eight features that he believes exemplify such practice:

1. a humanistic perspective
2. redefinition of problems in transactional terms
3. reformulation of assessment as competence clarification
4. redefinition of client and practitioner roles, with clients viewed primarily as resources and social worker as enabling agents
5. redefinition of the client social worker relationship
6. focus on life processes and life experiences
7. emphasis on using the environment
8. regular use of client feedback

Maluccio (1979) is commonly associated with renewing interest in the idea that there is therapeutic potential in life events, a concept first discussed by Bibring (1947) and Austin (1948). This approach to competence-based practice rests on the purposive use of life experiences as interventions. Seeking opportunities for enhancing client autonomy through activities and relationships is a major component in helping clients feel more competent. Helping clients mobilize their own resources as well as contracting around decision-making assists clients to increase control over their own lives. The competence-based approach to social work practice also emphasizes the role of the practitioner in changing select aspects of the client's environment to provide natural opportunities for growth.

Assessment

Assessment from the ecological social work practice approach most often begins with an evaluation of a client's whole situation to identify sources of stress. The goal of assessment is not necessarily to make a diagnostic classification of a client's difficulty as is done in other schools that examine mental illness as a disease entity. Rather, the concern is to deter-mine the needs and issues related to a client or client system's problems in living (Gitterman & Germain, 1981). The assessment of the unit of atten-tion is in itself a process, the beginning of intervention (Meyer, 1983, p. 177).

A principle to be considered during assessment is that the client and so-cial worker are partners in solving problems in living. Greene and Barnes (1998) have outlined the following concepts to use in an ecological assess-ment: Assessment requires the social worker to

- delineate the focal system, identifying that system, whether it be a person, housing complex, or neighborhood, that will receive primary at-tention
- comprehend the client's stress levels and the client's ability to cope, addressing the imbalance between demands and the use of resources to meet these demands
- understand the context and factors contributing to client efficacy, en-compassing a client's ability to act on the environment
- determine the extent and quality of client relationships or attach-ments, dealing with affectional ties, emotional and social exchanges among people and their micro- and mesoenvironments
- examine the nature of the client–social worker relationship and the climate for services to a range of clientele, including organizational and programmatic structure and tone
- explore large-scale or macrosystem societal context, involving insti-tutional resources, legal, health, educational, social, media, and techno-logical services

Treatment

Treatment or intervention from an ecological perspective has been viewed as "an extensive repertoire of techniques and skills designed to increase self-esteem, problem-solving, and coping skills; to facilitate pri-mary group functioning; and to engage and influence organizational struc-tures, social networks and physical settings" (Germain & Gitterman, 1979, p. 20). Life itself is seen as an arena for change—the social worker, when-ever possible, uses natural avenues to release the client's coping capacities and creative strivings (Table 8.4).

Client empowerment is perhaps the key element in the helping process. *Empowerment,* a process that fosters a development or an increase in indi-vidual's skills that permit interpersonal influence, encompasses a set of activities aimed at developing effective support systems and reducing in-stitutionally derived powerlessness (Solomon, 1976). The client's sense

Table 8.4.   Guidelines for the Ecological Approach to Social Work Intervention

View the person and environment as inseparable.
Be an equal partner in the helping process.
Examine transactions between the person and environment by assessing all
    levels of systems affecting a client's adaptiveness. Assess life situations and
    transitions that induce high stress levels.
Attempt to enhance a client's personal competence through positive relationships
    and life experiences.
Seek interventions that affect the goodness-of-fit among a client and his or her
    environment at all systems levels.
Focus on mutually sought solutions and client empowerment.

that he or she can master his or her problem is vital for problem-solving.
This, in turn, can increase a sense of competence and further empower the
person.

Greene and Barnes (1998) have outlined an approach to social work intervention aimed at improving goodness-of-fit between person-environment. They suggested that social workers who uses ecological-style
interventions need to

• choose strategies congruent with the client's environmental and
cultural context, encompassing problem-solving skills that are context-
specific
• direct interventions at any aspect of the ecosystem, recognizing that
life solutions may be found anywhere in the client's life space
• base interventions on the expertise and strengths of client, seeking
solutions that are empowering

REFERENCES

Ainsworth, M. D., & Bell, S. M. (1974). Mother-infant interaction and the develop-
    ment of competence. In K. J. Connolly and J. Bruner (Eds.), *The Growth of Com-
    petence.* New York: Academic.
Allen-Meares, P., & Lane, B. A. (1983). Assessing the adaptive behavior of children
    and youths. *Social Work, 28*(4), 297–301.
Aponte, H. J. (1976). The family-school interview: An eco–structural approach.
    Family Process, 15(3):303–311.
Aponte, H. J. (1979). The negation of values in therapy. *Family Process, 24,* 323–338.
Aponte, H. J. (1991). Training of therapists for work with poor and minorities. *Fam-
    ily Systems Application to Social Work, 5*(3/4), 23–39.
Austin, L. N. (1948). Trends in differential treatment in social casework. *Social Case-
    work, 29,* 203–211.
Bandler, B. (1963). The concept of ego-supportive psychotherapy. In H. Parad & R.

Miller (Eds.), *Ego-Oriented Casework: Problems and Perspectives* (pp. 60–73). New York: Family Service Association of America.

Berger, R., & Federico, R. (1982). *Human Behavior: A Social Work Perspective.* New York: Longman.

Bibring, G. (1947). Psychiatry and social work. *Social Casework, 28,* 203–211.

Biegel, D. E., Shore, B. K., & Gordon, E. (1984). *Building Support Networks for the Elderly.* Beverly Hills, CA: Sage.

Blumer, H. (1969). *Symbolic Interactionism: Perspective and Method.* Englewood Cliffs, NJ: Prentice-Hall.

Bosch, L. A. (1996). Needs of parents of young children with developmental delay: Implications for social work practice. *Families in Society, 77*(8), 477–487.

Bowlby, J. (1969). *Attachment and Loss* (Vol. 1). New York: Basic Books.

Bowlby, J. (1973a). Affectional bonds: Their nature and origin. In R. S. Weiss (Ed.), *Loneliness: The Experience of Emotional and Social Isolation* (pp. 38–52.) Cambridge, MA: MLT.

Bowlby, J. (1973b). *Attachment and Loss* (Vol. 2). New York: Basic Books.

Bowlby, J. (1980). *Attachment and Loss* (Vol. 3). New York: Basic Books.

Boxer, A. M., & Cohler, B. J. (1989). The life course of gay and lesbian youth: An immodest proposal for the study of lives. *Journal of Homosexuality, 17*(3–4), 315–355.

Bronfenbrenner, U. (1979). *The Ecology of Human Development.* Cambridge, MA: Harvard University Press.

Bronfenbrenner, U. (1989). Ecological systems theory. *Annals of Child Development, 6,* 187–249.

Butterfield, F. (1997). Study links violence rate to cohesion of community. *New York Times,* August, p. 11.

Chestang, L. W. (1972). Character Development in a hostile society (Occasional Paper No. 31). Chicago: School of Social Service Administration, University of Chicago.

Chestang, L. W. (1980). Character development in a hostile environment. In M. Brown (Ed.), *Life Span Development* (pp. 40–50). New York: Macmillan.

Coles, R. (1972). *Farewell to the South.* Boston: Little Brown.

Collins, A. H., & Pancoast, D. L. (1976). *Natural Helping Networks: A Strategy for Prevention.* Washington, DC: NASW Press.

Congres, E. P. (1994). The use of culturagrams to assess and empower culturally diverse families. *Families in Society, 5,* 531–538.

Coyle, G. L. (1930). *Social Process in Organized Groups.* New York: Richard R. Smith.

de Anda, D. (Ed.) (1997). *Controversial Issues in Multiculturalism.* Needham Heights, MA: Allyn & Bacon.

De Hoyos, G., & Jensen, C. (1985). The systems approach in American social work. *Social Casework, 66*(8), 490–497.

DeVos, G. A. (1982). Adaptive strategies in U.S. minorities. In E. E. Jones & S. J. Korchin (Eds.), *Minority Mental Health* (pp. 74–117). New York: Praeger.

Dies, L. P. (1955). *Nature and Nature's Man: The Ecology of Human Communication.* Ann Arbor: University of Michigan Press.

Draper, B. J. (1979). Black language as an adaptive response to a hostile environment. In C. B. Germain (Ed.), *Social Work Practice: People and Environment* (pp. 267–281). New York: Columbia University Press.

Dubos, R. (1959). *Mirage of Health.* New York: Harper & Row.

Eibl-Eibesfeldt, I. (1970). *Ethology: The Biology of Behavior.* New York: Holt, Rinehart & Winston.

Elwell, P., & Maltbie-Crannell, A. (1981). The impact of role loss upon coping resources and life satisfaction of the elderly. *Journal of Gerontology, 36*(March): 223–232.

Erikson, E. H. (1959). *Identity and the Life Cycle.* New York: Norton.

Ewalt, P. L., Freeman, E. M., Kirk, S. A., & Poole, D. L. (1996). *Multicultural Issues in Social Work.* Washington, DC: NASW Press.

Foote, N. N., & Cottrell, L. S. (1965). *Identity and Interpersonal Competence.* Chicago: University of Chicago Press.

Furstenberg, A. L., & Rounds, K. A. (1995). Self-efficacy as a target for social work intervention. *Families in Society, 76*(10), 587–595.

Garbarino, J. (1983). Social support networks: Rx for the helping professions. In J. J. Whittaker, J. Garbarino, & Associates (Eds.), *Social Support Networks: Informal Helping in the Human Services* (pp. 3–28). Hawthorne, NY: Aldine de Gruyter.

Gary, L. E. (1996). African-American men's perception of racial discrimination: A sociocultural analysis. In P. L. Ewalt, E. M. Freeman, S. A. Kirk, & D. L. Poole. (1996). *Multicultural Issues in Social Work* (pp. 218–240). Washington, DC: NASW Press.

Germain, C. B. (1968). Social study: past and future. *Social Casework, 49*, 403–409.

Germain, C. B. (1970). Casework and science: A historical encounter. In R. W. Roberts & R. H. Nee (Eds.), *Theories of Social Casework* (pp. 3–32). Chicago: University of Chicago Press.

Germain, C. B. (1973). An ecological perspective in casework practice. *Social Casework, 54*(6), 323–331.

Germain, C. B. (1976). Time: An ecological variable in social work practice. *Social Casework, 57*(7), 419–426.

Germain, C. B. (Ed.) (1979). *Social Work Practice: People and Environments.* New York: Columbia University Press.

Germain, C. B. (1987). Human development in contemporary environments. *Social Service Review, 61*(4), 565–580.

Germain, C. B. (1994). Human behavior and the social environment. In F. G. Reamer (Ed.), *The Foundations of Social Work Knowledge* (pp. 88–121). New York: Columbia University Press.

Germain, C. B., & Gitterman, A. (1980). *The Life Model of Social Work Practice.* New York: Columbia University Press.

Germain, C. B., & Gitterman, A. (1987). Ecological perspective. In A. Minahan (Editor-in-chief), *Encyclopedia of Social Work* (Vol. 1, 18th ed., pp. 488–499). Silver Spring, MD: National Association of Social Workers.

Germain, C. B., & Gitterman, A. (1986). The life model approach to social work practice revisited. In F. J. Turner (Ed.), *Social Work Treatment* (pp. 618–643). New York: Free Press.

Germain, C. B., & Gitterman, A. (1995). Ecological perspective. In R. L. Edwards

(Editor-in-chief), *Encyclopedia of Social Work* (Vol. 1, 19th ed., pp. 816–824). Silver Spring, MD: National Association of Social Workers.

Gitterman, A., & Germain, C. B. (1976). Social work practice: A life model. *Social Service Review, 50*(4), 3–13.

Gitterman, A., & Germain, C. B. (1981). Education for practice: Teaching about the environment. *Journal of Education for Social Work, 17*(3), 44–51.

Gitterman, A., & Shulman, L. (1986). *Mutual Aid Groups and the Life Cycle.* Itasca, IL: F. E. Peacock.

Goldstein, E. G. (1984). *Ego Psychology and Social Work Practice.* New York: Free Press.

Gordon, W. E. (1969). Basic constructs for an integrative and generative conception of social work. In G. Hearn (Ed.), *The General Systems Approach: Contributions toward a Holistic Conception of Social Work* (pp. 5–11). New York: Council on Social Work Education.

Green, J. (1995). *Cultural Awareness in the Human Services: A Multi-Ethnic Approach* (2nd ed.). Needham Heights, MA: Allyn & Bacon.

Greene, R. R. (1994). *Human Behavior Theory: A Diversity Framework.* Hawthorne, NY: Aldine de Gruyter.

Greene, R. R., & Barnes, G. (1998). The ecological perspective, diversity, and culturally competent social work practice. In R. R. Greene & M. Watkins (Eds.), *Serving Diverse Constituencies: Applying the Ecological Perspective* (pp. 63–96). Hawthorne, NY: Aldine de Gruyter.

Greene, R. R., & McGuire, L. (1998). Ecological perspective: Meeting the challenge of practice with diverse populations. In R. R. Greene & M. Watkins (Eds.), *Serving Diverse Constituencies: Applying the Ecological Perspective* (pp. 1–28). Hawthorne, NY: Aldine de Gruyter.

Greene, R. R., & Watkins, M. (Eds.) (1998). *Serving Diverse Constituencies: Applying the Ecological Perspective.* Hawthorne, NY: Aldine de Gruyter.

Guerin, P. J., & Pendagast, E. G. (1976). Evaluation of family system and genogram. In P. J. Guerin (Ed.), *Family Therapy, Theory and Practice.* New York: Gardner.

Hamilton, G. (1940). *Theory and Practice of Social Casework.* New York: Columbia University Press.

Hareven, T. L. (1982). The life course and aging in historical perspective. In T. K. Hareven & K. J. Adams (Eds.), *Aging and Life Course Transitions: An Interdisciplinary Perspective* (pp. 1–26.) New York: Guilford.

Harrison, A. O., Wilson, M. N., Pine, C. J., Chan, S. Q., & Buriel, R. (1990). Family ecologies of ethnic minority children. *Child Development, 61,* 347–362.

Hartmann, A. (1958). *Ego Psychology and the Problem of Adaptation.* New York: International Universities Press.

Hartmann, A. (1978). Diagrammatic assessment of family relationships. *Social Casework, 59,* 465–476.

Hartmann, A. (1979). The extended family. In C. G. Germain (Ed.), *Social Work Practice: People and Environment* (pp. 282–302). New York: Columbia University Press.

Hartmann, A., and Laird, J. (1987). Family practice. In A. Minahan (Editor-in-chief), *Encyclopedia of Social Work* (Vol. 1, 18th ed., pp. 575–589). Silver Spring, MD: National Association of Social Workers.

Hefferman, J., Shuttlesworth, G., & Ambrosino, R. (1988). *Social Work and Social Welfare*. St. Paul: West.

Hinde, R. A. (1989). Ethological and relationship approaches. *Annals of Child Development, 6,* 251–285.

Hoff, M. D., & Polack, R. J. (1993). Social dimensions of the environmental crisis: Challenges for social work. *Social Work, 38*(2), 204–211.

Holahan, C. J., Wilcox, B. L., Spearly, J. L., & Campbell, M. D. (1979). The ecological perspective in community mental health. *Community Mental Health Review, 4*(2), 1–9.

Hooyman, N. R. (1996). Curriculum and teaching: Today and tomorrow. In *White Paper on Social Work Education—Today and Tomorrow* (pp. 11–24). Cleveland, OH: Case Western University Press.

Irizarry, C., & Appel, Y. H. (1986). Growing up: Work with preteens in the neighborhood. In A. Gitterman & L. Shulman (Eds.), *Mutual Aid Groups and the Life Cycle* (pp. 111–139). Itasca, IL: F.E. Peacock.

Jung, M. (1996). Family-centered practice with single-parent families. *Families in Society, 77,* 583–590.

Kramer, K. D., & Nash, K. B. (1995). The unique social ecology of groups: Findings from groups for African-Americans affected by sickle cell disease. *Social Work with Groups, 18*(1), 55–65.

Lazarus, R. S. (1980). The stress and coping paradigm. In L. A. Bond & J. C. Rosen (Eds.), *Competence and Coping during Adulthood* (pp. 28–74). Hanover, NH: University Press of New England.

Lewin, K. (1931). The conflict between Aristotelian and Galilean modes of thought in contemporary psychology. *Journal of Genetic Psychology, 5,* 141–177.

Lewin, K. (1935). *A Dynamic Theory of Personality.* New York: McGraw-Hill.

Lewin, K. (1951). *Field Theory in Social Science.* New York: Harper & Brothers.

Lorenz, K. (1953). *King Solomon's Ring.* New York: Crowell.

Luria, A. R. (1978). *Cognitive Development: Its Cultural and Social Foundations.* Cambridge, MA; Harvard University Press.

Maluccio, A. N. (1979). Competence and life experience. In C. G. Germain (Ed.), *Social Work Practice: People and Environments* (pp. 282–302). New York: Columbia University Press.

Maluccio, A. N. (1981). *Promoting Competence in Clients.* New York: Free Press.

Maslow, A. H. (1970). *Motivation and Personality* (2nd ed.). New York: Harper & Row.

McAdoo, J. L. (1993). The role of african-American fathers: An ecological perspective. *Families in Society, 74*(1), 28–35.

Mead, G. H. (1934). *Mind, Self, and Society from the Standpoint of a Social Behaviorist.* Chicago: University of Chicago Press.

Mead, M. (1930). *Growing up in New Guinea.* New York: Mentor.

Meyer, C. H. (1973). Purpose and boundaries casework fifty years later. *Social Casework, 54,* 269–275.

Meyer, C. H. (1976). *Social Work Practice* (2nd ed). New York: Free Press.

Meyer, C. H. (Ed.) (1983). *Clinical Social Work in the Ecosystems Perspective.* New York: Columbia University Press.

Murphy, G., & Jensen, F. (1932). *Approaches to Personality.* New York: Coward-McCann.

Northen, H. (1988). *Social Work with Groups* (2nd ed.). New York: Columbia University Press.

Oxley, G. (1971). A life-model approach to change. *Social Casework, 52*(10), 627–633.

Pardeck, J. T. (1988). An ecological approach for social work practice. *Journal of Sociology and Social Welfare, 15*(2), 133–142.

Pennekamp, M., & Freeman, E. M. (1988). Toward a partnership perspective: Schools, families, and school social workers. *Social Work in Education, 10,* 246–259.

Perlman, H. H. (1957a). Freud's contribution to social work. *Social Service Review, 31,* 192–202.

Perlman, H. H. (1957b). *Social Casework: A Problem-Solving Process.* Chicago: University of Chicago Press.

Peterson, K. J. (1979). Assessment in the life model: A historical perspective. *Social Casework, 60,* 586–596.

Pinderhughes, E. (1983). Empowerment for our clients and for ourselves. *Social Casework, 64*(6), 331–338.

Pinderhughes, E. (1989). *Understanding Race, Ethnicity, and Power: The Key to Efficacy in Clinical Practice.* New York: Free Press.

Pinderhughes, E. (1995). Empowering diverse populations: Family practice in the 21st century. *Families in Society, 76*(3), 131–140.

Richmond, M. E. (1917). *Social Diagnosis.* New York: Russell Sage Foundation.

Rogers, C. R. (1961). *On Becoming a Person.* Boston: Houghton Mifflin.

Schwartz, N. (1977). Social group work: The interactionist approach. In J. B. Turner (Ed.), *Encyclopedia of Social Work* (Vol. 2, 17th ed., pp. 1328–1338). New York: National Association of Social Workers.

Searles, H. F. (1960). *The Nonhuman Environment.* New York: International Universities Press.

Selye, H. (1956). *The Stress of Life.* New York: McGraw-Hill.

Siporin, M. (1975). *Introduction to Social Work Practice.* New York: MacMillan.

Solomon, B. B. (1976). *Black Empowerment: Social Work in Oppressed Communities.* New York: Columbia University Press.

Strauss, J. B., & McGann, J. (1987). Building a network for children of divorce. *Social Work in Education, 9*(2), 96–105.

Stredt, E. (1968). Social work theory and implications of the practice methods. *Social Work Education Reporter, 16,* 22–46.

Suarez, Z. E., Lewis, E. A., & Clark, J. (1995). Women of color and culturally competent feminist social work practice. In N. Van Den Bergh (Ed.), *Feminist Practice in the 21st Century.* Washington, DC: NASW Press.

Swenson, C. (1979). Social networks, mutual aid and the life model of practices. In C. B. Germain (Ed.), *Social Work Practice: People and Environments* (pp. 215–266). New York: Columbia University Press.

Thomas, A., & Sillen, S. (Eds.) (1972). *Racism and Psychiatry.* New York: Brunner/Mazel.

Thompson, K. H., & Greene, R. R. (1994). Role theory and social work practice. In R. R. Greene (Ed.), *Human Behavior Theory: A Diversity Framework* (pp. 93–114). Hawthorne, NY: Aldine de Gruyter.

Tinetti, M. E., & Powell, L. (1993). Fear of falling and low self-efficacy: A cause of dependence in elderly persons. *Journal of Gerontology, 489,* Special Issue), 35–38.

Tran, T. V. (1993). Psychological traumas and depression in a sample of Vietnamese people in the United States. *Health and Social Work, 18*(3), 185–194.

Vygotsky, L. S. (1929). The problem of the cultural development of the child. *Journal of Genetic Psychology, 36,* 415–434.

White, R. W (1959). Motivation reconsidered: The concept of competence. *Psychological Review, 66,* 297–331.

Whittaker, J. (1983). Mutual helping in human services. In J. K. Whittaker, J. Garbarino, & Associates (Eds.), *Social Support Networks* (pp. 29–70). Hawthorne, NY: Aldine de Gruyter.

Whittaker, J., & Garbarino, J. (Eds.) (1983). *Social Support Networks: Informal Helping in the Human Services.* Hawthorne, NY: Aldine de Gruyter.

Zastrow, C., & Kurst-Ashman, K. (1987). *Understanding Human Behavior and the Social Environment.* Chicago: Nelson Hall.

GLOSSARY

Adaptive.   A goodness-of-fit between person-environment exchanges. Goodness-of-fit is more likely when the environment supports people's general well-being and people act with a greater degree of competence.

Attachment.   Mother-child bond.

Cohort theory.   An approach to development that suggests that the process of development is not the same for each group of people born in a particular year or era.

Competence.   A history of successful transactions with the environment. The ability to make confident decisions, to trust one's judgment, to achieve self-confidence, and to produce one's desired effects on the environment.

Coping skills.   Behaviors that effectively ameliorate, eliminate, or master stress.

Developmentally instigating characteristics.   Personal qualities that invite or discourage reactions from the environment, thereby fostering or discouraging growth.

Eclectic.   A framework that brings together and synthesizes concepts from many different disciplines.

Ecological map (eco-map).   A depiction of the family unit as it relates to other systems in its environment.

Ecology.   A science that studies the relationships of living organisms and their environments. How organisms adapt or achieve goodness-of-fit with their environment is the focus.

Empowerment.   A process whereby an individual gains power and increased interpersonal influence. Often achieved by building support systems and reducing societal discrimination.

Environment. Situational forces that work to shape the behavior and development of the individual in a particular setting.

Exosystem. A system comprising the linkages and processes occurring between two or more settings, at least one that does not ordinarily contain the developing person.

Field. The totality of coexisting facts that are viewed as mutually interdependent.

Genogram. A depiction of the extended family across generations.

Goodness-of-fit. The extent to which there is a match between the individual's adaptive needs and the qualities of the environment.

Habitat. Places or locations where individuals are found.

Life course. The timing of life events in relation to the social structures and historical changes affecting them.

Life model. A social work helping process that is based on the natural processes of growth through the life course. Emphasizes assisting the client to gain further control over his or her life, and is action-oriented.

Life space. The total psychological field, including the interdependent person and his or her environment.

Macrosystem. A system consisting of the overarching patterns of a given culture or broader social context.

Mesosystem. A system that encompasses the linkages and processes occurring between two or more settings containing the (developing) person.

Microsystem. A system comprising a pattern of activities and roles and interpersonal face-to-face relations in the immediate setting.

Niche. Statuses that are occupied by members of the community.

Oppression. Withholding of power by the dominant group(s) in society.

Phenomenological approach. A perspective that examines reality as it appears in the mind of the person.

Process. What happens over time or across encounters.

Relatedness. Attachment behaviors. Emotional and social exchanges among people. An individual's relationship with the natural environment.

Space. Physical settings, built world, and psychological or personal ideas. Active, coping use of the environment.

Stress. An imbalance between a person's perceived demands and his or her perceived capability to use resources to meet these demands.

Synergism.   When joint forces produce an effect greater than the sum of the individual effects.

Time.   Pacing, duration, and rhythm of the person-environment unit across evolutionary time and life course, encompassing biopsychosocial dimensions.

Transactions.   Reciprocal people-environment exchanges.

CRITIQUE

The Search for Social Work Coherence
The Ecological Perspective

GERALD T. POWERS

All the world's a stage, And all the men and women merely players. They have their exits and their entrances: And one man in his time plays many parts.
—William Shakespeare, *As You Like It*

All occupations seem to struggle with identity problems as they make the transition from a well-intentioned guild to that of a bona fide profession. Social work is no exception (Flexner, 1915). Among the attributes most commonly identified as the defining characteristics of a profession, two are particularly germane to the current discussion: (1) the existence of an abstract body of theoretical knowledge that can serve as the basis for a set of specialized and transferable practice skills, and (2) the ability to establish exclusive jurisdiction over an important area of human concern (Carr-Sanders, 1966; Greenwood, 1957; MacIver, 1966; Parsons, 1954; Wilensky, 1964). This critique examines the current status of the ecological perspective and its potential to guide the future of the social work practice within this context. Can the ecological perspective move the profession toward a clearer understanding of social work's professional identity and purpose (Wakefield, 1996b)? The most militant supporters of the perspective believe it deserves to be regarded as a true paradigm shift. To the perspective's severest critics, its conceptual usefulness is little more than an "illusion" (Wakefield, 1996a, p. 5).

Critics of the profession have questioned social work's claim to any exclusive jurisdiction based on technical expertise that sets it apart from the other helping professions such as psychology and psychiatry. It is social work's presumed failure to establish a clear-cut jurisdictional domain for its activities, and an accompanying set of appropriate technical competencies, that has encouraged many social workers to believe that the ecological perspective may finally provide the intellectual answer that they have long sought.

The ecological perspective addresses many of the concerns expressed by critics who question whether social work can legitimately claim exclusive professional jurisdiction over any meaningful area of service. While references to ecology can be found in the literature for numerous human service disciplines (Malo, 1994; Moos, 1974; Gustavsson & Balgopal, 1990; Toch, 1977; Hannan, 1989), no other helping profession appears to have embraced the ecological perspective as a means of defining its unique conceptual domain.

Professional behavior must be guided by a systematic body of abstract knowledge that informs the subject matter of professional concern (Goode, 1960). By that standard, the ecological perspective would appear to hold considerable promise. No one seems to question the ideological thrust of the perspective, nor whether its major tenets are congruent with the historical roots of the profession. The focus on transactions between people and their environments minimizes the tendency to think solely in linear terms and would seen to reduce the likelihood of blaming victims. In addition to all these generally acknowledged benefits, the perspective also appears to be flexible enough to accommodate a wide range of interventive modalities, especially those based on principles that emphasize strengths-based practice and resilience (White, 1959).

The most persistent concerns regarding the conceptual viability of the ecological perspective and its capacity to guide the profession into the twenty-first century seem to stem from its acknowledged status as a metaphor rather than a true theory. To be sure, metaphors are useful and bring into focus new understandings and new possibilities. However, the advocates of the ecological perspective will need to grapple with a number of thorny issues, including those that have important conceptual, research, practice, and value implications for the profession. It is to these three areas that the remainder of this chapter is devoted.

CONCEPTUAL IMPERATIVE

Following its introduction in the 1970s, the ecological perspective (Germain, 1973, 1979a,b), and the related practice life-model (Germain & Gitterman, 1980, 1996), gained considerable prominence in social work. No other conceptual frame of reference since the introduction of Freudian psychology has had as significant an impact on mainstream social work thinking. The claims for the ecological perspective are accompanied by a substantial and growing literature that currently permeates both the practice and educational establishments (Colinvaux, 1973; Dubos, 1978; Germain, 1981; Meyer, 1988; Moos, 1974).

Ecological thinking shifted the locus of attention from the individual or the environment to the unitary system as a whole. It focused attention on the lifelong process of person-environment transactions, a mutual adaptation of an organism and its ever-changing environment. Some social work theoreticians believe that these combined notions of mutuality and transaction of person-environment provide the foundation for a uniquely social work perspective of human behavior (Germain, 1991; Germain & Gitterman, 1995; Meyer, 1983). Such supporters argue that the ecological perspective provides a flexible, eclectic, framework capable of accommodating a wide range of apparently disparate practice modalities (Greene, 1991). Meyer and Mattaini (1998) contended that the ecological perspective was never intended as a framework designed to provide direct guidance with respect to specific practice situations, being too abstract to accomplish that end. Rather, "the purpose of the ecosystems perspective is to ensure that the practitioner pays attention to the multiple interacting elements that are always present in a case, particularly in assessment" (ibid., p. 14). Nonetheless, it is the insistence on viewing people and environments as interconnected that most clearly distinguishes the ecosystems point of view—a posture that some would argue is not only unique to social work, but also entirely consistent with the profession's most celebrated traditions (Germain & Gitterman, 1996).

In more recent iterations of the ecological perspective, a number of new analytical constructs have been added. Some are designed to address political issues embedded in the fabric of the larger macroenvironment—including the related concepts of coercive and exploitative power (Germain & Gitterman, 1995; Gitterman, 1991). Such phenomena are considered analogous to social pollution because they negatively impact people's lives—especially those in vulnerable and powerless groups. *Coercive power* is manifest in various forms of institutionalized oppression, such as racism and poverty. *Exploitative power* is associated with social stratification and occurs when abuses of power result in the victimization of vulnerable groups. Concepts such as these begin to address some of the implications of the ecological perspective in relation to the profession's broader policy agenda, especially those involving issues of diversity, empowerment, and social justice.

RESEARCH IMPERATIVE

It should be noted that the bulk of the literature on the ecological perspective is largely of a descriptive and anecdotal nature. There is very little, if any, empirical support for most of its major tenets—at least as they relate to the concerns of practicing social workers. There are numerous field studies that support ecological principles in the biological realm. In an effort to import ideas across disciplinary boundaries, however, it cannot be assume that what is true in the physical sciences will necessarily hold up when applied to the human condition. The ecological perspective cannot afford to hide behind the disclaimer of being nothing more than a metaphor, and at the same time expect to earn the kind of intellectual respectability it seeks. One of the most important indicators of a useful theory is its ability to generate research. Considering its popularity, the ecological perspective has been remarkably silent in this regard.

At the very least, the ecological perspective constitutes what Holzner and Marx (1979) refer to as a *frame of reference*:

> A frame of reference is a structure consisting of taken-for-granted assumptions, preferences for symbol systems, and analytical devices within which an observer's inquiry proceeds. This structure specifically defines the relationship of the observer to what he or she knows and represents. For a rational understandability of knowledge, it is necessary to signal the frame of reference. . . . We use frames of reference to orient ourselves to specific objects, to conceptualize what problems are and how they are constituted, and to determine their possible or permissible solutions. (p. 99)

Certainly, the ecological perspective contains most if not all of the identified requisites to qualify as a frame of reference. For the ecological perspective to advance its scientific credibility, the major tenets of this frame of reference will have to be subjected to rigorous empirical reality tests to validate the objective adequacy of its assertions. Such tests do not represent an unreasonable expectation if the ecological perspective hopes to sustain and vindicate its dominant position within the profession.

PRACTICE IMPERATIVE

The development of a practice framework based on metaphorical insights derived from another field poses some interesting challenges with respect to the transformation of knowledge. It is not surprising that one of the most persistent criticisms of the ecological perspective is its failure to provide any meaningful direction as to how concrete human problems can be resolved. In the professions, knowledge is brought into play for some instrumental purpose. The theoretical constructs of biological ecology, as well as systems theory, are known to have very strong explanatory power, but they were never intended to be employed as action theories designed to inform practice. The advocates of the ecological perspective have failed to establish a convincing case for its instrumental utility.

A review of the literature reveals numerous disclaimers regarding the prescriptive potency of the perspective. It is evident that most of its advocates would agree with the position that the perspective was never intended as a guide for practice. It is somewhat ironic that a framework that has so much to say regarding how human behavior should be viewed would have so little to offer with respect to how such behavior should be handled. Greif and Lynch (1983) attempted to put a positive spin on this apparent paradox by maintaining that "use of the eco-systems perspective avoids the limitation of methodological closure and permits more specific individualizing of the case through eclectic selection of one or more practice models or other interventive techniques"(p. 63).

Meyer and Mattaini (1998) take a more qualified position with respect to the presumed value of eclecticism. They suggest that the perspective functions at "a higher level of abstraction" than any particular practice theory (p. 7). Therefore, the essential issue is not the selection of a particular action theory per se, but whether that theory, when applied in practice, focuses on the entire transactional field. It is apparent in both of these positions that, when it comes to addressing specific practice situations, the ecological perspective is heavily dependent on the theoretical contributions of other practice paradigms. If the perspective insists on maintaining its methodological neutrality by serving as an integration and distribution hub for other practice modalities, then, at the very least, it would do well to articulate a functional set of guidelines that can instruct practitioners in their efforts to select and apply appropriate interventive techniques.

Advocates of the ecological perspective consider its limited ability to independently guide practice to be a serious shortcoming. Brower (1988) agreed that the framework has strong conceptual appeal in terms of its potential for assessment, that is, its ability to describe "how people interact with their environments" (p. 411). He is convinced, however, that the perspective is destined to play only a limited role in shaping the future of social work practice unless it develops it own repertoire of practice principles—that have immediate and real meaning to both clients and practitioners on a day-to-day basis.

Brower is not alone in this position. Taylor (1997) also maintained that the biological niche and related habitat constructs possess the potential to generate new practice principles, and that such principles are consonant with understanding sources of strength in the environment. He also argued that such initiatives "can lead to new knowledge for social work, lead to useful research, and suggest new possibilities for intervention" (p. 226). If such optimistic claims are true, developments of this nature hold great promise for addressing one of the perspective's most serious perceived limitations.

VALUE IMPERATIVE

The ecological metaphor as currently being applied in social work goes well beyond its origins as envisioned in biological ecology. That is understandable. There is certainly no a priori reason why a metaphor derived from one field must be restricted in its application in another. Nevertheless, the importation of constructs from other disciplines must be carried out with considerable caution. Take, for example, the concept of power—an important and central notion in both biological ecology and contemporary social work. In social work the term is most frequently used in reference to efforts on the part of one individual or group to exercise or gain control over another individual or group—as in the earlier discussion of exploitative and coercive power (Germain & Gitterman, 1995; Gitterman, 1991). Clearly, social workers see it as their moral responsibility to advocate on behalf of those who are being exploited or coerced. This is not the case in biological ecology, where power is viewed in a value-neutral context. In the animal kingdom, it is understood and accepted that one species will dominate another. Weaker animals succumb to the dominance of their stronger and healthier counterparts (Strickberger, 1990). Clearly, concepts such as exploitative and coercive power are antithetical to the precepts of biological ecology. Similarly, terms such as survival of the fittest evoke a like response among social workers whose espoused values place them at the service of the most marginalized (or least fit in ecological terms) members of society.

Unlike their academic counterparts, professions make no pretense of being value-free. All professions are ideologically grounded. Indeed, one of the most frequently cited attributes of a profession is the recurrent theme of self-regulation based on a clearly articulated code of ethics supported by public trust (Foote, 1953, p. 372). In the case of social work, that agenda includes a very strong commitment to advocacy on behalf of disadvantaged and oppressed groups. It is critical to keep this in mind as parallels are drawn between humans on the one hand and nonhumans or even nonsentient species on the other.

REFERENCES

Carr-Sanders, A. M. (1966). Professions: Their organization and place in society. In H. M. Volmer & D. L. Mills (Eds.), *Professionalization* (pp. 3–7). Englewood Cliffs, NJ: Prentice-Hall.

Colinvaux, P. (1973). *Introduction to Ecology*. New York: Wiley.

Dubos, R. (1978). Health and creative adaptation. *Human Nature, 1,* 74–82.

Flexner, A. (1915). Is social work a profession? In *Proceedings of the National Confer-*

ence of Charities and Corrections (pp. 576–590). Chicago, IL: Baltimore, MD: Russell Sage.

Foote, N. N. (1953). Professionalization of labor in Detroit. *American Journal of Sociology* (January), 372.

Germain, C. B. (Ed.) (1979a). *Social Work Practice: People and Environments, an Ecological Perspective.* New York: Columbia University Press.

Germain, C. B. (1979b). General systems theory and ego psychology, an ecological perspective. *Social Service Review, 52,* 535–550.

Germain, C. B. (1981). The ecological approach to people environment transactions. *Social Casework, 59,* 515–522.

Germain, C. B. (1991). *Human Behavior in the Social Environment: An Ecological View.* New York: Columbia University Press.

Germain, C. B., & Gitterman, A. (1980). *The Life Model of Social Work Practice.* New York: Columbia University Press.

Germain, C. B., & Gitterman, A. (1995). Ecological perspective. In R. L. Edwards (Ed.), *Encyclopedia of Social Work* (19th ed., Vol. 1, pp. 816–824). Washington, DC: NASW Press.

Germain, C. B., & Gitterman, A. (1996). *The Life Model of Social Work Practice* (2nd ed.). New York: Columbia University Press.

Gitterman, A. (1991). Introduction to social work practice with vulnerable populations and the life cycle. In A. Gitterman (Ed.), *Handbook of Social Work Practice with Vulnerable Populations* (pp. 1–34). New York: Columbia University Press.

Goode, W. J. (1960). Encroachment, charlatanism, and the emerging profession: Psychology, sociology and medicine. *American Sociological Review, 22,* 903.

Greene, R. R. (1991). The ecological perspective: An eclectic theoretical framework for social work practice. In R. R. Greene & P. H. Ephross (Eds.), *Human Behavior Theory and Social Work Practice* (pp. 261–296). Hawthorne, NY: Aldine de Gruyter.

Greenwood, E. (1957). Attributes of a profession. *Social Work, 2,* 45–55.

Greif, G. L., & Lynch, A. A. (1983). The eco-systems perspective. In C. H. Meyer (Ed.), *Clinical Social Work in the Eco-Systems Perspective* (pp. 35–71). New York: Columbia University Press.

Gustavsson, N. S., & Balgopal, P. R. (1990). Violence and minority youth: An ecological perspective. In A. R. Stiffman & L. E. Davis (Eds.), *Ethnic Issues in Adolescent Mental Health* (pp. 115–130). Newbury Park, NJ: Sage.

Hannan, M. T. (1989). *Organizational Ecology.* Cambridge, MA: Harvard University Press.

Holzner, B. & Marx, J. H. (1979). *Knowledge Application: The Knowledge System in Society.* Boston: Allyn & Bacon.

MacIver, R. (1966). Social significance of professional ethics. In H. M. Volmer & D. L. Mills (Eds.), *Professionalization* (pp. 51–54). Englewood Cliffs, NJ: Prentice-Hall.

Malo, C. (1994). Ex-partner, family, friends and relationships: Their role within the social network of long-term single mothers. *Journal of Applied Social Psychology, 24*(1), 60–81.

Meyer, C. H. (1983). The search for coherence. In C. H. Meyer (Ed.), *Clinical Social Work in the Eco-Systems Perspective* (pp. 5–34). New York: Columbia University Press.

Meyer, C. H. (1988). The eco-systems perspective. In R. A. Dorfman (Ed.), *Paradigms of Clinical Social Work* (pp. 275–294). New York: Brunner / Mazel.

Meyer, C. H., & Mattaini, M. A. (1998). The ecosystems perspective: Implications for practice. In M. A. Mattaini, C. T. Lowery, & C. H. Meyer (Eds.), *The Foundations of Social Work Practice* (2nd ed., pp. 3–19). Washington, DC: NASW Press.

Moos, R. H. (1974). Evaluating treatment environments: A social ecological approach. In D. Mechanic (Ed.), *Health, Medicine, and Society*. New York: Wiley.

Parsons, T. (1954). *A Sociologist Looks at the Legal Profession. Essays in Sociological Theory*. Glencoe, IL: Free Press.

Strickberger, M. W. (1990). *Evolution*. Boston: Jones and Bartlett.

Taylor, J. B. (1997). Niches and practice: Extending the ecological perspective. In D. Saleebey (Ed.), *The Strengths Approach in the Environment* (2nd ed., pp. 217–227). New York: Longman.

Toch, H. (1977). *Living in Prison: The Ecology of Survival*. New York: Free Press.

Wakefield, J. C. (1996a). Does social work need the eco-systems perspective? Part 1. Is the perspective clinically useful? *Social Service Review, 70*(1), pp. 5–32.

Wakefield, J. C. (1996b). Does social work need the eco-systems perspective? Part 2. Does the perspective save social work from incoherence? *Social Service Review, 70*(2), 183–213.

White, R. W. (1959). Motivation reconsidered: The concept of competence. *Psychological Review, 66*, 297–331.

Wilensky, H. (1964). The professionalization of everyone? *American Journal of Sociology, 70*(September), 137–158.

9

Social Construction

ROBERT BLUNDO and ROBERTA R. GREENE

Man is an animal suspended in the web of significance he himself has spun, and culture is the name given to this web of meaning.
—C. Geertz, *The Interpretation of Cultures*

Social constructionists are part of the postmodern movement, which devalues the search for universal laws and theories, emphasizes localized experiences, and recognizes differences (Fraser, Taylor, Jackson, & O'Jack, 1991; Sands & Nuccio, 1992). Social constructionists suggest that local or personal understandings help reduce stereotypes and promote firsthand understanding. Furthermore, they believe that personal meanings and views of social reality grow out of interaction and discourse in daily life experiences (Gergen & Gergen, 1983a,b). These theorists also recognize that individual and family meanings are "socially constituted within the context of the present sociopolitical juncture" (Lowe, 1991, p. 47). Therefore, social constructivist therapies have the potential "to relate to themes of justice, poverty, gender, politics, and power" (p. 47). Social constructionists also contend that their interest in multiple perspectives emphasizes communal belief systems, an emphasis that is useful in clinical practice (Lax, 1992; McNamee & Gergen, 1992).

The social constructionist perspective is one alternative way of looking at or approaching an understanding of what it means to be human within the context of an ongoing living process, what social work has attempted to understand by its hyphenated theme of the-person-in-the-environment. Roberta Imre's (1982) account of the state of the nature of social work knowledge represents one of the first substantial efforts within social work to alert social work to its underlying philosophical base or familiar—although covert—perspective for social work theory and practice, logical positivism, and modernist epistemology. At the same time, she alerted social work to the consequences of being unaware of this foundation for its theory and practice development.

Imre (1982) noted that "failure to recognize the existence of [this] underlying philosophical perspective allows it to operate sub rosa" with the consequence that its derivative theories and models are thus assumed to represent the only way of understanding and building a base for practice (p. 42). To appreciate the alternative perspective social constructionism offers requires that social workers

> Social constructionists are part of the philosophical change in the arts and sciences that addresses the local context of meaning and events.

make what Imre (1982) saw as "a conscious effort to shake [themselves] loose from conventional patterns of thought, which . . . [appears to those engaged in social work research and practice] to be the only way of viewing the world" (p. 42). She proposes that social work, "a profession intrinsically concerned with human beings, requires a philosophy of knowing capable of encompassing all that is human. . . . [Social work needs to address the question of] what it means to be human" (p. 44).

The social constructionist perspective challenges these familiar ways of constructing the world. This postmodern perspective offers a different way of considering individuals' "understanding" of who they are and how they relate to their experience of what appears to be a world totally independent of their own existence. It offers in its place an ongoing *process of language-in-use* as opposed to the mechanistic world of separate, autonomous interacting entities, which social work's present philosophical perspective has created. The challenge presented by the social constructionist perspective is to undo in a sense "reality" as we live it day to day. The idea of defamiliarizing ourselves with our routines or theories is not an easy task.

PERSON-ENVIRONMENT HISTORICAL CONTEXT: CHANGES IN SCIENTIFIC PARADIGM

Science is the constellation of facts, theories, and methods collected in current texts
—T. Kuhn, *The Structure of Scientific Revolutions*

Interventions in social work generally are thought of as social treatments process in which the social worker uses selective methods and techniques to enhance social functioning. These interventions may encompass forming supportive relationships, exploring and clarifying feelings, confronting issues, educating, or mobilizing and restructuring support systems (Northen, 1982). To understand the use of social constructionist theory as a guide to social work practice and its particular approach to intervention, it is first necessary to understand social work's interest in science and the scientific method. Thomas Kuhn (1970) suggested that the history of the philosophy of the social sciences is marked by the reconstruction of prior theory—the reevaluation of prior fact—and therefore is "an intrinsically revolutionary process" involving changes in the underlying scientific paradigm (p. 7). Because any particular scientific approach is taken for granted, changes in underlying paradigm are indeed revolutionary. For example, Copernicus destroyed time-honored ideas about terrestrial motion; Newton did the same in his explanation of gravity; and Einstein rewrote the laws of classical physics.

The social and psychological sciences have undergone a similar change process. The history of the social work profession's relationship to the philosophy of social science centers around a theoretical approach to questions such as, What is social reality like? How do people come to know about this reality and how is this knowledge transmitted? What is human nature basically like? What methodology do people use to study or observe social reality? (Burrell & Morgan, 1979; Martin & O'Connor, 1989).

Two perspectives on how to answer these questions have dominated the social sciences and have been infused into social work thinking. Burrell and Morgan (1979) suggested that most social sciences are either subjectivist, claiming that human consciousness exists primarily in the mind, or objectivist, believing that it has a real concrete existence. As an expression of Western culture and the era of science, social work presently reflects the faith in progress through systematic observation and analytic reasoning that, for example, has occurred in the study of the physical world and the technologies of medicine. Much of social work rests on the belief that, through the discovery of "objective" facts and universal laws, technology will be designed to take care of personal and social ills (Table 9.1). Bertrand Russell (1956) expressed this belief in the possibilities of science and technology when he proclaimed that the social sciences would discover the mathematics of human behavior as precise as the underlying working of machines. The rationalists and empiricists proposed this fundamental belief that truth is based on reason and logic. The study of humankind is scientific and people can thus be understood in the same logical terms as mechanical devices (Priest, 1990; Russell, 1956).

A steady commentary within social work has been concerned with the development of the knowledge base of social work, that is, the perspective through which the profession conceives the relationships of persons and their worlds. Much of this work has been a part of a controversy over the implications of positivism or the scientific method and possible alterna-

Table 9.1. Models of Ourselves and the Worlds These Selves Inhabit

Modernist or Medical Model

Basic assumptions taken for granted as truths about persons and their world:

- There is an independent and identifiable self with an identifiable personality that resides within a physical body.
- There is a separate world of others with whom this independent self comes and goes, interacting or being acted on.
- There is a separate reality of others who can be understood independently of the context of the moment, history, and biology.
- There is an independent reality whose data can be discovered or uncovered scientifically, which describe all humans in terms of normative and universal development as a person physically matures.

Basic consequences of objectivity and a knowable world of others:

- Humans are evaluated and adjudicated based on a standardized measure of normalcy produced by and reflecting the values and culture of the dominant group (in terms of political power to set the rules of conduct, thought, and expression) in a society.
- Based on the dominant forms of knowledge, the professional is sanctioned by the society to evaluate, judge, and assess others in terms of the standards of normalcy established by the dominant group's version of human development and their relationship with the world outside of them.
- The professional is considered the expert on the life being lived out by the person being evaluated. It is the professional who defines the appropriateness of this life based on "scientific" discoveries of normative development.
- The work done or intervention is oriented to changing the behaviors, feelings, and attitudes, which are not within the normative standards of the professional's model or theory of human development or practice, rather than human growth.
- The issues or challenges brought by the individual or family to the professional are translated into the language and labeling of the professional, who in turn interprets or translates the life of the person into his or her own model of practice. This interpretation is then presented to the designated client as the cause or reason for the client's issues, as well as the very nature of the issues (not conflict but boundary problems).
- The professional is considered and considers himself or herself as a "neutral" observer who proceeds to discover the model of development adhered to in the information solicited from those with whom he or she is working.
- The diagnosis or assessment often concerns an entity such as the "family system," which is assumed to exist independent of the constructions of its members. It is based on the assumption that something is broken, damaged, or nonfunctioning or is lacking within the "person" or the "family."

Basic consequences of the social constructionist, postmodern stance:

- Understanding can never be complete. It is continually influenced by the ongoing content of the work being done at the moment, the life experiences of those involved, including the professional, and models or theories of human development and conduct to which both have been exposed in all forms of social discourse.
- People are invited into a collaborative partnership. This position acknowledges that both have "expertise" that can be shared in the interest of the person seeking assistance.

continued

Table 9.1. (Continued)

- The nature of the "expertise" is in assisting the individual or family by providing a safe environment for exploring their own process in generating new possibilities, considering and trying on these new or recycled/retrieved possibilities from their own lived experiences.
- The individuals or families become their own "experts" in developing alternative understandings and processes for their lives.
- The professional is not considered to be neutral or objective in his or her understanding and interactions with those with whom the professional are working. It is the recognition of this that does create the "professional" stance.
- The work done is done in the language of those seeking assistance and not in the language of theories or models of human behavior.

---

tive perspectives (Bateson, 1979; H. Goldstein, 1981, 1986b; Gottschalk & Witkin, 1991; Gould, 1984; Haworth, 1984; Heineman, 1981, 1982; Imre, 1982). For example, Bernice Simon (1970) expressed concern that social work lacked the conceptual tools to produce a fundamental knowledge base encompassing the complexity of "man [sic] in movement with life" (p. 367). Germain (1970) asserted that this problem was a consequence of "our language, cultural habits of thought, and schooling," which prevented social workers from seeing the world in other than linear cause-and-effect (p. 19). Constructionist and feminist theorists particularly addressed the issue of linear cause-and-effect thinking and questioned the notion of objective discovery and reductionistic cataloging of the human condition and clinical intervention. Instead, they proposed a different concept of reality: one based on the context and meaning for both clients and social workers (Bricker-Jenkins & Hooyman, 1986; Hare-Mustin, 1990; Ruckdeschel, 1985; Saleebey, 1989, 1992; Scott, 1989; Tice, 1990; Weick, 1981, 1983, 1987).

Clearly, the mechanistic metaphor of objectivism has dominated the social sciences and social work. As a consequence, constructionist theorists believe that social work has reduced the complexity of persons living out their lives to either their intrapsychic malfunctions or social and societal causes. For example, Rodwell (1987) has claimed that general systems theory is an example of objectivist thinking, which assumes that scientific inquiry can produce a body of universal assumptions and facts that, in turn, facilitate and explain all human behavior. The consequence, according to constructionists, is that the environment may be seen as a separate entity that acts on the person or is acted on by the person in simple linear, billiard-ball fashion. The scientific method goes a step further and assumes that the unique complexity of any single person can be discovered through scientific study (Figure 9.1).

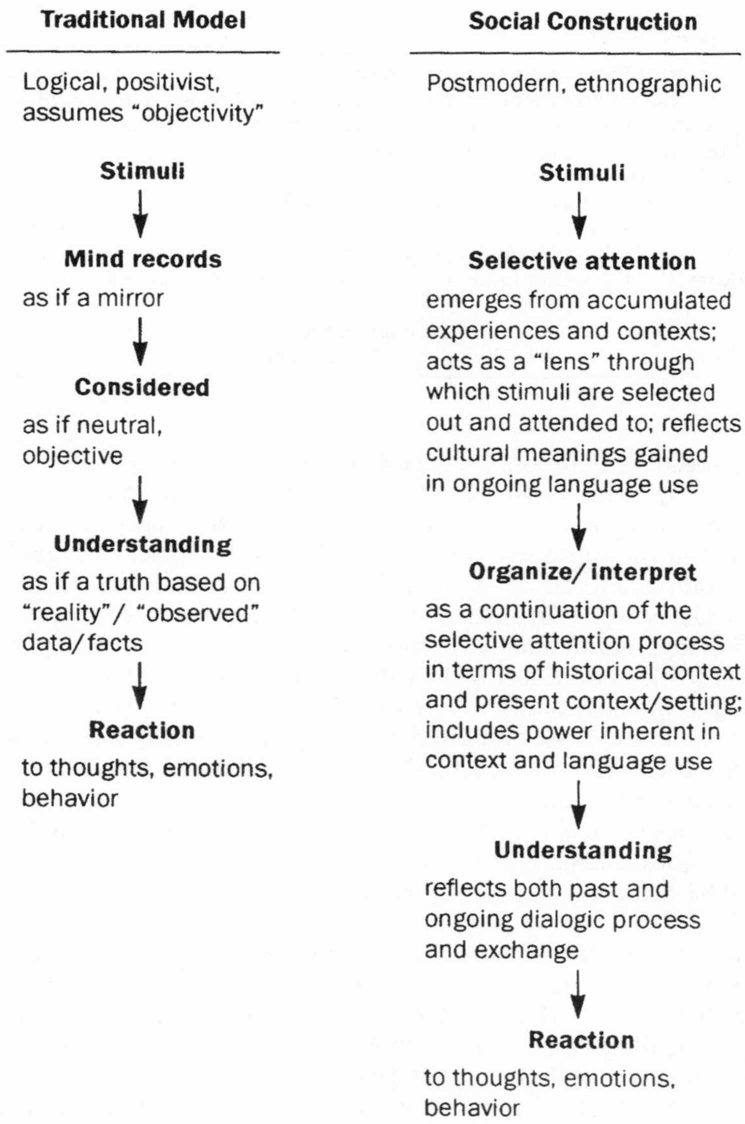

Traditional Model	Social Construction
Logical, positivist, assumes "objectivity"	Postmodern, ethnographic

Stimuli	**Stimuli**
↓	↓
Mind records	**Selective attention**
as if a mirror	emerges from accumulated experiences and contexts; acts as a "lens" through which stimuli are selected out and attended to; reflects cultural meanings gained in ongoing language use
↓	
Considered	
as if neutral, objective	
↓	↓
Understanding	**Organize/ interpret**
as if a truth based on "reality"/ "observed" data/facts	as a continuation of the selective attention process in terms of historical context and present context/setting; includes power inherent in context and language use
↓	
Reaction	
to thoughts, emotions, behavior	↓
	Understanding
	reflects both past and ongoing dialogic process and exchange
	↓
	Reaction
	to thoughts, emotions, behavior

Figure 9.1.   Contrasting models and their assumptions.

Constructionist theorists have tended to criticize the use of such classifications, categories, theories, and treatments (Gergen, 1982, Mahoney, 1991; Weick, 1983). Constructionists suggest that a fundamental reality cannot exist independently of the complexity of people's lives. In addition, constructionists have moved away from the objectivist's idea that the social worker is an expert who has access to universal truths through which he or she interprets and intervenes in the client's life. Although values, beliefs, and sociopolitical and ethical issues are assumed to be eliminated from the objectivist process of discovery through use of proper scientific control (Hudson, 1978, 1982), constructionists believe such values are at

> Constructionism represents a paradigm shift to naturalistic inquiry and reflective thinking.

the heart of the helping process. Constructionists reject the premise of objectivity because they believe that it forgoes the diversity of individuals, families, and communities, and the interweaving of a particular gender, race, religion, age, socioeconomic position, sexual preference, and life experience is thereby lost.

The emerging alternative perspective to the notion of objectivity and scientific inquiry within social work has been referred to using such labels as naturalistic, qualitative, heuristic, ethnographic, hermeneutic, phenomenological, postmodern, postpositivist, and constructivist or social constructionist. Although this new body of work has reflected differing emphases, these emphases have had in common a more dynamic and nondeterministic way of thinking of the complexity of human life (Fisher, 1991). For example, Ann Weick (1983, 1986) and Dennis Saleebey (1989, 1992) have based their work on the fundamental notion that human behavior cannot be isolated into component parts and predicted.

Howard Goldstein (1981, 1983, 1990a, 1990b) also has proposed an orientation toward social work knowledge that is concerned with the constructs with which individuals define their place in the world. He has suggested that the client's conceptualization of his or her life is contained within "the private metaphors and symbols used by the mind to explain the world as it is perceived" (p. xi). This is the basis for "starting where the client is," that is, for understanding the client's unique version of the world and his or her place in it. In addition, Carolyn Saari (1986a, 1986b, 1991) and Joseph Palombo (1992) incorporated a similar concept of meaning-making within human interaction into psychoanalytic and object-relations-oriented clinical theories.

However, there is not a single theory of constructivism or social constructionism conceived by one individual or academic discipline. It was not until recently that various theories and conceptualizations started to coalesce into patterns of ideas shared by members of different disciplines. As understood at present, this perspective represents a convergence of theories, concepts, and research from many areas of study (linguistics, sociology, anthropology, cognitive psychology, ethnology, philosophy, hermeneutics, neurobiology, developmental psychology, epistemology, and biology).

Mahoney (1991) has proposed viewing these diverse ideas as a "family

of theories" about mind and mentation, which share three basic commonalities, in that they

(1) emphasize the active and proactive nature of all perception, learning, and
knowing; (2) acknowledge the structural and functional primacy of abstract
(tacit) over concrete (explicit) processes in all sentient and sapient experience;
and (3) view learning, knowing, and memory as phenomena that reflect the
ongoing attempts of body and brain to organize (and endlessly reorganize)
their own patterns of action and experience. (p. 95)

The constructionist perspective taken by Mahoney (1991), Guidano
(1991), Hayek (1978), Weimer (1977), and others considers a personal reality to be a "co-creation" of the person and his or her social and physical
worlds. The basic sense of a person's being emerges from and is an expression of his or her unique individual history within the context of the
community of others and the physical world. This brief overview of the
kinds of contributions made to this family of theories by social constructionism demonstrates the diverse nature of the development of constructionist thought. At present, emphasis is on viewing language use in the
context of social interaction, including the interaction of social work intervention. The concern is with how, through language, each person weaves
a unique narrative or story about his or her life in the context of others and
societal constraints (Sarbin, 1986). For example, anthropologist Clifford
Geertz (1973) presented culture as a social system of shared symbols or language that provides the context for meaning and structure.

Given these increasingly popular ideas, social work must consider a
fundamental shift in thinking about what intervention entails and its implications for the diversity of individuals and groups with which social
work is concerned. The following provides the basic premises that underlie a social constructionist perspective of social work intervention and issues of diversity.

BASIC ASSUMPTIONS AND TERMINOLOGY

*The First Wave in psychotherapy was pathology-based. The Second Wave was prob-
lem-focused or problem-solving therapy. The Third Wave was solution-focused or so-
lution-oriented. The Fourth Wave is what is emerging now. Only no one has a good
name for it yet.*
                    —W. H. O'Hanlon, "Possibility Therapy: From Iatrogenic Injury
                                                    to Estrogenic Healing"

The social constructionists' approach to social work practice draws on
a multifaceted conceptual base that addresses how people think about and

organize their worlds (Berlin, 1980; Fisher, 1991; Mahoney, 1988). Social constructionists tend to make four assumptions:

1.   The manner in which people study the world is based on available concepts, categories, and scientific or research methods; these categories are a product of language.

2.   The various concepts and categories that people use vary considerably in their meanings and from culture to culture as well as over time.

3.   The popularity or persistence of certain concepts and categories depends on their usefulness, rather than on their validity; ideas tend to persist because of their prestige or congruence with cultural values.

4.   The way in which people describe or explain the world is a form of social action that has consequences; for example, the consequences of theories built on male experiences may deny women's values and processes (Gergen, 1985).

The basic assumptions of social construction theory are given in Table 9.2.

Social constructionists have proposed that no final, true explanation of the world, or client lives, can be found (Sluzki, 1990). Rather, there are multiple realities, and the purpose of inquiry is to gather conceptualizations of these realities manifested and considered in the social worker–client encounter. These constructs reflect the context of the lives of both client and therapist. Jenkins and Karno (1992) noted that "cross-cultural psychiatric literature of the past several decades has documented substantial cultural differences in conceptions of psychosis, display of emotion, behavioral

Table 9.2.   Constructivist Theory: Basic Assumptions

- People, as biological organisms, manifest a biological imperative to differentiate and categorize the stimuli they receive.
- People actively construct or create meaning over time through interaction with other people and action with the environment.
- Language is a particular form of action. Through language, people are able to contemplate and self-evaluate events and construct personal meanings.
- People are able to consider alternative meanings because those new versions of reality are less disruptive to their sense of personal integrity.
- Emotions and cognition are interrelated manifestations of personal meanings in the context of the person's life and the moment.
- The construction and reconstruction of the core of personal meanings is experienced by the person as a sense of self.
- The sense of self is reconstructed as the core of meanings or life narrative is rewritten.
- The formation of meaning and the use of language are a form of communal action. Therefore, people develop systems of meanings called *culture*. A *sociocultural system* is a meaning processing system through dynamic social exchange.

rules and norms" (p. 19). For example, the importance of the concept of *confianza* (trust) and the interpersonal space that reflects respect for some Puerto Rican clients must be understood by the social worker (Morales, 1992). Understanding must encompass an appreciation and recognition of communal processes and not classify client issues in an oppressive or pejorative manner (Fruggeri, 1992).

Meaning

Another fundamental premise of constructivist thinking is the idea that people construct meaning out of the jangle and dissonant chords of stimuli impinging at every moment (Gordon, 1964; Mahoney, 1988). Meaning denotes the implications, effect, tenor, and intent of its referent. In this sense, meaning represents a form of distinction. Meaning thus represents a person's ability to separate out and characterize the world. In this way, the person structures his or her world and attributes significance to the makeup of that structure. Meaning making represents a fundamental process by which people engage in and experience their existence in the world. Kelly (1955) observed that "man [*sic*] creates his own way of seeing the world in which he lives; the world does not create [perceptions] for him" (p. 12).

> Constructionists view language as a vehicle for the exchange of ideas and the creation of meaning.

Language and Narrative

Meanings about the self in the world occur through language—any means of conceptualizing, representing, and communicating experience. Metaphorical representations expressed in narrative form provide the means for organizing and structuring the person's life experience in language (Polkinghorne, 1988; Sarbin, 1986). The story a person constructs about his or her existence provides that person with a coherent understanding or meaning of his or her life as lived and a context from which to view the present and future.

Schank and Abelson (1990) suggested that these stories or scripts are means of coherently organizing experience into personally meaningful conceptualizations of one's life. The person approaches the world through the eyes of the organization of previous experiences expressed in the form of the metaphorical narrative. A story or script is thematic in that it contains not only content but a relationship between the details. In this way, a story acts as the context for understanding a familiar situation by recalling similar content and understanding novel situations by matching both details and the thematic nature of the story.

According to Lakoff and Johnson (1980) people will

define [their] reality in terms of metaphors and then proceed to act on the basis of the metaphors. [They] draw inferences, set goals, make commitments,
and execute plans, all on the basis of how [they] in part structure [their] experience, consciously or unconsciously, by means of metaphor. (p. 158)

Consider, for example, the emergent shift in the African-American conceptualization of understanding self in relation to an oppressive society,
which has been reflected in the change from the use of *Negro* to *black* and
later to *African-American*. These were not merely changes in words used
but changes revealed through the experiences of resisting oppressive and
discriminatory practices. These metaphors represent an emergent meaning out of a people's experience and provide a way of considering oneself
in relation to others on one's own terms.

EXPLAINING DEVELOPMENT ACROSS THE LIFE CYCLE

Stages

Constructionist theory is not a theory of universal stages such as Erikson's (1974). Stage theories are considered static insofar as they tend to represent the attitudes and beliefs of a culturally derived way of conceiving
of human development at a particular time in social history. On the other
hand, constructionist theory does not impose a culturally or temporally
bound model of human development. Rather, the theory provides the
social worker with a seemingly heterogeneous group (ethnic, religious,
geographical, political, and so forth), that is, a means to understand a *particular* individual within his or her sociocultural context (Table 9.3).

The notion of "time," a human creation with numerous meanings, has
been an added factor that is encompassed in thinking about the life of an
individual in our Western European culture. Specifically, in terms of the
usual discourse concerned with how life unfolds over time, social work has
assumed the traditional perspective. This has resulted in constructing categories assumed to be universal developmental stages such as childhood,
adolescents, and senior adults. The consequence is that social work practitioners assume these categories are existent, independent of their creation
and use within a community of language. On the other hand, social constructionists focus on "the ways in which people employ these categories
and descriptions [socially constituted through language use] to make sense
of life change [and] recast the objects of conventional life course studies—
phases, stages, and developmental sequences—as products of interpretive

Table 9.3.   Guidelines for Social Workers Using a Constructionist Approach

General Guidelines
- The social worker takes a stance of unconditional respect for the uniqueness of each client and the context of the client's life. The social worker recognizes that both he or she and clients respond to situations in idiosyncratic ways that reflect their experiential history, biological propensities, and the community of shared meanings embedded in the language of their day-to-day life.
- The social worker makes an effort to be aware of his or her preconceived ideas (both personal and theoretical) about who the client is, what the problem is, and how the client should be helped, and refrains from imposing those ideas on the client. The social worker takes the stance of open curiosity and interest in the client's life narrative and the issue as perceived by the client.
- The social worker acknowledges that the context of the therapeutic setting by its very structure and procedures reflects the values and beliefs of the community sanctioning the work to be done.
- The social worker respects the client's personal reality and the maintenance of this reality as a means of strengthening the integrity of his or her sense of self and the world as the client knows it.
- The social worker appreciates that the issues will be resolved as a result of a collaborative understanding, shared meanings, and the generation of alternative meanings. The social worker does not support unjust and prejudicial interpersonal or institutional actions. In these instances, the social worker seeks alternative meanings to alleviate a negative condition.
- Therapy involves an ongoing exchange of client–social worker meaning that shifts as new information is added. Meaning is generated through this communication. To help people with interpersonal functioning, it is important to assist them to take the perspective of the other person.
- The process of social work interventions is to provide a situation conducive for alternative meanings to be shared, understood, and used by the client and the social worker. Client-defined problems can be resolved as alternative meanings or perspectives emerge.

Specific Guidelines to Consider When Working with Clients
- Start where the person is and stay with the person. Always stay with the person and his or her agenda, respect where the person is in terms of the work you are doing together.
- Maintain a position of "not knowing." Although a paradox, it is significant to attempt to be self-aware and to be alert to our own selective attention and interpretations based on our personal life experiences as created in our language. It is also important to be alert to the theories and models of human behavior and pathology we incorporate into the lens through which we view those with whom we work.
- Don't assume. Don't assume that you understand what a person is saying or meaning.
- Check it out. Always ask for the person's explanations, understanding, or meaning.
- Construct a narrative or story. We all are engaged in the process of constructing stories or narratives that explain ourselves and our worlds to ourselves and others. Meaning is created within these stories or narratives of our lives

continued

Table 9.3. (Continued)

and the world we live in. This includes the social worker in the moment with the person with whom the practitioner is working.

- Work with the client's internal context. Where the person is at the moment in terms of internal thoughts, emotions, expectations, and motivations, all of which are changing over time and reflect the present external context.
- Work with the client's external context. The circumstances of the person's life and what social workers refer to as their "environment" in which the person has lived and is living, including you the social worker, your agency, social policy and values, and economic factors.
- Create new meaning. We human beings are always constructing meaning or "making meaning" out of our being engaged in the process of living. It is on the bases of these constructed meanings or the meaning-making process that we think, believe, experience affect, and behave.
- Engage clients in collaboration. Collaboration engages others from a position of equality and joint participation in a meaningful (to both members) partnership focused on the enhancement of that person's life on the person's terms.

practice, not objectively meaningful "things" in their own right" (Gubrium, Holstein, & Buckholdt, 1994, pp. 2–3).

The conventional Western European-centered discourse concerned with notions of a life course or human development is expressed through the cultural/social metaphors of a community of people. This language both creates and at the same time represents "an abstract image or notion evident in particular vocabularies and social rituals that is taken to stand over and above lived experience and simultaneously represents experience to

> Social constructionists do not subscribe to the idea of fixed developmental stages. Rather, the self is dynamic and emerges and grows through communal discourse.

those concerned. [These] constructs, such as 'community, personality, or social role,' . . . provide a means of structuring and apprehending lives" (Gubrium et al., 1994, p. 24).

Human behavior theory can be understood as constructed categories social workers use to characterize the expected life experience of those with whom they are engaged. The life courses that emerge are not mere representations of inherent patterns of experiences as much as they are formulations of just what the speakers understand their experience to be (Gubrium et al., 1994, p. 30). For example, the idea of the concept labeled "child" and what that might mean depends on the dialogic context of the moment and carries with it the social and cultural history of a particular community expressed through its language use. Therefore the "meaning" that is construed within a specific narrative or dialogic process is "neither an objective feature of a particular chronological time in life nor a property of the term itself" (Gubrium et al., 1994, p. 31). These developmental concepts such as "child," "adolescent," or the "elderly" are social "objects" constructed over time, always in transition within differential contexts. They do not exist "out there" to be found or discovered. Rather, they represent "ways of doing things with words to produce meaningful realities and formulate the social world" including the sense of "self" we consider the center of our Western cultural world (Gubrium et al., 1994, p. 31). Therefore, what social work considers "real" about human existence, such as naturally occurring developmental phases with normative consequences is, according to the social constructionist perspective, constituted through narratives reflective of social and cultural communities.

Biological Propensities

The social constructivist perspective asserts that people are active creators of their experience and not mere passive recorders of an external world. The world does not consist of things out there to be passively seen, experienced, and learned. The experience of "out there" is the result of a person's biological structure "bringing forth a world" (Maturana & Varela, 1987).

From this perspective, there is no such thing as a single or universal view of reality, but a reality constructed as an outcome of the biological structure and as a manifestation of a person's system of beliefs and social context at the moment (Watzlawick, 1984). Within the uniqueness of personal constructs it must be recognized that "phenomenological day-to-day [contexts] of race, language, class, gender, and age emerge in each individual's recognition of himself or herself and the individual's relationship with his or her world" (Rivera & Erlich, 1992, p. 7). Both social worker and client reflect in their actions the diversity of their respective experiences.

From their beginnings, people act on the world, creating distinctions out of the enormous complexity of biological stimuli its structure is capable of organizing. These distinctions and classifications that emerge from people's actions are known as *knowledge* (Efran, Lukens, & Lukens, 1990; Maturana & Varela, 1987). Knowledge and meaning participate in the emerging patterns of experience as they form the forever-evolving perspective or core meanings from which the sense of order and consistency of one's own self and world are created and maintained. A person construes himself or herself in the world in a particular way by selectively attending, perceiving, interpreting, and integrating stimuli as meanings are generated consistent with the evolving core of meanings. This core is the emerging sense of self in the world. It is within the context of this most central and dominant core of meanings, as the individual's personal reality is constructed, that thoughts, affect, and behavior arise. A fundamental consequence of this biological imperative is that each individual occupies a unique reality reflecting his or her own biological propensities, history of personal experience, and the myths and traditions of community:

> Each person comes into the world with unique sensitivities or temperaments (von Glaserfeld, 1984; Markus, 1977; Nisbett & Ross, 1980; Pepitone, 1949; Schacter, 1964; Weimer, 1977). People are biologically "wired" differently (Mahoney, 1991). For example, one child may sleep through the night, respond with an inviting smile, and act at ease with contact, whereas another child may awaken during the night, act fretful or cry, and stiffen when approached. The parent or caretaker will have his or her own interactional style that will result in a unique encounter between him or her and the child. A particular caretaker may respond to the first child with satisfaction and intimacy but respond to the second child with less satisfaction and connectedness. Thus the biological disposition may set the possibilities for the experience between the caretaker and each child, and the consequence will be a part of the evolving relationship between them and, later, others. (Guidano, 1991)

In addition to caregiving behaviors, Tiefer (1987) has suggested that human sexuality is another behavior that can be examined from a social constructionist perspective. She contended that a universal norm or single social-historical context cannot be used to define or understand human sexuality. Rather, biological sexuality is the necessary precondition to a set of potentialities transformed by societies.

Mind and Knowledge

The biological process we call *mind* fills in and elaborates on the sensations available to people. The mind enables a person to maintain a sense of consistency and steadiness in the midst of the shifting and changing world (Guidano, 1987). People are continually involved in the process of creating notions about their world to anticipate and predict its circumstances. According to Popper (1959), a person survives as a result of his or her ability to solve problems. The person can be thought to be continually constructing and reconstructing theories about his or her world (Weimer, 1977).

In turn, the theory or theories of the world form the context from which a person selects to see and interpret his or her world. From this perspective, knowing the self and the world is acting on the sensations encountered at any particular moment (Maturana & Varela, 1987). The person knows by organizing the stimuli based on their previous organizations, stories, or scripts within the context of the moment.

> People create a world of meaning through their interpretation of stimuli.

The Self

Humans cannot know the world except through the self-referential context of perceived distinctions or meanings (Guidano, 1991). It is through the "eyes" of constructed meanings that each person views himself or herself and the world. Meanings are founded on the distinctions each person makes of the stimuli he or she engages. As a consequence of the embedded nature of constructs in language and discourse, people take for granted the reality of the world as differentiated and expressed in language and thus perceived (Stewart, Franz, & Layton, 1988). It is difficult for people to imagine it otherwise. It is on the bases of meanings attached to these perceived differences that decisions are made and actions are taken that affect people. A significant example is a person's skin color. Rivera and Erlich (1992) provided a poignant example of the strength of constructs in limiting understanding and of their power to act on others:

> Middle-class Asians, Latinos, or African Americans are still viewed as minorities because of a most easily identified characteristic: skin color. Good clothes and an elegant briefcase are not much help when you need a cab in the middle of the night in Chicago or Washington, D.C. (p. 6)

In a similar manner, a person can experience a complex social occurrence from his or her unique perspective and interpret its meaning differently than anyone else. The history of personal experiences evolves over time, creating a perspective of idiosyncratic expectancy based on the accumulated picture of one's self in relation to the world, that is, a perspective that should reflect the diversity of an individual's personal life history. The basic concepts that account for these processes and their consequences are meaning, language and narrative, mind and knowing.

Adaptiveness: Knowledge and Power

Client stories generally tend to be directed by the knowledge of the dominant culture and may describe oppressive experiences (Polanyi, [1958] 1964; White, 1993). The way in which such knowledge is construed may give some individuals and groups power to dominate others (Foucault, 1965, 1978, 1980). According to Poster (1989), "to begin a discourse is to enter into a political world" (p. 50). One such argument about the political nature of knowledge concerns the then revised third edition of the *Diagnostic and Statistical Manual of Mental Disorders* (DSM-III-R) published by the American Psychiatric Association (1987; now in the fourth edition, 1994) Carolyn Cutler (1991) contended that DSM-III-R reflects the differential power-based relationship between the social worker and the client. She states that this differential relationship is "based on the clinician's desire to see clients as other than themselves" (p. 157). Consequently, the client so labeled often becomes depersonalized and powerless (Rosenhan, 1984).

Tomm (1990) argued against pathologizing people through labeling and segregating, whereas Amundson (1991) has suggested that when considering classification and or labeling of clients, practitioners remember that "'truth' is often historical, that social practices evolve and that psychology and psychiatry ride on the back of, rather than stand apart from, culture" (p. 30). For example, use of the term *learning disabled* invites a person who is so labeled to view himself or herself as less than whole, and avoids an examination of contextually oriented interventions (Stewart & Nodrick, 1990).

How a practitioner defines truth or insight supports particular social / political arrangements (Efran et al., 1990; Kleinman, 1973). When knowledge is seen as universal or essential, it can be institutionalized in oppressive ways (Lowe, 1991). The practitioner listens within his or her own "convictions, and puts them in a cultural context. . . . [Therefore, the helping process always] stems from the therapist's personal history, cultural context, and theoretical orientation" (Cecchin, 1992, p. 93). Hence, therapists must "become responsible for their own actions and opinions . . . to dare to use their resources to intervene, to construct rituals, to reframe situations, behaviors, and ideas for both the client and themselves" (pp. 92–93).

For example, de Amorin and Cavalcante (1992) used a combination of constructionist narrative and puppet drama to counter the stories of stigmatized individuals—developmentally disabled adults—who faced myths of deficiency:

> Using a social constructionist perspective in our work we have encouraged persons labeled as "developmentally disabled" to reconstruct their personal narratives, socially re-examining the misconceptions and / or myth-conceptions that have caused their segregation. (p. 149)

UNDERSTANDING CULTURAL DIFFERENCES: CROSS-CULTURAL SOCIAL WORK

The social constructionist perspective suggests that persons are always creating and recreating a world of meaning, which is referred to as a *process of construction*. This ongoing and evolving process results in freedom of interpretation, misinterpretation, and innovation, while simultaneously these constructions are manifestations of language use within a culture. In this manner, social traditions and categorizations expressed through language are shared through dialogic processes by participants in a specific cultural tradition (Geertz, 1973). Thus, constructions of meaning are embedded within the cultural traditions symbolized within the language in use. How one then sees oneself and the world is bounded within the cultural traditions constructed in language use and, likewise, exposed to alteration and change through the process of language use within a locality.

> Humans live in a world of socially constructed meaning called *culture*.

Polanyi (1958) described language as central to our existence and how we come to "know" ourselves and our worlds:

> We are born into a language, and we are also born into a set of beliefs about the nature of things. And, once brought up in our beliefs, we embrace them with sufficient conviction to participate in imposing them on the next generation. (p. 75)

Therefore, the focus of concern is with the emergence of language within communities.

The social constructionist concept of culture is the expression of historically shared meanings of a community of people. The meanings emerge within the context of human interaction and are continually transformed during that transaction. Culture does not exist as an entity, even though people often speak of culture as if it had a permanent and unchangeable form. A social constructivist perspective recognizes "cultures as texts . . . [which therefore are] differently read, differently construed, by men and women, young and old, expert and nonexpert, even in the least complex societies" (Keesing, 1987, p. 161).

Culture thus is not recognized as a monolithic stereotype of groups of people. Attempts to draw broad cultural pictures of peoples do injustice to any particular individual who does not match this stereotypical version of a culture. For example, although it might be said that Puerto Rican people inhabit the world of two spiritual belief systems—the Roman Catholic Church and *Botanicas,* that is, the practices of visiting the *espiritistas* (spiritist mediums) for health and personal problems—it cannot be assumed that every individual would use either belief system as other members of their community might (Delgado, 1977). Social constructionists recognize the importance of social workers being aware of these beliefs and values especially in terms of the particular meaning for the client. Depending on the significance of either system, social workers would be able to acknowledge and work with these values and beliefs in support of the work in which they and their clients are engaged.

UNDERSTANDING HOW HUMAN BEINGS FUNCTION
AS MEMBERS OF FAMILIES, GROUPS,
AND COMMUNITIES

The traditional focus of social work theory building and practice—person in the social environment—takes as the natural order of things a somewhat autonomous individual residing with other autonomous individuals, each individual coordinating his or her "will" with those others creating "families," "communities," and "societies." This conceptualization of the self-contained "individual" is assumed to be the "natural order of things of this world" or "reality" and is one of the principles or beliefs on which social work theories of human life and development have been built over time through scientific research and practice.

Social constructionists ask that social work take an uneasy look into this taken-for-granted sense of reality and what seems so sensibly and self-evidentially a "self" and a "world" in which this self resides as a basically autonomous agent. A social constructionist perspective or stance contends that this "reality" of self-in-the-world that is experienced as if primordial can be viewed as a process, socially co-constructed and reconstructed through language. The person-in-the-environment exists through ongoing social discourse as people are engaged with each other and their institutions. It reflects historical roots of a people and culture as well as the transitions in that historical retelling through social discourse. It reflects power differentials as well as values of members within and between groups. It is through the confluence of the activities of everyday interactions that lives are constituted through meaning and structure. What is construed as a "society" or "community" is constituted through communicative acts of participants in a locality.

Myths and Traditions of the Community

Language expresses the mind's construction of a person's life in the world. Language is a communal act and reflects both human biology and the communal relationships between persons. People are born physically helpless and dependent on a caretaker, who in turn has come of age within a community of other people with whom he or she shares a language. Through relationships, an infant acquires not only the means of using the caretaker's language but the meanings embedded in that language. Language expresses the myths and traditions of the family and community of which the growing child is a part. As a result, language provides individuals with the means of organizing the world and their relationship with others in terms of the experiences of their shared community. These shared experiences, values, and beliefs of the community, present and past, are contained in the language and in the stories or traditions used by the person to understand himself or herself and the world in which he or she lives.

Each person is continually constructing a life narrative reflective of both his or her own unique life experiences and the prevailing theories about possible lives that are a part of that person's communal traditions (Bruner, 1987; Schank & Abelson, 1990). Each person lives a life that is original and yet is within the broadest boundaries of the community of shared possibilities of a life to be lived. Although the context of an individual's life or culture can thus constrain change, people also bring about change through social discourse and a reconstruction of ideas and beliefs (Gelfand & Fandetti, 1986; Malinowski, 1954; Myerhoff, 1978).

> Humans create their community and institutions through language and shared stories, values, and ideas.

DIRECT PRACTICE IN SOCIAL WORK

The narrative view holds that it is the process of developing a story about one's life that becomes the basis of all identity and thus challenges any underlying concept of a unified or stable self.
        —W. D. Lax, "Postmodern Thinking in a Clinical Practice"

The Self and Change

The social work profession's attempt to understand the consequences of the practitioner intervention or client change has had at its core the traditions of a mechanistic scientific theory. This perspective assumes that there is a reality that can be objectively measured, tested, and verified independent of the observer and context. Underlying varied methodologies and techniques is the assumption that interventions are concrete entities that somehow exist independently of a particular encounter or context. Problems exist as if they are entities to be discovered, identified, and measured through objective investigation and testing. Once a problem is objectively studied and understood, then the correct solution can be applied.

Schon (1983) has referred to this basic premise as the myth of technical rationality. A consequence of this scientific perspective is that it fails to provide a body of knowledge for understanding the processes involved in what transpires during the encounter between the social worker and the client (Gordon, 1983; Stiles, 1988). Schon's (1983) work has demonstrated that expert technical understanding—that is, methodology—can result in misunderstanding the essence of the client's situation. It is the contention of Rice and Greenberg (1984) that this "preoccupation with the role of the therapist and theoretical orientation used has led to . . . losing sight of the mechanisms of change with the client. It is the client who changes" (p. 18). To understand the change processes, social work must concern itself with the client.

A consistent theme in the literature is that change necessitates transformations of meaning about the self and the world, although the theories of explanation and methodology differ. For example, Rogers and Dymond (1957) described change as the emergence into awareness of new perspectives of self (p. 425). Sanville (1987) contended that change is the creation and re-creation of the self throughout one's life, and intervention is the vehicle for freeing this process in the client. In her text on clinical social work treatment, Saari (1986b) stated that intervention involves the client's "organizing of old meanings into newly constructed consciousness [or] new meanings" (p. 27).

> Social workers who use social constructionist philosophy believe client change comes about as the client reconstructs his or her story and develops new meaning.

Significant changes within the person are the consequence of transformations in the fundamental core of meanings about the self in relationship to others and within the context of one's life. The person experiences himself or herself to be the same person in encounters from day to day and over a lifetime (Shotter, 1993). Simultaneously, the context of that person's life is in constant flux as each forthcoming encounter has yet to be experienced. To alter the fundamental core of meanings is to alter the person's felt experience of what it is to be his or her self and to be in his or her world. Alternative versions of how a person should be or how that person should live a life challenge the individual's experience of a sense of self and reality.

Language is not only a means to change: It is the means by which persons categorize, explain, and predict their world. Therefore, from this point of view, the client's hesitation, reluctance, or uncertainty to take on the social worker's perspective is not resistance, but client maintenance of the continuity of experience. Language also is an action and, in many instances, contains power differentials between people. For example, Elliot Liebow's (1967) work *Tally's Corner* challenged the dominant culture's belief that the poor population has demonstrated an inability to defer gratification. Although viewed as an important sociological "fact," Liebow suggested that this statement does not reflect the issues of poverty or the lives of these particular people. Rather, this sociological language of the dominant culture blames the poor population for their plight. According to Lee (1980), language used by social workers can be an aggressive and demeaning act toward their clients. She commented that "how we talk and think about a client or, perhaps more importantly, a 'class' of clients, determines how we act toward the client" (p. 580). It is not unusual for social workers in community mental health settings to use their professional jargon in referring to clients who do not cooperate with the rules and process of treatment. Such clients often are described as "resistant," "uncooperative," "not ready for treatment," or "borderline," as illustrated in the following case study:

> During a clinical conference in a mental health clinic in a large city in the Northeast, social workers were insistent that a particular female client was definitely a passive-dependent personality and resisting treatment because she would not recognize the importance of taking specific assertive actions the social worker had decided were needed. All the social workers at the meeting knew that these actions were the "healthy" thing for her to do and concurred with her pathology. Then, one social worker pointed out that she was from a small rural town in the South and had lived there for 30 years before moving. This social worker, having lived in a town similar to that of the client, pointed out that the client and her family might view what was being asked of the client as being "uppity" and therefore unacceptable. The social worker was able to identify this issue with the client and their work took a different turn. Later, the client talked about her sessions, and confided that she had felt both pressured and stuck during the earlier part of their work together.

It is evident from this discussion that it is not only the client's construction of meaning but the social worker's personal and professional meanings that must be revealed if a truly collaborative exchange is to occur.

Interventions: Changed Meanings

White and Epston (1990) noted that "persons who seek therapy frequently experience an incapacity to intervene in a life that seems unchanging; they are stymied in their search for new possibilities and alternative meanings" (p. 36). An acceptable outcome of intervention would be the generation of alternative narratives that "enable [a person] to perform new meanings, bringing with them desired possibilities—new meanings that [the person] will experience as more helpful, satisfying, and open-ended" (p. 15). According to Shafer (1983), psychoanalysts are "people who listen to the narrations of analysands and help them to transform these narrations into others that are more complete, coherent, convincing, and adoptively useful than those they have been accustomed to constructing" (p. 240). That is, therapists coauthor a new version of the original story, also known as *restorying*. The social worker's role is to ask questions that bring forth "alternative landscapes" and facilitate the "re-authoring" process (White, 1993, p. 41). All interventions are a variation on this process.

The social constructionist approach requires that practitioners adopt a not-knowing position (Anderson & Goolishian, 1988, 1992, p. 29). A practitioner must be diligent about his or her own assumptions about the client. Although the social worker must be aware of preconceived theoretical positions, he or she should rely on the client's views and explanations. This perspective is particularly congruent with James Green's (1995) model of cross-cultural practice. Practitioners may not place people in predetermined social categories, but must take the stance of learner to achieve cultural congruence with clients (Gergen & Gergen, 1983a,b).

The constructivist perspective views intervention, then, as an opportunity for the social worker and client to explore together the narratives the client has evolved to give meaning to his or her life. The social worker must appreciate that his or her own understanding about the client reflects personal narratives or contexts. It is through language that collaboration is expressed in personal meanings and exchanged in conversation. From this perspective, intervention is not a treatment as much as it is a dialogue in which multiple meanings are shared and from which cultural meanings are drawn from both client and social worker. Change, then, is a rewriting of the personal narrative so that a person sees himself or herself and the world from a different perspective.

At times, the client seeks assistance because he or she has identified a personal struggle ensuing from living, for instance, a bicultural life. Such was the situation for a twenty-year-old Puerto Rican woman attending college. She had attempted to come to terms with her family and their opposition to her decision to move out of the neighborhood and start a career. The issue was not one of autonomy and individuality, which the dominant culture had decided was the "natural" order of things, nor was it what was best for her or who was right or wrong. Rather, the struggle was how to maintain what was important to her about her family and culture and, at the same time, express different values she had come to embrace while growing up in the United States. Issues of dating, marriage, and living on her own were only a few with which she had to come to terms in her efforts to maintain good relations with her family and also live a life that differed from her family and community's expectations. The issue for the social worker is that of appreciating and understanding the client's struggle in the language of the client. In this example, the social worker participates with the client in rewriting her cultural history as she has lived it and as she may live it in her life.

Restorying People's Lives

Social constructionists have suggested that it is important to value a client's experiences "without trying to rid clients of those [seemingly negative] experiences directly" (O'Hanlon, 1993, p. 14). The focus is on client ideas, beliefs, frames of reference, and language, and how these relate to the presenting issue. Clients are urged not to blame themselves, but to change their stance toward the problem (Anderson, 1991; Auerswald, 1986; Durrant & Coles, 1991; Goldstein, 1986a).

One way of restorying, that is, developing new meanings, is through deconstruction (Derrida, 1976, 1978). *Deconstruction* is a technique in which the practitioner disrupts typical frames of references, listens for multiple meanings, and reconstructs negative meanings (White, 1993, p. 34). Feminist therapists Hare-Mustin and Marecek (1988) have contended that practitioners must challenge dominant norms related to gender through nontraditional forms of intervention such as deconstruction. In addition, Laird (1989), a family-focused theorist who wrote about restorying women's self constructions, contended that, generally, women's stories have not been told by women but have been defined by men. The deconstruction of and retelling of women's lives is at the heart of the feminist movement (see Chapter 10). Similarly, Taggart (1989) argued that the struggle by women to define themselves has been held back by "the standard theories [that] routinely construct" the female position (p. 100). He believed that limited socially constructed knowledge about women, particularly women's roles in families, needs to be addressed in family therapy approaches.

An example of deconstruction is a cartoon of the Holocaust drawn by Spiegelman (1991) and entitled *Maus*. In the cartoon, in which the Nazis are portrayed as cats and Jewish people as mice, Spiegelman shocks the reader out of any sense of familiarity with the events described. Instead, he approaches the unspeakable through the diminutive; thus, externalizing events generates what might be thought of as "counter-language" (White, 1993, p. 39).

The Social Worker's Role

The social worker listens to the client's story with curiosity and openness, acknowledges his or her own assumptions and beliefs, and attempts to refrain from quickly interpreting the client's story. In addition, the social worker does not assume that he or she knows what the client means. This form of sensitivity protects the social worker from potentially stereotyping the client's culture. This intervention approach stems from the perspective that any time practitioners set up predetermined assumptions about a group, they are evaluating those particular clients on the basis of an artificial stereotype—not all Italians are the same, not all blacks are the same. Familiarity, even if based on the latest descriptions of a particular culture, holds the danger of becoming a template by which clients are measured.

Constructionists appreciate differences, but in terms of the particular meanings expressed by the clients. Contained in the meanings is a particular person's experience with gender, race, socioeconomic and religious background, and so forth, and experience within the context of all levels of social structure: family, neighborhood, community, region, and country. Understanding client meaning also includes understanding the client's relationships with other groups and social systems.

The social worker starts where the client is and remains open to the client's story. In addition, the social worker is a collaborator, learning anew with each client what it is like to be, for example, *this* African-American male, *this* American-Indian female, *this* southern white female, this northern Jewish male, or this white Methodist male. The uneasy task is to initially take a learning stance with the client rather than portraying oneself as an expert who knows all about diversity and what the problem is. This task can be uncomfortable until the practitioner recognizes that it is his or her responsibility to hear the client's story. The social worker's ability lies in enabling the communication to inform him or her about who the person is and how the person understands himself or herself in the particular context of systems or community. The collaboration continues as the social worker and client reassure themselves that there is a mutual level of understanding of how the client lives his or her life, and what work might need to be done to meet the client's needs.

Overall, social constructivism addresses the fundamental issue of diversity as it is expressed in the life of a particular person or group of persons with whom the social worker is engaged. It is diversity as it is lived, reflecting the temporal and contextual meanings for a particular client or client group. Social constructivism recognizes that the agency, its structure, and its organizational values and goals may not necessarily reflect the client's needs. Agencies, policies, and theoretical perspectives reflect the value-laden social scripts of how to get help and where to get help (Freire, 1993). The structures of time, physical setting, and proper procedures all represent a fundamental belief in what is the "normal" or "right" way to live a life. Those who are a part of the dominant culture or those who successfully function within that culture do not recognize the embedded values as anything but reality.

Social constructionist perspectives challenge the social worker to move away from the comfort of knowing and from technique to join with clients in discovering meanings and beliefs that the social worker, client, or both have assumed to be the only way to live. Diversity is an important and compelling example of the significance of differences. As each person respects another's version of life, he or she can recognize that there are multiple perspectives by which one can live.

REFERENCES

American Psychiatric Association (1987). *Diagnostic and Statistical Manual of Mental Disorders* (DSM—III-R). Washington, DC: Author.

American Psychiatric Association (1994). *Diagnostic and Statistical Manual of Mental Disorders* (DSM—IV). Washington, DC: Author.

Amundson, J. (1991). Diagnosis and treatment in another light. *Calgary Participator, 1*(3), 30.

Anderson, H., & Goolishian, H. (1988). Human linguistic systems. *Family Process, 27,* 371–395.

Anderson, H., & Goolishian, H. (1992). The client is the expert: A not-knowing approach to therapy. In S. McNamee & K. J. Gergen (Eds.), *Therapy as Social Construction* (pp. 25–39). Newbury Park, CA: Sage.

Anderson, T. (1991). *The Reflecting Team: Dialogues and Dialogues about the Dialogues.* New York: Norton.

Auerswald, E. H. (1986). Thinking about thinking in family therapy. In H. C. Fishman & B. L. Rosman (Eds.), *Evolving Models for Family Change* (pp. 13–27). New York: Guilford.

Bateson, G. (1979). *Mind and Nature: A Necessary Unity.* New York: Bantam.

Berlin, S. B. (1980). Cognitive-behavioral approaches. In A. Rosenblatt & D. Waldfogel (Eds.), *Handbook of Clinical Social Work* (pp. 1095–1119). San Francisco: Jossey-Bass.

Bricker-Jenkins, M., & Hooyman, N. (Eds.) (1986). *Not for Women Only: Social Work Practice for a Feminist Future.* Silver Spring, MD: National Association of Social Workers.

Bruner, J. (1987). Life as narrative. *Social Research, 54*(1), 11–22.

Burrell, G., & Morgan, G. (1979). *Sociological Paradigms and Organizational Analysis.* Portsmouth, NH: Heinemann.

Cecchin, G. (1992). Constructing therapeutic possibilities. In S. McNamee & K. J. Gergen (Eds.), *Therapy as Social Construction* (pp. 86–95). Newbury Park, CA: Sage.

Cutler, C. (1991). Deconstructing the DSM-III. *Social Work, 36,* 154–157.

de Amorin, A., & Cavalcante, G. F. (1992). Narrations of the self: Video production in a marginalized subculture. In S. McNamee & K. J. Gergen (Eds.), *Therapy as Social Construction* (pp. 149–165). Newbury Park, CA: Sage.

Delgado, M. (1977). Puerto Rican spiritualism and the social work profession. *Social Casework, 58*(8), 451–458.

Derrida, J. (1976). *Of Grammatology to G. C. Spivak.* Baltimore, MD: Johns Hopkins University Press.

Derrida, J. (1978). *Writing and Difference.* Chicago: University of Chicago Press.

Durrant, M., & Coles, C. (1991). Michael White's cybernetic approach. In T. C. Todd & M. D. Selekman (Eds.), *Family Therapy Approaches with Adolescent Substance Abusers* (pp. 137–174). Boston: Allyn & Bacon.

Efran, J. S., Lukens, M. D., & Lukens, R. J. (1990). *Language Structure and Change: Frameworks of Meaning in Psychotherapy.* New York: Norton.

Erikson, E. H. (1974). *Dimensions of a New Identity.* New York: Norton.

Fisher, D. D. V. (1991). *An Introduction to Constructivism for Social Workers.* New York: Praeger.

Foucault, M. (1965). *Madness and Civilization*. New York: Vintage.

Foucault, M. (1978). *The History of Sexuality: An Introduction* (Vol. 1). New York: Vintage.

Foucault, M. (1980). *Power/Knowledge: Selected Interviews and Writings*. New York: Pantheon.

Fraser, M., Taylor, M. J., Jackson, R., & O'Jack, J. (1991). Social work and science: Many ways of knowing. *Social Work, 27*(4), 5–15.

Freire, P. (1993). *Pedagogy of the Oppressed*. New York: Continuum.

Fruggeri, L. (1992). Therapeutic process as the social construction of change. In S. McNamee and K. J. Gergen (Eds.), *Therapy as Social Construction* (pp. 40–53). Newbury Park, CA: Sage.

Geertz, C. (1973). *The Interpretation of Cultures*. New York: Basic Books.

Gelfand, D. E., & Fandetti, D. V. (1986). The emergent nature of ethnicity: Dilemmas in assessment. *Social Casework, 67*(9), 542–550.

Gergen, K. J. (1982). *Toward Transformation in Social Knowledge*. New York: Springer.

Gergen, K. J. (1985). The social constructionist movement in modern psychology. *American Psychologist, 40*(3), 266–275.

Gergen, K. J., & Gergen, M. J. (1983a). Narratives of the self. In T. R. Savin & K. E. Scheibe (Eds.), *Studies in Social Identity*. New York: Praeger.

Gergen, K. J., & Gergen, M. J. (1983b). The social construction of helping relationships. In J. D. Fisher & B. DePaulo (Eds.), *New Directions in Helping* (Vol. 1). New York: Academic.

Germain, C. B. (1970). Casework and science: A historical encounter. In R. Roberts & R. Nee (Eds.), *Theories of Social Casework* (pp. 3–32). Chicago: The University of Chicago Press.

Goldstein, H. (1981). *Social Learning and Change: A Cognitive Approach to Social Services*. Columbia: University of South Carolina Press.

Goldstein, H. (1983). Starting where the client is. *Social Casework, 64*(5), 267–275.

Goldstein, H. (1986a). A cognitive humanistic approach to the hard-to-reach client. *Social Casework, 67*(1), 27–36.

Goldstein, H. (1986b). Toward the integration of theory and practice: A humanistic approach. *Social Work, 31*(5), 352–357.

Goldstein, H. (1990a). Strength of pathology: Ethical and rhetorical contrasts in approaches to practice families in society. *Families in Society, 71*(5), 267–275.

Goldstein, H. (1990b). The knowledge base of social work practice: theory, wisdom analogue of art. *Families in Society, 71*(1).

Gordon, W. (1964). Notes on the nature of K. In H. Bartless (Ed.), *Building Social Work: A Report of a Conference* (pp. 1–15). New York: National Association of Social Workers.

Gordon, W. (1983). Social work revolution or evolution? *Social Work 28*(3), 181–185.

Gottschalk, S. S., & Witkin, S. L. (1991). Rationality in social work: A critical examination. *Journal of Sociology and Social Welfare, 18*(4), 121–135.

Gould, K. H. (1984). Original works of Freud on women: Social work references. *Social Casework, 65*(2), 94–101.

Green, J. (1995). *Cultural Awareness in the Human Services*. Englewood Cliffs, NJ: Prentice-Hall.

Gubrium, J. F., Holstein, J. A., & Buckholdt, D. R. (1994). *Constructing the Life Course.* New York: General Hall.

Guidano, V. F. (1987). *Complexity of the Self.* New York: Guilford.

Guidano, V. F. (1991). *The Self in Process: Towards a Post-Rationalist Cognitive Therapy.* New York: Guilford.

Hare-Mustin, R. T. (1990). Sex, lies and headaches: The problem is power. In T. J. Goodrich (Ed.), *Women and Power: Perspectives for Family Therapy* (pp. 61–83). New York: Norton.

Hare-Mustin, R. T., & Marecek, J. (1988). The meaning of difference: Gender theory, past modernism and psychology. *American Psychologist, 43,* 445–464.

Haworth, G. (1984). Social work research, practice and paradigms. *Social Service Review, 61,* 343–357.

Hayek, F. A. (1978). *New Studies in Philosophy, Politics, Economics and the History of Ideas.* Chicago: University of Chicago Press.

Heineman, M. B. (1981). The obsolete scientific imperative in social work research. *Social Service Review, 58,* 371–397.

Heineman, M. B. (1982). Author's reply. *Social Service Review, 56,* 312.

Hudson, (1978). First axioms of treatment. *Social Work, 23,* 65–66.

Hudson, (1982). Scientific imperatives in social work research and practice. *Social Service Review, 56,* 242–258.

Imre, R. W. (1982). *Knowing and Caring: Philosophical Issues in Social Work.* Lanham, MD: University Press of America.

Jenkins, J. H., & Karno, M. (1992). The meaning of expressed emotion: Theoretical issues raised by cross-cultural research. *American Journal of Psychiatry, 149*(1), 9–21.

Keesing, R. M. (1987). Anthropology as interpretive quest. *Current Anthropology, 28,* 161–176.

Kelly, G. A. (1955). *The Psychology of Personal Constructs.* New York: Norton.

Kleinman, A. M. (1973). Medicine's symbolic reality on a central problem in the philosophy of medicine. *Inquiry, 16,* 206–213.

Kuhn, T. S. (1970). *The Structure of Scientific Revolutions* (2nd ed.). Chicago: University of Chicago Press.

Laird, J. (1989). Women and stories: Restoring women's self-constructions. In M. McGoldrick, C. M. Anderson, & F. Walsh (Eds.), *Women in Families: A Framework for Family Therapy* (pp. 427–450). New York: Norton.

Lakoff, G., & Johnson, M. (1980). *Metaphors We Live By.* Chicago: University of Chicago Press.

Lax, W. D. (1992). Postmodern thinking in a clinical practice. In S. McNamee & K. J. Gergen (Eds.), *Therapy as Social Construction* (pp. 69–85). Newbury Park, CA: Sage.

Lee, J. A. B. (1980). The helping professional's use of language in describing the poor. *American Journal of Orthopsychiatry, 50,* 500–584.

Liebow, E. (1967). *Tally's Corner.* Boston: Little Brown.

Lowe, R. (1991). Postmodern themes and therapeutic practices: Notes towards the definition. *Dulwich Centre Newsletter, 3,* 41–53.

Mahoney, M. J. (1988). The cognitive sciences and psychotherapy: Patterns in a developing relationship. In K. S. Dobson (Ed.), *The Handbook of Cognitive-Behavioral Therapies* (pp. 357–386). New York: Guilford.

Mahoney, M. J. (1991). *Human Change Processes: The Scientific Foundations of Psychotherapy.* New York: Basic Books.

Malinowski, B. (1954). *Magic, Science, and Religion.* New York: Doubleday.

Markus, H. (1977). Self-schemata and processing information about the self. *Journal of Personality and Social Psychology, 35,* 63–78.

Martin, P. Y., & O'Connor, G. G. (1989). *The Social Environment: Open Systems Applications.* New York: Longman.

Maturana, H., & Varela, F. (1987). *The Tree of Knowledge.* Boston: New Science Library.

McNamee, S., & Gergen, K. J. (Eds.) (1992). *Therapy as Social Construction.* Newbury Park, CA: Sage.

Morales, J. (1992). Community social work with Puerto Rican communities in the United States: One organizer's perspective. In F. G. Rivera & J. L Erlich (Eds.), *Community Organization in a Diverse Society* (pp. 91–112). Boston: Allyn & Bacon.

Myerhoff, B. (1978). *Number Our Days.* New York: Dutton.

Nisbett, R., & Ross, L. (1980). *Human Inference: Strategies and Shortcoming of Social Judgment.* Englewood Cliffs, NJ: Prentice-Hall.

Northen, H. (1982). *Clinical Social Work.* New York: Columbia University Press.

O'Hanlon, W. H. (1993). Possibility therapy: From iatrogenic injury to estrogenic healing. In S. Gilligan & R. Price (Eds.), *Therapeutic Conversations* (pp. 3–17). New York: Norton.

Palombo, J. (1992). Narratives, self-cohesion, and the patient's search for meaning. *Clinical Social Work Journal, 20,* 249–270.

Pepitone, A. (1949). Motivation effects in social perception. *Human Relations, 3,* 57–76.

Polanyi, M. ([1958] 1964). *Personal Knowledge.* Chicago: University of Chicago Press.

Polkinghorne, D. E. (1988). *Narrative Knowing and the Human Sciences.* Albany, NY: State University of New York Press.

Popper, K. R. (1959). *The Logic of Scientific Discovery.* London: Hutchison.

Poster, M. (1989). *Critical Theory and Poststructuralism: In Search of a Context.* Ithaca, NY: Cornell University Press.

Priest, S. (1990). *The British Empiricists.* New York: Penguin.

Rice, L. N., & Greenberg, L. S. (Eds.) (1984). *Patterns of Change: An Intensive Analysis of Psychotherapy Process.* New York: Guilford.

Rivera, F. G., & Erlich, J. L. (1992). Introduction: Prospects and challenges. In F. G. Rivera & J. L. Erlich (Eds.), *Community Organization in a Diverse Society* (pp. 1–26). Boston: Allyn & Bacon.

Rodwell, M. K. (1987). Naturalistic inquiry: An alternative model for social work assessment. *Social Service Review,* 231–246.

Rogers, C. R., & Dymond, R. F. (Eds.) (1957). *Psychotherapy and Personality Change.* Chicago: University of Chicago Press.

Rosenhan, D. L. (1984). On being sane in insane places. *The Invented Reality.* New York: Norton.

Ruckdeschel, R. A. (1985). Qualitative research as a perspective. *Social Work Research & Abstracts, 21,* 17–21.

Russell, B. (1956). *Logic and Knowledge.* London: Allen & Unwin.

Saari, C. (1986a). The created relationship: Countertransferences and the therapeutic culture. *Clinical Social Work Journal, 14*(1), 39–51.

Saari, C. (1986b). *Clinical Social Work Treatment: How Does It Work?* New York: Gardner.

Saari, C. (1991). *The Creation of Meaning in Clinical Social Work.* New York: Guilford.

Saleebey, D. (1989). The estrangement of knowing from doing: Profession in crisis. *Social Work, 70*, 556–563.

Saleebey, D. (1992). Introduction: Power to the people. In D. Saleebey (Ed.), *The Strengths Perspective in Social Work Practice* (pp. 3–17). New York: Longman.

Sands, R. G., & Nuccio, K. (1992). Postmodern feminist theory and social work. *Social Work, 37*(6), 489–502.

Sanville, J. (1987). Creativity and constructing of the self. *Psychoanalytic Review, 74*, 263–279.

Sarbin, T. R. (1986). *Narrative Psychology.* New York: Praeger.

Schacter, S. (1964). The interaction of cognitive and physiological determinants on emotional state. In L. Berkowitz (Ed.), *Advances in Experimental Social Psychology* (Vol. 1). New York: Academic.

Schank, R. C., & N. Abelson, R. P. (Eds.) (1990). *Scripts, Plans, Goals and Understanding.* Hillsdale, NJ: Erlbaum.

Schon, D. (1983). *The Reflective Practitioner: How Professionals Think in Action.* New York: Basic Books.

Scott, D. (1989). Meaning construction and social work practice. *Social Service Review, 39*–51.

Shafer, R. (1983). *The Analytic Attitude.* New York: Basic Books.

Shotter, J. (1993). Identity and belonging. In N. Coupland & J. F. Nussbaum (Eds.), *Discourse and Lifespan Identity* (pp. 5–27). Newbury Park, CA: Sage.

Simon, B. (1970). Social casework theory: An overview. In R. Roberts & R. Nee (Eds.), *Theories of Social Casework* (pp. 353–394). Chicago: University of Chicago Press.

Sluzki, C. E. (1990). Negative explanations drawing distinctions, raising dilemmas, collapsing time externalization of problems: A note on some powerful conceptual tools. *Residential Treatment for Children and Youth, 7*(3), 33–37.

Spiegelman, A. (1991). *Maus.* New York: Pantheon.

Stewart, B. & Nodrick, B. (1990). The learning disabled lifestyle: From reification to liberation. *Family Therapy Case Studies, 5*(1), 60–73.

Stewart, A. J., Franz, C., & Layton, L. (1988). The changing self: Using personal documents to study lives. *Journal of Personality, 56*(1), 41–73.

Stiles, W. B. (1988). Psychotherapy process—Outcome correlations may be misleading. *Psychotherapy, 25*, 27–35.

Taggart, M. (1989). Epistemological equality as the fulfillment of family therapy. In M. McGoldrick, C. M. Anderson, & F. Walsh (Eds.), *Women in Families: A Framework for Family Therapy* (pp. 97–106). New York: Norton.

Tice, K. (1990). Gender and social work education: Directions for the 1990's. *Journal of Social Work Education, 26*(2), 134–144.

Tiefer, L. (1987). Social constructionism and the study of human sexuality. In P. Shaver & C. Hendrick (Eds.), *Sex and Gender* (pp. 70–93). Newbury Park, CA: Sage.

Tomm, K. (1990). A critique of the DSM. *Dulwich Centre Newsletter, 3,* 5–8.

von Glaserfeld, E. (1984). An introduction to radical constructivism. In P. Watzlawick (Ed.), *The Invented Reality: Contributions to Constructivism* (pp. 18–20). New York: Norton.

Watzlawick, P. (1984). *The Invented Reality: How Do We Know What We Believe We Know?* New York: Norton.

Weick, A. (1981). Reframing the person-in-environment perspective. *Social Work, 26,* 140–143.

Weick, A. (1983). Issues in overturning a medical model of social work practice. *Social Work, 28,* 467–471.

Weick, A. (1986). The philosophical contest of a health model of social work. *Social Casework, 67,* 551–559.

Weick, A. (1987). Reconceptualizing the philosophical perspective of social work. *Social Service Review, 61,* 218–230.

Weimer, W. B. (1977). A conceptual framework for cognitive psychology: Motor theories of the mind. In R. Shaw & J. Bransford (Eds.), *Perceiving, Acting, and Knowing* (pp. 267–311). Hillsdale, NJ: Erlbaum.

White, M. (1993). Deconstruction and therapy. In S. Gilligan & R. Price (Eds.), *Therapeutic Conversation* (pp. 22–61). New York: Norton.

White, M., & Epston, D. (1990). *Narrative Means to Therapeutic Ends.* New York: Norton.

GLOSSARY

Biological propensities. Each person's inborn sensitivities and temperament. The core of the self.

Culture. The expression of historically shared meanings of a community of people. People create culture through the use of language within a locality.

Deconstruction. A social worker's technique that disrupts a client's typical frames of references, listens for multiple meanings, and reconstructs negative meaning.

Human behavior theory. constructed categories social workers use to characterize the expected life experience of those with whom they are engaged.

Intervention. the client's 'organizing of old meanings into newly constructed consciousness or new meanings. Change necessitates transformations of meaning about the self and the world.

Language. A means of conceptualizing, representing, and communicating experiences. Language is a communal act.

Meaning. A person knows the world through his or her perception, interpretation, and characterization of stimuli. Meaning represents a person's ability to separate out and characterize the world.

Mind. A biological process that elaborates on people's sensations.

Not-knowing-position.   A social worker's learning stance in which he or she hears a client's views and explanations.

Person-in-the-environment.   Person-environment is a mental construct created through ongoing social discourse as people are engaged with each other and their institutions. It reflects historical roots of a people, culture as well as power differentials, and the values of members within and between groups.

Reality.   A socially constructed view. There is no final, true explanation of the world.

Self.   The person I experience in myself from day to day over a lifetime.

Story.   A person's way of coherently organizing experiences into personally meaningful conceptualizations of his or her life.

Theory or theories of the world.   What forms the context from which a person selects in order to see and interpret his or her world.

CRITIQUE

How Useful Is the Social Constructionist Approach?

The following critiques of the usefulness of the social constructionist approach in terms of its application particularly in the 1990s. It reflects on
the theory for social work practice and education in a world of shifting paradigms. Social constructionism is a recent conceptualization that dates back
to the 1960s and the work of Wittgenstein (1963) and Berger and Luckmann's (1967) classic book *The Social Construction of Reality: A Treatise in the
Sociology of Knowledge*. Social constructionists understand knowledge and
meaning as socially created within a cultural context (Dean & Fleck-Henderson, 1992). To paraphrase Gergen (1985), a social constructionist approach is a theoretical conceptualization that asserts that most of human life
exists in the way we know it because of social and interpersonal influences.

In constructivism, which is based on the work of Kelly (1969), Gilligan
(1982), and others, knowledge development is proactive; That is, humans
are active participants in creating meaning and knowledge based on their
realities (Granvold, 1996). Although *social constructionism* and *constructivism* are distinct metatheories (Franklin, 1995), most authors use these
terms interchangeably. Dean (1993) agreed with this interchange for the
sake of simplicity, but delineated the two. Both perspectives suggest that
reality is socially or psychologically constructed. However, the perspectives differ in that constructivism places emphasis "on the limits on our
abilities to know another and the need to construct meaning together"
(p. 56), whereas the social constructionist perspective emphasizes the role
of culture, especially language, narratives, and sociohistorical factors, in
the construction of reality (Franklin, 1995). Perhaps as the discourse on
these two theoretical perspectives is strengthened, there may be more dis-
criminating writings based on their commonalities and differences.

Fundamental assumptions of social constructionism include language as the main vehicle for understanding reality, cultural assumptions, and historical precedents (Witkin, 1990). Fletcher (1998) clearly stated that language is never neutral but rather "a powerful means of constructing an ideological world view that furthers the interest of dominant groups." In a practice approach guided by social constructionism, the use of language is critical to establishing the meaning of problems. Client concerns are understood as intersubjective linguistic creations that are shaped through the dialogue between clinicians and clients (Guterman, 1994). Two important components of this dialogue are life narratives, which help individuals find meaning in their personal experiences, and history and mythology, which help construct collective meaning (Gilmartin, 1997).

As Gordon (1997) explained, social constructionism has displaced the universal "grand narratives," which are construed as the truth, with smaller "local" narratives, which represent the experiences of a particular locale. Indeed, community workers have long used this conceptualization in their approach to understanding the structures and dynamics of local communities. Language derives its meaning from social processes that occur within the context of culture. A related concept is that understanding individual and social phenomena is closely related to cultural and historical patterns of viewing the world and its structure of power relationships. Dean (1993) warned that those in power can determine and define our categories and assumptions. At the macro level, the importance of language and its interpretation within the sociocultural-political arena is exemplified daily in the mass media. For example, although Saddam Hussein's speeches on the United Nations embargo against Iraq are perceived as defiant and aggressive by most Western powers, they are welcomed as patriotic statements by most Iraqi people.

Guterman (1994) has criticized clinical psychology, psychiatry, and social work for their strong underpinnings in positivist epistemologies, which tend to "pathologize" clients. Yet, this criticism does not consider social work orientations such as empowerment, feminist theories, the dual perspective, strengths perspective, and a growing body of social work knowledge based on a social constructionist perspective. Witkin (1990) stated that social constructivism provides another interpretation of reality and complements social work well based on a number of shared dimensions—particularly, the person-in-environment perspectives and the quest for social and moral justice.

LEARNING FROM A SOCIAL CONSTRUCTIONIST VIEWPOINT

The social constructionist approach may create uncertainty among students not accustomed to questioning reality or among those used to "cookbook recipes." Hardcastle (1993), recognizing students' struggles with uncertainty, stated that students must be offered the experience to learn and grow in a safe, open space to graduate practitioners with an orientation that aims at treating the client as the expert and at understanding clients' meanings of reality.

Another contribution of the social constructionist approach to teaching and learning is the respect for personal knowledge and how this knowledge can be transmitted to students in the supervisory relationship (Dean, 1989). In supervision, guided by the constructionist framework, there is a recognition that both supervisor and supervisee bring different ways of knowing and understanding to the relationship that enrich the learning process. In this way, rigid hierarchical supervisory relationships are avoided (Edwards & Keller, 1995). Dean and Fleck-Henderson (1992) formulated three goals in teaching about theory and practice with clients: (1) help students think critically about reality, that is, "breed in our students a mistrust of fixed notions about reality" (p. 8); (2) help students understand the existence of different world views; and (3) help students see meaning-making as "an activity that is shared and social" (p. 9).

Dean (1993) identified the following six classroom activities demonstrating the constructivist approach to teaching and learning treatment techniques:

1. Students learn the art of interviewing through questioning. Through this activity, students use different questions as a means of conducting a "therapeutic conversation," which is guided by the client's views.

2. Students experiment with the co-creation of meaning. Students witness new understandings and meanings through conversation. Simultaneously, clients also realize new "meanings in their concerns" through the interview process.

3. Students learn a collaborative approach with clients. The constructivist approach does not recognize the therapist as the expert. Clients are enlisted in making the choices that will guide the therapeutic sessions, thus releasing the social worker from directing the interview or treatment process.

4. Students learn to tolerate "not understanding." When the clinician is considered the expert and projects his or her own experiences onto the client, there is less understanding of the client. To have a dialogue, there must be a clear distinction of client and social worker viewpoints.

5. Students learn to listen to narratives. As a classroom activity, students learn by watching videotaped interviews with classmates to determine how much they can shape the conversation.

6. Students learn to be reflective about their practice. By abandoning the idea of a "single reality or objective truth" that will serve as an evaluation tool of practice, students learn to be reflective and become disciplined in making these reflections known to others.

Social work educators have acknowledged that agency practice is often driven by third-party payments and, with it the need to "assess," "diagnose," and "label." Therefore, it would be a disservice to students and the profession if the profession did not prepare students to meet those demands. A reconciliation of these two conflicting views of the client situation is offered by Dean and Fleck-Henderson (1992): Students learn how meaning is co-constructed and how assessment is influenced by the context created between the client and the practitioner. As a result, assessment develops out of a genuine, dynamic exchange of "stories," "views," and "narratives," elicited during the dialogue between client and practitioner.

PRACTITIONER USE OF SOCIAL CONSTRUCTION

Practitioners use many of the concepts of the social constructionist approach more often than they realize. The skill of starting where the client is, paying attention to gut-level feelings, rejecting the concept of total objectivity, and the importance of the client's accounts of her or his experience are examples of how ingrained aspects of this framework are integrated into practice. Witkin (1990) emphasized the contributions of this theory in social work education in a number of areas, such as the role of "social theory and the linguistic representation of knowledge" (p. 40), critical thinking, historical and cultural relativity, and moral and value implications of social actions.

Inherent in this approach is the understanding that practitioners do not have to name or categorize problems or challenges to be helpful to clients. Rather, practitioners co-construct meanings with the client's help. Anderson and Goolishian (1990) discussed a position of "not knowing," requiring the clinician to be conscious of his or her own opinions. By taking this position, social workers need to adopt a learning stance, be willing to change previously held views, and to consider the client's narrative as the current reality. In this type of helping relationship, the practitioner is not an "expert" but a co-discoverer of the client's realities (Gallant, 1993). Thus, a social constructionist perspective redefines the client-practitioner relationship to one that is based on a more mutual, personalized knowledge (Gergen, Hoffman, & Anderson, 1996).

The social constructionist perspective can assist social workers to analyze and respond to socially defined challenges both they and their clients face, particularly clients who may be among a population-at-risk. In an analysis of the Cuban-American "success story" and the Asian "model minority" as portrayed in the popular media, Vidal de Haymes (1997) concluded that these socially constructed views have a negative effect on the sense of solidarity among minority groups. These views tend to favor the agenda of the culture of failure, pointing out that certain minority groups' lack of success is the result of their own cultural deficiencies. The focus of attention is shifted to the victims rather than to the inequalities in the social structures. Recognizing the power of socially constructed images, Paulo Freire (1970) offered the explanation that, through the process of internalized oppression, the oppressed takes on the characteristics of the oppressor.

Social constructivism as well as feminist theories recognize that individuals, groups, and communities experience oppression differently. For example, societal oppression of women based on gender affects all women (Davis, 1993). In a different context, Gilmartin (1997) addressed the oppressive and devastating effects of stigmatization of former psychiatric patients as the result of strong stereotypical societal images of this population. Gilmartin suggested that the liberating processes for former psychiatric patients emerged by "reconstructing life events through personal narratives in order to integrate these events into the life story in meaningful ways" (p. 86).

GROUP INTERVENTIONS

The concept that meaning is socially constructed through the use of dialogue or conversations also permeates the practice literature (Berger & Luckmann, 1967; Middleman & Wood, 1993). For example, Brower (1996) described the usefulness of a constructivist perspective in working with small groups. In this group model, the group moves from a beginning stage lacking external meaning; that is, members are unclear about their own purpose for membership in the group and the group lacks clear goals for itself. In the next stage, the leader provides his or her vision for the group and members usually begin to question the leader's vision as they feel more comfortable in the group situation. The next stage developed by group members is marked by a schema that represents a shared understanding of the values, norms, rules, roles, and so on that govern the group experience. The current author recommends two constructivist techniques: narratives and role plays. Overall, a number of authors (Balgopal & Vassil, 1983; Brower, 1996; Franklin, 1995; Neimeyer & Neimeyer, 1987) have supported the use of a constructivist perspective in working with small groups.

In an approach based on social constructionism, practitioners examine the historical, economic, and sociocultural factors affecting surrounding clients' challenges. Furthermore, it is clearly understood that clients bring different worldviews to their situations, such as illness, unemployment, or ability (Brown, 1995). The social construction of societal phenomena has been expanded to the point that social movements have come together to find solutions based on those social definitions. It was not until the baby boom generation started to grow older that society moved from conceptualizing older adults from "them" to "us." The Gray Panthers, the feminist movement, and the AIDS movement are just a few examples in recent history.

Moreover, Pugliesi (1992) has contended that social constructionism is essential in feminist therapy when working with women who exhibit psychological distress. McQuaide and Ehrenreich (1998), in their study on women in prison, used constructivist and feminist perspectives to understand the personal histories and experiences, shared experiences of gender, race, and ethnicity, and the effect of imprisonment on women's lives to create intervention strategies that are positive and that enhance the construction of the female self-image.

Fiene (1991) in discussing the construction of self among Appalachian women, pointed out the importance of two dimensions in assessing human behavior: (1) understanding the way individuals conceive the reality of their lives and (2) appreciating the effect of contextual factors on individual and family development. This type of assessment brings understanding about the interplay between community mores and individual behavior. As a result, social work practice that results from this conceptualization is based on "individual, family, and community strengths that may not be recognized without an appreciation of the client group's world view" (p. 58).

FAMILY THERAPY

The use of social construction is well documented in the field of family therapy (Atwood & Zebersky, 1995; Gergen, 1985; Goolishian & Anderson, 1992; Lax, 1989). The literature has indicated that social constructivist family therapy uses such techniques as engaging in conversation versus monologue (Real, 1990), listening to family stories, understanding the various meaning systems (Atwood & Zebersky, 1995), identifying and amplifying exceptions (Real, 1990), and engaging in mutual discovery (Mailick & Vigilante, 1997).

Clearly, the social constructivist perspective has challenged many practice assumptions including the influence of positivism on human behavior theories, the way problems are defined, the construction of the helping process, the client and practitioner roles, and approaches to outcome research. Simultaneously, it has offered practitioners the opportunity to engage in creating knowledge with clients and to formulate an array of guiding principles for practice. Application of this perspective may prove difficult in agencies in which more traditional perspectives are expected of the practitioners. Furthermore, at all levels of practice (micro, meso, macro), the social constructivist perspective requires a commitment to challenge the supposed "truth" sponsored by people in positions of power, such as a parent, school principal, council person, and religious leader, or an agency board of directors, policymakers, media images, or international consortium.

Students are also subject to experience discomfort with this approach. Dean (1993) pointed out that some students might have difficulty in making the transition from a realist perspective to that of the constructionist perspective. She recommended that the curriculum must have a balance between constructivist and realist positions. The teaching of the social constructionist approach should assist students in recognizing social and economic injustice and in understanding the richness of societal voices in a diverse society.

The main discourse of a social constructionist approach takes place outside traditional social work journals, even though social workers do write about this approach in other professional media. If the profession conceives perspectives such as strengths, feminist, empowerment, and ethnic sensitive practice as sharing many of the underpinnings of social constructionism, then we may conclude that many social workers are not only active in conceptualizing this approach but also applying it to their practice and teaching modalities.

A concluding thought—a topic that could lead into a whole other paper—relates to the extent to which a social constructionist approach, which is so closely based on a dialogue between clients and practitioners and a deep understanding of others' realities, will be effective with the "Net Generation" (Tapscott, 1998) whose main source of reference will be digital technology.

REFERENCES

Anderson, H., & Goolishian, H. (1990). Supervision as a collaborative conversation: Questions and reflections. In H. Brandau (Ed.), *Von der supervision zur systemischen vision*. Salzburg, Austria: Otto Muller Verlag.

Atwood, J. D., & Zebersky, R. (1995). Using social construction therapy with the REM family. *Journal of Divorce and Remarriage, 24*(2), 133–162.

Balgopal, P. R., & Vassil, T. V. (1983). *Groups in Social Work: An Ecological Perspective*. New York: Macmillan.

Berger, P., & Luckmann, T. (1967). *The Social Construction of Reality: A Treatise in the Sociology of Knowledge*. London: Penguin.

Brower, A. M. (1996). Group development as constructed social reality revised: The constructivism of small groups. *Families in Society, 77*(6), 336–344.

Brown, P. (1995). Naming and framing: The social construction of diagnosis and illness. *Journal of Health and Social Behavior (Suppl.)*, 34–52.

Davis, L. V. (1993). Feminism and constructivism: Teaching social work practice with women. *Journal of Teaching in Social Work, 8*(1/2), 147–163.

Dean, R. (1989). Ways of knowing in clinical practice. *Clinical Social Work Journal, 17*(2), 116–127.

Dean, R. (1993). Teaching a constructive approach to clinical practice. In J. Laird (Ed.), *Revisioning Social Work Education: A Social Constructionist Approach* (pp. 55–76). New York: Haworth.

Dean, R., & Fleck-Henderson, A. (1992). Teaching clinical theory and practice through a constructivist lens. *Journal of Teaching in Social Work, 6*(1), 3–20.

Edwards, T. M., & Keller, J. F. (1995). Partnership discourse in marriage and family therapy supervision: A heterarchical alternative. *Clinical Supervisor, 13*(2), 141–153.

Fiene, J. I. (1991). The construction of self by rural low-status Appalachian women. *Affilia: Journal of Women and Social Work, 6*(2), 45–60.

Fletcher, J. (1998). *Relational Practice: A Feminist Reconstruction of Work*. Available at: http://www.si.unich.edu/icos/jni-rev4.html

Franklin, C. (1995). Expanding the vision of the social constructionist debates: Creating relevance for practitioners. *Families in Society, 76*, 395–406.

Freire, P. (1970). *Pedagogy of the Oppressed*. New York: Seabury.

Gallant, J. P. (1993). New ideas for the school social worker in the counseling of children and families. *Social Work in Education, 15*(2), 119–126.

Gergen, K. J. (1985). Social constructionist inquiry: Context and implications. In K. J. Gergen & K. E. Davis (Eds.), *The Social Construction of the Person* (pp. 3–18), New York: Springer-Verlag.

Gergen, K. J., Hoffman, L., & Anderson, H. (1996). Is diagnosis a disaster?: A constructionist trialogue. Available at: http:www.swarthmore.edu/socsci/kgergen1/-text5.html

Gilligan, C. (1982). *In a Different Voice*. Cambridge, MA: Harvard University Press.

Gilmartin, R. M. (1997). Personal narrative and the social reconstruction of the lives of former psychiatric patients. *Journal of Sociology and Social Welfare, 24*(2), 77–101.

Goolishian, A., & Anderson, H. (1992). Strategy and intervention versus nonintervention: A matter of theory? *Journal of Marital and Family Therapy 18*(1), 5–15.

Gordon, L. (1997). Therapeutic theory and social context: A social constructionist perspective. *British Journal of Guidance and Counseling, 25*(1), 5–16.

Granvold, D. K. (1996). Constructivist psychotherapy. *Families in Society, 77*(6), 345–357.

Guterman, J. T. (1994). A social constructionist position for mental health counseling. *Journal of Mental Health Counseling, 16*, 226–244.

Hardcastle, J. (1993). The Student as Consumer. In J. Laird (Ed.), *Revisioning Social Work Education: A Social Constructionist Approach* (pp. 183–197). New York: Haworth.

Kelly, G. (1969). Man's construction of his alternatives. In R. Maher (Ed.), *Clinical Psychology and Personality, the Second Papers of George Kelly*. New York: Wiley.

Lax, W. D. (1989). Systematic family therapy with young children and their families: Use of the reflecting team. *Children in Family Therapy: Treatment and Training,* 56–60.

Mailick, M. D., & Vigilante, F. W. (1997). The family assessment wheel: A social constructionist perspective. *Families in Society, 78*(4), 361–370.

McQuaide, S., & Ehrenreich, J. H. (1998). Women in prison: Approaches to understanding the lives of a forgotten population. *Affilia: Journal of Women and Social Work, 13*(2), 233–243.

Middleman, R. R., & Wood, G. G. (1993). So much for the bell curve: Constructionism, power/conflict, and the structural approach to direct practice in social work. *Journal of Teaching in Social Work, 8*(1/2), 129–146.

Neimeyer, R. A., & Neimeyer, G. J. (1987). *Personal Construct Therapy Casebook.* New York: Springer.

Pugliesi, K. (1992). Women and mental health: Two traditions of feminist research. *Women & Health, 19*(2/3), 43–68.

Real, T. (1990). The therapeutic use of self in constructionist/systemic therapy. *Family Process, 29*(3), 255–272.

Tapscott, D. (1998). *Growing Up Digital: The Rise of the Net Generation.* New York: McGraw Hill.

Vidal de Haymes, M. (1997). The golden exile: The social construction of the Cuban American success story. *Journal of Poverty, 1*(1), 65–79.

Witkin, S. L. (1990). The implications of social constructionism for social work education. *Journal of Teaching in Social Work, 4*(2), 37–48.

Wittgenstein, L. (1963). *Philosophical Investigations.* Oxford: Blackwell.

10

Feminist Theories and Social Work Practice

REBECCA MORRISON VAN VOORHIS

Every woman needs lipstick with staying power.
And mascara that won't run if she sheds a few tears.
Which she's likely to do at a sad movie.
Or if she hears from an old friend.
Or if she has to put her kids to bed hungry.
Because she can't buy food
Because she doesn't have a job
Or even the skills to get one.
And her welfare is about to run out
And the chances of getting a child support check are nil
And she's just about at the end of her rope
And then that waterproof mascara will really come in handy.
        —The Women's Fund of Central Indiana

Social work and feminism have been interwoven since the emergence of the social work profession (Wetzel, 1976). Women have long constituted the bulk of the client population for social workers. Therefore, social work needs to have a feminist view, according to Wetzel (1986). "Clearly, our foremothers who helped define the profession of social work were much concerned with disenfranchised groups and women's issues" (Land, 1995, p. 4). Yet several feminists have reported that women's issues described in the social work literature usually have not been informed by feminist theory (Sands & Nuccio, 1992; Simon, 1988; Van Den Bergh, 1995). This chapter explores the contributions that feminist theories can provide to enhance social work practice.

HISTORY OF FEMINIST THEORY

Feminism, which gained widespread recognition as the result of the women's movement of the 1960s and 1970s, is often equated with social action because of the activism of the women's movement. However, feminism is also a mode of analysis that has attracted many scholars. Since the 1970s, multiple feminist models have been developed for "understanding women's lives and experiences, the nature of inequality between the sexes, and the structuring of gender" (Land, 1995, pp. 5–6). The emergence of multiple feminist theories in the last three decades is likely in response to the plethora of masculinist theories on human behavior that were established in the first part of the twentieth century. Historically, "perceptions of reality based on marginalized people (that is, women, ethnic minorities, and poor people) tended to be overlooked and excluded" (Nicholson, 1990, cited in Van Den Bergh, 1995, p. xii.). The existence of multiple feminist theories also suggests the diversity among women and the inability of one theory to fit all women. As social workers, Sandra Butler and Claire Wintram (1991) noted, "feminist theories are neither monolithic nor static; it is their diversity and dynamism that are worthy of attention" (p. 6).

From the early formulation of the liberal feminist perspective through the contemporary array of feminist theories, there has been a growing recognition of the need for social change. As Collins (1990) pointed out, it is a "journey from silence to language to action" (p. 112). Initially, the need for social change focused on the lack of opportunities for women because they were not recognized as equal to men in the capacity to reason. The array of feminist perspectives as a new millennium dawns shows the growing recognition of the diversity among women related to color, sexual orientation, age, ability, and class. Although feminist perspectives share a common goal of seeking to render women visible and to engage in activism to change oppressive conditions, their diversity provides a number of viewpoints to inform social work practice.

> Feminism is not a monolithic perspective. It has numerous branches each with its own approach to person-environment.

THEORETICAL DEVELOPMENT

Feminist theory has three main historical branches: liberal, radical, and socialist. These three schools of thought represent different philosophical roots that inform their feminist analysis as well as different approaches to address inequality based on gender. Of these three primary feminist perspectives, radical feminist theory also has two significant offshoots: cultural, and lesbian feminism. In addition, womanism, which is a reaction to liberal feminism, and postmodern feminism, which is a reaction to cultural feminist theory, provide important frameworks for feminist analysis. Each of these feminist theories provides a perspective from which social workers may analyze women's experiences and develop actions to address aspects of inequality. Although each of these feminist theories is described separately, this separation is rather artificial, because there are overlaps among feminist schools of thought. Therefore, social workers are encouraged to draw from several feminist theories to enhance practice effectiveness with a diverse array of girls and women.

Liberal

Liberal feminist theory is the best known feminist perspective and often is what people mean when they refer to *feminist* theory. Liberal feminist theorists believe that men and women are essentially the same because the capacity to reason is the defining characteristic of being human and is not gender specific. Therefore, gender differences in areas such as physical capacities are not seen as important and should not be the basis for determining resources and opportunities. Liberal feminists believe that it is the disparity in social conditions, not innate differences in the capacity to reason, that have interfered with women's achievements.

Liberal feminists have focused their attention on the denial of equal opportunity to women that is based on gender. They seek equal treatment of men and women in the public sector, in areas such as education, employment, credit, property rights, and housing. Liberal feminism is well-known for its advocacy of equal pay for equal work. Numerous other achievements have benefited the status of all women, including legalizing abortion, outlawing gender discrimination and marital rape, defining and contesting sexual harassment, including women in all affirmative action programs, and establishing policies on maternity and family leave. For example, social workers use a liberal feminist perspective when establishing job training programs that prepare women to compete with men for jobs in nontraditional areas such as construction, law enforcement, and firefighting.

Within liberal feminism there are classic liberals and welfare liberals. Classic liberals view government as responsible for (1) protecting civil liberties and (2) providing equal opportunity for all people. Welfare liberals believe that the state should take a larger role by regulating the market to provide a minimum level of economic justice for all people (Saulnier, 1996). Social workers often use welfare liberal feminism to seek policies that provide for the economic needs of women, particularly those with young children, through federally funded welfare programs.

The differences between classic liberals and welfare liberals lead to different views on policies such as affirmative action. Liberal feminists who favor "making the playing field more even" through affirmative action programs represent the welfare liberal perspective. Liberal feminists who oppose affirmative action believe that such policies violate the liberal feminist argument that women and men are fundamentally equal and therefore should be treated equally.

Liberal feminists formed the National Organization for Women during the women's movement of the 1960s and 1970s. Liberal feminist thought is perhaps most well-known for the Equal Rights Amendment, that was proposed as an amendment to the U.S. Constitution.

Radical

Radical feminists view male supremacy as the oldest form of oppression. Radical feminist thinkers emerged from the antiwar and civil rights movements of the 1960s. The initial theorizing by radical feminists was a reaction against the Left and the civil rights movement for their male dominance and antifeminist stance.

The hallmark of radical feminist theory is the view that a woman's personal problems are political and are grounded in sexist power imbalances. Borrowing from the belief of the Left that individual alienation and powerlessness had political origins, radical feminist theorists asserted that social action could transform both the society and a person's own well-being. Consciousness-raising was developed to enable women to learn to recognize the political origins of personal problems and also to transform both the self and the society. Thus, social workers use the radical feminist perspective in developing groups for women who have been battered to help them learn that their actions do not justify being beaten. This group intervention also builds awareness that women may identify with their oppressor or believe that they are responsible for their maltreatment.

In contrast to liberal feminists, who have accepted women's subordinate roles in the family, radical feminists have focused on women's exploitation in the family (Saulnier, 1996). Radical feminist theorists claim that both families and societies are organized along lines that give men more power. For example, Francine, a client of a social work agency that provides housing and economic development services, had depended on her husband to provide for their family. As the husband's drug addiction grew, he used not only his income to buy drugs, but began taking money from Francine's purse, whose earnings came from providing afterschool child care. When the bills could no longer be paid, they lost their home. Francine moved her three children into the basement of a friend's home. With the help of the neighborhood center's social worker, Francine obtained temporary housing for her family, divorced her husband, and has taken on several part-time jobs to provide for the needs of her three children.

Radical feminist writings have addressed the need for revolutionary changes to free women from domination and psychological control (Echols, 1989; Dworkin, 1988, 1989; Firestone, 1970). Furthermore, radical feminists regard a woman's so-called consent to being used as a prostitute or pornographic object as the result of conditioning. Because radical feminist thinkers believe that sexism is pervasive, they also believe that social change is necessary. Outspoken against the traditional ways of helping women to adapt to sexist structures, radical feminists have challenged these very structures. Reforms, such as the gradual increase in child care or the legalization of abortion, do not effectively address the underlying sexism in society. To challenge the sexist core, radical change is needed, such as the social provision of child care and the end of marriage. Social workers often use a radical feminist perspective to organize shelters for women who have experienced violence in the home as well as to secure court protection from further violence. Social workers also develop treatment programs for male perpetrators to stop

> The various branches of feminism differ in how social and political action shape their therapeutic approach.

the violence against women and also advocate an end to the societal tolerance of male violence by establishing and enforcing legal sanctions against perpetrators of violence against women.

Cultural

Cultural feminism emerged as an offshoot of radical feminism in the 1980s, when the United States had swung toward conservatism and there was a strong resurgence in the belief that a woman is responsible for her own plight. Cultural feminist thinkers view women as profoundly different from men and seek to celebrate traits, such as nurturing and caregiving, that are attributed to women. They view such traits as superior to the male traits of competitiveness and independence.

While cultural feminist thinkers believe in gender differences, some believe that gender differences are innate, while others believe that gender differences are socially constructed (Saulnier 1996). Cultural feminists share a common concern for relationships that provide a sense of community among women.

Gilligan (1982, 1995; Brown & Gilligan, 1992; Gilligan, Rogers, G., & Tolman, 1991), a contemporary proponent of the cultural feminist theory, has focused on the conditions that support or impede the building of relational connections for girls and women. Her study findings have supported a relational theory about the psychosocial development of girls. Her theory challenges the theories espoused by Erikson (1950) and Kohlberg (1981; see Chapter 4), which present development as a process of separation, disconnection, and independence. Cultural feminists have suggested that theories such as those of Erikson and Kohlberg may apply to an understanding of the development of American males, but are not generalizable to American females.

Cultural feminist thinkers also believe that there are many ways of knowing (Belenky, Clinchy, Goldberger, & Tarule, 1986). Culturalists believe that there are limits to what can be known through logic and seek recognition for knowledge that is gained through intuition or emotion. Drawing from the cultural feminist perspective, social workers seek to understand a woman's experience through listening to her story with all its meaning for her, instead of making a clinical interpretation of the woman's reality.

Because of their beliefs in gender differences and their desire to foster connectedness among women, cultural feminists seek to create a distinctly female culture. Giving attention to literature, art, and music that celebrates women's nurturing and relationship-building has led to the development of women's culture. Feminist bookstores, women's music, film, and art festivals, and other feminist cultural events have contributed to the advancement of women's culture. Although initial ventures to focus on aspects of women's culture were launched with little capital and much sweat equity, contemporary women's events have often attracted funding from mainstream arts organizations, and feminist sections are now a mainstay of bookstores across the country. Feminist art, music, and literature have not supplanted traditional culture; however, cultural feminists can be credited with having firmly established women's culture.

Cultural feminism has been well-received by social work clinicians. Gilligan's work and the writings of theorists (Jordan, Kaplan, Miller, Stiver, & Surrey, 1991) at Wellesley's Stone Center in Massachusetts often guide the clinical social worker's interventions with women who are depressed or anxious, or who suffer from eating disorders or the aftermath of sexual trauma. Social work treatment for such conditions focuses both on achieving a self that is connected to others rather than separate or autonomous and developing mutually empathic relationships to replace relationships that have been disrupted or have lacked mutual caring.

Socialist

Socialist feminists focus on women as a class who are not recognized in the capitalist system of production. Because society has made women responsible for activities in the home, women may lack access to money. Their child rearing and other responsibilities for maintaining their homes are not included in the capitalist system in which money is exchanged for activities that contribute to production.

Unlike radical feminists, who addressed the psychological consequences of patriarchy, socialist feminists stress the social and economic aspects of patriarchal structures. Socialist feminists engage in a materialist analysis of women's exploitation in relation to the means of production and reproduction. Socialist feminist thinkers also focus on alienation that results from systems of stratification based on sex and class.

Some socialist feminists see capitalism and patriarchy as unified and some see them as separate forms of oppression. For example, Hartmann (1981) views capitalism as enhancing sexism by separating wage work from home work and requiring women to do the home work. Those who regard capitalism and patriarchy as one unified system of oppression recognize many facets such as sex and class, which intersect. For example, Young (1981) sees marginalization of women as a secondary labor force as an essential trait of capitalism.

Socialist feminists have criticized capitalist family policy because it focuses on ensuring that men receive a "family wage" to support their families. Such family policy protects the traditional family structure, which is headed by a male breadwinner, because it excludes all other family structures from having access to a family wage. Specifically, socialist feminists advocate for policies that will ensure that poor women and single mothers will receive a family wage so they can care for their families. To ensure support for all family types, socialist feminists also advocate for public support for families.

Although some socialist feminists want women to be paid for work in the home, other socialist feminists fear that such practice will keep women segregated in the home. Thus, socialist feminists have become known for their advocacy for public responsibility for household work. Child care and housework must be defined as a societal, and not a parental, responsibility if oppression based on gender is to be eliminated. For example, defining child care as a societal responsibility will lead social workers to advocate for public funding for all child care, instead

> Feminist social work practice places a high value on enhancing the rights of the oppressed, particularly women.

of continuing to make it the parents' responsibility to care for one's children or pay for their care.

Beneath the socialist feminists' advocacy for public policies that show public responsibility for childcare and housework is the core belief that all forms of oppression should be eliminated. Societal policies and structures should ensure that "one individual's self-actualization . . . does not occur at the expense of another" (Nes & Iadicola, 1989, p. 16).

BASIC ASSUMPTIONS AND CONCEPTS

Several basic assumptions of feminist theories are shared with social work (Table 10.1). Among them is the need to analyze social structures to assess their oppressive effect on individuals. Feminist theorists have a common starting point, which is the view that patriarchal social structures privilege men as a group and afford them opportunities and resources that are not equally available to women as a group. While assessing and intervening in social structures is not new for social workers, this feminist stance does challenge practitioners to evaluate whether theories of human behavior that guide their practice have included the social context in the construction of the theory.

Feminists use oppression to describe the social condition of women as a group while also recognizing that some women have more privileges than others due to class, color, sexual orientation, and so forth. Thus, feminists do not believe that the oppression of women is the only form of oppression, but do maintain that oppression affects all women. As hooks (1989) stated, sexist oppression is a "form of domination we are most likely to encounter in an ongoing way in everyday life" (p. 21). Social workers should realize that despite the pervasiveness of the oppression of women, many women do not recognize it. According to Frye (1983), this oppression goes unrecognized because the divisions of race and class tend to obscure the commonality of oppression for women. Furthermore, recognizing the oppression of women also frightens some women who do not want to be seen as critical of men.

Feminist theories do not separate knowledge from values as has been true for traditional masculine theories. A feminist perspective ensures that knowledge and values are integrated, unlike the positivist paradigms that historically have guided the practice of social work and claim to separate knowledge from values.

Like social workers, feminists believe in the uniqueness of the individual, including unique ways of knowing. Wetzel (1986) pointed to the respect given by feminist thinkers to nonobjective ways of knowing, such as intuition, and personal and subjective experiences. Giving respect to the

Table 10.1. Basic Assumptions of Feminism

- Social structures privilege men as a group and oppress women as a group.
- Knowledge and values are integrated.
- Knowledge is unitary, holistic, global, rather than linear or dualistic.
- There are many ways of knowing, including nonobjective, intuitive sources of information.
- Psychosocial development focuses on attachment and relatedness.
- Gender differences should not be equated with female inferiority.
- Personal problems and sociopolitical conditions are interrelated.
- Empowerment includes both individual and social change.

many ways of knowledge building has brought attention to women's experience and knowledge. The silence of women's voices has been broken because feminists have insisted on alternatives to logical positivism (see Chapter 1).

Feminists believe that it is necessary for women, despite their diversity, to recognize their fundamental unity as a distinct biological sex. "Women as members of this sex share both the bodily experience of femaleness and the social condition imposed on them by virtue of their sex" (GlenMaye, 1998, p. 30). Fostering a sexual class identification among women, instead of focusing on an individual identity, is a cornerstone of feminist thought.

> Feminist practitioners focus on how large-scale political issues are played out on the personal or local level.

Feminists believe in personal power and seek egalitarian environments in the family and public arena in which each person has the power to be and to become and no one group has power over another.

Furthermore, partnership in collective social and political action to reduce oppressive conditions for women has become a hallmark of feminism, which has also long been central to social work practice. Although feminist theories differ in their views of actions needed to address inequality, all espouse social action. As Sands and Nuccio (1992) have concluded, "Regardless of whether a feminist has a liberal, socialist, radical, or other perspective, she has a desire to change the social and political order so that women will no longer be oppressed" (p. 492).

BIOPSYCHOSOCIAL INTERACTIONS

Liberal feminist theory insists on the *essential* biological similarity between men and women. Because all people are rational, liberal feminists have criticized society for denying women equal rights through the prevailing use of physical capacities rather than intellectual capacities to determine a woman's place in society. Based on John Locke's (1977) theory of the rationality of man, liberal feminist thinkers have argued that people should be judged on their capacity to reason, rather than on their physical abilities.

Radical theorists, and some cultural theorists, believe there are *innate* differences between men and women. For example, men are seen as innately more aggressive and women as innately more nurturing (see Chapter 11). Other feminists see differences between men and women but regard socialization—not biology—as the cause of these differences. For example, women are conditioned to meet men's needs and thus may appear to accept patriarchal structures. "According to socialist feminists, the differences between men and women are not a reflection of differences in their natures per se but rather are a product of the [patriarchal social] system" (Nes & Iadicola, 1989, p. 15). Still other feminist thinkers view biological and social factors as so interconnected that attributing cause of women's subordination to one or the other is not possible. Although they do not agree on the cause of gender differences, feminist theorists are united in their view that gender differences should not be equated with female inferiority.

A major feminist tenet that perhaps best represents the social work focus on the interaction of biopsychosocial factors is the belief that *the personal is political*. This feminist view maintains that individual problems are inextricably linked to sexist power imbalances. Furthermore, "behavior which is conceived as being dysfunctional or deviant by our society often reflects behavior of less-privileged groups, such as women" (Land, 1995, p. 7). Thus, psychological problems experienced by women, such as depression, are viewed as the consequence of conditions such as the societal expectations for women of reproduction, child care, and housework as well as limitations that women have faced in roles outside the home.

The cultural feminist thinkers have focused on human development, particularly gender differences in development. In contrast to the writings of Erikson (1950) and Kohlberg (1981), which emphasized the development of separation and autonomy, Gilligan (1982, 1995; Gilligan et al., 1991) has focused her research on the development of the capacity for connectedness and caring in females. Her work has examined the development of girls and has given particular attention to the conditions in families, schools, and communities that support or impede the development and maintenance of relationships as girls grow from infancy into adulthood. Jean Baker Miller (1976), another early cultural feminist thinker, examined the importance of attachment and relatedness in women's functioning in her work *Toward a New Psychology of Women*. Miller and Gilligan's works have served as the basis for the theory building and research on the functioning of girls and women at Wellesley's Stone Center. The Stone Center's "Self-in-Relation" theory examines the distinctiveness of female development and sharply contrasts it with the traditional masculine theories that stress the development of a detached self (Jordan, Kaplan, Miller, Stiver, & Surrey, 1991). Contemporary social workers often draw on this perspective in organizations serving girls, such as Girls, Inc., as well as in clinical practice with women.

PERSON-IN-ENVIRONMENT

Feminist theories are person-in-situation oriented. A key feminist principle is to think holistically and see the unity of all things. Feminist perspectives focus on the interactions between personal traits and the surrounding context(s). To understand the internal psychic structure of women, and women's concepts of self, the effect of external and oppressive structures on women's psychological development must be acknowledged. This knowledge may then assist clinicians in understanding how the therapeutic relationship can address women's needs (Land, 1995, p. 7).

Postmodern feminism provides the strongest focus on the context and the inseparability of the environment and the person. Emphasizing context and examining the social and cultural construction of meanings, postmodern feminists maintain that nothing can be understood separate from its context. The centrality of this principle concerning the wholeness of person and environment is epitomized in the feminist mantra, *the personal is political*, which refers to the interrelationship of all events in both the private sphere and public sector. Furthermore, feminist thinkers do not dichotomize relevant variables such as person and situation or personal and political; rather they see the centrality of connectedness (Wetzel, 1986).

UNDERSTANDING DIVERSITY AMONG WOMEN

Originally, feminists focused on the similarities among women and the inequities between men and women. This focus on the patriarchal bias in traditional theories and social structures led to advocacy by liberal feminists for equal opportunities for women in employment and education, as well as efforts by radical feminists to free women from child care and housework. Critics have claimed that liberal and radical feminists over-look the diversity among women as a result of both race and economic re-sources (Faludi, 1991). Because women of color and poor women have long been in the work force, the goals of both liberal and radical feminists are frequently perceived as irrelevant to sizable groups of women. Socialist feminists do address oppression that results from both class and gender, because their theory considers both capitalism and patriarchy in its analy-sis of the oppression of women. However, critics have suggested that so-cialist feminists have failed to address the experiences of women of color that result from racism, rather than capitalism or sexism.

Because of the criticisms that the three original feminist theories over-look the diversity of women, several additional feminist frameworks have been developed. Lesbian feminist theory analyzes the intersection of gen-der and sexual orientation and womanism examines the intersection of race, gender, and class. In addition to these two feminist theories that ad-dress multiple forms of oppression, postmodern feminist theory stresses the uniqueness of the individual woman's perceptions and experiences.

Lesbian feminism arose as a challenge to both heterosexism and sexism in our culture. Lesbian feminism opposes the imposition of any form of sex-ual orientation on all people. Lesbian feminism is a political perspective that criticizes institutionalized heterosexual preference and ought not to be equated with genital sexual activity (Saulnier, 1996).

Lesbian feminism views heterosexuality and patriarchy as equally op-pressive systems that maintain male supremacy and the oppression of women. Lesbian feminists, such as Charlotte Bunch (1987) distrust hetero-sexuality, as it is institutionalized, because men are viewed as intrinsically more valuable than women (Bunch, 1993). "Above all, lesbian feminist theory is a critique of a hierarchy—the system that allows for some people to be held as intrinsically more valuable based on the sex of their partner" (Saulnier, 1996, p. 90).

Lesbian feminists theorize that heterosexism, which is the belief that heterosexuality is superior, is both an outgrowth of patriarchy and a key support that maintains patriarchal structures (Calhoun, 1994). A recent de-bate that involves lesbian feminists concerns the use of the terms *homo-phobia* and *heterosexism.* Some are concerned that homophobia, which means an irrational fear and hatred of lesbians and gay men, is sometimes used when what is being referred to really represents heterosexism. A se-rious concern about the possible misuse of the homophobia term pertains to its use by the helping professions. As pointed out by Kitzinger and Perkins (1993), homophobia explains the problem in individual terms rather than focusing on the social etiology of conditions, such as an indi-vidual's dislike of homosexual persons. Furthermore, when the focus is on disordered individuals, the solution focuses on fixing those individuals rather than changing the biased social structures that foster the homophobia exhibited by individual people.

No doubt lesbian feminism is most well-known for its cry for the "woman-identified woman." Such women define themselves independently from men and look to other women, not men, for help in understanding what it means to be a woman. As Bunch (1987) asserted: "A woman-identified woman is a feminist who adopts a lesbian-feminism ideology and enacts that understanding in her life, whether she is a lesbian sexually or not" (p. 198). Claiming the right to define oneself can be a radical act for many women who have been carefully socialized in families and schools to conform to both patriarchal and heterosexual norms. As stated by Frye (1983), "Definition is another face of power" (p. 105). One aspect of self-definition is the right to define one's sexuality. Lesbian feminists argue that no woman "will ever be free to choose to be anything until all women are free to choose to be lesbians" (Saulnier, 1996, p. 79).

Urging women to abandon their caretaking of men has caused lesbian feminism to be viewed as a threat to the social order. Bunch (1987) captures this as a

> threat to the ideological, political, personal, and economic basis of male superiority. The lesbian threatens the ideology of male supremacy by destroying the lie about female inferiority, weakness, passivity, and by denying women's "innate" need for men. Lesbians literally do not need men. (p. 164)

With their challenge to both the institution of heterosexual marriage and the pervasive social structures that privilege heterosexual men, lesbian feminists clearly seek radical change in the social order.

While separatism has been advocated by some lesbian feminists, many regard that as a practical impossibility. Furthermore many argue that separatism is politically unwise. Phelan (1994) argues cogently for the need for lesbians to remain a part of the larger social order no matter how badly society treats lesbians. As she notes, lesbians really cannot flee to another place where they will belong and be allowed to live without oppression. She concludes that the only way to truly be accepted is to remain within the dominant society and challenge the barriers to belonging in the dominant culture.

Womanism seeks to focus attention on the interlocking oppressions of gender and race rather than having them dealt with separately. Historically black women have been very involved in seeking rights, opportunities, and services for women. Many contemporary black women support feminist ideals and want equal attention to be given to issues of race. Many feminists of color, such as Anzaldua (1990), hooks (1984), Espin (1994) and Lorde (1984) have stated that feminism is not for white middle-class women only and should be seen as relevant for women of color. To ensure treatment relevance, Comas-Diaz (1987) states that feminism must be culturally embedded to be effective with women of color. Thus, instead of dichotomizing race and gender, womanists promote a "both and" worldview that addresses racism and sexism as interlocking systems.

> Feminist theory represents a range of views and seeks to be inclusive to diversity of ideas and aspirations among women.

Womanists recognize all aspects of the self and differ from feminists who privilege gender over other aspects of the self, such as race or class. In direct practice, "Self- assertion and reaffirmation of multiple identities not only empower women of color, but also facilitate the development of a more integrated and less dysfunctionally fragmented sense of identity" (Comas-Diaz, 1994, p. 291). Recognizing all parts of the self also leads womanists to seek new ways of valuing difference that lead to coalitions that work together as equals, not continuing patterns in which some have more power.

At the core of the womanist perspective is social change in which solutions to social problems are sought. Theorizing is secondary and clearly informed by activism. Womanists are concerned that abstract philosophical ideas are overvalued and can result in activism being sacrificed in the quest to develop obscure theories. Womanism includes both a social agenda for change and a personal agenda for self-healing. Recognizing the multiple group membership for women of color, Comas-Diaz developed an approach called "psychotherapeutic decolonization" (1994, p. 287), which addresses both the individual healing and the transformation of oppressive conditions. Social workers can use Comas-Diaz's approach to help women of color with:

- Recognizing the systemic and societal context of colonialism and oppression, thus, becoming aware of the colonized mentality.
- Correcting cognitive errors that reinforce the colonized mentality, for example, working through dichotomous thinking (superior-inferior, the colonized is good, the colonizer is bad, etc.) and acknowledging ambivalence (toward self and others).
- Self-asserting and reaffirming racial and gender identity, as well as developing a more integrated identity.
- Increasing self-mastery and achieving autonomous dignity.
- Working toward transformation of self and / or the colonized condition (e.g., improving the condition of women, men, and children of color). (p. 291)

Practitioners who use this approach with individual women of color can aid these clients to define themselves independently of the idealized white female standard. Social workers may also help individual women of color to see ways that they can mold their environment and not simply be shaped into the oppressors' mold.

Postmodern feminist theory focuses on socially constructed meanings held by particular women. Because postmodern feminists place high value on socially constructed meanings and definitions of one's reality, they seek to understand the perceptions and meanings of specific women. Thus, postmodernists oppose the development of theories because they do not believe that it is possible to develop "propositions concerning reality that are to be generalized and ubiquitously applied" (Van den Bergh, 1995, p. xiii).

Diversity is of utmost interest to postmodern feminists. Furthermore, postmodern feminists view categories such as race, gender, and class as reductive and leading to superficiality in understanding the meaning of human experiences. Thus, woman is not a universal construct and no one speaks for all women. Postmodern feminists specify which women are being addressed and speak about particular women, not universal woman. With their focus on diversity, postmodern feminists seek to avoid having the interests of women of higher status dominate, which is a major criticism of many feminists who presume to speak for all women (Sands & Nuccio, 1992).

UNDERSTANDING HOW HUMAN BEINGS FUNCTION AS MEMBERS OF FAMILIES, GROUPS, ORGANIZATIONS, AND COMMUNITIES

Families

Although feminist thinkers initially focused only on the public arena in their examination of sexual inequality, with the emergence of both radical and cultural feminists, the focus has expanded to include the private sphere of the family. A feminist perspective on the family has spawned several feminist approaches to family assessment and treatment that social workers can use in their work with families. Authors of these feminist family therapy approaches were leading women in the family therapy field who recognized the need to expand treatment approaches to ensure that women are not encouraged to adapt to oppressive family structures or processes (Walters, Carter, Papp and Silverstein, 1988; McGoldrick, Anderson, and Walsh, 1989). Although the women who published these books represent different schools of family therapy, they shared a common focus: to address women's needs in families and ensure that family therapy does not ignore or sacrifice women's needs for the "good of the family." Additional attention to the family has been given by feminists who are concerned with the power differential between men and women in families. Thus, feminist social workers have sometimes opposed family treatment for problems such as battering because of the greater power possessed by men than women.

Groups

Women's groups have become a primary way of building feminist consciousness. In the 1970s, consciousness-raising groups for women became well-known for their effect on women's understanding of their common experiences as women and the bonding that occurred among women in the groups. According to Land (1995), the purpose of consciousness-raising groups "was akin to many empowerment-oriented self-help groups today" (p. 5). Or as described by Vourlekis (1991), consciousness raising develops "a new, shared view of 'reality' that alters each individual's previously circumscribed view. Members of oppressed groups . . . may have self- attributed and self-blamed for difficulties in their life, to the exclusion of recognizing other influential social circumstances" (p. 143). For example, women who have been battered often blame themselves and explain violent episodes as triggered by a failure to cook or serve their spouse's dinner the way he wants it, or clean the house before he got home, or put away the laundry the way he wants it done, or keep "my mouth shut." Social workers often use groups to aid women who have been battered to stop blaming themselves for the violence and develop a new understanding of intimate violence that holds the person responsible for his violent behavior.

Contemporary social workers develop support groups for women that foster bonding among women and a sharing of experiences that are common to women. In these support groups, the social worker and other women validate women's shared pain and shared strength. Such support groups have helped to give voice to women's experiences with alcohol abuse, overeating, homelessness, single parenting, battering, and sexual assault. For example, a social work group for women who were homeless helped women realize their common experiences—being abandoned by men, and being unable to obtain affordable housing in safe neighborhoods—and strengths as women who were determined to find sufficient work to provide for their children, get their children educated, and nurture their children through loving relationships. Perhaps, most significantly, the women encouraged one another to believe in themselves instead of continuing to believe that the solution to homelessness is finding a man to take care of them.

Community Organizing

Developing a sense of community has been important for women to build ties with other women, understand sexual inequality and oppression, and organize actions to achieve social justice for women. The cultural feminists have focused on building a women's community with a distinctive culture comprising feminist literature, films, music, and art.

In contrast to the cultural feminists, who focus on creating a specific women's culture, most feminist community organizing has focused on making existing communities safe for women and having all aspects of the community accessible to women. Thus, numerous political and social action activities have been organized to reduce gender inequality and achieve social justice in every community.

In the 1970s, community organizing efforts to *Take Back the Night* led to community recognition of the need for increased safety measures to ensure women's security and freedom from sexual assault. Similarly, women organized community advocacy groups to lobby for the right to reproductive choice that led to legalized abortion rights. Contemporary feminist community organizing has led to vigils, marches, and abortion escort services to protect a woman's reproductive choice. Another example of feminist community organizing involves the efforts made to organize support for the election of women to public offices. Although much remains to be done to achieve equitable representation by women, considerable progress has been made in the election of women since the early 1970s.

APPLYING THE THEORY: DIRECT PRACTICE INTERVENTIONS

Although social work and feminism have long shared core principles, only in recent years has direct social work practice begun to systematically apply feminist principles in areas such as substance abuse, eating disorders, sexual trauma, intimate violence, depression, and other family or mental health problems. Table 10.2 describes how the practitioner can use feminist theory to inform practice.

Using a feminist approach will lead social workers to understand and acknowledge their own values because feminists do not believe that treatment is value-free. In addition to acknowledging one's values, feminist practitioners make other appropriate disclosures to their clients. This contrasts to traditional psychotherapy, which views therapist self-disclosure as inappropriate:

Many feminist clinicians believe that their clients may learn from the clinician's experience as a woman living in a male-dominated society; hence, elements of self-disclosure, especially in situations where the personal is political, are used with greater frequency in feminist clinical practice. (Land, 1995, p. 9)

For example, a social worker's disclosure that she will not tolerate violence in her life provides a model for her clients.

Feminists believe that self-disclosure helps to reduce the power imbalance in the therapeutic relationship. Achieving an egalitarian relationship is a desired goal for a feminist practitioner. Such a relationship is consonant with the social work principle of client self- determination. Considerable attention has been given to equality in the treatment relationship by several social work feminist writers (Bricker-Jenkins & Hooyman, 1986; Bricker-Jenkins, Hooyman, & Gottlieb, 1991; Collins, 1986; Doninelli & McLeod, 1989; Land, 1995; Lundy, 1993; Nes & Iadicola, 1989; Van Den Bergh, 1995). Rebalancing the relationship between client and practitioner requires sustained effort to prevent slipping into the traditional asymmetry in the treatment relationship. Van Den Bergh (1995) stressed the importance of building a partnership between the social worker and her clients in which understanding of client needs and goals to pursue are co-created. She further suggested that "partnership" may be a more appropriate goal for the feminist treatment relationship than "equality" between practitioners and clients. *Partnership building* shows that the practitioner recognizes that most clients will not perceive themselves as equal to the professional.

> The feminist practitioner addresses societal role expectations when exploring seemingly individual or private concerns.

Although feminist theories are probably best known for their use in advocacy efforts to win rights and opportunities for women, social workers can also use feminist theory to guide their work with individuals, families, and groups. Feminist practitioners recognize the unity of personal and social change. As hooks (1989) asserted,

[Feminism] is that political movement which most radically addresses the person—the personal—citing the need for transformation of self, of relationships, so that we might be better able to act in a revolutionary manner, challenging and resisting domination, transforming the world outside the self. (p. 22)

Thus, feminist treatment is "concerned with the psychological effects of social forces. . . . [I]t emphasizes the social construction of women's psychology and the necessity of attending to the social world in order to un-

Table 10.2.   Guide for Feminist Practitioners

- Recognize the power inherent in the therapeutic relationship
- Understand one's values and their impact on the treatment of women
- Use self-disclosure to help clients learn from the practitioner's experience as a woman
- Address the invisibility of women's experience
- Build women's awareness about the impact of male dominance in their lives
- Recognize survival behaviors of women that are sometimes mistaken for pathological responses
- Understand the privileging of traditional masculine qualities, such as independence and autonomy, and the pathologizing of female traits, such as nurturing
- Assess psychological effects of oppressive social conditions
- Recognize women's anger and facilitate its expression in clear, direct statements
- Assess the political aspects of a woman's personal experiences due to structural factors that lead to the universal experience of oppression for women
- Address the differing aspects of social injustice among women resulting from color, class, sexual orientation, ability, age, and so forth
- Empower women both individually and collectively to change oneself and the surrounding conditions and structures that oppress women.

derstand and restore the integrity of the psychic world" (Espin, 1994, p. 269). In essence, analyzing how a client is affected by oppression distinguishes feminist treatment from other forms of treatment.

Because of the attention given to social factors that affect the functioning of women clients, feminists do not seek individual solutions for client situations that are essentially rooted in social, political, or economic conditions. Thus, in feminist treatment, all the threads of the social context are included. The core feminist principle that "the personal is political" significantly influences the work of the feminist practitioner. Espin (1994) argues that feminism "presupposes that changes in the lives of women necessitate changes in the basic structure of society" (p. 270). Moreover, a feminist social worker helps "clients distinguish the situations in their lives for which they are personally responsible from circumstances and intrapsychic attitudes that reflect broader social problems" (Espin, 1994).

Feminist practitioners look for public issues that may contribute to private problems when assessing and planing interventions for women clients. Feminists have argued that many of the psychological problems women experience result from the "gender-based power imbalance in our society and the related inferior status assigned to women" (Burden & Gottlieb, 1987, p. 47). Thus, "changing the conditions of oppression under which women live is both a promoter and a consequence of psychological healing" (Espin, 1994, p. 273).

Feminist practitioners understand survival behaviors triggered by what Root (1992) calls insidious trauma, which is caused by poverty, racism, sexism, and so forth. These survival behaviors must not be mistaken for pathological responses. As Espin (1994) stated:

> Anyone who has a sense of the connections between life stress and mental health understands that "mental health" is not an exclusively intrapsychic and individual/existential concept. To be subjected to the constant stresses of racism and sexism has a definite impact on a person's mental health. Attempts at restoring a person's well-being (or "mental health") that do not include a consideration of all stressors in a person's life are obviously doomed to failure. (p. 268)

Furthermore, feminist practitioners keep a vigilant eye on revisions to the American Psychiatric Association's *Diagnostic and Statistical Handbook of Mental Disorders (DSM)* to prevent categories that define women as pathological.

A central tenet of feminist treatment is to empower women. *Empowerment* seeks to increase a client's power so that she can take action to improve her situation and gain control over her life (Gutierrez, DeLois, & GlenMaye, 1995). Empowerment begins by focusing on the personal experience of a woman and encouraging her to tell her life story in her own language. Such intervention can be very empowering because "the power to name their own experience in their own language has been previously denied to women, oppressed by silence or being forced to use the language of the oppressor" (GlenMaye, 1998, p. 37). Feminist social workers assist female clients to recognize their own perceptions, needs, and feelings through the lens of their own experience. Empowering interventions help women clients to see ways they can be active in solving their own problems. Such interventions strengthen a woman's capacity to have her needs met and prevent being caught in a lifelong role of victim.

Feminist social work practice also engages clients in examining the impact of male dominance on their own lives as well as the lives of other women (Bricker-Jenkins & Hooyman, 1986; MacKinnon, 1982). Such awareness is often facilitated in women's groups that examine gender power imbalances in both the family and the public sphere of women's lives. While developing women's awareness of power issues and the role of power in her daily experience no longer often carries the 1970s' label of "consciousness-raising," that still remains the outcome of such social work intervention. As Bartky (1990) recognized, "Coming to have a feminist consciousness . . . [w]e begin to understand why we have such depreciated images of ourselves and why so many of us are lacking any genuine conviction of personal worth" (p. 21).

Feminist practitioners validate women's anger and encourage its expression in ways that are healthy for their clients. Anger is recognized as an appropriate response to oppressive conditions and is also seen as a strength that aids women to survive. Harriet Lerner's *Dance of Anger* (1985) provided an excellent analysis of the various unproductive ways that women are socialized to express anger, including the "bitch" category and the "nice lady syndrome." While being "bitchy" is readily recognized as being angry, most would not perceive that being nice in situations that elicit anger is another form of unproductive anger. As Lerner (1985) stated, by remaining nice, women "stay silent—or become tearful, self-critical, or 'hurt'" (p. 5). Feminist practitioners help "nice ladies" learn to express their anger in clear statements to prevent depression and produce change in both a woman's interpersonal relationships and in the larger social milieu. It is important to recognize that feminist treatment does not *make* women angry as is often claimed by those who oppose feminists. However, women who are in individual or group treatment with feminist practitioners often discover their deep-seated anger as they become aware of the effects of oppression and power inequities in their lives. Other women may shift from depression to anger as they realize that their deep sadness stems from their inability to get ahead in patriarchal structures.

Feminist social workers who work with families seek empowerment of women and the protection of children and *not* family preservation at any cost. Feminist family interventions address imbalances of power that traditionally have defined women as subservient caretakers. Assisting families to restructure so that responsibilities for nurturing are shared and ensuring that women receive as well as give in intimate relationships are vital interventions for the well-being of women and their families. Achieving mutuality in relationships is important for women because "many women either have been or are in relationships . . . in which they do the nurturing, supporting, and empowering, but are not nurtured, supported, or empowered in return" (Rubenstein & Lawler, 1990, p. 34). Of course, feminist practitioners combine their work with individual families with community organizing for publicly provided child care and elder care. Such societal support for families is needed to permit mothers as well as fathers to engage in roles outside the family while also ensuring the well-being of all family members.

The case of Susan illustrates the use of feminist principles in social work assessment and intervention:

Susan became pregnant the summer after graduation from high school. The baby's father stopped coming around after he learned that Susan was pregnant, leaving Susan to face the baby's birth alone. Although she had not planned on becoming pregnant, Susan decided to keep the baby and raise it alone. While she could accept herself as a mother, she struggled with being a single mother who lacked the needed resources to care for herself and her baby. She felt like a double failure for not being able to keep the baby's father faithful to her and secondly for being financially unable to take care of herself. Furthermore, she had just left high school, where she had been encouraged, like her male peers, to go out into the world and contribute to it. Now pregnancy was the only thing that defined her in the eyes of her community. Now she should settle down and be a mother; no more plans for further training or a career. Such a contrast to the baby's father, who got into an apprentice program to become an electrician and was earning enough money to get his own apartment before the baby was even born.

After the baby was born, Susan continued to live with her mother. However, Susan's mother seemed to be constantly angry with Susan and frequently criticized her care of the baby. She also insisted that Susan stop going out with her friends and remain home in the evenings. Susan had expected more support from her mother because like Susan, she had been a single mother with full responsibilities for raising her children. So after a few months, Susan moved out and went to live with her father and his wife.

While she found her father to be less judgmental than her mother, he was not financially able to support her and the baby. Furthermore, her anger with the baby's father prevented her from negotiating child support and visitation with him. She was determined to keep the baby away from him, because Susan didn't want the baby to be around his new girlfriend who lived with him. To support herself, Susan got a job as a clerk at Wal-Mart. Her stepmother agreed to care for the baby when Susan was at work, but soon tired of this confining responsibility. She asked Susan to make other arrangements for the baby's care, and her mother and sister stepped in for a while, but Susan could not find someone to provide child care regularly. After missing work twice because she did not have anyone to care for the baby, Susan was fired. She was crushed, because she never thought Wal-Mart would fire her for having to stay home to care for her baby. She wondered what they expected her to do? Surely they would not want her to take the baby to work!

Having been fired from the only job that she had ever had, Susan began to feel trapped. Who would hire her after she had been fired? Who would care for her baby, if she could find another job? How would she ever make enough money to be able to get her own apartment where she and the baby could live? Maybe her baby would be better off living with someone who could provide for her? Feeling more and more hopeless, Susan found her stepmother's bottle of sleeping pills and swallowed them.

Susan awoke to find herself being referred by the psychiatrist to an intensive day therapy program at the local community mental health center. While she was still pretty groggy, she wondered how a therapy program would help her with her problems. She wanted to ask the psychiatrist about this, but he had gone. A social worker came in to discuss the treatment plans with Susan and engaged Susan and her father in making a plan to prevent further suicide attempts. It helped Susan to hear the social worker talking about the energy Susan had been spending on caring for the baby and trying to provide for them financially. Susan faintly smiled when the social worker praised her for her dedication as a mother and said that she knew the baby was benefiting from her loving care even though the baby could not express her thanks in words. Before she left, the social worker said that it would be important to the clinicians in the therapy program to understand what it is like for Susan as a young mother because many women find it hard to live up to the expectations everyone has for mothers. Sometimes new mothers become angry about all their responsibilities for the baby's care, especially when the father is not available. She also mentioned that often new mothers think they shouldn't feel angry, because it was their own fault that they got pregnant . . . because a nice, smart girl doesn't have sex with her boyfriend, unless she's on birth control, and they're really, really in love. The social worker said that our society has unreasonable expectations for mothers and should provide public funding for child care so that women can have time to pursue other parts of life while still being parents. Susan was surprised that the social worker seemed to know so much about her, because she really hadn't said anything. The social worker concluded by telling Susan that the staff in the day therapy program would work with her to find ways to aid her to pursue the plans she had for her life—the ones she made before the unplanned pregnancy. Susan thought about how nobody in her family had shown any interest in her plans after she became pregnant. They just talked about her responsibilities for the baby. She guessed she would give the day therapy program a try tomorrow.

In the day therapy program, Susan found herself participating in several groups that were mostly comprised of women. During the first couple of days, she listened to the experiences that the other women described. She was surprised that they, too, said that they "had gotten involved with men that they believed cared about them and then were deeply hurt when these guys dumped them." Like Susan, several were left to care for a baby alone. The social worker said that she understood how they felt sad because they had believed the boy who once said, "I love you." The social worker said that she felt sad because no one explains to girls that it is more important to love herself first.

Being left by their baby's fathers to care for their babies alone, Susan really identified with the other women who were forced to take whatever help they could get from their families. Having to live with relatives produced strains on family relationships and left these women feeling like a burden on their loved ones. Susan listened as the social worker validated their hurt and disappointment at the lack of support from their children's fathers and the difficulty of having to move back in with family members. The social worker also commented on the frustration of being unable to find good jobs and reliable child care at affordable prices. Susan felt that a few of the women had worse experiences than hers, because their boyfriends and husbands sometimes abused them. Susan realized that these women stayed with abusive men because their families couldn't take them in and they didn't have enough money to get a place on their own. Susan was surprised when the social worker spoke up and said that no woman deserves to be hit. The social worker also asked the woman who had a black eye if they could talk after the group session about getting her and her children into a shelter for women that have been battered.

One evening Susan couldn't stop thinking about the social worker's comment that afternoon that most men, like her baby's father, do not have to move back in with a parent when they father babies, nor do they lose their jobs because they don't stay home to care for their babies. The next day, she arrived at the therapy group ready to tell her story. She started by saying how much the social worker's comments got her thinking about how different her life had been from the baby's father since the baby had been born. She talked about feeling really angry that she hadn't been able to go on after high school to get the training for computer design work in the automobile plant where her dad worked. She said that it just wasn't fair that women are expected to give up everything to take care of their children or if they did try to do something, they still had to be totally responsible for their children's care. Lots of heads nodded as they listened to Susan. She told the group that she never dreamed that she'd end up like her mother—raising her child alone. She guessed that maybe her mother's anger was the result of having been left to raise three young children, and now that they were all out of school, she had wanted to start a life of her own. Then Susan got pregnant and needed to live with her mom, which probably was a setback for both of them. Susan wondered whether her mother might even feel guilty about Susan's getting pregnant—after all she had done as a mother, she no doubt wanted to protect her only daughter from the life of pain that she had endured. The social worker said that she thought that both Susan and her mother were brave women who showed a lot of strength in being able to care for their children despite receiving so little support. She also said that it sounded important to help Susan find ways to get the training for the work that she had planned to do after high school.

In the next group session, the social worker asked each member to talk about goals that she or he wanted to achieve. When it was Susan's turn, the social worker asked her if she would like to work toward some of the plans she had for her life when she was finishing high school. Although Susan felt scared about how she would manage everything, she said that it would be wonderful to get the training for computer design work. Together with the social worker, she began to get information on the training program and the application process. The social worker also talked with her about getting child support from the baby's father so she could afford child care and have health insurance for the baby. With the social worker, she rehearsed how she would ask for child support and was pleased with how well she did telling him directly that she needed him to support his child. In the past, she knew she had either stayed silent when she felt angry with him or screamed at him. This time, she felt really good because she told him exactly what she needed.

Susan began to receive child support for the baby the next month and was scheduled to start the computer design training program in the fall. With the child support, she was able to secure child care for her toddler. Susan felt a growing confidence that she would be able to manage as a mother and still fulfill her high school career plan. During a follow-up phone call with her social worker from the day therapy program, Susan said that she was managing everything pretty well, but kept thinking that it shouldn't be so hard for women. The social worker suggested that she might like to join in an effort to get public funding for child care so that no woman has to choose between caring for her children and going to school or working outside the home. Susan thought that would be a big help for mothers like herself, but she said that she had never talked to any politician and doubted that any would listen to someone like her. Her social worker reminded her that she had felt the same way about the baby's father, and had been quite effective in telling him what she needed and getting him to respond. So, Susan decided to plan very carefully what she wanted to say to her state representative and with some coaching from her social worker, she rehearsed her requests for publicly funded child care for all children and tax support to help young mothers get housing so they do not have to depend on family members to take care of them—or worse, remain with abusive men rather than become homeless. Susan and her social worker met together with Susan's representative, and he listened attentively to her story and her ideas for child care and housing. When Susan finished, he asked her to testify before the legislative committee that was considering state child care funding for children of working parents. Testify—Susan was stunned and looked at the social worker with panic in her eyes. Her social worker quickly translated the representative's request by telling Susan that he was asking her to tell her story, and he said that was exactly what he meant when he said that he wanted her to testify. Susan realized that she was getting better about speaking up—first to the baby's father, then to her state representative, and now to a whole legislative committee! Her high school plans never included anything like this, but she was beginning to realize that girls never learned anything about some of the more important things in life while they were in school. (I am grateful to Sherri Moulden for providing the background information for this case study as well as her insight concerning the effects of sexism on individual women like Susan.)

CONCLUSION

L and (1995) believes that feminist practice has moved into the core of social work practice because of its attention to human rights. To support her belief that feminist practice is now a mainstream practice approach, she cites topics such as sexual exploitation of therapy clients, domestic violence, incest, rape, and sexual harassment, which are now included in the essential knowledge base for social work practice. She then concludes that it is not feminist scholarship that has adapted to fit into the mainstream, but rather

feminists have acted as a part of the conscience of ethical social work practice, helping move mainstream thought away from destructive paradigms
toward new ones that are influenced by feminist thought. (p. 14)

REFERENCES

American Psychiatric Association (1994). *Diagnostic and Statistical Handbook of Mental Disorders* (4th ed). Washington, DC: Author.
Anzaldua, G. (Ed.). (1990). Making face, making soul—Haciendo caras: Creative
and critical perspectives by feminists of color. San Francisco: Aunt Lute Foundation.
Bartky, S. L. (1990). *Femininity and Domination: Studies in the Phenomenology of Oppression*. New York: Routledge.
Belenky, M. F., Clinchy, B. M., Goldberger, N. R., & Tarule, J. M. (1986). *Many Ways
of Knowing: The Development of Self, Voice, and Mind*. New York: Basic Books.
Bricker-Jenkins, M., & Hooyman, N. R. (1986). A feminist world view: Ideological
themes from the feminist movement. In M. Bricker-Jenkins & N. R. Hooyman
(Eds.), *Not for Women Only: Social Work Practice for a Feminist Future* (pp. 7–22).
Silver Spring, Maryland: National Association of Social Workers.
Bricker-Jenkins, M., Hooyman, N. R., & Gottlieb, N. (Eds.) (1991). *Feminist Social
Work Practice in Clinical Settings*. Newbury Park, CA: Sage.
Brown, L. M., & Gilligan, C. (1992). *Meeting at the Crossroads: Women's Psychology
and Girls' Development*. New York: Ballantine.
Bunch, C. (1987). *Passionate Politics: Feminist Theory in Action*. New York: St. Mar-
tin's.
Bunch, C. (1993). Women's subordination through the lens of sex / gender and sex-
uality: Radical feminism. In A. Jaggar & P. Rothenberg (Eds.), *Feminist Frame-
works: Alternative Accounts of the Relations between Women and Men* (3rd ed., pp.
174–178). New York: McGraw-Hill.
Burden, D., & Gottlieb, N. (1987). Women's socialization and feminist groups. In
Claire Brody (Ed.), *Women's Therapy Groups: Paradigms of Feminist Treatment*
(pp. 24–39). New York: Springer.
Butler, S., & Wintram, C. (1991). *Feminist Group Work*. Newbury Park, CA:
Sage.
Calhoun, C. (1994). Separating lesbian theory from feminist theory. *Ethics, 104,* 558–
581.
Collins, B. (1986). Defining feminist social work. *Social Work, 31,* 214–219.
Collins, P. H. (1990). *Black Feminist Thought: Knowledge, Consciousness and the Poli-
tics of Empowerment*. Boston: Unwin Hyman.
Comas-Diaz, L. (1987). Feminist therapy with Hispanic / Latina women: Myth or
reality? *Women and Therapy, 6*(4), 39–61.
Comas-Diaz, L. (1994). An integrative approach. In L. Comas-Diaz & B. Greene
(Eds.), *Women of Color: Integrating Ethnic and Gender Identities in Psychotherapy*
(pp. 287–318). New York: Guilford.
Doninelli, L., & McLeod, E. (1989). *Feminist Social Work*. London: Macmillan.

Dworkin, A. (1988). *Letters from a War Zone*. New York: Dutton.

Dworkin, A. (1989). *Pornography: Men Possessing Women*. New York: Dutton.

Echols, A. (1989). *Daring to Be Bad: Radical Feminism in America 1967–1975*. Minneapolis: University of Minnesota Press.

Erikson, E. (1950). *Childhood and Society*. New York: Norton.

Espin, O. M. (1994). Feminist approaches. In L. Comas-Diaz & B. Greene (Eds.), *Women of Color: Integrating Ethnic and Gender Identities in Psychotherapy* (pp. 265–286). New York: Guilford.

Faludi, S. (1991). *Backlash: The Undeclared War against American Women*. New York: Crown Publishers.

Firestone, S. (1970). *The Dialectic of Sex*. New York: Bantam.

Frye, M. (1983). *The Politics of Reality*. Trumansburg, NY: Crossing.

Gilligan, C. (1982). *In a Different Voice: Psychological Theory and Women's Development*. Cambridge, MA: Harvard University Press.

Gilligan, C. (1995). Hearing the difference: Theorizing connection. *Hypatia, 10*(2), 120–127.

Gilligan, C., Rogers, A. G., & Tolman, D. L. (Eds.) (1991). *Women, Girls and Psychotherapy: Reframing Resistance*. New York: Harrington Park.

GlenMaye, L. (1998). Empowerment of women. In L. M. Gutierrez, R. J. Parsons, & E. O. Cox (Eds.), *Empowerment in Social Work Practice* (pp. 29–51). Pacific Grove, CA: Brooks/Cole.

Gutierrez, L. M., DeLois, K. A., & GlenMaye, L. (1995). Understanding empowerment practice: Building on practitioner-based knowledge. *Families in Society, 76*, 534–542.

Hartman, H. (1981). The unhappy marriage of Marxism and feminism: Towards a more progressive union. In L. Sargent (Ed.), *Women and Revolution* (pp. 1–42). Boston: South End.

hooks, b. (1984). *Feminist Theory: From Margin to Center*. Boston: South End.

hooks, b. (1989). *Talking Back: Thinking Feminist, Thinking Black*. Boston: South End.

Jordan, J. V., Kaplan, A. G., Miller, J. B., Stiver, I. P., & Surrey, J. L. (1991). *Women's Growth in Connection*. New York: Guilford.

Kitzinger, C. & Perkins, R. (1993). *Changing Our Minds: Lesbian Feminism and Psychology*. New York: New York University Press.

Kohlberg, L. (1981). *The Philosophy of Moral Development*. San Francisco: Harper & Row.

Land, H. (1995). Feminist clinical social work in the 21st century. In N. Van Den Bergh (Ed.), *Feminist Practice in the 21st Century* (pp. 3–19). Washington, DC: NASW Press.

Lerner, H. G. (1985). *The Dance of Anger*. New York: Harper & Row.

Locke, J. (1977). Second treatise on civil government. In Samuel Stumpf (Ed.), *Philosophy: History and Problems* (2nd ed., pp. 202–207). New York: McGraw-Hill.

Lorde, A. (1984). *Sister Outsider: Essays and Speeches*. Trumansburg, NY: Crossing.

Lundy, M. (1993). Explicitness: The unspoken mandate of feminist social work. *Affilia, 8*(2), 184–199.

MacKinnon, C. A. (1982). Feminism, Marxism, method, and the state: An agenda for theory. *Signs, 7*(3), 515–544.

McGoldrick, M., Anderson, C. M., & Walsh, F. (1989). *Women in Families: A Framework for Family Therapy*. New York: Norton.

Miller, J. B. (1976). *Toward a New Psychology of Women*. Boston: Beacon.

Nes, J. A., & Iadicola, P. (1989). Toward a definition of feminist social work: A comparison of liberal, radical, and socialist models. *Social Work, 34*, 12–21.

Phelan, S. (1994). *Getting Specific: Postmodern Lesbian Politics*. Minneapolis: University of Minnesota Press.

Root, M. P. P. (1992). The impact of trauma on personality: The second reconstruction. In L. S. Brown & M. Ballou (Eds.), *Personality and Psychopathology: Feminist Reappraisals* (pp. 229–265). New York: Guilford.

Rubenstein, H., & Lawler, S. K. (1990). Toward the psychosocial empowerment of women. *Affilia, 5*(3), 27–38.

Sands, R. G., & Nuccio, K. (1992). Postmodern feminist theory and social work. *Social Work, 37*, 489–494.

Saulnier, C. F. (1996). *Feminist Theories and Social Work: Approaches and Applications*. Binghamton, NY: Haworth.

Simon, B. (1988). Social work responds to the women's movement. *Affilia, 3*(4), 60–68.

Van Den Bergh, N. (1995). Feminist social work practice: Where have we been . . . Where are we going? In N. Van Den Bergh (Ed.), *Feminist Practice in the 21st Century* (pp. xi–xxxix). Washington, DC: NASW Press.

Vourlekis, B. S. (1991). Cognitive theory for social work practice. In R. R. Greene & P. H. Ephross (Eds.), *Human Behavior Theory and Social Work Practice* (pp. 123–150). Hawthorne, NY: Aldine de Gruyter.

Walters, M., Carter, B., Papp, P., & Silverstein, O. (1988). *The Invisible Web: Gender Patterns in Family Relationships*. New York: Guilford.

Wetzel, J. W. (1976). Interaction of feminism and social work in America. *Social Casework, 57*, 227–236.

Wetzel, J. W. (1986). A feminist world view conceptual framework. *Social Casework, 67*, 166–173.

Young, I. (1981). The unhappy marriage of Marxism and feminism: Towards a more progressive union. In L. Sargent (Ed.), *Women and Revolution: A Discussion of the Unhappy Marriage of Marxism and Feminism* (pp. 1–42). Boston, MA: South End.

GLOSSARY

Consciousness-Raising. Becoming aware of social and political factors that influence a woman's daily experience and recognizing the patriarchal messages and gender-based roles that have been internalized and resulted in self-doubt, negative views of oneself, and self-blame for the difficulties in one's life.

Cultural Feminism. Seeks to build a sense of community among women in which gender differences are recognized and traits attributed to women, such as nurturing and caregiving, are recognized as superior to traditionally masculine traits, such as competitiveness and independence.

Deconstruction. Process of analyzing the cultural and ideological construction of meanings, theories, and social orders.

Dualistic Thinking. Dichotomizing factors into two categories that are viewed as opposing each other.

Empowerment. Assisting a woman to gain the necessary skills, knowledge or influence to have her needs met, enhance her control over her life, and seek change in the social, interpersonal, and political environments that impact her wellbeing.

Global Perspective. Holistic thinking that focuses on the connectedness among all things, including seemingly disparate factors.

Heterosexism. Belief system that heterosexuality is superior.

Homophobia. An irrational fear and hatred of homosexual people.

Identification with the Oppressor. A process of conditioning to accept a subordinate position, discard one's goals and desires, and adopt and espouse the desires and views of the oppressor.

Lesbian. Women whose sexual and affectional orientation is for women.

Lesbian Feminism. Challenges the organization of society around both heterosexual and male dominance.

Liberal Feminism. Focuses on the denial of equal access to society's resources for girls and women.

Many Ways of Knowing. Knowledge can be constructed through such processes as intuition, inductive reasoning, and personal experience, as well as the traditional rational, deductive, linear approach.

Objectification of Women. Focusing on the physical beauty and sexual attractiveness of women and thereby viewing them as objects.

Patriarchy. A society or organization that is organized around the supremacy of men and the dependency of women and children.

The Personal Is Political. The belief that individual problems are inextricably linked to sexist power imbalances.

Postmodern Feminism. Recognizes the multiple voices of women; deconstructs traditional theories and opposes generalized propositions and universal constructs concerning women's reality; focuses on the socially constructed meanings and definitions of reality that are held by a specific woman.

Psychotherapeutic Decolonization. A treatment approach that addresses individual healing and the transformation of oppressive conditions.

Radical Feminism. Focuses on the subjugation of girls and women due to both family and societal structures that are designed to meet male needs.

Self-in-Relation Theory. A perspective that addresses the development of con-

nectedness in human relationships across the life cycle and the situational conditions that foster growth in relatedness and connection.

Sexism.   Discrimination against women or behavior, conditions, or attitudes that
foster stereotypes about women and their social roles.

Socialist Feminism.   Focuses on the intersection of class and gender through the
economics of capitalism and the patriarchal social structures that maintain
women's subordinate position.

Woman-Identified Woman.   Feminists who define themselves independently
from men, look to other women for help in understanding what it means to be a
woman, and seek an authentic essence apart from the stereotypes and expectations of patriarchal society.

Womanism.   Feminism that focuses on the interlocking oppressions of gender
and race that are inextricable from each other theoretically and experientially
and seeks social change to remedy social problems.

CRITIQUE

Feminist Theory and Social Work
Lost in Space?

CAROL T. TULLY

The year 1998 marked the celebration of the sesquicentennial of the Seneca Falls, New York, convention—the first meeting to champion the rights of women in the United States and the sowing of the first seeds of feminism in this country. Following the Seneca Falls adoption of the Declaration of Sentiments, based on the U.S. Constitution, women began to reevaluate their roles (Gilligan, 1982). Emerging in the late nineteenth century from the growing concern about women's rights debated at Seneca Falls came such organizations as the Women's Christian Temperance Union (WTCU), the Young Women's Christian Association (YWCA), the National Consumer's League, and other groups dedicated to women's needs. Such organizations were viewed as necessary because of the growing realization that men dominated society (D'Emilio & Freedman, 1988).

The suffragette movement of the early 1900s culminated in the 1920 passage of the nineteenth Amendment to the U.S. Constitution, which allowed women the right to vote. This first wave of the women's movement—as it has come to be known—provided some political and social gains for women, but men still dominated. World War II provided women an opportunity to leave their homes and go to work while the country's men went to war. But once victory was proclaimed, women and men returned to their traditional roles: the men moved back into the corporations, the women back to their homes. And during the 1950s, that seemed acceptable.

But then came the 1960s. African-Americans were demanding equal rights, lesbians and gays were coming out of the closet, students were taking over college administrative buildings, and women were entering the second wave of the women's movement: feminism. The slogan that the "personal is the political" became the rallying cry for women who again began to explore roles other than those traditionally associated with being a woman. Such included redefining what it meant to be a woman in terms of marriage, motherhood, employment, health care, sexual orientation, and other aspects of current prevailing views about women's roles. It was from this fertile era that concepts related to feminist social work practice emerged.

The 1960s provided an ideal backdrop for the early development of feminist social work practice, but the implementation of feminist social work practice waited until the mid-1970s (Acker, 1987; Bricker-Jenkins & Lockett, 1995; Van Den Bergh & Cooper, 1986). What has happened to those principles of feminist social work practice in the intervening twenty years? This critique explores the principles of feminist social work practice and explains how and where those principles exist in social work of the late 1990s. Have the constructs blossomed into a well-developed feminist theory, have they been lost in space, or have they been incorporated into ther emerging social work practice paradigms like the empowerment perspective?

FEMINISM, FEMINIST THEORY, AND SOCIAL WORK PRACTICE

Feminism as a concept is one that is multidimensional. Traditionally it as been defined as having three major forms: radical feminism, socialist feminism, and liberal feminism. *Radical feminism* is a belief in an omnipresent patriarchy that undergirds all forms of gender oppression, supports racism and classism, and must be eradicated before women will have equal social and political freedom. Thus, fundamental changes in the social structure that will ensure the elimination of patriarchy and male domination must be implemented. *Socialist feminism* is a belief in capitalism as the cause for gender, race, and class discrimination and oppression. Thus, to ensure equality, alliances between women and men to eliminate capitalism and reconcile feminism with Marxism need to occur. *Liberal feminism* (or bourgeois feminism) is a belief that equality between the sexes and races can be obtained with no changes to the existing capitalist and political systems. Equality can be accomplished within the existing systems with modifications to beliefs and mores as opposed to structural changes (Acker, 1987; Einstein, 1984; Sands & Nuccio, 1992).

Equipped with newly conceptualized constructs of feminism, scholars sought ways to incorporate these into a theoretical orientation. A *theory* is a set of interrelated statements and constructs about how parts of the empirically testable world operate or function. As such, these statements should lead to hypotheses capable of being measured. Feminist theory then provides a conceptual framework for exploring the subordination of women to men, its antecedent roots and perpetuation, and how the world would function were women and men equal. The nature of the constructs related to feminism are connected to the development of views that will provide data on how one perceives gender roles and has at its core a dual focus. First, feminist theory seeks to determine and understand gender inequity and, second, it seeks to create change (Acker, 1987).

There has been a general acceptance that the overall views of feminism and feminist theory fit well with the values, goals, and skills of professional social work. Wetzel (1986) noted that concern about women's rights and feminism and social work all emerged historically around the same time, both share similar values, and both seek to and are essential in the creation of social change. She further stated that both feminism and social work are interested in the well- being and development of humans, are actively involved in society, care about an individual's dignity and self-worth, seek to remove obstacles that prevent self-realization, seek to prevent or eliminate oppression and discrimination, and recognize the reality of common human needs.

To further support the natural linkages between feminist thought and social work practice is the reality that the majority of social work practitioners and clients are women (Wetzel, 1986). Additionally, a feminist worldview examines the unity of all events, knowledge, and living things; supports the uniqueness of the individual; and champions personal power and responsibility (Wetzel, 1986). Feminist social work practice has specific ideological themes that include a dedication to the end of patriarchy, the reconceptualization of empowerment, the elimination of false dichotomies and categories, a dedication to the concept of the personal is the political, the fundamental belief of renaming, validation of the nonrational, valuing the process as a product, and a respect for difference (Bricker-Jenkins & Lockett, 1995; Sands & Nuccio, 1992; Van Den Bergh & Cooper 1986; Wetzel, 1986).

The basic assumptions of feminist thought and their relationship to social work practice were delineated by Bricker-Jenkins (1989). She explored the basic philosophy, values, and goals of feminist practice and concluded that feminist social work practice assumes a prowoman posture, supports self-actualization through the political, and realizes self-actualization is not accomplished individually but rather in concert with others. In the area of human behavior and the social environment, there is an appreciation of diversity; a reliance on the interdependence of all things; a dedication to health and strength; and the belief that reality is socially constructed, multifaceted, and ever-changing. In relation to practice methods and relationships, the personal is not separate from the political, nonviolent relationships and structures are valued, and there is an emphasis on an individual's transformation.

It seems that feminist thought, sometimes referred to as feminist theory or feminist standpoint theory, has a natural fit with professional social work practice. But if the links are so strong, has the feminist framework been used? And how have the constructs and assumptions of feminism emerged and evolved in social work practice during the latter part of the 1970s?

FEMINISM AND SOCIAL WORK PRACTICE: LOST IN SPACE?

When trying to assess the implementation of any conceptual framework in social work there are three traditional means of gathering data: searching for existing books on the topic, seeking out scholarly articles and papers that use the constructs, and talking to social work practitioners. All three methods were used in gathering information for this critique.

Books written about the feminist perspective and feminism flourished during the 1970s and 1980s. The demand for such content was so intense that bookstore chains expanded their offerings to include a new section on their shelves called "Women's Studies." Even the Library of Congress subject headings were revised to accurately reflect the new content area (Westbrook, 1986). Authors explored women's social and political lives through writing in a variety of fields including the arts, social sciences, humanities and fine arts, history, and medicine. Social workers contributed to the increasing literature through such books as Weick and Vandiver's (1982) *Women, Power, and Change,* Van Den Bergh and Cooper's (1986) *Feminist Visions for Social Work,* and Bricker-Jenkins & Hooyman's (1986) *Not for Women Only: Social Work Practice for a Feminist Future.* Each of these is an edited volume, so there are many voices providing input into social work and the feminist perspective. Whereas other disciplines have continued to produce the majority of content related to feminism and women's studies (McFeely, 1990; Westbrook, 1986), some few social workers are still actively involved with the development of feminist thought and social work practice (Taylor & Daly, 1995; Van Den Bergh, 1995). Their edited volumes borrow from and add to the work being created in other disciplines, creating a pragmatic application of feminist thought to professional social work. So, although social workers have not written a great number of books on the topic, and none is written by a sole author that articulates a single theoretical approach to the application of feminist thought to social work practice, feminism and its ideals are part of the social work library.

Because writing books is a time-consuming activity, often taking more than two years to get a book from the conceptual stage to press, journal articles provide another form of scholarly productivity and are another indicator of the current status of a particular theory. *An Author's Guide to Social Work Journals* (National Association of Social Workers, 1997) provides the reader with a listing of more than 170 ($n = 177$) journals related to social work. Of these, only a few are related only to women ($n = 7$, 3.95%), and none relies solely on the use of feminist thought as a determinant for publication. A ten-year review (late 1980s–late 1990s) of what have been described as the "premier" journals of the profession (e.g., *Social Work, Social Service Review, Child Welfare, Journal of Social Work Education, Clinical Social Work Journal*) revealed that feminism and the use of feminist theory are found in only a few articles. That is not to say that feminism and feminist theory are not being used in the development of knowledge—far from it. Since the late 1980s, the current author has collected more than two hundred articles on the topic of feminism, feminist methodology, feminist theory, feminist philosophy, symbolic feminism, postmodern feminist thought, and others. Yet those who are not in the profession of social work are writing the vast majority of these articles. Furthermore, those in social work who are publishing articles related to feminism and women's studies continue to publish in smaller, specialty journals that identify as being accepting of such submissions (e.g., *Affilia, Feminist Studies*, and *Signs*).

Given that writing journal articles and getting them published appears to also be time-consuming (it can take more than one year to get an article written, accepted, and published), it seemed that the best test of the use of a particular theory or conceptual framework would be how social work practitioners actually used the constructs. To gather information from this population, the current author interviewed social work educators and social work practitioners from the New Orleans, Louisiana, area. Granted, New Orleans may present a biased view, but it does have a large percentage of both licensed social workers and social work educators available for inquiry. Data from these two groups revealed that, like books and journal articles on the use of feminist theory in social work practice, the constructs of the view that were used were not identified as feminist theory per se, but rather as pieces of the theory had been incorporated into other frameworks.

Although a feminist perspective was a topic of discussion by some social work educators in some baccalaureate- and master's-level classes, it was not presented in a unified manner as an important professional theoretical perspective and was presented unevenly throughout the curricula. For example, those educators with a feminist worldview presented the content, whereas those not possessing such a viewpoint either ignored the content altogether or glossed over it in favor of other, more traditional theoretical perspectives.

Those practicing social work agreed that few practiced from what they would identify as a totally feminist perspective, preferring instead to include pieces of feminism's ideology and assumptions into a more eclectic

approach to social work practice. The pieces of feminist ideology that social workers find most comfortable to use with other more traditional
theoretical approaches include the use of empowerment concepts, narratives, renaming, and spirituality. Whereas social work practitioners seem
less likely to include ideas of ending the patriarchal system, they do seem
willing to discuss the construct of the personal is the political. None advocated a radical or socialist feminist approach, preferring the more middle-
of-the-road liberal feminism.

Just as there are social work authors writing about feminism and social
work practice and educators teaching feminism and feminist theory, there
are social work practitioners who practice from a feminist perspective
(Bricker-Jenkins & Lockett, 1995; Sands & Nuccio, 1992; Van Den Bergh,
1995). But is feminist thought currently a major paradigm of thought and
practice within the profession of social work? The answer is no. Social
work scholars who wish to write in this field seem limited to less traditional presses (although National Association of Social Workers has done
an adequate job of ensuring this content in its book offerings) and journals
and seem to find better avenues for publication beyond the bounds of the
professional social work literature. It is possible that the development of
theory needs to come first from the philosophy of science and then go on
to implementation by professions. However, in the more than twenty years
of the existence of a frame of reference related to feminist thought, it would
seem social work is slow to embrace a conceptual framework that has such
congruence with the values, skills, and knowledge of the profession.

The one glimmer of feminist light in social work practice is that many
of its major constructs and tenets are gradually being picked up and used
by other emerging paradigms and conceptual frameworks. The best current example is that of the empowerment perspective. Major tenets and
constructs of the empowerment viewpoint seem to have their basis in feminist thought. Whether this is good or bad cannot be determined. But what
is evident is that social work practice has missed an excellent opportunity
to develop and implement a perspective that is uniquely suited to the profession. Unless we embrace this perspective, feminist theory and social
work practice will be lost in space.

REFERENCES

Acker, S. (1987). Feminist theory and the study of gender and education. *International Review of Education, 33*(4), 419–435.
Bricker-Jenkins, M. (1989). Foundations of feminist social work practice: The
changes and the changed are one. Dissertation Abstracts International, 5104A
(University Microfilms No. 9015943).

Bricker-Jenkins, M., & Hooyman, N. R. (Eds.) (1986). *Not for Women Only: Social Work Practice for a Feminist Future*. Washington, DC: NASW Press.

Bricker-Jenkins, M., & Lockett, P. W. (1995). Women: Direct practice. In R. L. Edwards (Editor-in-chief), *Encyclopedia of Social Work* (Vol. 3, 19th ed., pp. 2529–2539). Washington, DC: NASW Press.

D'Emilio, J., & Freedman, E. B. (1988). *Intimate Matters: A History of Sexuality in America*. New York: Harper & Row.

Einstein, H. (1984). *Contemporary Feminist Thought*. London: Unwin.

Gilligan, C. (1982). *In a Different Voice: Psychological Theory and Women's Development*. Cambridge, MA: Harvard University Press.

McFeely, M. D. (1990). *Women's Studies: A Bibliography of Reference Sources*. Athens: University of Georgia Libraries.

National Association of Social Workers (1997). *An Author's Guide to Social Work Journals* (4th ed.). Washington, DC: NASW Press.

Sands, R. G., & Nuccio, K. (1992). Postmodern feminist theory and social work. *Social Work, 37*(6), 489–494.

Taylor, P., & Daly, C. (1995). *Gender Dilemmas in Social Work: Issues Affecting Women in the Profession*. Washington, DC: NASW Press.

Van Den Bergh, N. J. (Ed.) (1995). *Feminist Practice in the 21st Century*. Washington, DC: NASW Press.

Van Den Bergh, N. J., & Cooper, L. B. (Eds.) (1986). *Feminist Visions for Social Work*. Washington, DC: NASW Press.

Weick, A., & Vandiver, S. T. (Eds.) (1982). *Women, Power, and Change*. Washington, DC: NASW Press.

Westbrook, L. (1986). *Women and Women's History* (University of Georgia Libraries Series No. 23). Athens: University of Georgia Libraries.

Wetzel, J. W. (1986). A feminist world view conceptual framework. *Social Casework, 67*, 166–176.

11

Genetics, Environment, and Development

JOYCE G. RILEY

Human beings carry within them chemically encoded information that makes each a member of the human species and each a unique individual. This information is shuffled, reshuffled, and changed by natural and unnatural events and through heredity influences the next generation of people. *Genetics* is the study of heredity (Brennan, 1985). It "is the process of asking and answering questions about the characteristics and continuity of life" (Knowles, 1985, p. 4).

Heredity affects each of us on many levels, as individuals, as members of families, and as members of the larger community (Knowles, 1985). Genetic disorders can interfere with the ability to fulfill individual roles in society. As taxpayers, people may support programs that conduct research on or provide services for genetic disabilities. As social work professionals, people may help individuals or families struggling to cope with a genetically influenced problem.

Newman and Newman ([1979] 1987) describe two types of heredity. The first encompasses those attributes people all share as members of the human species. These include things as abstract as "the readiness to learn and the inclination to participate in social interaction" as well as the ability to walk upright (p. 109). The second type of heredity encompasses those characteristics or traits such as hair color or blood type that are passed through a specific gene pool from one generation to another. These are the things that distinguish us as individuals and link us to our parents and grandparents.

Mendel (1822–1884), an Austrian monk, was able to deduce many principles of inheritance through his experiments with pea plants. Because of his major contributions to this field, he is often called the "father of genetics" (Gardner and Snustad, 1984). The title of "father of human genetics" is usually given to Archibald Garrod, a British physician (Knowles, 1985).

389

He is recognized for demonstrating genetic control of biochemical reactions in the body that he called "inborn errors of metabolism."

Since the time of these early investigators, the body of knowledge about human genetics has expanded tremendously. Increasingly, information appears in magazines, in newspapers, and on television linking conditions such as heart disease, cancer, addictive disorders, and mental health problems to genetic factors. The catalog of genetic diseases includes more than three hundred observed defects of the hemoglobin (oxygen-carrying pigment of the red blood cell) molecule alone (Baskin, 1984). The prospect of genetic engineering, the ability to replace or repair defective genes, leaves some excitedly anticipating future interventions. For others, genetic engineering causes concern about the moral and ethical implications of this technology.

The Human Genome Project is a fifteen-year undertaking that was begun in 1990 with an anticipated completion date of 2005. A major aspect of this project is to identify all the estimated 80,000 genes in human DNA. According to the Genome Database, the public repository for human genome mapping information, over 7000 genes had been mapped to specific chromosomes as of August 1998. Mapping requires the identification of unique genome markers and their localization to specific chromosomal sites (Rowen, Mahairas, & Hood, 1997). The current development of technology is expected to move the process forward quickly.[1]

Social workers and other helping professionals have, and will continue to have, a major role in developing ways of translating this knowledge and technology into methods of helping people understand and cope with their specific problems (Hamilton & Noble, 1983). Rauch (1988a,b) provides insight into why it is important for social workers to be knowledgeable about genetic disorders and the influence of genes on development and behavior:

• In the framework of a biopsychosocial model, social workers use family and individual histories to evaluate client situations.

• Social workers provide services to persons and families affected by disabilities and chronic conditions that often have contributing genetic factors or origins.

• Social workers must be able to provide accurate information and make referrals to appropriate genetic services for their clients with genetic concerns.

BASIC TERMS AND ASSUMPTIONS

Social work in the ecological perspective focuses on transactions between human beings and their environments. The ecological perspective emphasizes the biological concept of adaptation or the active efforts of the species to achieve goodness-of-fit with its environment over evolutionary time. How individuals "survive, develop, and achieve reproductive success" within their environments is also encompassed in goodness-of-fit (Germain, 1979). For social workers to understand these complex processes, information on the basic terms and assumptions of genetics and the relationship between heredity and environment is necessary (Table 11.1).

Deoxyribonucleic acid (DNA) molecules are the smallest units of genetic information (Newman and Newman, [1979] 1987). DNA forms long twisted double chains (double helixes) of nucleotides that make up *chromosomes.* Genes are elements of genetic information (ibid.) and each gene is located in a definite position on a particular chromosome (*Dorland's Medical Dictionary,* 1989). Genes are identified as sequences of nucleotides and thousands of genes make up each chromosome. Humans have a total of 46 chromosomes or 23 pairs. Of the 23 pairs of chromosomes, half of each pair come from the mother, through the ovum or egg, and half come from the father, through the sperm (Wymelenberg, 1990). The egg and sperm cells are called *gametes.*

All 23 pairs of chromosomes have been visually identified and have been numbered from 1 to 23. Twenty-two of the pairs are made up of chromosomes of equal size and similar arrangement of genes. These matched

Table 11.1. Basic Assumptions: Genetics, Environment, and Development

- Human beings carry within them chemically encoded information that makes each a member of the human species and each a unique individual.
- People differ because each person has undergone a complex series of transactions between a unique set of genes and a unique sequence of environments.
- Many genetic conditions are a result of a multiplicity of factors both genetic and environmental.
- Some conditions have a genetic predisposition and are more susceptible to environmental influences.
- Environmental factors can either promote or prevent the expression of some diseases.
- Genetic information is encompassed in the biopsychosocial model social workers use to evaluate client situations.
- Genetic disorders can interfere with an individual's ability to fulfill his or her roles in society.
- Some genetic disorders are found more frequently in certain ethnic groups or among persons who have origins from specific geographic regions.
- Genetic disorders may stress a family's abilities to cope.
- Social workers have a major role in translating genetic knowledge and technology into methods of helping people that are congruent with the client's cultural stance and value base.
- Interventions in genetic counseling are aimed at enhancing the adaptive capacities and strengthening coping mechanisms of client families.

pairs of chromosomes are called *autosomes* (Rauch, 1988b). The 23rd pair is identified as the *sex chromosomes* (Figure 11.1). In this pair, females have two X chromosomes and males have a X and a Y (Newman & Newman, 1987). The mother can produce ova or gametes that contain only X chromosomes, so it is the father who determines the sex of the baby. The father contributes either an X gamete for a female (XX) or a Y gamete for a male (XY). The presence of a Y chromosome is necessary for maleness; its presence induces development of the testis (Gardner & Snustad, 1984).

It is possible for chromosomes to develop abnormalities, which can occur spontaneously or from exposure to environmental elements (Brennan, 1985). For example, exposure to X-rays or workplace hazards has been identified as having damaging effects on the reproductive process. The

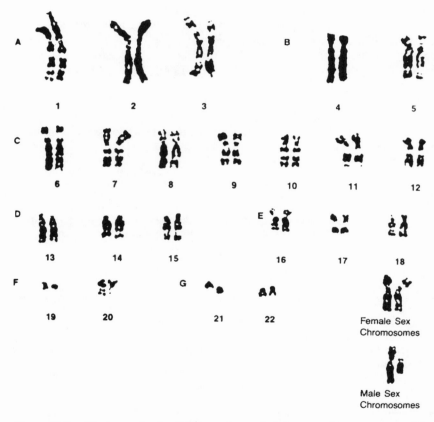

Figure 11.1. Photograph of a full complement of human chromosomes with both male and female sex chromosomes shown. (Courtesy of the March of Dimes Birth Defect Foundation.)

results can cause an abnormal complement of chromosomes to be transmitted in the gametes during the fertilization process. Often the serious damage caused by these aberrant chromosomes will result in spontaneous abortions, stillbirths, or infant deaths (Gardner & Snustad, 1984). This is understandable since there are thousands of genes on a chromosome and even if only a small segment of a chromosome is damaged it will involve many genes. Social workers are concerned both about reproductive issues and the health and safety of people in the workplace.

Down syndrome is the most common cause of mental retardation in the United States (Rauch, 1988b). It is also the most common disability associated with aberrant chromosomes, and occurs in about 1 in 700 births (Brennan, 1985). It is caused by the presence of three number 21 chromosomes (trisomy 21) instead of the normal pair. Besides being mentally retarded the child also may have a range of other conditions such as congenital heart defects, intestinal disorders, webbing between the fingers and toes, ears low set and malformed, elongated upper eye folds, and a small head with a flattened face. Social workers functioning in children's services may work with families grappling with this disorder.

The age of the mother is associated with the risk of giving birth to an infant with Down syndrome (Brennan, 1985). Only 1 in 2000 births results in infants with Down syndrome for mothers in their early twenties. This figure jumps to 1 in 50 births for mothers over age 45. Previously, the age of the father was not thought to be a factor, but more recent studies indicate that as many as a third of Down syndrome births may be due to the father (Brennan, 1985). It appears that paternal risk of contributing to this condition increases after age 55.

Cri-du-chat (cat cry) syndrome is an example of a deficiency in a chromosome (Gardner & Snustad, 1984). It is named after the catlike cry made by infants with the disorder. The infants have very small heads and are severely retarded. This syndrome is associated with a missing portion of one of the number 5 chromosomes.

Syndromes related to altered numbers of sex chromosomes have also been identified. In Klinefelter syndrome, the male offspring have two X chromosomes (XXY) (Brennan, 1985). The extra X chromosome can be derived from the father or the mother. Persons with this disorder have male genitalia and are usually sterile. They develop secondary sex characteristics such as enlarged breasts, tend to be of lower intelligence, and account for about 1% of the males institutionalized for mental defects (Brennan, 1985).

Persons with three X chromosomes have been found. These females are usually of normal intelligence and fertility, but do appear to have a higher risk of mental defects and decreased fertility (Brennan, 1985). On the other hand, persons with Tumer's syndrome have only an X chromosome

(XO) with no corresponding X or Y. Only about 5% of the XO conceptions survive to birth (Brennan, 1985). Survivors have female characteristics, a characteristic webbing of the neck, mental retardation, and infantile sexual development leading to sterility (Nagle, 1984).

When an egg and sperm unite to begin the process of developing a new human being, each contributes 23 chromosomes, bringing the total back to 46 individual or 23 pairs of chromosomes. As cells divide to form gametes, the chromosomes separate independently such that there are 223 possible combinations of chromosome separation for any individual's gametes (Newman & Newman, 1987, p. 109).

Another opportunity for variation called *crossing over* arises during *meiosis*. Meiosis is the cell division that occurs during maturation of the gametes. During meiosis, the chromosomes pair up with their matching regions aligned. Crossing over happens when the aligned matched chromosomes exchange paired segments, resulting in a new combination of genes on each chromosome (Rauch, 1988b). When variation resulting from crossing over and the chance union of a sperm and an ovum from two adults is considered, the number of possible combinations becomes staggering.

Each gene found on the 22 pairs of matched chromosomes, or autosomes, has the possibility of two or more forms or states. One is contributed by the mother and one by the father. It is possible that both parents may contribute the same form of the gene or each may contribute a different form. "These alternative states [of the gene] are called *alleles*. . . . If both alleles are the same, the gene is said to be *homozygous*. If the alleles are different, the gene is *heterozygous*" (Newman & Newman, 1987, p. 111). Alleles represent coded information that serve as the genes determining some particular characteristic such as eye color or blood type (Nagle, 1984).

Changes can occur in genetic material that result in altered or new alleles for a gene. This abrupt change is called a *mutation* (Brennan, 1985). Somatic mutations are those that occur to genes in the nonreproductive cells of the body; they cannot be passed on to offspring (Nagle, 1984). Changes to the gamete genes are called *germinal mutations* and can be passed on to progeny if the mutated gene is part of the fertilization process. Mutations are a spontaneous and naturally occurring phenomenon present in all organisms (Nagle, 1984). They can be caused by things normally found in the environment or by things artificially introduced by humans. DDT is a manufactured pesticide that was banned from use because it caused gene mutations. Almost all alternative inherited traits, including most genetic diseases, are the result of gene mutations (Nagle, 1984).

Ecological theory sensitizes social workers to concerns about air and water pollution, and exposure of people to toxic materials in workplaces, schools, dwellings, and communities. Increasingly, social workers interested in improving human environments are participating in efforts to effect change in public policy, attitudes, and values (Germain & Gitterman, 1987).

The genetic information represents the *genotype* of the individual. As indicated before, the genotype may be homozygous or heterozygous. It is the genotype that influences the actual appearance or observable nature of the individual, and this observable characteristic is the *phenotype* (Nagle, 1984). Similarity in observable characteristics among people who are relatives is a function of their genetic similarity to the degree that heredity or genetics is important in influencing phenotype (Plomin, DeFries, & Fulkner, 1988).

Different alleles can contribute to the phenotype in varying degrees. If an allele is *dominant*, it will be expressed as the phenotype or observable characteristic whether it is paired with a similar allele (homozygous) or with a different allele (heterozygous). People who do not have the observable characteristic do not have the dominant allele for this trait and therefore cannot pass it on to their children (Gardner & Snustad, 1984). The allele that is masked by the dominant gene is *recessive*. The recessive allele will appear as the phenotype only when the allelic pair is homozygous.

A simplified example of this would be in the transmission of the trait of eye color. Brown is the dominant allele and blue is recessive. Therefore the

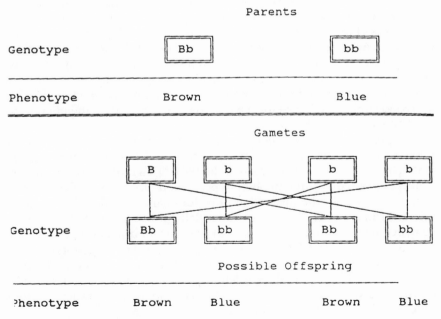

Figure 11.2. Possible outcomes from a mating of a blue-eyed parent and a parent heterozygous for brown eyes.

phenotype brown will appear when the gene pair is homozygous or heterozygous for brown. Because blue is recessive, it will appear as the phenotype only when the gene pair is homozygous for blue. Figure 11.2 shows the possible outcomes from the mating of a heterozygous brown-eyed person and a blue-eyed person.

Another example of the dominant-recessive genetic relationship of a physical characteristic in humans is earlobe shape (Brennan, 1985). Earlobes can generally be described as attached or free. This trait is controlled by a single autosomal gene with two alleles. The free form of the allele is dominant over the attached form. Therefore, persons with the phenotype attached earlobes are homozygous for the trait. On the other hand persons with the phenotype free earlobes can be heterozygous or homozygous for the trait.

Some characteristics transmitted through these genetic processes are not as innocuous as eye color or earlobe shape. Serious physical abnormalities and developmental problems have been linked to genetic transmission. Conditions such as cystic fibrosis, phenylketonuria (PKU), sickle-cell anemia, and Tay-Sachs disease are associated with recessive genes (Nagle, 1984; Zanden, 1985). Huntington's disease or Huntington's chorea and achondroplastic dwarfism are linked with dominant genes (Nagle, 1984). All of these genetically linked conditions have the potential to disrupt the developmental process of the individual and shorten life expectancy.

Patterns of inheritance or genotypic influence on phenotype are not always as clear-cut as those described above. Both alleles in a heterozygous gene pair can sometimes be expressed in the phenotype (Gardner & Snustad, 1984). In this case, the alleles are said to be *codominant*. An example of this in humans is blood type. When the type A allele and the type B allele for blood come together to form a heterozygous gene pair, the phenotype for this pair is type AB blood.

It is possible for some genes to have more than two forms or alleles. When this is the case, the inheritance of the trait is described as being regulated by a *multiple allelic system* (Nagle, 1984). This multiple allelic system results in a range of different phenotypes. Blood type is controlled by three different alleles. In the discussion of codominance, A and B alleles were said to form type AB blood. The third allele for blood type is O. It acts as recessive when paired with A or B. Therefore blood phenotypes A and B can be homozygous AA/BB or heterozygous AO/BO for genotype. Type O blood will appear as a phenotype only when the genotype is homozygous OO. Because of the three allelic system and the codominance relationship between alleles A and B, human blood is expressed in four different phenotypes: A, B, AB, and O.

Another phenomenon that affects phenotypic presentation is *pleiotropy* (Nagle, 1984). In this case a gene will produce multiple phenotypic effects or influence the observable characteristics in more than one body structure. Pyknodysostosis is caused by an abnormal recessive allele that has pleiotropic effects. It results in shortened stature, formation of fragile bones, a large skull, receding chin, abnormally formed lower jaw, and shortened fingers and toes. In cystic fibrosis, also caused by a recessive gene, the lungs, pancreas, and sweat and mucus glands are affected.

There are also situations in which one pair of genes that is separate and independent for inheritance will obscure or conceal the influence of another pair of genes on phenotype (Brennan, 1985). This effects is called *epistasis* and is different from dominance because separate gene pairs and not just different alleles of the same gene pair are involved. Albinism is caused by a pleiotropic recessive gene pair that controls the production of melanin pigment in the body. When the gene pair is homozygous for the recessive allele, the individual will present the appearance or phenotype of an albino regardless of the number of genes present for dark skin, eyes, or hair. The mechanism necessary to produce the pigment for these phenotypes is not functioning.

Expressivity and *penetrance* are terms used to help explain the variable effects of genes on phenotype. Some traits are represented by an array of phenotypes that range from mild to severe (Nagle, 1984). This range of degrees to which a genotype exhibits a phenotype is known as *variable expressivity.* Cystic fibrosis, a recessive gene disorder involving the lungs, may affect one child at birth while another may stay healthy until later childhood or early adolescence (Rauch, 1988b).

Alleles of a specific gene may have *reduced penetrance.* This occurs when the appropriate genotype fails to produce the expected phenotype (Nagle, 1984). Penetrance can be expressed numerically as a percentage of the full potential (Brennan, 1985). For example, a dominant gene with 50% penetrance would show up as the phenotype only half the time in those having the gene. Normally, we would expect the phenotype to show up 100% of the time when a dominant gene is present. Dominant traits with reduced penetrance are retinoblastoma, an inherited defect that results in eye tumors with 80% penetrance, and polydactyl, an inherited condition of extra digits with 90% penetrance (Nagle, 1984). Reduced penetrance and variable expressivity reflect the fact that genes cannot produce a phenotypic effect if the proper environmental conditions do not exist, and that phenotype is sometimes influenced by more than one independent gene pair (Brennan, 1985).

Because females have two X chromosomes, the genes on their sex chromosomes can be homozygous or heterozygous just as they are on the autosomes (Ehrman & Probber, 1983). The Y chromosome is smaller and less biochemically active than the X chromosome; it does not contain matching genes to form pairs with those found on the X chromosome (Ehrman &

Probber, 1983). This condition is known as *hemizygosity.* In males, because of this hemizygous condition, all alleles on the X chromosome, whether dominant or recessive, are expressed in the phenotype or observable characteristic (Nagle, 1984).

Genes that are carried on the X chromosome are said to be *sex-linked.* Many of the genes linked to the X chromosome have an abnormal recessive allele. More than 200 traits have been linked to the X chromosome in humans (Gardner & Snustad, 1984). Some of these are color blindness, hemophilia (a blood-clotting disorder), juvenile muscular dystrophy, degeneration of the optic nerve, juvenile glaucoma (hardening of the eyeball), abnormality of the mitral valve of the heart, and nearsightedness.

When a characteristic such as color blindness appears in males, it has always been inherited from the mother. Fathers can contribute only Y chromosomes to their male offspring. When female children exhibit the recessive characteristic, they have always inherited the trait from both their father and their mother. The father will express the phenotype for the trait; the mother does not need to have the observable characteristic, but must carry the allele for the trait.

If a characteristic was linked to a gene located on the Y chromosome, it would appear only in males and would be passed directly from father to son. These are labeled *holandric* genes. Only the male determining genes had previously been identified on the Y chromosome (Brennan, 1985). Because the inheritance pattern is so obvious, the existence of a large number of holandric genes probably would have led to more being described (Gardner & Snustad, 1984). However, recent research on the nonrecombining region of the human Y chromosome suggests the Y chromosome may not be the "functional wasteland" scientists previously believed (Lahn & Page, 1997). The importance of the Y chromosome in many men with infertility caused by spermatogenic failure, who are otherwise healthy, has been brought to light by recent genetic studies (Vogt et al., 1996; Pryor et al., 1997).

Some traits are called *sex-influenced* rather than sex-linked. In this case, gender controls the dominant-recessive relationship of autosomally inherited genes (Nagle, 1984). An allele that is dominant in a male will be recessive in a female. The phenotype can appear in either sex, but is more prevalent in the gender where it is expressed as dominant. Baldness is a sex-influenced characteristic. It is dominant in males and recessive in females, and is displayed in an array of phenotypes (variable expressivity) from severe to mild in both genders.

Traits that can be expressed as a phenotype in only a specific sex are designated *sex-limited* (Brennan, 1985). High milk production could never be demonstrated in a male, but the allele for this trait could be passed to male and female offspring by both or either parent. The development of secondary sex characteristics is normally active in only one sex. These genes are located on the autosomes, but are limited in their phenotypic expression by the sex chromosomes.

To complicate further the recognition of genotype in phenotype, some characteristics are controlled by more than one pair of genes. There is a cumulative effect of the *polygenes* on the phenotype (Brennan, 1985). The cumulative effects of the polygenes allow for a range of expressed phenotypes from one extreme to the other. Examples of human characteristics influenced by polygenes are skin color, height, and intelligence. Because of the range of possible phenotypes, a unit of measure is often used as a descriptor or classification. As a result, the study of characteristics controlled by polygenes has become known as *quantitative genetics* (Brennan, 1985).

PERSON-IN-ENVIRONMENT

Many abnormalities and developmental characteristics are influenced by polygenes. The severity or level of malfunction will vary from individual to individual. These conditions can also be classified as *multifactorial* because they are influenced by a multiplicity of factors both genetic and environmental (Nagle, 1984). There may be a threshold at which the cumulative affect of the associated genes will cause the abnormality to appear as the phenotype or physical characteristic. On the other hand, environmental factors such as nutritional status, exposure to stress, and general health of the individual can exert significant influence on the severity of the presentation (Nagle, 1984). Some conditions, although not well understood, that are known to have multigenetic causation are diabetes mellitus, clubfoot, cleft lip and palate, and incomplete closure of the lower spine (spina bifida).

Some conditions are described as having a *genetic predisposition,* and are even more susceptible to environmental influence. Environmental factors can either promote or prevent the expression of diseases such as hypertension, peptic ulcers, heart disease, and some forms of cancer (Nagle, 1984).

This leads us to one undeniable conclusion: "People differ. This is so because each person has undergone a complex series of transactions between a unique set of genes and a unique sequence of environments" (Loehlin, 1989, p. 1285). When considering genetics and environment and their contributions to human differences, some investigators use an additive model while others claim they must be analyzed as interactions (Smith, 1985). The interactive model assumes genetics and environment are inseparable (Overton, 1973). The additive model assumes the components can each be identified and separately analyzed for its contribution.

Lerner (1986) relates Anne Anastasi's interactive approach on the relationship of heredity and environment to development. Anastasi's work on this topic first appeared in the *Psychological Review* in 1958. According to her view, heredity and environment are inseparable because "there would be no one in an environment without heredity, and there would no place to see the effects of heredity without environment" (p. 83). Development is the result of a "multiplicative interaction" between heredity and the environment. Both act indirectly, and always with each other, on influencing outcome.

Anastasi conceived the influence of heredity on development along a continuum ranging from "least indirect" to "most indirect." Characteristics that would fall on the continuum closest to "least indirect" are those more directly influenced by heredity, or less likely to be affected by environmental intervention. Sex, eye color, blood type, or a serious disability such as Tay-Sachs disease, for example, would fall near that end of the continuum. Predisposition to a disorder would fall farther along the continuum toward "most indirect." As discussed earlier, environment plays an important role in promoting or suppressing the expression of such a disorder.

Conversely, Anastasi perceived environment contributing to development on a continuum from broad to narrow pervasiveness. A broadly pervasive environmental factor would affect many dimensions of an individual's functioning over a long period of time. Family life would be an example of broadly pervasive environmental factor. She also divided environmental effects into two broad categories, organic and stimulative. *Organic effects* are associated with physical assaults or changes to the body. *Stimulant effects* are those environmental conditions that arouse behavioral responses. Social class would act as a stimulant effect. It is through this interactive process that heredity and the environment produce development in the individual.

Behavioral genetics is an applied form of quantitative genetics (Plomin & Daniels, 1987). Quantitative genetics examines the phenotypic variability brought about by genetic and environmental differences among individuals (Plomin, DeFries, & Fulkner, 1988). Plomin (1983), in a special section of *Child Development*, describes developmental behavioral genetics as a "truly interdisciplinary field . . . just beginning to emerge." He goes on to say, "The perspective of behavioral genetics can give developmentalists a new way to look at their research problems, recognizing both genetic and environmental sources of observed individual differences" (p. 258). Genetic influence on complex behavior does not fit the deterministic model of a single-gene effect, but rather is multifactorial, involving many genes, each with small effects (Plomin, 1989).

Behavioral genetics seeks to identify the relative contribution of heredity and environment in explaining individual differences using such methods as model fitting, multivariate analysis, analysis of genetic change over the life cycle, as well as continuity during development (Plomin, 1989). The major research designs used by behavioral geneticists are adoption and twin studies (Plomin & Daniels, 1987). These research designs have been developed to more clearly delineate between genetic and environmental contributions to phenotype.

The twin design compares similarities and differences between identical or monozygotic (developing from a single fertilized egg) twins and same-sex fraternal or dizygotic (developing from two eggs separately fertilized) twins (Hoffman, 1985; Plomin & Daniels, 1987). If genes do not influence the trait or behavior being studied, than the greater genetic similarity of identical twins will not make them more alike than fraternal twins for the given trait. Since identical twins have the same genotype, any differences within the pair can be attributed to nongenetic factors.

The adoptive design hopes to differentiate between the influence of shared heredity and shared environment when it examines genetically related individuals adopted apart and reared in uncorrelated environments (Plomin & Daniels, 1987). The rarest and most dramatic form of this design is when identical twins adopted apart at birth are studied. Measures obtained from children adopted at birth or near birth are sometimes compared to those of their biological parents, who did not interact with them (Hoffman, 1985).

Areas researched by behavioral genetics include intellectual factors, personality factors, and psychopathology (Plomin, 1989). In each area, genetic influence on individual differences in behavior has been found. Some of these findings have generated controversy, particularly around research topics such as IQ, academic achievement, and criminal behavior. Behavioral genetic research on psychopathology is very active at this time. Schizophrenia continues to receive a lot of attention, as well as manic depression and alcoholism. The understanding of the genetic contribution to these problems is important because it can lead to understanding biochemical imbalances caused by genetic error. In turn, these biochemical imbalances may respond to appropriate pharmacological intervention.

On the other hand, these same behavioral genetic studies suggest that nongenetic factors or environment are responsible for more than half the variation in more complex behaviors (Plomin, 1989). Take the case of schizophrenia; even among identical twins who have the same genotype, both twins have the condition only 40% of the time. Likewise, studies on personality factors have shown about half of the variation is attributable to environment (Eaves, Eysenck, & Martin, 1989). Interestingly, it appears that unshared environment is more important than shared environment in the development of personality and psychopathology (Eaves et al., 1989;

Plomin et al., 1988). "That is, whatever homes and teachers do to influence behavior in a systematic way, it is clear that even twins and siblings in the same family have their own unique experiences that contribute to their personality" (Eaves et al., 1989, p. 406).

EXPLAINING DEVELOPMENT ACROSS THE LIFE CYCLE

Even before conception, the exposure of parents to environmental hazards, such as ionizing radiation or chemicals that damage the genes or chromosomes in the reproductive cells, has a bearing on developmental outcome for the offspring. Everyday items such as adhesives, gasoline additives, industrial chemicals, insecticides, medicines, paints, and solvents contain chemical mutagens (Nagle, 1984). This, coupled with the genotypes of both parents and the possible natural errors that can occur in the production of gametes, sets the stage for the expression of genetic disorders during the life span.

The months between conception and birth may be the most important time in the developmental process. Particularly during the first three months, the developing fetus is vulnerable to environmental insults. From the eighteenth day after conception to about the ninth week, when the embryo is recognized as a fetus, the basic pattern of all the organ systems begins to develop (Wymelenberg, 1990). It is during this time that a genetic regulatory function promotes cell differentiation and organ systems formation (Nagle, 1984). "At all stages of development, it is clear that different portions of DNA are active in each type of cell and tissue. . . . [G]enes act in sequence during development so that a given gene may start one event which in turn activates other genes, leading to a series of developmental steps" (Ehrman & Probber, 1983, p. 18).

A classic example of what can happen when this critical sequence of development is disrupted is in the misuse of thalidomide, a sleep inducer, by pregnant women (Nagle, 1984). Although perfectly safe for other adult use, when taken by pregnant women during the third to fifth week of pregnancy, it results in babies being born with seriously deformed arms and legs. This suggests that the controlling genes must operate correctly when the differentiation of the limb buds is taking place or deformity will result. Substances that cause these developmental malformations are called *teratogens*.

Today, alcohol is a major teratogen contributing to birth defects (Nagle, 1984). No safe level of alcohol consumption during pregnancy has been established. It is best for women even trying to conceive to abstain from alcohol. The deleterious effects on the infant of heavy alcohol consumption during pregnancy were well established by studies during the 1970s and early 1980s (Abel, 1980; Streissguth, Landesman, Dwyer, Martin, and Smith, 1980; Palmer, Ouellette, Warner, and Leichtman, 1974). The condition is called fetal alcohol syndrome (FAS) (Nagle, 1984). It is denoted by a pattern of recognizable defects in the infant. These include distorted facial features, growth deficiency, and mental retardation. Social workers often must deal with the resulting physical and social problems caused by this syndrome.

The effects of genes both normal and abnormal, can have delayed onset (Nagle, 1984). Most delays are measured from the date of birth, but "the entire developmental process from the moment of fertilization involves the activity of genes whose expressions are delayed until appropriate times" (Nagle, 1984, p. 212). Some problems such as Down syndrome and defects such as spina bifida are readily apparent at birth. Other problems will appear during the first year of life, for example, sickle-cell anemia and Tay-Sachs disease. Early childhood will see the advent of such conditions as muscular dystrophy and juvenile diabetes. Adulthood will set the stage for the onset of other genetic disorders such as Huntington's disease, some forms of diabetes, glaucoma, and some forms of cancer.

As stated earlier, environmental factors influence the occurrence and severity of many genetically linked conditions. particularly those described as genetically predisposed. Stress in the form of life change events, infection, trauma, or exposures in the physical environment can occur at any time during the life cycle, precipitating a latent genetic disorder. The social, psychological, and physical aspects of a person's development, at any stage of the life cycle, are so intimately related that dysfunction in any one dimension can lead to a request for help or referral for service.

UNDERSTANDING CROSS-CULTURAL DIFFERENCES

The emphasis in this chapter has been on differences between individuals rather than between groups. However, some genetic disorders are found more often in certain ethnic groups or among persons who have their origins from specific geographic regions. Because there is often a need to develop a culturally relevant approach to these condition, several examples will be discussed in this section.

Tay-Sachs, one of the most disabling deadly genetic diseases, is found chiefly among Jews of European (Ashkenazi Jews) ancestry (Wymelenberg, 1990). This is a recessively inherited condition. At birth the infant appears perfectly normal, and it is not until about six months that the loss of motor abilities begin (Brennan, 1985). Death occurs by age four, following the loss of sight, controlled movement, and other nervous function. The lack of an enzyme, hexoseaminidase A, results in fatty deposits building up on nerve cells causing loss of function. In 1970, 50 to 100 babies with this disorder were born each year (Wymelenberg, 1990). The availability of testing and counseling programs has reduced this number to less than 10 a year, indicating the importance of culturally sensitive genetic counseling programs.

Sickle-cell anemia results from the production of an abnormal type of hemoglobin by the body due to the presence of two alleles for sickle hemoglobin (HbS) (Brennan, 1985). It gets its name from the abnormally shaped red blood cells that have a sickle or crescent shape. These distorted blood cells are not effective oxygen carriers, and have a tendency to hang up in small capillaries, causing reduced blood supply and pain. Persons with this condition experience sickling crises that cause episodes of severe pain lasting for as brief a period as an hour to as long as a week (Rauch, 1988b). To reduce these episodes, persons with the disease tend to lead a restrictive life-style. They must avoid emotional and physical stress, illness, injury, or situations that increase the body's need for oxygen such as exercise or high altitudes.

The severity of sickle-cell disease can vary greatly (Rauch, 1988b). Some people are almost symptom free, while others suffer serious consequences such as stroke, deterioration of hip joints, and even death from blockage of blood supply to vital organs such as the heart. There is also a related condition called sickle-cell trait (Brennan, 1985). A person with sickle-cell trait has one allele for normal hemoglobin (HbA) and one HbS allele. They produce both normal and abnormal hemoglobin and have few or no symptoms.

Because the HbS allele also provides a resistance to malarial infection to those who carry it, the HbS gene is found most often in persons who live or have their origins in a risk area for malaria (Brennan, 1985). Therefore, persons most likely to have sickle-cell trait or disease come from equatorial Africa and less commonly the Mediterranean area and India (Nagle, 1984). In the United States, it is most often found among persons of African-American decent. One in 12 carries the trait and 1 in 500 has the disease (Rauch, 1988b).

Thalassemia, another blood disorder, is most common to people of Mediterranean descent, primarily Italian and Greek (Wymelenberg, 1990). This represents a series of conditions that result in reduced hemoglobin in the blood and anemia, the most common being Cooley's anemia (Brennan, 1985). Children with the disease appear normal at birth but soon become listless, prone to infection, and grow slowly (Wymelenberg, 1990). They need frequent blood transfusions that eventually lead to iron accumulations in the organs and heart failure.

UNDERSTANDING HOW PEOPLE FUNCTION
AS MEMBERS OF FAMILIES, GROUPS,
ORGANIZATIONS, AND COMMUNITIES

"A person may be viewed as a biopsychosocial system who, from birth, is a member of a family and an extended family and who subsequently becomes a member of friendship, educational, recreational, religious, and cultural groups, and civic associations" (Northen, 1988, p. 9). Genetic disorders that impair cognitive or motor development or result in chronic illness or any form of dysfunction will have a detrimental effect on the individual's ability to take on the roles and responsibilities necessary to participate as an effective member of these groups.

Rauch (1988b) discusses the impact of a family dealing with a new infant diagnosed as having a genetic disorder:

> The infant with a genetic disorder presents its family with extraordinary stress, both chronic and acute. Initially, the parents interact with their atypical baby during a time when they may be fatigued, angry, depressed, worried and overwhelmed by the diagnosis. Although many families cope beautifully, the risk is high that the interaction established between an infant with reduced adaptive capacities and stressed parents will be negative. For that reason, infants with a genetic disorder are considered to be vulnerable. They are at higher risk than healthy children for the development of psychological problems and are more likely to be abused. (p. 39)

All of these factors increase the probability that intervention will be needed, and that the family will be brought to the attention of social services for assistance. Ideally, support should be made routinely available to these stressed families so severe dysfunction such as abuse will not develop.

A myriad of services is needed by families and their impaired members to compensate for or overcome difficulties in functioning brought on by genetic disorders. Rehabilitation programs are often needed to surmount lags in cognitive and motor development, or the limitations of handicapping conditions. Special education is frequently needed to deal with circumstances such as hearing impairment, learning disabilities, mental retardation, or a range of other problems. Job training, sheltered workshops, and specialized housing are sometimes needed to help individuals become productive members of the community. The social worker often is the professional providing both counseling and case management services to such families.

As individuals and families struggle to adapt, they need to focus on their strengths and learn to identify and draw on resources within themselves and in the community. Through this process, they will enhance their coping mechanisms, feel more in control of their life situation, and achieve their highest level of performance.

DIRECT PRACTICE IN SOCIAL WORK: INTERVENING
IN THE PERSON-ENVIRONMENT SITUATION TO
ENHANCE PSYCHOSOCIAL FUNCTIONING

A s public awareness grows and more conditions are found to be associated with genetic causes, social workers will have increased opportunities to work with people and families dealing with genetically based
disorders. In a recent survey of active members of the NASW Maryland
Chapter (Rauch & Tivoli, 1989), about 20% of the respondents indicated
they had worked with clients who had themselves initiated requests for
genetic counseling or information. Most were concerned about the risk for
an inherited condition or were making decisions about reproductive issues. Yet more than half of the social workers surveyed did not know
where to refer a client with genetic concerns, and about a third did not
know if genetic consultation was available to their agencies.

Increased use of genetic screening has expanded the need for and use of
genetic counseling. Genetic screening can be categorized into three main
types: adult screening, newborn screening, and prenatal testing (Wymelenberg, 1990). Adult screening can identify carriers when an accurate, reliable test is available. An example of when this type of testing has
effectively decreased the incidence of a disease is in the case of Tay-Sachs.
Similar screenings for sickle-cell anemia and thalassemia have not been
successful mainly because of inadequate educational efforts, lack of confidentiality, and concern about stigmatization (Wymelenberg, 1990). Another aspect of adult screening is identifying those who have the disorder, but
are still asymptomatic. Ideally, this type of screening would allow preventive intervention. However, in many cases, effective intervention is not yet
available, and this type of testing will only relieve or confirm anxiety
(Rauch, 1988a). Such is the case for children of parents with Huntington's
disease, a dominant gene disorder that does not appear until adulthood.

Newborn screening can be very beneficial in preventing the deleterious
effects of about 12% of inherited metabolic diseases (Wymelenberg, 1990).
Early detection is important in preventing long-lasting, cumulative damage incurred by the untreated disease. Phenylketonuria (PKU) is an inherited condition in which an enzyme needed to break down phenylalanine,
found in dietary protein, is absent (Brennan, 1985). The build-up of phenylalanine in the infant's body causes abnormal brain development, resulting in varying degrees of retardation. Blood taken from the heel of the
infant shortly after birth allows these infants to be identified. Although
there is no cure for PKU, the effects of the disease can be controlled by placing the infant on a phenylalanine-free diet (Brennan, 1985). By age six, the
child no longer needs to be on such a rigid diet.

More than ten other disorders of this type can be identified by similar testing methods. Among the conditions that can be identified this way are homocystinuria (high levels of homocystine in the blood), galactosemia (an inability to digest milk sugar), and maple sugar urine disease (improper amino acid metabolism giving a maple syrup odor to the urine) (Wymelenberg, 1990). As with PKU, if left undetected and untreated they cause mental retardation and they can be controlled by diet. Simple low-cost tests make it feasible to test every newborn; in many states these tests are required by law.

Prenatal testing or testing during pregnancy is helpful in identifying some genetic disorders in the developing fetus. These tests mainly rely on biochemical assessments to identify the disease, but more recently analysis of fetal DNA can account for cystic fibrosis, sickle-cell anemia, and thalassemia (Wymelenberg, 1990). The range of available prenatal tests includes the following.

Amniocentesis involves the withdrawal of fluid from the amniotic sack with a needle, through the abdominal and uterine walls of the mother, during the fourteenth or fifteenth week of the pregnancy (Nagle, 1984). Living cells found in the amniotic fluid are then cultured for two to three weeks so biochemical appraisals and chromosome studies can be done. Tay-Sachs disease or Down syndrome can be distinguished in a fetus using this method.

Fetal blood testing is also done by inserting a needle through the abdomen of the mother and into the umbilical cord to remove blood (Wymelenberg, 1990). This procedure cannot be done until the sixteenth week of the pregnancy. Hemophilia, an inherited clotting disorder, can be uncovered with this test.

Chorionic villus sampling takes a small piece of the chorionic villus, which is part of the placenta, either by way of a catheter inserted through the birth canal or a needle through the mother's abdomen (Wymelenberg, 1990). Enough live cells are present in this tissue that a culture does not need to be done and it can be done early as the ninth week of pregnancy.

Ultrasound is used to guide the needle placement in the previously described tests. It is also useful as a diagnostic tool for skeletal disorders and disorders of the nervous system indicated by abnormal head size (Wymelenberg, 1990).

Maternal serum alpha-fetoprotein screen (MSAFP) tests the level of alpha-fetoprotein (AFP) produced by the fetus in the mother's blood (Wymelenberg, 1990). A high level of AFP in early pregnancy suggests the presence of spina bifida.

Negative test findings bring relief to the expectant parents. Positive results often place them in a position of needing to make a decision about whether to terminate the pregnancy. Today very little help in correcting these serious defects is yet available. Many couples, when faced with the outcome of a seriously impaired child, opt to end the pregnancy and try again for a healthy baby. For this reason, tests that provide information early in the pregnancy have an obvious advantage. As technology in this area continues to develop, more treatments will become an option.

An area of social work practice that is directly affected by increased knowledge of genetic influences on health and behavior is the field of adoption. The acknowledged right of adoptees to know about their biological background and possible genetic risks to themselves or their own children makes genetic histories an important part of the adoption records (Rauch, 1988a).

Social workers also participate in multidisciplinary teams providing genetic counseling. Team members may include a physician with special training in genetics (medical geneticist), a nurse, a social worker, and perhaps a psychologist (Hamilton & Noble, 1983). The social worker would be responsible for doing a psychosocial assessment and gathering family background information (Rauch, 1988a; Hamilton & Noble, 1983).

Hamilton and Noble (1983) describe the multiple purposes of genetic counseling, according to the American Society of Human Genetics:

> Genetic counseling includes helping the family or individual: (1) comprehend medical facts, including diagnosis, the probable course of the disorder, and the available management; (2) understand the genetic and nongenetic aspects of the disorder and the risk of recurrence; (3) understand available options for subsequent family planning; (4) choose the course of action most appropriate to their individual needs and (5) make the best possible family adjustments to that disorder in an affected member or to the risk of recurrence of the disorder. (p. 19).

The following case study captures the range of emotions experienced by clients as they try to cope with what seems to be an unmanageable situation. In this particular client, guilt, denial, grief, anger, confusion, and frustration are seen.

> Joann L., a social worker who functioned as a member of a genetic team, had dealt with Mrs. M. throughout the initial genetic testing on Mrs. M.'s 4-year-old son. Soon after the diagnosis was established and explained in depth—a diagnosis that carried little life hope for the child's life—Joann received a long letter from Mrs. M. In it, Mrs. M. asked many questions that revealed her confusion and pain. She expressed her disappointment in her child and in her husband, and her belief that she had failed them. In part, the letter read, "Why was my son born like this? Why did it happen to us? Was it because I was unhappy in my marriage? Was it because of poor nutrition during pregnancy? Was it because I took water pills and vitamins, or because I drank a half gallon of milk every day? Was it the way I slept? Does it run in the family? Will he ever recover? Will he be able to have normal children?

Will he be a complete man physically, mentally, sexually? Will I ever know the truth?"

The contents of the letter made it clear to Joann that Mrs. M. needed additional clarification about the genetic diagnosis that had already been explained to her. Joann spent a good deal of time trying to help Mrs. M. understand the information. Within a few months, Joann received another letter from Mrs. M. that contained many of the same questions asked in the first letter, questions that Joann thought had been thoroughly answered by the genetic team. Clearly, Mrs. M. was struggling to make sense of a painful, confusing reality that threatened her concept of herself as a mother, a wife, and a person. (Hamilton and Noble, 1983, pp. 19–20)

Social workers can be very effective in helping clients rally existing coping mechanisms or build new ones to deal with the situation. The following list, developed from Hamilton and Noble (1983), provides specific ways the social worker can assist the client or family.

- Help client break down the problem into manageable units. Mobilize the family into meaningful activity such as participating in a support group.
- Link families up with appropriate support services such as financial assistance, medical equipment and care, and special education programs.
- Clarify and reinforce medical information provided by other health professionals.
- Facilitate communication and decision making within the family
- Assist the family in developing a healthy self-concept.

Social workers in all fields need to be aware of existing genetic counseling services in their community, be able to identify those clients with genetic service needs, and make appropriate referrals when necessary (Rauch & Tivoli, 1989).

NOTE

1. For more information on the project, use the U.S. government–sponsored Internet site www.ornl.gov/TechResources?Human Genome/home.html. This site gives information on whether a gene for a disorder, disease, or trait has been identified, and provides information on counseling, support, and treatment.

REFERENCES

Abel, E. L. (1980). Fetal alcohol syndrome: Behavioral teratology. *Psychological Bulletin, 87,* 29–50.

Baskin, Y. (1984). *The Gene Doctors*. New York: Morrow.

Brennan, J. R. (1985). *Pattern of Human Heredity*. Princeton, NJ: Prentice-Hall.

Eaves, L. J., Eysenck, H. J., & Martin, N. G. (1989). *Genes: Culture and Personality*. San Diego: Academic.

Ehrman, L., & Probber, J. (1983). Fundamentals of genetic and evolutionary theories. In J. L. Fuller & E. C. Simmel (Eds.), *Behavior Genetics* (pp. 1–31). Hillsdale, NJ: Lawrence Erlbaum.

Gardner, E. J., & Snustad, D. P. (1984). *Principles of Genetics* (7th ed.). New York: Wiley.

Germain, C. B. (Ed.) (1979). *Social Work Practice: People and Environments*. New York: Columbia University Press.

Germain, C. B., & Gitterman, A. (1987). Ecological perspectives. In A. Minahan (Editor-in-chief), *Encyclopedia of Social Work* (18th ed. pp. 488–499). Silver Spring, MD: National Association of Social Workers.

Hamilton, A. K., & Noble, D. N. (1983). Assisting families through genetic counseling. *Social Casework, 64,* 18–25.

Hoffman, L. W. (1985). The changing genetics / socialization balance. *Journal of Social Issues, 41,* 127–148.

Knowles, R. V. (1985). *Genetics, Society, and Decision*. Columbus, OH: Charles E. Merrill.

Lahn, B. T., & Page, D. C. (1997). Functional coherence of the Y chromosome. *Science, 278,* 675–679.

Lerner, R. M. (1986). *Concepts and Theories of Human Development* (2nd ed.). New York: Random House.

Loehlin, J. C. (1989). Partitioning environmental and genetic contributions to behavioral development. *American Psychologist, 44,* 1285–1292.

Nagle, J. J. (1984). *Heredity and Human Affairs* (3rd ed.). St. Louis: Mosby.

Newman, B., & Newman, P. R. ([1979] 1987). *Development through Life: A Psycho Social Approach*. Homewood, IL: Dorsey.

Northen, H. (1988). *Social Work with Groups* (2nd ed.). New York: Columbia University Press.

Overton, W. F. (1973). On the assumptive base of the nature-nurture controversy: Additive versus interactive conceptions. *Human Development, 16,* 74–89.

Palmer, R. H., Ouellette, E. M., Warner, L., & Leichtman, S. R. (1974). Congenital malformations in offspring of a chronic alcoholic mother. *Pediatrics, 53,* 490–494.

Plomin, R. (1983). Developmental behavioral genetics. *Child Development, 54,* 253–259.

Plomin, R. (1989). Environment and gene. *American Psychologist, 44,* 105–111.

Plomin, R., & Daniels, D. (1987). Why are children in the same family so different from one another? *Behavioral and Brain Sciences, 10,* 1–60.

Plomin, R., DeFries, J. C., & Fulkner, D. W. (1988). *Nature and Nurture during Infancy and Early Childhood*. New York: Cambridge University Press.

Pryor, J. L., Kent-First, M., Muallem, A., Van Bergen, A. H., Nolten, W. E., Meisner, L., & Roberts, K. P. (1997). Microdeletions in the Y chromosome of infertile men. *New England Journal of Medicine, 336*(8), 534–539.

Rauch, J. B. (1988a). Social work and the genetics revolution: Genetic services. *Social Work, 33,* 389–394.

Rauch, J. B. (1988b). *Genetic Content for Graduate Social Work Education: Human Behavior and the Social Environment.* Washington, DC: Council on Social Work Education.

Rausch, J. B., & Tivoli, L. (1989). Social workers' knowledge and utilization of genetic services. *Social Work, 34,* 55–56.

Rowen, L., Mahairas, G., & Hood, L. (1997). Sequencing the human genome. *Science, 278,* 675–679.

Smith, N. W. (1985). Heredity and environment revisited. *Psychological Record, 35,* 173–176.

Streissguth, A. P. Landesman-Dwyer, S., Martin, J. C., and Smith, D. W. (1980). Teratogenic effects of alcohol in humans and laboratory animals. *Science, 209,* 253–361.

Vogt, P. H., Edelmann, A., Kirsch, S., Henegariu, O., Hirschmann, P., Kiesewetter, F., Koen, F. M., Schill, W. B., Farah, S., Ramos, C., Hartmann, M., Meschede, D., Behre, H. M., Castel, A., Nieschiag, E., Weidner, W., Grone, H. J., Jung, A., Engel, W., & Haidl, G. (1996). Human Y chromosome azoospermia factors (AZF) mapped to different subregions in Yq11. *Human-Molecular Genetics, 5*(7), 933–943.

Wymelenberg, S. (1990). *Science and Babies.* Washington, DC: National Academy Press.

Zanden, J. W. V. (1985). *Human Development.* New York: Knopf.

GLOSSARY

Alleles.   Alternative states of a gene.

Autosomes.   The 22 pairs of chromosomes that do not include the sex chromosomes.

Behavioral genetics.   An applied form of quantitative genetics, recognizing both genetic and environmental sources of observed individual differences.

Chromosome.   Each human cell, not including the gametes, contains 46 or 23 pairs, and each contains a specific sequence of genes.

Codominant.   Both alleles in a heterozygous gene pair are expressed in the phenotype.

Crossing over.   Occurs during meiosis when the aligned matched chromosomes exchange paired segments resulting in a new combination of genes on each chromosome.

Deoxyribonucleic acid (DNA).   Chemical that makes up the genes that make up the chromosomes.

Dominant.   An allele that will be expressed as the phenotype or observable characteristic, masking the paired (recessive) abele.

Epistasis.   One pair of genes that is separate and independent for inheritance will obscure or conceal the influence of another pair of genes on phenotype; this is different from dominance because separate gene pairs and not just different alleles of the same gene pair are involved.

Expressivity.   The degree to which a gene is expressed in the phenotype.

Gametes.   The egg and sperm cells.

Gene.   A unit of heredity, each located in a specific position on a chromosome.

Genetic predisposition.   Denotes a condition or disease that has a genetic component, but is susceptible to environmental influence; environmental factors can either promote or prevent the expression of the condition.

Genetics.   The study of heredity.

Genotype.   Genetic information in each cell.

Germinal mutations.   Changes to the gamete genes; can be passed on to progeny if the mutated gene is part of the fertilization process.

Hemizygosity.   A condition in which only one allele is present where there would normally be two; males are hemizygous for the X-linked genes.

Heterozygous.   A condition in which the genotype is represented by two different alleles.

Holandric.   Found on or related to the Y chromosome.

Homozygous.   A condition in which the genotype is represented by alleles that are the same.

Meiosis.   Cell division in the formation of the gametes, leaving half the number of chromosomes in each egg or sperm.

Multifactorial.   When referring to phenotype, caused by many factors, usually a combination of many genes and environmental factors.

Multiple allelic system.   A condition in which there are three or more alleles for the gene, as in blood type.

Mutation.   Changes that occur in genetic material that result in altered or new alleles for a gene.

Organic effects.   Environmental factors that relate to physical assaults or changes to the body.

Penetrance.   The percentage of individuals who demonstrate the expected phenotype from a given genotype; can be expressed numerically as a percentage of the full potential.

Phenotype.   The observable characteristic influenced by the genotype and the environment.

Pleiotropy.   When a gene produces multiple phenotypic effects or influences the observable characteristics in more than one body structure.

Polygenes.　When many genes affect the same characteristic in a cumulative way and are represented in a range of presentations of phenotype, e.g., skin color.

Quantitative genetics.　The study of characteristics controlled by polygenes; it examines the phenotypic variability brought about by genetic and environmental differences among individuals.

Recessive.　The allele that is masked by the dominant gene.

Sex chromosomes.　The X and Y chromosomes, they are involved in the determination of the sex of the individual.

Sex-influenced.　An autosomal gene in which one allele will act in a dominant manner in one sex and recessively in the other.

Sex-limited.　Autosomal genes that produce phenotypes that can be expressed only in one sex or the other, although they can be transmitted through both sexes, e.g., beard growth pattern in males and milk production in females.

Sex-linked.　Genes that are carried on the X or Y chromosomes.

Somatic mutations.　Changes that occur to genes in the nonreproductive cells of the body; they cannot be passed on to offspring.

Stimulant effects.　Environmental conditions that arouse behavioral responses.

Teratogens.　Substances that cause malformations during uterine development.

CRITIQUE

Nature and Nurture

JOAN ESTERLINE LAFUZE[1]

This critique has three goals. The first is to address the continuing controversy surrounding nature and nurture from the perspective of behavioral genetics, especially related to psychiatric disorders. The second is to evaluate the incongruities between what seems realistic and what we expect in regard to influences on behavior. The third is to challenge social workers to fill expanded roles in use of genetic information as proposed from a perspective outside social work.

A FOCUS ON NATURE AND NURTURE THROUGH BEHAVIORAL GENETICS

Behavioral genetics is a modern expression that captures the age-old dialogue about the roles of the inherent makeup of an individual or population (nature) and the environment (nurture) as they influence who a person is and what he/she does. Just as the nature versus nurture dialogue has bounced back and forth between "sides," so does the issue of behavioral genetics.

A 1994 article in *Science* presents the wide range of perspectives on behavioral genetics (Mann, 1994). One such example involves the expression of anger and whether it is a manifestation of nature or nurture. The authors state concern that the findings of such a study can be misused to support biased arguments that blame people for their own problems or to support a return to practices related to eugenics. The opposite position is one of confidence that emerging techniques can make it possible to discover genes to account for behavioral patterns.

Through this and other recent articles that explore the risks and benefits of employing behavioral genetics as a tool for understanding, diagnosing and counseling people with psychiatric disorders, several points are worth noting:

1.   Almost all psychiatric disorders are multifactorial. Not only are several different genes likely to be involved, but also there is almost certainly a great deal of interplay between genetic and environmental influences (Plomin and Rutter, 1998).

2.   Environment runs a tremendous gamut. Environmental factors that have been investigated include viral exposure, nutritional deficiencies, and obstetric complications (Schultz & Andreasen, 1999). Even such a seemingly small factor as which side the fetus lies on in the womb is an environmental issue (Mann, 1994).

3.   Genetic techniques are complex. Therefore, finding effects of a gene or behavior is neither a simple nor a straightforward finding. An article focused on a tryptophan hydroxylase (TPH) gene marker for suicidality and alcoholism in a cohort of Finnish males concludes as follows:

> The linkage and association results presented herein indicate that the TPH intron 7 polymorphism, or another mutation(s) nearby, is involved in suicidality, alcoholism, and socialization. No other specific genetic components of suicidality have been identified, although the recent report of familial transmission of suicidal behavior is consistent with our findings. Since suicidality and alcoholism are likely to be complex, multifactorial phenotypes, TPH may turn out to be one of several genes involved. (Neilsen et al., 1998)

Note that the authors couch their findings in very tentative language. They provide no basis for conclusion or for applying these findings to a specific situation.

4.   Just as the genetic effects of behavioral and nonbehavioral traits are complex, the implications for genetic counseling are just as complex. In multifactorial disorders, a single gene may have limited or even no predictive value in the ultimate phenotype (Sherman et al., 1997, p. 1272).

5.   Heritability (a term to describe the role of genes in terms of the proportion of variation in the population due to genetic (factors) is correlated to the population being studied rather than a fixed property of a trait (Owen and McGuffin, 1997).

6.   Correlation is *not* cause. At best, the results of such (genetic) studies can only raise the possibility of "genetic influences" by providing correlations between similarities in phenotype (the observed manifestations of a trait or condition) and the closeness of genetic relationship between individuals. They cannot be used to determine which genes, or even the number of genes, are responsible for human behavioral differences. Also, of greater importance, these studies cannot show the existence of a causal link between genes and behaviors (Billings, Beckwith, & Alper, 1992).

7.   Genes associated with disease are *not* necessarily bad. If the situation were that simple, the goal could simply be finding the "bad" gene and getting rid of it (Rutter and Plomin, 1997). What might be problematic in some circumstances could be helpful in another. (See Riley's comments in Chapter 13 about the protective benefits of the sickle cell anemia trait.)

A closing commentary regarding these issues related to behavioral genetics must be that as important as it is to be aware of all of the research in genetics and environment and the intricate interplay between the two, it is also important to know that there will not be quick, easy answers on which to base conclusions. It is the nature of scientific inquiry to avoid conclusions and to use answers as stepping stones to new questions.

RELATING WHAT WE KNOW TO WHAT WE EXPECT

This section consists of an informal conversation that rests on what this author considers commonsense observations that link our knowledge and wisdom about genetic information to expectations for behavior and attitudes. The discussion rests on the assumption that knowledge is not simple. It also suggests that there is much we do not know. For example, schizophrenia is a devastating illness with diverse clinical presentations. Although there is evidence of increased risk associated with genetic familial tendencies, the exact nature of the genetic susceptibility is unclear, and the role of various environmental factors has been and continues to be studied (Schultz & Andreasen, 1999).

Historically, these facts were unknown. The causes of schizophrenia were largely attributed to environmental factors, particularly to faulty family dynamics that specifically blamed the mother. The term "schizophrenogenic mother" described a prevailing causal theory for the illness. The mother was defined as being dominant, overprotective but basically rejecting of the child (Park, 1982). Excellent correlation was noted between the fact that mothers of persons diagnosed with schizophrenia interacted differently with them, and such differences in interaction were assumed to be the cause of schizophrenia. Research later showed that the mother who could cause schizophrenia in her offspring did not exist. A great deal of harm may have been caused by unwarranted blaming attacks (which had no scientific merit) on this group of mothers (Neil, 1990).

One such mother relates that she was told that she was "toxic" to her daughter. Her reflection on those times and events was that although she never believed that she had caused her daughter's illness, it hurt her to know that the professionals believed that she had (Gardner, 1993). Heeding such mismatches between assumed knowledge and truth in the past can help us avoid making similar mistakes currently.

Anecdotal accounts by persons who suffer from psychiatric disorders and those who relate closely with them often mention the presence in the person who has the disorder of corresponding extraordinary talents that are not disordered. Such strengths are important to consider. A woman who has had a diagnosis of schizophrenia for a number of years consulted with a specialist for services not related to schizophrenia. The person in charge of billing asked to see her insurance card and commented on examining it that she must have a disability. The woman seeking treatment replied quickly, "Yes, but I also have ability."

EXPANDED ROLES FOR SOCIAL WORKERS

Social workers need to play an expanded role in the area of genetic counseling. This vision is based on the fact that social workers are well suited to be the professional link between society and persons within that society who have genetic disorders. Social workers need to connect with the basic scientific information, medical clinicians, and the social science researchers who provide material to be considered in terms of causes, treatments, and potential prevention techniques and technologies. It is the social worker who translates and applies what is known to basic human needs:

1.   Social workers can encourage high-trust relationships between professional providers and those who seek services and their caregivers. High-trust relationships are based on mutual honesty, mutual respect, and mutual regard. In seeking to build on strengths, the social worker can advocate for systems that respect persons' abilities and strengths before considering disability or dysfunction.

2.   Social workers need to know the basics of genetics and the role of behavioral genetics not only to counsel persons regarding what we know, but also about what we don't know, and what we cannot predict in terms of outcomes.

3.   Social workers can lead persons who suffer and their families to programs of hope, empowerment, and recovery (Hall & Nelson, 1996; Corrigan & Garman, 1997; Burland, 1998). It is very important that the person who is ill is perceived and supported as a person of potential contribution, and not as a problem or burden. Supporting person's strengths, abilities, and potential contributions is, perhaps, as important as being sensitive to potential "abuse" of disabled persons by those who are overwhelmed by the burden of care, particularly in the face of systems that fail to provide

needed services. Empowerment of persons who are ill and their families comes through education and support. Educating consumers, family members, the public, and other providers is a primary responsibility of social workers.

4. Social workers can educate and advocate for healthy interdependence between all people. Seeing all persons as having strengths and weaknesses and as having potential for both giving and receiving caring support can keep the world of professionals from making unwarranted judgments and punitive restrictions on anyone.

James Thurber wrote, "Let us not look back in anger, nor forward in fear, but let us look around us in awareness." It is easy to look backward at the misunderstandings and injustices that have been done, and become angry. It is easy to look forward and become afraid, especially with the kind of fear that is rooted in confusion about what is to be believed and what is not. But Thurber challenges us (regardless of why we are interested in genetics, environment, and development and regardless of our views regarding nature and / or nurture) to become fully aware of the importance and implications of those elements of understanding that make critical differences in persons' lives.

NOTE

1. The author acknowledges support from the Indiana consortium for Mental Health Services Research (ICMHSR), Institute of Social Research of Indiana University.

REFERENCES

Billings, P. R., Beckwith, J., & Alper, J. S. (1992). The genetic analysis of human behavior: A new era? *Social Science and Medicine, 35*, 227–238.

Burland, J. (1998). Family-to-Family: A trauma-and-recovery model of family education. *New Directions for Mental Health Services, 77*, 33–41.

Corrigan, P. W., & Garman, A. N. (1997). Considerations for research on consumer empowerment and psychosocial interventions. *Psychiatric Services, 48*, 347–352.

Gardner, A. (1993). A mother's story. In Mental Illness: A Family Perspective. Indianapolis, IN: National Alliance for Mentally Ill (NAMI).

Hall, G. B., & Nelson, G. (1996). Social networks, social support, personal empowerment, and the adaptation of psychiatric consumers / survivors: Path analytic models. *Social Science and Medicine, 43*, 1743–1754.

Mann, C. C. (1994). Behavioral genetics in transition. *Science, 264*, 1686–1689.

Neil, J. (1990). Whatever became of the schizophrenogenic mother? *American Journal of Psychotherapy, 44,* 499–505.

Neilsen, D. A., Virkkunen, M., Lappalainen, J., Eggert, M. Brown, G. L., Long, J. C., Goldman, D., & Linnoila, M. (1998). A tryptophan hydroxylase gene marker for suicidality and alcoholism. *Archives of General Psychiatry, 55,* 593–602.

Owen, M. J., & McGuffin, P. (1997). Genetics in psychiatry. *British Journal of Psychiatry, 17,* 201–202.

Park, G. (1982). Re-searching the schizophrenogenic mother. *Journal of Nervous and Mental Diseases, 170,* 452–462.

Plomin, R., & Rutter, M., (1998). Child development, molecular genetics, and what to do with genes once they are found. *Child Development, 69,* 1223–1242.

Rutter, M., & Plomin, R. (1997). Opportunities for psychiatry from genetic findings. *British Journal of Psychiatry, 17,* 209–219.

Schultz, S. K., & Andreasen, N. C. (1999). Schizophrenia. *Lancet, 353,* 1425–1430.

Sherman, S. L., DeFries, J. C., Gottesman, I. I., Loehlin, J. C., Meyer, J. M., Pelias, M. Z., Rice, J., & Waldman, I. (1997). Recent developments in human behavioral genetics: Past accomplishments and future directions. *American Journal of Human Genetics, 60,* 1265–1275.

Index

Abelson, R. P., 318
Accommodation, 186
Active construction of personal knowl-
    edge, 179
Adaptation
    biopsychological functioning and,
        40–43
    in cognitive stages, 186
    ecological perspective and, 275–277,
        280
    psychoanalytic theory and, 86–87
    psychological health and, 86–87
    social constructionist theory and,
        324–325
Adaptive systems, 232–234
Administration, 54
Adoption, 401, 408
Africentricity, 9
Aging, 190–191
Alcohol, birth defects and, 402–403
Allen, J., 41
American Academy of Psychothera-
    pists Tape Library, 159
American Psychiatric Association, 41,
    324, 371
American Society of Human Genetics,
    408
Amniocentesis, 407
Amundson, J., 325
Anal retentiveness, 86
Anal stage, 86, 118–119
Anastasi, Anne, 400
Anderson, H., 344

Anderson, R. E., 52, 215
Andrada, P. A., 130–131
Anthropology, 264–265
Antifeminism, 88
Anxiety, 83
Anzaldua, G., 363
Appel, Y. H., 286
Assessment
    of client strengths, guidelines for,
        42–43
    cognitive theory and, 195–196
    defined, 22
    ecological perspective and, 290–291
    general systems theory and, 240–241
    positivist theory and, 22–23
    postmodern theory and, 23–24
Assimilation, 186
Attitude, 158–159
Attributions, 184–185
Austin, L. N., 290
Author's Guide to Social Work Journals,
    An, 386
Autonomy, 118–119
Autosomes, 391–392

Bandura, A., 182–183
Barker, R., 250, 253
Barnes, G., 291
Bartky, S. L., 370
Bartlett, H. M., 17
Bateson, G., 226
Beck, A. T., 177
Becoming a Person (Rogers), 154

Behavioral genetics, 400–402
Belief systems, religious, 63–69
Berger, P., 341
Berger, R., 230
Berlin, S., 196–197
Bern, S. L., 126
Bertalanffy, L., 216, 221
Bibring, G., 290
Bicultural environment, 277
Biculturalism, 235
Biegel, D. E., 281
Biestek, F. B., 145
Binet, A., 185
Biological development, 36–37
Biological time, 277
Biopsychological functioning
    adaptation and, 40–43
    biological development and, 36–37
    direct practice in social work and,
        39–40
    psychological development and, 38–
        39
    sociocultural development and, 37–
        38
Biopsychosocial interactions, 359–360
Birth defects, 402–403
Blank slate, 271
Blood type, 396
Blumer, H., 266
Boyd, T. A., 67
Brain research, 207
Briar, S., 6
Bricker-Jenkins, M., 383–384
Bromley, M. C., 242
Bronfenbrenner, U., 113, 259, 270–271,
    274, 280
Buckley, W., 223, 230, 232–233
Bullis, R., 67
Bunch, Charlotte, 362–364
Burnside, I., 130
Burrell, G., 311
Bush, J. A., 218
Butler, R. N., 129
Butler, Sandra, 352

Canda, E. R., 67
Caroff, P., 41

Carroll, M., 65
Carter, I., 215
Carter, L., 52
Casework
    cognitive theory, 197, 200
    ecological perspective, 286–288
    feminist theories, 371–375
    general systems theory, 242–243
    genetic theories, 405, 408–409
    Perlman's view of, 20
    person-centered approach, 159–162
    social work and, 20
Causality, 187, 268
Cavalcante, G. F., 325
Chestang, L., 235
Chin, R., 215, 237, 241
Chorionic villus sampling, 407
Chromosomes, 391–399
Circular questioning, 24
Classification, 187
Client strengths, guidelines for assess-
    ing, 42–43
Client-centered therapy, 147
Clock time, 277
Closed systems, 228
Code of Social Work Ethics (NASW),
    44–47, 66
Codominant genes, 396
Coercive power, 303
Cognition, 178–181
Cognitive dissonance, 189
Cognitive domain, 178
Cognitive processes, 181–185
Cognitive revolution, 176–177
Cognitive science, 104
Cognitive stages, 185–188
Cognitive structures, 182–185
Cognitive theory
    in adulthood, 189
    assessment and, 195–196
    assumptions, basic, 178–181
    brain research and, 207
    casework, 197, 200
    in childhood, 185–189
    cognitive process and, 181–185
    cognitive structures and, 182–185
    concepts, 181–185

critique, 206–211
cross-cultural practice in social work
  and, 191–193
development across life cycle and,
  185–191
direct practice in social work and,
  194–200
families and, 193–194
functioning of humans and, 193–194
genetic science and, 207
groups and, 194
historical context, 174–178
information process models of, 177
intervention and, 196–200
in old age, 189–191
person-in-environment perspective
  and, 174–176
Piaget and, 176–177, 185–188
policy-practice curriculum and, 207–
  208
self and, 182–183
social work and, 173–174, 177–178,
  208–211
stages of cognitive development
  and, 185–188
terminology, basic, 203–205
Cohen, J., 80–81
Cohort theory, 271
Coles, R., 275
Collins, P. H., 352
Comas-Diaz, L., 364
Communication, family, 225–227
Communities
  feminist theories and, 367–368
  organization of, 54
  person-centered approach and, 155
  social constructionist theory and,
    327–328
Competence, 111, 272–273
Complementarity of roles, 225
Complex adaptive systems, 232–234
Compton, B., 221
Compulsion, 119
Concepts, defined, 182
Conceptual imperative, 302–303
Concrete operational stage, 187
Congres, E. P., 284

Congruence, 148, 158
Consciousness, 79–80
Conservation, 187
Constructionism, 11 (*see also* Social
  constructionist theory)
Contextualized theories, 8
Cooper, S., 43
Coping skills, 276
Corbett, Lucille, 65
Corey, G., 128–129
Cornett, C., 39–40
Council on Social Work Education
  (CSWE), 15, 32, 66
Coyle, G. L., 284
Cri-du-chat (cat cry) syndrome, 393
Crises, 115–124
Critical theory, 9
Critique
  Cognitive theory and, 206–211
  ecological perspective, 301–306
  ego psychology, 143–144
  feminist theories, 381–386
  general systems theory, 250–256
  genetic theories, 414–418
  human behavior theory, 13–14
  moral development, 143–144
  person-centered approach, 166–170
  psychoanalytic theory, 102–105
  social constructionist theory, 341–
    347
Cross-cultural invariance theory, 192
Cross-cultural practice in social work
  cognitive theory and, 191–193
  ecological perspective and, 277–279
  ego psychology and, 124–126
  general systems theory and, 234–236
  genetic theories and, 403–404
  human behavior theory and, 43–47
  person-centered approach and, 153–
    154
  psychoanalytic theory and, 87–89
  social constructionist theory and,
    325–326
Crossing over, 394
CSWE, 15, 32, 66
Culturagram, 284–285
Cultural feminist theory, 356–357

Cultural time, 277
Culture, 234–235, 326 (*see also* Cross-
    cultural practice in social work)
Cutler, Carolyn, 324–325
Cystic fibrosis, 396, 397

Dance of Anger (Lerner), 371
Darwinian theory, 77
de Amorin, A., 325
De Hoyos, G., 221
Dean, R., 21, 341–344, 347
"Decade of the Brain" (federal research
    initiative), 207
Declaration of Sentiments, 381
Deconstructionism, 332
Dementia, 191–192
Demographics, 283–284
Denial, 83
Deoxyribonucleic acid (DNA), 390–
    391, 402
Despair, 123–124
Determinism, 79, 179–180
Development across life cycle
    cognitive theory and, 185–191
    ecological perspective and, 270–277
    ego psychology and, 114–124
    general systems theory and, 229–234
    genetic theories and, 402–403
    human behavior theory and, 32–36
    life span development and, 33–36
    person-centered approach and, 151–
        153
    personality and, 107–109
    positivist theory and, 32–36
    postmodern theory and, 34–36
    psychoanalytic theory and, 84–87
    social constructionist theory and,
        319–325
Developmental model, 84–87
Developmental theory (*see* Develop-
    ment across life cycle; *specific
    types*)
Developmentally instigating character-
    istics, 271
*Diagnostic and Statistical Manual of
    Mental Disorders* (DSM), 371
Diagnostic and Statistical Manual of

Mental Disorders Fourth Edition
    (DSM-IV), 41, 191
*Diagnostic and Statistics Manual of Men-
    tal Disorders Third Edition, Revised*
    (DSM-III-R), 324
Differentiation, 112, 225
Direct practice in social work
    biopsychosocial functioning and,
        39–40
    cognitive theory and, 194–200
    ecological perspective and, 288–292
    ego psychology and, 127–131
    feminist theories and, 367–375
    general systems theory and, 239–243
    genetic theories and, 406–409, 417–
        418
    intervention and, 18–21
    person-centered approach and, 156–
        162
    psychoanalytic theory and, 80–81,
        91–93
    social constructionist theory and,
        328–333
    theoretical framework for, 1–2
    theory and, 1
Disdain, 123
Dissonance, 189
Diversity, 333, 361–365 (*see also* Cross-
    cultural practice in social work)
DNA, 390–391, 402
Dominant genes, 395–397
Down syndrome, 393, 403
Draper, B. J., 279
Dream analysis, 80, 92
Drive theory, 83–84, 105
DSM, 371
DSM-III-R, 324
DSM-IV, 41, 191
Dual perspective, 234–235
Duncan, B. L., 25
Dymond, R. F., 329
Dynamic model, 83–84
Dysfunctional communication, 227
Dysfunctional families, 229

Eclectic orientation, 25
Eco-map, 282–284

Ecological perspective
adaptation and, 275–277, 280
anthropology and, 264–265
assessment and, 290–291
assumptions, basic, 268–270
casework, 286–288
competence and, 272–273
conceptual imperative for, 302–303
critique, 301–306
cross-cultural practice in social work
and, 277–279
development across life cycle and,
270–277
direct practice in social work and,
288–292
ecology and, 261, 264
ego psychology and, 265
ethology and, 264
evolutionary biology and, 264
families and, 281–284
functioning of humans and, 280–288
general systems theory and, 267
Gestalt school of psychology and,
265–266
groups and, 284–288
habitat and, 274
humanistic psychology and, 266–
267
intervention and, 291–292
life course and, 271–272
life span development and, 35
niche and, 274
overview, 259–261
person-centered approach and, 168
person-in-environment perspective
and, 261–268
power and, 267–268, 279
practice imperative for, 304–305
relatedness and, 272
research imperative for, 303–304
role of social worker and, 394–395
role theory and, 266
roles and, 273–274
social work and, 259–261, 302–303
stress theory and, 265
terminology, basic, 268–270, 298–
300

theoretical foundations, 261–263
value imperative for, 306
view of, 9
Ecology, 261, 264
Economic model, 79
Ego, 82–83
Ego defenses, 83
Ego identity, 109, 113–114, 118
Ego psychologists, 109
Ego psychology
assumptions, basic, 110–114
background information, 107–109
critique, 143–144
cross-cultural practice in social work
and, 124–126
development across life cycle and,
114–124
direct practice in social work and,
127–131
ecological perspective and, 265
families and, 126–127
functioning of humans and, 126–127
gender identity and, 125–126
groups and, 126–127, 129–131
moral development and, 137–144
person-in-environment perspective
and, 109–110
personality and, 107–109
psychoanalytic theory and, 73, 77–78
social work and, 107–109
terminology, basic, 110–114, 133–136
Electra complex, 86
Ellis, A., 177–178
Emery, G., 208
Empathy, 142, 148, 157
Empirical knowledge, 11
Empowerment, 167, 291–292, 371
Energy, 228
Environment
bicultural, 277
defined, 273–274
families and, 227–229
Epigenesis, 112
Epistasis, 397
Epistemological approaches, changes
in, 3–4 (*see also specific types*)
Epston, D., 330

Equilibrium, 228–229, 250
Erikson, Eric, 73, 78, 107–131, 137–144,
    319, 356, 361 (*see also* Ego psychol-
    ogy)
Eriksonian theory (*see* Ego psychology)
Erlich, J. L., 324
Espin, O. M., 363, 369–370
Ethnosystem, 236
Ethology, 264
Eurocentric models, 9
Evolutionary biology, 264
Evolutionary time, 277
Ewalt, P., 20
Existential philosophy, 146
Exosystem, 280
Expectancies, 184–185
Exploitative power, 303
Expressivity, 397
External resources, 276
Eye color, 395–396

Faith, 64, 67 (*see also* Spirituality)
Falck, H. S., 51
Families
    cognitive theory and, 193–194
    communication and, 225–227
    definitions of, 50, 222
    dysfunctional, 229
    ecological perspective and, 281–284
    ego psychology and, 126–127
    environment and, 227–229
    feminist theories and, 365
    functional, 229
    functioning of humans and, 48–50
    general systems theory and, 224,
        230–232, 238–239
    genetic theories and, 405
    human behavior theory and, 48–50
    kibbutz and, 143
    organizational properties of, 223–225
    person-centered approach and, 154–
        155
    postmodern theory and, 49
    psychoanalytic theory and, 89–90
    roles of, 225
    social constructionist theory and,
        346–347

as social systems, 222, 231
    social work and, 48–50
    structure of, 223–225
Family development, 224, 230–232
Family services field, 53
Family therapy, 241–243, 346–347
FAS, 403
Federico, R., 230
Feedback, 226
Feminist theories
    assumptions, basic, 358–359
    biopsychosocial interactions and,
        359–361
    casework, 371–375
    communities and, 365–367
    concepts, basic, 358–359
    critique, 381–386
    cultural, 355–356
    direct practice in social work and,
        367–375
    diversity in, 361–365
    families and, 365
    functioning of humans and, 365–367
    groups and, 366
    historical perspective, 352, 381–382
    lesbian feminism and, 362, 363
    liberal, 353–354, 382
    partnership building and, 368
    person-in-environment perspective
        and, 361
    positivist theory and, 358
    postmodern, 365
    power and, 11, 370
    psychoanalytic theory and, 88
    radical, 354–355, 381
    social work and, 351, 375, 383–387
    socialist, 357–358, 382
    terminology, basic, 378–380
    theoretical development of, 352–358
    womanism and, 363–364
Feminist Visions for Social Work (Van
    Den Bergh), 384
Fetal alcohol syndrome (FAS), 403
Fetal blood testing, 407
Fidelity, 121
Field, 266
Fiene, J. I., 346

Findlay, P. C., 219
Fischer, J., 146
Fixation, 85
Flavell, J. H., 185
Fleck-Henderson, A., 42, 343–344
Fleming, R. C., 184
Fletcher, J., 342
Formal operational stage, 187–188
Frame of reference, 304
Free association, 92
Freedom, 148
Freeman, D., 68
Freire, Paulo, 345
Freud, Sigmund, 73–93, 102–105, 118–119, 121 (*see also* Psychoanalytic theory)
Freudian theory (*see* Psychoanalytic theory)
Frye, M., 359
Functional families, 229
Functioning of humans
    cognitive theory and, 193–194
    ecological perspective and, 280–288
    ego psychology and, 126–127
    families, 48–50
    feminist theories and, 365–367
    general systems theory and, 236–239
    genetic theories and, 405
    groups, 51–52
    human behavior theory and, 8, 47–52
    person-centered approach and, 154–155
    psychoanalytic theory and, 89–91
    social constructionist theory and, 327–328
    understanding, 47–48
Functioning whole, 112

Galaway, B., 221
Gametes, 391
Garrod, Archibald, 389
Garvin, C. D., 52
Geertz, C., 316
Gender differences, 353
Gender identity, 125–126

General systems theory
    assessment and, 240–241
    assumptions, basic, 224–229
    casework, 242–243
    critique, 250–256
    cross-cultural practice in social work and, 234–236
    development across life cycle and, 229–234
    direct practice in social work and, 239–243
    ecological perspective and, 267
    families and, 224, 230–232, 238–239
    functioning of humans and, 236–239
    intervention and, 241
    person-in-environment perspective and, 219–221
    psychoanalytic theory and, 220
    social learning theory and, 254–255
    in social sciences, 251–252
    social work and, 4, 6, 215, 252–254
    structure, 223–225
    terminology, basic, 224–229, 247–249
Generativity versus stagnation, 122–123
Genetic counseling, 408
Genetic model, 84–87
Genetic predisposition, 399
Genetic science, 207
Genetic screening, 406–408
Genetic theories
    assumptions, basic, 390–399
    casework, 405, 408–409
    childhood and, 127
    chromosomes and, 391–399
    codominant genes and, 396
    critique, 414–418
    cross-cultural practice in social work and, 403–404
    development across life cycle and, 402–403
    direct practice in social work and, 406–409, 417–418
    dominant genes and, 395–397
    expectations and, 416–417
    families and, 405
    functioning of humans and, 405

Genetic theories (*cont.*)
  HbS allele and, 404
  Hemizygosity and, 397–398
  heredity and, 389
  heterozygous genes and, 394–397
  holandric genes and, 398
  homozygous genes and, 394–397
  nature versus nurture and, 414–416
  overview, 389–390
  person-in-environment perspective
    and, 399–402
  recessive genes and, 395–397
  role of social worker and, 417–418
  scientific perspectives and, 104
  social work and, 389–390
  terminology, basic, 390–399, 411–413
Genital stage, 86, 119, 121
Genogram, 283
Genome Database, 390
Genotype, 395
Genuineness, 158
Gergen, K. J., 35–36, 341
Germain, C. B., 17, 43, 74, 232, 261, 276,
  313
Germinal mutation, 394
Gestalt school of psychology, 265–266
Gibbs, J. T., 154
Gillespie, J., 252–253
Gilligan, C., 88, 126, 143, 341, 356,
  360–361
Gilmartin, R. M., 345
Gitterman, A., 17, 43, 276
Glantz, M. D., 209
Goal formulation, 154
God representation, 64, 67 (*see also*
  Spirituality)
Goldberg, G., 52
Goldstein, E., 31, 275
Goldstein, H., 315
Goodness-of-fit, 269, 278
Goolishian, H., 344
Gordon, L., 342
Gordon, W. E., 220
Gorey, K. M., 252
Gould, K. H., 88
Green, J., 44, 331
Greene, R. R., 291

Greif, G. L., 305
Griffin, J., 67
Group Psychology and the Analysis of Ego
  (Freud), 90
Groups
  cognitive theory and, 194
  ecological perspective and, 284–288
  ego psychology and, 126–127, 129–
    131
  feminist theories and, 366–367
  functioning of humans and, 51–52
  human behavior theory and, 51–52
  intervention with older, 129–131
  person-centered approach and, 155
  platica, 130–131
  psychoanalytic theory and, 90–91
  social constructionist theory and,
    345–346
  social work and, 51–52
Guba, E. G., 3–4
Guidano, V. F., 316
Guterman, J. T., 342

Habitat, 274
Hale, W., 35
Hamilton, A. K., 408–409
Hamilton, N. G., 74, 77
Hardcastle, J., 343
Hare-Mustin, R. T., 332
Hartmann, A., 281–282, 284
Hartmann, H., 357
Hayek, F. A., 316
HbS allele, 404
Hearn, G., 221, 230
Helping process, 20–22
Helping relationship, 148–149
Hemizygosity, 397–398
Heredity (*see* Genetic theories)
Herr, J. J., 239
Heterosexism, 362
Heterosexuality, 363
Heterozygous genes, 394–397
Hierarchical reorganization, 114
Hierarchy, 225
Historical moment, 124–125
Holandric genes, 398
Hollis, F., 74

Holon, 223
Holzner, B., 304
Homeostasis, 228
Homophobia, 363
Homosexuality, 88–89, 126, 363
Homozygous genes, 394–397
hooks, b., 358, 363, 368
Hooyman, N. R., 44, 384
Horror of time concept, 93
Human behavior theory (*see also specific types*)
    biopsychological functioning and, 36–43
    critique, 13–14
    cross-cultural social work practice and, 43–47
    development across life cycle and, 32–36
    families and, 48–50
    functioning of humans and, 8, 47–52
    groups and, 51–52
    limitations of, 8
    organizations and, 53–55
    psychoanalytic theory and, 73–75
    social constructionist theory and, 321–322
    social work and, 3–8, 31–32, 49
    social work methods and, 21–26
    working knowledge of, 15–16
Human development, 32–36 (*see also* Development across life cycle; *specific theories*)
Human Genome Project, 390
Human services field, 53
Humanistic philosophy, 146, 266–267
Hussein, Saddam, 342

Id, 81–82
Identification
    confusion, 121
    defined, 83
    ego, 109, 113–114, 118
    Freud's view of, 83, 86
    gender, 125–126
    psychosocial, 114
    sexual, 88–89, 116, 126
Identity, defined, 121

Identity formation, 114
Identity versus identity confusion, 121
Imre, R. W., 310
Individual development, 229–230
Individual dysfunction, 23–24
Individual-in-the-mass, 127
Individual-within-his-family, 127
Industry versus inferiority, 120
Inertia, 120
Inferiority, 120
Information exchange, 175
Information-processing models, 177
Inhibition, 119
Input, 226
Insight, 128
Institute of Mental Health, 129
Institutional racism, 277–278
Integrity versus despair, 123–124
Intelligence, 187
Intentionality, 187
Interdisciplinary cooperation, 207–208
Internal locus of evaluation, 152
Internal resources, 276
Internal-External Change Balance, 15
Interpretation, 92, 128
Intervention
    cognitive theory and, 196–200
    direct practice in social work and, 18–21
    ecological perspective and, 291–292
    general systems theory and, 241
    group, 129–131
    person-in-environment perspective and, 17
    positivist theory and, 25
    social constructionist theory and, 330–331, 345–346
Intimacy versus isolation, 121–122
Introjection, 83
Intuitive knowledge, 11–12
Irizarry, C., 286
Isolation, 121–122

Jackson, D. D., 226
Jenkins, J. H., 317–318
Jensen, C., 221

Johnson, H., 41
Justice, social and economic, 278

Kadushin, A., 81, 146
Kagan, J., 185, 189
Karno, M., 317–318
Kearney, J., 221
Keith-Lucas, A., 66
Keller, J. F., 242
Kelly, G., 318, 341
Kibbutz, 143
Kitzinger, C., 363
Klinefelter syndrome, 393
Knowing-in-practice, 12
Knowledge, 11–12, 179, 322–325
Kohlberg, L., 137–144, 356, 361 (*see also*
    Moral development)
Korte, A. O., 130–131
Kuhn, T., 215, 311

Land, H., 235, 352, 366, 375
Lang, N., 52
Language, 318–319, 329, 342
Latency stage, 86, 120
Latent content, 92
Learning disabled, 325
Lee, J. A. B., 329–330
Leibniz, G., 253
Leighninger, L., 220
Lerner, Harriet, 371
Lerner, R. M., 400
Lesbian feminism, 362–363
Lewandowski, C. A., 67
Lewin, K., 266
Lewis, R., 236
Liberal feminist theory, 353–354, 382
Lieberman, F., 74
Liebow, Elliot, 329
Life course, 35, 271–272
Life cycle approach, 112 (*see also* Devel-
    opment across life cycle)
Life space, 266
Life span development, 33–36
Lineal orienting questions, 24
Locke, John, 360
Loevinger, J., 137
Lorde, A., 363–364

Luckmann, T., 341
Lukes, C. A., 235
Lynch, A. A., 305

MacDonald, G., 252–253
Macrosystem, 280
Mahler, M. S., 102
Mahoney, M. J., 315–316
Maluccio, A. N., 290
Manifest content, 92
Mann, X., 93
Marecek, J., 332
Markstrom-Adams, C., 126
Marx, J. H., 304
Marx, Karl, 253
Marxism, 9
Maslow, A. H., 153, 266
Maternal serum alpha-fetoprotein
    screen (MSAFP), 407
Mattanin, M. A., 303, 305
Mead, G. H., 266
Mead, Margaret, 264
Meaning, 318
Mediating role of cognition, 179–181
Medical model, 74, 220
Meiosis, 394
Mendel, G., 389
Mental health, 86–87
Mesosytem, 280–281
Meyer, C., 19–20, 22, 31, 216, 220, 253,
    303, 305
Microsystem, 280–281
Middleman, R. R., 52
Midlife crisis, 122–123
Miller, H., 6
Miller, Jean Baker, 360–361
Miller, S., 235
Mind, 323
Minuchin, S., 231
Moral development
    background information, 138
    critique, 143–144
    ego psychology and, 137–144
    Kohlberg's framework for, 138–141
    social work and, 137, 141–144
Morgan, G., 311
Morphogenesis, 232

MSAFP, 407
Multifactorial conditions, 399
Multiple allelic system, 396
Mutation, gene, 394

Narrative, 318–319
NASW, 44–47, 66
National Association of Social Workers
    (NASW), 44–47, 66
National Organization for Women,
    354
Nature versus nurture, 414–416
Newborn screening, 406–407
Newman, B., 389
Newman, P. R., 389
Niche, 274
Noble, D. N., 408–409
Nondeterministic view, 178–179
Nondirective counseling, 147
Nonpassive warmth, 148, 157
Normative crisis, 128
Normative event, 116
North American Association of Christ-
    ian Social Workers, 66
Northern, H., 51
Norton, D. G., 218, 234–235
Not for Women Only (Bricker-Jenkins
    and Hooyman), 384
Nuccio, K., 359
Nurius, P. S., 183

Object permanence, 186–187
Object relations theory, 78–79
Oedipal stage, 86
Oedipus conflict, 86, 119
Open systems, 228
Optimistic view, 178–179
Oral stage, 85, 118–120
Organic effects, 400
Organismic valuing processes, 150–
    153
Organizations
    defined, 223
    families and, 223–225
    human behavior theory and, 53–55
    social work and, 53–55
Output, 226

Palombo, J., 315
Paradigm, 3–4, 13, 19–20
Partnership building, 368
Pathology-Health Balance, 15
Patriarchy, 360–362
Payne, M., 253
Penetrance, 397
Perkins, R., 362
Perlman, H. H., 20, 266
Person-centered approach
    assumptions, basic, 148–151
    casework, 159–162
    community and, 155
    critique, 166–170
    cross-cultural practice in social work
        and, 153–154
    development during life cycle and,
        151–153
    direct practice in social work and,
        155–162
    ecological perspective and, 168
    families and, 154–155
    feminist social work practice and,
        168–169
    functioning of humans and, 154–155
    in future, 169–170
    groups and, 155
    person-in-environment perspective
        and, 146–148
    Rogers and, 145–146
    role of social worker and, 158–162
    self and, 151–152
    strengths perspective and, 167
    terminology, basic, 148–151, 164–
        165
    therapeutic conditions and, 157–158
Person-environment exchanges, 9
Person-in-environment perspective
    cognitive theory and, 174–176
    ecological perspective and, 261–268
    ego psychology and, 109–110
    feminist theories and, 361
    general systems theory and, 219–221
    genetic theories and, 399–402
    intervention and, 17
    person-centered approach and, 146–
        148

Person-in-environment perspective
    (*cont.*)
  positivist theory and, 20
  postmodern theory and, 17–21
  psychoanalytic theory and, 75–79
  social constructionist theory and,
      310–316
  social learning theory and, 254–255
  social work and, 1–2, 16–18, 31–32
Personal is political concept, 359–361
Personal order, 111
Personal problem-solving model, 196,
    198–199
Personal-Societal Impact Balance, 15
Personality, 107–109, 156–158, 266
Phallic stage, 86
Phelan, S., 363
Phenomenal self, 152
Phenomenological theories, 151, 266
Phenotype, 395
Phenotypes, 396–397
Phenylketonuria (PKU), 396, 406–407
Piaget, Jean, 176–177, 185–188
Pinderhughes, E., 154, 279
PKU, 396, 406–407
Platica group, 130–131
Pleasure principle, 82
Pleiotropy, 396–397
Plomin, R., 400
Polanyi, M., 326
Policy-practice curriculum, 207–208
Polsky, H., 238
Poor fit between person and environ-
    ment, 175
Positivist theory
  assessment and, 22–23
  development across life cycle and,
      32–36
  feminist theories and, 358
  intervention and, 25
  person-in-environment perspective
      and, 20
  social work and, 6
  theoretical assumptions of, 11
  view of, 9
Possible self, 183
Postmodern theory

  assessment and, 23–24
  Dean and, 21
  Development across life cycle and,
      34–36
  families and, 49
  feminist, 365–366
  life span development and, 34–36
  person-in-environment perspective
      and, 17–21
  power and, 11
  renaming, 25–26
  social work and, 12, 31–32
  spirituality and, 65
  view of, 11–13
Power
  coercive, 303
  ecological perspective and, 267–268,
      279
  exploitative, 303
  feminist theories and, 11, 370
  Pinderhughes's definition of, 279
  postmodern theory and, 11
  social constructionist theory and,
      324–325
Practice imperative, 304–305
Practitioner-Client Control Balance, 15
Pragmatism, 207–208
Preconscious mental processes, 79
Prelogical thinking, 187
Prenatal testing, 407–408
Preoperational stage, 187
Primary process thinking, 82
Privileges, 9–11
Problem-solving sequence, 196, 198–
    199
Process
  of construction, 325–326
  of language-in-use, 310
  orientation, 269
  working through, 92–93
Projection, 83
Propositions, 182
Psychiatric disorders, 416–417
PsychINFO database, 251–252
Psycho-historical side, 114
Psychoanalytic theory
  adaptation and, 86–87

antifeminism and, 88
assumptions, basic, 79–84
contemporary, 77–78
critique, 102–105
cross-cultural practice in social work
    and, 87–89
development across life cycle and,
    84–87
developments in, new, 102–105
direct practice in social work and,
    80–81, 91–93
ego psychology and, 73, 77–78
families and, 89–90
feminist theories and, 88
functioning of humans and, 89–91
general systems theory and, 220
groups and, 90–91
homosexuality and, 88–89
human behavior theory and, 73–75
person-in-environment perspective
    and, 75–79
scientific perspectives on, 103–105
social work and, 4, 6
terminology, basic, 79–84, 97–101
Psychological development, 38–39
Psychological health, 86–87
Psychological time, 277
Psychosexual development, 116
Psychosexual stages, 84–86
Psychosocial crises, 115–124
Psychosocial development, 116
Psychosocial identity, 114
Psychosocial theory, 12
Pugliesi, K., 346
Pyknodysostosis, 397

Racism, institutional, 277–278
Radical feminist theory, 354–355, 382
Rationalization, 83
Rauch, J. B., 405
Reaction formation, 83
Reality principle, 82
Reality testing, 83
Recessive genes, 395–397
Reciprocal causality, 268
Reciprocal determinism, 179–180
Reduced penetrance, 397

Reductionism, 76
Reflection-about-action, 12
"Reflections on Dual Perspective"
    (Miller), 235
Reflexive questions, 24
Regression, 83, 85
Rejection, 121
Relatedness, 272
Relational models, 102–103, 105
Relief and Aid and Charity Organiza-
    tion Societies, 48
Religion, 64, 67 (*see also* Spirituality)
Representational intelligence, 187
Repression, 83
Repudiation, 121
Research imperative, 303–304
Resistance, 92
Resources, external and internal, 276
Restorying people's lives, 330–332
Reversibility, 187
Reynolds, B., 40, 65–66, 219, 259–260
Rhodes, S. L., 231
Richmond, Mary, 20, 74, 219, 259
Riley, M. W., 113
Rivera, F. G., 324
Rizzuto, A., 64
Robbins, S. P., 15
Rodwell, M. K., 313
Rogers, Carl, 145–162, 166–170, 266, 329
    (*see also* Person-centered approach)
Role of social worker (*see also* Cross-
    cultural practice in social work;
    Direct practice in social work;
    Social work)
    ecological perspective and, 394–395
    genetic theories and, 417–418
    person-centered approach and, 158–
    162
    social constructionist theory and,
    332–333
Role theory, 266
Roles, 225, 273–274
Root, M. P. P., 370
Rowe, W., 155
Rules, 226
Rusk, G. S., 25
Russell, Bertrand, 311

Saari, C., 315, 329
Saleeby, D., 14–15, 39, 315
Sanders, C. L., 218
Sands, R. G., 359
Sanville, J., 329
Satir, V., 227
Schank, R. C., 318
Schemata, 182
Schiele, J. H., 9
Schizophrenia, 416–417
Schon, D., 12, 328
Schwartz, W., 18
Scientific perspectives, 103–105
Scientific thinking, 187
Screening, genetic, 406–408
Searles, H. F., 265
Secondary process thinking, 82
Self
    change and, 328–330
    cognitive theory and, 182–183
    person-centered approach and, 151–
        152
    possible, 183
    social constructionist theory and,
        324
Self-awareness, 129
Self-concept, 182
Self-efficacy, 182–183, 265
Self-esteem, 273
Self-evaluation, 150–152
Selye, H., 265
Seneca Falls (New York) convention,
    382
Sensorimotor stage, 186–187
Seriation, 187
Sex chromosomes, 392–393
Sex-influenced traits, 398
Sex-limited traits, 398–399
Sexism, 360
Sexual orientation, 88–89
Shafer, R., 330
Shame, 118–119
Sheldon, B., 252–253
Shulman, L., 81
Sickle-cell anemia, 396, 403–404, 406
Significant interaction, 113
Siporin, M., 221

Smith, E., 67–68
Social addresses, 274
Social Construction of Reality, The (Ber-
    ger and Luckmann), 341
Social constructionist theory
    adaptation and, 324–325
    assumptions, basic, 316–319, 341–
        342
    biological propensities of, 322–323
    communities and, 327–328
    critique, 341–347
    cross-cultural practice in social work
        and, 325–326
    culture and, 326
    development across life cycle and,
        319–325
    direct practice in social work and,
        328–333
    families and, 346–347
    functioning of humans and, 327–328
    groups and, 345–346
    guidelines for, 320
    human behavior theory and, 321–
        322
    intervention and, 330–331, 345–346
    knowledge and, 324–325
    learning from, 342–344
    overview, 309–310
    person-in-environment and, 310–
        316
    power and, 324–325
    restorying people's lives and, 330–
        332
    role of social worker and, 332–333
    self and, 324
    social work and, 255–256, 309–310,
        344–345
    terminology, basic, 316–319, 339–
        340
Social diagnosis, 20
Social Diagnosis (Richmond), 74
Social learning theory, 254–255
Social network analysis, 281–282
Social order, 111
Social planning, 54–55
Social policy, 68
Social sciences, 251–252

Social systems, 222
Social time, 277
Social work (*see also* Cross-cultural
  practice in social work; Direct
  practice in social work)
 casework and, 20
 cognitive theory and, 173–174, 177–
  178, 208–211
 contemporary, 18
 criteria for effective, 15
 ecological perspective and, 259–261,
  302–303
 ego psychology and, 107–109
 families and, 48–50
 feminist, 168–169
 feminist theories and, 351, 375, 382–
  386
 general systems theory and, 4, 6,
  215, 252–254
 genetic theories and, 389–390
 groups and, 51–52
 helping process and, 20–22
 human behavior theory and, 3–8,
  31–32, 49
 macro versus micro, 255–256
 methods, 19–26
 moral development and, 137, 141–144
 organizations and, 53–55
 paradigm of, 19–20
 person-in-environment perspective
  and, 1–2, 16–18, 31–32
 policy-practice curriculum and, 207–
  208
 positivist theory and, 6
 postmodern theory and, 12, 31–32
 psychanalytic theory and, 4, 6
 purpose of, 19
 social constructionist theory and,
  255–256, 309–310, 344–345
 spirituality, in social work, 65–69
 spiritually sensitive, 63–69
 strengths perspective and, 26, 42
 theory and, 1–2, 6–7, 251
 values inherent to, 15
Social Work Abstracts, 251–252
Social worker's role (*see* Role of social
  worker)

Socialist feminist theory, 357–358, 382
Socialization process, 83, 87–88
Society for Spirituality and Social
  Work, 66
Sociocultural development, 37–38
Sociological unconscious, 112
Solomon, B. B., 218, 236
Solovey, A. D., 25
Somatic order, 111
Spencer, M. B., 126
Spiegelman, A., 332
Spina bifida, 403
Spirit, 64
Spirituality, 63–69
Spiritually sensitive social work prac-
  tice, 63–69
Stage theories, 34–36, 319, 321
"Stages and Sequence" (Kohlberg), 142
Stagnation, 122–123
Steady state, 229
Stein, I., 220, 241
Stimulant effects, 400
Strategic questions, 24
Strengths perspective
  empowerment and, 167
  person-centered approach and, 167
  social work and, 26, 42
Stress, 270, 403
Stress theory, 265
Structural model, 81–83
Structure, defined, 223
Structured approach, 20–21
Sublimation, 83
Subsystems, 223–224, 250
Suffragette movement, 381
Superego, 83, 112
Swenson, C., 281
Synergy, 228, 269–270
Systems boundaries, 227–228
Systems theory (*see* General systems
  theory)

Tabula rasa, 271
Taggart, M., 332
Take Back the Night movement, 367
Tally's Corner (Liebow), 329
Target population, 210

Tay-Sach's disease, 396, 403–404
Taylor, J. B., 305
Tension, 81, 229
Teratogens, 402
Thalassemia, 404, 406
Theoretical framework, value of, 6–7
Theory (*see also specific types*)
  concerns about, 8
  contextualized, 8
  critique of, 13–14
  definitions of, 4–5, 250, 382
  direct practice in social work and, 1
  evaluating, 14–15
  paradigm and, 3–4, 13
  social work and, 1–2, 6–7, 251
  views on, different, 8–13
Therapeutic conditions, 157–158
Thinking paradigm, 13
Thomas, R. M., 143
Thurber, James, 418
Tiefer, L., 323
Time, 277
Time-limited psychotherapy, 93
Tomm, K., 24, 325
Topographic model, 79–81
Toward a New Psychology of Women
    (Miller), 361
TPH gene, 415
Transactional approach, 9, 240, 268–
    270
Transference, 93
Treatment (*see* Intervention)
Triangles (communication exchanges),
    227
Tryptophan hydroxylase (TPH) gene,
    415
Tumer's syndrome, 393–394
Twin studies, 401

Ultrasound, 407
Unconditional positive regard, 148, 157
Unconscious mental processes, 79–80

Unconsciousness, 111–112
Undoing, 83

Value imperative, 306
Van Den Bergh, N., 235, 368, 384
Vandiver, S. T., 384
Variable expressivity, 397
Vidal de Haymes, M., 344
Vourlekis, B. S., 366

Wakefield, J. C., 254
Warning signs of problems, 196–197
Way of Being, A (Rogers), 154
WCTU, 381
Weakland, J. H., 239
Weick, A., 220, 315, 384
Weimer, W. B., 316
Wellesley's Stone Center, 356
Wellness theory, 43
Werner, H. D., 193, 195
Wetzel, J. W., 351, 358, 383
White, M., 330
Whittaker, J., 289
Will, 119
Wintram, Claire, 352
Withdrawal, 118
Witkin, S. L., 43, 344
Wittgenstein, L., 341
Woman, Power, and Change (Weick and
    Vandiver), 384
Womanism, 363–364
Women's Christian Temperance Union
    (WCTU), 381
Wood, K. M., 78
Working through process, 92–93

X chromosomes, 392–394, 397–398

Y chromosomes, 392–394, 397–398
Young Women's Christian Association
    (YWCA), 381
YWCA, 381